D0555405

# The Independent Study Catalog c.1

## NUCEA's Guide to Independent Study Through Correspondence Instruction 1986–1988

Editors
Barbara C. Ready
Raymond D. Sacchetti

**The Catalog Committee of the Division of Independent Study, NUCEA**

Mary Beth Almeda, University of California Extension; Chair
Kathryn R. Allen, University of Texas
Mary T. Andrews, University of Missouri
Robert W. Batchellor, University of Illinois
James K. Broomall, Allegany Community College
David F. Holden, University of Tennessee

**Division of Independent Study, Administrative Committee Officers**

Monty E. McMahon, University of Nebraska; Chair
Becky S. Duning, Auburn University; Chair-Elect
Rebecca C. Monley, University of North Dakota; Secretary
Nancy G. Williams, University of Alabama; Immediate Past Chair

**Administrative Committee**

Robert W. Batchellor, University of Illinois
Nancy R. Colyer, University of Kansas
Norman Loewenthal, University of North Carolina
Phyllis J. Luebke, Oklahoma State University
Harold Markowitz, University of Florida
David F. Mercer, Pennsylvania State University
Deborah L. Nelson, University of Minnesota
Joyce E. Nielsen, Western Illinois University
Von V. Pittman Jr., University of Iowa
Roger G. Young, University of Missouri

A Peterson's Guides Publication for the National University Continuing Education Association

ISBN 0-87866-379-7
ISSN 0733-6020

Cover design by Janice Conklin

Printed in the United States of America

The membership of the National University Continuing Education Association (NUCEA) consists of universities, colleges, and related organizations and their professional staffs who are dedicated to lifelong learning and public service. Through continuing education programs, NUCEA members make their institutional and community resources available to youth and adults, individuals and groups, volunteer organizations, government units, and private industry. They are devoted to the enrichment of living by making continuing education available—and attractive—to individuals in every segment of the population.

10   9   8   7   6   5   4   3   2   1

Additional copies of this book may be ordered prepaid ($8.95 plus $1.25 postage/ handling) from: NUCEA Book Order Department, Peterson's Guides, P.O. Box 2123, Princeton, New Jersey 08543-2123.

---

For information about other Peterson's publications, please see the listing at the back of this volume.

# CONTENTS

*In parentheses following each institution's name is each division of instruction offered by the institution for courses listed in this Guide, as follows: E = Elementary, H = High School, C = College, G = Graduate, NC = Noncredit.*

*Contents*

Correspondence study is individual instruction by mail. It is flexible, convenient, and personalized. Students can enroll at any time, study at home, and set their own pace. Work is done on a one-to-one basis with faculty experts who design the instructional materials, guide course study, and prepare specific responses to the submitted work.

## The Nature of Correspondence Study

Correspondence study helps a wide range of people meet their educational needs and objectives. Individuals who are unable to come to the classroom, or who prefer to study at their own pace, can earn credit toward a degree or toward a professional certificate. Adults with work and family responsibilities can gain new job skills and learn about new subjects for personal enrichment or satisfaction. With an increased choice of courses, students can:

- Solve campus scheduling problems
- Meet prerequisites
- Gain advanced standing
- Explore new subjects
- Study while away from campus
- Accelerate their programs

**Credit courses** are offered for every academic level from elementary school (including preschool) through graduate work, although the emphasis is on high school and undergraduate courses.

**Noncredit courses** and courses offered for certification purposes are also available from most NUCEA institutions.

Additional study opportunities for off-campus students include telecourses, courses by newspaper, group study, credit by examination, and external degree programs. (See the sections on "Special Study Opportunities" and "External Degree Programs," page 6.)

Correspondence study is demanding. Since the printed word and written exchanges are the principal learning media, it is essential that students have reasonably strong reading and writing skills. While the flexibility of correspondence study is one of its distinct advantages, it is also one of its greatest hazards. Many people who enroll in correspondence courses do not finish them. Being on their own, unsupported by the discipline of the traditional classroom, correspondence students *must* have the initiative and self-reliance to develop good study habits, work independently, and establish and maintain a regular schedule of study.

In general, students who complete correspondence courses feel that they have learned as much as—if not more than—they would have in a traditional course, but they often feel that the experience has been more rigorous. Those who are able to take responsibility for their own education find correspondence study rewarding and satisfying. Anyone contemplating enrollment in correspondence study should give careful consideration to both the advantages and drawbacks of the correspondence study method before enrolling.

## Accreditation

Members of the National University Continuing Education Association (NUCEA) are primarily degree-granting institutions of higher education accredited by one of the six regional accrediting associations that hold membership in the Council on Postsecondary Accreditation (COPA) or, with the approval of the Board of Directors, by any other accrediting agency that holds membership in COPA. In addition, member institutions must have substantial programs in continuing education.

Approximately 300 colleges and universities in the United States currently have met the requirements for membership in NUCEA. Of these, over 70 have established correspondence courses which are included in the accreditation of the institution offering the courses. Some high school courses are approved by state educational agencies.

With three exceptions, all of the institutions included in this directory are accredited by one of the six regional accrediting associations. The exceptions are NUCEA members that are not degree-granting institutions. The Graduate School, USDA, is a non-degree-granting institution that offers a continuing education program for working adults. Its courses are designed to meet the specific needs of federal employees, but most are applicable to the private sector as well. Home Study International is the extension division for the Association of Seventh-day Adventist Colleges and Universities in North America. These schools are accredited by their regional accrediting associations. Home Study International is accredited by the National Home Study Council. The Massachusetts Department of Education offers high school and noncredit courses as required by legislative mandate. The courses are reviewed by the Massachusetts Board of Education.

In addition, Canada does not have a system of regional accreditation; rather, qualified degree-granting institutions are chartered by their respective provincial governments—the nearest Canadian equivalent to U.S. accreditation. The Canadian university in this book, Athabasca University, has such a charter.

The six U.S. regional accrediting associations that hold membership in COPA are the New England Association of Schools and Colleges, the Middle States Association of Colleges and Schools, the North Central Association of Colleges and Schools, the Northwest Association of Schools and Colleges, the Southern Association of Colleges and Schools, and the Western Association of Schools and Colleges. The National Home Study Council, which also holds membership in COPA, is the specialized accrediting body for institutions and organizations that have been established primarily to offer programs for home study.

## NUCEA Standards

Institutions listed in the Guide support the *Standards of the Division of Independent Study of NUCEA*. The standards are guidelines for conducting effective programs of independent study and improving their quality. They are also intended to assist units of independent study in the internal and external evaluation of their programs. The standards serve as goals toward which independent study programs should strive, and they address all aspects of program operation: mission, instruction, services, faculty, administration, staff, and research and evaluation.

## Admission

In general, correspondence study courses listed in this Guide are open to all individuals, regardless of age or previous educational experience. Applications are usually accepted without entrance examinations or proof of prior educational experience. However, some institutions may impose certain requirements before they will accept correspondence study credit, and some courses or programs may require previous study or experience. *Students should determine the requirements of the resident institution or of the particular program for which they intend to earn credit before enrolling in a correspondence study course.* An institution's catalog will list both general admission requirements and prerequisites for individual courses.

## Enrollment, Registration Forms, and Catalogs

Usually, to enroll in a correspondence course, the student simply fills in the registration form provided by the institution and sends a check or money order to cover tuition and fees, as listed in the catalog.

After reviewing the course names shown in this Guide, prospective students may obtain registration forms and catalogs, providing descriptions of the courses, from all NUCEA member institutions listed in this Guide. In addition, some institutions offer detailed information about individual courses, such as a course outline, which will be sent upon request. To obtain these materials, the contact name and address or telephone number shown at the top of each institution's entry in the "Institutions and Correspondence Courses Offered" section should be used.

## Time Requirements

Courses are not tied to an academic year. Students can enroll at their convenience and work at their own pace. An enrollment is valid for a certain period, often for twelve months, and most institutions provide for extensions of time. Some institutions, however, do have regulations prohibiting rapid completion of a course to ensure the validity of the learning experience and to enable the instructor to respond to the student's work before the final examination. (Such regulations are listed in the institutional catalog.) Within these broad limits, students determine the time it will take to complete their program of study.

## The Mechanics of Correspondence Study

While each institution has somewhat different policies and procedures, correspondence study generally follows the pattern outlined below.

1. **Study Materials.** A study guide that includes a list of required textbooks and materials, supplementary information, specific learning assignments, and all other details necessary for successful completion of the course is sent to a student as soon as the enrollment process is complete. (Details of the enrollment procedures are contained in the institutional catalog.)

2. **Textbooks.** The required textbooks and other course materials may be obtained in a number of ways, depending upon the procedures of the particular institution. They are either ordered at the time of enrollment and sent at the same time as the study guide, ordered from a designated bookstore after the receipt of the study guide, or obtained from local sources. Audiovisual aids, if any, are usually sent with the study guide, and charges for these are indicated in the catalogs of the individual institutions.

3. **Study Assignments.** The study guide divides the course into segments, usually called "lessons" or "assignments." Each lesson directs certain study activities, such as readings, self-check exercises, occasional field trips, interviews, and any other activities that are appropriate to the subject area of the course. These are done in preparation for the successful completion of the next step.

4. **Assignments for Evaluation.** After the study activities in each lesson are completed, a written assignment is submitted for evaluation. This varies widely from course to course, and sometimes even within the same course. A written assignment may consist of prescribed objective or essay questions, a report, a paper, or any other example of written work. In some instances, the student has the opportunity to submit a cassette, answering questions or performing orally.

   These assignments are evaluated and returned as soon as possible. The instructor expresses a judgment of the quality of the assignment, most often with descriptive comments and a grade.

5. **Examinations.** Credit courses usually require one or two examinations that must be taken under the supervision of an authorized proctor. Generally, students are able to arrange for supervision of the examination at an institution near their home. In some cases, noncredit courses also require final examinations. Examination forms are sent directly to the proctor, and the completed examination is returned to the institution by the proctor after it has been administered to the student. Specific details are given in the catalog or the study guide of the enrolling institution.

6. **Records and Transcripts.** A record of a completed correspondence course is maintained by each institution. For credit courses, the student's grade is recorded, and transcripts of the credit earned may be requested from the institution. Generally, a small charge is assessed for each transcript. For noncredit and certificate courses, some institutions award a certificate of completion or Continuing Education Units (CEUs).

## Credit

**Limits of Correspondence Study Credit.** Students who wish to apply credit earned through correspondence study to a college degree or a high school diploma should consult the resident institution **before enrolling in a correspondence study course.** Most institutions have limitations on the number and kinds of correspondence study credits that they will accept.

Some accredited colleges and universities offer a college degree or high school diploma mainly or entirely by correspondence. Students interested in external degree or diploma programs should contact the institution of their choice and inquire if such a program is available.

**College Credit.** Academic credit is measured in semester or quarter hours. The equivalent value of semester and quarter hours is as follows:

| | | |
|---|---|---|
| 1⅓ semester hours | = | 2 quarter hours |
| 2 semester hours | = | 3 quarter hours |
| 2⅔ semester hours | = | 4 quarter hours |
| 3 semester hours | = | 4½ quarter hours |
| 3⅓ semester hours | = | 5 quarter hours |

**Grades and Transcripts for College Courses.** Each institution follows its regular grading policies in evaluating the work of independent students. When a course is completed, a grade report is sent to the student, the grade is recorded at the institution, and a transcript will be sent to any address designated by the student in a written request. Most institutions charge for additional transcripts.

**Transfer of Credit.** Credit earned in correspondence study courses taken from a regionally accredited institution is normally transferable from one institution to another; however, since policies and degree requirements vary among universities and colleges, students are urged to consult appropriate officials of the institution from which they expect to receive a degree to ascertain whether credit is transferable. If course work is taken from an institution that is not regionally accredited, the transferability of the course work for credit to another institution may be more difficult.

**High School Credit.** Most institutions offering credit for high school courses tailor their credit units to coincide with the method most common in the state system they serve. Generally, courses are offered for one-half unit of credit (equal to one semester of course work in a regular classroom) or for one-quarter credit, depending on the state system.

High schools that offer a diploma by correspondence award credit on a semester basis of one-half unit of credit per course. Prior approval of correspondence work should be obtained from the resident high school to ensure acceptance of the credit.

**Enrollment in Credit Courses on a Noncredit Basis.** Most NUCEA member universities and colleges accept enrollments in credit courses on a noncredit basis and take special interest in students who are studying for personal satisfaction without regard to credit.

**The Continuing Education Unit or CEU.** The Continuing Education Unit (CEU) is used to recognize and measure achievement in noncredit courses. The CEU is defined as 10 contact hours of participation in an organized continuing education experience under responsible sponsorship, capable direction, and qualified instruction. Individuals interested in receiving CEUs for noncredit courses listed in this Guide should request information from the institutions offering the courses.

## Financial Considerations

The costs associated with taking a correspondence course vary from course to course and from one college or university to another. Each institution sets its own pricing structure, based upon the expenses associated with a course and the institution's overall fee policies.

In general, a person can expect direct charges for tuition, textbooks, and other necessary course materials, and sometimes for postage and handling fees.

**Tuition.** Tuition for college and university credit courses is most often figured on the basis of a set amount per credit hour, regardless of whether the institution uses the semester or quarter unit of measurement. (Example: Accounting 101 offered for 3 credits at $30 per credit requires a tuition of $90, to be sent with the registration: 3 x $30 = $90.)

Tuition for noncredit and high school courses is usually stated as a flat fee for the course rather than in terms of a set amount per credit hour. For such courses, no computation is needed in completing a registration form.

Tuition rates for credit courses at NUCEA member institutions currently range from a low of $20 to a high of $90 per credit unit. Rates for high school and noncredit courses also vary widely and change frequently. Before enrolling, any interested person should check the catalog of the individual institution for current rates.

**Textbooks.** In most cases, the cost of textbooks is not included in the cost of the course, and students must purchase their own books. The catalog of the enrolling institution or the study guide that is mailed to a student who enrolls will indicate exactly how the texts can be obtained and the exact or approximate cost. The cost can vary widely, depending upon the number and kinds of texts. In a few instances, the study guide is also the text.

**Course Materials.** Course materials always include a study guide, which is usually provided as part of the initial cost. In addition, workbooks, procedure manuals, kits, audiotapes, phonograph records, filmstrips or slides, photographs, or various other audiovisual aids may be required, in which case the cost is borne by the student. Although these items are sometimes quite expensive, they often cost only a few dollars. In some cases, the material is loaned to the student, who pays a deposit that is partially refunded when the material is returned. Details about costs for course materials will be listed in the institution's catalog or in the study guide.

**Postage.** In all cases, students bear the cost for postage on items that they mail. Some institutions levy a postage fee for items mailed to their students, such as course materials and returned assignments. Rates for domestic postage are not high, but rates for postage to foreign countries can be a major expense, with total foreign postage for course materials and returned assignments being as much as $50. When possible, students going to foreign countries should enroll before they leave the United States, taking their textbooks and course materials with them in order to avoid both postage and tariff expenses. An institution's catalog will identify policies and costs for foreign enrollments.

**Handling and Special Fees.** Some institutions charge a handling fee to help them defray the cost for processing materials and registration. The fee range is from $2 to $20. In addition, rental fees, usually small, are sometimes charged for special course materials.

**Payment Plans.** Most institutions require at the time of registration full payment of all charges due. The preferred method of payment is a check or money order. In a few instances, textbooks are paid for separately. Some institutions accept credit cards, and a few have some form of partial or deferred payment plan, but the number of institutions that offer these options is small. It is necessary to examine the catalog or bulletin of the institution to determine its payment policies.

## Financial Aid

Financial aid is not as readily available for correspondence study students as it is for traditional classroom students. However, the sources listed below can occasionally provide some financial aid, and students who require aid should explore all applicable possibilities.

**Employers.** Many employers provide educational benefits to their employees. These are generally administered through the personnel or benefits department of the organization.

**Unions.** Unions have been negotiating educational benefits into many of their contracts. The union's business manager would be the person to provide information.

**Veterans' and Military Benefits.** All of the federal veterans' assistance acts have had provisions for financial assistance for college and university correspondence study, usually under the term independent study. The amount and type of assistance varies, and it is best to check with a local Veterans Administration office for specific details.

Active-duty military personnel have two specific options available to them for financial assistance. The first is "in-service" VA benefits. Under specified conditions, a person on active duty may be eligible for financial assistance under the Veterans' Readjustment Benefits Act of 1966, as amended, the Post–Vietnam Era Veterans' Educational Assistance Program (Public Law 94-502, as amended), or the Veterans' Educational Assistance Act of 1984 (Public Law 98-525).

The second is "tuition assistance," which comes from the military person's respective service. In either case, the Educational Service Officer of the base, post, or ship can provide information.

In addition to the federal government's VA tuition assistance plans, some states have educational benefits for veterans. Questions and inquiries should be directed to the state veterans or military affairs offices.

**Vocational Rehabilitation.** Nearly all states provide financial benefits for the education of persons with some form of handicap. A number of states include correspondence study in the forms of education allowable for benefits. Any inquiries should be directed to a state's department of vocational rehabilitation.

**Institutional Aid.** A small number of colleges and universities have a limited amount of financial aid available for correspondence study. Guide users should carefully examine the catalogs of the institutions for financial aid information or consult the office of financial aid.

## Special Study Opportunities

While the focus of this Guide is on correspondence courses, other related opportunities are frequently offered by independent study programs. To obtain details, you will need to contact an institution's independent study office.

Some institutions use periodic or regular **television** or **radio** broadcasts to supplement independent study instruction. Courses having **newspaper components** are also occasionally offered. These courses are generally limited both by time of offering and by geographical area. Some correspondence courses also use **audiocassette tape recordings, laboratory kits,** and **computer programs** as instructional tools.

Such opportunities as **credit by examination, tutorial study,** and **directed study** are also available at some institutions. Credit by examination allows students to receive degree credit for successful scores on the various tests of the College-Level Examination Program (CLEP) or the ACT Proficiency Examination Program (PEP) or on institutionally administered tests. Tutorial study makes it possible for students to arrange for correspondence instruction in courses not otherwise offered by the correspondence method. Directed study allows the student to substitute special projects or submissions for the assignments usually required in a course. Some correspondence courses include **optional class meetings.** Others lend themselves well to **group study** projects for the benefit of friends or associates who wish to study the same subject. In some instances such projects may include visits with the instructor or other experts. These variations of the traditional correspondence format are especially helpful for students with special needs.

In many states correspondence courses serve as a way of meeting requirements for **professional certification** or recertification. Teachers constitute one major group that has benefited in this way, though persons in other professions should also determine if correspondence study might allow them to complete requirements in their fields. Some institutions offer entire **series of correspondence courses** in specific subject areas, sometimes in relation to vocational or professional requirements. Often a certificate of completion is awarded to individuals who complete the full series.

## External Degree Programs

Related in concept to correspondence courses are **external degree programs,** which are now offered by numerous colleges and universities in the United States. These flexible programs make it possible for students to complete all degree requirements with little or no attendance on campus. Correspondence courses are one of several ways that requirements toward external degrees may be met. A useful directory of external degree programs is the American Council on Education's *Guide to External Degree Programs in the United States.* Check for this and other references at your local library or bookstore.

# Special Advice and Counseling

As a prospective nontraditional student in correspondence study, you face three major questions that institutions have helped traditional students answer but to which you must find the answers yourself: (1) Why am I taking this course? (2) What options are available to me for taking this course? (3) How do I study?

Anyone contemplating independent study should determine the answers to these questions before enrolling in a correspondence course. In some instances, the correspondence study offices of the colleges and universities can answer a few questions, particularly in reference to their own institution. However, it is best to get official information from the admissions office, the academic department in which you wish to take a course, or the counseling service of the college or university. In addition, it is vitally important that you seek formal counseling and advice from the institution's counseling service, particularly when college or high school credit is involved. Very few of the correspondence study offices have the personnel to answer questions or to advise you, and in many cases they are not authorized to do so.

The section below offers you help in finding answers to the three basic questions.

**Question 1.  Why am I taking this course?**

If the course is for college or high school credit, you must ask:
a. Will any college or high school accept the course credit and apply it toward my graduation?
b. How many credits by correspondence will be accepted toward graduation?
c. Will my institution accept credit for correspondence work transferred from another institution?
d. Will credits earned by correspondence be accepted in my area of concentration?

If the course is being taken for certification and not for degree purposes, you should ask:
a. What are the certification requirements?
b. Will the course be acceptable to the certifying agency?
c. How many credits can be earned or how much work can be done by correspondence?

**Question 2.  What options are available to me for taking this course?**

Some institutions offer optional ways of taking their courses or of earning degree credit. For these, you should ask:
a. Is the pass-fail option acceptable to my college or certifying agency?
b. Is credit by examination acceptable?
c. Is credit for experiential learning available and acceptable?
d. Are the external degree programs that some institutions offer by correspondence acceptable to other colleges, employers, and certifying agencies?

**Question 3.  How do I study?**

Since successful correspondence study requires really good study habits, you should take the time to evaluate your own approach to studying before you enroll. Assess your study habits and decide, with as much objectivity as possible, how well you think you can study on your own.

**Schedule.** It is extremely important to set aside a regularly scheduled time for study. If you have not been involved in academic pursuits recently, you may find that your career, family, hobbies, or social and civic commitments leave little time for studying. In order to make room for study in your schedule, you may have to sacrifice other activities. To help you decide how to do this, keep a record for a week or two of how you spend your time, and see what you are willing to give up. Since you won't have the built-in pacing of classes and preestablished deadlines set by instructors, you may find it hard to make progress unless you set up a definite study schedule.

Try to schedule this study for a time when you will be mentally fresh and able to devote at least one hour to your work. Think of the hour as "reserved time," but don't get discouraged if you can't always keep the schedule. After all, one of the advantages of correspondence study is its flexibility. Just keep in mind that regularly scheduled study is the ideal, and make it your goal. If you miss too many study periods, revise your schedule.

**Where to Study.** You'll find it easier to focus on your work if you arrange an appropriate environment for study. You will need a place that is quiet and free from reminders of other responsibilities. You might consider a public library if your home does not offer a suitable place.

**Reading Skills.** The abilities to read with comprehension and to retain what you read are necessary for real learning to take place, especially in correspondence study. These skills can be developed by concentrating on what you read and by taking frequent pauses to organize and review the material in your mind. At the end of a study session, you should review everything you have read, making special notes of important points learned in that session.

**Writing Skill.** Writing is also an essential skill. Written assignments provide the main channel of communication between you and your instructor. In your written assignments, you collect and synthesize what you've learned, demonstrating to your instructor that you are progressing according to plan. An elementary skill in writing is prerequisite to taking a correspondence course, but it is also a skill that is developed further in most courses.

In preparing written assignments, you must pay careful attention to instructions and be sure you understand what is being asked. Are you willing to work at preparing a good answer? You may need to develop a brief outline of your responses or draft your answer and check it over before preparing a final copy. Organization, grammar, and writing style are important in most correspondence study courses. If your skills in these areas need improvement, you may need to do extra work in a writing handbook.

If you do not understand some point, inquiries can be made only by mail. Responses to your instructor's comments on your lessons, requests for clarification of comments, and all other exchanges between you and your instructor will take time. This written interaction with your instructor can be very rewarding, but you must be willing to take the initiative, and you must have a great deal of patience in order to make it worthwhile.

Completing a correspondence course is not always easy. It requires a great deal of self-discipline and work. However, the benefits you derive can also be great. In addition to the mastery of subject matter, the study skills you develop should help you to undertake other difficult educational tasks with more confidence.

## Division of Independent Study, NUCEA

The Division of Independent Study is one of five divisions within the Council on Continuing Education Delivery Systems of the National University Continuing Education Association (NUCEA). Over 70 of the Association's 300 or so members offer correspondence study programs, and the Division of Independent Study provides the professional base for the various staff members of these programs.

The purpose of the Division of Independent Study is to provide a means of developing guidelines for programs of high quality and to offer professional training for staff members. The division also acts to promote the concept of correspondence study, encourage research, and offer a forum for the exchange of information.

*The Independent Study Catalog: NUCEA's Guide to Independent Study Through Correspondence Instruction* is one of the major projects of the division. The intent of this book is to offer a composite picture of the college- and university-based correspondence study opportunities that are currently available through 71 of the NUCEA member institutions. The Guide provides in convenient form the title and course number, sponsoring department, credit value, and level of instruction of each correspondence course.

The National University Continuing Education Association is the premier association concerned with the postsecondary continuing education movement in the United States. It currently has a membership of approximately 300 colleges, universities, and other educational institutions, all of which have a commitment to the part-time student.

The purposes of the Association are:

1. To provide a means by which institutions may cooperate to advance the concept of lifelong, continuing education
2. To encourage institutions to communicate and cooperate
3. To provide leadership in research and professional judgment
4. To maintain liaison with other agencies and organizations
5. To publish journals, newsletters, and educational materials
6. To provide information as a representative of university extension interests

# HOW TO USE THIS GUIDE

*The Independent Study Catalog: NUCEA's Guide to Independent Study Through Correspondence Instruction* is just that, a "guide" to colleges and universities providing correspondence instruction and to the courses offered by those institutions. There are three ways of using the Guide:

## Finding Courses

1. **Finding Courses from a Particular Institution.** If you have already decided to study at a particular institution listed in this book, simply find the institution's page number in the Contents, turn to its entry in the "Institutions and Correspondence Courses Offered" section, and review the courses offered.

   Each institution's entry lists elementary school courses, if any, first, followed by high school, college, graduate, and noncredit courses offered; these five kinds of courses are discussed on page 11. For each kind of course, course names are grouped together by academic or subject-matter area. To the right of each course name is the department offering the course, the number of the course, the number of credits earned by its successful completion, and the level of instruction; the codes for credits and levels of instruction are explained on page 12.

2. **Finding Courses Through the Index.** To locate a course in a particular category, turn to the Index. Listed there alphabetically are broad subject-matter areas, representing major academic disciplines, with more specific areas grouped under them in two levels of subordination. The name of an area is followed by the **code number of each institution** offering one or more courses in that area, plus a **code letter for each kind of course** the institution offers in that area (E = Elementary, H = High School, C = College, G = Graduate, N = Noncredit; see the following section entitled "Kinds of Courses"). Institutional code numbers and their corresponding institutional names are listed numerically and alphabetically in the Contents, on the inside back flap, and on the pages in the "Institutions and Correspondence Courses Offered" section of this book.

   After finding a subject-matter area of interest in the Index, make a note of its **NCES number** (to left of area name) and the code number of each institution offering a course in that area. Note also the code letter, indicating the kind of course offered, that is attached to an institution's number. Identify the institution and page number in the Contents, and turn to the institution's entry. Or turn directly to its entry in the "Institutions and Correspondence Courses Offered" section, where the code numbers and corresponding institutional names are listed numerically and alphabetically at the beginning of institutional entries and—in dictionary fashion—at the top of pages. When using the Index, you may also wish to keep the back cover foldout open, in order to quickly identify the institution corresponding to a given code number.

   To find the specific course name(s) in an institution's entry, locate the section for the kind of course indicated by the code letter, then run down the numerical listing of NCES numbers (first column) until you find the one that corresponds to the subject-matter area of interest. You will find the name of each course offered by the institution in that category, the department offering it, the number of the course, the number of credits earned by its successful completion, and the level of instruction. The abbreviations used for department names are explained on page 12.

3. **Finding a Specific Subject-Matter Area.** If you have difficulty locating a subject-matter area in the Index, refer to the Alphabetical Listing of Subject-Matter Areas, which precedes the Index. Then turn to the Index and follow the instructions above.

This Guide does not and cannot provide all of the information needed to actually enroll in a course. To do that, the prospective student must use the address at the top of an institution's entry to request a copy of the correspondence study catalog and specific information about enrolling. Some institutions offer detailed information about individual courses, such as an outline of the course, which will be sent upon request.

In general, course selection should follow an assessment of the purpose for which the course is needed: (1) for credit to apply toward a degree or diploma; (2) for personal development, without regard to credit; or (3) for certification in a professional program.

Students who expect to apply credit earned through correspondence study to a degree or a diploma should contact the resident institution for counseling and advice in order to ensure that the credit will be accepted. (See the sections on "Credit," page 3, and "Special Advice and Counseling," page 7.)

(See the sections on "Credit," page 3, and "Special Advice and Counseling," page 7.)

## Kinds of Courses

Five kinds of correspondence study courses are listed in this Guide:

1. **Elementary School Courses.** One institution (Home Study International) offers correspondence courses for preschool through grade eight.

2. **High School Courses.** Courses covering virtually every area of high school study are offered by NUCEA member institutions. A few institutions offer high school diplomas by correspondence, but in most cases correspondence credit is accepted by the local high school, which issues the diploma. Students should have approval from the diploma-granting institution before enrolling in a correspondence study course.

3. **College Courses.** A great variety of courses offering undergraduate credit are provided.

4. **Graduate Courses.** Only a few institutions offer courses for graduate credit only, although some offer courses that are applicable toward credit at either the upper-division collegiate **or** graduate level. Some institutions will not accept correspondence study courses as credit toward a graduate degree.

5. **Noncredit Courses.** Courses designed to meet the job-related, professional, cultural, or personal needs of individuals who do not desire credit are offered by most NUCEA institutions. In addition, most courses that are offered for credit can **also** be taken on a noncredit basis.

In addition to offering single courses, some institutions offer complete programs of courses to meet certification, vocational, or professional needs. Students should consult an institution's catalog to obtain specific information.

In general, vocational courses are not listed in the Guide. Individuals who are interested in this type of study can secure information about such courses from institutions that are members of the National Home Study Council. The NHSC is the accrediting association for private, proprietary correspondence schools and publishes the **Directory of Accredited Home Study Schools.** A free copy of this directory can be obtained from the National Home Study Council, 1601 Eighteenth Street, NW, Washington, D.C. 20009. Send the Council a postcard stating your request, with your name, address, and zip code printed clearly on it.

## Course Information and Abbreviations

All information in the section entitled "Institutions and Correspondence Courses Offered" has been supplied by the institutions themselves in response to a 1985 NUCEA survey. If any part of the usual data does not appear with a course listing, it was not supplied by the college or university, and students are advised to write directly to the institution for further information.

**NCES Code Numbers.** The first number appearing on a line with the name of a course in an institution's entry is the National Center for Education Statistics (NCES) number, as determined by the institution offering the course. This number derives from the taxonomy, or system of numerical classification, of educational subject matter prepared by the National Center for Education Statistics and published as **A Classification of Educational Subject Matter** by the U.S. Government Printing Office in 1978. This taxonomy is also used as a basis for the alphabetical listing of subject-matter areas and the subject-matter index in the Guide, although only those portions of it that relate to courses in this book are shown.

01 = Agriculture and renewable natural resources
02 = Architecture and environmental design
03 = Arts, visual and performing
04 = Business
05 = Communication
06 = Computer science and data processing
07 = Education

08 = Engineering and engineering technology
09 = Health care and health sciences
10 = Home economics
11 = Industrial arts, trades, and technology
12 = Language, linguistics, and literature
13 = Law
14 = Libraries and museums
15 = Life sciences and physical sciences
16 = Mathematical sciences
17 = Military sciences
18 = Philosophy, religion, and theology
19 = Physical education, health education, and leisure
20 = Psychology
21 = Public administration and social services
22 = Social sciences and social studies

**Course Names and Numbers.** Wherever possible, course names have been written in full, with the name of the department offering the course and the course number appearing to the right. However, because of space limitations, it has been necessary to abbreviate long course names. If there is any question about the specific content of a course, students should write directly to the institution offering the course, referring to the department and course number.

**Credit Code.** The credits earned by successful completion of courses listed in this Guide are indicated by the number of credits followed, usually, by S or Q to indicate the specific number of semester or quarter credit hours. (Example: 2S = 2 semester hours.) One or more of the following codes may also be used:

TN = Tenth unit
QT = Quarter unit
TH = Third unit
HF = Half unit
2T = Two-thirds unit
TQ = Three-quarters unit
1U = One unit
NC = Noncredit
VC = Credit varies

**Level of Instruction.** The level of instruction for each course listed in this Guide is indicated by one of the following codes:

L   = Lower-division collegiate
U   = Upper-division collegiate
B   = Upper-division collegiate **or** graduate
G   = Graduate
V   = Vocational certificate
D   = Developmental or remedial
H   = High school
E   = Elementary

**Department Name Abbreviations.** The name of the department offering a course has usually been abbreviated and is shown to the right of the course name, although the names of some departments are written in full (e.g., Art = Art). In some instances, the same abbreviation may be used for the name of two different departments (e.g., Fin = Finance **or** Finnish), but the title of the course should make the correct department name clear. The following list defines abbreviations appearing in this Guide:

| | |
|---|---|
| A&S | Anthropology and Sociology |
| AAC | Athletic Administration and Coaching |
| AAM | Academy of Adventist Ministers |
| Acc, Acct, Acctg, Acta | Accounting |
| ACS | Agronomic Crop Sciences, American Cultural Studies |
| Admn | Administration |

| | |
|---|---|
| AdmSt | Administrative Studies |
| AdSci | Administrative Science |
| ADT | Automotive Diesel Technology |
| Adv | Advertising |
| AE | Aerospace Engineering, Architectural Engineering |
| AEB | Agriculture, Economics, and Business |
| AEd | Adult Education, Art Education |
| AEdSF | Adult Education and Social Foundations |
| Aero | Aerospace |
| AF | Aviation Flight Management |
| AfAmS | Afro-American Studies |
| AFHE | Administration, Foundations, and Higher Education |
| AG, AmGvt | American Government |
| Agcr, Agri | Agriculture |
| AgEc, AgEcn, AgEco, AgrEc | Agricultural Economics |
| AgEd | Agricultural Education |
| AgEng | Agricultural Engineering |
| Agro, Agron | Agronomy |
| AgSci | Agricultural Science |
| AH | Allied Health |
| AH, AmH, AmHis | American History |
| AHC | Allied Health Careers |
| AInSt | American Indian Studies |
| AJ | Administration of Justice |
| Alc | Alcoholism |
| Alg | Algebra |
| AmCul | American Culture |
| AmL | American Literature |
| AmS, AmSt | American Studies |
| AnHis | Ancient History |
| AnSc, AnSci, AS | Animal Sciences |
| Ant, Anth, Anthr, Anthy | Anthropology |
| AOM | Administrative Office Management |
| ApSt | Applied Studies |
| Arab | Arabic |
| ArAEg | Aerospace and Aeronautical Engineering |
| Arch | Architecture |
| Archy | Archaeology |
| ArHis, ArtH | Art History |
| ArPlg | Architecture and Planning |
| ArsIn | Arson Investigation |
| ASBE | Administrative Systems and Business Education |
| Asian | Asian Languages and Literature |
| AsSt | Asian Studies |
| Ast, Astr, Astro | Astronomy |
| Atmo, AtmSc, AtS | Atmospheric Sciences |
| Athl | Athletics |
| ATS | Advanced Technical Studies |
| Avi, Avn | Aviation |
| | |
| BA, BAd, BAdm, BuAd, BusAd | Business Administration |
| Bact | Bacteriology |
| BC, BuC, BuCom | Business Communications |
| BCEd | Business Career and Education |
| Bdcst, Brdcs | Broadcasting |
| BDEOA | Business-Distributive Education and Office Administration |
| BEcn, BusEc | Business and Economics |
| BEd, BusEd | Business Education |

| | |
|---|---|
| BEOA | Business Education and Office Administration |
| Bio, Biol | Biology |
| Bioch | Biochemistry |
| BiSci, BlSc | Biological Sciences |
| Bk, Bkp | Bookkeeping |
| BL, BLaw, BuL, BuLaw, BusL, BusLw | Business Law |
| BlgIn | Building Inspection |
| BLog | Business Logistics |
| BlS | Black Studies |
| Bmet | Biometeorology |
| BMT | Business Management Technology |
| BMt | Business Management |
| BOA | Business Office Administration |
| BOE | Business and Office Education |
| Bot, Botny | Botany |
| BPA | Business and Public Administration |
| BTWr | Business and Technical Writing |
| Bus, Buss | Business |
| BusAr | Business Arithmetic |
| BusEc | Business Economics |
| BusEd | Business Education |
| BusEn | Business English |
| BusHS | Business, high school level |
| BVEd | Business and Vocational Education |
| | |
| C&I, CI, CrIns, CuIns | Curriculum and Instruction |
| CA&S | Communication Arts and Sciences |
| CAC | Computer-assisted Courses |
| CarEd | Career Education |
| CCJ | Corrections and Criminal Justice |
| CE | Civil Engineering, Consumer Economics |
| Ce, Chem | Chemistry |
| CE, ChmEg | Chemical Engineering |
| CEd, CntEd, ConEd | Continuing Education |
| CEE | Civil and Environmental Engineering |
| CESHP | Continuing Education, Science/Health Professions |
| CET | Civil Engineering Technology |
| ChD | Child Development |
| ChEd | Child Education |
| ChFam | Child and Family Studies |
| Chi | Chinese, Chinese Studies |
| Cit, Citz | Citizenship |
| Civ | Civics |
| CivEg, CivEn | Civil Engineering |
| CJ, CJus, CJust, Cr, CrJ, CrJu, CrmJ | Criminal Justice |
| CJC | Criminal Justice and Criminology |
| Clas, Class, Clsx | Classics |
| ClCiv | Classical Civilization |
| CLEE | Corrections and Law Enforcement Education |
| CLit, CmLit, ComLi | Comparative Literature |
| ClLL | Classical Languages and Literature |
| ClP | Clinical Psychology |
| ClrPr | Clerical Practice |
| ClTx, CTe | Clothing and Textiles |
| CmDis, ComD | Communicative Disorders |
| CmpSc, Comp, CompS, ComSc, CpSc, CSc, CSs | Computer Science |

| | |
|---|---|
| COAS | College of Arts and Sciences |
| Com, Comms, Commu | Communications |
| ComEg | Computer Engineering |
| Comm | Commerce |
| CommS, ComS | Communication Studies |
| Comp | Composition and Communication, Computer Science |
| CorLa | Correlated Language Arts |
| CP | Career Planning |
| CPo | Comparative Politics |
| CpScM | Computer Science and Mathematics |
| CPsy | Child Psychology |
| CR | Career Resources |
| CR, Crim | Criminology |
| CRK | Clerical Record Keeping |
| CrW | Creative Writing |
| CSLP | Civil Service License Preparation |
| Curr | Curriculum |
| | |
| DA | Dental Assisting |
| Dan | Danish |
| DC | Dental Charting |
| DCT | Dental Chairside Techniques |
| Dem | Democracy |
| DeP | Developmental Psychology |
| Des, Dsgn | Design |
| DesT | Design Technology |
| DGTS | Division of General and Technology Studies |
| DisEd | Distributive Education |
| DLT | Dental Laboratory Technology |
| DM | Diet Management |
| DOP | Dental Office Procedures |
| DP | Data Processing |
| Dr, DrEd, DriEd | Driver Education |
| DRad | Dental Radiology |
| DySc | Dairy Science |
| | |
| EAsLL | East Asian Languages and Literature |
| Eco, Econ | Economics |
| EconM | Economics and Mathematics |
| Ed | Education |
| EdAd, EdAdm | Educational Administration |
| EdBus | Business Education |
| EdF, EdFdn | Educational Foundations |
| EdFA | Educational Foundations and Administration |
| EdFM | Educational Foundations and Media |
| EdGS | Educational Guidance Counseling and Student Services |
| EdP, EdPsy, EPy | Educational Psychology |
| EdPSF | Educational Psychology and Social Foundations |
| EdRes | Educational Research |
| EdSE | Education: Special |
| EdThP | Educational Theory and Policy |
| Educ | Education |
| EduM | Educational Studies–Media |
| EE, EEg | Electrical Engineering |
| EED | Education: Emotional Disorders |
| EG | Engineering Graphics |
| Eg, Engin, Engr | Engineering |
| EH, EngHS | English, high school level |

| | |
|---|---|
| EIn, EngIn | Engineering: Industrial |
| ElEd, Elem | Elementary Education |
| ElIns | Electrical Inspection |
| Elt | Electronics |
| ElT | Electronics Technology |
| EMch, EMech, EngrM, EnMec | Engineering Mechanics |
| Eng, Engl | English |
| EngAS | Engineering and Applied Science |
| EnglL | English Literature |
| EngLL | English Language and Literature |
| EnGra | Engineering Graphics |
| EngrM | Engineering Mechanics |
| EngrT | Engineering Technology |
| EngSc, EnSci | Engineering Science |
| EnSt, EnvSt | Environmental Studies |
| Entm, Ento, Entom | Entomology |
| EntSc | Entomological Science |
| EnvD | Environmental Design |
| EnvSB | Environmental Study Board |
| EnvSc, ESci | Environmental Science |
| EPA | Educational Policies and Administration |
| EPR | Educational Psychology and Research |
| ErSci, ESci | Earth Science |
| ESI | Engineering Systems: Industrial |
| Esk | Eskimo |
| ESLR | Educational Systems and Learning Resources |
| Etiq | Etiquette |
| EuH | European History |
| EVI | Education: Visually Impaired |
| ExtEd | Extension Education |
| | |
| Fa, FnArt | Fine Arts |
| FamHS | Family Studies, high school level |
| Famil | Family |
| FamLC, FLC | Family Living Center |
| FamSc | Family Science |
| FCMed | Family and Community Medicine |
| FdAcg | Fundamentals of Accounting |
| FDC | Family Day Care |
| FdNut, F&N, FN | Food and Nutrition |
| Fin, Finan, Finc, Fnce | Finance |
| Fin, Finn | Finnish |
| FinL | Finance Law |
| FL, FLan, ForL, ForLa, ForLg, FornL | Foreign Languages |
| FLHS | Family and Local History Studies |
| Flklr, Folk | Folklore |
| FMHCS | Family Management and Housing and Consumer Science |
| FmTng | Fireman Training |
| FND | Food, Nutrition, and Dietetics |
| FNIM | Food, Nutrition, and Institution Management |
| FOM | Fundamentals of Mathematics |
| For, Fores | Forestry |
| ForES | Forestry and Environmental Studies |
| ForLL | Foreign Languages and Literature |
| ForM | Forestry Management |
| Fors | Forensics |
| FoS | Food Studies |
| FPro | Fire Protection |

| | |
|---|---|
| Fr, Frech, Fren, Frnch | French |
| FrC | Fruit Culture |
| FrEng | Freshman English |
| FRM | Family Resource Management |
| FrSci | Fire Science |
| FSc | Food Science |
| FScN, FSN | Food Science and Nutrition |
| FSHA | Food Service and Housing Administration |
| FSHN | Food Science and Human Nutrition |
| FSoS | Family Social Science |
| FSS | Food Services for Supervisors |
| FueEg | Fuels Engineering |
| | |
| GB, GBu, GenBs | General Business |
| GBA | General Business Administration |
| GBio | General Biology |
| GC | General College, General Computers |
| GEB | General Education B (Science) |
| GEC | General Education C (Social Sciences) |
| GED | General Educational Development |
| GeGe | Geography/Geology |
| Gen | Genetics |
| Genea | Genealogy |
| GenEg, GEngr | General Engineering |
| GenS, GenSt, GStd | General Studies |
| GenT | General Technology |
| Geo, Geog, Ghy, Grg | Geography |
| Geo, Geol, Gly | Geology |
| Geo, Geom | Geometry |
| GeoSc | Geological Science |
| Geosc | Geosciences |
| Ger, Germ, Germn, GL, | |
| Grmn | German |
| Geron | Gerontology |
| GHum | General Humanities |
| GIBM | Growth in Basic Mathematics |
| GInt | Government and International Studies |
| GnKno | General Knowledge |
| GnMth | General Mathematics |
| Gov, Govmt, Govt | Government |
| Graph | Graphic Arts |
| GrBks | Great Books |
| Grk | Greek |
| GRP | Graded Reading Program |
| GS | General Science |
| GSS | General Social Science |
| Guid, Guida | Guidance |
| | |
| H, Hea, Heal, Hlth, Hth | Health |
| H&FL | Home and Family Living |
| H&HS | Health and Human Services |
| H&R | Hobbies and Recreation |
| H&S | Health and Safety |
| HCA | Health Care Administration |
| HDev, HuDev | Human Development |
| HDFL | Human Development and Family Life |
| HE, HeaEd, HEd, HEdu, | |
| HelEd, HlEd | Health Education |
| HeaSc, HeS, HlSci, HSci | Health Sciences |
| Heb, Hebr | Hebrew |

| | |
|---|---|
| HEc, HEco, HmEc, HomeE | Home Economics |
| HFL | Home and Family Life |
| HFS | Hotel and Food Service, Housing and Food Service |
| HFT | Hospitality, Food, Tourism |
| His, Hist, Histo | History |
| HLang | High School Languages |
| HM | Home Management |
| HMath | High School Mathematics |
| HNF | Human Nutrition and Foods |
| HNFSM | Human Nutrition and Food Service Management |
| HoA | Hotel Administration |
| HOM | History of Mathematics |
| HomLv | Home Living |
| Hort | Horticulture |
| HPE&R, HPER, HPRe | Health, Physical Education, and Recreation |
| HPES | Health, Physical Education, and Sports |
| HPSc | History and Philosophy of Science |
| HRIM | Hotel, Restaurant, and Institutional Management |
| HRM | Human Resource Management |
| HRP | Health, Recreation, and Physical Education |
| HS | Home Study |
| HsHCA | Hospital and Health Care Administration |
| HSMgt | Health Systems Management |
| HSSci | High School Science |
| HSSSt | High School Social Studies |
| HSU | Health Science Unit |
| Hum, Hums | Humanities |
| HuN | Human Nutrition |
| | |
| IA | Introductory Algebra |
| ICS | Intercultural Studies |
| ID | Interior Design |
| ID, IDS, Int | Interdisciplinary Studies |
| IE, IndEg, InEg | Industrial Engineering |
| IEd, IndEd, InEd | Industrial Education |
| IEOR | Industrial Engineering/Operations Research |
| IFS | Individual and Family Studies |
| IM | Instructional Media |
| IMSE | Industrial and Management Systems Engineering |
| InArt, IndA | Industrial Arts |
| InCo | Interpersonal Communication |
| InDec | Interior Decoration |
| IndTc | Industrial Technology |
| Ins | Insurance |
| InSci | Instructional Science |
| IntBu | International Business |
| IntEn | Interior Environment |
| IntRe | International Relations |
| IR | Industrial Relations |
| Irr | Irrigation |
| IS | Individual Study |
| ISCS | Intermediate Science Curriculum Study |
| Ital | Italian |
| | |
| Jap, Jpn | Japanese |
| JMC | Journalism and Mass Communications |
| Jou, Jour, Journ, Jrnl | Journalism |

| | |
|---|---|
| JrEng | Junior English |
| JusAd | Justice Administration |
| Just | Justice |
| JwSt | Jewish Studies |
| | |
| La | Latin |
| LA | Landscape Architecture |
| LA&S | Liberal Arts and Sciences |
| LabSt, LS | Labor Studies |
| LAEP | Landscape Architecture and Environmental Planning |
| LAm, LAS | Latin American Studies |
| Lang | Languages |
| LanHS | Languages, high school level |
| Lat | Latin |
| LEA | Law Enforcement Administration |
| LegS, LSt | Legal Studies |
| LeiSt | Leisure Studies |
| LET | Law Enforcement Technology |
| LfSci | Life Sciences |
| LgRl | Legal Relations |
| LibSc, LibSi | Library Sciences |
| LibSt | Liberal Studies |
| Ling | Linguistics |
| LiS | Literary Studies |
| Lit | Literature |
| LMT | Library Media Technology |
| | |
| MAF | Marriage and Family |
| Man, Mgmt | Management |
| ManEc | Management Economics |
| ManSc | Management Science |
| Mar, Mkt, Mktg, Mrkt | Marketing |
| Mat, Math, Ms | Mathematics |
| MatHS | Mathematics, high school level |
| MathS | Mathematical Sciences |
| MCE | Mathematics and Consumer Economics |
| MComm | Mass Communications |
| MdvSt | Medieval Studies |
| ME | Mechanical Engineering |
| MEAS | Mathematics, Engineering, and Applied Sciences |
| Mech | Mechanics |
| MedT | Medical Terminology |
| Met, Meteo, Metr | Meteorology |
| MetEg | Metallurgical Engineering |
| MgtFn | Management/Finance |
| Micro | Microbiology |
| Milit | Military Sciences |
| Misc | Miscellaneous Studies |
| MLang | Modern Languages |
| MSci | Marine Science |
| Multi | Multidisciplinary Studies |
| Mus, Musc | Music |
| Museo | Museology |
| MWPE | Men/Women Physical Education |
| | |
| NatrS | Natural Sciences |
| NELL | Near Eastern Languages and Literature |
| NF | Nutrition and Foods |

| | |
|---|---|
| NFS | Nutrition and Food Science |
| Nor, Norw | Norwegian |
| Nrsng, Nurs | Nursing |
| NucEg | Nuclear Energy |
| NucSc | Nuclear Science |
| Nutr, Nutrn | Nutrition |
| NutSc | Nutritional Sciences |
| | |
| OAd, OAdm, OfAdm, OffAd | Office Administration |
| Ocean | Oceanography |
| OR | Outdoor Recreation |
| OrgB | Organizational Behavior |
| OrStu | Oriental Studies |
| OT | Occupational Therapy |
| | |
| PA, PAd, PAdm | Police Administration |
| PAdm, PbAd, PuAdm, PubAd | Public Administration |
| PAIR | Personnel Administration and Industrial Relations |
| PBM | Personal Business Management |
| PC, PCl | Pest Control |
| PCD | Principles of Curriculum Design |
| PCG | Psychology, Counseling and Guidance |
| PCn | Peer Counseling |
| PE, PEd, PEdu, PhEd, PhyEd | Physical Education |
| PerDe, PerDv | Personal Development |
| Persi | Persian |
| PGS | Psychology (General Studies) |
| Pharm | Pharmacology, Pharmacy |
| Phi, Phil, Philos | Philosophy |
| Photo | Photography |
| Phs, Phycs, Phys | Physics |
| PhSc, PhSci, PhySc, PS | Physical Sciences |
| PIAD | Problems in American Democracy |
| PlEd | Paralegal Education |
| PlS, PlSci | Plant Sciences |
| PlSc, Pol, PolS, PolSc, PolSi, PoSci, PS, PSci | Political Science |
| Plsh | Polish |
| PMR | Physical, Medical Rehabilitation |
| PNG | Petroleum and Natural Gas |
| Polic | Police Science |
| Port | Portuguese |
| PPath | Plant Pathology |
| PPe | Psychology of Personality |
| PrArt | Practical Arts |
| PreS | Preschool |
| PrPM | Procurement and Property Management |
| PSS | Plant and Soil Science |
| Psy, Psyc, Psych | Psychology |
| Pt | Petroleum |
| PTher | Physical Therapy |
| PubHl | Public Health |
| PuR | Public Relations |
| PvMed | Preventive Medicine |
| | |
| QBA | Quantitative Business Analysis |
| QM, QMeth | Quantitative Methods |
| QMB | Quantitative Methods of Business |

| | |
|---|---|
| R&TC | Research and Training Center in Mental Retardation |
| RadTV | Radio/Television |
| RcPk, RecPk | Recreation and Parks |
| RE, RlEs, RlEst | Real Estate |
| Read | Reading |
| Rec | Recreation |
| RecEd | Recreation Education |
| RecLe | Recreation and Leisure |
| RecPA | Recreation and Park Administration |
| REF | Research and Foundations |
| Rehab | Rehabilitation Studies |
| REI | Real Estate and Insurance |
| Rel, Relig, RelS, Rlgn | |
| RlSt | Religion (Religious Studies) |
| Res | Resources |
| Rhet | Rhetoric |
| RHIM | Restaurant, Hotel, and Institutional Management |
| RngSc | Range Science |
| RNR | Renewable Natural Resources |
| Rom | Romance Languages |
| RS | Reading and Study Skills |
| Rus, Russ | Russian |
| RuSoc | Rural Sociology |
| | |
| Sales | Salesmanship |
| SAT | SAT Review |
| Sc, Sci, Scien | Science |
| Scan, Scand | Scandinavian Languages |
| ScEd | Science Education |
| SDA, SpDrA | Speech and Dramatic Arts |
| SEAs, SEAS | Southeast Asian Studies |
| SecEd | Secondary Education |
| Secr, SecTr | Secretarial Training |
| SEd | Safety Education |
| SelfD | Self-Development |
| Sfty | Safety |
| Shhnd, Shthd | Shorthand |
| SHS | Speech and Hearing Sciences |
| Slav | Slavic Languages and Literature |
| SMT | Social Management of Technology |
| SoAn | Sociology/Anthropology |
| Soc, Soci, Socio | Sociology |
| SocHS | Social Studies, high school level |
| SocS, SoS, SoSc, SoSci | Social Science |
| SocSt, SoStu, SS, SSt | Social Studies |
| SocW, SocWk, SoW, SoWk, | |
| SWk | Social Work |
| SoEng | Sophomore English |
| SoJu | Society and Justice |
| SoP | Social Psychology |
| SOP | Secretarial Office Procedure |
| SoWel | Social Welfare |
| Sp | Speech and Theater |
| Span | Spanish |
| Spch, Speec, Sph | Speech |
| SpCHR | Speech Communications and Human Relations |
| SpDrA | Speech and Dramatic Arts |
| Spe | Speech Communication |

| | |
|---|---|
| SpE, SpEd, SplEd | Special Education |
| SPEA | School of Public and Environmental Affairs |
| SrEng | Senior English |
| SSt | Social Studies, Southern Studies |
| SST | Security Safety Technology |
| Sta, Stat | Statistics |
| STC | School of Technical Careers |
| StSki, StSkl, Study, | |
| StuSk | Study Skills |
| Sup | Supervision |
| Sur | Surveying |
| Swed | Swedish |
| | |
| TAM | Theoretical and Applied Mechanics |
| TchPr | Teacher Preparation |
| TCom | Telecommunications |
| Tech | Technology |
| TEd | Teacher Education |
| Th, Thea, Theat | Theater |
| ThArt | Theater Arts |
| Theo | Theology |
| Thy | Therapy |
| Trans | Transportation |
| Trg | Trigonometry |
| TV | Television |
| Type, Typew, Typg | Typewriting |
| | |
| UC | University College |
| UConj | University Conjoint Courses |
| UnStu | University Studies |
| UrPl | Urban Planning |
| USGov | United States Government |
| USHis | United States History |
| | |
| VEd, Voc, VocEd | Vocational Education |
| VetSc | Veterinary Sciences |
| VisAr | Visual Arts |
| VocT, VoTec | Vocational and Technical Education, Vocational Technology |
| VTIE | Vocational, Trade, and Industrial Education |
| | |
| WCiv | Western Civilization |
| WGS | World Geography Studies |
| WHS | World History Studies |
| Wildl, WlfSc | Wildlife Science |
| WmSt, WnStu, WomS, WomSt, | |
| WSt | Women's Studies |
| Writ, Writi | Writing |
| WshMg | Watershed Management |
| | |
| YthLd | Youth Leadership |
| | |
| Zoo, Zool, Zoolo | Zoology |

# INSTITUTIONS AND CORRESPONDENCE COURSES OFFERED

# ① ADAMS STATE COLLEGE

Mr. Donald F. Eden
Director of Extension Division
Adams State College
Alamosa, Colorado 81102
Phone: 303-589-7671

Enrollment on a noncredit basis accepted in all credit courses. Gifted high school students are permitted to enroll in undergraduate courses for credit. Overseas enrollment accepted for college courses.

| NCES No. | Course Title | Dept. | Course No. | Credits | Level |
|---|---|---|---|---|---|
| | **College courses** | | | | |
| 070516 | Math for elem teachers | Math | 108A | 3S | L |
| 070516 | Math for elem teachers | Math | 108B | 3S | L |
| 160301 | Arithmetic | Math | 103 | 3S | L |
| 160302 | Algebra | Math | 104 | 3S | L |
| 160406 | Differential equations | Math | 327 | 3S | U |
| 161201 | Math for business majors | Math | 206A | 3S | L |
| 161201 | Math for business majors | Math | 206B | 3S | L |

# ② ARIZONA STATE UNIVERSITY

Ms. Shari Westbrook
Admissions Clerk
Correspondence Study Office
ASB 112, Off-Campus Academic Services
Arizona State University
Temple, Arizona 85287
Phone: 602-965-6563

Only in exceptional cases are gifted high school students permitted to enroll in undergraduate courses for credit. Overseas enrollment accepted.

| NCES No. | Course Title | Dept. | Course No. | Credits | Level |
|---|---|---|---|---|---|
| | **College courses** | | | | |
| 040601 | Business communications | Bus | AD233 | 3S | L |
| 040604 | Business report writing | Bus | AD431 | 3S | U |
| 040904 | Principles of management | Mgmt | MG301 | 3S | U |
| 0499 | Elmnts of bus enterprise | Bus | AD101 | 3S | L |
| 0499 | Business law | Bus | AD305 | 3S | U |
| 0499 | Business law | Bus | AD306 | 3S | U |
| 051199 | Urban communication | Commu | CO494 | 3S | U |
| 051199 | Intercultural communicats | Commu | CO363 | 3S | U |
| 051199 | Crisis communication | Commu | CO478 | 3S | U |
| 051199 | Death and dying | Commu | CO494 | 3S | U |
| 051199 | Woman and communications | Commu | CO494 | 3S | U |
| 051199 | Communication and aging | Commu | CO479 | 3S | U |
| 051199 | Medical communication | Commu | CO494 | 3S | U |
| 051299 | Nonverbal communication | Commu | CO330 | 3S | U |
| 051299 | Sktch skls for spch clncn | SHS | CD294 | 1S | L |
| 070302 | Comm behav in elem school | Educ | CO415 | 3S | U |
| 070303 | Prin & curr of sec schls | Educ | SE311 | 3S | U |
| 070520 | Educational psychology | Educ | ED310 | 3S | U |
| 070520 | St: principles of beh mod | EdP | ED494 | 3S | U |
| 070610 | Reading in content areas | Educ | RD467 | 2S | U |
| 070610 | Practicum rdg in content | Educ | RD480 | 1S | U |
| 0708 | Orientation to ed ex chil | SpE | 311 | 3S | U |
| 070805 | Intro to learnng disabilt | SpE | 361 | 3S | U |
| 070805 | Mthds of rmdtng lrng dsab | SpE | 494 | 3S | U |
| 070806 | Mental retardation | Educ | SP312 | 3S | U |
| 070811 | Nature of stuttering | SHS | 494 | 3S | U |
| 0799 | Exploration of education | Educ | ED111 | 3S | L |
| 100313 | Human nutrition | HmEc | FO141 | 3S | L |
| 100602 | Family relationships | HmEc | FA331 | 3S | U |
| 120299 | Books for children | LiS | LI494 | 3S | U |
| 120307 | C S Lewis | EnglL | 345 | 3S | U |
| 1210 | Elementary French | Frnch | FR101 | 4S | L |
| 1210 | Elementary French | Frnch | FO102 | 4S | L |
| 1210 | Intermediate French | Frnch | FR201 | 4S | L |
| 1210 | Intermediate French | Frnch | FR202 | 4S | L |
| 1211 | Elementary German | Ger | 101 | 4S | L |
| 1211 | Elementary German | Ger | 102 | 4S | L |
| 1225 | Elementary Spanish | Span | SP101 | 4S | L |
| 1225 | Elementary Spanish | Span | SP102 | 4S | L |
| 1225 | Intermediate Spanish | Span | SP201 | 4S | L |
| 1225 | Intermediate Spanish | Span | SP202 | 4S | L |
| 1225 | Spanish conversation | Span | SP313 | 3S | U |

| NCES No. | Course Title | Dept. | Course No. | Credits | Level |
|---|---|---|---|---|---|
| 1507 | Ideas of physics | Phs | 370 | 3S | U |
| 160302 | Intermediate algebra | Math | MA106 | 3S | L |
| 160302 | College algebra | Math | MA117 | 3S | L |
| 160602 | Plane trigonometry | Math | MA118 | 3S | L |
| 160901 | Mathematical analysis | Math | MA210 | 3S | L |
| 2099 | Intro to psychology | Psych | PG100 | 3S | L |
| 2099 | Prsnlty thry and research | Psych | PG315 | 3S | U |
| 2099 | Abnormal psychology | PGS | PG466 | 3S | U |
| 220201 | Principles of economics | Econ | EC201 | 3S | L |
| 220201 | Principles of economics | Econ | EC202 | 3S | L |
| 220423 | Japan | Hist | HI477 | 3S | U |
| 220423 | Japan | Hist | HI478 | 3S | U |
| 220423 | Asian civilizations | Hist | HI305 | 3S | U |
| 220423 | Asian civilizations | Hist | HI306 | 3S | U |
| 220426 | Hitler—man and legend | Hist | HI434 | 3S | U |
| 220432 | United States history | Hist | HI103 | 3S | L |
| 220432 | United States history | Hist | HI104 | 3S | L |
| 220432 | American urban history | Hist | HI419 | 3S | U |
| 220432 | American urban history | Hist | HI420 | 3S | U |
| 220432 | The West in 20th century | Hist | HI369 | 3S | U |
| 220432 | The American Southwest | Hist | HI425 | 3S | U |
| 220433 | Western civilization | Hist | HI102 | 3S | L |
| 220453 | Modern American cltrl his | Hist | HI304 | 3S | U |
| 220453 | Contemporary America | Hist | HI411 | 3S | U |
| 220501 | American national govt | PolSc | PO300 | 3S | U |
| 220501 | Az constitution and govt | PolSc | PO311 | 2S | U |
| 220505 | The US and Japan | Hist | HI471 | 3S | U |
| 220602 | The justice system | CrJ | CR100 | 3S | U |
| 220602 | The police function | CrJ | CR306 | 3S | U |
| 220602 | Justice theory | CrJ | CR100 | 3S | U |
| 220602 | Rsrch in justice studies | CrJ | CR301 | 3S | U |
| 220605 | Courtship and marriage | Socio | SO305 | 3S | U |
| 220615 | Women's roles | Socio | SO464 | 3S | U |
| 220699 | Socio of deviant behavior | Socio | SO340 | 3S | U |
| 220699 | Intro to sociology | Socio | SO101 | 3S | L |

# ③ ATHABASCA UNIVERSITY

Student Services Office
Athabasca University
Box 10000
Athabasca, Alberta TOG 2RO
Canada
Phone: 403-645-6111

Enrollment on a noncredit basis accepted in all credit courses. Only in exceptional cases are gifted high school students permitted to enroll in undergraduate courses for credit. No overseas enrollment accepted. All programs are offered through home study. All students have a telephone tutor.

| NCES No. | Course Title | Dept. | Course No. | Credits | Level |
|---|---|---|---|---|---|
| | **College courses** | | | | |
| 030399 | Hist pop music 1: 1900-40 | Hum | 285 | 3U | L |
| 030399 | Hist pop music 2: 1940-70 | Hum | 286 | 3U | L |
| 040108 | Intro financial acctg | Acctg | 253 | 3U | L |
| 040108 | Intermediate fin acctg I | Acctg | 351 | 3U | U |
| 040108 | Intermediate fin acctg II | Acctg | 352 | 3U | U |
| 040111 | Intro managerial acctg | Acctg | 254 | 3U | L |
| 040111 | Intermed managerial acctg | Acctg | 354 | 3U | U |
| 040301 | Intro to financial mgmt | Fnce | 370 | 3U | U |
| 040312 | Canadian public finance | PubAd | 390 | 3U | U |
| 040901 | Business policy | Admn | 404 | 3U | U |
| 040903 | Commu & problem solving | Comm | 377 | 3U | U |
| 040903 | Organizational behaviour | OrgBl | 364 | 3U | U |
| 040904 | Administrative principles | Admn | 232 | 3U | L |
| 040999 | Motivation and management | Admn | 319 | 6U | U |
| 040999 | Small business management | Admn | 373 | 3U | U |
| 041001 | Intro to marketing | Mktg | 398 | 3U | U |
| 0411 | Intro personnel mgmt | OrgB | 386 | 3U | U |
| 051103 | Intro interpersonal commu | Comm | 229 | 3U | L |
| 051103 | Prac interpersonal commu | Comm | 329 | 3U | U |
| 051103 | Interpersonal commu, mgmt | Comm | 243 | 3U | L |
| 060799 | Intro BASIC programming | CmpSc | 203 | 3U | L |
| 060799 | Fortran programming | CmpSc | 220 | 3U | L |
| 060799 | Computer prog with Pascal | CmpSc | 268 | 3U | L |
| 0699 | Science projects | Sci | 314 | 3U | U |
| 070509 | Prin tchng/lrng hlth prof | ApSt | 382 | 3U | U |
| 090703 | Environmental impact asmt | EnvSt | 347 | 3U | U |

| NCES No. | Course Title | Dept. | Course No. | Credits | Level |
|---|---|---|---|---|---|
| 090999 | Research in nursing | ApSt | 325 | 3U | U |
| 120201 | Comp lit & great authors | Engl | 339 | 6U | U |
| 120201 | Comp Canadian literature | Engl | 350 | 6U | U |
| 120299 | Images of man in mod lit | Engl | 301 | 3U | U |
| 120299 | Shakespeare 1 | Engl | 324 | 3U | U |
| 120299 | Trends in mod Brit drama | Engl | 332 | 3U | U |
| 120299 | Lit of Canadian West | Engl | 337 | 6U | U |
| 120299 | Plays of Ibsen & Shaw | Engl | 392 | 3U | U |
| 120299 | Nineteenth-cen Engl novel | Engl | 395 | 6U | U |
| 120299 | Shakespeare 2 | Engl | 396 | 3U | U |
| 120299 | Twentieth-cent Engl novel | Engl | 397 | 6U | U |
| 120299 | History of drama | Engl | 300 | 3U | U |
| 120299 | Literature for children | Engl | 305 | 3U | U |
| 120299 | American literature I | Engl | 344 | 3U | U |
| 120307 | Literary forms & technol | Engl | 210 | 6U | L |
| 120307 | Intro to Canadian lit | Engl | 302 | 6U | U |
| 120310 | Writing skills | Engl | 255 | 3U | L |
| 120310 | Advanced composition | Engl | 353 | 3U | U |
| 1210 | Ensemble: Fr for beginner | Frnch | 103 | 6U | L |
| 1210 | Sur le vif: 1st-yr French | Frnch | 242 | 6U | L |
| 1210 | Allez France: 2nd-yr Fren | Frnch | 361 | 6U | U |
| 1210 | Français pour tous | Frnch | 312 | 3U | U |
| 1210 | Directed studies in Frnch | Frnch | 398 | 3U | U |
| 1210 | Surv 20th-cent Frnch lit | Frnch | 363 | 3S | U |
| 1302 | Commercial law | LgRl | 369 | 3U | U |
| 150304 | World ecology | Bio | 201 | 6U | L |
| 150316 | Wild flowers | Bio | 321 | 3U | U |
| 150324 | Le corps humain (Fr) | Bio | 104 | 3U | L |
| 150326 | Human genetics | Bio | 341 | 3U | U |
| 150399 | Human sexuality | Bio | 378 | 3U | U |
| 150399 | Human physiology | Bio | 230 | 6U | L |
| 150401 | Chemical principles | Chem | 209 | 6U | L |
| 150408 | Organic chemistry | Chem | 320 | 3U | U |
| 1505 | Understanding the earth | Geol | 231 | 6U | L |
| 150599 | Our physical resources | Geol | 313 | 3U | U |
| 1599 | Science projects | Sci | 314 | 3U | U |
| 1603 | Algebra & analytic geom | Math | 101 | 3U | L |
| 160401 | Intro to calculus | Math | 265 | 3U | L |
| 160401 | Intro to calculus II | Math | 266 | 3U | L |
| 160406 | Ordinary diff equations | Math | 376 | 3U | U |
| 160602 | Trigonometry | Math | 102 | 3U | L |
| 1608 | Intro to statistics | Math | 215 | 3U | L |
| 161101 | Business mathematics | Math | 244 | 3U | L |
| 161199 | Research in nursing | ApSt | 325 | 3U | U |
| 1699 | Science projects | Sci | 314 | 3U | U |
| 180405 | East meets West | Hum | 360 | 3U | U |
| 1805 | Critical thinking | Phil | 252 | 3U | U |
| 2001 | Psych as natural science | Psych | 289 | 3U | L |
| 2001 | General psychology | Psych | 290 | 3U | L |
| 200104 | Behaviour principles | Psych | 322 | 3U | U |
| 2002 | Biological psychology | Psych | 402 | 3U | U |
| 200406 | Learning | Psych | 387 | 3U | U |
| 200406 | Intro learng disabilities | Psych | 389 | 3U | U |
| 200408 | Cognitive psychology | Psych | 355 | 3U | U |
| 200501 | Abnormal psychology | Psych | 335 | 3U | U |
| 200504 | Intro child development | Psych | 228 | 3U | L |
| 200504 | Social psych/adult devmt | Psych | 381 | 3U | U |
| 200504 | Psych de l'enfant (Fr) | Psych | 257 | 3U | L |
| 200802 | Counseling girls & women | Psych | 343 | 3U | U |
| 200802 | Intro to counseling | Psych | 388 | 3U | U |
| 210113 | Public policy | PubAd | 403 | 3U | U |
| 210199 | Canadian public admin | PubAd | 390 | 3U | U |
| 210199 | Administrative law | LgRl | 331 | 3U | U |
| 2201 | Intro human diversity | Anthr | 207 | 6U | L |
| 220103 | Ethnography: princ in pra | Anthr | 382 | 3U | U |
| 220199 | Anthropology & the city | Anthr | 394 | 3U | U |
| 220199 | Patterns/process in anthr | Anthr | 334 | 3U | U |
| 220199 | The Inuit way | Anthr | 307 | 3U | U |
| 220201 | Macroeconomics | Econ | 246 | 3U | L |
| 220201 | Microeconomics | Econ | 247 | 3U | L |
| 220305 | Intro to physical geog | Geog | 261 | 3U | L |
| 220305 | Lab-intro to phys geog | Geog | 262 | 3U | L |
| 220399 | Man & environment | Geog | 317 | 6U | U |
| 220402 | Can-Amer relations | Hist | 342 | 3U | U |
| 220406 | From Sumer to Athens | Hum | 248 | 3U | L |
| 220406 | Rome & early Christianity | Hum | 249 | 3U | L |
| 220407 | Era of world wars | Hist | 264 | 3U | L |
| 220409 | Western family in history | Hist | 399 | 3U | U |
| 220425 | Canadian his: 1500-1867 | Hist | 224 | 3U | L |
| 220425 | Canadian his: 1867-presnt | Hist | 225 | 3U | L |
| 220425 | Hist of Canadian West | Hist | 338 | 6U | U |
| 220425 | Hist Canadian labour | Hist | 336 | 6U | U |

| NCES No. | Course Title | Dept. | Course No. | Credits | Level |
|---|---|---|---|---|---|
| 220426 | Revolutionary Europe | Hist | 263 | 3U | L |
| 220433 | World War II | Hist | 367 | 3U | U |
| 220472 | Hist women in North Amer | Hist | 325 | 6U | U |
| 2205 | Power, control & lib dem | PolSc | 214 | 3U | L |
| 220599 | Canadian govt & politics | PolSc | 309 | 3U | L |
| 2206 | Intro sociology | Socio | 289 | 6U | L |
| 2206 | Sociological perspective | Socio | 315 | 6U | U |
| 2206 | Intro modern society | Socio | 288 | 3U | U |
| 220605 | Family in world perspec | SoAn | 384 | 3U | U |
| 220605 | Sociology of the family | Socio | 316 | 3U | U |
| 220606 | Contemp socio theory | Socio | 337 | 3U | U |
| 220610 | Sociology of deviance | Socio | 365 | 3U | U |
| 220611 | Sociology of work | Socio | 321 | 3U | U |
| 220614 | Canadian urban developmnt | Geog | 310 | 6U | U |
| 220699 | Sex roles | SoAn | 385 | 3U | U |
| 220699 | Technology and change | Hum | 259 | 3U | L |
| 2299 | Intro human communities | LibSt | 202 | 6U | L |
| 2299 | Making sense of society | SoSc | 226 | 6U | L |
| 2299 | Res methods in social sci | SoSc | 366 | 3U | U |
| 2299 | Perspectives on women | WmSt | 267 | 3U | U |

④ **AUBURN UNIVERSITY**

Becky S. Duning
Director, Independent Study Program
Mell Hall
Auburn University
Auburn, Alabama 36849
Phone: 205-826-5103

Enrollment on a noncredit basis accepted in all credit courses. Overseas enrollment accepted for college and noncredit courses. Gifted high school students may enroll in undergraduate courses with principal's recommendation.

| NCES No. | Course Title | Dept. | Course No. | Credits | Level |
|---|---|---|---|---|---|
| | **College courses** | | | | |
| 040601 | Written business commu | Engl | 415 | 3Q | U |
| 040604 | Bus & prof report writing | Engl | 315 | 3Q | U |
| 050402 | Technical writing | Engl | 304 | 3Q | U |
| 0701 | Development of voc ed | VEd | 541 | 5Q | U |
| 0706 | Org of inst in vo-tech ed | VEd | 574 | 5Q | U |
| 0708 | Probs in tchg disadv adlt | VEd | 591 | 5Q | U |
| 0799 | Learning res in voc ed | VEd | 556 | 5Q | U |
| 100313 | Nutrition and man | NF | 112 | 3Q | L |
| 100602 | Structure & func of fam | HmEc | 270 | 4Q | L |
| 100603 | Maturity & aging | Psych | 507 | 5Q | U |
| 120307 | Survey of English lit | Engl | 253 | 5Q | L |
| 120307 | The short story | EnglLL | 325 | 5Q | U |
| 1503 | Perspectives in biology | Bio | 105 | 5Q | L |
| 160302 | College algebra | Math | 140 | 5Q | L |
| 1604 | Precalculus with trig | Math | 160 | 5Q | L |
| 190104 | Hist & principles of PE | HSci | 201 | 3Q | L |
| 1905 | Health science | HSci | 195 | 2Q | L |
| 1905 | Community health | HSci | 296 | 3Q | L |
| 190704 | Recreation leadership | HSci | 386 | 3Q | U |
| 190799 | Principles of recreation | HSci | 282 | 3Q | L |
| 200901 | Industrial psychology | Psych | 561 | 5Q | U |
| 2099 | Psychology | Psych | 211 | 5Q | L |
| 210301 | Criminal justice | PolSc | 336 | 3Q | U |
| 220201 | Economics I | Econ | 200 | 5Q | L |
| 220201 | Economics II | Econ | 202 | 5Q | L |
| 220302 | Economic geography | Geog | 302 | 5Q | U |
| 220399 | Principles of geography | Geog | 102 | 5Q | L |
| 220426 | European hist 1500-1815 | Hist | HY207 | 5Q | L |
| 220427 | History of Latin America | Hist | HY300 | 5Q | U |
| 220428 | History of Alabama | Hist | HY381 | 5Q | U |
| 220432 | Hist of the US to 1865 | Hist | HY202 | 5Q | L |
| 220432 | Am syst & Jacksonian dem | Hist | HY403 | 5Q | U |
| 220432 | Hist of the US since 1865 | Hist | HY202 | 5Q | L |
| 220499 | History of the West | Hist | HY371 | 5Q | U |
| 220501 | Intro to American govt | PolSc | 209 | 5Q | L |
| 220511 | American st & local govt | PolSc | 210 | 5Q | L |
| 220601 | Community organization | Agri | 362 | 5Q | U |
| 220602 | Criminology | Socio | 302 | 5Q | U |
| 220608 | Rural social organization | Socio | 561 | 5Q | U |
| 220613 | Social problems | Socio | 202 | 5Q | L |
| 220699 | Introduction to sociology | Socio | 201 | 5Q | L |
| 220699 | Minority groups | Socio | 304 | 5Q | U |

④ *Auburn University*

| NCES No. | Course Title | Dept. | Course No. | Credits | Level |
|---|---|---|---|---|---|
| | **Noncredit courses** | | | | |
| 051103 | Interpersonal communica | Psych | | NC | L |
| 100603 | Planning retirement | Psych | | NC | L |
| 100702 | Dietary mgr indep study | NF | DM | NC | L |
| 100702 | Dietary mgr suppmtl pract | NF | DMSP | NC | L |

⑤ **BALL STATE UNIVERSITY**

Dr. M. E. Ratliff
Director, Independent Study
Carmichael Hall, School of Continuing Education
Ball State University
Muncie, Indiana 47306
Phone: 317-285-1581

Gifted high school students are permitted to enroll in undergraduate courses for credit. No overseas enrollment accepted.

| NCES No. | Course Title | Dept. | Course No. | Credits | Level |
|---|---|---|---|---|---|
| | **College courses** | | | | |
| 0304 | Intro to theater | ThArt | 100 | 4Q | L |
| 0304 | Modern drama | ThArt | 310 | 4Q | L |
| 030402 | History of theater | ThArt | 410 | 4Q | L |
| 0401 | Elem of accty 1 | Accty | 201 | 3Q | L |
| 040107 | Elem of accty 2 | Accty | 202 | 3Q | L |
| 040107 | Elem of accty 3 | Accty | 203 | 3Q | L |
| 040203 | Records administration | BEOA | 253 | 4Q | L |
| 0407 | Prin of insurance | Ins | 370 | 4Q | U |
| 040903 | Operations management | Mgmt | 282 | 4Q | L |
| 040904 | Mgt principles | Mgmt | 280 | 4Q | L |
| 041103 | Mgt of human resources | Mgmt | 281 | 4Q | L |
| 041106 | Industrial supervision | Mgmt | 283 | 4Q | L |
| 050102 | Advertising fund print me | Journ | 250 | 4Q | L |
| 0506 | Mass communications media | Journ | 100 | 4Q | L |
| 050602 | Intro to journalistic wri | Journ | 120 | 4Q | L |
| 050608 | Feature and column writin | Journ | 312 | 4Q | U |
| 100206 | Personal finance | Fin | 110 | 4Q | L |
| 120201 | World literature | Engl | 205 | 4Q | L |
| 1203 | English comp 1 | Engl | 103 | 4Q | L |
| 1203 | English comp 2 | Engl | 104 | 4Q | L |
| 1501 | Mysteries of the sky | Astro | 100 | 4Q | L |
| 150201 | Climate | Geog | 331 | 4Q | U |
| 150202 | Weather 1 | Geog | 230 | 4Q | L |
| 1505 | Geol nat parks | Geol | 203 | 4Q | L |
| 150501 | Geomorphology | Geol | 210 | 4Q | L |
| 150501 | Geomorphology of North Am | Geol | 411 | 4Q | U |
| 150599 | World political geog | Geog | 470 | 4Q | U |
| 150599 | Historical geology | Geog | 102 | 4Q | L |
| 1506 | Oceanography | Geol | 420 | 4Q | U |
| 150702 | Intro to energy space sci | Phycs | 100 | 4Q | L |
| 160802 | Elem statistics | Psych | 241 | 4Q | L |
| 180301 | Ethics | Philo | 202 | 4Q | L |
| 1804 | Intro to philosophy | Philo | 100 | 4Q | L |
| 190303 | Intro to sport in Am life | ID | 205 | 4Q | L |
| 200103 | General psychology | Psych | 100 | 4Q | L |
| 2103 | Intro Am crim justice | CJC | 101 | 4Q | L |
| 210301 | Intro to corrections | CJC | 260 | 4Q | L |
| 210301 | Probation and parole | CJC | 361 | 4Q | U |
| 210304 | Data and theory crim deli | CJC | 210 | 4Q | L |
| 210304 | Proc adult and juven offe | CJC | 211 | 4Q | L |
| 210304 | Fund of law enforcement | CJC | 230 | 4Q | L |
| 2202 | Elements of economics 1 | Econ | 200 | 4Q | L |
| 2202 | Elements of economics 2 | Econ | 201 | 4Q | L |
| 220201 | Survey of econ ideas | Econ | 116 | 4Q | L |
| 2203 | Global geog for teachers | Geog | 105 | 3Q | L |
| 2203 | Global geog | Geog | 150 | 4Q | L |
| 220301 | Geog of cultural environ | Geog | 121 | 4Q | L |
| 220302 | Econ geog and contemp iss | Geog | 120 | 4Q | L |
| 220305 | Elem of physical geog | Geog | 110 | 4Q | L |
| 220305 | Phy geog earth sci teache | Geog | 111 | 4Q | L |
| 220306 | Indiana crossroads Americ | Geog | 255 | 4Q | L |
| 220306 | Geog of US and Canada | Geog | 350 | 4Q | U |
| 220306 | Geog of Europe | Geog | 355 | 4Q | U |
| 220399 | Earth sea and sky geo vie | Geog | 101 | 4Q | L |
| 220399 | Agri and rural geography | Geog | 324 | 4Q | U |
| 2204 | Intro hist bus in US | Hist | 110 | 4Q | L |
| 220402 | Natl vs sect US 1820-1860 | Hist | 405 | 4Q | U |
| 220409 | Hist Am popular cultures | Hist | 222 | 4Q | L |
| 220421 | Found of US 1492-1829 | Hist | 201 | 4Q | L |
| 220421 | Colonial and tran-Applach | Hist | 418 | 4Q | U |
| 220422 | The world in recent times | Hist | 153 | 4Q | L |
| 220426 | Birth of modern world | Hist | 152 | 4Q | L |
| 220427 | The Spanish borderlands | Hist | 327 | 4Q | U |
| 220428 | History of Indiana | Hist | 415 | 4Q | U |
| 220432 | Dev of the United States | Hist | 202 | 4Q | L |
| 220432 | Recent past in the US | Hist | 203 | 4Q | L |
| 220432 | Recent US hist 1941-pres | Hist | 413 | 4Q | U |
| 220432 | Trans-Mississippi frontie | Hist | 419 | 4Q | U |
| 220432 | Indians in US history | Hist | 421 | 4Q | U |
| 220452 | Roots of Western traditio | Hist | 151 | 4Q | L |
| 220501 | Am national govt | PolSc | 130 | 4Q | L |
| 220501 | Urban govt in US | PolSc | 238 | 4Q | L |
| 220509 | Public opinion pol proces | PolSc | 370 | 4Q | U |
| 220511 | Comparative state politic | PolSc | 237 | 4Q | L |
| 220511 | Metropolitan problems | PolSc | 438 | 4Q | U |
| 2206 | Prin of sociology | Soc | 100 | 4Q | L |
| 220605 | The family | Soc | 424 | 4Q | U |
| 220610 | Soc of deviant behavior | Soc | 241 | 4Q | L |
| 220613 | Social problems | Soc | 242 | 4Q | L |
| 220699 | Sociology of the future | Soc | 222 | 4Q | L |

⑥ **BRIGHAM YOUNG UNIVERSITY**

Mr. Scott Froerer
Administrator of Student Services
Independent Study
206 Harmon Continuing Education Building
Brigham Young University
Provo, Utah 84604
Phone: 801-378-2868

Enrollment on a noncredit basis accepted in all credit courses. Gifted high school students are permitted to enroll in undergraduate courses for credit. Overseas enrollment accepted.

| NCES No. | Course Title | Dept. | Course No. | Credits | Level |
|---|---|---|---|---|---|
| | **High School courses** | | | | |
| 020103 | Inter design & decoration | HomLv | 6 | HF | H |
| 030302 | Beginning guitar pt 1 | Music | 3 | HF | H |
| 030302 | Beginning guitar pt 2 | Music | 4 | HF | H |
| 030403 | Intro to the theater | EngLL | 47 | HF | H |
| 040104 | Bookkeeping 1 pt 1 | Bus | 2 | HF | H |
| 040104 | Bookkeeping 1 pt 2 | Bus | 3 | HF | H |
| 040111 | Understanding 1981 taxes | Bus | 6 | HF | H |
| 040199 | Business law pt 1 | Bus | 11 | HF | H |
| 040199 | Business law pt 2 | Bus | 12 | HF | H |
| 040205 | Shorthand: Gregg Pt 1 | Bus | 8 | HF | H |
| 040205 | Shorthand: Gregg Pt 2 | Bus | 9 | HF | H |
| 040207 | Beginning typing Pt 1 | Bus | 4 | HF | H |
| 040207 | Beginning typing Pt 2 | Bus | 5 | HF | H |
| 0403 | Finance and credit | Bus | 35 | HF | H |
| 040502 | Starting your own busnss | Bus | 29 | HF | H |
| 040502 | Ldg and supv in busnss | Bus | 32 | HF | H |
| 040999 | Work experience | Bus | 1 | HF | H |
| 041001 | Merchandising | Bus | 17 | HF | H |
| 041001 | Gen merchandise retailing | Bus | 38 | HF | H |
| 041003 | Creative selling | Bus | 20 | HF | H |
| 041003 | Basic salesmanship | Bus | 19 | HF | H |
| 041099 | Wholesaling & phys distri | Bus | 18 | HF | H |
| 041099 | Petroleum marketing | Bus | 39 | HF | H |
| 0411 | Survival today | SoSci | 23 | HF | H |
| 0413 | Real estate | Bus | 40 | HF | H |
| 0501 | Advertising services | Bus | 33 | HF | H |
| 050101 | Advertising | Bus | 21 | HF | H |
| 050102 | Display and promotion | Bus | 22 | HF | H |
| 050199 | Communications in mrktng | Bus | 25 | HF | H |
| 050499 | Man & mass media pt 1 | EngLL | 36 | HF | H |
| 0509 | Psych & hum rel in mrktng | Bus | 27 | HF | H |
| 051101 | Intro to pub speaking 1 | EngLL | 45 | HF | H |
| 061101 | Computer literacy | CmpSc | 1 | HF | H |
| 0799 | Eff study & adjst to coll | SoSci | 25 | HF | H |
| 090101 | General health | HSci | 1 | HF | H |
| 090272 | Home nursing pt 1 | HomLv | 14 | HF | H |
| 090302 | The drug scene | Sci | 5 | HF | H |
| 1001 | Fashion merchandising | Bus | 34 | HF | H |
| 100103 | Clothing selection & care | HomLv | 4 | QT | H |
| 100104 | Basic clothg constr pt 1 | HomLv | 1 | HF | H |

| NCES No. | Course Title | Dept. | Course No. | Credits | Level |
|---|---|---|---|---|---|
| 1003 | Food marketing | Bus | 36 | HF | H |
| 100309 | Food services | Bus | 37 | HF | H |
| 100311 | Food and your future | HomLv | 5 | HF | H |
| 100401 | Practical decision making | SoSci | 22 | HF | H |
| 100601 | Child development pt 1 | HomLv | 7 | HF | H |
| 100601 | Child development pt 2 | HomLv | 8 | HF | H |
| 100699 | Preprg fr resp parenthood | HomLv | 16 | HF | H |
| 110104 | House wiring | IndEd | 4 | HF | H |
| 110205 | Leathercraft | IndEd | 1 | HF | H |
| 110406 | Upholstry repair | IndEd | 2 | HF | H |
| 110412 | Small engine repair | IndEd | 6 | HF | H |
| 110413 | Auto fundamentals Pt 1 | IndEd | 7 | HF | H |
| 110413 | Auto fundamentals Pt 2 | IndEd | 8 | HF | H |
| 110413 | Auto body repair | IndEd | 5 | HF | H |
| 110503 | Keys to drawing accuracy | Art | 3 | HF | H |
| 110504 | General photography | Sci | 18 | HF | H |
| 110599 | General art Pt 1 | Art | 1 | HF | H |
| 110599 | General art Pt 2 | Art | 2 | HF | H |
| 120305 | 9th grade English Pt 1 | EngLL | 1 | HF | F |
| 120305 | 9th grade English Pt 2 | EngLL | 2 | HF | H |
| 120305 | Business English | EngLL | 9 | HF | H |
| 120305 | Basic spelling skills | EngLL | 42 | HF | H |
| 120307 | The year 2100 | EngLL | 18 | QT | H |
| 120307 | Self-esteem | EngLL | 12 | QT | H |
| 120307 | Bible as literature | EngLL | 22 | HF | H |
| 120307 | Steps to reading literatu | EngLL | 10 | HF | H |
| 120308 | 12th-grade English Pt 2 | EngLL | 8 | HF | H |
| 120308 | Remedial develqt reading | EngLL | 26 | HF | H |
| 120308 | Recreational reading | EngLL | 27 | HF | H |
| 120308 | Reading comp for ind stu | EngLL | 23 | HF | H |
| 120310 | 10th-grade English pt 1 | EngLL | 3 | HF | H |
| 120310 | 10th-grade English pt 2 | EngLL | 4 | HF | H |
| 120310 | 11th-grade English pt 1 | EngLL | 5 | HF | H |
| 120310 | 12th-grade English pt 1 | EngLL | 7 | HF | H |
| 120310 | Comp expo writing | EngLL | 31 | HF | H |
| 120310 | Comp narr description | EngLL | 32 | HF | H |
| 120310 | Creative writing | EngLL | 33 | HF | H |
| 120310 | College writing pt 1 | EngLL | 34 | HF | H |
| 120310 | Editing & proofreading | EngLL | 43 | HF | H |
| 120310 | 11th-grade English pt 2 | EngLL | 6 | HF | H |
| 120399 | Review of fundamentals | EngLL | 20 | HF | H |
| 1207 | Begining Chinese Mandarin | ForLg | 7 | HF | H |
| 1225 | Spanish Pt 1 | ForLg | 3 | HF | H |
| 1225 | Spanish Pt 2 | ForLg | 4 | HF | H |
| 150301 | Biology Pt 1 | Sci | 1 | HF | H |
| 150301 | Biology Pt 2 | Sci | 2 | HF | H |
| 150304 | Ecology Pt 1 | Sci | 3 | HF | H |
| 150304 | Ecology Pt 2 | Sci | 4 | HF | H |
| 150324 | Taxidermy | Sci | 6 | HF | H |
| 150401 | Chemistry Pt 1 | Sci | 16 | HF | H |
| 150401 | Chemistry Pt 2 | Sci | 17 | HF | H |
| 150799 | Nonmath physics Pt 1 | Sci | 9 | HF | H |
| 150799 | Nonmath physics Pt 2 | Sci | 10 | HF | H |
| 150799 | Elements of psychology | SoSci | 31 | QT | H |
| 1509 | Earth & space sci Pt 1 | Sci | 13 | HF | H |
| 1509 | Earth & space sci Pt 2 | Sci | 14 | HF | H |
| 160301 | Remedial arithmetic Pt 1 | Math | 1 | HF | H |
| 160301 | Remedial arithmetic Pt 2 | Math | 2 | HF | H |
| 160301 | Rem arith using a cal pt1 | Math | 18 | HF | H |
| 160301 | Rem arith using a cal pt2 | Math | 19 | HF | H |
| 160302 | 1st course algebra Pt 1 | Math | 5 | HF | H |
| 160302 | 1st course algebra Pt 2 | Math | 6 | HF | H |
| 160302 | 2nd course algebra Pt 1 | Math | 7 | HF | H |
| 160302 | 2nd course algebra Pt 2 | Math | 8 | HF | H |
| 160399 | Computerized rem math 1 | Math | 13 | HF | H |
| 160399 | Computerized rem math 2 | Math | 14 | HF | H |
| 160401 | Calculus with anal geomet | Math | 15 | HF | H |
| 160401 | Calculus with anal geomet | Math | 16 | HF | H |
| 160601 | Plane geometry Pt 1 | Math | 9 | HF | H |
| 160601 | Plane geometry Pt 2 | Math | 10 | HF | H |
| 160602 | Trigonometry Pt 1 | Math | 11 | HF | H |
| 160602 | Trigonometry Pt 2 | Math | 12 | HF | H |
| 161101 | Mathematics in marketing | Bus | 26 | HF | H |
| 161201 | Bus & consumer math pt 1 | Math | 3 | HF | H |
| 161201 | Bus & consumer math pt 2 | Math | 4 | HF | H |
| 190102 | Fitness for living | PhyEd | 3 | HF | H |
| 190102 | Jogging | PhyEd | 139 | HF | H |
| 190103 | Tennis | PhyEd | 4 | HF | H |
| 190103 | Bowling | PhyEd | 5 | HF | H |
| 200199 | Elements psychology Pt 2 | SoSci | 32 | QT | H |
| 200499 | Undstdg & improvg memory | SoSci | 26 | HF | H |
| 200502 | Educ & career planning | SoSci | 20 | HF | H |
| 200799 | Dating–romance & reason | SoSci | 16 | HF | H |
| 2099 | Project self-discovery | SoSci | 39 | HF | H |
| 220201 | Economic problems | SoSci | 19 | HF | H |
| 220208 | Consumer economics | SoSci | 18 | HF | H |
| 220432 | US history–foreign polic | SoSci | 5 | QT | H |
| 220432 | US history–government | SoSci | 6 | QT | H |
| 220432 | American government Pt 1 | SoSci | 12 | HF | H |
| 220432 | American government Pt 2 | SoSci | 13 | HF | H |
| 220432 | US hist: liberty/soc chng | SoSci | 1 | HF | H |
| 220432 | US hist: Amer chrt/ec | SoSci | 2 | HF | H |
| 220432 | US Hist: consti/demo gov | SoSci | 3 | HF | H |
| 220433 | World hist-modern era | SoSci | 7 | QT | H |
| 220433 | World hist: Europe/Asia | SoSci | 8 | HF | H |
| 220433 | World hist: Ltn Am/Mid Ea | SoSci | 9 | HF | H |
| 220499 | How to climb yr fam tree | SoSci | 21 | HF | H |
| 220499 | Current events | SoSci | 38 | HF | H |
| 220601 | Sociology 1 | SoSci | 27 | HF | H |
| 220615 | Sociology 2 | SoSci | 28 | HF | H |

**College courses**

| NCES No. | Course Title | Dept. | Course No. | Credits | Level |
|---|---|---|---|---|---|
| 010602 | Heredity | Bio | 276 | 3S | L |
| 010602 | Heredity | Zool | 276 | 3S | L |
| 030403 | Intro to the theatre | ThArt | 115 | 3S | L |
| 030403 | Playwriting | ThArt | 378R | 3S | U |
| 030502 | 19th-century European art | ArHis | 309 | 3S | U |
| 030603 | Modern art | Art | 310 | 3S | U |
| 0399 | Intro to the humanities | Hum | 101 | 3S | L |
| 040108 | Elementary accounting | Acctg | 201 | 3S | L |
| 040108 | Elementary accounting | Acctg | 202 | 3S | L |
| 040108 | Mathematics of business | Acctg | 232 | 3H | L |
| 040109 | Intro to commercial law | Acctg | 242 | 3S | L |
| 040205 | Shorthand 1 | IM | 111 | 4S | L |
| 040207 | Production typewriting | IM | 203 | 3S | L |
| 040311 | Financial management | Bus | 301 | 3S | U |
| 040601 | Business communications | IM | 320 | 3S | U |
| 041004 | Marketing management | Bus | 341 | 3S | U |
| 050605 | Magazine writing | Commu | 427 | 3S | U |
| 050608 | News writing | Commu | 211 | 3S | L |
| 0509 | Public relations | Commu | 235 | 3S | U |
| 051102 | Analysis of communication | Commu | 100 | 3S | L |
| 051104 | Organ comm & hum develop | Commu | 217 | 3S | L |
| 051107 | Public speaking | Commu | 102 | 3S | L |
| 051107 | Argumentation | Comms | 202 | 3S | L |
| 060103 | Elem computer application | CmpSc | 103 | 2S | L |
| 060799 | Intro comp programming | CmpSc | 142 | 2S | L |
| 070199 | Youth agencies & organiza | YthLd | 344 | 2S | U |
| 070199 | Yth mtgs, activts & con | YthLd | 371 | 2S | U |
| 070199 | Boy Scout leadership | YthLd | 372R2 | 2S | U |
| 070199 | Explorer leadership | YthLd | 372R3 | 2S | U |
| 070199 | Techniques of outdoor adv | YthLd | 378 | 2S | U |
| 070299 | The professional teacher | SecEd | 37665 | 1S | U |
| 070299 | The professional teacher | EdAd | 452 | 1S | U |
| 070301 | Early chil learn experien | ElEd | 515R9 | 2S | U |
| 070309 | Adult education | EdAd | 500 | 2S | U |
| 070309 | Community education | EdAd | 604 | 2S | U |
| 070401 | 5 stps to effctv tutoring | InSci | 51520 | 2S | U |
| 070402 | Creativity in the classrm | SecEd | 37611 | 1S | U |
| 070402 | Improv student behavior | SecEd | 37634 | 1S | U |
| 070402 | Form useful instruc objec | SecEd | 37645 | 1S | U |
| 070402 | Questions that turn stdts | SecEd | 37646 | 1S | U |
| 070402 | Intro to test & appraisal | EdPsy | 501 | 3S | U |
| 070402 | Teaching reading | SecEd | 37652 | 1S | U |
| 070402 | Professional teacher | SecEd | 37665 | 1S | U |
| 070404 | Working with pict & displ | InSci | 51156 | 1S | U |
| 070404 | Projected images multi co | InSci | 51557 | 1S | U |
| 070404 | Using other instru techni | InSci | 51558 | 1S | U |
| 070404 | Improving your teaching | InSci | 515R7 | 1S | U |
| 070512 | Children's literature | ElEd | 340 | 2S | U |
| 070512 | Apply struc tutor mod rdg | InSci | 51522 | 2S | U |
| 070512 | Apply struc tutor adv rdg | InSci | 51524 | 2S | U |
| 070512 | Tutor model rdg sec educ | InSci | 51532 | 2S | U |
| 070512 | Screen stud mat read plac | ElEd | 51410 | 1S | U |
| 070512 | Shakespeare | Engl | 282 | 3S | L |
| 070512 | English fundamentals | Engl | 327 | 3S | U |
| 070512 | Am lit 1914 to mid-centry | Engl | 363 | 3S | U |
| 070516 | Apply struc mod bsc math | InSci | 51525 | 2S | U |
| 070516 | Metric measurements | ElEd | 515R8 | 1S | U |
| 070516 | Metric measurements | SecEd | 515R8 | 1S | U |
| 070599 | Equity in education | EdPsy | 51516 | 2S | U |
| 070602 | Life plan & decision makg | CarEd | 115 | 2S | L |
| 070602 | Career exploration | CarEd | 116 | 1S | L |
| 070602 | Employment strategy | CarEd | 317 | 2S | U |

| NCES No. | Course Title | Dept. | Course No. | Credits | Level |
|---|---|---|---|---|---|
| 070610 | Companion rdg program | InSc | 51518 | 1S | U |
| 070611 | Struc tut tchg Eng 2d lan | InSci | 51531 | 2S | U |
| 070613 | Org adm driver safety ed | HSci | 444 | 2S | U |
| 070613 | Drvr & safety ed workshop | Hlth | 502R | VC | U |
| 070699 | Individ curriculum projec | ElEd | 51515 | TH | U |
| 070699 | Individ curriculum projec | SecEd | 51515 | TH | U |
| 070701 | How to eliminate self-def | EdPsy | 515R1 | 1S | U |
| 070701 | Resolving studt hostility | EdPsy | 515R5 | 2S | U |
| 070701 | Obtaining stu coop class | EdPsy | 51543 | 1S | U |
| 070701 | Counsel guidance services | EdPsy | 545 | 2S | U |
| 070803 | Educ of exceptional child | EdPsy | 205 | 3S | L |
| 070803 | Behav mod tech tchr exce | EdPsy | 51550 | 2S | U |
| 070806 | Educ severely mntly retrd | EdPsy | 519 | 3S | U |
| 070899 | Implem public law ed hand | EdPsy | 51551 | 1S | U |
| 070902 | Community relationships | YthLd | 332 | 3S | U |
| 071001 | Help stud learn by inquir | SecEd | 37647 | 1S | U |
| 071101 | Simulation and games | SecEd | 37656 | HF | U |
| 071103 | Evaluating stud learning | SecEd | 37635 | 1S | U |
| 071199 | Measuring student effect | SecEd | 37620 | 1S | U |
| 071201 | Selecting effective instr | SecEd | 37660 | 1S | U |
| 080704 | Eng mech/mech of material | CivEn | 203 | 3S | L |
| 080707 | Elem structural theory | CivEn | 321 | 3S | U |
| 0810 | Intro to engineering grph | Tech | 111 | 3S | L |
| 081104 | Eng mechanics/dynamics | CivEn | 204 | 3S | L |
| 0899 | Technology & society | Engin | 200 | 3S | L |
| 090272 | Family health management | Nurs | 288 | 2S | L |
| 090403 | Drug use and abuse | HSci | 460 | 2S | U |
| 090504 | First aid & safety instr | HSci | 121 | 2S | L |
| 090504 | School hlth for ele tchrs | HSci | 361 | 3S | U |
| 090504 | School hlth for sec tchrs | HSci | 362 | 2S | U |
| 090702 | Consumer health | HSci | 370 | 2S | U |
| 090702 | Community health | HSci | 451 | 2S | U |
| 090799 | Safety education | HSci | 325 | 2S | U |
| 090902 | Personal health | HSci | 129 | 1S | L |
| 090902 | Personal health | HSci | 130 | 2S | L |
| 0999 | Hlth & the aging process | Hlth | 563 | 2S | U |
| 100101 | General textiles | ClTx | 260 | 3S | L |
| 100104 | Flat pattern designing | ClTx | 145 | 1S | L |
| 100206 | Personal finance | Bus | 200 | 2S | L |
| 100206 | Family financial manage | FLC | 304 | 3S | U |
| 100302 | Essentials of nutrition | FSN | 115 | 2S | L |
| 100399 | Special problems food sci | FSN | 494R | VC | U |
| 100601 | Child development | FamLC | 210 | 3S | L |
| 100601 | Parenting | FLC | 303 | 3S | U |
| 100601 | Developing parenting skil | FLC | 380R | 3S | U |
| 100602 | Topics in child dev fam | FamSc | 495R | VC | U |
| 110104 | Basic electricity | InArt | 101 | 3S | L |
| 110599 | Intro to hand lettering | Art | 109 | 2S | L |
| 120305 | Vocabulary building | Engl | 225 | 2S | L |
| 120305 | Modern American usage | Engl | 322 | 3S | U |
| 120305 | Study in English grammars | Engl | 328 | 3S | U |
| 120307 | Fundmntls of literature | Engl | 251 | 3S | L |
| 120307 | Vital themes in Amer lit | Engl | 260 | 3S | L |
| 120307 | Masterpieces of Engl lit | Engl | 270 | 3S | L |
| 120307 | The English novel | Engl | 333 | 3S | U |
| 120307 | The American novel | Engl | 336 | 3S | U |
| 120307 | Modern poetry | Engl | 366 | 2S | U |
| 120307 | Engl lit from 1780-1832 | Engl | 374 | 3S | U |
| 120307 | Lit for adolescents | Engl | 420 | 2S | U |
| 120307 | Bible as literature | Engl | 350 | 3S | U |
| 120307 | The short story | Engl | 359 | 3S | U |
| 120307 | Children's nonfiction lit | ElEd | 515R6 | 1S | U |
| 120307 | Fiction drama poetry | Engl | 250 | 3S | L |
| 120307 | Eminent authors | Engl | 395R | VC | U |
| 120308 | Wrtg for chldrn & adolesc | Engl | 217 | 2S | L |
| 120308 | Coll developmental readng | GenSt | 1211 | 2S | L |
| 120308 | Rdg skls for law students | GenSt | 1212 | 2S | L |
| 120308 | System approach to readng | InSci | 51517 | 2S | U |
| 120310 | Creative writing | Engl | 218 | 3S | L |
| 120310 | Writing personal history | Engl | 220 | 3S | L |
| 120310 | Writing about literature | Engl | 314 | 3S | L |
| 120310 | Critical & interprtv wrtg | Engl | 312 | 3S | U |
| 120310 | Exposition & report wrtg | Engl | 315 | 3S | U |
| 120310 | Technical writing | Engl | 316 | 3S | U |
| 120310 | Writing of fiction | Engl | 318R | 3S | U |
| 120310 | Writing of poetry | Engl | 319R | 3S | U |
| 120399 | Study habits | GenSt | 111 | 1S | L |
| 120399 | Basic read & write review | Engl | 105 | 3S | L |
| 120399 | Freshman English | Engl | 115 | 4S | L |
| 120399 | Stdy skill for coll rdg | GenSt | 214R | 1S | L |
| 1210 | Interm French read & conv | Frnch | 201 | 4S | L |
| 1211 | Second-year German | Ger | 201 | 4S | L |

| NCES No. | Course Title | Dept. | Course No. | Credits | Level |
|---|---|---|---|---|---|
| 1211 | Third-yr Ger grammar-comp | Ger | 321 | 3S | U |
| 1213 | First-yr biblical Hebrew | Heb | 131 | 4S | L |
| 1216 | Latin for genealogists | La | 121 | 3S | L |
| 1225 | Third-yr Span gram & comp | Span | 321 | 3S | U |
| 1225 | Third-yr Span gram & comp | Span | 322 | 3S | U |
| 1225 | Introductory Spanish | Span | 100A | 2S | L |
| 1225 | Survey of Hispanic Am lit | Span | 451 | 3S | U |
| 1225 | Second-yr Spanish | Span | 201 | 4S | L |
| 140199 | How to use the library | LibSc | 111 | 1S | L |
| 1501 | Descriptive astronomy | Phys | 127 | 3S | L |
| 150302 | Principles of biology | Bio | 100 | 3S | L |
| 150304 | Conservation of nat rescs | Bio | 400 | 2S | U |
| 150311 | General microbiology | Micro | 221 | 3S | U |
| 150329 | Ichthyology | Zool | 443 | 2S | U |
| 150399 | Plant kingdom | Bio | 105 | 3S | L |
| 150401 | Elementary coll chemistry | Chem | 100 | 3S | L |
| 150504 | Life of the past | Geol | 103 | 3S | L |
| 150599 | Intro to geology | Geol | 101 | 3S | L |
| 150599 | Landforms & their origin | Geol | 306 | 3S | U |
| 1508 | Physical science | PhSci | 100 | 3S | L |
| 160101 | Math & the humanities | Math | 307 | 3S | U |
| 160101 | History of mathematics | Math | 300 | 3S | U |
| 160301 | Concepts of mathematics | Math | 306 | 3S | U |
| 160301 | Basic concepts of math | Math | 305 | 4S | U |
| 160302 | Intermediate algebra | Math | 100 | 2S | L |
| 160302 | Foundations of algebra | Math | 301 | 3S | U |
| 160302 | College algebra | Math | 110 | 5H | L |
| 160406 | Intro ordinary diffent eq | Math | 321 | 3S | U |
| 160412 | Intro to calculus | Math | 119 | 4S | L |
| 1606 | Topics in geometry | Math | 451R | 3S | U |
| 160602 | Trigonometry | Math | 111A | 2S | L |
| 160603 | Analytic geometry | Math | 111B | HF | L |
| 160603 | Analytic geom-calculus 1 | Math | 112 | 4S | L |
| 160603 | Analytic geom-calculus 2 | Math | 113 | 4S | L |
| 160603 | Analyt geom-calculus 3 | Math | 214 | 3S | L |
| 160699 | Survey of geometry | Math | 302 | 3S | U |
| 160706 | Elementary probability | Stat | 341 | 3S | U |
| 160801 | Prin of statistics 1 | Stat | 221 | 3S | L |
| 160801 | Prin of statistics 2 | Stat | 222 | 4S | L |
| 160801 | Prin of statistics 3 | Stat | 223 | 1S | L |
| 160802 | Applied social statistics | Socio | 205 | 3S | L |
| 161108 | Psychological statistics | Psych | 301 | 4S | U |
| 180504 | Logic and language | Philo | 205 | 3S | L |
| 181202 | The New Testament | Relig | 211 | 2S | L |
| 181202 | The New Testament | Relig | 212 | 2S | L |
| 181202 | The Old Testament | Relig | 301 | 2S | U |
| 181202 | The Old Testament | Relig | 302 | 2S | U |
| 181202 | The doctrine & covenants | Relig | 324 | 2S | U |
| 181202 | The doctrine & covenants | Relig | 325 | 2S | U |
| 181299 | The pearl of great price | Relig | 327 | 2S | U |
| 181299 | Writings of Isaiah | Relig | 304 | 2S | U |
| 181299 | Intro to Book of Mormon | Relig | 122 | 2S | L |
| 181299 | Intro to Book of Mormon | Relig | 121 | 2S | L |
| 181603 | Gospel in prin & practice | Relig | 231 | 2S | L |
| 181603 | Gospel in prin & practice | Relig | 232 | 2S | L |
| 181603 | Intro to genealogy | Relig | 261 | 2S | L |
| 181603 | Teach of the living proph | Relig | 333 | 2S | U |
| 181603 | LDS chrch hist after 1844 | Relig | 342 | 2S | U |
| 181603 | LDS church hist to 1844 | Relig | 341 | 2S | U |
| 181603 | The writings of John | Relig | 392R1 | 1S | U |
| 181603 | Spec topics in chur hist | Relig | 540R | 3S | U |
| 181603 | Interntl LDS Church hist | Relig | 343 | 2S | U |
| 181603 | The international church | Relig | 344 | 2S | U |
| 181603 | Gspl prin in youth progrm | Relig | 393R1 | 1S | U |
| 181603 | Presidents of the church | Relig | 393R2 | 1S | U |
| 181603 | Genealogy & the LDS fmly | Relig | 393R3 | 1S | U |
| 181608 | Sharing the Gospel | Relig | 130 | 2S | L |
| 190102 | Fitness for living | PhyEd | 129 | HF | L |
| 190102 | Jogging | PhyEd | 139 | HF | L |
| 190102 | Intermediate swimming | PhyEd | 172 | HF | L |
| 190108 | Mgt of athletic intra pro | PhyEd | 351 | 3S | U |
| 190199 | Sociology & psych of spor | PhyEd | 450 | 2S | U |
| 190311 | Football: fundmtl coachin | PhyEd | 344 | 2S | U |
| 190311 | Basketball: fndtl coach | PhyEd | 341 | 2S | U |
| 190401 | Social dance: beginning | PhyEd | 180 | HF | L |
| 190499 | Aerobic dance | PhyEd | 130 | HF | L |
| 190512 | Sex roles in fam & societ | FLC | 306 | 3S | U |
| 190705 | Family recreation | RecEd | 314 | 2S | U |
| 200104 | General psychology | Psych | 111 | 3S | L |
| 200199 | Understnd & improv memry | Psych | 495R1 | 1S | U |
| 200199 | Psychology statistics | Psych | 301 | 4S | U |
| 2003 | Environmental psychology | Psych | 359 | 3S | U |

| NCES No. | Course Title | Dept. | Course No. | Credits | Level |
|---|---|---|---|---|---|
| 200404 | How to motivate students | EdPsy | 515R4 | 1S | U |
| 200504 | Child psychology | Psych | 320 | 3S | U |
| 200504 | Adolescent psychology | Psych | 321 | 3S | U |
| 200504 | Adult psychology | Psych | 322 | 3S | U |
| 200504 | Developmental psychology | FamSc | 310 | 3S | U |
| 200505 | Personal & social adjust | Psych | 240 | 3S | L |
| 200507 | Exceptional children | Psych | 346 | 3S | U |
| 200509 | Personality | Psych | 341 | 3S | U |
| 200599 | Emotional cont/self-consl | EdPsy | 515R2 | 1S | U |
| 200701 | Develop hlthy self-image | Psych | 395R2 | 2S | U |
| 200702 | Interprsnl growth group | Psych | 357 | 3S | U |
| 200702 | Interprsnl growth group | Socio. | 357 | 3S | U |
| 200703 | Organizational psychology | Psych | 330 | 3S | U |
| 200799 | Intro to social psychol | Psych | 350 | 3S | U |
| 200799 | Intro sociology | Socio. | 111 | 3S | L |
| 200804 | The community educ philos | RecEd | 585 | 2S | U |
| 210101 | Intro public admin | PolSc | 330 | 3S | U |
| 220206 | Econmy, society & pub pol | Econ | 110 | 3S | L |
| 220216 | Microecon for bus decisns | ManEc | 200 | 3S | L |
| 220306 | North America | Geog | 450 | 3S | U |
| 220307 | Trvl plng rates & tariffs | Geog | 350 | 3S | U |
| 220399 | Intro to geography | Geog | 101 | 3S | L |
| 220399 | Travel & tourism patterns | Geog | 250 | 3S | L |
| 220399 | Tour operation | Geog | 352 | 3S | L |
| 220424 | England | Hist | 335 | 3S | U |
| 220424 | British resch Eng/Wales 16 | Hist | 391R4 | 3S | U |
| 220424 | Brtsh resch Scotlnd/Ireld | Hist | 391R6 | 3S | U |
| 220426 | France | Hist | 332 | 3S | U |
| 220426 | 19th-century Europe | Hist | 322 | 3S | U |
| 220426 | The European family | Hist | 326 | 3S | U |
| 220428 | Utah | Hist | 366 | 3S | U |
| 220431 | USSR & Eastern Europe | Hist | 331 | 3S | U |
| 220432 | The United States | Hist | 120 | 3S | L |
| 220432 | The United States | Hist | 121 | 3S | L |
| 220432 | California | Hist | 365 | 2S | U |
| 220432 | American heritage | SocSc | 100 | 3S | L |
| 220432 | Northeast US and Canada | Hist | 391R1 | 3S | U |
| 220432 | Southern states | Hist | 391R2 | 3S | U |
| 220432 | Middle states | Hist | 391R3 | 3S | U |
| 220432 | Practicum | Genea | 480R1 | 2S | U |
| 220432 | Seminar | Genea | 480R2 | 2S | U |
| 220432 | Writing family history | Hist | 397R1 | 3S | U |
| 220432 | Oral hist interviewing | Hist | 422 | 3S | U |
| 220433 | Modern world history | Hist | 111 | 3S | L |
| 220433 | Wrld civilization to 1500 | Hist | 110 | 3S | L |
| 220499 | Directed readings | Hist | 498R | VC | U |
| 220499 | Cultural hist of the US | Hist | 390R1 | 3S | U |
| 220499 | Cultural hist Scotld/Irel | Hist | 390R2 | 3S | U |
| 220499 | Paleography/English | Hist | 400R1 | 2S | U |
| 2205 | Theories of human freedom | PolSc | 308 | 3S | U |
| 220501 | Amer govt and politics | PolSc | 110 | 3S | L |
| 220509 | Moral foundations of poli | PolSc | 302 | 3S | U |
| 220511 | State-local govt politics | PolSc | 311 | 3S | U |
| 220607 | Intro to social psycholog | Socio | 350 | 3S | U |
| 220613 | Soc aspects of mental hlt | Socio | 389 | 3S | U |
| 220613 | Modern social problems | Socio | 112 | 3S | U |
| 220699 | Mthds of rsch in sociolog | Socio | 300 | 3S | U |
| 220699 | Stress & coping behavior | Socio | 390R3 | 1S | U |
| 220699 | Sociology of aging | Socio | 365 | 2S | U |

| NCES No. | Course Title | Dept. | Course No. | Credits | Level |
|---|---|---|---|---|---|
| | **Noncredit courses** | | | | |
| 030302 | Fun guitar for all part 1 | Cultu | 76 | NC | |
| 030302 | Fun guitar for all part 2 | Cultu | 77 | NC | |
| 040902 | Way to become success mgr | Bus | 70 | NC | |
| 041004 | Salesmanship for managers | Bus | 73 | NC | |
| 041004 | Improving manager skills | Bus | 74 | NC | |
| 0499 | Interviewing: improving | Bus | 71 | NC | |
| 0499 | Legal decision, law & emp | Bus | 72 | NC | |
| 0499 | Employment strategy | Bus | 80 | NC | |
| 070701 | Stress coping in law fam | JusAd | 70 | NC | |
| 070701 | Elim self-defeatg behavor | PerDv | 71 | NC | |
| 070701 | Changing undesired emotio | PerDv | 72 | NC | |
| 070701 | Dvlp self-image with gosp | PerDv | 73 | NC | |
| 100401 | Practical decision making | PerDv | 70 | NC | |
| 100401 | Help teen make career dec | Famil | 76 | NC | |
| 100601 | Early child lrng exp home | Famil | 71 | NC | |
| 100601 | Nurt childs nat curiosity | Famil | 72 | NC | |
| 100601 | Prep child to succ in sch | Famil | 70 | NC | |
| 100604 | Help yourself: self-impro | PerDv | 74 | NC | |
| 100604 | Handle conflict at home | PerDv | 75 | NC | |
| 110599 | Keys to drawing accuracy | Cultu | 72 | NC | |
| 120308 | Tutor child: rdg skills 1 | Famil | 73 | NC | |

| NCES No. | Course Title | Dept. | Course No. | Credits | Level |
|---|---|---|---|---|---|
| 120308 | Tutor child: rdg skills 2 | Famil | 74 | NC | |
| 120310 | Remedial spelling | GenSt | 15R1 | NC | D |
| 120310 | Remedial grammar | GenSt | 15R2 | NC | D |
| 120310 | Children's creative writ | Famil | 75 | NC | |
| 120399 | English at home part 1 | Lang | 85-1 | NC | |
| 120399 | English at home part 2 | Lang | 85-2 | NC | |
| 120399 | English at home part 3 | Lang | 85-3 | NC | |
| 120399 | Building your vocabulary | Famil | 77 | NC | |
| 1207 | Comp intro Mandar Chinese | CAC | 75 | NC | |
| 1215 | Comp intro Japanese | CAC | 76 | NC | |
| 1225 | Intro Spanish | Lang | 80 | NC | |
| 160199 | Review of basic math | Math | 99 | NC | L |
| 160301 | Computerized rem math pt1 | CAC | 13 | NC | |
| 160301 | Computerized rem math pt2 | CAC | 14 | NC | |
| 160302 | Beginning algebra | Math | 98 | NC | L |
| 190102 | Hooked on aerobics | Hlth | 71 | NC | |
| 200599 | Spirit roots human relats | PerDv | 76 | NC | |
| 220424 | British rsch 1: survey | Genea | 73-1 | NC | |
| 220424 | British rsch 1: Brit Pt 1 | Genea | 73-2 | NC | |
| 220424 | Brit rsch 2: Scot rsch 1 | Genea | 74-1 | NC | |
| 220424 | Brit rsch 2: Irish rsch 1 | Genea | 74-3 | NC | |
| 220427 | Mexican research English | Genea | 81-1 | NC | |
| 220427 | Mexican research Spanish | Genea | 81-2 | NC | |
| 220432 | N Am rsch 2: NE states Ca | Genea | 72-1 | NC | |
| 220432 | N Am rsch 2: midwest sts | Genea | 72-3 | NC | |
| 220432 | 8 steps to find your root | Genea | 70 | NC | |

⑦ **CALIFORNIA STATE UNIVERSITY, SACRAMENTO**

Mr. Kenneth D. Kerri
Professor of Civil Engineering
Office of Water Programs
California State University, Sacramento
6000 J Street
Sacramento, California 95819
Phone: 916-454-6142

Enrollment on a noncredit basis accepted in all credit courses. Gifted high school students are permitted to enroll in undergraduate courses for credit. Overseas enrollment accepted. Correspondence courses are prepared for persons interested in the operation and maintenance of drinking-water and wastewater facilities.

| NCES No. | Course Title | Dept. | Course No. | Credits | Level |
|---|---|---|---|---|---|
| | **College courses** | | | | |
| 081304 | Oper wastewater treatment | CivEg | X12A | 6S | L |
| 081304 | Oper wastewater treatment | CivEg | X12B | 6S | L |
| 081304 | Oper wastewater treatment | CivEg | X12C | 6S | L |
| 081304 | Water treatment plant opr | CivEg | X18A | 6S | L |
| 081304 | Water treatment plant opr | CivEg | X18B | 6S | L |
| 081304 | Water supply system opera | CivEg | X17 | 6S | L |

⑧ **CENTRAL MICHIGAN UNIVERSITY**

Ms. Ann Marie N. Bridges
Coordinator, Office of Independent Study
Continuing Education and Community Services
Rowe Hall 125
Central Michigan University
Mt. Pleasant, Michigan 48859
Phone: 517-774-7140

Enrollment on a noncredit basis accepted in some credit courses. Only in exceptional cases are gifted high school students permitted to enroll in undergraduate courses for credit. Overseas enrollment accepted for college courses. Enrollment period is for nine months. One three-month extension is permitted upon written request. VISA/MasterCard accepted.

| NCES No. | Course Title | Dept. | Course No. | Credits | Level |
|---|---|---|---|---|---|
| | **College courses** | | | | |
| 030499 | Hist of drama/theatre I | ThArt | 386 | 3S | L |
| 030499 | Hist of drama/theatre II | ThArt | 387 | 3S | L |
| 030599 | Understanding art | Art | 125 | 2S | L |
| 040101 | Financial accounting | Acctg | 201 | 3S | L |
| 040111 | Managerial accounting | Acctg | 221 | 3S | L |

| NCES No. | Course Title | Dept. | Course No. | Credits | Level |
|---|---|---|---|---|---|
| 051103 | Persuasion | InCo | 365 | 3S | L |
| 051108 | Foundations comm theory | InCo | 251 | 3S | L |
| 060801 | Assembly language program | CmpSc | 210 | 3S | L |
| 070516 | Arithmetic in elem school | Educ | 320 | 2S | L |
| 071103 | Measurement & evaluation | Educ | 570 | 3S | L |
| 120101 | Contrastive appl linguist | ForLL | 510 | 3S | U |
| 120307 | English literature | EngLL | 235 | 3S | L |
| 120307 | English literature | EngLL | 236 | 3S | L |
| 120307 | American literature | EngLL | 251 | 3S | L |
| 120307 | American literature | EngLL | 252 | 3S | L |
| 120307 | Shakespeare | EngLL | 349 | 3S | L |
| 1210 | Intermediate French I | Frnch | 201 | 4S | L |
| 1210 | Intermediate French II | Frnch | 202 | 4S | L |
| 1210 | French lit 20th century | Frnch | 409 | 3S | L |
| 1211 | Elementary German | Ger | 101 | 4S | L |
| 1225 | Spanish lit to 18th cent | Span | 304 | 3S | L |
| 150304 | Ecology | Bio | 340 | 3S | L |
| 150316 | Nature study | Bio | 229 | 3S | L |
| 150399 | Conserva of nat resources | Bio | 240 | 3S | L |
| 150399 | Human animal | Bio | 328 | 3S | L |
| 150399 | Human ecology | Bio | 338 | 3S | L |
| 150799 | Physics for poets | Phys | 100 | 3S | L |
| 160102 | Hist of elementary math | Math | 253 | 2S | U |
| 160102 | History of mathematics | Math | 573 | 3S | U |
| 160302 | College algebra | Math | 106 | 3S | L |
| 160602 | Plane trigonometry | Math | 106 | 3S | L |
| 160801 | Intro to statistics | Math | 282 | 3S | L |
| 161101 | Mathematics for business | Math | 116 | 3S | L |
| 161101 | Mathematics for business | Math | 216 | 3S | L |
| 190104 | Foundations of phys ed | PhyEd | 106 | 2S | L |
| 190104 | Hist of phys ed & sports | PhyEd | 515 | 3S | L |
| 190405 | History of dance | Dance | 530 | 3S | U |
| 190502 | Community health | HEd | 317 | 3S | L |
| 190505 | Environmental health | HEd | 252 | 3S | L |
| 190509 | Personal health | HEd | 106 | 3S | L |
| 190599 | Safety education | HEd | 209 | 2S | L |
| 190701 | Playgrounds/community ctr | Rec | 402 | 3S | L |
| 190701 | Admin of recreation parks | Rec | 505 | 3S | U |
| 190703 | Camp counseling | Rec | 220 | 3S | L |
| 200699 | Intro to psych statistics | Psych | 311 | 3S | L |
| 220102 | Cultural anthropology | Anthr | 170 | 3S | L |
| 220106 | Physical anthropology | Anthr | 171 | 3S | L |
| 220201 | Principles of economics 1 | Econ | 201 | 3S | L |
| 220201 | Principles of economics 2 | Econ | 202 | 3S | L |
| 220301 | Cultures of the world | Geog | 121 | 3S | L |
| 220399 | Weather | Geog | 201 | 4S | L |
| 220432 | Westward movement in Amer | Hist | 322 | 3S | L |
| 220499 | Western civilization | Hist | 101 | 3S | L |
| 220499 | Western civilization | Hist | 102 | 3S | L |
| 220501 | Intro: Am govt & politics | PolSc | 105 | 3S | L |
| 220503 | Comparative politics: Eur | PolSc | 240 | 3S | L |
| 220599 | Intro to political sci | PolSc | 100 | 3S | L |
| 220602 | Criminology | Socio | 421 | 3S | L |
| 220604 | Juvenile delinquency | Socio | 222 | 3S | L |
| 220605 | The family | Socio | 411 | 3S | L |
| 220606 | Introductory sociology | Socio | 100 | 3S | L |
| 220607 | Social psychology | Socio | 201 | 3S | L |
| 220699 | Intro to human sexuality | Socio | 213 | 3S | L |
| 220699 | Educational sociology | Socio | 311 | 3S | L |
| 220699 | Socio of health/illness | Socio | 312 | 3S | L |
| 220699 | Religion in society | Socio | 319 | 3S | L |
| 220699 | Minorities | Socio | 323 | 3S | L |

⑨ **COLORADO STATE UNIVERSITY**

Ms. Patricia Morris
Correspondence Program Coordinator
C102 Rockwell Hall
Colorado State University
Fort Collins, Colorado 80523
Phone: 303-491-5288

Enrollment on a noncredit basis accepted in some credit courses. Gifted high school students are permitted to enroll in undergraduate courses for credit. Overseas enrollment accepted.

| NCES No. | Course Title | Dept. | Course No. | Credits | Level |
|---|---|---|---|---|---|
| **College courses** | | | | | |
| 010407 | Basic nutrition for pets | AnSci | AN322 | 2S | U |
| 010603 | Ind study/pesticides | Agri | A495 | 3S | U |
| 0110 | Natl forest rec mangmt | For | OR435 | VC | B |
| 011299 | Hunter educ for instructr | For | FW355 | 2S | U |
| 020199 | Ecology & env issues | Fores | NR130 | 3S | L |
| 070309 | Ind study/adult education | Educ | AD495 | VC | B |
| 070899 | Educational psychology | Educ | ED355 | 3S | U |
| 070899 | Exceptionality & hum rel | Educ | ED428 | 3S | U |
| 0709 | Evaluation of achievement | Educ | ED452 | 2S | B |
| 100313 | Nutrition & preschool chl | HmEc | FN160 | 2S | L |
| 100401 | Decision making: pers/fam | HmEc | HC330 | 3S | U |
| 100601 | Play behavior | HmEc | HD430 | 2S | B |
| 100602 | Ind & family development | HmEc | HD101 | 3S | L |
| 100699 | Practicum I | HmEc | HD286 | 2S | L |
| 100699 | Adm of human dvlpmt ctrs | HmEc | HD438 | 3S | B |
| 120299 | Western American lit | Engl | E179 | 3S | L |
| 190108 | Beg Phys Ed-tennis | PhyEd | PE100 | 1S | L |
| 220431 | Imperial Russia | Hist | HY440 | 3S | B |
| 220470 | Afro-Amer hist 1619-1865 | Hist | HY250 | 3S | L |
| **Graduate courses** | | | | | |
| 050602 | Seminar: grantsmanship | InArt | IS692 | 3S | G |
| 070309 | Adult education | Educ | AD520 | 3S | G |
| 070799 | Guidance:multicult&sp pop | Educ | ED551 | 3S | G |
| 070899 | Educ exceptional student | Educ | ED528 | 2S | G |
| **Noncredit courses** | | | | | |
| 010407 | Basic nutrition for pets | AnSci | CE521 | NC | |
| 010603 | Pesticides: how & why | Agri | CE102 | NC | |
| 0110 | Natl forest rec mangmt | For | 140-6 | NC | |
| 020103 | Oriental carpets & rugs | HmEc | 1342 | NC | |
| 070309 | Program development | Educ | 3107 | NC | |
| 070309 | Administration | Educ | 3108 | NC | |
| 070309 | Adult development | Educ | 3109 | NC | |
| 070309 | Adult basic education | Educ | 3111 | NC | |
| 070309 | Adult learner | Educ | 3112 | NC | |
| 070309 | Adult teaching | Educ | 3113 | NC | |
| 080999 | Fund of electrical systms | EngAS | 3205 | NC | |

⑩ **EASTERN KENTUCKY UNIVERSITY**

Mr. Kenneth D. Tunnell
Dean of Extended Programs
Perkins 217
Eastern Kentucky University
Richmond, Kentucky 40475
Phone: 606-622-2001

Enrollment on a noncredit basis accepted in all credit courses. Gifted high school students are permitted to enroll in undergraduate courses for credit. Overseas enrollment accepted.

| NCES No. | Course Title | Dept. | Course No. | Credits | Level |
|---|---|---|---|---|---|
| **High School courses** | | | | | |
| 120305 | English grammar | Engl | 11 | HF | H |
| 120305 | English grammar | Engl | 12 | HF | H |
| 120307 | American literature | Engl | 11A | HF | H |
| 120307 | American literature | Engl | 11B | HF | H |
| 120307 | British literature | Engl | 12A | HF | H |
| 120307 | British literature | Engl | 12B | HF | H |
| 190502 | Personal/community health | Hea | 1 | HF | H |
| 220201 | Economics | Econ | 12 | HF | H |
| 220399 | World geography | Geog | 10A | HF | H |
| 220399 | World geography | Geog | 10B | HF | H |
| 220432 | American history | Hist | 11A | HF | H |
| 220432 | American history | Hist | 11B | HF | H |
| 220433 | World history | Hist | 10A | HF | H |
| 220433 | World history | Hist | 10B | HF | H |
| 220501 | Government | Gov | 12 | HF | H |
| 220502 | Civics | Civ | 9 | HF | H |
| 220606 | Sociology | Socio | 12 | HF | H |
| **College courses** | | | | | |
| 030302 | Enjoyment of music | Music | 271 | 3S | L |
| 040299 | Introduction to business | OAd | 101 | 3S | L |
| 040299 | Business communications | OAd | 201 | 3S | U |
| 040308 | Money and banking | Econ | 324 | 3S | U |

| NCES No. | Course Title | Dept. | Course No. | Credits | Level |
|---|---|---|---|---|---|
| 041001 | Marketing | Mktg | 300 | 3S | U |
| 041303 | Real estate principles | RlEst | 310 | 3S | U |
| 041306 | Real estate finance | RlEst | 330 | 3S | U |
| 050199 | Advertising | Mktg | 320 | 3S | U |
| 06 | Computers and modern wld | ComSc | 102 | 3S | U |
| 120201 | Survey of world lit 1 | Engl | 211 | 3S | L |
| 120201 | Survey of world lit 2 | Engl | 212 | 3S | L |
| 120305 | English composition 1 | Engl | 101 | 3S | L |
| 120305 | English composition 2 | Engl | 102 | 3S | L |
| 120307 | American literature 1 | Engl | 350 | 3S | U |
| 150399 | Economic plants | Bio | 300 | 3S | U |
| 160199 | Understanding arithmetic | Math | 201 | 3S | L |
| 160302 | Introductory algebra | Math | 105 | 3S | L |
| 160302 | College algebra | Math | 107 | 3S | L |
| 160602 | Trigonometry | Math | 108 | 3S | L |
| 190502 | Personal/community health | Hea | 281 | 2S | L |
| 190511 | Safety and first aid | Hea | 202 | 2S | L |
| 200199 | Psychology as a social sc | Psych | 202 | 3S | L |
| 200501 | Abnormal psychology | Psych | 308 | 3S | U |
| 2103 | Police administration | PAd | 101 | 3S | L |
| 2103 | Prin & proc in admin jus | PAd | 110 | 3S | U |
| 2103 | Delinq & juv jus system | PAd | 311 | 3S | U |
| 2103 | Introduction to security | SaCor | 110 | 3S | U |
| 2103 | Alcohol and other drugs | SaCor | 232 | 3S | U |
| 2103 | Introduction to security | PAd | 110 | 3S | U |
| 220201 | Principles of economics 1 | Econ | 230 | 3S | L |
| 220201 | Principles of economics 2 | Econ | 231 | 3S | L |
| 220302 | Economic geography | Geog | 330 | 3S | U |
| 220308 | Urban geography | Geog | 421 | 3S | U |
| 220399 | Cons, technol & env probl | Geog | 402 | 3S | U |
| 220405 | History of science | Sci | 310 | 3S | U |
| 220432 | American civiliz to 1877 | Hist | 202 | 3S | L |
| 220432 | American civ since 1877 | Hist | 203 | 3S | L |
| 220433 | Preindustrial world civ | GSS | 246 | 3S | L |
| 220433 | Industrialism in wrld civ | GSS | 247 | 3S | L |
| 220499 | South in American history | Hist | 406 | 3S | U |
| 220499 | Kentucky history | Hist | 516 | 3S | U |
| 220501 | Intro to American govt | PolSc | 101 | 3S | L |
| 220501 | Amer state & local govt | PolSc | 230 | 3S | L |
| 220599 | Government of Kentucky | PolSc | 332 | 3S | U |

## (11) EASTERN MICHIGAN UNIVERSITY

Mr. Michael McPhillips
Coordinator of Independent Study
329 Goodison Hall
Eastern Michigan University
Ypsilanti, Michigan 48197
Phone: 313-487-1081

Enrollment on a noncredit basis accepted in all credit courses. Gifted high school students are permitted to enroll in undergraduate courses for credit. Overseas enrollment is not encouraged; each case is judged on an individual basis. Fifteen semester hours of credit, via correspondence, may be applied to an Eastern Michigan University degree. Our most unique course is Basic Technological Concepts, IDT 150, designed to impart technological literacy and an understanding of the social impact of technology.

| NCES No. | Course Title | Dept. | Course No. | Credits | Level |
|---|---|---|---|---|---|
| | **College courses** | | | | |
| 041106 | Basic supervision | Mgmt | 281 | 3S | L |
| 110299 | Wire manufact technology | Tech | 479 | 3S | U |
| 120302 | History English language | Engl | 421 | 3S | B |
| 120305 | Modern English syntax | Engl | 402 | 3S | B |
| 120307 | Shakespeare | EngLL | 210 | 3S | L |
| 120307 | Shakespeare | EngLL | 305 | 3S | L |
| 120310 | Expository writing | Engl | 325 | 3S | L |
| 160302 | Intermediate algebra | Math | 104 | 3S | L |
| 220432 | Trends in US history | Hist | 123 | 3S | L |
| 220612 | Basic technolog/concept | Tech | 150 | 3S | L |
| 220615 | Culture Latino groups US | LAS | 215 | 3S | L |
| 220699 | Introduction to sociology | Socio | 105 | 3S | L |

## (12) EAST TENNESSEE STATE UNIVERSITY

Dr. Creg S. Bishop
Associate Professor of Environmental Health
East Tennessee State University
P.O. Box 22960-A
Johnson City, Tennessee 37614
Phone: 615-929-4462

Enrollment on a noncredit basis accepted in all credit courses. Gifted high school students are permitted to enroll in undergraduate courses for credit. Overseas enrollment accepted for college courses.

| NCES No. | Course Title | Dept. | Course No. | Credits | Level |
|---|---|---|---|---|---|
| | **College courses** | | | | |
| 090799 | Basic mathematics | 818 | 4927 | 3S | B |
| 090799 | Insect & rodent control | 818 | 4937 | 2S | B |
| 090799 | Waterborne-disease contrl | 818 | 4947 | 2S | B |
| 090799 | Food-borne-disease contrl | 818 | 4957 | 2S | B |
| 090799 | Community health analysis | 818 | 4967 | 3S | B |
| 090799 | Communicable disease cont | 818 | 4977 | 2S | B |
| 090799 | Environmental protection | 818 | 4987 | 3S | B |
| 090799 | Principles-epidemiology | 818 | 4997 | 2S | B |
| 090799 | Environtl sanitation surv | 818 | 4917 | 3S | B |

## (13) GOVERNORS STATE UNIVERSITY

Ms. Odessa Nolin
Continuing Education Coordinator
Independent Study by Correspondence
Governors State University
Stuendel Road
University Park, Illinois 60466
Phone: 312-534-5000 Ext. 2121

Enrollment on a noncredit basis accepted in some credit courses. Overseas enrollment accepted for college courses. Courses are to be completed within one trimester (14 1/2 weeks). If the student lives within a 50-mile radius of Governors State University, one orientation session is required.

| NCES No. | Course Title | Dept. | Course No. | Credits | Level |
|---|---|---|---|---|---|
| | **College courses** | | | | |
| 040312 | Public finance | Econ | 404 | 3U | B |
| 040903 | Organizational behavior | Mgmt | 401 | 3U | B |
| 070199 | Educ of minorities in US | Educ | 535 | 3U | B |
| 120310 | Writing principles | Engl | 310 | 3U | B |
| 1509 | Environmental science | ESci | 316 | 3U | B |
| 190501 | Alchlm: stdy in addiction | Alc | 340 | 3U | B |
| 2101 | Intro to public administr | PAdm | 301 | 3U | B |
| 220428 | Hist of Il & its constit | Hist | 50A | 3U | B |
| 220614 | Principles of urban studi | Socio | 310 | 3U | B |
| 2299 | Survey of social science | SoSc | 311 | 3U | B |
| 2299 | Ethnic cultre & politics | ICS | 541 | 3U | B |
| | **Graduate courses** | | | | |
| 120307 | Black literature | Engl | 512 | 3U | G |
| 220420 | African civilization | ICS | 548 | 3U | G |
| 220470 | Hispanic experience in US | ICS | 540 | 3U | G |
| 220472 | Women in American history | Hist | 550 | 3U | G |
| 220599 | Urban politics | PolS | 538 | 3U | G |
| 2299 | Urban dynamics | SocW | 530 | 3U | G |

## (14) HOME STUDY INTERNATIONAL

President of Home Study International
Home Study International
6940 Carroll Avenue
Takoma Park, Maryland 20912
Phone: 202-722-6572

Enrollment on a noncredit basis accepted in some credit courses. Gifted high school students are permitted to enroll in undergraduate courses for credit. Overseas enrollment accepted.

| NCES No. | Course Title | Dept. | Course No. | Credits | Level |
|---|---|---|---|---|---|
| | **Elementary courses** | | | | |
| 040207 | Elementary typing | ETypg | 6 | | E |
| 040207 | Elementary typing | ETypg | 7 | | E |
| 040207 | Elementary typing | ETypg | 8 | | E |
| 09 | Science health 1st sem | EHlth | 71 | | E |
| 09 | Science health 2nd sem | EHlth | 72 | | E |
| 09 | Science health 1st sem | EHlth | 81 | | E |
| 09 | Science health 2nd sem | EHlth | 82 | | E |
| 120399 | Language 1st sem | EEngl | 71 | | E |
| 120399 | Language 2nd sem | EEngl | 72 | | E |
| 120399 | Language 1st sem | EEngl | 81 | | E |
| 120399 | Language 2nd sem | EEngl | 82 | | E |
| 161199 | Mathematics 1st sem | EMath | 71 | | E |
| 161199 | Mathematics 2nd sem | EMath | 72 | | E |
| 161199 | Mathematics 1st sem | EMath | 81 | | E |
| 161199 | Mathematics 2nd sem | EMath | 82 | | E |
| 1899 | Bible 1st sem | ERlgn | 71 | | E |
| 1899 | Bible 2nd sem | ERlgn | 72 | | E |
| 1899 | Bible 1st sem | ERlgn | 81 | | E |
| 1899 | Bible 2nd sem | ERlgn | 82 | | E |
| 2299 | Social studies 1st sem | EHist | 71 | | E |
| 2299 | Social studies 2nd sem | EHist | 72 | | E |
| 2299 | United States history 1s | EHist | 81 | | E |
| 2299 | United States history 2s | EHist | 82 | | E |
| | **High School courses** | | | | |
| 030302 | Music apprec 1st sem | SMusc | 15 | HF | H |
| 030302 | Music apprec 2nd sem | SMusc | 15 | HF | H |
| 040102 | Bookkpng & acctg 1st sem | SAcct | 3 | HF | H |
| 040102 | Bookkpng & acctg 2nd sem | SAcct | 4 | HF | H |
| 040207 | Typing 1st sem | STypg | 7 | HF | H |
| 040207 | Typing 2nd sem | STypg | 8 | HF | H |
| 100104 | Clothing construction | SHmEc | 16 | HF | H |
| 100702 | Foods | SHmEc | 17 | HF | H |
| 100799 | Home planning | SHmEc | 18 | HF | H |
| 120299 | Adventist literature | SEngl | 13 | HF | H |
| 120305 | English I 1st sem | SEngl | 1 | HF | H |
| 120305 | English I 2nd sem | SEngl | 2 | HF | H |
| 120305 | English II 1st sem | SEngl | 3 | HF | H |
| 120305 | English II 2nd sem | SEngl | 4 | HF | H |
| 120307 | American lit 1st sem | SEngl | 9 | HF | H |
| 120307 | American lit 2nd sem | SEngl | 10 | HF | H |
| 120307 | English lit 1st sem | SEngl | 11 | HF | H |
| 120307 | English lit 2nd sem | SEngl | 12 | HF | H |
| 120399 | Selected Amer writings | SEngl | 7 | HF | H |
| 120399 | Structure of writing | SEngl | 8 | HF | H |
| 1210 | French II 1st sem | SFren | 3 | HF | H |
| 1210 | French II 2nd sem | SFren | 4 | HF | H |
| 1211 | German II 1st sem | SGrmn | 7 | HF | H |
| 1211 | German II 2nd sem | SGrmn | 8 | HF | H |
| 1225 | Spanish I 1st sem | SSpan | 13 | HF | H |
| 1225 | Spanish I 2nd sem | SSpan | 14 | HF | H |
| 1503 | Biology 1st sem | SBiol | 5 | HF | H |
| 1503 | Biology 2nd sem | SBiol | 6 | HF | H |
| 1504 | Chemistry 1st sem | SChem | 7 | HF | H |
| 1504 | Chemistry 2nd sem | SChem | 8 | HF | H |
| 160302 | Algebra I 1st sem | SMath | 5 | HF | H |
| 160302 | Algebra I 2nd sem | SMath | 6 | HF | H |
| 160302 | Algebra II | SMath | 11 | 1U | H |
| 160601 | Geometry 1st sem | SMath | 9 | HF | H |
| 160601 | Geometry 2nd sem | SMath | 10 | HF | H |
| 161202 | Consumer math 1st sem | SMath | 3 | HF | H |
| 161202 | Consumer math 2nd sem | SMath | 4 | HF | H |
| 1899 | Breakthru w God 1st sem | SRlgn | 1 | HF | H |
| 1899 | Breakthru w God 2nd sem | SRlgn | 2 | HF | H |
| 1899 | God's church 1st sem | SRlgn | 5 | HF | H |
| 1899 | God's church 2nd sem | SRlgn | 6 | HF | H |
| 1899 | God's Word | SRlgn | 9 | HF | H |
| 1899 | God's Word | SRlgn | 10 | HF | H |
| 1899 | God's world | SRlgn | 13 | HF | H |
| 1899 | God's world | SRlgn | 14 | HF | H |
| 190515 | Health | SHlth | 15 | HF | H |
| 220432 | American hist 1st sem | SHist | 7 | HF | H |
| 220432 | American hist 2nd sem | SHist | 8 | HF | H |
| 220433 | World history 1st sem | SHist | 3 | HF | H |
| 220433 | World history 2nd sem | SHist | 4 | HF | H |
| 220501 | American govt 2nd sem | SHist | 10 | HF | H |
| 220501 | American govt 1st sem | SHist | 9 | HF | H |
| | **College courses** | | | | |
| 030302 | Music appreciation | Musc | 204 | 3S | L |

| NCES No. | Course Title | Dept. | Course No. | Credits | Level |
|---|---|---|---|---|---|
| 040207 | Typing 1st sem | Secr | 105 | 2S | L |
| 040207 | Typing 2nd sem | Secr | 106 | 2S | L |
| 051109 | Speech | Spch | 101 | 3S | L |
| 070299 | Admin of the elem school | Educ | 350 | 3S | U |
| 070509 | Health education | Educ | 260 | 3S | L |
| 070599 | The teaching of reading | Educ | 354 | 3S | U |
| 071103 | Evaluation in teaching | Educ | 360 | 3S | U |
| 100601 | Adolescent growth and dev | Psyc | 344 | 3S | U |
| 100601 | Child development | Psyc | 242 | 3S | L |
| 100601 | Exploring early childhood | Psyc | 254 | 2S | L |
| 120299 | American lit 1st sem | Engl | 221 | 2S | L |
| 120299 | American lit 2nd sem | Engl | 222 | 2S | L |
| 120307 | English lit 1st sem | Engl | 241 | 2S | L |
| 120307 | English lit 2nd sem | Engl | 242 | 2S | L |
| 120310 | Freshman comp 1st sem | Engl | 101 | 3S | L |
| 120310 | Freshman comp 2nd sem | Engl | 102 | 3S | L |
| 1210 | French II 1st sem | Fren | 103 | 2S | L |
| 1210 | French II 2nd sem | Fren | 104 | 2S | L |
| 1211 | German II 1st sem | Grmn | 103 | 2S | L |
| 1211 | German II 2nd sem | Grmn | 104 | 2S | L |
| 1211 | Intermed German 1st sem | Grmn | 201 | 3S | L |
| 1211 | Intermed German 2nd sem | Grmn | 202 | 3S | L |
| 1212 | Greek I 1st sem | Grek | 201 | 2S | L |
| 1212 | Greek I 2nd sem | Grek | 202 | 2S | L |
| 1212 | Intermed Greek 1st sem | Grek | 311 | 3S | U |
| 1212 | Intermed Greek 2nd sem | Grek | 312 | 3S | U |
| 1212 | Greek II 1st sem | Grek | 203 | 2S | L |
| 1212 | Greek II 2nd sem | Grek | 204 | 2S | L |
| 1225 | Spanish I 1st sem | Span | 101 | 2S | L |
| 1225 | Spanish I 2nd sem | Span | 102 | 2S | L |
| 1225 | Spanish II 1st sem | Span | 103 | 2S | L |
| 1225 | Spanish II 2nd sem | Span | 104 | 2S | L |
| 1509 | Scientfc stdy of creation | Biol | 311 | 2S | U |
| 160302 | College algebra | Math | 121 | 4S | L |
| 180999 | Bible doctrines 1st sem | Rlgn | 321 | 2S | U |
| 180999 | Bible doctrines 2nd sem | Rlgn | 322 | 2S | U |
| 180999 | World religions | Rlgn | 300 | 2S | U |
| 180999 | Adventist history | Rlgn | 230 | 3S | L |
| 181406 | Life & tchngs of Jesus 1s | Rlgn | 201 | 2S | L |
| 181406 | Life & tchngs of Jesus 2s | Rlgn | 202 | 2S | L |
| 1899 | Bible survey 1st sem | Rlgn | 101 | 2S | L |
| 1899 | Bible survey 2nd sem | Rlgn | 102 | 2S | L |
| 1899 | Corinthian Epistles | Rlgn | 340 | 2S | U |
| 1899 | Old Testmt prophets—earl | Rlgn | 335 | 3S | U |
| 1899 | Old Testmt prophets—late | Rlgn | 336 | 3S | U |
| 1899 | Philos of Adventist educ | Educ | 210 | 3S | L |
| 1899 | Prophetic guidance | Rlgn | 360 | 2S | U |
| 1899 | Revelation | Rlgn | 312 | 2S | U |
| 1899 | Science & Chrstian belief | Rlgn | 314 | 1S | U |
| 1899 | Work of the Bible instruc | AEd | | 1U | L |
| 1899 | Literature evangelism | AEd | | 2U | L |
| 190599 | Health principles | Hlth | 100 | 2S | L |
| 2099 | General psychology | Psyc | 120 | 3S | L |
| 220299 | Macroeconomics | Econ | 331 | 3S | U |
| 220303 | Geography 1st sem | Geog | 351 | 2S | U |
| 220303 | Geography 2nd sem | Geog | 352 | 2S | U |
| 220432 | US history 1st sem | Hist | 201 | 3S | L |
| 220432 | US history 2nd sem | Hist | 202 | 3S | L |
| 220499 | Church history 1st sem | Hist | 311 | 3S | U |
| 220499 | Church history 2nd sem | Hist | 312 | 3S | U |
| 220499 | Hist of civiliz 1st sem | Hist | 101 | 3S | L |
| 220499 | Hist of civiliz 2nd sem | Hist | 102 | 3S | L |
| 220499 | American history | Hist | 304 | 3S | U |
| 220501 | Govt in the United States | Hist | 203 | 3S | L |
| 220699 | Sociology | Soci | 204 | 3S | L |

⑮ **INDIANA STATE UNIVERSITY**

Dr. Clair D. Woodward
Director of Independent Study
Alumni Center 124
Indiana State University
Terre Haute, Indiana 47809
Phone: 812-237-2555

Enrollment on a noncredit basis accepted in all credit courses. Only in exceptional cases are gifted high school students permitted to enroll in undergraduate courses for credit. Overseas enrollment accepted for college and noncredit courses. ISU pays return postage on lessons. Enrollment active for one year. If study is terminated within one month,

ISU refunds full tuition less $10. The two noncredit courses, entitled Basic Supervision and Management (course numbers BSBM 1 and 2), are widely used by hospitals, nursing homes, government agencies, and similar institutions in training supervisory personnel. Sample lessons available upon request.

| NCES No. | Course Title | Dept. | Course No. | Credits | Level |
|---|---|---|---|---|---|
| | **College courses** | | | | |
| 0399 | Arts in civilization | Art | 151 | 3S | L |
| 040601 | Business communications | BDEOA | 330 | 3S | U |
| 040604 | Business report writing | BDEOA | 336 | 2S | U |
| 040604 | Business report writing | BDEOA | 336 | 3S | U |
| 040708 | Risk and insurance | Fin | 340 | 3S | U |
| 041308 | Real estate II | Fin | 346 | 3S | U |
| 050605 | Magazine writing | Jrnl | 318 | 3S | U |
| 050608 | Newswriting | Jrnl | 116 | 3S | L |
| 051106 | Parliamentary procedures | Comm | 251 | 1S | L |
| 0599 | Survey of broadcasting | Comm | 218 | 3S | L |
| 0599 | Writing for brdcst media | Comm | 218 | 3S | L |
| 070899 | Foundations of spec educ | SpEd | 162 | 3S | L |
| 100206 | Personal finance mgmt | Fin | 108 | 2S | L |
| 120305 | English grammar | Engl | 310 | 3S | U |
| 120307 | Intro to literature | Engl | 130 | 2S | L |
| 120307 | Intro to literature | Engl | 130 | 3S | L |
| 120307 | Intro to the short story | Engl | 231 | 2S | L |
| 120307 | Lit for younger children | Engl | 280 | 3S | L |
| 120307 | The Bible as literature | Engl | 334 | 3S | U |
| 120310 | Intro to fiction writing | Engl | 220 | 3S | L |
| 120310 | Expository writing | Engl | 305 | 2S | U |
| 120310 | Expository wrtng–technic | Engl | 305T | 2S | U |
| 160299 | Basic elementary math I | Math | 104 | 3S | L |
| 160302 | Intermediate algebra | Math | 111 | 4S | L |
| 160399 | Basic elementary math III | Math | 304 | 3S | U |
| 160801 | Principles of statistics | Math | 241 | 3S | L |
| 161101 | Math of finance | Math | 212 | 3S | L |
| 161199 | Fundamentals & applicatns | Math | 201 | 3S | L |
| 190104 | Hist & principles of PE | MWPE | 201 | 2S | L |
| 190109 | Org & admin of phys educ | MWPE | 441 | 3S | U |
| 190504 | Adv first aid & emer care | H&S | 211 | 2S | L |
| 190511 | Intro to general safety | H&S | 323 | 3S | U |
| 190599 | Traffic & transp safety | H&S | 325 | 3S | U |
| 190599 | Ath trng & emer first aid | MWPE | 292 | 3S | L |
| 200199 | General psychology | Psych | 101 | 3S | L |
| 200501 | Abnormal psychology | Psy | 368 | 3S | U |
| 200504 | Developmental psychology | EdPsy | 221 | 3S | L |
| 200509 | Psy of personality & adjt | EdPsy | 426 | 3S | U |
| 200799 | Intro to social psycholgy | Socio | 240 | 3S | L |
| 200804 | Educational psychology | EdPsy | 322 | 3S | U |
| 200804 | Adolescent psychology | EdPsy | 422 | 3S | U |
| 210499 | Intro to soc wlfr/soc wrk | SocWk | 290 | 3S | L |
| 210499 | Child welfare services | SocWk | 392 | 2S | U |
| 220301 | Political geography | Geog | 432 | 3S | U |
| 220301 | Global geography | Geog | 330 | 3S | U |
| 220302 | Intro to economic geog | Geog | 213 | 3S | L |
| 220305 | Man's physical environmnt | Geog | 111 | 3S | L |
| 220305 | Intro to earth & sky sci | Geog | 113 | 3S | L |
| 220308 | Urban geography | Geog | 431 | 3S | U |
| 220399 | Conservation of nat resrs | Geog | 433 | 3S | U |
| 220432 | The US since 1865 | Hist | 202 | 3S | L |
| 220433 | Studies in world civlztn | Hist | 101 | 3S | L |
| 220433 | Studies in world civlztn | Hist | 102 | 3S | L |
| 220602 | Criminology | Crim | 200 | 3S | L |
| 220602 | Correctional institutions | Crim | 430 | 3S | U |
| 220602 | Criminal investigations | Crim | 435 | 3S | U |
| 220605 | Courtship & marriage | Socio | 260 | 3S | L |
| 220606 | Principles of sociology | Socio | 120 | 3S | L |
| | **Noncredit courses** | | | | |
| 040299 | Basic mgmt & supervision | CntEd | BSBM1 | NC | |
| 040299 | Basic mgmt & supervision | CntEd | BSBM2 | NC | |

## (16) INDIANA UNIVERSITY

Mr. Frank R. DiSilvestro
Director of Independent Study Program
Owen Hall
Indiana University
Bloomington, Indiana 47405
Phone: 812-335-3693

Gifted high school students are permitted to enroll in undergraduate courses for credit. Overseas enrollment accepted.

| NCES No. | Course Title | Dept. | Course No. | Credits | Level |
|---|---|---|---|---|---|
| | **High School courses** | | | | |
| 0106 | Plant science 1st sem | Scien | 21H | HF | H |
| 0106 | Plant science 2nd sem | Scien | 22H | HF | H |
| 030302 | Music history & lit | Music | 01M | HF | H |
| 030501 | Drawing and storytelling | Art | 23A | HF | H |
| 030501 | Basic art level 1 | Art | 03A | HF | H |
| 030502 | Art history & appreciatn | Art | 31H | HF | H |
| 030502 | Creative vision | Art | 31T | HF | H |
| 040108 | Beginning accounting 1 | BusEd | 21B | HF | H |
| 040108 | Beginning accounting 2 | BusEd | 22B | HF | H |
| 040108 | Advanced accounting sem 1 | BusEd | 31B | HF | H |
| 040205 | Beginning shorthand sem 1 | BusEd | 25S | HF | H |
| 040207 | Typewriting 1st sem | BusEd | 21T | HF | H |
| 040207 | Typewriting 2nd sem | BusEd | 22T | HF | H |
| 040299 | Office procedures | BusEd | 31P | HF | H |
| 040601 | Business English | BusEd | 31E | HF | H |
| 0499 | Gen bus 1st sem | BusEd | 11G | HF | H |
| 0499 | Gen bus 2nd sem | BusEd | 12G | HF | H |
| 0499 | Salesmanship | DisEd | 31S | HF | H |
| 0499 | Gen merchandising retail | DisEd | 31M | HF | H |
| 050699 | Journalism | Engl | 01J | HF | H |
| 051103 | Speech | Engl | 09S | HF | H |
| 0599 | Mass media | Engl | 01M | HF | H |
| 060705 | Intr BASIC programming 1 | Multi | 33C | HF | H |
| 060705 | Intr BASIC programming 2 | Multi | 34C | HF | H |
| 061101 | Computer literacy | Multi | 01C | HF | H |
| 061104 | Beginning data processing | BusEd | 31D | HF | H |
| 070703 | Voc info career planning | Multi | 01V | HF | H |
| 070703 | Voc info self-discovery | Multi | 02V | HF | H |
| 0801 | Princ flight/space travel | Scien | 01A | HF | H |
| 090901 | Human dev & family health | Hlth | 12H | HF | H |
| 090999 | Health & safety education | Hlth | 11B | HF | H |
| 100202 | Consumer education | HmEc | 41C | HF | H |
| 100313 | Foods and nutrition | HmEc | 11N | HF | H |
| 100402 | Family management | HmEc | 02F | HF | H |
| 100503 | Housing & interior design | HmEc | 41H | HF | H |
| 100601 | Child development | HmEc | 31C | HF | H |
| 100699 | Pers adj/marr/fam living | HmEc | 01F | HF | H |
| 110503 | Drafting 1st semester | IndA | 11M | HF | H |
| 110503 | Drafting 2nd semester | IndA | 12M | HF | H |
| 110503 | Architectural drafting | IndA | 21A | HF | H |
| 120299 | Experience of drama | Engl | 31D | HF | H |
| 120305 | Adv grammar & composition | Engl | 01V | HF | H |
| 120305 | Basic vocabulary | Engl | 01V | HF | H |
| 120305 | English II grammar & comp | Engl | 30W | HF | H |
| 120307 | Freshman English 1st sem | Engl | 11E | HF | H |
| 120307 | Freshman English 2nd sem | Engl | 12E | HF | H |
| 120307 | Sophomore English 1st sem | Engl | 21E | HF | H |
| 120307 | Sophomore English 2nd sem | Engl | 22E | HF | H |
| 120307 | American lit 1st sem | Engl | 31L | HF | H |
| 120307 | American lit 2nd sem | Engl | 32L | HF | H |
| 120307 | Women writers | Engl | 33L | HF | H |
| 120307 | Eng lit 1st sem | Engl | 41L | HF | H |
| 120307 | Eng lit 2nd sem | Engl | 42L | HF | H |
| 120307 | Four American novels | Engl | 73L | QT | H |
| 120307 | Children's literature | Engl | 81K | QT | H |
| 120307 | Literature of the future | Engl | 82L | QT | H |
| 120307 | Mythology | Engl | 83L | QT | H |
| 120307 | Mysteries | Engl | 84L | QT | H |
| 120307 | The Bible and literature | Engl | 51B | HF | H |
| 120307 | The short story | Engl | 81L | QT | H |
| 120308 | Developmental reading | Engl | 01R | HF | H |
| 120310 | Senior-year composition | Engl | 41W | HF | H |
| 120310 | Creative writing-fiction | Engl | 05W | HF | H |
| 120310 | Basic composition | Engl | 81W | QT | H |
| 120310 | Advanced composition | Engl | 91W | QT | H |
| 120399 | Vocabulary improvement | Engl | 81V | QT | H |
| 120399 | How to study in college | Engl | 91S | QT | H |
| 1210 | First-yr French 1st sem | Fren | 11F | HF | H |
| 1210 | First-yr French 2nd sem | Fren | 12F | HF | H |
| 1210 | Second-yr French 1st sem | Fren | 21F | HF | H |
| 1210 | Second-yr French 2nd sem | Fren | 22F | HF | H |
| 1211 | First-yr German 1st sem | Ger | 11G | HF | H |
| 1211 | First-yr German 2nd sem | Ger | 12G | HF | H |
| 1211 | Second-yr German 1st sem | Ger | 21G | HF | H |
| 1211 | Second-yr German 2nd sem | Ger | 22G | HF | H |
| 1216 | First-yr Latin 1st sem | Latin | 11L | HF | H |
| 1216 | First-yr Latin 2nd sem | Latin | 12L | HF | H |

| NCES No. | Course Title | Dept. | Course No. | Credits | Level |
|---|---|---|---|---|---|
| 1216 | Second-yr Latin 1st sem | Latin | 21L | HF | H |
| 1216 | Second-yr Latin 2nd sem | Latin | 22L | HF | H |
| 1225 | First-yr Spanish 1st sem | Span | 11S | HF | H |
| 1225 | First-yr Spanish 2nd sem | Span | 12S | HF | H |
| 1225 | Second-yr Spanish 1st sem | Span | 21S | HF | H |
| 1225 | Second-yr Spanish 2nd sem | Span | 22S | HF | H |
| 130799 | Business law | BusEd | 31L | HF | H |
| 1499 | Library & research skills | Engl | 23L | HF | H |
| 150399 | General biology 1st sem | Scien | 21B | HF | H |
| 150399 | General biology 2nd sem | Scien | 22B | HF | H |
| 150401 | Phys sci-introd chemistry | Scien | 21P | HF | H |
| 1507 | Phys sci-introd physics | Scien | 22P | HF | H |
| 150799 | Physics 1st sem | Scien | 41P | HF | H |
| 150799 | Physics 2nd sem | Scien | 42P | HF | H |
| 1509 | Earth science 1st sem | Scien | 11E | HF | H |
| 1509 | Earth science 2nd sem | Scien | 12E | HF | H |
| 160199 | Basic math 1st sem | Math | 11M | HF | H |
| 160199 | Basic math 2nd sem | Math | 12M | HF | H |
| 160302 | Algebra 1st sem | Math | 11A | HF | H |
| 160302 | Algebra 2nd sem | Math | 12A | HF | H |
| 160302 | Advanced algebra I | Math | 21A | HF | H |
| 160302 | Advanced algebra II | Math | 22A | HF | H |
| 160401 | Calculus 1st sem | Math | 41C | HF | H |
| 160601 | Plane geometry 1st sem | Math | 21G | HF | H |
| 160601 | Plane geometry 2nd sem | Math | 22G | HF | H |
| 160602 | Trigonometry | Math | 41T | HF | H |
| 161201 | Business mathematics | Math | 11B | HF | H |
| 161202 | Consumer mathematics | Math | 03C | HF | H |
| 200199 | Psychology | SocSt | 01P | HF | H |
| 200406 | Understand-improve memory | Engl | 81S | HF | H |
| 220201 | Economics | SocSt | 41E | HF | H |
| 220399 | World geography 1st sem | SocSt | 21G | HF | H |
| 220399 | World geography 2nd sem | SocSt | 22G | HF | H |
| 220432 | United States history 1 | SocSt | 31A | HF | H |
| 220432 | United States history 2 | SocSt | 32A | HF | H |
| 220433 | World history 1st sem | SocSt | 11W | HF | H |
| 220433 | World history 2nd sem | SocSt | 12W | HF | H |
| 220501 | United States govt I | SocSt | 41G | HF | H |
| 220501 | US govt II–current probs | SocSt | 42G | HF | H |
| 220699 | Sociology | SocSt | 01S | HF | H |
| 220699 | Males & females in Am soc | SocSt | 05S | HF | H |
| 2299 | Intro to social science | SocSt | 11X | HF | H |

**College courses**

| NCES No. | Course Title | Dept. | Course No. | Credits | Level |
|---|---|---|---|---|---|
| 030399 | Music for the listener | Music | M174 | 3S | L |
| 030399 | Rudiments of music 1 | Music | T109 | 3S | L |
| 030501 | Textiles | HmEc | H203 | 3S | L |
| 030502 | Intro to African art | FnArt | A250 | 3S | L |
| 030603 | Ancient & medieval art | InArt | A101 | 4S | L |
| 040101 | Intro to accounting I | Bus | A201 | 3S | L |
| 040101 | Intro to accounting II | Bus | A202 | 3S | L |
| 040106 | Cost accounting | Bus | A325 | 3S | U |
| 040109 | Prins of hospital acctg | Bus | A203 | 3S | L |
| 040109 | Intermed hospital acctg | Bus | A233 | 3S | L |
| 040109 | Hosp budget & cost analys | Bus | A333 | 3S | U |
| 040109 | Fund accounting | Bus | A335 | 3S | U |
| 040114 | Intro to taxation | Bus | A328 | 3S | U |
| 040114 | Advanced income tax | Bus | A339 | 3S | U |
| 040199 | Intermediate acctg theory | Bus | A211 | 3S | L |
| 040199 | Intermediate acctg probs | Bus | A212 | 2S | L |
| 040199 | Adv financial acctg I | Bus | A322 | 3S | U |
| 040199 | Prof aspects of acctg | Bus | A434 | 3S | U |
| 040299 | Administrative systems | Bus | C300 | 3S | U |
| 040302 | Personal finance | Bus | F260 | 3S | L |
| 040304 | Mgt comm banks & fin inst | Bus | I446 | 3S | U |
| 040306 | Investment | Bus | F420 | 3S | U |
| 040312 | Bus enterprise & pub pol | Bus | G406 | 3S | U |
| 040601 | Business communications | Bus | C204 | 3S | L |
| 040708 | Prin of risk & insurance | Bus | N300 | 3S | U |
| 0408 | Internat'l business admin | Bus | D300 | 3S | U |
| 0408 | Environ anal for int bus | bus | D419 | 3S | U |
| 040902 | Retail management | Bus | M419 | 3S | U |
| 040903 | Org behav & leadership | Bus | Z300 | 3S | U |
| 040903 | Org behav & ldrship-hosp | Bus | Z300H | 3S | U |
| 040904 | Financial management | bus | F301 | 3S | U |
| 040904 | Operations management | Bus | P301 | 3S | U |
| 041001 | Intro to marketing | Bus | M300 | 3S | U |
| 041303 | Prins of real estate | Bus | R300 | 3S | U |
| 0499 | Business admin: intro | Bus | X100 | 3S | L |
| 0499 | Job search techniques | Bus | X425 | 1S | U |
| 0499 | Basic career development | COAS | Q294 | 1S | L |
| 0499 | Principles of urban econ | Bus | G330 | 3S | U |

| NCES No. | Course Title | Dept. | Course No. | Credits | Level |
|---|---|---|---|---|---|
| 050605 | Writing for publication | Jrnl | C327 | 3S | U |
| 051103 | Interpersonal communicatn | Speec | S122 | 2S | L |
| 051107 | Public speaking | Speec | S121 | 2S | L |
| 0599 | Intro to mass communicats | Jrnl | C200 | 3S | L |
| 0599 | Citizen and the news | Jrnl | C300 | 3S | U |
| 060705 | COBOL & file processing | CmpSc | C203 | 3S | L |
| 060705 | COBOL programming | CmpSc | C303 | 1S | L |
| 060707 | Foundations digital comp | CmpSc | C251 | 3S | L |
| 060799 | Intr to computer programg | CmpSc | C201 | 4S | L |
| 070401 | Math in elementary school | Educ | E343 | 3S | U |
| 070401 | Prins of secondary educ | Educ | S485 | 3S | U |
| 070401 | Prins: jr hi & mid sch ed | Educ | S486 | 3S | U |
| 070503 | Self-instruction in art | Educ | M135 | 1S | L |
| 070503 | Self-instruction in art | Educ | M135 | 2S | L |
| 070503 | Self-instruction in art | Educ | M135 | 3S | L |
| 070503 | Self-instruction in art | Educ | M135 | 4S | L |
| 070503 | Self-instruction in art | Educ | M135 | 5S | L |
| 070503 | Art expers–elem teacher | Educ | M333 | 2S | U |
| 070516 | Math for elem teachers 1 | Math | T101 | 3S | L |
| 070516 | Math for elem teachers 2 | Math | T102 | 3S | L |
| 070516 | Math for elem teachers 3 | Math | T103 | 3S | L |
| 070704 | Human dev opps college st | Educ | U205 | 3S | L |
| 070899 | Intr to exceptional child | Educ | K205 | 3S | L |
| 090115 | Nutrition thru life cycle | Nurs | B215 | 3S | L |
| 090118 | Pharmacology | Nurs | B219 | 3S | L |
| 090255 | Dynamics of nursing I | Nurs | J355 | 3S | U |
| 090255 | Dynamics of nursing II | Nurs | J356 | 3S | U |
| 090255 | Dynamics of nursing III | Nurs | J357 | 3S | U |
| 090255 | Dynamics of nursing IV | Nurs | J358 | 3S | U |
| 090255 | Framework nursing practic | Nurs | B400 | 1S | U |
| 090255 | Acute health disruptions | Nurs | J304 | 3S | U |
| 090255 | Health disruptions | Nurs | J305 | 3S | U |
| 090255 | Chronic health disruption | Nurs | J408 | 2S | U |
| 090255 | Human sex & health profes | Nurs | K380 | 3S | U |
| 090255 | Mental health disruptions | Nurs | P306 | 3S | U |
| 090699 | Leadership in nursing | Nurs | L473 | 2S | U |
| 090999 | Med terms from Greek-Lat | Clas | C209 | 2S | L |
| 100313 | Human nutrition | HmEc | H231 | 3S | L |
| 100699 | Marriage & family interac | HmEc | H258 | 3S | L |
| 110699 | Prins of transportation | Bus | T300 | 3S | U |
| 120199 | Intro to study of lang | Ling | L103 | 3S | L |
| 120201 | Introduction to film | CmLit | C190 | 3S | L |
| 120201 | Mod lit & other arts: int | CmLit | C255 | 3S | L |
| 120204 | Literary interpretation | Engl | L202 | 3S | L |
| 120204 | Crit stdy: Eng lit to 170 | Engl | L211 | 3S | L |
| 120204 | Cr stdy Eng lit snce 1700 | Engl | L212 | 3S | L |
| 120305 | Intro to the English lang | Engl | G205 | 3S | L |
| 120305 | English grammar review | Engl | W202 | 1S | L |
| 120307 | Classical mythology | Clas | C205 | 3S | L |
| 120307 | Introduction to drama | Engl | L203 | 3S | L |
| 120307 | Introduction to fiction | Engl | L204 | 3S | L |
| 120307 | Introduction to poetry | Engl | L205 | 3S | L |
| 120307 | Intro to Shakespeare | Engl | L220 | 3S | L |
| 120307 | Late Shakespeare plays | Engl | L314 | 3S | U |
| 120307 | American fiction to 1900 | Engl | L355 | 3S | U |
| 120307 | American drama | Engl | L363 | 3S | U |
| 120307 | Children's literature | Engl | L390 | 3S | U |
| 120307 | 19th-century Brit fiction | Engl | L348 | 3S | U |
| 120307 | 20th-century Amer fiction | Engl | L358 | 3S | U |
| 120307 | Women and literature | Engl | L207 | 3S | L |
| 120308 | Reading/learning techs 1 | Educ | X150 | 1S | D |
| 120308 | Read/learn tech 3: human | Educ | X152A | 1S | D |
| 120308 | Read/learn tech 3: soc sc | Educ | X152B | 1S | D |
| 120308 | Read/learn techs 3: scien | Educ | X152C | 1S | D |
| 120308 | Literary masterpieces I | Engl | L213 | 3S | L |
| 120308 | Literary masterpieces II | Engl | L214 | 3S | L |
| 120308 | Amer lit since 1914 | Engl | L354 | 3S | U |
| 120309 | Effective oral communicat | Speec | S124 | 3S | L |
| 120309 | Bus & prof speaking | Speec | S223 | 3S | L |
| 120309 | Freedom of speech | Speec | S339 | 3S | U |
| 120310 | Elementary composition | Engl | W131 | 3S | L |
| 120310 | Prof writing skills | Engl | W231 | 3S | L |
| 120310 | Advanced expository writg | Engl | W350 | 3S | U |
| 120310 | Creative writing: poetry | Engl | W203A | 3S | L |
| 120310 | Creative writing: prose | Engl | W203B | 3S | L |
| 120310 | Creative wrtg: poet/prose | Engl | W203C | 3S | L |
| 120310 | Intro creative writing | Engl | W103 | 3S | L |
| 120310 | Crit review writing-film | Engl | W119 | 1S | L |
| 120399 | Intr: wrtg & lit study I | Engl | L141 | 4S | L |
| 120399 | Intr: wrtg & lit study II | Engl | L142 | 4S | L |
| 120399 | Intr wrtg & lit: murder | Engl | L141A | 4S | L |
| 120399 | Vocabulary acquisition | Engl | W205 | 1S | L |

| NCES No. | Course Title | Dept. | Course No. | Credits | Level |
|---|---|---|---|---|---|
| 1210 | Elementary French 1 | Frnch | F100 | 4S | L |
| 1214 | Elementary Italian I | Ital | M100 | 4S | L |
| 1214 | Elementary Italian II | Ital | M150 | 4S | L |
| 1216 | Elementary Latin I | Clas | L100 | 4S | L |
| 1216 | Elementary Latin II | Clas | L150 | 4S | L |
| 1225 | 2nd yr Spanish reading I | Span | S216 | 3S | L |
| 1225 | 2nd yr Spanish reading II | Span | S266 | 3S | L |
| 130299 | Leg environment of bus | Bus | L201 | 3S | L |
| 130299 | Commercial law II | Bus | L303 | 3S | U |
| 130403 | Amer juvenile justice sys | CrJu | P475 | 3S | U |
| 131004 | Occupationl hlth & safety | LabSt | L240 | 3S | L |
| 131099 | Labor law | LabSt | L201 | 3S | L |
| 150102 | The solar system | Astro | A100 | 3S | L |
| 150103 | Stellar astronomy | Astro | A105 | 3S | L |
| 150199 | Introduction to astronomy | Astro | A110 | 3S | L |
| 150201 | Weather and climate | Geog | G109 | 3S | L |
| 150399 | Contemporary biology | Bio | N100 | 3S | L |
| 150599 | Earth sci: matls/process | Geol | G103 | 3S | L |
| 150799 | Physics in modern world I | Phys | P101 | 4S | L |
| 150799 | Energy | Phys | P110 | 2S | L |
| 150799 | Energy and technology | Phys | P120 | 3S | L |
| 160199 | Excursions into math | Math | M110 | 3S | L |
| 160203 | Finite mathematics | Math | M118 | 3S | L |
| 160302 | Basic algebra | Math | M014 | 4S | D |
| 160399 | Pre-calculus mathematics | Math | M125 | 3S | L |
| 160401 | Brief surv of calculus I | Math | M119 | 3S | L |
| 160602 | Trigonometric functions | Math | M126 | 2S | L |
| 160603 | Analyt geom & calc I | Math | M215 | 5S | L |
| 160603 | Analyt geom & calc II | Math | M216 | 5S | L |
| 160899 | Statistical techniques | Psych | K300 | 3S | U |
| 180202 | Nature of scient inquiry | HPSc | X201 | 3S | L |
| 180399 | Elementary ethics | Philo | P140 | 3S | L |
| 180401 | Ancient Greek philosophy | Philo | P201 | 3S | L |
| 180499 | Women in phil thouglt | Phil | P282 | 3S | L |
| 1808 | Intro to philosophy | Philo | P100 | 3S | L |
| 181104 | Intro to relig in West | Relig | R152 | 3S | L |
| 190106 | Org & curr str phy e K-12 | HPER | P497 | 3S | U |
| 190502 | Health probs in community | HPER | H366 | 3S | U |
| 190508 | Nutritional ecology | HmEc | H220 | 3S | L |
| 190509 | Personal health | HPER | H363 | 3S | U |
| 190513 | Organiz of health educ | HPER | H464 | 2S | U |
| 190702 | Leisure services arm forc | HPER | R317 | 3S | U |
| 190703 | Recreation and leisure | HPER | R160 | 3S | L |
| 190703 | Recreational sports progr | HPER | R324 | 3S | U |
| 200199 | Introd psychology I | Psych | P101 | 3S | L |
| 200199 | Introd psychology II | Psych | P102 | 3S | L |
| 200501 | Abnormal psychology | Psych | P324 | 3S | U |
| 200508 | Psy: childhood & adolesc | Psych | P316 | 3S | U |
| 200509 | Psychology of personality | Psych | P319 | 3S | U |
| 200799 | Social psychology | Psych | P320 | 3S | U |
| 200804 | Psych measurement–schools | Educ | P407 | 3S | U |
| 210103 | Personnel mgt in pub sect | SPEA | V373 | 3S | U |
| 210103 | Managing human resources | SPEA | V366 | 3S | U |
| 210199 | Policy in state govt | SPEA | V445 | 3S | U |
| 210199 | Contemp issues in pub aff | SPEA | V450 | 3S | U |
| 210304 | Fndtns criminal investig | CrJu | P320 | 3S | U |
| 210399 | Amer juvenile justice sys | CrJu | P475 | 3S | U |
| 220101 | Human origins & prehist | Anthr | A105 | 3S | L |
| 220102 | Intro to cultures/Africa | Anthr | E310 | 3S | U |
| 220102 | Culture and society | Anthr | E105 | 3S | L |
| 220201 | Intro to microeconomics | Econ | E103 | 3S | L |
| 220201 | Intro to macroeconomics | Econ | E104 | 3S | L |
| 220206 | Public finance: survey | Econ | E360 | 3S | U |
| 220213 | Intro to managerial econ | Bus | G300 | 3S | U |
| 220299 | Intro stat theory ec/bus | Econ | E270 | 3S | L |
| 220301 | Intro to human geography | Geog | G110 | 3S | L |
| 220305 | Phys systems–environment | Geog | G107 | 3S | L |
| 220306 | World regional geography | Geog | G120 | 3S | L |
| 220399 | Environmental conservatn | Geog | G315 | 3S | U |
| 220399 | Meteorology & phys clima | Geog | G304 | 3S | U |
| 220409 | Amer soc hist 1865-presen | Hist | A317 | 3S | U |
| 220420 | History of Africa II | Hist | E432 | 3S | U |
| 220421 | Colonial & revol America | Hist | A301 | 3S | U |
| 220423 | Mod East Asian civiliz | Hist | H207 | 3S | L |
| 220426 | Europe in 20th century I | Hist | B361 | 3S | U |
| 220426 | Europe in 20th century II | Hist | B362 | 3S | U |
| 220426 | French Rev & Napoleon | Hist | B356 | 3S | U |
| 220426 | Europe: Renaissance/Napol | Hist | H103 | 3S | L |
| 220426 | Europe: Napoleon/present | Hist | H104 | 3S | L |
| 220427 | Lat-Am culture & civiliz | Hist | H211 | 3S | L |
| 220428 | Survey Indiana history | Hist | A363 | 3S | U |
| 220432 | American history I | Hist | H105 | 3S | L |
| 220432 | American history II | Hist | H106 | 3S | L |
| 220433 | World in 20th century I | Hist | H101 | 3S | L |
| 220450 | Ancient Greek culture | Clas | C101 | 3S | L |
| 220450 | Roman culture | Clas | C102 | 3S | L |
| 220451 | Hist backgrd–contemp prob | Hist | H111 | 3S | L |
| 220470 | Hist of Black Americans | Hist | A364 | 3S | U |
| 220472 | Women in American history | Hist | H225 | 3S | L |
| 220499 | The American West | Hist | A318 | 3S | U |
| 220499 | History of Indiana | Hist | A333 | 2S | U |
| 220499 | American military history | Hist | H220 | 3S | L |
| 220499 | American labor history | LabSt | L101 | 3S | L |
| 220499 | Directed labor study | LabSt | L495 | VC | U |
| 220504 | Intro to world politics | PolSc | Y109 | 3S | L |
| 220507 | Pol parties & int groups | PolSc | Y301 | 3S | U |
| 220509 | Intro to Amer politics | PolSc | Y103 | 3S | L |
| 220510 | Intro to political theory | PolSc | Y105 | 3S | L |
| 220599 | Labor & political system | LabSt | L203 | 3S | L |
| 220599 | Union org & govt | LabSt | L270 | 3S | L |
| 220599 | Sex discrimination & law | PolSc | Y200 | 3S | L |
| 220599 | Black politics | PolSc | Y325 | 3S | U |
| 220599 | Intro to world politics | Pol | Y109 | 3S | L |
| 220601 | The community | Soc | S309 | 3S | U |
| 220603 | Population & human ecol | Soc | S305 | 3S | U |
| 220605 | Sociology of the family | Soc | S316 | 3S | U |
| 220606 | Soc analysis of society | Soc | S100 | 3S | L |
| 220606 | Principles of sociology | Soc | S161 | 3S | L |
| 220606 | Social theory | Soc | S340 | 3S | U |
| 220610 | Deviant bhvr/soc control | Soc | S320 | 3S | U |
| 220610 | Ther of norm violatg behv | CrJu | P200 | 3S | L |
| 220612 | Social change | Soc | S215 | 3S | L |
| 220612 | Social organization | Soc | S210 | 3S | L |
| 220613 | Social problems | Soc | R121 | 3S | L |
| 220614 | Urban sociology | Soc | S461 | 3S | U |
| 220699 | Society & the individual | Soc | S230 | 3S | L |
| 220699 | Sociology of religion | Soc | S313 | 3S | U |
| 220699 | Sociology of work | Soc | S315 | 3S | U |
| 220699 | Social stratification | Soc | S317 | 3S | U |
| 220699 | Sociology of sex roles | Soc | S338 | 3S | U |
| 220699 | Sociology of law | Soc | S424 | 3S | U |
| 2299 | Introduction to folklore | Flklr | F101 | 3S | L |
| 2299 | Intro to Amer folklore | Flklr | F220 | 3S | L |
| 2299 | Intro to philos of sci | HPSc | X303 | 3S | U |
| 2299 | Int to scientific reason | HPSc | X200 | 3S | L |
| 2299 | Connections:tech & change | HPSc | X355 | 3S | U |
| 2299 | Topics: interdisciplinary | Flklr | F404 | 3S | U |

**Noncredit courses**

| NCES No. | Course Title | Dept. | Course No. | Credits |
|---|---|---|---|---|
| 040301 | Small business finance 1 | Bus | Bus 9 | NC |
| 040301 | Small business finance 2 | Bus | Bus10 | NC |
| 040306 | Securities & investing | PF | 1 | NC |
| 040599 | Owning/mging small bus | Bus | Bus 6 | NC |
| 041005 | Adver/promoting sm bus | Bus | Bus 7 | NC |
| 0499 | Bus topics for artists | Bus | Bus 8 | NC |
| 050699 | Labor journalism | LS | 1 | NC |
| 0607 | Intro computer literacy | CmpSc | Comp1 | NC |
| 0608 | Intro BASIC programming 1 | CmpSc | Comp2 | NC |
| 0608 | Intro BASIC programming 2 | CmpSc | Comp3 | NC |
| 070703 | Employ search strat: pers | CP | 4 | NC |
| 070703 | Employ search strat: jobs | CP | 5 | NC |
| 090308 | Rec ther for bdrdn/handcp | CP | CP6 | NC |
| 090399 | Motivating nurs home res | CP | CP7 | NC |
| 090399 | Soc servs health care fac | CP | CP11 | NC |
| 100699 | Preparation for retiremnt | CP | 2 | NC |
| 120305 | Adv grammar & composition | RS | RS3 | NC |
| 120399 | Understndg/improvg memory | RS | 4 | NC |
| 131401 | Appraisal ltd ed prints | ISA | ISA 1 | NC |
| 131401 | Appraisal oriental rugs | ISA | ISA 4 | NC |
| 131401 | Appraisal apprec res cont | ISA | ISA 5 | NC |
| 131401 | Appraisal paintings | ISA | ISA 7 | NC |
| 131401 | Appraisal antique jewelry | ISA | ISA10 | NC |
| 160199 | Overcoming math anxiety | GIBM | 3 | NC |
| 160399 | Arithmetic for algebra I | GIBM | 1 | NC |
| 160399 | Arithmetic for algebra II | GIBM | 2 | NC |
| 190311 | Pressure defense basketba | Athl | Ath 1 | NC |
| 1999 | Intro to collectibles | H&R | 2 | NC |
| 1999 | Finding your roots | H&R | 3 | NC |
| 220502 | English & government | Cit | 1 | NC |
| 220502 | Our Constitution & govt | Cit | 2 | NC |

## (17) LOUISIANA STATE UNIVERSITY

Mr. Don Hammons
Director, Department of Independent Study
Office of Independent Study
Louisiana State University
Baton Rouge, Louisiana 70803
Phone: 504-388-3171

Enrollment on a noncredit basis accepted in all credit courses. Gifted high school students are permitted to enroll in undergraduate courses for credit. Overseas enrollment accepted.

| NCES No. | Course Title | Dept. | Course No. | Credits | Level |
|---|---|---|---|---|---|
| | **High School courses** | | | | |
| 030599 | Art | Art | 121 | HF | H |
| 030599 | Art | Art | 122 | HF | H |
| 040104 | Bookkeeping | Bus | 231 | HF | H |
| 040104 | Bookkeeping | Bus | 232 | HF | H |
| 040205 | Shorthand | Bus | 221 | HF | H |
| 040207 | Typewriting | Bus | 211 | HF | H |
| 040207 | Typewriting | Bus | 212 | HF | H |
| 040299 | Clerical practice | Bus | 241 | HF | H |
| 041299 | Data processing | Bus | 251 | HF | H |
| 0499 | General business | Bus | 201 | HF | H |
| 0499 | General business | Bus | 202 | HF | H |
| 061101 | Computer literacy | Math | 171 | HF | H |
| 0810 | Drafting technology | InArt | 161 | HF | H |
| 100202 | Consumer education | HmEc | 153 | HF | H |
| 100312 | Nutrition education | HmEc | 155 | HF | H |
| 100699 | Home and family | HmEc | 151 | HF | H |
| 120399 | English I | Engl | 311 | HF | H |
| 120399 | English I | Engl | 312 | HF | H |
| 120399 | English II | Engl | 321 | HF | H |
| 120399 | English II | Engl | 322 | HF | H |
| 120399 | English III | Engl | 331 | HF | H |
| 120399 | English III | Engl | 332 | HF | H |
| 120399 | English IV | Engl | 341 | HF | H |
| 120399 | English IV | Engl | 342 | HF | H |
| 120399 | Business English | Engl | 351 | HF | H |
| 120399 | Business English | Engl | 352 | HF | H |
| 1210 | French | Frnch | 141 | HF | H |
| 1210 | French | Frnch | 142 | HF | H |
| 1225 | Spanish | Span | 145 | HF | H |
| 1225 | Spanish | Span | 146 | HF | H |
| 1503 | Biology | Biol | 511 | HF | H |
| 1503 | Biology | Biol | 512 | HF | H |
| 150899 | General science | Sci | 501 | HF | H |
| 150899 | General science | Sci | 502 | HF | H |
| 160301 | Mathematics I | Math | 401 | HF | H |
| 160301 | Mathematics I | Math | 402 | HF | H |
| 160301 | Mathematics II | Math | 441 | HF | H |
| 160301 | Mathematics II | Math | 442 | HF | H |
| 160302 | Algebra I | Math | 411 | HF | H |
| 160302 | Algebra I | Math | 412 | HF | H |
| 160302 | Algebra II | Math | 431 | HF | H |
| 160302 | Algebra II | Math | 432 | HF | H |
| 160602 | Trigonometry | Math | 451 | HF | H |
| 161201 | Business math | Math | 421 | HF | H |
| 161201 | Business math | Math | 422 | HF | H |
| 161202 | Consumer mathematics | Math | 461 | HF | H |
| 161202 | Consumer mathematics | Math | 462 | HF | H |
| 190599 | Health | HEd | 131 | HF | H |
| 190599 | Health | HEd | 132 | HF | H |
| 220299 | Free enterprise | SoSci | 661 | HF | H |
| 220399 | World geography | SoSci | 601 | HF | H |
| 220399 | World geography | SoSci | 602 | HF | H |
| 220432 | American history | SoSci | | HF | H |
| 220433 | World history | SoSci | 621 | HF | H |
| 220501 | American government | SoSci | | HF | H |
| 220611 | Sociology | SoSci | | HF | H |
| 220612 | Sociology | SoSci | | HF | H |
| 2299 | Civics | SoSci | 611 | HF | H |
| 2299 | Civics | SoSci | 612 | HF | H |
| | **College courses** | | | | |
| 010199 | Coop in agriculture | Agri | 4020C | 3S | U |
| 010406 | Elements of dairying | DySc | 1048C | 3S | L |
| 020902 | Home planning | ID | 3721C | 3S | U |
| 030399 | Music appreciation | Music | 1751C | 3S | L |
| 030399 | Music appreciation | Music | 1752C | 3S | L |
| 030399 | Music history | Music | 4451C | 3S | U |

| NCES No. | Course Title | Dept. | Course No. | Credits | Level |
|---|---|---|---|---|---|
| 030399 | Music history | Music | 4452C | 3S | U |
| 030499 | Introduction to theater | Spch | 1020C | 3S | L |
| 030499 | Argumentation & debate | Spch | 2063C | 3S | L |
| 030499 | Stage costuming | Spch | 4122C | 3S | U |
| 040101 | Intro financial acctg | Acctg | 2001C | 3S | L |
| 040101 | Intermediate acctg Pt I | Acctg | 2021C | 3S | L |
| 040101 | Intermediate acctg Pt II | Acctg | 3021C | 3S | U |
| 040101 | Advanced acctg | Acctg | 3022C | 3S | U |
| 040103 | Auditing | Acctg | 3222C | 3S | U |
| 040106 | Cost analysis & control | Acctg | 3121C | 3S | U |
| 040111 | Intro managerial acctg | Acctg | 2101C | 3S | L |
| 040114 | Income-tax acctg | Acctg | 3221C | 3S | U |
| 040201 | Office management | OAdm | 3400C | 3S | U |
| 040203 | Records management | BAdm | 3200C | 3S | U |
| 040205 | Beginning shorthand | OAdm | 2100C | 3S | L |
| 040207 | Beginning typewriting | OAdm | 2000C | 3S | L |
| 040207 | Intermediate typing | OAdm | 2001C | 3S | L |
| 040207 | Advanced typing | OAdm | 3000C | 3S | U |
| 040301 | Basic business finance | Fin | 3715C | 3S | U |
| 040308 | Money and banking | Econ | 3500C | 3S | U |
| 040399 | Business law | Fin | 3201C | 3S | U |
| 040399 | Commercial transactions | Fin | 3202C | 3S | U |
| 040399 | Principles of real estate | Fin | 3351C | 3S | U |
| 040601 | Business communication/ | BAdm | 2071C | 3S | L |
| 040705 | Life and health insurance | Fin | 3441C | 3S | U |
| 040709 | Property & liability ins | Fin | 3442C | 3S | U |
| 040799 | Risk and insurance | Fin | 3440C | 3S | U |
| 040901 | Mgmt prin & policies | Mgmt | 3159C | 3S | U |
| 040901 | Bus policies & problems | Mgmt | 3190C | 3S | U |
| 040903 | Human behavior in orgn | Mgmt | 4164C | 3S | U |
| 040999 | Business communication | Mgmt | 2071C | 3S | L |
| 040999 | Operations & info systems | Mgmt | 3115C | 3S | U |
| 040999 | Collective bargaining | Mktg | 3127C | 3S | U |
| 041001 | Prins of marketing | Mktg | 3401C | 3S | U |
| 041004 | Sales management | Mktg | 4423C | 3S | U |
| 041004 | Retailing management | Mktg | 4431C | 3S | U |
| 041004 | Marketing management | Mktg | 4451C | 3S | U |
| 041099 | Consumer anal & behavior | Mktg | 3411C | 3S | U |
| 041099 | Marketing research | Mktg | 3413C | 3S | U |
| 041099 | Mkt comm selling & advtg | Mktg | 4421C | 3S | U |
| 041107 | Personnel-human resources | Mgmt | 4167C | 3S | U |
| 041299 | Operations & info systems | QM | 3115C | 3S | U |
| 0499 | Intro to business | Bus | 1001C | 3S | L |
| 060701 | FORTRAN programming | CmpSc | 1240C | 3S | L |
| 060701 | COBOL programming | CmpSc | 2270C | 3S | L |
| 070199 | Intro to study of educ | Educ | 2000C | 3S | L |
| 070514 | School libraries | Educ | 3553C | 3S | U |
| 070599 | Books & AV for children | Educ | 3551C | 3S | U |
| 070801 | Char of excep children | Educ | 3700C | 3S | U |
| 070806 | Intro to mentally retardd | Educ | 3750C | 3S | U |
| 071199 | Evaluation of instruction | Educ | 3200C | 2S | U |
| 0810 | Engineering graphics | Engr | 1001C | 2S | L |
| 0810 | Machine drawing | Engr | 2162C | 2S | L |
| 081104 | Dynamics | ME | 3133C | 3S | U |
| 100103 | Clothing and human behavr | HmEc | 1030C | 3S | L |
| 100312 | Intro to human nutrition | HmEc | 1010C | 3S | L |
| 100602 | Changing home & family | HmEc | 1050C | 3S | L |
| 1199 | Intro to voc education | VTIE | 2070C | 3S | L |
| 120305 | English grammar | Engl | 2210C | 3S | L |
| 120307 | English lit to 1798 | Engl | 2020C | 3S | L |
| 120307 | Engl lit 1798-pres | Engl | 2022C | 3S | L |
| 120310 | English composition | Engl | 1001C | 3S | L |
| 120310 | English composition | Engl | 1002C | 3S | L |
| 120310 | Advanced composition | Engl | 2001C | 3S | L |
| 120310 | Technical writing | Engl | 2002C | 3S | L |
| 120399 | Intro to fiction | Engl | 2025C | 3S | L |
| 120399 | Intro to drama & poetry | Engl | 2027C | 3S | L |
| 120399 | Major American writers | Engl | 2070C | 3S | L |
| 1210 | Elementary French | Frnch | 1001C | 5S | L |
| 1210 | Intermediate French | Frnch | 2051C | 3S | L |
| 1210 | Intermediate French | Frnch | 2053C | 3S | L |
| 1211 | Intermediate German | Ger | 2053C | 3S | L |
| 1211 | Reading in German lit | Ger | 2055 | 3S | L |
| 1216 | Elementary Latin | Latin | 1001C | 5S | L |
| 1216 | Intermediate Latin | Latin | 2051C | 5S | L |
| 1216 | Vergil | Latin | 2055C | 3S | L |
| 1225 | Elementary Spanish | Span | 1001C | 5S | L |
| 1225 | Intermediate Spanish | Span | 2051C | 3S | L |
| 1225 | Intermediate Spanish | Span | 2053C | 3S | L |
| 1225 | Readings in Spanish lit | Span | 2055C | 3S | L |
| 150103 | Stellar astronomy | Astro | 1102C | 3S | L |
| 150199 | The solar system | Astro | 1101C | 3S | L |

| NCES No. | Course Title | Dept. | Course No. | Credits | Level |
|---|---|---|---|---|---|
| 1503 | Human physiology | Biol | 2160C | 3S | L |
| 150399 | General biology | Bio | 1001C | 3S | L |
| 150399 | General biology | Bio | 1002C | 3S | L |
| 150599 | Geology | Geo | 1001C | 3S | L |
| 150799 | General physics | Phys | 2001C | 3S | L |
| 150799 | General physics | Phys | 2002C | 3S | L |
| 150899 | Physical science | PhSc | 1001C | 3S | L |
| 150899 | Physical science | PhSc | 1002C | 3S | L |
| 160302 | Algebra | Math | 1021C | 3S | L |
| 160302 | Algebra and applications | Math | 1015C | 3S | L |
| 160302 | Linear algebra | Math | 2085C | 3S | L |
| 160305 | Introductory coll math I | Math | 1009C | 3S | L |
| 160305 | Introductory coll math II | Math | 1010C | 3S | L |
| 160401 | Analyt geom & calculus II | Math | 1452C | 5S | L |
| 160401 | Multidimensional calculus | Math | 2057C | 3S | L |
| 160602 | Plane trigonometry | Math | 1022C | 3S | L |
| 160603 | Analyt geom & calculus I | Math | 1450C | 5S | L |
| 160801 | Statistcl methods/models | QM | 2000C | 3S | L |
| 160802 | Intro to business science | QM | 2001C | 3S | L |
| 160802 | Statistical analysis | QM | 3001C | 3S | U |
| 160803 | Foun for operations resch | QM | 3002C | 3S | U |
| 161103 | Calculus with bus & econ | Math | 1431C | 3S | L |
| 161103 | Finite math—bus & econ | Math | 1435C | 3S | L |
| 180301 | Intro to philosophy | Philo | 1011C | 3S | L |
| 180502 | Elementary logic | Philo | 1021C | 3S | L |
| 180502 | Intro to logic theory | Philo | 2010C | 3S | L |
| 190502 | Personal & comm health | HPRe | 1600C | 2S | L |
| 190511 | Occupational safety | InEd | 2051C | 3S | L |
| 190512 | Human sexuality | HPRe | 2600C | 3S | L |
| 190599 | Community safety educ | HPRe | 4602C | 3S | U |
| 200199 | Intro to psychology | Psych | 2000C | 3S | L |
| 200505 | Psychology of adjustment | Psych | 2004C | 3S | L |
| 200599 | Child psychology | Psych | 2076C | 3S | L |
| 200599 | Adolescent psychology | Psych | 2078C | 3S | L |
| 200804 | Educational psychology | Psych | 2060C | 3S | L |
| 210304 | Intro to law enforcement | CJ | 1107C | 3S | L |
| 210304 | Judicial process | CJ | 2132C | 3S | L |
| 210304 | Correctional process | CJ | 2133C | 3S | L |
| 220102 | Culture growth | Anthr | 1003C | 3S | L |
| 220199 | General anthropology | Anthr | 1001C | 3S | L |
| 220201 | Econ prins & problems | Econ | 2010C | 3S | L |
| 220201 | Econ prins & problems | Econ | 2020C | 3S | L |
| 220201 | Economic principles | Econ | 2030C | 3S | L |
| 220209 | Dev of econ system in US | Econ | 1010C | 3S | L |
| 220211 | Labor economics | Econ | 4210C | 3S | U |
| 220212 | Economics of consumption | Econ | 3310C | 3S | U |
| 220299 | Macroecon anal & policy | Econ | 2035C | 3S | L |
| 220299 | Econ of govt regulation | Econ | 4440C | 3S | U |
| 220301 | Human geography | Geog | 1001C | 3S | L |
| 220301 | Human geography | Geog | 1003C | 3S | L |
| 220406 | History of Western civ | Hist | 1001C | 3S | L |
| 220406 | History of Western civ | Hist | 1003C | 3S | L |
| 220421 | Colonial Amer 1607-1763 | Hist | 4051C | 3S | U |
| 220421 | The American Revolution | Hist | 4052C | 3S | U |
| 220424 | English history | Hist | 2012C | 3S | L |
| 220424 | English history | Hist | 2011C | 3S | L |
| 220426 | Mod European history | Hist | 2021C | 3S | L |
| 220426 | Mod European history | Hist | 2022C | 3S | L |
| 220428 | History of Louisiana | Hist | 2071C | 3S | L |
| 220432 | American history | Hist | 2055C | 3S | L |
| 220432 | American history | Hist | 2057C | 3S | L |
| 220432 | Recent American history | Hist | 4059C | 3S | U |
| 220432 | Recent American history | Hist | 4060C | 3S | U |
| 220432 | The antebellum South | Hist | 4071C | 3S | U |
| 220432 | The new South | Hist | 4072C | 3S | U |
| 220501 | American government | PolSc | 2051C | 3S | L |
| 220503 | Intro to comparative pol | PolSc | 2053C | 3S | L |
| 220507 | Pol parties in the US | PolSc | 4031C | 3S | U |
| 220602 | Criminology | Socio | 4461C | 3S | U |
| 220602 | Criminology | SocW | 3007C | 3S | U |
| 220605 | Marriage and family relat | Socio | 2505C | 3S | L |
| 220608 | Rural sociology | Socio | 2351C | 3S | L |
| 220613 | Current social problems | Socio | 2501C | 3S | L |
| 220699 | Introductory sociology | Socio | 2001C | 3S | L |

**Noncredit courses**

| NCES No. | Course Title | Dept. | Course No. | Credits | Level |
|---|---|---|---|---|---|
| 040101 | Basic accounting | Acct | 0000 | NC | V |
| 061101 | Computer literacy | CmpSc | 44 | NC | D |
| 061101 | BASIC programming | CmpSc | 45 | NC | V |
| 120310 | English composition | Engl | 0001C | NC | L |
| 150704 | Electricity–alt current | InArt | 0002 | NC | V |
| 150704 | Electricity–dir current | InArt | 0001 | NC | V |

| NCES No. | Course Title | Dept. | Course No. | Credits | Level |
|---|---|---|---|---|---|
| 160301 | Refresher math | Math | 0000 | NC | D |
| 160301 | Arithmetic for college | Math | 0091C | NC | D |
| 160302 | Intro to college algebra | Math | 0092C | NC | D |
| 210302 | Firefighter I | FmTng | I | NC | V |
| 210302 | Firefighter II | FmTng | II | NC | V |
| 210302 | Firefighter III | FmTng | III | NC | V |
| 210302 | Fire service inspector I | FmTng | 0000 | NC | V |
| 210302 | Fire service officer | FmTng | 32 | NC | V |

## ⑱ MASSACHUSETTS DEPARTMENT OF EDUCATION

Ms. Ellen H. Maddocks
Supervisor of Correspondence Instruction
Bureau of Student, Community, and Adult Services
Massachusetts Department of Education
1385 Hancock Street
Quincy, Massachusetts 02169
Phone: 617-770-7582

Enrollment on a noncredit basis accepted in some credit courses. No overseas enrollment accepted.

| NCES No. | Course Title | Dept. | Course No. | Credits | Level |
|---|---|---|---|---|---|
| **High School courses** | | | | | |
| 040104 | Bookkeeping | Acctg | BUS1 | 1U | H |
| 040207 | Typewriting | Bus | BUS2 | HF | H |
| 040502 | Small-business mgt | Bus | BUS4 | HF | H |
| 0804 | Automotive engines | EngAS | AUT1 | HF | H |
| 0804 | Automotive chassis | EngAS | AUT2 | HF | H |
| 090901 | Modern health | HSci | SCI2 | 1U | H |
| 100202 | Consumer economics | Econ | SS10 | HF | H |
| 100503 | Interior design | Graph | ART2 | 1U | H |
| 110503 | Basic drawing techniques | Graph | ART1 | HF | H |
| 120305 | English for everyone | EngLL | ENG2 | 1U | H |
| 120308 | Improving your reading | EngLL | ENG10 | 1U | H |
| 120399 | English IX | EngLL | ENG3 | 1U | H |
| 120399 | English X | EngLL | ENG4 | 1U | H |
| 120399 | English XI: general | EngLL | ENG6 | 1U | H |
| 120399 | English XI: college prep | EngLL | ENG5 | 1U | H |
| 120399 | English XII: general | EngLL | ENG8 | 1U | H |
| 120399 | English XII: college prep | EngLL | ENG7 | 1U | H |
| 1210 | French I | Frnch | LAN3 | 1U | H |
| 1216 | Latin I | CILL | LAN1 | 1U | H |
| 1216 | Latin II | CILL | LAN2 | 1U | H |
| 1225 | Spanish I | Span | LAN7 | 1U | H |
| 1225 | Spanish II | Span | LAN8 | 1U | H |
| 130799 | Business law | Bus | BUS3 | HF | H |
| 1503 | General biology | Bio | SCI1 | 1U | H |
| 150401 | Chemistry | Chem | SCI4 | 1U | H |
| 160302 | Elementary algebra | Math | MATH5 | 1U | H |
| 160302 | Intermediate algebra | Math | MATH6 | 1U | H |
| 160601 | Geometry | Math | MATH7 | 1U | H |
| 161201 | Business mathematics | Bus | MATH3 | 1U | H |
| 161299 | General mathematics | Math | MATH4 | 1U | H |
| 200102 | General psychology | Psych | SS8 | 1U | H |
| 220432 | Amer history coll prep | Hist | SS5 | 1U | H |
| 220432 | American history general | Hist | SS11 | 1U | H |
| 220433 | World history | Hist | SS6 | 1U | H |
| 220501 | Problems of democracy | Hist | SS7 | 1U | H |

**Noncredit courses**

| NCES No. | Course Title | Dept. | Course No. | Credits | Level |
|---|---|---|---|---|---|
| 080903 | Basic electronics | EEg | EEG5 | NC | D |
| 080999 | Basic television | EEg | EEG4 | NC | D |
| 080999 | Transistors | EEg | EEG6 | NC | D |
| 110405 | Building custodian's prep | CSLP | CSLP2 | NC | D |
| 120309 | Vocabulary building | Eng | ENG1 | NC | D |
| 120399 | High school equiv prep | GED | GED1 | NC | D |
| 1318 | Law and the legal system | Law | SS4 | NC | D |
| 160199 | The metric system | Math | MATH2 | NC | D |
| 160301 | Everyday review math | Math | MATH1 | NC | D |
| 160399 | High school equiv prep | GED | GED1 | NC | D |
| 2199 | Basic civil service train | CSLP | CSLP1 | NC | D |
| 220502 | Prep for naturalization | Pol | CSLP6 | NC | D |
| 220506 | Practical politics | PolSc | SS1 | NC | D |
| 2299 | High school equiv prep | GED | GED1 | NC | D |

## ⑲ MISSISSIPPI STATE UNIVERSITY

Dr. C. K. Lee
Director, Independent Study Office
Continuing Education
Mississippi State University
P.O. Drawer 5247
Mississippi State, Mississippi 39762
Phone: 601-325-3473

Enrollment on a noncredit basis accepted in some credit courses. Only in exceptional cases are gifted high school students permitted to enroll in undergraduate courses for credit. Overseas enrollment accepted for high school and college courses.

| NCES No. | Course Title | Dept. | Course No. | Credits | Level |
|---|---|---|---|---|---|
| | **High School courses** | | | | |
| 0499 | General business | Buss | | 1U | H |
| 0601 | Computer science | ComSc | | HF | H |
| 070515 | General science | Scien | | 1U | H |
| 0901 | Modern health I | Scien | | HF | H |
| 0901 | Modern health II | Scien | | HF | H |
| 100699 | Personal & family relatns | HmEc | | HF | H |
| 120307 | English I | Engl | | 1U | H |
| 120307 | English II | Engl | | 1U | H |
| 120307 | English III | Engl | | 1U | H |
| 120307 | English IV | Engl | | 1U | H |
| 1210 | French III pt 1 | ForLa | | HF | H |
| 1210 | French III pt 2 | ForLa | | HF | H |
| 1210 | French IV pt 1 | ForLa | | HF | H |
| 1210 | French IV pt 2 | ForLa | | HF | H |
| 1216 | Latin I | ForLa | | 1U | H |
| 1216 | Latin II | ForLa | | 1U | H |
| 1225 | Spanish III | ForLa | | 1U | H |
| 1225 | Spanish IV | ForLa | | 1U | H |
| 1503 | Fundamentals of biology I | Scien | | HF | H |
| 1503 | Fundamentals of biology 2 | Scien | | HF | H |
| 160199 | General mathematics I | Math | | 1U | H |
| 160199 | General mathematics II | Math | | 1U | H |
| 160199 | Senior math | Math | | 1U | H |
| 160199 | Consumer math | Math | | 1U | H |
| 160302 | Algebra I | Math | | 1U | H |
| 160302 | Algebra II | Math | | 1U | H |
| 160601 | Plane geometry | Math | | 1U | H |
| 160601 | Solid geometry | Math | | HF | H |
| 160602 | Trigonometry | Math | | HF | H |
| 220201 | Economics | SoStu | | HF | H |
| 220399 | World geography | SoStu | | HF | H |
| 220432 | American history | SoStu | | 1U | H |
| 220433 | World history | SoStu | | 1U | H |
| 220499 | Mississippi history | SoStu | | HF | H |
| 220501 | American government | SoStu | | HF | H |
| 220599 | Civics | SoStu | | HF | H |
| 220599 | Problems in American demo | SoStu | | HF | H |
| | **College courses** | | | | |
| 011202 | Game conservation & mgt | Wildl | 4513 | 3S | U |
| 011299 | Env prob: forest water | Wildl | 4143 | 3S | U |
| 040101 | Accounting principles I | Acctg | 1413 | 3S | L |
| 040101 | Accounting principles II | Acctg | 1423 | 3S | L |
| 040106 | Cost accounting | Acctg | 2213 | 3S | L |
| 040203 | Filing records and mgmnt | Bus | 2052 | 2S | U |
| 040206 | Secretarial procedures | Bus | 3113 | 3S | U |
| 040299 | Office management | Bus | 3133 | 3S | U |
| 040301 | Business finance | Bus | 2223 | 3S | U |
| 040308 | Money and banking | Bus | 2113 | 3S | U |
| 041001 | Principles of marketing | Mktg | 2313 | 3S | U |
| 041099 | Retailing | Mktg | 2223 | 3S | U |
| 0601 | Basic comp concepts & app | ComSc | 1103 | 3S | L |
| 070504 | Tchg of basic bus subjcts | Bus | 4213 | 3S | U |
| 070516 | Tcng math: elem & jr high | Elem | 5453 | 3S | U |
| 070520 | Learning theories classrm | Psych | 4133 | 3S | U |
| 070701 | Basic course in guidance | Guid | 4103 | 3S | U |
| 070705 | Guid ser & mental health | Guid | 4113 | 3S | U |
| 070899 | Work/parents of excpt ch | SpEd | 5113 | 3S | U |
| 070899 | Tchg the disadvantaged ch | SpEd | 5123 | 3S | U |
| 071199 | Measurement & evaluation | Psych | 4313 | 3S | U |
| 0810 | Graphic communications | EnGra | 1113 | 3S | L |
| 090114 | Elem microbiology | Bio | 1113 | 3S | U |
| 090199 | Science of public health | Bio | 1123 | 3S | L |
| 100399 | Indiv & family nutrition | HmEc | 3213 | 3S | U |
| 100799 | Purch food & equip instit | HmEc | 5293 | 3S | U |

| NCES No. | Course Title | Dept. | Course No. | Credits | Level |
|---|---|---|---|---|---|
| 1210 | Intermediate French | Lang | 1133 | 3S | L |
| 1210 | Intermediate French | Lang | 1143 | 3S | L |
| 1225 | Intermediate Spanish | Lang | 1133 | 3S | L |
| 1225 | Intermediate Spanish | Lang | 1143 | 3S | L |
| 150199 | Descriptive astronomy | Phys | 1063 | 3S | L |
| 150899 | Physical science survey | Phys | 1013 | 3S | L |
| 150899 | Physical science survey | Phys | 1023 | 3S | L |
| 160202 | Structure real number sys | Math | 1513 | 3S | L |
| 160204 | Informal geometry & meas | Math | 1523 | 3S | L |
| 160302 | College algebra | Math | 1153 | 3S | L |
| 160399 | Mathematics | Math | 1053 | 3S | L |
| 160401 | Finite math & intro calcu | Math | 1263 | 3S | L |
| 160401 | Calculus I | Math | 1713 | 3S | L |
| 160401 | Calculus II | Math | 1723 | 3S | L |
| 160602 | Trigonometry | Math | 1253 | 3S | L |
| 180302 | Intro to business statist | Bus | 1513 | 3S | L |
| 180302 | Intro to ethics | Philo | 1123 | 3S | L |
| 180302 | Intro to Old Testament | Relig | 1213 | 3S | L |
| 180302 | Intro to New Testament | Relig | 1223 | 3S | L |
| 180302 | World religions I | Relig | 2203 | 3S | U |
| 180302 | World religions II | Relig | 2213 | 3S | U |
| 181101 | Intro to philosophy | Philo | 1103 | 3S | L |
| 190399 | Prin of elem health & PE | PhyEd | 3123 | 3S | U |
| 190502 | Community recreation | PhyEd | 3362 | 2S | U |
| 190502 | Community hygiene | PubHl | 1003 | 3S | L |
| 190503 | Consumer education | PhyEd | 2163 | 3S | U |
| 190504 | Communicable disease | PubHl | 2003 | 3S | U |
| 190511 | General safety methods | PhyEd | 3433 | 3S | U |
| 190599 | Health education | PhyEd | 3233 | 3S | U |
| 190599 | Foodborne-disease control | PubHl | 2013 | 3S | U |
| 190599 | Vectorborne-disease contr | PubHl | 2023 | 3S | U |
| 190599 | Waterborne-disease contr | PubHl | 2033 | 3S | U |
| 20 | General psychology | Psych | 1013 | 3S | L |
| 200504 | Human growth & developmt | Psych | 1053 | 3S | L |
| 200599 | Psychology of adolescence | Psych | 1073 | 3S | L |
| 200804 | Prin of educational psych | Psych | 2123 | 3S | U |
| 220201 | Prin of economics I | Econ | 1113 | 3S | L |
| 220201 | Prin of economics II | Econ | 1123 | 3S | L |
| 220432 | Early US history | Hist | 1063 | 3S | L |
| 220432 | Modern US history | Hist | 1073 | 3S | L |
| 220499 | Early Western world | Hist | 1013 | 3S | L |
| 220499 | Modern Western world | Hist | 1023 | 3S | L |
| 220499 | Mississippi history | Hist | 3333 | 3S | U |
| 220501 | American government | Govt | 1013 | 3S | L |
| 220502 | Comparative government | Govt | 1513 | 3S | L |
| 220505 | International relations | Govt | 1313 | 3S | L |
| 220602 | Intro to criminal justice | SocWk | 3103 | 3S | U |
| 220604 | Juvenile delinquency | SocWk | 4233 | 3S | U |
| 220605 | Marriage and family | Socio | 1503 | 3S | L |
| 220606 | Intro to sociology | Socio | 1003 | 3S | L |
| 220699 | Current issues in correct | SocWk | 4303 | 3S | U |

## ⑳ MURRAY STATE UNIVERSITY

Mr. Donald E. Jones
Dean of Continuing Education
Center for Continuing Education
Murray State University
15th at Main
Murray, Kentucky 42071
Phone: 502-762-4159

Gifted high school students are permitted to enroll in undergraduate courses for credit. The Center for Continuing Education does not encourage overseas enrollment but will make individual exceptions for those in military service.

| NCES No. | Course Title | Dept. | Course No. | Credits | Level |
|---|---|---|---|---|---|
| | **College courses** | | | | |
| 0104 | Animal science | Agri | 100 | 3S | L |
| 0104 | Poultry science | Agri | 121 | 3S | L |
| 0104 | Swine science | Agri | 326 | 3S | U |
| 0106 | Crop science | Agri | 240 | 3S | L |
| 0109 | Introduction to forestry | Agri | 269 | 3S | L |

| NCES No. | Course Title | Dept. | Course No. | Credits | Level |
|---|---|---|---|---|---|
| 040101 | Prin of accounting I | Acctg | 200 | 3S | L |
| 040101 | Prin of accounting II | Acctg | 201 | 3S | L |
| 040114 | Federal income tax | Acctg | 302 | 3S | U |
| 0402 | Prin of office administra | OAd | 360 | 3S | U |
| 040203 | Records management | OAd | 235 | 3S | L |
| 040299 | Admin Supervision | OAd | 260 | 3S | L |
| 051399 | Cable TV opr and mgt | TV | 558 | 3S | U |
| 120310 | Composition I | Engl | 101 | 3S | L |
| 120310 | Composition II | Engl | 102 | 3S | L |
| 120310 | Tech writing/ind technol | Engl | 225 | 3S | L |
| 1307 | Business law I | LSt | 240 | 3S | L |
| 1307 | Business law II | LSt | 540 | 3S | U |
| 160302 | College algebra | Math | 101 | 4S | L |
| 160302 | Trigonometry | Math | 104 | 3S | L |
| 1901 | Intro to phys education | PhyEd | 175 | 3S | L |
| 2001 | General psychology | Psy | 180 | 3S | L |
| 2105 | Personal health | Heal | 191 | 2S | L |
| 2105 | First aid and safety | Heal | 195 | 2S | L |
| 2105 | School health | Heal | 598 | 3S | U |
| 2105 | Intro to recreation | Rec | 101 | 3S | L |
| 2204 | Civil War and Reconstruc | Hist | 534 | 3S | U |
| 2204 | Modern Europe | Hist | 201 | 3S | L |
| 2204 | Amer experience to 1865 | Hist | 221 | 3S | L |
| 2204 | Amer experience snc 1865 | Hist | 222 | 3S | L |
| 220426 | Europe since 1914 | Hist | 503 | 3S | U |
| 2205 | American national govt | Pol | 140 | 3S | L |
| 2205 | State and local govt | Pol | 240 | 3S | L |
| 2206 | Introductory sociology | Socio | 133 | 3S | L |
| 2206 | Social problems | Socio | 231 | 3S | L |
| 2206 | The family | Socio | 331 | 3S | L |

## ㉑ OHIO UNIVERSITY

Dr. Richard W. Moffitt
Director of Independent Study
303 Tupper Hall
Ohio University
Athens, Ohio 45701
Phone: 614-594-6721

Enrollment on a noncredit basis accepted in all credit courses. Gifted high school students are permitted to enroll in undergraduate courses for credit. Overseas enrollment accepted for college courses. Students may enroll in individual courses or complete selected two- or four-year degrees through the Independent Study External Student Program.

| NCES No. | Course Title | Dept. | Course No. | Credits | Level |
|---|---|---|---|---|---|
| | **College courses** | | | | |
| 030302 | Hist and lit of music | Music | 321 | 4Q | L |
| 030302 | Jazz history | Music | 428 | 3Q | U |
| 030502 | History of art | ArHis | 211 | 4Q | L |
| 040101 | Financial accounting | Acctg | 201 | 4Q | L |
| 040102 | Accounting info systems | Acctg | 203 | 4Q | L |
| 040111 | Managerial accounting | Acctg | 202 | 4Q | L |
| 040301 | Managerial finance | Fin | 325 | 4Q | U |
| 040502 | Small-business administra | BusAd | 445 | 4Q | U |
| 040599 | Bus and its environment | BusAd | 101 | 4Q | L |
| 040601 | Business communication | Mgmt | 325J | 4Q | U |
| 040604 | Business report writing | BMT | 260 | 4Q | L |
| 040902 | Management | Mgmt | 300 | 4Q | U |
| 040903 | Introd to management | Mgmt | 200 | 4Q | L |
| 040999 | Production management | BusAd | 310 | 4Q | U |
| 040999 | Security administration | SST | 240 | 3Q | L |
| 041004 | Marketing principles | Mktg | 301 | 4Q | U |
| 041099 | Consumer surv in mktplace | Mktg | 101 | 4Q | L |
| 0411 | Admin of personnel | HRM | 420 | 4Q | U |
| 041108 | Occup safety and health | SST | 120 | 3Q | L |
| 051103 | Fund of human communica | InCo | 101 | 3Q | L |
| 051104 | Parliamentary procedure | InCo | 210 | 2Q | L |
| 051108 | Intro to communica theory | InCo | 234 | 5Q | L |
| 0513 | Intro to telecommunica | TCom | 106 | 4Q | L |
| 0599 | Intro to mass communica | Jrnl | 105 | 4Q | L |
| 0599 | Intro to mass communica | TCom | 105 | 4Q | L |
| 0599 | Introd to mass communica | InCo | 105 | 4Q | L |

| NCES No. | Course Title | Dept. | Course No. | Credits | Level |
|---|---|---|---|---|---|
| 060503 | Info and data systems sec | SST | 230 | 3Q | L |
| 061103 | Computer science survey | CmpSc | 120 | 5Q | L |
| 070512 | Children's literature | Educ | 321L | 4Q | U |
| 070516 | Elem topics in math | Math | 121 | 5Q | L |
| 070516 | Elem topics in math | Math | 120 | 5Q | L |
| 070703 | Career & life planning | EdGS | 201 | 3Q | L |
| 070799 | Life & career exper analy | EdGS | 102 | 4Q | L |
| 0799 | Effective study skills | UC | 110 | 2Q | L |
| 080102 | Priv pilot ground instruc | Avn | 110 | 4Q | L |
| 080102 | Comm pilot ground instruc | Avn | 310 | 4Q | U |
| 080102 | Instrument ground instruc | Avn | 350 | 4Q | U |
| 080699 | Intro to chemical engrg | ChmEg | 200 | 4Q | L |
| 090704 | Bio and the future of man | Zool | 390 | 5Q | U |
| 090705 | Occup safety and health | SST | 120 | 3Q | L |
| 100199 | Elementary textiles | HmEc | 315 | 4Q | U |
| 100202 | Family consumer economics | HmEc | 390 | 3Q | U |
| 100299 | Consumer surv in mktplace | Mktg | 101 | 4Q | L |
| 100313 | Introd to nutrition | HmEc | 128 | 4Q | L |
| 100501 | Furnishing today's home | HmEc | 180 | 3Q | L |
| 120201 | Humanities: Great Books | Hum | 107 | 3Q | L |
| 120201 | Humanities: Great Books | Hum | 108 | 3Q | L |
| 120201 | Humanities: Great Books | Hum | 109 | 3Q | L |
| 120201 | Intro to mod lit III | Engl | 206 | 5Q | L |
| 120201 | Spanish lit in English | Span | 336A | 4Q | U |
| 120201 | Spanish lit in English | Span | 336B | 4Q | U |
| 120202 | Interpretation of fiction | Engl | 201 | 5Q | L |
| 120202 | Interpretation of poetry | Engl | 202 | 5Q | L |
| 120202 | Interpretation of drama | Engl | 203 | 5Q | L |
| 120202 | Mystery fiction | Engl | 210 | 4Q | L |
| 120202 | Shakespeare—histories | Engl | 301 | 5Q | U |
| 120202 | Shakespeare—comedies | Engl | 302 | 5Q | U |
| 120202 | Shakespeare—tragedies | Engl | 303 | 5Q | U |
| 120202 | Med and Ren English lit | Engl | 312 | 5Q | U |
| 120202 | Res and neoclass Engl lit | Engl | 313 | 5Q | U |
| 120202 | Am lit to the Civil War | Engl | 321 | 5Q | U |
| 120202 | Am lit since the Civil Wr | Engl | 322 | 5Q | U |
| 120202 | 20th-cent Brit and Am lit | Engl | 331 | 5Q | U |
| 120202 | Romantic & Victorian lit | Engl | 314 | 5Q | U |
| 120307 | Women & men in literature | Engl | 153A | 5Q | L |
| 120308 | Speed readg & comprehensn | UC | 112 | 2Q | L |
| 120310 | Fundamental usage skills | Engl | 150 | 4Q | L |
| 120310 | Frsh comp:writing/reading | Engl | 152 | 5Q | L |
| 120310 | Advanced composition | Engl | 308J | 4Q | U |
| 120310 | Creative writing–poetry | Engl | 309A | 5Q | U |
| 120310 | Creative writing–fiction | Engl | 309B | 5Q | U |
| 120310 | Fr comp: writng & rhetric | Engl | 151 | 5Q | L |
| 1211 | Elementary German | Ger | 111 | 4Q | L |
| 1211 | Elementary German | Ger | 112 | 4Q | L |
| 1211 | Elementary German | Ger | 113 | 4Q | L |
| 1212 | Beginning Greek | Greek | 111 | 4Q | L |
| 1212 | Beginning Greek | Greek | 112 | 4Q | L |
| 1212 | Beginning Greek | Greek | 113 | 4Q | L |
| 1216 | Beginning Latin | Latin | 111 | 4Q | L |
| 1216 | Beginning Latin | Latin | 112 | 4Q | L |
| 130299 | Law of commercial transac | BusL | 357 | 4Q | U |
| 130399 | Constit, crim & civil law | LET | 120 | 3Q | L |
| 130402 | Criminal investigation | LET | 260 | 3Q | L |
| 1307 | Law of mgmt process | BusL | 356 | 4Q | U |
| 130799 | Law and society | BusL | 255 | 4Q | L |
| 130902 | Law of prop and real est | BusL | 442 | 4Q | U |
| 131004 | Occup safety and health | SST | 120 | 3Q | L |
| 131004 | Fire safety and fire code | SST | 201 | 4Q | L |
| 140899 | Circulation & pub comm | LMT | 102 | 4Q | L |
| 1501 | The universe | PhySc | 100B | 4Q | L |
| 150316 | Principles of biology | Bot | 101 | 4Q | L |
| 150316 | Plant biology | Bot | 102 | 5Q | L |
| 150323 | Principles of biology | Zool | 101 | 5Q | L |
| 150323 | Introduction to zoology | Zool | 150 | 6Q | L |
| 150399 | Bioethic prob in biol/med | Zool | 384 | 5Q | U |
| 150399 | Biol and future of man | Zool | 390 | 5Q | U |
| 150399 | Human biology | Zool | 103 | 5Q | L |
| 150401 | Principles of chemistry | Chem | 121 | 4Q | L |
| 150401 | Principles of chemistry | Chem | 122 | 4Q | L |
| 150408 | Organic chemistry | Chem | 301 | 3Q | U |
| 150408 | Organic chemistry | Chem | 302 | 3Q | U |
| 150799 | Introduction to physics | Phys | 201 | 3Q | L |
| 150799 | Introduction to physics | Phys | 202 | 3Q | L |
| 150799 | Introduction to physics | Phys | 203 | 3Q | L |
| 1508 | Physical world | PhySc | 101 | 4Q | L |
| 150899 | Physical world | PhySc | 121 | 3Q | L |
| 1603 | Basic mathematics | Math | 101 | 4Q | L |
| 160302 | Algebra | Math | 113 | 5Q | L |

| NCES No. | Course Title | Dept. | Course No. | Credits | Level |
|---|---|---|---|---|---|
| 160303 | Elem topics in math | Math | 120 | 5Q | L |
| 160303 | Elem topics in math | Math | 121 | 5Q | L |
| 160306 | Elem linear algebra | Math | 211 | 5Q | L |
| 160401 | Intro to calculus | Math | 163A | 5Q | L |
| 160401 | Analytic geom and calc | Math | 263A | 5Q | L |
| 160401 | Analytic geom and calc | Math | 263B | 5Q | L |
| 160401 | Intro to calculus | Math | 163B | 3Q | L |
| 160499 | Intro to math (precalc) | Math | 115 | 5Q | L |
| 1606 | Foundations of geometry | Math | 330 | 5Q | U |
| 160603 | Plane analytic geometry | Math | 130 | 3Q | L |
| 160603 | Analytic geom and calc | Math | 263A | 5Q | L |
| 160603 | Analytic geom and calc | Math | 263B | 5Q | L |
| 160699 | Elementary applied math | Math | 118 | 4Q | L |
| 160701 | Finite mathematics | Math | 250B | 5Q | L |
| 160802 | Elem stat for behav sci | Psych | 121 | 5Q | L |
| 161101 | Intro to bus statistics | QBA | 201 | 4Q | L |
| 180101 | Philosophy of art | Philo | 232 | 3Q | L |
| 180302 | Introduction to ethics | Philo | 130 | 4Q | L |
| 180303 | Bioethic prob in bio/med | Zool | 384 | 5Q | U |
| 180401 | Hist of West phil: ancien | Philo | 310 | 5Q | U |
| 180501 | Principles of reasoning | Philo | 120 | 4Q | L |
| 180605 | Philosophy of culture | Philo | 350 | 5Q | U |
| 180609 | Philosophy of religion | Phil | 260 | 4Q | L |
| 1808 | Fundamentals of philo | Philo | 101 | 5Q | L |
| 1808 | Introduction to philo | Philo | 301 | 3Q | U |
| 190104 | Hist and prin of phys ed | HPES | 404 | 4Q | U |
| 190106 | Org and adm of phys ed | HPES | 406 | 4Q | U |
| 1902 | Kinesiology | HPES | 302 | 4Q | U |
| 1902 | Kinesiology | Zool | 352 | 4Q | U |
| 1902 | Kinesiology | Zool | 302 | 4Q | U |
| 190502 | Personal and comm health | Hlth | 202 | 4Q | L |
| 2001 | General psychology | Psych | 101 | 5Q | L |
| 2003 | Environmental psychology | Psych | 335 | 5Q | U |
| 200501 | Abnormal psychology | Psych | 332 | 4Q | U |
| 200504 | Studies of children | Educ | 200 | 4Q | L |
| 200508 | Psych of adulthood/aging | Psych | 374 | 4Q | U |
| 200509 | Psychology of personality | Psych | 333 | 4Q | U |
| 2006 | Elem stat for behav sci | Psych | 121 | 5Q | L |
| 200799 | Social psych of justice | Psych | 337 | 4Q | U |
| 200804 | Educational psychology | Psych | 275 | 4Q | L |
| 210302 | Fire safety & fire codes | SST | 201 | 3Q | L |
| 210303 | Occup safety and health | SST | 120 | 3Q | L |
| 210304 | Introd to law enforc tech | LET | 100 | 3Q | L |
| 210304 | Const, crim and civil law | LET | 120 | 3Q | L |
| 210304 | Interview & report writg | LET | 130 | 3Q | L |
| 210304 | Criminal investigation | LET | 260 | 3Q | L |
| 210305 | Physical security systems | SST | 110 | 3Q | L |
| 210305 | Occup safety and health | SST | 120 | 3Q | L |
| 210305 | Loss prev in mod retail | SST | 210 | 3Q | L |
| 210305 | Anal of sec needs–survey | SST | 220 | 3Q | L |
| 210305 | Inf and data systems sec | SST | 230 | 3Q | L |
| 210305 | Security administration | SST | 240 | 3Q | L |
| 210305 | Current prob in security | SST | 250 | 3Q | L |
| 210305 | Spec area stud: terrorism | SST | 290A | 3Q | L |
| 210305 | Spec area stud: law/secur | SST | 290B | 3Q | L |
| 210305 | Current prob in security | SST | 250 | 3Q | L |
| 220201 | Prin of macroeconomics | Econ | 104 | 4Q | L |
| 220201 | Prin of microeconomics | Econ | 103 | 4Q | L |
| 220204 | Money and banking | Econ | 360 | 4Q | L |
| 220205 | Macroeconomics | Econ | 304 | 4Q | U |
| 220211 | Labor economics | Econ | 320 | 4Q | U |
| 220213 | Microeconomics | Econ | 303 | 4Q | U |
| 220214 | International economics | Econ | 340 | 4Q | U |
| 220301 | Elements of cultural geog | Geog | 121 | 4Q | L |
| 220305 | Elements of physical geog | Geog | 101 | 5Q | L |
| 220408 | Early Christianity | Hist | 354 | 4Q | U |
| 220421 | American hist to 1828 | Hist | 211 | 4Q | L |
| 220426 | Western civ: Ren to 1648 | Hist | 101 | 4Q | L |
| 220426 | Western civ: 1848–pres | Hist | 103 | 4Q | L |
| 220426 | Western civ: 1648-1848 | Hist | 102 | 4Q | L |
| 220428 | Ohio history to 1851 | Hist | 317A | 4Q | U |
| 220428 | Ohio history since 1851 | Hist | 317B | 4Q | U |
| 220432 | Hist of US 1828-1900 | Hist | 212 | 4Q | L |
| 220432 | Hist of US since 1900 | Hist | 213 | 4Q | L |
| 220453 | Western civ: 1848-present | Hist | 103 | 4Q | U |
| 220470 | Intro to black media | AfAmS | 150 | 4Q | L |
| 220501 | American national govt | PolSc | 101 | 4Q | L |
| 220511 | State politics | PolSc | 304 | 5Q | U |
| 220602 | Criminology | Socio | 362 | 4Q | U |
| 220606 | Intro to sociology | Socio | 101 | 5Q | L |
| 220609 | Elem research techniques | Socio | 351 | 4Q | U |
| 220699 | Sociology of aging | Socio | 334 | 4Q | U |

㉒ **OKLAHOMA STATE UNIVERSITY**

Dr. Charles E. Feasley
Director of Correspondence Study Department
001P Classroom Building
Oklahoma State University
Stillwater, Oklahoma 74078
Phone: 405-624-6390

Enrollment on a noncredit basis accepted in all credit courses. Only in exceptional cases are gifted high school students permitted to enroll in undergraduate courses for credit. Overseas enrollment accepted. All course materials delivered inside the United States are sent by insured, return-postage-guaranteed mail. Book service is offered through the Independent and Correspondence Study Department.

| NCES No. | Course Title | Dept. | Course No. | Credits | Level |
|---|---|---|---|---|---|
| **High School courses** | | | | | |
| 040101 | Accounting IA | Acctg | IA | HF | H |
| 040101 | Accounting IB | Acctg | IB | HF | H |
| 040601 | Business English | Bus | I | HF | H |
| 070602 | Salesmanship IA | Bus | IA | HF | H |
| 070602 | Salesmanship IB | Bus | IB | HF | H |
| 120201 | World lit IA | EngLL | 1AW | HF | H |
| 120201 | World lit IB | EngLL | 1BW | HF | H |
| 120307 | Mystery fiction | Engl | | HF | H |
| 120307 | The short story | Engl | | HF | H |
| 120307 | Science fiction | Engl | | HF | H |
| 120308 | English IA | EngLL | 1A | HF | H |
| 120308 | English IB | EngLL | 1B | HF | H |
| 120308 | English IIA | EngLL | 2A | HF | H |
| 120308 | English IIB | EngLL | 2B | HF | H |
| 120308 | English IIIA | EngLL | 3A | HF | H |
| 120308 | English IIIB | EngLL | 3B | HF | H |
| 120308 | English IVA | EngLL | 4A | HF | H |
| 120308 | English IVB | EngLL | 4B | HF | H |
| 160302 | Algebra IA | Math | 1AA | HF | H |
| 160302 | Algebra IB | Math | 1AA | HF | H |
| 160601 | Plane geometry IA | Math | 1AG | HF | H |
| 160601 | Plane geometry IB | Math | 1BG | HF | H |
| 180302 | Technology & change | Philo | I | HF | H |
| 220208 | Consumer economics IA | SocSt | IA | HF | H |
| 220208 | Consumer economics IB | SocSt | IB | HF | H |
| 220399 | Geography IA | Geog | 1A | HF | H |
| 220399 | Geography IB | Geog | 1B | HF | H |
| 220421 | American history IA | Hist | 1BA | HF | H |
| 220433 | World history IA | Hist | IA | HF | H |
| 220433 | World history IB | Hist | IB | HF | H |
| 220450 | Ancient & medieval hst IA | Hist | 1AAN | HF | H |
| 220450 | Ancient & medieval hst IB | Hist | 1BAN | HF | H |
| 220499 | American history IB | Hist | 1BA | HF | H |
| **College courses** | | | | | |
| 010406 | Ecology of agri animals | AnSci | 3903 | 3S | U |
| 010407 | Livestock feeding | AnSci | 2123 | 3S | L |
| 010601 | Problems in agronomy | Agri | 4470 | 3S | U |
| 010701 | Fundaments of soil scienc | Agron | 2124 | 4S | L |
| 030399 | Music appreciation | Musc | 2580C | 3S | L |
| 030402 | Intro theater in Wstn civ | ThArt | 2413 | 3S | L |
| 030402 | Theater history I | ThArt | 4453 | 3S | L |
| 030402 | Theater history II | ThArt | 4463 | 3S | L |
| 030602 | Western humanities: modrn | IDS | 2223 | 3S | L |
| 040101 | Principles of accounting | Acctg | 2103 | 3S | L |
| 040101 | Principles of accounting | Acctg | 2203 | 3S | L |
| 040599 | Small-business management | Mktg | 4113 | 3S | U |
| 040601 | Written communication | Bus | 3113 | 3S | U |
| 040604 | Int tech & report writing | Eng | 3323 | 3S | U |
| 041001 | Marketing | Mktg | 3213 | 3S | U |
| 041003 | Sales management | Mktg | 3513 | 3S | U |
| 041023 | Production/operation mgmt | Mgmt | 3223 | 3S | U |
| 050605 | Feature writing/news/mag | Journ | 4113 | 3S | U |
| 060802 | Programming in FORTRAN | CmpSc | 2113 | 3S | L |
| 0701 | School in American soc | CIEd | 2112 | 3S | L |
| 070102 | Philosophy of education | Educ | 3713 | 3S | U |
| 070199 | History of education | Educ | 4123 | 3S | U |
| 070401 | Human learng in ed psych | Educ | 4223 | 3S | U |
| 070403 | Teaching discipline | Educ | 5720 | 1S | U |
| 070403 | Teacher training | Educ | 5740 | 1S | U |
| 070404 | Evaluation: elemen school | Educ | 4052 | 2S | U |
| 070404 | Organize for individ inst | Educ | 5720A | 1S | U |
| 070511 | Trade & industrial educ | Educ | 3203 | 3S | U |
| 070516 | Math for teachers | Math | 2413 | 3S | L |

| NCES No. | Course Title | Dept. | Course No. | Credits | Level |
|---|---|---|---|---|---|
| 070516 | Structure concepts/teach | Math | 2513 | 3S | L |
| 070811 | Spch-lang path for tchrs | SpEd | 3213 | 3S | U |
| 071203 | Educational media | Educ | 3122 | | U |
| 080603 | Thermodynamics | ChmEg | 2213 | 3S | L |
| 080901 | Digital electronics | EEg | 2650A | 3S | L |
| 080901 | Linear integrated circuit | EEg | 2050 | 3S | L |
| 080903 | Elements of elec/electron | EEg | 1103 | 3S | U |
| 080904 | Fiber optics | EEg | 4050A | 3S | U |
| 080906 | Electronic instrum/measur | GenT | 2650C | 3S | L |
| 082303 | Radiological safety | NucEg | 3233 | 3S | U |
| 082599 | Intro to petrol industry | EngAS | 1113 | 3S | L |
| 082599 | Properties of petroleum | EngAS | 1234 | 4S | L |
| 0899 | Elementary dynamics | EngAS | 2122 | 2S | L |
| 0899 | Technical drawing | VisAr | 1153 | 3S | L |
| 090121 | Radiation biology | NucEg | 2650B | 3S | L |
| 090504 | First aid | HSci | 2602 | 2S | L |
| 090901 | Personal & comm hlth sci | HSci | 2603 | 3S | L |
| 100304 | Intro to nutrition | HmEc | 1113 | 3S | L |
| 100402 | Resource mgt ind/family | HmEc | 2413 | 3S | L |
| 100503 | Housing for cont living | HmEc | 2313 | 3S | L |
| 100601 | Child & family developmnt | HmEc | 2113 | 3S | L |
| 120201 | The short story | Lit | 3333 | 3S | U |
| 120201 | Shakespeare | Lit | 3883 | 3S | U |
| 120201 | Period study Am colonial | Engl | 4943 | 3S | U |
| 120201 | Readings in the novel | Lit | 4853 | 3S | U |
| 120202 | Introduction to new media | Lit | 3200 | 3S | L |
| 120204 | Intro to lit & critic wrt | EngLL | 2413 | 3S | U |
| 120305 | English grammar | Engl | 4013 | 3S | U |
| 120307 | Intro to technical writng | Engl | 2333 | 3S | L |
| 120310 | Freshman composition I | Engl | 1113 | 3S | L |
| 120310 | Freshman composition II | Engl | 1323 | 3S | L |
| 120310 | Short fiction writing | Engl | 3033 | 3S | U |
| 120310 | Poetry writing | Engl | 3043 | 3S | U |
| 1210 | Elementary French I | Frnch | 1115 | 5S | L |
| 1211 | Elementary German I | Germn | 1115 | 5S | L |
| 130799 | Business law I | Law | 3213 | 3S | U |
| 130799 | Business law II | Law | 3323 | 3S | U |
| 130799 | Const law & insurance | Law | 3563 | 3S | U |
| 1409 | Children's literature | LibSc | 4023 | 3S | U |
| 150101 | Cosmos | Astro | 4010 | 3S | U |
| 150103 | Elementary astronomy | Astro | 1104 | 4S | U |
| 150202 | Descriptive meteorology | Geog | 2013 | 3S | L |
| 150301 | Biological sciences | Bio | 1114 | 4S | L |
| 150307 | Heredity & man | Bio | 3003 | 3S | U |
| 150599 | General geology | Geol | 1014 | 4S | L |
| 150599 | Energy & the way we live | Geol | 4990 | 3S | U |
| 150600 | Intro to oceanography | Geog | 3113 | 3S | L |
| 160199 | Metric system | Math | 4910A | 1S | U |
| 160301 | Basic math wth calculator | Math | 4910B | 2S | U |
| 160302 | Intermediate algebra | Math | 1213 | 3S | L |
| 160302 | College algebra | Math | 1513 | 3S | L |
| 160401 | Elementary calculus | Math | 2713 | 3S | L |
| 160602 | College algebra & trig | Math | 1715 | 5S | L |
| 160602 | Trigonometry | Math | 1613 | 3S | L |
| 160606 | Differential equations | Math | 2613 | 3S | L |
| 160802 | Elem statistics for bus | Stat | 2023 | 3S | L |
| 1801 | Western humanities (mod) | IDS | 2223 | 3S | L |
| 180302 | Philos & quality of life | Philo | 3300 | 3S | U |
| 180599 | Intro critical thinking | Philo | 1313 | 3S | L |
| 190512 | Human sexuality | HmEc | 1113 | 3S | L |
| 200102 | History of psychology | Psych | 3273 | 3S | U |
| 200104 | Psych & human problems | Psych | 2313 | 3S | L |
| 200199 | Intro to psychology | Psych | 1113 | 3S | L |
| 200507 | Excep child psychology | Psych | 3202 | 2S | U |
| 200599 | Psych found of childhood | Psych | 3113 | 3S | U |
| 200599 | Psychology of adolescence | Psych | 3213 | 3S | U |
| 210302 | Structural fire protectn | EngAS | 2143 | 3S | L |
| 210302 | Fire protection mgt | EngAS | 2153 | 3S | L |
| 220199 | North American cultures | Anthr | 3823 | 3S | U |
| 220201 | Intro to macroeconomics | Econ | 2013 | 3S | L |
| 220215 | Economics of soc issues | Econ | 1113 | 3S | L |
| 220301 | Intro to geog behavior | Geog | 1113 | 3S | L |
| 220305 | Physical geography | Geog | 1114 | 4S | L |
| 220306 | Geography of Oklahoma | Geog | 3653 | 3S | U |
| 220399 | Geog of music | Geog | 4223 | 3S | U |
| 220423 | Modern Japan | Hist | 3423 | 3S | U |
| 220423 | Traditional Japan | Hist | 3980A | 3S | U |
| 220426 | European hist to 1714 | Hist | 1613 | 3S | L |
| 220426 | European hist since 1714 | Hist | 1623 | 3S | L |
| 220428 | Oklahoma history | Hist | 2323 | 3S | L |
| 220432 | American history to 1865 | Hist | 1483 | 3S | L |
| 220432 | American hist since 1865 | Hist | 1493 | 3S | L |
| 220432 | The Great Plains exper | Hist | 3980B | 3S | U |
| 220432 | Survey of American hist | Hist | 1103 | 3S | L |
| 220450 | Ancient Greece | Hist | 3023 | 3S | U |
| 220450 | Ancient Rome | Hist | 3033 | 3S | U |
| 220501 | American government | PolSc | 1013 | 3S | L |
| 220604 | Juvenile delinquency | Socio | 3523 | 3S | U |
| 220606 | Principles of sociology | Socio | 1113 | 3S | L |
| 220612 | Social ecol & life proc | Soc | 4433 | 3S | U |
| 220613 | Social problems | Soc | 2123 | 3S | L |
| 220613 | Death and dying | Soc | 3823 | 3S | U |
| 220615 | Soc of American family | Soc | 3723 | 3S | U |

**Noncredit courses**

| NCES No. | Course Title | Dept. | Course No. | Credits | Level |
|---|---|---|---|---|---|
| 020599 | Earth-sheltered housing | Arch | | NC | |
| 040101 | Basic accounting A | Acctg | | NC | |
| 040101 | Basic accounting B | Acctg | | NC | |
| 050605 | Feature writing/news/mag | Journ | | NC | |
| 060701 | BASIC prog for beginners | CmpSc | | NC | |
| 082303 | Radiological safety | NucEg | | NC | |
| 082599 | Intro to petroleum indust | EngAS | | NC | |
| 089900 | Hydraulic calc of sprklrs | EngAS | | NC | |
| 160301 | Intro hand-held calculatr | Math | | NC | |
| 210302 | Industrial fire pump inst | EngAS | | NC | |
| 220499 | Oklahoma history IA | Hist | | NC | |
| 220499 | Genealogical research | Hist | | NC | |

## ㉓ OLD DOMINION UNIVERSITY

Ms. Barbara K. Wallace
Director of Off-Campus Instruction
Office of Continuing Education
Old Dominion University
Education Building, Room 145
Norfolk, Virginia 23508
Phone: 804-440-3163

Enrollment on a noncredit basis accepted in some credit courses. Gifted high school students are permitted to enroll in undergraduate courses for credit. Overseas enrollment accepted for college and noncredit courses.

| NCES No. | Course Title | Dept. | Course No. | Credits | Level |
|---|---|---|---|---|---|
| | **Noncredit courses** | | | | |
| 090255 | Fluid electrolyte acid ba | CESHP | 0162 | NC | U |
| 090255 | NSG diagnosis documentat | CESHP | 0762 | NC | U |
| 090255 | Pharmacology vol I NSG | CESHP | 0150 | NC | U |
| 090255 | Pharmacology vol II NSG | CESHP | 0151 | NC | U |
| 090255 | Pharmacology vol III NSG | CESHP | 0153 | NC | U |
| 090255 | Basic EKG | CESHP | 0799 | NC | U |
| 090255 | Coronary artery disease | CESHP | 0801 | NC | U |
| 090504 | Poisonings | CESHP | 0800 | NC | U |
| 090706 | Update maternal-child hea | CESHP | 0256 | NC | U |

## ㉔ OREGON STATE SYSTEM OF HIGHER EDUCATION

Dr. Paul A. Wurm
Head, Independent Study
Office of Independent Study
Portland State University
P.O. Box 1491
Portland, Oregon 97207
Phone: 800-547-8887 Ext 4865

Gifted high school students are permitted to enroll in undergraduate courses for credit. Overseas enrollment accepted. Enrollment period is twelve months. A six-month extension is permitted upon request and payment of required fee. Many courses available through credit-by-examination format. Call or write for detailed course listing. Telephone registrations accepted with Visa or MasterCard.

| NCES No. | Course Title | Dept. | Course No. | Credits | Level |
|---|---|---|---|---|---|
| | **High School courses** | | | | |
| 040101 | Intro to accounting | BusAd | 1 | HF | H |
| 040101 | Intro to accounting | BusAd | 2 | HF | H |
| 040302 | Personal finance I | BusAd | 3 | HF | H |
| 040302 | Personal finance II | BusAd | 4 | HF | H |
| 040601 | Business English | Engl | 14 | HF | H |

| NCES No. | Course Title | Dept. | Course No. | Credits | Level |
|---|---|---|---|---|---|
| 120305 | English review | Engl | 1 | HF | H |
| 120305 | Tenth-grade English III | Engl | 3 | HF | H |
| 120305 | Eleventh-grade English V | Engl | 5 | HF | H |
| 120305 | Twelfth-grade English VII | Engl | 7 | HF | H |
| 120305 | Corrective English | Engl | 13 | HF | H |
| 120307 | Tenth-grade English IV | Engl | 4 | HF | H |
| 120307 | Eleventh-grade English VI | Engl | 6 | HF | H |
| 120307 | Twelfth-grade Eng VIII | Engl | 8 | HF | H |
| 1503 | Biology I | Bio | 1 | HF | H |
| 1503 | Biology II | Bio | 2 | HF | H |
| 1509 | General science I | GS | 1 | HF | H |
| 1509 | General science II | GS | 2 | HF | H |
| 160301 | General math I | Math | 1 | HF | H |
| 160301 | General math II | Math | 2 | HF | H |
| 160302 | Elements of algebra I | Math | 3 | HF | H |
| 160302 | Elements of algebra II | Math | 4 | HF | H |
| 160601 | Geometry I | Math | 5 | HF | H |
| 160601 | Geometry II | Math | 6 | HF | H |
| 190509 | Health education I | H | 1 | HF | H |
| 190509 | Health education II | H | 2 | HF | H |
| 220432 | US history I | Hist | 1 | HF | H |
| 220432 | US history II | Hist | 2 | HF | H |
| 220433 | World history I | Hist | 3 | HF | H |
| 220433 | World history II | Hist | 4 | HF | H |
| 220501 | Government | Gov | 1 | HF | H |
| 2299 | Global studies I | GbS | 1 | HF | H |
| 2299 | Global studies II | GbS | 2 | HF | H |

**College courses**

| NCES No. | Course Title | Dept. | Course No. | Credits | Level |
|---|---|---|---|---|---|
| 010406 | Animal science | AnSci | 121 | 3Q | L |
| 020299 | Housing and arch phil | Arch | 178 | 3Q | L |
| 030501 | Basic drawing | Art | 291 | 3Q | L |
| 040101 | Intermed finan acctg I | BusAd | 317 | 4Q | U |
| 040101 | Intermed finan acctg II | BusAd | 318 | 4Q | U |
| 040101 | Intermed finan acctg III | BusAd | 319 | 4Q | U |
| 040103 | Auditing | BusAd | 427 | 4Q | B |
| 040106 | Cost accounting | BusAd | 421 | 4Q | U |
| 040109 | Acctg not-for-profit inst | BusAd | 423 | 4Q | B |
| 040205 | Stenography | BusEd | 111 | 3Q | L |
| 040205 | Stenography | BusEd | 112 | 3Q | L |
| 040205 | Stenography | BusEd | 113 | 3Q | L |
| 040206 | Medical terminology | AH | 200 | 3Q | L |
| 040299 | Med ofc and hos procedure | SST | 240 | 3Q | L |
| 040999 | Transportation management | Mgmt | 410 | 3Q | U |
| 060404 | Intro to microcomputers | CmpSc | 410 | 3Q | U |
| 060705 | Intro to FORTRAN | CmpSc | 133 | 3Q | L |
| 060705 | Intro to COBOL | CmpSc | 199 | 4Q | L |
| 060705 | Adv FORTRAN programming | CmpSc | 421 | 4Q | U |
| 060806 | Intro to computer systems | CmpSc | 199 | 3Q | L |
| 070506 | Calc and comp in elem sch | CmpSc | 407 | 2Q | B |
| 070509 | Elem sch health education | HE | 440 | 3Q | U |
| 070509 | Health instruction | HE | 441 | 3Q | U |
| 070610 | Reading in high school | Educ | 469 | 3Q | U |
| 0804 | Intern combust eng theory | DPT | 101 | 3Q | L |
| 0804 | Physics elect & magnetism | DPT | 121 | 3Q | L |
| 080706 | Highway materials | CET | 229 | 3Q | L |
| 120201 | World literature | Engl | 107 | 3Q | L |
| 120201 | World literature | Engl | 108 | 3Q | L |
| 120201 | World literature | Engl | 109 | 3Q | L |
| 120201 | Contemporary literature | Engl | 384 | 3Q | U |
| 120201 | Contemporary literature | Engl | 385 | 3Q | U |
| 120307 | Survey of English lit | Engl | 101 | 3Q | L |
| 120307 | Survey of English lit | Engl | 102 | 3Q | L |
| 120307 | Survey of English lit | Engl | 103 | 3Q | L |
| 120307 | Shakespeare | Engl | 201 | 3Q | L |
| 120307 | Shakespeare | Engl | 202 | 3Q | L |
| 120307 | Shakespeare | Engl | 203 | 3Q | L |
| 120307 | Survey of American lit | Engl | 253 | 3Q | L |
| 120307 | American fiction | Engl | 366 | 3Q | U |
| 120310 | English composition | Writ | 121 | 3Q | L |
| 120310 | English composition | Writ | 122 | 3Q | L |
| 120310 | English composition | Writ | 123 | 3Q | L |
| 120310 | Short story writing | Writ | 324 | 3Q | U |
| 120310 | Poetry writing | Writ | 341 | 3Q | U |
| 120310 | Poetry writing | Writ | 342 | 3Q | U |
| 120399 | American folklore | Engl | 419 | 3Q | B |
| 1210 | First-year French | Fr | 101 | 4Q | L |
| 1210 | First-year French | Fr | 102 | 4Q | L |
| 1210 | First-year French | Fr | 103 | 4Q | L |
| 1211 | First-year German | GL | 101 | 4Q | L |
| 1211 | First-year German | GL | 102 | 4Q | L |
| 1211 | First-year German | GL | 103 | 4Q | L |

| NCES No. | Course Title | Dept. | Course No. | Credits | Level |
|---|---|---|---|---|---|
| 130199 | Courts and justice | AJ | 112 | 3Q | L |
| 130199 | Corrections and justice | AJ | 113 | 3Q | L |
| 130199 | Organ of justice agencies | AJ | 461 | 3Q | U |
| 130199 | Admin of justice agencies | AJ | 462 | 3Q | U |
| 130199 | Supervision justice pers | AJ | 463 | 3Q | U |
| 130199 | Police and justice | AJ | 111 | 3Q | L |
| 130402 | Crim law & legal reason | AJ | 444 | 3Q | U |
| 130402 | Leg aspct arst srch seiz | AJ | 445 | 3Q | U |
| 130402 | Fifth amend & court procd | AJ | 446 | 3Q | U |
| 150202 | Intro to atmosphere | AtS | 300 | 3Q | U |
| 150202 | Weather analysis lab | AtS | 430 | 3Q | U |
| 1505 | General geology | Geol | 101 | 3Q | L |
| 1505 | General geology | Geol | 102 | 3Q | L |
| 1505 | General geology | Geol | 103 | 3Q | L |
| 1505 | Geology of Oregon | Geol | 352 | 3Q | U |
| 150599 | Geologic history of life | Geol | 301 | 3Q | U |
| 1506 | Intro to oceanography | Geol | 353 | 3Q | U |
| 150799 | General physics | Phys | 201 | 3Q | L |
| 150799 | General physics | Phys | 202 | 3Q | L |
| 150799 | General physics | Phys | 203 | 3Q | L |
| 1599 | Foundations of phys sci | GS | 105 | 3Q | L |
| 1599 | Foundations of phys sci | GS | 106 | 3Q | L |
| 1599 | Foundations of phys sci | GS | 104 | 3Q | L |
| 160302 | Intermediate algebra | Math | 100 | 4Q | L |
| 160302 | College algebra | Math | 101 | 4Q | L |
| 160306 | Intro linear algebra | Math | 411 | 3Q | U |
| 160401 | Elements of calculus | Math | 106 | 4Q | L |
| 160401 | Calculus | Math | 200 | 4Q | L |
| 160401 | Calculus | Math | 201 | 4Q | L |
| 160602 | Trigonometry | Math | 102 | 4Q | L |
| 181002 | Intro to world religions | Relig | 101 | 3Q | L |
| 190509 | Personal health problems | HE | 250 | 3Q | L |
| 200199 | Psych as a social science | Psych | 204 | 3Q | L |
| 200199 | Psych as a natural sci | Psych | 205 | 3Q | L |
| 200501 | Abnormal psychology | Psych | 434 | 3Q | U |
| 200504 | Developmental psychology | Psych | 407 | 3Q | U |
| 220102 | Native North Americans | Anthr | 317 | 3Q | U |
| 220102 | Native Central Americans | Anthr | 318 | 3Q | U |
| 220102 | Native South Americans | Anthr | 318 | 3Q | U |
| 220201 | Principles of economics | Econ | 213 | 4Q | L |
| 220201 | Principles of economics | Econ | 214 | 4Q | L |
| 220305 | Introductory geography | Geog | 105 | 3Q | L |
| 220305 | Introductory geography | Geog | 106 | 3Q | L |
| 220305 | Introductory geography | Geog | 107 | 3Q | L |
| 220406 | Hist of Western civiliz | Hist | 150 | 3Q | L |
| 220406 | Hist of Western civiliz | Hist | 151 | 3Q | L |
| 220406 | Hist of Western civiliz | Hist | 152 | 3Q | L |

**Noncredit courses**

| NCES No. | Course Title | Dept. | Course No. | Credits | Level |
|---|---|---|---|---|---|
| 030599 | Kiln construction | Art | 044 | NC | |
| 040103 | Municipal auditing review | BusAd | T-71 | NC | |
| 040103 | Audits state/local govt | BusAd | T-73 | NC | |
| 040109 | Intro to fund accounting | BusAd | T-74 | NC | |
| 120305 | Corrective English | Writ | 10 | NC | |
| 220502 | Prep for citizenship | PolSc | 01 | NC | |

㉕ **PENNSYLVANIA STATE UNIVERSITY**

Dr. David Mercer
Director of Independent Learning
128 Mitchell Building
Pennsylvania State University
University Park, Pennsylvania 16802
Phone: 814-865-5403

Only in exceptional cases are gifted high school students permitted to enroll in undergraduate courses for credit. Overseas enrollment accepted. In addition to individual courses, several extended associate degrees are offered through independent learning. Please call or write for additional information. MasterCard and VISA accepted.

| NCES No. | Course Title | Dept. | Course No. | Credits | Level |
|---|---|---|---|---|---|
| | **High School courses** | | | | |
| 090709 | Modern health | HSSci | 001A | HF | H |
| 090709 | Modern health | HlSci | 002A | HF | H |
| 120305 | Basic English | HLang | 010 | HF | H |
| 120307 | Ninth-grade English | HLang | 001N | HF | H |
| 120307 | Ninth-grade English | HLang | 002N | HF | H |
| 120307 | Tenth-grade English | HLang | 003A | HF | H |

| NCES No. | Course Title | Dept. | Course No. | Credits | Level |
|---|---|---|---|---|---|
| 120307 | Tenth-grade English | HLang | 004A | HF | H |
| 120307 | Eleventh-grade English | HLang | 005A | HF | H |
| 120307 | Eleventh-grade English | HLang | 006A | HF | H |
| 120307 | Twelfth-grade English | HLang | 007A | HF | H |
| 120307 | Twelfth-grade English | HLang | 008A | HF | H |
| 120308 | Improv of reading skills | HLang | 025 | HF | H |
| 120308 | Improv of reading skills | HLang | 026 | HF | H |
| 160302 | Elementary algebra | HMath | 001A | HF | H |
| 160302 | Advanced algebra | HMath | 011A | HF | H |
| 160302 | Advanced algebra | HMath | 011B | HF | H |
| 160302 | Modern 4th-year math | HMath | 017 | HF | H |
| 160302 | Modern 4th-year math | HMath | 018 | HF | H |
| 160302 | Elementary algebra | HMath | 001B | HF | H |
| 160601 | Geometry | HMath | 003A | HF | H |
| 160601 | Geometry | HMath | 004A | HF | H |
| 160602 | Trigonometry | HMath | 007 | HF | H |
| 190699 | Driver education | HDrEd | 001 | HF | H |
| 220432 | American history | HSSSt | 005P | HF | H |
| 220432 | American history | HSSSt | 006P | HF | H |
| 220433 | World history | HSSSt | 003A | HF | H |
| 220433 | World history | HSSSt | 004A | HF | H |

**College courses**

| NCES No. | Course Title | Dept. | Course No. | Credits | Level |
|---|---|---|---|---|---|
| 030402 | Principles of playwriting | Thea | 440 | 3S | U |
| 030501 | Intro visual arts & studi | Art | 1 | 3S | L |
| 0399 | Survey of Western art | ArtH | 110 | 3S | L |
| 040101 | Intro financial acctg | Acctg | 101 | 3S | L |
| 040111 | Managerial accounting | Acctg | 104 | 3S | L |
| 040302 | Personal finance | Fin | 108 | 3S | L |
| 040306 | Security markets | Fin | 204 | 3S | L |
| 040311 | Introduction to finance | Fin | 100 | 3S | L |
| 040604 | Business writing | Engl | 219 | 3S | L |
| 040902 | Problems of small bus | BA | 250 | 3S | L |
| 040903 | Intro organizatl behavior | Mgmt | 321 | 3S | U |
| 040904 | Survey of management | Mgmt | 100 | 3S | L |
| 041007 | Physical distribution | BLog | 301 | 3S | U |
| 041007 | Transport systems | BLog | 304 | 3S | U |
| 041104 | Industrial relations | LS | 100 | 3S | L |
| 041299 | Elementary bus statistics | QBA | 101 | 3S | L |
| 041299 | Elementary bus statistics | QBA | 102 | 3S | L |
| 050101 | Advertising and public rl | Journ | 240 | 3S | L |
| 051002 | Intro radio news | Journ | 297G | 3S | U |
| 070199 | History of education US | EdThP | 430 | 3S | L |
| 070306 | Vocational education | VocEd | 1 | 3S | L |
| 070306 | Safety ed for voc ed teac | IEd | 106 | 3S | L |
| 070499 | Observ/exp preschl childn | IFS | 330A | 1S | U |
| 070499 | Observ/exp preschl childn | IFS | 330B | 3S | U |
| 070708 | Ed psy for prof effect | EdPsy | 020 | 3S | L |
| 070899 | Orienta exceptl children | SplEd | 105 | 3S | L |
| 080703 | Fluid flow | CE | 861 | 3S | L |
| 080901 | Signals and circuits I | EE | 251 | 3S | L |
| 080901 | Signals and circuits II | EE | 352 | 3S | U |
| 0810 | Engineering drawing | EG | 1 | 2S | L |
| 0810 | Intro engineering graphic | EG | 10 | 1S | L |
| 0810 | Engineering design graph | EG | 11 | 1S | L |
| 0810 | Spatial analysis | EG | 12 | 2S | L |
| 0810 | Advan engineering drawing | EG | 803 | 3S | L |
| 0811 | Elementary mechanics | EMch | 811 | 3S | L |
| 081103 | Strength & prop of metals | EMch | 813 | 3S | L |
| 081104 | Dynamics | EMch | 12 | 3S | L |
| 081104 | Statics | EMch | 11 | 3S | L |
| 081302 | Community noise fundamtls | CmDis | 297 | 3S | L |
| 081302 | Community noise fundamtls | CmDis | 497 | 3S | B |
| 081304 | Water pollution control | CE | 370 | 3S | U |
| 081599 | Industrial organ and admn | IE | 315 | 3S | U |
| 081999 | Strength of materials | EMch | 13 | 3S | L |
| 082006 | Product design | ME | 810 | 3S | L |
| 082099 | Kinematics | ME | 805 | 3S | L |
| 0899 | Engineering orientation | Engr | 2 | 1S | L |
| 090276 | Hlth efts ionizg radiatio | Nucle | 497G | 4S | U |
| 090276 | Hlth efts ionizg radiatio | Nucle | 297G | 3S | L |
| 100309 | Nutr component food svcs | Nutr | 801 | 3S | L |
| 100313 | Elementary nutrition | Nutr | 150 | 2S | L |
| 100313 | Diet therp/nutr care dise | Nutr | 252 | 4S | L |
| 100399 | Nutrition of the family | Nutr | 251 | 3S | L |
| 100601 | Infancy and early childhd | IFS | 229 | 3S | L |
| 100701 | San/hskpng hlth care facl | HFS | 802 | 3S | L |
| 100702 | Food service supervision | HFS | 860 | 4S | L |
| 100702 | Food bev labor cost cntrl | Hrlm | 337 | 3S | U |
| 100702 | Hosp food oper syst | HFS | 875 | 4S | L |
| 100799 | San hskpng/com food serv | HSF | 802 | 3S | L |
| 120201 | Mastrpcs Wstn lit snc Ren | CLit | 2 | 3S | L |

| NCES No. | Course Title | Dept. | Course No. | Credits | Level |
|---|---|---|---|---|---|
| 120202 | Masterpieces Wstn lit/Ren | CLit | 1 | 3S | L |
| 120305 | English language analysis | Engl | 100 | 3S | L |
| 120307 | Amer lit Civ War to WWI | Engl | 232 | 3S | L |
| 120307 | Understanding literature | Engl | 101 | 3S | L |
| 120310 | Basic writing skills | Engl | 004 | 3S | L |
| 120310 | Rhetoric and composition | Engl | 015 | 3S | L |
| 1210 | Elementary French I | Fr | 1 | 4S | L |
| 1210 | Elementary French II | Fr | 2 | 4S | L |
| 1211 | Basic German | Ger | 001 | 4S | L |
| 1211 | Basic German | Ger | 002 | 4S | L |
| 1211 | Intermediate German | Ger | 003 | 4S | L |
| 1212 | Greek lit translation I | Class | 26 | 3S | L |
| 1212 | Greek lit translation II | Class | 27 | 3S | L |
| 1216 | Latin lit Eng translation | Class | 34 | 3S | L |
| 1220 | Elementary Russian | Rus | 5 | 3S | L |
| 1225 | Intermediate Spanish | Span | 3 | 4S | L |
| 1307 | Legal envir of business | BLaw | 243 | 3S | L |
| 150202 | Weather and man | Meteo | 002 | 2S | L |
| 150202 | Tropical meteorology | Meteo | 452 | 3S | U |
| 150202 | Applic of stat to meteoro | Meteo | 474 | 3S | U |
| 150301 | Man and environment | BiSci | 3 | 3S | L |
| 150307 | Genetics/ecol & evolution | BlSc | 2 | 3S | L |
| 150399 | Physiology | Biol | 41 | 3S | L |
| 150401 | Chemical principles | Chem | 12 | 3S | L |
| 150408 | Organic chemistry | Chem | 34 | 3S | L |
| 150706 | Optic laboratory | Phys | 204P | 1S | L |
| 150799 | General physics | Phys | 203 | 3S | L |
| 150799 | General physics | Phys | 202A | 4S | L |
| 150899 | Physical science | PhSc | 7 | 3S | L |
| 160103 | Insights into mathematics | Math | 36 | 3S | L |
| 160199 | General view of math | Math | 35 | 3S | L |
| 160203 | Finite mathematics | Math | 17 | 3S | L |
| 160302 | Intermediate algebra | Math | 4 | 3S | L |
| 160302 | College algebra | Math | 5 | 3S | L |
| 160303 | Number systems | Math | 200 | 3S | L |
| 160306 | Elem linear algebra | Math | 18 | 3S | L |
| 160306 | Elementary linear algebra | Math | 18 | 3S | L |
| 160401 | Techniques of calculus I | Math | 110 | 4S | L |
| 160401 | Techniques of calculus II | Math | 111 | 2S | L |
| 160401 | Calculus with analyt geom | Math | 140 | 4S | L |
| 160406 | Differential equations | Math | 250 | 3S | L |
| 160602 | Plane trigonometry | Math | 6 | 3S | L |
| 160801 | Elementary statistics | Stat | 200 | 4S | L |
| 180404 | Introduction to philosphy | Phil | 2 | 3S | L |
| 180499 | Basic problems of philos | Phil | 4 | 3S | L |
| 180501 | Introduction to logic | Phil | 1 | 3S | L |
| 180502 | Element of symb logic | Phil | 12 | 3S | L |
| 181304 | Intro to religion of West | RlSt | 4 | 3S | L |
| 181304 | Religions of the East | RlSt | 3 | 3S | L |
| 1899 | Intro study of religion | RlSt | 1 | 3S | L |
| 1899 | Relig in Am lfe & thought | RlSt | 19 | 3S | L |
| 190104 | Hist or prin of hl ph ed | PhEd | 140 | 3S | L |
| 190107 | Admn hlth/phys ed in schl | PhEd | 491 | 3S | U |
| 190108 | Adapted physical educatn | PhEd | 400 | 3S | U |
| 190110 | Measurmt eval in hlth/PE | PhEd | 490 | 2S | U |
| 190301 | Intramural athletics | PhEd | 489 | 3S | U |
| 190311 | Meth prin of ath coaching | PhEd | 493 | 2S | U |
| 190501 | Drugs in society | HlEd | 43 | 1S | L |
| 190503 | Prin healthful living | HlEd | 60 | 3S | L |
| 190503 | Consumer health | HlEd | 57 | 1S | L |
| 190503 | Intr:hlth aspt/hum sexlty | HlEd | 046 | 1S | L |
| 190504 | Man and disease | HlEd | 19 | 1S | L |
| 190706 | Leisure in human experien | RcPk | 120 | 3S | L |
| 200505 | Mental health | Psy | 37 | 3S | L |
| 210499 | Child maltreatment | IFS | 297B | 1S | L |
| 210599 | Funct plan of park | RcPk | 434 | 3S | U |
| 220102 | Cultural anthropology | Anthy | 45 | 3S | L |
| 220199 | Introductory anthropology | Anthy | 1 | 3S | L |
| 220201 | Principles of economics | Econ | 14 | 3S | L |
| 220204 | Intro microecon anal pol | Econ | 2 | 3S | L |
| 220204 | Intro macroecon anal pol | Econ | 4 | 3S | L |
| 220211 | Labor economics | Econ | 315 | 3S | U |
| 220426 | Western heritage I | Hist | 1 | 3S | L |
| 220428 | Colonial Pennsylvania | Hist | 150 | 3S | L |
| 220432 | Hist of the US since 1865 | Hist | 21 | 3S | L |
| 220432 | Hist of US to 1865 | Hist | 20 | 3S | L |
| 220499 | Hist of American worker | Hist | 156 | 3S | L |
| 220501 | Gov and pol of Am states | PlSc | 425 | 3S | U |
| 220503 | Comparative pol West Eur | PlSc | 20 | 3S | L |
| 220504 | Govt & poltics in mod soc | PlSc | 3 | 3S | L |
| 220511 | Amer local govt & admin | PlSc | 417 | 3S | U |
| 220604 | Urbanization of man | SoSc | 1 | 3S | L |

| NCES No. | Course Title | Dept. | Course No. | Credits | Level |
|---|---|---|---|---|---|
| 220605 | Sociology of the family | Soc | 30 | 3S | L |
| 220606 | Intro to sociology | Soc | 1 | 3S | L |
| 220607 | Introductory social psych | Soc | 3 | 3S | L |
| 220614 | Urban sociology | Soc | 15 | 3S | L |
| 2299 | Urbanization of man | SoSc | 1 | 3S | L |
| 2299 | Intro to American studies | AmSt | 100 | 3S | L |
| | **Noncredit courses** | | | | |
| 020101 | Planned rdg & arch detail | AE | 1901 | NC | |
| 030402 | Theater: fund-raising | Thea | 5203 | NC | |
| 030402 | Theater: mgt finan/facilt | Thea | 5204 | NC | |
| 030402 | Theater: audience dvlpt | Thea | 5205 | NC | |
| 030499 | Organizational structure | Thea | 5202 | NC | |
| 030499 | Volunteer & staff dev | Thea | 5206 | NC | |
| 030699 | Craft fair primer | Art | 5211 | NC | |
| 040604 | Technical writing | Engl | 5832 | NC | |
| 041106 | Basic supervision | IE | 601 | NC | |
| 041106 | Advanced supervision | IE | 602 | NC | |
| 0509 | Dynamics volunteer progrm | HDev | 5703 | NC | |
| 081302 | Community noise fundamtls | CmDis | 5401 | NC | |
| 082501 | Petro & naturl gas explor | PNG | 952 | NC | |
| 082599 | Oil & gas production prac | P N G | 953 | NC | |
| 090276 | Hlth efcts ionizing radia | Nucle | 5534 | NC | |
| 100304 | Fat chance: eating & nutr | Nutr | 7385 | NC | |
| 100701 | Sanitation & housekeeping | HFS | 5701 | NC | |
| 160301 | Basic math | Math | 5951 | NC | |
| 190799 | Beginning stamp collectng | LA | 5834 | NC | |
| 190799 | Begin stamp collect/adult | LA | 5836 | NC | |
| 190799 | Intermed stamp collect I | LA | 5837 | NC | |
| 190799 | Intermed stamp collect II | LA | 5838 | NC | |

## ㉖ PURDUE UNIVERSITY

Mrs. Shirley M. Davis
Director, Division of Media-Based Programs
116 Stewart Center
Purdue University
West Lafayette, Indiana 47907
Phone: 317-494-7231

Overseas enrollment accepted. Programs are limited to professional noncredit certification/CEU credits.

| NCES No. | Course Title | Dept. | Course No. | Credits | Level |
|---|---|---|---|---|---|
| | **Noncredit courses** | | | | |
| 010403 | Pest control technology | Entm | | NC | V |
| 090411 | Pharmacy correspondence | Pharm | | NC | V |
| 090905 | Central service tech trng | CntEd | | NC | V |
| 090905 | Central service mgmt & sp | CntEd | | NC | V |
| 100702 | Food service mgt & supv | RHIMI | | NC | V |
| 100702 | Food purchasing & procur | RHIMI | | NC | V |
| 100702 | Prof cooking & food serv | RHIMI | | NC | V |
| 100702 | Computer app in food serv | RHIMI | | NC | V |

## ㉗ ROOSEVELT UNIVERSITY

Mr. Arny Reichler
Director of External Degree Program
Evelyn T. Stone College of Continuing Education
Roosevelt University
430 South Michigan Avenue
Chicago, Illinois 60605
Phone: 312-341-3866

Enrollment on a noncredit basis accepted in all credit courses. Only in exceptional cases are gifted high school students permitted to enroll in undergraduate courses for credit. Overseas enrollment accepted for college courses. Students may enroll at any time and are given six months to complete the course.

| NCES No. | Course Title | Dept. | Course No. | Credits | Level |
|---|---|---|---|---|---|
| | **College courses** | | | | |
| 0306 | Pro-seminar | BGS | 201 | 6S | U |
| 0306 | Advanced pro-seminar | BGS | 301 | 3S | U |
| 0306 | Seminar in humanities | BGS | 392 | 6S | U |
| 0306 | Adv seminar humanities | BGS | 398 | 3S | U |

| NCES No. | Course Title | Dept. | Course No. | Credits | Level |
|---|---|---|---|---|---|
| 0306 | Senior thesis | BGS | 399 | 3S | U |
| 060199 | Bus app IBM PC/XT | CpSc | 341 | 3S | U |
| 060705 | COBOL programming | CpSc | 213 | 3S | U |
| 060705 | Adv COBOL programming | CpSc | 219 | 3S | U |
| 060705 | Advanced BASIC | CpSc | 242 | 3S | U |
| 060903 | Intro programming tech | CpSc | 202 | 3S | U |
| 060904 | Systems analysis & design | CpSc | 208 | 3S | U |
| 061104 | CPSC data processing | CpSc | 101 | 3S | U |
| 090602 | Health systems adm I | PbAd | 351 | 3S | U |
| 090699 | Health services economics | PbAd | 356 | 3S | U |
| 090702 | Adm urban disease problem | PbAd | 354 | 3S | U |
| 090710 | Admin health mgmt II | PbAd | 352 | 3S | U |
| 090901 | Admin health planning III | PbAd | 353 | 3S | U |
| 120310 | Composition I | Engl | 101 | 3S | L |
| 120310 | Composition II | Engl | 102 | 3S | L |
| 120310 | Composition III | Engl | 103 | 3S | L |
| 1599 | Seminar natural sciences | BGS | 391 | 6S | U |
| 2001 | General psychology | Psych | 103 | 3S | L |
| 200501 | Abnormal psychology | Psych | 201 | 3S | U |
| 200504 | Childhood & Adolescence | Psych | 254 | 3S | U |
| 200509 | Personality | Psych | 360 | 3S | U |
| 2007 | Social psychology | Psych | 220 | 3S | U |
| 2101 | Intro to public admin | PbAd | 301 | 3S | U |
| 210113 | Public policy & admin | PbAd | 371 | 3S | U |
| 210304 | Adm law enforcement adm | PbAd | 345 | 3S | U |
| 210401 | Social welfare programs | SWk | 250 | 3S | U |
| 220305 | Physical geography I | Geog | 101 | 3S | L |
| 220305 | Physical geography II | Geog | 102 | 3S | L |
| 220308 | Urban geography | Geog | 305 | 3S | U |
| 220399 | Political geography | Geog | 309 | 3S | U |
| 220399 | Urban environment | Geog | 350 | 3S | U |
| 220409 | American social history | Hist | 326 | 3S | U |
| 220428 | History of Chicago | Hist | 305 | 3S | U |
| 220499 | US labor history | Hist | 327 | 3S | U |
| 220499 | Urban civilization | Hist | 380 | 3S | U |
| 2205 | Intro political science | PolSc | 200 | 3S | U |
| 2206 | Introduction to sociology | Soc | 101 | 3S | L |
| 220601 | Community organization | Soc | 346 | 3S | U |
| 220602 | Criminology | Soc | 331 | 3S | U |
| 220603 | Human ecology | Soc | 348 | 3S | U |
| 220604 | Juvenile delinquency | Soc | 335 | 3S | U |
| 220610 | Deviant behavior | Soc | 230 | 3S | U |
| 220612 | Intro social organization | Soc | 315 | 3S | U |
| 220614 | Urban society | Soc | 245 | 3S | U |
| 220615 | Sociology of women | Soc | 237 | 3S | U |
| 220699 | Housing | Soc | 347 | 3S | U |
| 220699 | Methods of social researc | Soc | 375 | 3S | U |
| 2299 | Seminar in social science | BGS | 390 | 6S | U |
| 2299 | Adv sem in social sci | BGS | 396 | 3S | U |
| | **Graduate courses** | | | | |
| 200509 | Understanding personality | MGS | 435 | 2S | G |
| 2099 | Application of psychology | MGS | 437 | 2S | G |
| 2099 | Assess indiv group styles | MGS | 436 | 2S | G |

## ㉘ SAINT JOSEPH'S COLLEGE

Mr. Harry W. Osgood
Acting Dean
Continuing Education/Extension Degree Program
Saint Joseph's College
White's Bridge Road
North Windham, Maine 04062
Phone: 207-892-6766

Overseas enrollment accepted for college courses.

| NCES No. | Course Title | Dept. | Course No. | Credits | Level |
|---|---|---|---|---|---|
| | **College courses** | | | | |
| 040101 | Principals of accounting | Bus | Ac101 | 3S | L |
| 040101 | Principals of accounting | Bus | Ac102 | 3S | L |
| 040904 | Intro to management | Bus | Mg201 | 3S | L |
| 040999 | Sales management | Bus | Mk304 | 3S | U |
| 041001 | Marketing | Bus | Mk201 | 3S | U |
| 041004 | Marketing management | Bus | Mk401 | 3S | U |
| 041099 | Retailing | Bus | Mk303 | 3S | U |
| 0411 | Personnel management | Bus | Mg302 | 3S | U |
| 041104 | Labor relations | Bus | Mg304 | 3S | U |
| 0501 | Advertising | Bus | Mk301 | 3S | U |

| NCES No. | Course Title | Dept. | Course No. | Credits | Level |
|---|---|---|---|---|---|
| 070199 | History of American ed | Ed | Ed402 | 3S | U |
| 0702 | Ed administration | Ed | Ed434 | 3S | U |
| 070309 | Adult learning I | Ed | Ed308 | 3S | U |
| 070309 | Adult learning I | Ed | Ed309 | 3S | U |
| 0711 | Measurements & evaluation | Ed | Ed401 | 3S | U |
| 090601 | Mgmt in hlth care facil | HCA | HC300 | 3S | U |
| 090601 | Financial mgmt in HCA I | HCA | HC441 | 3S | U |
| 090601 | Financial mgmt in HCA II | HCA | HC442 | 3S | U |
| 090602 | Am health care systems I | HCA | HC305 | 3S | U |
| 090602 | Am health care systems II | HCA | HC306 | 3S | U |
| 090699 | Decis-mkng in hlth cr adm | HCA | HC406 | 3S | U |
| 0907 | Public health I | HCA | HC423 | 3S | U |
| 0907 | Public health II | HCA | HC424 | 3S | U |
| 090703 | Environmental health | HCA | ES202 | 3S | U |
| 090704 | Human ecology | HCA | ES201 | 3S | U |
| 090904 | Legal aspects of HCA | HCA | HC453 | 3S | U |
| 090904 | Ethics in health care | HCA | HC455 | 3S | U |
| 120307 | American literature I | Engl | 203 | 3S | U |
| 120307 | American literature II | Engl | 204 | 3S | U |
| 120310 | English composition I | Engl | 106 | 3S | L |
| 120310 | English composition II | Engl | 107 | 3S | L |
| 1307 | Business law I | Bus | Ba301 | 3S | U |
| 1307 | Business law II | Bus | Ba302 | 3S | U |
| 1804 | Intro to philosophy | Phil | 201 | 3S | U |
| 181002 | Comparative religions | Phil | HU302 | 3S | U |
| 2001 | Intro to psychology | Psy | 101 | 3S | L |
| 2001 | Topics in psychology | Psy | 204 | 3S | U |
| 200404 | Psychology of motivation | Psy | 302 | 3S | U |
| 200501 | Abnormal psychology | Psy | 303 | 3S | U |
| 200503 | Behavior modification | Psy | 316 | 3S | U |
| 200509 | Psychology of personality | Psy | 301 | 3S | U |
| 2007 | Social psychology | Soc | 201 | 3S | U |
| 200804 | Educational psychology | Ed | Ed301 | 3S | U |
| 200901 | Industrial psychology | Psy | 402 | 3S | U |
| 200999 | Human relations in bus | Psy | 309 | 3S | U |
| 220201 | Intro to microeconomics | Bus | BA201 | 3S | L |
| 220201 | Intro to macroeconomics | Bus | BA202 | 3S | L |
| 220432 | Hist of the United States | Hist | 201 | 3S | L |
| 220432 | Hist of the United States | Hist | 202 | 3S | L |
| 220433 | Western civilization | Hist | 101 | 3S | L |
| 220433 | Western civilization | Hist | 102 | 3S | L |
| 220601 | Modern community | Soc | 304 | 3S | U |
| 220602 | Criminology | Soc | 307 | 3S | L |
| 220605 | The family | Soc | 303 | 3S | U |
| 220606 | Principles of sociology | Soc | 201 | 3S | L |
| 220613 | Social problems | Soc | 301 | 3S | U |

## ㉙ SAVANNAH STATE COLLEGE

Mrs. Bernita L. Greene
Program Coordinator for Correspondence Study
Correspondence Study Office
Savannah State University
P.O. Box 20372
Savannah, Georgia 31404
Phone: 912-356-2243

Overseas enrollment accepted. Credit for courses completed in this program or in similar programs at recognized institutions will be accepted if not more than 45 quarter hours were earned in correspondence; not more than 50% of the required courses in the major or minor were completed in correspondence; and correspondence courses were not taken by students who had completed 135 hours or more.

| NCES No. | Course Title | Dept. | Course No. | Credits | Level |
|---|---|---|---|---|---|
| | **College courses** | | | | |
| 040308 | Money, credit & banking | Bus | 323 | 5Q | U |
| 040314 | Business finance | Bus | 320 | 5Q | U |
| 041299 | Quantitative analysis | Bus | 332 | 5Q | U |
| 0499 | Introduction to business | Bus | 105 | 5Q | L |
| 130399 | Amer constitutional law | PolSc | 311 | 5Q | U |
| 160302 | College algebra | Mat | 107 | 5Q | U |
| 160599 | Bus & econom statistics | Bus | 331 | 5Q | U |
| 200599 | Psych basis for hum behav | Soc | 201 | 5Q | U |
| 220299 | Introduction to economics | Bus | 200 | 5Q | U |
| 220399 | World & human geography | Soc | 111 | 5Q | L |

| NCES No. | Course Title | Dept. | Course No. | Credits | Level |
|---|---|---|---|---|---|
| 220426 | US & Afro-Am snc Civ War | His | 203 | 5Q | U |
| 220426 | His of early modrn Europe | His | 331 | 5Q | U |
| 220426 | His of early modrn Europe | His | 332 | 5Q | U |
| 220432 | US & Afro-Am thr Civ War | His | 202 | 5Q | U |
| 220433 | History of Western civil | His | 101 | 5Q | L |
| 220433 | History of Western civil | His | 102 | 5Q | L |
| 220501 | Government | PolSc | 200 | 5Q | U |
| 220599 | Black politics | PolSc | 390 | 5Q | U |
| 220599 | American political proc | PolSc | 405 | 5Q | U |
| 220605 | The family | Soc | 315 | 5Q | U |
| 220613 | Social problems | Soc | 350 | 5Q | U |
| 220699 | Introduction to sociology | Soc | 201 | 5Q | U |

## ㉚ SOUTHERN ILLINOIS UNIVERSITY AT CARBONDALE

Dr. Mary Jane Sullivan
Coordinator of Individualized Learning
Division of Continuing Education
Southern Illinois University at Carbondale
Washington Square C
Carbondale, Illinois 62901
Phone: 618-536-7751

Enrollment on a noncredit basis accepted in all credit courses. Only in exceptional cases are gifted high school students permitted to enroll in undergraduate courses for credit. Overseas enrollment accepted for college courses.

| NCES No. | Course Title | Dept. | Course No. | Credits | Level |
|---|---|---|---|---|---|
| | **College courses** | | | | |
| 030301 | Appl tech information | ATS | 416 | 3U | U |
| 030501 | Survey of 20th-cen art | ArHis | 346 | 3S | U |
| 060499 | Computer sys applications | Elt | 224 | 3U | L |
| 061101 | Computers in society | CompS | 102 | 3U | L |
| 090999 | Medical terminology | AHC | 105 | 2U | L |
| 110303 | Intro to electronics | Elt | 100 | 3U | L |
| 110601 | Primary flight theory | AF | 200 | 3U | L |
| 161299 | Technical mathematics | STC | 105 | 2U | L |
| 180502 | Elementary logic | GeC | 208 | 3U | L |
| 220203 | Insurance | Fin | 327 | 3U | U |
| 220208 | Consumer problems | ATS | 340 | 3U | U |
| 220305 | Understanding the weather | Geog | 330 | 3S | U |
| 220453 | Modern American history | GeB | 301 | 3U | U |
| 220507 | Political parties | PolSc | 319 | 3S | U |

## ㉛ TEXAS TECH UNIVERSITY

Ms. Kay Simonton
Correspondence Office Supervisor
Continuing Education
Texas Tech University
P.O. Box 4110
Lubbock, Texas 79409
Phone: 806-742-1513

Enrollment on a noncredit basis accepted in all credit courses. Gifted high school students are permitted to enroll in undergraduate courses for credit. Overseas enrollment accepted.

| NCES No. | Course Title | Dept. | Course No. | Credits | Level |
|---|---|---|---|---|---|
| | **High School courses** | | | | |
| 010107 | Gen agriculture sem 1 | Agri | 1S1 | 1S | H |
| 010107 | Gen agriculture sem 2 | Agri | 1S2 | 1S | H |
| 040108 | Accounting | Acctg | 1S1 | 1S | H |
| 040108 | Accounting | Acctg | 1S2 | 1S | H |
| 040599 | General business | Bus | 1S1 | 1S | H |

| NCES No. | Course Title | Dept. | Course No. | Credits | Level |
|---|---|---|---|---|---|
| 040599 | General business | Bus | 1S2 | 1S | H |
| 040999 | Bus mgmt & ownership | Mgmt | 1S1 | 1S | H |
| 040999 | Bus mgmt & ownership | Mgmt | 1S2 | 1S | H |
| 041003 | Salesmanship | Bus | 1S1 | 1S | H |
| 041003 | Salesmanship | Bus | 1S2 | 1S | H |
| 050606 | Journalism I: history | Jrnl | 1S2 | 1S | H |
| 060199 | Computer math I | Comp | 2S1 | 1S | H |
| 060199 | Computer math I | Comp | 2S2 | 1S | H |
| 060199 | Computer math II | Comp | 3S1 | 1S | H |
| 060199 | Computer math II | Comp | 3S2 | 1S | H |
| 060199 | Computer science I | Comp | 4S1 | 1S | H |
| 060199 | Computer science I | Comp | 4S2 | 1S | H |
| 061101 | Intro computer programing | Comp | 1S1 | 1S | H |
| 061104 | Bus data processing | Comp | 1S2 | 1S | H |
| 100601 | Child development | HmEc | 1S1 | 1S | H |
| 100604 | Project self-discovery | HFL | 2S1 | HF | H |
| 100699 | Home & family living | HmEc | 2S1 | 1S | H |
| 120299 | Humanities | Hum | 1S1 | HF | H |
| 120305 | English I sem 1 | Engl | 1S1 | 1S | H |
| 120305 | English I sem 2 | Engl | 1S2 | 1S | H |
| 120305 | English II sem 1 | Engl | 1S2 | 1S | H |
| 120305 | English II sem 2 | Engl | 1S2 | 1S | H |
| 120305 | English III sem 1 | Engl | 3S1 | 1S | H |
| 120305 | English III sem 2 | Engl | 3S2 | 1S | H |
| 120305 | English IV sem 1 | Engl | 4S1 | 1S | H |
| 120305 | English IV sem 2 | Engl | 4S2 | 1S | H |
| 120305 | Correlated lang arts I | CorLa | 1S1 | HF | H |
| 120305 | Correlated lang arts I | CorLa | 1S2 | HF | H |
| 120305 | Correlated lang arts II | CorLa | 2S1 | HF | H |
| 120305 | Correlated lang arts II | CorLa | 2S2 | HF | H |
| 120305 | Correlated lang arts III | CorLa | 3S1 | HF | H |
| 120305 | Correlated lang arts III | CorLa | 3S2 | HF | H |
| 120305 | Correlated lang arts IV | CorLa | 4S1 | HF | H |
| 120305 | Correlated lang arts IV | CorLa | 4S2 | HF | H |
| 120307 | Life & lit of Southwest | Engl | 1S1 | 1S | H |
| 1210 | French I | Fren | 1S1 | 1S | H |
| 130799 | Business and consumer law | Bus | 1S1 | 1S | H |
| 1503 | Biology I | Bio | 1S1 | 1S | H |
| 1503 | Biology I | Bio | 1S2 | 1S | H |
| 1507 | Physics | Phys | 1S1 | 1S | H |
| 1507 | Physics | Phys | 1S2 | 1S | H |
| 1508 | Physical science | Phys | 1S1 | 1S | H |
| 1508 | Physical science | Phys | 1S2 | 1S | H |
| 160302 | Algebra I | Math | 1S1 | 1S | H |
| 160302 | Algebra I | Math | 1S2 | 1S | H |
| 160302 | Algebra II | Math | 2S1 | 1S | H |
| 160302 | Algebra II | Math | 2S2 | 1S | H |
| 160302 | Pre-algebra | PAlg | 1S1 | 1S | H |
| 160302 | Pre-algebra | PAlg | 1S2 | 1S | H |
| 160401 | Elementary analysis | Math | 1S1 | 1S | H |
| 160601 | Geometry | Math | 1S1 | 1S | H |
| 160601 | Geometry | Math | 1S2 | 1S | H |
| 160602 | Trigonometry | Math | 1S1 | 1S | H |
| 160603 | Analytical geometry | Geom | 2S1 | HF | H |
| 161202 | Fundamentals of math | Math | 1S1 | 1S | H |
| 161202 | Math of consumer econom | Math | 1S1 | 1S | H |
| 181202 | Bible sem 1 | Relig | 1S1 | 1S | H |
| 181202 | Bible sem 2 | Relig | 1S2 | 1S | H |
| 190509 | Health education | HSci | 1S1 | 1S | H |
| 2001 | Psychology | Psych | 1S1 | 1S | H |
| 2201 | Anthropology | Anthr | 1S1 | 1S | H |
| 220215 | Economics with free enter | Econ | S1 | 1S | H |
| 220428 | Advanced Texas studies | Hist | 1S1 | 1S | H |
| 220432 | United States history | Hist | S1 | 1S | H |
| 220432 | United States history | Hist | S2 | 1S | H |
| 220433 | World history | Hist | 2S1 | 1S | H |
| 220433 | World history | Hist | 2S2 | 1S | H |
| 220501 | United States government | PolSc | S1 | 1S | H |
| 2206 | Sociology | Socio | 1S1 | 1S | H |

**College courses**

| NCES No. | Course Title | Dept. | Course No. | Credits | Level |
|---|---|---|---|---|---|
| 010102 | Agricultural finance | Agri | 3302 | 3S | U |
| 010104 | The agriculture industry | Agri | 1111 | 3S | L |
| 010199 | Agricultural economics | Agri | 1301 | 3S | L |
| 010699 | Weed control | Agri | 4323 | 3S | U |
| 010704 | Soil fertility | Agri | 4335 | 3S | U |
| 040101 | Elementary accounting I | Acctg | 2300 | 3S | L |
| 040101 | Elementary accounting II | Acctg | 2301 | 3S | L |
| 040199 | Personal finance | Acctg | 2320 | 3S | L |
| 040199 | Corporation finance | Acctg | 3320 | 3S | U |
| 040199 | Using accounting info | Acctg | 2303 | 3S | L |
| 040304 | Prin of money/bankg/credt | Acctg | 3323 | 3S | U |

| NCES No. | Course Title | Dept. | Course No. | Credits | Level |
|---|---|---|---|---|---|
| 040306 | Investments | Bus | 4324 | 3S | U |
| 040707 | Life & health insurance | Ins | 3327 | 3S | U |
| 040999 | Managerial communication | Mgmt | 3373 | 3S | U |
| 041001 | Introduction to marketing | Mktg | 3350 | 3S | U |
| 041299 | Intro business statistics | Bus | 2445 | 4S | L |
| 041307 | Real estate invest analys | Fin | 4335 | 3S | U |
| 041399 | Real estate fundamentals | RIEs | 3332 | 3S | U |
| 050606 | Hist of Amer journalism | Jrnl | 3350 | 3S | U |
| 0509 | Principles of public rela | Adv | 3311 | 3S | U |
| 0599 | Intro to mass communicatn | Commu | 1300 | 3S | L |
| 070103 | Foundations of ed soc | Educ | 4323 | 3S | U |
| 070199 | History & philos of educ | Educ | 4314 | 3S | U |
| 070303 | Student discipline | EdSE | 3100 | 1S | U |
| 070403 | Substitute teaching | EdSE | 3100 | 1S | U |
| 070610 | Children's literature | Educ | 4350 | 3S | U |
| 070610 | Teaching Engl in sec schs | Engl | 4336 | 3S | U |
| 081103 | Mechanics of solids | Chem | 3303 | 3S | U |
| 081104 | Statics | Chem | 330 | 3S | U |
| 100304 | Food and nutrition | HmEc | 1301 | 3S | L |
| 100503 | Intr housing & interiors | HmEc | 1380 | 3S | L |
| 100602 | Courtship and marriage | HmEc | 2322 | 3S | L |
| 120201 | Masterpieces of lit | Engl | 2301 | 3S | L |
| 120201 | Masterpieces of lit | Engl | 2302 | 3S | L |
| 120204 | Short story | Engl | 3331 | 3S | U |
| 120204 | American novel | Engl | 3325 | 3S | U |
| 120204 | Modern American drama | Engl | 4343 | 3S | U |
| 1203 | Essentials of Eng usage | Engl | 1300 | 3S | L |
| 120302 | Hist of the Engl language | Engl | 4372 | 3S | U |
| 120310 | Essentials of rhetoric | Engl | 1301 | 3S | L |
| 120310 | Advanced college rhetoric | Engl | 1302 | 3S | L |
| 130799 | Business law I | Bus | 3391 | 3S | U |
| 130799 | Business law II | Bus | 3392 | 3S | U |
| 130799 | Oil & gas law | Bus | 3395 | 3S | U |
| 1505 | Man & his earth | Geo | 1308 | 3S | L |
| 160302 | College algebra | Math | 1320 | 3S | L |
| 160401 | Intro to math analysis | Math | 1330 | 3S | L |
| 160401 | Intro to math analysis | Math | 1331 | 3S | L |
| 160401 | Analyt geom & calculus I | Math | 1551 | 5S | L |
| 160401 | Analyt geom & calculus II | Math | 1552 | 5S | L |
| 160401 | Calculus I | Math | 1317 | 3S | L |
| 160401 | Calculus II | Math | 1318 | 3S | L |
| 160401 | Calculus III | Math | 2350 | 3S | L |
| 160602 | Trigonometry | Math | 1321 | 3S | L |
| 160603 | Analytical geometry | Math | 1316 | 3S | L |
| 161108 | Statistical methods | Psych | 3304 | 3S | U |
| 1804 | Beginning philosophy | Phil | 2300 | 3S | L |
| 180502 | Logic | Phil | 2310 | 3S | L |
| 181202 | Intro to New Testament | Relig | 1302 | 3S | L |
| 181299 | Intro to Old Testament | Relig | 1301 | 3S | L |
| 190501 | Risk taking behaviors | HlEd | 3308 | 3S | U |
| 190504 | Chron dis/quality of life | HSci | 2201 | 2S | L |
| 190504 | Reducing risks of disease | HlEd | 2202 | 2S | L |
| 190509 | Patterns of healthful liv | HSci | 1303 | 3S | L |
| 190512 | Health aspects sexuality | HlEd | 2207 | 2S | L |
| 190701 | Process of rec programmng | Rec | 3301 | 3S | U |
| 190701 | Manag leisure servs organ | Rec | 4308 | 3S | U |
| 190706 | Hist sports & recreation | Hist | 3338 | 3S | U |
| 200102 | History of psychology | Psych | 4316 | 3S | U |
| 200403 | Human learning | Psych | 4319 | 3S | U |
| 2005 | General psychology | Psych | 1301 | 3S | L |
| 200501 | Abnormal psychology | Psych | 4305 | 3S | U |
| 200504 | Child psychology | Psych | 2301 | 3S | L |
| 200504 | Adolescent psychology | Psych | 2305 | 3S | L |
| 200505 | Mental health | Psych | 2302 | 3S | L |
| 200509 | Personality | Psych | 3306 | 3S | L |
| 2007 | Intro social psychology | Psy | 3304 | 3S | U |
| 220102 | Cultural anthropology | Anthr | 2302 | 3S | L |
| 220201 | Principles of economics I | Econ | 2311 | 3S | L |
| 220201 | Prin of economics II | Econ | 2312 | 3S | L |
| 220306 | Regional geog of world | Geog | 2351 | 3S | L |
| 220428 | History of Texas | Hist | 3310 | 3S | U |
| 220432 | History of US to 1877 | Hist | 2300 | 3S | L |
| 220432 | History of US since 1877 | Hist | 2301 | 3S | L |
| 220433 | Western civilization I | Hist | 1300 | 3S | L |
| 220433 | Western civilization II | Hist | 1301 | 3S | L |
| 220501 | Amer govt organization | PolS | 2301 | 3S | L |
| 220501 | American public policy | PolS | 2302 | 3S | L |
| 220608 | Rural sociology | Socio | 3361 | 3S | U |
| 220613 | Current social problems | Socio | 2320 | 3S | L |

**Noncredit courses**

| NCES No. | Course Title | Dept. | Course No. | Credits | Level |
|---|---|---|---|---|---|
| 0711 | SAT review | SAT | S1 | NC | |

## ③② UNIVERSITY OF ALABAMA

Dr. Nancy G. Williams
Director of Independent Study
Independent Study Department
University of Alabama
P.O. Box 2967
University, Alabama 35486
Phone: 205-348-7642

Enrollment on a noncredit basis accepted in some credit courses. Gifted high school students are permitted to enroll in undergraduate courses for credit. Overseas enrollment accepted.

| NCES No. | Course Title | Dept. | Course No. | Credits | Level |
|---|---|---|---|---|---|
| | **High School courses** | | | | |
| 040104 | General business | Bus | 1A | HF | H |
| 040104 | General business | Bus | 1B | HF | H |
| 090101 | Modern health | HSci | 1A | HF | H |
| 090101 | Modern health | HSci | 16 | HF | H |
| 120307 | Ninth-grade English | Engl | 9A | HF | H |
| 120307 | Ninth-grade English | Engl | 9B | HF | H |
| 120307 | Tenth-grade English | Engl | 10A | HF | H |
| 120307 | Tenth-grade English | Engl | 10B | HF | H |
| 120307 | Eleventh-grade English | Engl | 11A | HF | H |
| 120307 | Eleventh-grade English | Engl | 11B | HF | H |
| 120307 | Twelfth-grade English | Engl | 12A | HF | H |
| 120307 | Twelfth-grade English | Engl | 12B | HF | H |
| 120307 | Basic grammar review | Engl | 13 | HF | H |
| 1211 | Beginning German | Ger | 1A | HF | H |
| 1211 | Beginning German | Ger | 1B | HF | H |
| 1211 | Second-year German | Ger | 2A | HF | H |
| 1211 | Second-year German | Ger | 2B | HF | H |
| 1508 | Physical science | PhySc | 9a | HF | H |
| 1508 | Physical science | PhySc | 9b | HF | H |
| 160301 | General mathematics | Math | 13A | HF | H |
| 160301 | General mathematics | Math | 13B | HF | H |
| 160302 | Algebra I | Math | 9A | HF | H |
| 160302 | Algebra I | Math | 9B | HF | H |
| 160302 | Algebra II | Math | 11A | HF | H |
| 160302 | Algebra II | Math | 11B | HF | H |
| 160304 | Unified geometry | Math | 10A | HF | H |
| 160304 | Unified geometry | Math | 10B | HF | H |
| 160602 | Trigonometry | Math | 12 | HF | H |
| 161202 | Consumer mathematics | Math | 14 | HF | H |
| 220403 | Economics | Hist | 12A | HF | H |
| 220428 | Alabama history | Hist | 9A | HF | H |
| 220428 | Alabama history | Hist | 96 | HF | H |
| 220432 | American history | Hist | 11A | HF | H |
| 220432 | American history | Hist | 11B | HF | H |
| 220433 | World history | Hist | 10A | HF | H |
| 220433 | World history | Hist | 10B | HF | H |
| 220501 | Government | PolSc | 12B | HF | H |
| | **College courses** | | | | |
| 030399 | Intro to listening | Music | 121C | 3S | L |
| 030399 | Intro to study of music | Music | 421C | 3S | U |
| 030402 | Theatre history | ThArt | 451C | 3S | U |
| 030402 | Theatre history | ThArt | 452C | 3S | L |
| 040101 | Prin of accounting I | Acctg | 201C | 3S | L |
| 040101 | Prin of accounting II | Acctg | 202C | 3S | L |
| 040104 | Intermediate accounting I | Acctg | 310C | 3S | U |
| 040104 | Intermediate acctg II | Acctg | 311C | 3S | U |
| 040106 | Cost accounting | Acctg | 361C | 3S | U |
| 040109 | Acctg: nonprofit organizs | Acctg | 456C | 3S | U |
| 040114 | Income tax procedure | Acctg | 371C | 3S | U |
| 040301 | Business finance | Bus | 302C | 3S | U |
| 040306 | Investments | Bus | 414C | 3S | U |
| 040308 | Money and banking | Bus | 301C | 3S | U |
| 040312 | Public finance | Bus | 423C | 3S | U |
| 040399 | Transportation | Bus | 351C | 3S | U |
| 040601 | Written bus communication | Bus | 206C | 2S | L |
| 040604 | Written bus communication | Bus | 372C | 2S | U |

| NCES No. | Course Title | Dept. | Course No. | Credits | Level |
|---|---|---|---|---|---|
| 040712 | Personal ins planning | Bus | 341C | 3S | U |
| 040905 | Organ theory & behavior | Mgmt | 300C | 3S | U |
| 041001 | Marketing | Mktg | 300C | 3S | U |
| 041099 | Retail management | Mktg | 321C | 3S | U |
| 041099 | Sales management | Mktg | 338C | 3S | U |
| 041099 | Promotional strategy | Mktg | 444C | 3S | U |
| 041099 | Essen of multinatnl mktg | Mktg | 455C | 3S | U |
| 041099 | Marketing research | Mktg | 473C | 3S | U |
| 041099 | Salesmanship | Mktg | 337C | 3S | U |
| 041099 | Consumer behavior | Mktg | 313C | 3S | U |
| 041104 | Collective bargaining | Mgmt | 430C | 3S | U |
| 041199 | Intro human resources mgt | Mgmt | 301C | 3S | U |
| 041199 | Personnel management | Mgmt | 310C | 3S | U |
| 041199 | Management group behavior | Mgmt | 320C | 3S | U |
| 041301 | Real estate appraisal | Bus | 432C | 3S | U |
| 041303 | Principles of real estate | Bus | 431C | 3S | U |
| 041306 | Real estate finance | Bus | 436C | | U |
| 050499 | Intro to mass communica | Commu | 101C | 3S | L |
| 050499 | Mass media law & regula | Commu | 401C | 3S | L |
| 070799 | Guidance for teachers | Educ | 411C | 3S | U |
| 080699 | Process calculations | ChmEg | 252C | 3S | L |
| 080699 | Thermodynamics calculatns | ChmEg | 253C | 3S | L |
| 090699 | Intro to health system | HSci | 370C | 3S | U |
| 090699 | Anal of health-care mgmt | HSci | 371C | 3S | U |
| 100206 | Personal finance | HmEc | 404C | 3S | U |
| 100299 | Consumer protection | HmEc | 401C | 3S | U |
| 100299 | Consumer behavior | CEd | 313C | 3S | U |
| 100399 | Nutrition: birth thru adol | HmEc | 302C | 3S | U |
| 100401 | Decision mkg & fam resour | HmEc | 201C | 3S | L |
| 100401 | Household equipment | HmEc | 240C | 3S | L |
| 100601 | Child devel: school age | HmEc | 301C | 3S | U |
| 100601 | Child devel: adolescence | HmEc | 302C | 3S | U |
| 100602 | Marriage and the family | HmEc | 262C | 3S | L |
| 100699 | Human development | HmEc | 101C | 3S | L |
| 120299 | Greek & Roman mythology | Clas | 222C | 2S | L |
| 120307 | English literature | EngLL | 205C | 3S | L |
| 120307 | English literature | EngLL | 206C | 3S | L |
| 120307 | American literature | EngLL | 209C | 3S | L |
| 120307 | American literature | EngLL | 210C | 3S | L |
| 120307 | Major American writers | EngLL | 340C | 3S | U |
| 120307 | Major American writers | EngLL | 341C | 3S | U |
| 120307 | Contemporary American lit | EngLL | 345C | 3S | U |
| 120307 | Southern literature | EngLL | 347C | 3S | U |
| 120307 | Eng Bible as literature | EngLL | 363C | 3S | U |
| 120307 | Shakespeare | EngLL | 366C | 3S | U |
| 120307 | The English novel | EngLL | 387C | 3S | U |
| 120307 | The modern short story | EngLL | 390C | 3S | U |
| 120307 | The Age of Browning | EngLL | 485C | 3S | U |
| 120307 | The Age of Hardy | EngLL | 486C | 3S | U |
| 120307 | Modern British fiction | EngLL | 491C | 3S | U |
| 120310 | English composition | Engl | 101C | 3S | L |
| 120310 | English composition | Engl | 102C | 3S | L |
| 120399 | American folklore | Hum | 221C | 3S | L |
| 120399 | Popular culture in Amer | Hum | 222C | 3S | L |
| 120399 | The American experience | Hum | 300C | 3S | U |
| 120399 | Independent study reading | Hum | 421C | 3S | U |
| 1210 | Intermediate French | Frnch | 201C | 3S | L |
| 1210 | Intermediate French | Frnch | 202C | 3S | L |
| 1211 | Elementary German | Ger | 101C | 4S | L |
| 1211 | Elementary German | Ger | 102C | 4S | L |
| 1211 | Intermediate German | Ger | 201C | 3S | L |
| 1211 | Intermediate German | Ger | 202C | 3S | L |
| 1211 | Intermed scientific Ger | Ger | 209C | 3S | L |
| 1211 | Intermed scientific Ger | Ger | 210C | 3S | L |
| 1211 | German for reading profic | Ger | 103C | 3S | L |
| 1211 | German for reading profic | Ger | 104C | 3S | L |
| 1216 | Elementary Latin | Latin | 101C | 3S | L |
| 1216 | Elementary Latin | Latin | 102C | 3S | L |
| 1225 | Intermediate Spanish | Span | 201C | 3S | L |
| 1225 | Intermediate Spanish | Span | 202C | 3S | L |
| 1225 | Advanced grammar & comp | Span | 356C | 3S | U |
| 1225 | Survey of Spanish lit | Span | 371C | 3S | U |
| 1225 | Survey of Spanish lit | Span | 372C | 3S | U |
| 1225 | Spanish civilization | Span | 364C | 3S | U |
| 130499 | Intro to criminal justice | Socio | 200C | 3S | L |
| 130499 | Intro to law enforcement | Socio | 201C | 3S | L |
| 130499 | Intro to corrections | Socio | 202C | 3S | L |
| 130499 | Criminal investigation | Socio | 240C | 3S | L |
| 130499 | Intro to private security | Socio | 260C | 3S | L |
| 130499 | Org & man con in crim jus | Socio | 330C | 3S | U |
| 130499 | Crime prev & control | Socio | 460C | 3S | U |
| 130799 | Law, business & society | Law | 200C | 3S | L |

| NCES No. | Course Title | Dept. | Course No. | Credits | Level |
|---|---|---|---|---|---|
| 130999 | Real & pers property law | Law | 407c | 3S | U |
| 140199 | Library research | LibSc | 140C | 2S | U |
| 1501 | Introduction to astronomy | Astro | 101C | 3S | U |
| 150103 | Obser astronomy with lab | Astro | 102C | 3S | U |
| 150399 | Heredity | Bio | 209C | 3S | L |
| 150399 | Human reproduction | Bio | 210C | 2S | L |
| 150399 | Hum anatomy & physiology | Bio | 213C | 3S | L |
| 150399 | Hum anatomy & physiology | Bio | 214C | 3S | L |
| 150399 | History of biology | Bio | 281C | 2S | L |
| 150399 | Medical etymology | Bio | 209C | 2S | L |
| 150799 | Desc physics non-sci majr | Phys | 115C | 3S | L |
| 150799 | Desc physics non-sci majr | Phys | 116C | 3S | L |
| 160302 | College algebra | Math | 109C | 3S | L |
| 160302 | High school algebra | Math | 001C | 1U | L |
| 160399 | Intro college mathematics | Math | 111C | 3S | L |
| 160399 | Plane geometry | Math | 002C | 1U | L |
| 160401 | Calculus & analytic geom | Math | 126C | 4S | L |
| 160401 | Calculus | Math | 227C | 4S | L |
| 160401 | Introduction to calculus | Math | 121C | 3S | L |
| 160403 | Analytic geom & calculus | Math | 125C | 4S | L |
| 160602 | Analytic trigonometry | Math | 115C | 3S | L |
| 160801 | Statistical methods I | Stat | 250C | 3S | L |
| 160801 | Statistical methods II | Stat | 251C | 3S | L |
| 180322 | Ethics | Philo | 200C | 3S | L |
| 180599 | Intro to deductive logic | Philo | 101C | 3S | L |
| 1807 | Intro to philosophy | Philo | 100C | 3S | L |
| 180902 | New Testm: earlier commun | Rel | 112C | 3S | L |
| 180902 | New Testm: later commun | Rel | 212C | 3S | L |
| 181102 | Intro religious studies | Rel | 100C | 3S | L |
| 190199 | Phys ed in elem school | PEdu | 363C | 3S | U |
| 190509 | Personal health | HEd | 270C | 3S | L |
| 1999 | Intro health, PE & recrea | HPER | 191C | 2S | L |
| 200199 | Intro to psychology | Psych | 101C | 3S | L |
| 200505 | Psychology of adjustment | Psych | 207C | 3S | L |
| 2099 | Elementary statistic meth | Psych | 211C | 3S | L |
| 2099 | Applied psychology | Psych | 228C | 3S | L |
| 210401 | Soc services for delinq | PubAd | 308C | 3S | U |
| 210401 | Family & child welfare | PubAd | 310C | 3S | U |
| 220199 | General anthropology I | Anthr | 101C | 3S | L |
| 220199 | General anthropology II | Anthr | 102C | 3S | L |
| 220201 | Prin of economics I | Econ | 101C | 3S | L |
| 220201 | Prin of economics II | Econ | 102C | 3S | L |
| 220202 | Hist of economic concepts | Econ | 450C | 3S | U |
| 220299 | Amer economic institution | Econ | 160C | 3S | L |
| 220305 | Survey of physicl geogra | Geog | 103C | 3S | L |
| 220306 | World regional geography | Geog | 105C | 3S | L |
| 220399 | Geography of Anglo-Amer | Geog | 243C | 3S | L |
| 220399 | Geography of Europe | Geog | 246C | 3S | L |
| 220408 | Hist of Chris chu to 1500 | Hist | 235C | 3S | L |
| 220408 | Hist Chris chu since 1500 | Hist | 236C | 3S | L |
| 220408 | Religion in Amer South | Rel | 221C | 3S | L |
| 220421 | US hist: colonial period | Hist | 220C | 3S | L |
| 220424 | England to 1688 | Hist | 247C | 3S | L |
| 220424 | England since 1688 | Hist | 248C | 3S | L |
| 220427 | Colonial Latin American | Hist | 237C | 3S | L |
| 220427 | Mod Latin Amer since 1808 | Hist | 238C | 3S | L |
| 220428 | Hist of Alabama to 1865 | Hist | 225C | 3S | L |
| 220428 | Hist of Ala since 1865 | Hist | 226C | 3S | L |
| 220431 | Russia to 1894 | Hist | 361C | 3S | U |
| 220431 | Rus & Sov Union snce 1894 | Hist | 362C | 3S | U |
| 220432 | Wstrn movemnt in Amer his | Hist | 321C | 3S | U |
| 220432 | The US since 1945 | Hist | 318C | 3S | U |
| 220432 | Western civiliz to 1648 | Hist | 101C | 3S | L |
| 220432 | Western civ since 1648 | Hist | 102C | 3S | L |
| 220433 | Comparative world civiliz | Hist | 110C | 3S | L |
| 220453 | US in twentieth century | Hist | 222C | 3S | L |
| 220499 | US in nineteenth century | Hist | 221C | 3S | L |
| 220501 | Intro to American govt | PolSc | 101C | 3S | L |
| 220501 | Intro to public policy | PolSc | 103C | 3S | L |
| 220511 | State & local government | PolSc | 211C | 3S | L |
| 220599 | International politics | PolSc | 204C | 3S | L |
| 220599 | Public administration | PolSc | 206C | 3S | L |
| 220602 | Criminology | Socio | 301C | 3S | U |
| 220605 | The family | Socio | 206C | 3S | L |
| 220613 | Analysis of social prob | Socio | 102C | 3S | L |
| 220615 | Minority peoples | Socio | 215C | 3S | L |
| 220699 | Intro to sociology | Socio | 101C | 3S | L |
| 220699 | Human relations—industry | Socio | 355C | 3S | U |

**Noncredit courses**

| NCES No. | Course Title | Dept. | Course No. | Credits | Level |
|---|---|---|---|---|---|
| 220502 | Citizenship | Hist | NC | NC | |

(33) **UNIVERSITY OF ALASKA**

Dr. Keith Edmonds
Director of Correspondence Study
115 Eielson Building
University of Alaska
403 Salcha Street
Fairbanks, Alaska 99701
Phone: 907-474-7222

Gifted high school students are permitted to enroll in undergraduate courses for credit. Overseas enrollment accepted. Overseas students need excellent English skills and dependable mail service. External degrees are not offered. New correspondence courses are developed on a continuing basis, and students are encouraged to request a brochure.

**College courses**

| NCES No. | Course Title | Dept. | Course No. | Credits | Level |
|---|---|---|---|---|---|
| 040101 | Elementary accounting I | Acctg | 101C | 3S | L |
| 040101 | Elementary accounting II | Acctg | 102C | 3S | L |
| 040306 | Pract guide to mod invest | BA | 170C | 3S | L |
| 040601 | Business correspondence | OO | 071c | 2S | D |
| 041308 | Real estate/property law | BA | 223C | 3S | L |
| 0501 | Principles of advertising | Jrnl | 326C | 3S | U |
| 050699 | Intro to mass comm | Jrnl | 101C | 3S | L |
| 051103 | Fund of oral communicatn | Sph | 111C | 3S | L |
| 0607 | BASIC programming | CmpSc | 106C | 3S | L |
| 070102 | Philosophy of education | Educ | 422C | 3S | U |
| 070102 | Human development | Educ | 312C | 3S | U |
| 0704 | Introduction to education | Educ | 201C | 3S | L |
| 070401 | Comm in cross-cult clrms | Educ | 350c | 3S | U |
| 070516 | Teaching metrics in class | Educ | 467C | 2S | U |
| 0708 | Exceptional learner | Educ | 393C | 3S | U |
| 0711 | Measurement & evaluation | Educ | 330C | 3S | U |
| 071201 | Microcomputer applic clrm | Educ | 429C | 3S | U |
| 0825 | Fundamentals of petroleum | Pt | 101C | 3S | L |
| 100313 | Science of nutrition | HmEc | 203C | 3S | L |
| 110601 | Private pilot ground schl | Avi | 100C | 4S | L |
| 120103 | Nature of language | Ling | 101C | 3S | L |
| 120299 | Women's exper modern fict | Engl | 193C | 3S | L |
| 120307 | Frontier lit of Alaska | Engl | 350C | 3S | U |
| 120310 | Methods of written comm | Engl | 111C | 3S | L |
| 120310 | Intermediate exposition | Engl | 211C | 3S | L |
| 120310 | Creative writing: poetry | Engl | 293C | 3S | L |
| 120310 | Technical writing | Engl | 312C | 3S | U |
| 1217 | Elem Inupiaq Eskimo I | Esk | 111C | 5S | L |
| 1217 | Elem Inupiaq Eskimo II | Esk | 112C | 5S | L |
| 130701 | Business law I | BA | 331C | 3S | U |
| 130702 | Business law II | BA | 332C | 3S | U |
| 150304 | Natural history of Alaska | Bio | 104C | 3S | L |
| 150408 | Chemistry | Chem | 104C | 3S | L |
| 1505 | General geology | Geol | 101C | 3S | L |
| 160199 | The metric system | Math | 100C | 1S | L |
| 160302 | College algebra | Math | 107C | 3S | L |
| 160302 | Elementary algebra I | Math | 075C | 3S | D |
| 160302 | Elementary algebra II | Math | 076C | 3S | D |
| 160401 | Calculus I | Math | 200C | 4S | L |
| 160401 | Calculus II | Math | 201C | 4S | L |
| 160602 | Trigonometry | Math | 108C | 3S | L |
| 161299 | Basic mathematics | Math | 051C | 3S | D |
| 200104 | Intro to psychology | Psych | 101C | 3S | L |
| 200504 | Developmental psychology | Psych | 240C | 3S | L |
| 200799 | Drugs & drug dependence | Psych | 370C | 3S | U |
| 210304 | Intro to criminal justice | Just | 110C | 3S | L |
| 210304 | Criminal law | Just | 352C | 3S | U |
| 220102 | General anthropology | Anth | 101C | 3S | L |
| 220199 | Anth of Alaskan natives | Anth | 242C | 3S | L |
| 220305 | Elements of physical geog | Geog | 205C | 3S | L |
| 220399 | Geography of Alaska | Geog | 302C | 3S | U |
| 220432 | History of the US I | Hist | 131C | 3S | L |
| 220432 | History of the US II | Hist | 132C | 3S | L |
| 220453 | History of Western civ I | Hist | 101C | 3S | L |
| 220453 | History of Western civ II | Hist | 102C | 3S | L |
| 220499 | History of Alaska | Hist | 341C | 3S | U |
| 220499 | Maritime hist of Alaska | Hist | 345C | 3S | U |
| 220499 | Polar exploration & lit | Hist | 380C | 3S | U |
| 220603 | Population & ecology | Socio | 207C | 3S | L |
| 220605 | Sociology of the family | Socio | 242C | 3S | L |
| 220613 | Social problems | Socio | 201C | 3S | L |
| 220699 | Drugs & drug dependence | Socio | 370C | 3S | U |

## (34) UNIVERSITY OF ARIZONA

Dr. Michael Offerman
Assistant Director of Continuing Education
Babcock Building, Suite 1201
University of Arizona
1717 East Speedway
Tucson, Arizona 85719
Phone: 602-621-3021

Gifted high school students are permitted to enroll in undergraduate courses for credit. Overseas enrollment accepted for high school and college courses.

| NCES No. | Course Title | Dept. | Course No. | Credits | Level |
|---|---|---|---|---|---|
| | **High School courses** | | | | |
| 040104 | Elementary accounting | Acct | 11A | HF | H |
| 040104 | Elementary accounting | Acct | 11B | HF | H |
| 120310 | Composition | Eng | 11A | HF | H |
| 120310 | Expository writing | Eng | 11B | HF | H |
| 120310 | Current literature | Eng | 12A | HF | H |
| 120310 | Creative writing | Eng | 12B | HF | H |
| 120310 | Language and usage | Eng | 9-12A | HF | H |
| 120310 | Vocabulary study | Eng | 11-12 | HF | H |
| 1509 | Basic earth science | Sci | 10A | HF | H |
| 1509 | Basic earth science | Sci | 10B | HF | H |
| 160301 | General math | Math | 9A | HF | H |
| 160301 | General math | Math | 9B | HF | H |
| 160302 | Elementary algebra | Math | 9C | HF | H |
| 160302 | Elementary algebra | Math | 9D | HF | H |
| 160601 | Plane geometry | Math | 10A | HF | H |
| 160601 | Plane geometry | Math | 10B | HF | H |
| 160602 | Plane trigonometry | Math | 11A | HF | H |
| 200599 | Elementary psychology | SocSt | 12 | HF | H |
| 220399 | World geography | Geo | 10A | HF | H |
| 220399 | World geography | Geo | 10B | HF | H |
| 220428 | Arizona history | Hist | 11-12 | HF | H |
| 220432 | US history | Hist | 12 | HF | H |
| 220432 | US history to 1865 | Hist | 11A | HF | H |
| 220432 | US history from 1865 | Hist | 11B | HF | H |
| 220501 | Amer political process | Govt | 12 | HF | H |
| 220501 | US government | Govt | 11-12 | HF | H |
| 220511 | Arizona government | Govt | 11-12 | HF | H |
| 220606 | Elementary sociology | SocSt | 12 | HF | H |
| 229999 | Free enterprise | SocSt | 12 | HF | H |
| | **College courses** | | | | |
| 010499 | Feeds and feeding | AnSci | 4134A | 1U | L |
| 010499 | Feeds and feeding | AnSci | 4134B | 2U | L |
| 0114 | Conserv of nat resources | RNR | 4135 | 3U | L |
| 040101 | Principles of accounting | Acctg | 4200A | 3U | L |
| 040101 | Principles of accounting | Acctg | 4200B | 3U | L |
| 040203 | Records management | BCEd | 4379 | 3U | U |
| 040399 | Risk management | Fin | 4453 | 3U | U |
| 040601 | Intro to bus commun | BCEd | 4373 | 3U | L |
| 041099 | Creative advertising | Mrkt | 4364 | 3U | U |
| 041099 | Public relations | Mrkt | 4366 | 3U | U |
| 041199 | Personnel management | Mgmt | 4330 | 3U | U |
| 070103 | Social found and administr | EdFA | 4350 | 3U | U |
| 090903 | Sec sch health education | Hlth | 4180 | 3U | L |
| 090903 | Intro to health sci educ | Hlth | 4178 | 3U | U |
| 090999 | International health pblm | Hlth | 4433 | 3U | U |
| 090999 | Safety ed & accident prev | Hlth | 4435 | 3U | U |
| 100601 | Child development | HEco | 4223 | 3U | L |
| 100602 | Family relations | HmEc | 4337 | 3U | U |
| 100699 | Education for marriage | HEco | 4137 | 3U | L |
| 120305 | Modern grammar & usage | Engl | 4406 | 3U | U |
| 120307 | Modern literature | Engl | 4261 | 3U | L |
| 120307 | English literature | Engl | 4370B | 3U | U |
| 120308 | Major American writers | Engl | 4265 | 3U | L |
| 120308 | Shakespeare | Engl | 4431A | 3U | U |
| 120308 | Shakespeare | Engl | 4431B | 3U | U |
| 120308 | American Romanticism | Engl | 4482 | 3U | U |
| 1210 | Elementary French | Frech | 4101A | 2U | L |
| 1210 | Elementary French | Frech | 4101B | 2U | L |
| 1210 | Intermediate French | Frech | 4201A | 2U | L |
| 1210 | Intermediate French | Frech | 4201B | 2U | L |

| NCES No. | Course Title | Dept. | Course No. | Credits | Level |
|---|---|---|---|---|---|
| 1211 | Elementary German | Ger | 4101A | 2U | L |
| 1211 | Elementary German | Ger | 4101B | 2U | L |
| 1211 | Intermediate German | Ger | 4201A | 2U | L |
| 1225 | Elementary Spanish | Span | 4101A | 2U | L |
| 1225 | Second-semester Spanish | Span | 4101B | 2U | L |
| 1225 | Third-semester Spanish | Span | 4201A | 2U | L |
| 1225 | Fourth-semester Spanish | Span | 4201B | 2U | L |
| 1225 | Commercial & tech Spanish | Span | 4371A | 2U | U |
| 1225 | Commercial & tech Spanish | Span | 4371B | 2U | U |
| 1299 | Literature of India | OrStu | 4444A | 3U | U |
| 150202 | Intro meteorology/climate | Atmo | 4171 | 3U | L |
| 150316 | Plants useful to man | GBio | 4412 | 2U | U |
| 150321 | General plant pathology | PPath | 4205 | 3U | L |
| 1505 | Intro to geology | GeoSc | 4101A | 3U | L |
| 1505 | Intro to geology | GeoSc | 4101B | 3U | L |
| 1599 | Insects and man | Ento | 4151 | 3U | L |
| 160302 | Intermediate algebra | Math | 4116 | 3U | L |
| 160302 | College algebra | Math | 4117 | 3U | L |
| 160401 | Calculus | Math | 4125A | 3U | L |
| 160401 | Elements of calculus | Math | 4123 | 3U | L |
| 160401 | Calculus | Math | 4125B | 3U | L |
| 160602 | Trigonometry | Math | 4118 | 2U | L |
| 160899 | Intro to statistics | Math | 4160 | 3U | L |
| 160999 | Finite mathematics | Math | 4119 | 3U | L |
| 161199 | Survey of math thought | Math | 4101A | 2U | L |
| 161199 | Survey of math thought | Math | 4101B | 2U | L |
| 161199 | Modern elem mathematics | Math | 4105A | 3U | L |
| 161199 | Modern elem mathematics | Math | 4105B | 3U | L |
| 180499 | Intro to philosophy | Phil | 4111 | 3U | L |
| 180502 | Intro to logic | Phil | 4112 | 3U | L |
| 1807 | Intro to moral & soc phil | Phil | 4113 | 3U | L |
| 190513 | Elem sch health education | Hlth | 4181 | 2U | L |
| 200599 | Child development | EdPsy | 4301 | 3U | U |
| 200599 | Adolescent development | EdPsy | 4302 | 3U | U |
| 200805 | Learning in the schools | EdPsy | 4310 | 3U | U |
| 2099 | Intro to psych statistics | Psych | 4245 | 3U | L |
| 220199 | Intro to phys anth & arch | Anthr | 4100 | 3U | U |
| 220199 | Prehistic peopl of the SW | Anthr | 4205 | 3U | L |
| 220199 | Intro to Asian civiliz | Anthr | 4170A | 3U | L |
| 220199 | Intro to Asian civiliz | Anthr | 4170B | 3U | L |
| 220199 | Cultural anthropology | Anthr | 4200 | 3U | L |
| 220199 | Native peoples of the SW | Anthr | 4206 | 3U | L |
| 220199 | Intro to cult anth & ling | Anthr | 4102 | 3U | U |
| 220201 | Principles of economics | Econ | 4201A | 3U | L |
| 220201 | Principles of economics | Econ | 4201B | 3U | L |
| 220204 | Money and banking | Econ | 4330 | 3U | U |
| 220423 | Oriental humanities | OrStu | 4140A | 3U | L |
| 220423 | Intro to Asian civiliz | OrStu | 4170A | 3U | L |
| 220423 | Modern Chinese history | OrStu | 4476A | 3U | U |
| 220423 | Modern Chinese history | OrStu | 4476B | 3U | U |
| 220423 | Intro to Asian civiliz | Hist | 4170A | 3U | L |
| 220423 | Intro to Asian civiliz | Hist | 4170B | 3U | L |
| 220423 | History of China | OrStu | 4375B | 3U | U |
| 220423 | Modern Chinese history | OrStu | 4476 | 3U | U |
| 220423 | Intro to Asian civiliz | OrStu | 4170B | 3U | U |
| 220424 | History of England | Hist | 4117A | 3U | L |
| 220424 | History of England | Hist | 4117B | 3U | L |
| 220426 | French Revolut & Napoleon | Hist | 4420 | 3U | U |
| 220432 | Intro to hist of Wstn wld | Hist | 4101A | 3U | L |
| 220432 | Intro to hist of Wstn wld | Hist | 4101B | 3U | L |
| 220432 | Hist of the United States | Hist | 4130A | 3U | L |
| 220432 | Hist of the United States | Hist | 4130B | 3U | L |
| 220432 | US: 1945 to present | Hist | 4440 | 3U | U |
| 220432 | History of Am foreign rel | Hist | 4449B | 3U | U |
| 220470 | American ethnic history | Hist | 4452 | 3U | U |
| 220499 | History of China | Hist | 43756 | 3U | U |
| 220499 | Modern Chinese history | Hist | 4476A | 3U | U |
| 220499 | Modern Chinese history | Hist | 4476B | 3U | U |
| 220501 | Am national government | PolSc | 4102 | 3U | L |
| 220505 | Intro to internatl relat | PolSc | 4150 | 3U | L |
| 220511 | Am state & local govt | PolSc | 4103 | 3U | L |
| 220511 | Arizona government | PolSc | 4214B | 1U | L |
| 220599 | Nat & state constitutions | PolSc | 4110 | 3U | L |
| 220599 | Soviet foreign policy | PolSc | 4451 | 3U | U |
| 220601 | Intro to sociology | Soc | 4100 | 3U | L |
| 220602 | Criminology | Soc | 4342 | 3U | U |
| 220603 | World population | Soc | 4289 | 3U | L |
| 220604 | Juvenile delinquency | Soc | 4341 | 3U | U |
| 220613 | American social problems | Soc | 4201 | 3U | L |
| 220614 | Minority rel & urban soc | Soc | 4160 | 3U | L |
| 220699 | Sociology of the family | Soc | 4321 | 3U | U |
| 2299 | Intro to black studies | BIS | 4220 | 3U | L |

## (35) UNIVERSITY OF ARKANSAS

Mr. William E. Manning
Director of the Department of Independent Study
#2 University Center
University of Arkansas
Center for Continuing Education
Fayetteville, Arkansas 72701
Phone: 501-575-3647

Gifted high school students are permitted to enroll in undergraduate courses for credit. Overseas enrollment accepted.

| NCES No. | Course Title | Dept. | Course No. | Credits | Level |
|---|---|---|---|---|---|
| | **High School courses** | | | | |
| 040104 | Accounting | Acctg | 11A | HF | H |
| 040104 | Accounting | Acctg | 11B | HF | H |
| 040201 | Secretarial office proced | SOP | 11A | HF | H |
| 040201 | Secretarial office proced | SOP | 11B | HF | H |
| 040203 | Records management | AdSci | NL | HF | H |
| 040205 | Shorthand | Shhnd | 12A | HF | H |
| 040205 | Shorthand | Shhnd | 12B | HF | H |
| 040207 | Typing | Type | 11A | HF | H |
| 040207 | Typing | Type | 11B | HF | H |
| 040601 | Business communications | Engl | 1 SEM | HF | H |
| 0810 | Industrial arts drafting | InArt | 12A | HF | H |
| 0810 | Industrial arts drafting | InArt | 12B | HF | H |
| 120201 | World literature | Engl | 1STSE | HF | H |
| 120201 | World literature | Engl | 2NDSE | HF | H |
| 120305 | Grammar | Engl | 11 | HF | H |
| 120305 | Grammar | Engl | 12 | HF | H |
| 120305 | Remedial language arts | Engl | 1 SEM | HF | H |
| 120305 | Advanced language arts | Engl | 1 SEM | HF | H |
| 120307 | Literature | Engl | 11 | HF | H |
| 120307 | Literature | Engl | 12 | HF | H |
| 120308 | Vocab improv and read dev | Engl | 1 SEM | HF | H |
| 120399 | Grammar and literature | Engl | 9A | HF | H |
| 120399 | Grammar and literature | Engl | 9B | HF | H |
| 120399 | Grammar and literature | Engl | 10A | HF | H |
| 120399 | Grammar and literature | Engl | 10B | HF | H |
| 120399 | Grammar and literature | Engl | 11A | HF | H |
| 120399 | Grammar and literature | Engl | 11B | HF | H |
| 120399 | Grammar and literature | Engl | 12A | HF | H |
| 120399 | Grammar and literature | Engl | 12B | HF | H |
| 1210 | French | FornL | Ia | HF | H |
| 1210 | French | FornL | Ib | HF | H |
| 1216 | Latin | FornL | 9A | HF | H |
| 1216 | Latin | FornL | 9B | HF | H |
| 1216 | Latin | FornL | 10A | HF | H |
| 1216 | Latin | FornL | 10B | HF | H |
| 1225 | Spanish | FornL | 9A | HF | H |
| 1225 | Spanish | FornL | 9B | HF | H |
| 1299 | Introduction to mythology | Engl | 1 SEM | HF | H |
| 150399 | Biology | Sci | 10A | HF | H |
| 150399 | Biology | Sci | 10B | HF | H |
| 160301 | Remedial arithmetic | Math | I | HF | H |
| 160301 | Remedial arithmetic | Math | II | HF | H |
| 160302 | Algebra | Math | 9A | HF | H |
| 160302 | Algebra | Math | 9B | HF | H |
| 160302 | Advanced algebra | Math | 11A | HF | H |
| 160302 | Advanced algebra | Math | 11B | HF | H |
| 160601 | Geometry | Math | 10a | HF | H |
| 160601 | Geometry | Math | 10b | HF | H |
| 161101 | Business mathematics | Math | I | HF | H |
| 161101 | Business mathematics | Math | II | HF | H |
| 161199 | Vocational mathematics | Math | I | HF | H |
| 161199 | Vocational mathematics | Math | II | HF | H |
| 190509 | Physiology and hygiene | Sci | 11B | HF | H |
| 220201 | Economics | SocSt | 12 | HF | H |
| 220302 | Commercial geography | SocSt | 9A | HF | H |
| 220302 | Commercial geography | SocSt | 9B | HF | H |
| 220306 | United States geography | SocSt | 10A | HF | H |
| 220306 | United States geography | SocSt | 10B | HF | H |
| 220432 | United States history | SocSt | 11A | HF | H |
| 220432 | United States history | SocSt | 11B | HF | H |
| 220433 | World history | SocSt | 10A | HF | H |
| 220433 | World history | SocSt | 10B | HF | H |
| 220501 | American government | SocSt | 12A | HF | H |
| 220501 | American government | SocSt | 12B | HF | H |
| 220502 | Civics | SocSt | 9A | HF | H |
| 220502 | Civics | SocSt | 9B | HF | H |
| 2206 | Sociology | SocSt | | HF | H |

| NCES No. | Course Title | Dept. | Course No. | Credits | Level |
|---|---|---|---|---|---|
| | **College courses** | | | | |
| 0101 | Agricultural economics | Agri | 2103 | 3S | L |
| 010404 | Principles of genetics | AnSci | 3123 | 3S | U |
| 010699 | Plant geography | Bot | 3513 | 3S | U |
| 0114 | Conservation of nat resou | Geog | 3003 | 3S | U |
| 030402 | Intro to dramatic art | SpDrA | 2223 | 3S | L |
| 030499 | Origins of modern theater | SpDrA | 5753 | 3S | U |
| 040101 | Principles of acctg I | Acctg | 2013 | 3S | L |
| 040101 | Principles of acctg II | Acctg | 2023 | 3S | L |
| 040601 | Business communications | Mgmt | 2323 | 3S | L |
| 040904 | Intro to management | Mgmt | 1033 | 3S | L |
| 051104 | Parliamentary procedure | SpDrA | 2351 | 1S | L |
| 051303 | Writing for television | SpDrA | 4833 | 3S | U |
| 070401 | Intro to childhood educ | ElEd | 1103 | 3S | L |
| 070401 | Prin & meth in middle sch | SecEd | 4043 | 3S | U |
| 070404 | Teaching science | ElEd | 3303 | 3S | U |
| 070499 | Meth & mat sch & comm rec | Rec | 3813 | 3S | U |
| 070511 | Drafting | VocEd | 1603 | 3S | L |
| 070511 | Industrial design I | VocEd | 3603 | 3S | U |
| 070512 | Children's literature | ElEd | 2273 | 3S | L |
| 070512 | Reading & other lang arts | ElEd | 3333 | 3S | U |
| 070516 | Teaching math | ElEd | 4413 | 3S | U |
| 070516 | Teaching math | SecEd | 4223 | 3S | U |
| 070519 | Meth & mats phy ed el sch | PhyEd | 3373 | 3S | U |
| 070522 | Teaching of social stud | SecEd | 4232 | 2S | U |
| 071103 | Secon tests & measurement | SecEd | 4723 | 3S | U |
| 081102 | Mechanics of fluids | EngSc | 3203 | 3S | U |
| 081104 | Statics | EngSc | 2003 | 3S | L |
| 081104 | Dynamics | EngSc | 3003 | 3S | U |
| 081199 | Mechanics of materials | EngSc | 3103 | 3S | U |
| 0899 | Engineering statistics | InEg | 3313 | 3S | U |
| 0899 | Engr economics analysis | InEg | 3413 | 3S | U |
| 090599 | Personal health & safety | HelEd | 1103 | 3S | L |
| 100313 | Nutrition in health | HmEc | 1213 | 3S | L |
| 120201 | Intro to literature | Engl | 1113 | 3S | L |
| 120201 | Masterpieces Wstrn lit | Engl | 1123 | 3S | L |
| 120307 | Engl lit from beg to 1700 | Engl | 2113 | 3S | L |
| 120307 | Engl lit from 1700 to pre | Engl | 2123 | 3S | L |
| 120310 | Composition | Engl | 1013 | 3S | L |
| 120310 | Composition—continuation | Engl | 1023 | 3S | L |
| 120310 | Essay writing | Engl | 2013 | 3S | L |
| 120310 | Intermediate composition | Engl | 3003 | 3S | U |
| 120399 | Vocabulary building | Engl | 1153 | 3S | L |
| 1210 | Elementary French | Frnch | 1003 | 3S | L |
| 1210 | Advanced grammar & comp | Frnch | 4003 | 3S | U |
| 1210 | Elementary French | Frnch | 1013 | 3S | L |
| 1210 | Intermediate French | Frnch | 2003 | 3S | L |
| 1210 | Intermediate French | Frnch | 2013 | 3S | L |
| 1211 | Intro to German | Ger | 1003 | 3S | L |
| 1211 | Intro to German | Ger | 1013 | 3S | L |
| 1211 | Modern German prose | Ger | 2003 | 3S | L |
| 1225 | Elementary Spanish | Span | 1003 | 3S | L |
| 1225 | Elementary Spanish | Span | 1013 | 3S | L |
| 1225 | Spanish readings | Span | 3133 | 3S | U |
| 1225 | Intermediate Spanish | Span | 2003 | 3S | L |
| 1225 | Intermediate Spanish | Span | 2013 | 3S | L |
| 1225 | Advanced grammar & comp | Span | 4003 | 3S | U |
| 1302 | Business law I | Acctg | 2222 | 2S | L |
| 1302 | Business law II | Acctg | 2322 | 2S | L |
| 150307 | Genetics | Bot | 3203 | 3S | U |
| 150316 | Survey of botany | Bot | 1913 | 3S | L |
| 150317 | Bacteria in human affairs | Bact | 2003 | 3S | L |
| 150399 | Nature study | Bot | 1022 | 2S | L |
| 1509 | Man and his environment | Bot | 2533 | 3S | L |
| 1599 | Conservation of nat resou | Zoolo | 3133 | 3S | U |
| 160199 | Patterns in math | Math | 1103 | 3S | L |
| 160302 | College algebra | Math | 1203 | 3S | L |
| 160401 | Calculus I | Math | 2555 | 5S | L |
| 160401 | Calculus II | Math | 2565 | 5S | L |
| 160401 | Calculus III | Math | 2573 | 3S | L |
| 160408 | Finite math | Math | 2053 | 3S | L |
| 160602 | Plane trigonometry | Math | 1213 | 3S | L |
| 161101 | Math of finance | Math | 1503 | 3S | L |
| 180403 | Intro to philosophy | Philo | 2003 | 3S | L |
| 180599 | Logic | Philo | 2203 | 3S | L |
| 190106 | Organ & admin of phy ed | PhyEd | 4213 | 3S | U |
| 190110 | Tests & measure in phy ed | PhyEd | 3313 | 3S | U |
| 200501 | Abnormal psychology | Psych | 3023 | 3S | U |
| 200503 | Applied psychology | Psych | 2023 | 3S | L |
| 200504 | Infancy and early childhd | Psych | 3033 | 3S | U |

| NCES No. | Course Title | Dept. | Course No. | Credits | Level |
|---|---|---|---|---|---|
| 200504 | Childhood and adolescence | Psych | 3093 | 3S | U |
| 200599 | Exceptional children | Psych | 4013 | 3S | U |
| 200603 | Psychological tests | Psych | 4053 | 3S | U |
| 200804 | Educational psychology | Psych | 4033 | 3S | U |
| 200902 | Personnel psychology | Psych | 3043 | 3S | U |
| 2099 | General psychology | PolSc | 2003 | 3S | L |
| 210403 | Problems of child welfare | SoWel | 3633 | 3S | U |
| 220102 | Intro to anthropology | Anthr | 2023 | 3S | L |
| 220104 | Indians of North America | Anthr | 3213 | 3S | U |
| 220201 | Principles of economics I | Econ | 2013 | 3S | L |
| 220201 | Prin of economics II | Econ | 2023 | 3S | L |
| 220202 | Economic dev of the US | Econ | 1123 | 3S | L |
| 2203 | Emerging nations | Geog | 2103 | 3S | L |
| 2203 | Developed nations | Geog | 2203 | 3S | L |
| 220302 | Economic geography | Geog | 2023 | 3S | L |
| 220305 | Physical geography | Geog | 1003 | 3S | L |
| 220399 | Human geography | Geog | 1123 | 3S | L |
| 220399 | United States & Canada | Geog | 3253 | 3S | U |
| 220406 | Cultural hist of Germany | Ger | 2013 | 3S | L |
| 220406 | Inst ideas of Wstrn man | WCiv | 1003 | 3S | L |
| 220406 | Study of civ 1650-present | WCiv | 1013 | 3S | L |
| 220421 | Col & Rev Amer 1607-1783 | Hist | 4403 | 3S | U |
| 220427 | Latin American civilizatn | Span | 4223 | 3S | U |
| 220432 | The Amer Repub 1492-1877 | Hist | 2003 | 3S | L |
| 220432 | US as wld power 1877-1965 | Hist | 2013 | 3S | L |
| 220470 | American Negro history | Hist | 3403 | 3S | U |
| 220471 | Hist of the Amer Indian | Hist | 3103 | 3S | U |
| 220501 | American national govt | PolSc | 2003 | 3S | L |
| 220511 | State and local govt | PolSc | 2203 | 3S | L |
| 220599 | Intro to political science | PolSc | 1503 | 3S | L |
| 220602 | Criminology | Socio | 3023 | 3S | U |
| 220603 | Population problems | Socio | 3013 | 3S | U |
| 220605 | Marriage and the family | Socio | 2043 | 3S | L |
| 220606 | General sociology | Socio | 2013 | 3S | L |
| 220613 | Social problems | Socio | 2033 | 3S | L |
| 220614 | Black ghetto | Socio | 4123 | 3S | U |
| 220614 | Urban sociology | Socio | 3153 | 3S | U |
| **Noncredit courses** | | | | | |
| 040203 | Business records control | AdSci | 1 | NC | |
| 040203 | Business records control | AdSci | 2 | NC | |
| 041303 | Principles of real estate | | NC-1 | NC | |

## ㊱ UNIVERSITY OF CALIFORNIA EXTENSION

Ms. A. Theresa McNally
Program Coordinator of Independent Study
Independent Study
University of California Extension
2223 Fulton Street
Berkeley, California 94720
Phone: 415-642-4124

Enrollment on a noncredit basis accepted in all credit courses. Gifted high school students are permitted to enroll in undergraduate courses for credit. Overseas enrollment accepted.

| NCES No. | Course Title | Dept. | Course No. | Credits | Level |
|---|---|---|---|---|---|
| **High School courses** | | | | | |
| 010599 | Horticulture | Agri | AG901 | | H |
| 030302 | Hist & appreciation music | Music | MU900 | | H |
| 030501 | Begin drawing & painting | VisAr | A901 | | H |
| 040101 | Accounting 2nd semester | Bus | B906 | | H |
| 049900 | General business | Bus | B907 | | H |
| 100699 | Marriage & family living | HmEc | H903 | | H |
| 110504 | Photography | VisAr | P900 | | H |
| 120202 | The short story | Engl | E908 | | H |
| 120202 | The novel | Engl | E911 | | H |
| 120305 | Ninth-grade English | Engl | E900 | | H |
| 120305 | Ninth-grade English | Engl | E901 | | H |
| 120305 | Tenth-grade English | Engl | E902 | | H |
| 120305 | Tenth-grade English | Engl | E903 | | H |
| 120305 | Eleventh-grade English | Engl | E904 | | H |
| 120305 | Eleventh-grade English | Engl | E905 | | H |
| 120305 | Twelfth-grade English | Engl | E906 | | H |
| 120305 | Twelfth-grade English | Engl | E907 | | H |
| 120305 | Business English | Engl | E912 | | H |

| NCES No. | Course Title | Dept. | Course No. | Credits | Level |
|---|---|---|---|---|---|
| 120305 | Basic English | Engl | E915 | | H |
| 120308 | Improving reading skills | Engl | E913 | | H |
| 120310 | Composition | Engl | E909 | | H |
| 120399 | Effective study methods | StSkl | ST900 | | H |
| 1210 | First-year French | Frnch | F900 | | H |
| 1210 | First-year French | Frnch | F901 | | H |
| 1210 | Second-year French | Frnch | F902 | | H |
| 1211 | First-year German | Ger | G900 | | H |
| 1211 | First-year German | Ger | G901 | | H |
| 1211 | Second-year German | Ger | G902 | | H |
| 1211 | Second-year German | Ger | G903 | | H |
| 1216 | First-year Latin | Latin | L900 | | H |
| 1216 | First-year Latin | Latin | L901 | | H |
| 1216 | Second-year Latin | Latin | L902 | | H |
| 1216 | Second-year Latin | Latin | L903 | | H |
| 1225 | First-year Spanish | Span | S900 | | H |
| 1225 | First-year Spanish | Span | S901 | | H |
| 1225 | Second-year Spanish | Span | S902 | | H |
| 1225 | Second-year Spanish | Span | S903 | | H |
| 1503 | Biology optional lab | Bio | SC903 | | H |
| 1503 | Biology with lab | Bio | SC904 | | H |
| 1503 | Biology | Bio | SC901 | | H |
| 1503 | Biology | Bio | SC902 | | H |
| 150799 | Physics with laboratory | Phys | SC905 | | H |
| 150799 | Physics with laboratory | Phys | SC906 | | H |
| 150799 | Descriptive physics | Phys | SC907 | | H |
| 150799 | Descriptive physics | Phys | SC908 | | H |
| 160103 | General mathematics | Math | M914 | | H |
| 160103 | General mathematics | Math | M915 | | H |
| 160301 | Business & consumer math | Math | M917 | | H |
| 160301 | Business & consumer math | Math | M918 | | H |
| 160301 | Basic math | Math | M912 | | H |
| 160302 | Elementary algebra | Math | M900 | | H |
| 160302 | Elementary algebra | Math | M901 | | H |
| 160302 | 2nd year algebra 1st sem | Math | M908 | | H |
| 160302 | 2nd year algebra 2nd sem | Math | M909 | | H |
| 160601 | Plane geometry | Math | M904 | | H |
| 160601 | Plane geometry | Math | M905 | | H |
| 160602 | Trigonometry | Math | M910 | | H |
| 190509 | Health science | HSci | SC900 | | H |
| 190603 | Driver education | DrEd | D900 | | H |
| 200104 | Psychology | Psych | SS911 | | H |
| 220201 | Economics | Econ | SS909 | | H |
| 220399 | World geography | Geog | SS901 | | H |
| 220399 | World geography | Geog | SS902 | | H |
| 220432 | American history | Hist | SS905 | | H |
| 220432 | American history | Hist | SS906 | | H |
| 220433 | World history | Hist | SS903 | | H |
| 220433 | World history | Hist | SS904 | | H |
| 220502 | Civics | PolSc | SS900 | | H |
| 220599 | Modern problems | Socio | SS908 | | H |
| 220606 | Sociology | Socio | SS910 | | H |
| 2299 | Career planning | SocSt | SS912 | | H |
| **College courses** | | | | | |
| 030301 | Elementary counterpoint | Music | 6 | 3S | L |
| 030302 | Introduction to music | Music | 27 | 4S | L |
| 030302 | Introduction to harmony | Music | 5 | 3S | L |
| 030399 | History of jazz | Music | 7 | 3S | L |
| 030501 | Two-dimensional design | VisAr | 416 | 2S | U |
| 030501 | Italic lettering | VisAr | 424 | 2S | U |
| 030501 | Beginning drawing | VisAr | 5 | 2S | L |
| 030502 | Fundamental discoveries | VisAr | 415 | 2S | U |
| 030502 | Collage | VisAr | 419 | 2S | U |
| 030502 | Acrylic painting | VisAr | 417 | 2S | U |
| 030599 | Individual study in art | VisAr | 457 | 2S | U |
| 030603 | Intro to modern painting | ArHis | 11 | 1S | L |
| 030603 | Intro to contemporary art | ArHis | 13 | 1S | L |
| 030603 | Ancient art: Egypt | ArHis | 152A | 4Q | U |
| 030603 | Ancient art: Greece I | ArHis | 152E | 4Q | U |
| 030603 | Ancient art: Greece II | ArHis | 152F | 4Q | U |
| 040101 | Acctg: intermediate I | Bus | 148 | 3S | L |
| 040101 | Acctg: intermediate II | Bus | 149 | 3S | U |
| 040101 | Administrative accounting | Bus | 125 | 3S | U |
| 040101 | Intro to accounting II | Bus | 2 | 3S | L |
| 040101 | Accounting: advanced I | Bus | 152 | 3S | U |
| 040101 | Accounting: advanced II | Bus | 153 | 3S | U |
| 040103 | Auditing | Bus | 126 | 4S | U |
| 040106 | Cost accounting | Bus | 124 | 3S | U |
| 040109 | SEC comm acct rules & reg | Bus | 422.1 | 3S | U |
| 040114 | Federal tax: individuals | Bus | 167 | 3S | U |
| 040114 | Fed tax: partners & corps | Bus | 179 | 3S | U |

| NCES No. | Course Title | Dept. | Course No. | Credits | Level |
|---|---|---|---|---|---|
| 040114 | Calif personal income tax | Bus | 170 | 1S | U |
| 040306 | Evaluating capital invest | Bus | 430.2 | 2S | U |
| 040306 | Investment management | Bus | 430 | 2S | U |
| 040601 | Business communications | Bus | 109 | 4Q | U |
| 040903 | Leadership & org devel | Bus | 176 | 3S | U |
| 040904 | Mgmt theory & policy | Bus | 158 | 3S | U |
| 040904 | Finance planning & mgmt | Bus | 135 | 3S | U |
| 040905 | Intro to bus org & mgmt | Bus | 492.8 | 3S | U |
| 040999 | Small business management | Bus | 105 | 3S | U |
| 040999 | Choosing small bus comput | Bus | 402 | 3S | U |
| 040999 | Purchasing: basic prin | Bus | 453 | 3S | U |
| 041001 | Marketing | Bus | 160 | 3S | U |
| 041103 | Mgr's guide to behavior | Bus | 490.5 | 2S | U |
| 041103 | Mgrs guide to human behav | Bus | 490.5 | 2S | U |
| 041104 | Industrial relations | Bus | 173 | 3S | U |
| 041104 | Labor relations | Bus | 451.9 | 3S | U |
| 041106 | Office mgmt & control | Bus | 492.9 | 3S | U |
| 041106 | Effective supervision | Bus | 411 | 3S | U |
| 041199 | Effective personnel admin | Bus | 424 | 3S | U |
| 041203 | Production management | Bus | 157 | 3S | U |
| 041301 | Residential appraisal | Bus | 408 | 3S | U |
| 041303 | Real estate principles | Bus | 406.8 | 3S | U |
| 041305 | Real estate economics | Bus | 406.9 | 3S | U |
| 041306 | Real estate finance | Bus | 407 | 3S | U |
| 041308 | Land titles | Bus | 405.8 | 3S | U |
| 041308 | Real estate law | Bus | 405.9 | 3S | U |
| 041309 | Real estate practice | Bus | 406 | 3S | U |
| 0499 | Principles of purchasing | Bus | 453 | 3S | U |
| 050608 | Introduction to news writ | Jrnl | 100 | 3S | U |
| 050699 | Tech writing & editing | EngAS | 412 | 3S | U |
| 050699 | Publications production | EngAS | 413 | 3S | U |
| 051303 | Screenwriting: film & TV | Engl | 401 | 3S | U |
| 060705 | Introductory FORTRAN | CmpSc | 114 | 3S | U |
| 060705 | Introductory COBOL | CmpSc | 6 | 3S | L |
| 060705 | Introductory Pascal | CmpSc | 13 | 3S | L |
| 060705 | Intro to program BASIC | CmpSc | 11 | 3S | L |
| 060904 | Systems analysis & design | CmpSc | 422 | 3S | U |
| 061104 | Business computer systems | Bus | 482.5 | 3S | U |
| 061104 | Concepts of data processg | CmpSc | 42 | 3S | L |
| 070199 | History of education | Educ | 105 | 3S | U |
| 070302 | Elementary education | Educ | 126 | 3S | U |
| 070404 | Adult ed matls & methods | Educ | 355.1 | 2S | U |
| 070499 | Adult ed principles | Educ | 355.4 | 2S | U |
| 070506 | Elem curriculum comp sci | Educ | 391 | 3S | U |
| 070512 | The reading program | Educ | 147 | 3S | U |
| 070512 | Literature in elem school | Educ | 148 | 3S | U |
| 070512 | Language in elem school | Educ | 155 | 3S | U |
| 070516 | Math for elem teachers | Educ | 157 | 3S | U |
| 070516 | Elem curriculum arith/sci | Educ | 331 | 3S | U |
| 070701 | Counseling & guidance | Educ | 362.3 | 3S | U |
| 080901 | Intro to electrical engr | EngAS | 40 | 3S | L |
| 080903 | Intro to electronics | EngAS | 40 | 3S | L |
| 080999 | Designing with oper ampls | EngAS | 408 | 2S | U |
| 081199 | Engineering mechanics | EngAS | 36 | 2S | L |
| 0812 | Digital integrtd circuits | EngAS | 480 | 3S | U |
| 082602 | Surveying | EngAS | 4 | 2S | L |
| 0899 | Intro to control systems | EngAS | 171A | 4Q | U |
| 090799 | Childbirth education | PubHl | 420 | 3S | U |
| 090799 | Sound mind sound society | PubHl | 406 | VC | U |
| 100302 | Clinical nutrition | NutSc | 105A | 3S | U |
| 100311 | Survey of nutritional sci | NutSc | 12 | 3S | L |
| 100313 | Nutrition | NutSc | 103 | 3S | U |
| 100603 | Death and dying | Nrsng | 403 | 3Q | U |
| 110504 | Photography | Graph | 4 | 2S | L |
| 120302 | English language history | Engl | 436 | 3S | U |
| 120305 | First-yr reading & comp | Engl | 1A | 4S | L |
| 120305 | First-yr reading & comp | Engl | 1B | 4S | L |
| 120305 | Freshman comp & lit | Engl | 2A | 3S | L |
| 120305 | Freshman comp & lit | Engl | 2B | 3S | L |
| 120307 | Shakespeare | Engl | 117S | 4S | U |
| 120307 | American lit 1914 to 1940 | Engl | 146 | 4S | U |
| 120307 | The hero and the city | Engl | 179 | 3S | U |
| 120307 | Mystery fiction | Engl | 103.9 | 3S | U |
| 120307 | English novel | Engl | 125A | 4S | U |
| 120307 | English novel | Engl | 125B | 4S | U |
| 120307 | American fiction to 1900 | Engl | 135A | 3S | U |
| 120307 | Amer fiction 1900 to pres | Engl | 135B | 3S | U |
| 120307 | Western novel 19th cent | Engl | 152.1 | 3S | U |
| 120307 | Western novel 20th cent | Engl | 152.2 | 3S | U |
| 120310 | Advanced Engl composition | Engl | 119.1 | 3S | U |
| 120310 | Writing to grow | Engl | 425 | 2S | U |
| 120310 | Individ projects writing | Engl | 445 | 2S | U |
| 120399 | Grammar & composition | Engl | 22 | 3S | L |
| 1210 | French: elem course I | Frnch | 25 | 3S | L |
| 1210 | French: elem course II | Frnch | 26 | 3S | L |
| 1211 | Readings: German culture | Ger | 137 | 3S | U |
| 1211 | German: elem course I | Ger | 36 | 3S | U |
| 1211 | German: elem course II | Ger | 37 | 3S | U |
| 1211 | German: elem course III | Ger | 38 | 3S | U |
| 1211 | Intermed German: course I | Ger | 39 | 3S | L |
| 1212 | Myths of Greece & Rome | Clas | 25 | 2S | L |
| 1214 | Elementary Italian I | Ital | 15 | 3S | L |
| 1214 | Elementary Italian II | Ital | 16 | 3S | L |
| 1225 | Spanish: elem course I | Span | 30 | 3S | L |
| 1225 | Spanish: elem course II | Span | 31 | 3S | L |
| 1225 | Spanish: elem course III | Span | 32 | 3S | L |
| 1225 | Spanish: interm course I | Span | 33 | 3S | L |
| 1225 | Span in bus & professions | Span | 401 | 2S | U |
| 1299 | Icelandic lit: part I | Scand | 156 | 2S | U |
| 1299 | Icelandic lit: part II | Scand | 157 | 2S | U |
| 1299 | Elementary mod Icelandic | Scand | 180 | 3S | U |
| 1299 | Intermed modern Icelandic | Scand | 181 | 3S | U |
| 130799 | Intro to business law | Bus | 18 | 3S | U |
| 130799 | Advanced business law | Bus | 410.2 | 2S | U |
| 150199 | Intro to gen astronomy | Astro | 10 | 4S | L |
| 150307 | Survey of gen genetics | Gen | 102 | 3S | U |
| 150316 | Plants in California | Bot | 113 | 3S | U |
| 150316 | Plants and civilization | Bot | 15 | 3S | U |
| 150323 | Modern biology | Zoo | 4 | 3S | L |
| 150327 | Pest control course br 1 | EntSc | 401 | 3S | U |
| 150327 | Pest control course br 2 | EntSc | 402 | 3S | U |
| 150399 | Intro human physiology | Zoo | 1 | 3S | U |
| 150401 | Introductory chemistry | Chem | 25 | 4Q | L |
| 150403 | Introductory biochemistry | Bioch | 105 | 3S | U |
| 150408 | Organic chemistry | Chem | 18A | 2S | L |
| 150408 | Organic chemistry | Chem | 18B | 2S | L |
| 150409 | Physical chemistry | Chem | 100 | 3S | U |
| 150410 | Surface chem/phys-bio sys | Chem | 137 | 3S | U |
| 150501 | Marine geology | Geol | 105 | 4Q | U |
| 150501 | Geology of California | Geol | 109 | 4Q | U |
| 150501 | Intro physical geology | Geol | 3 | 3S | L |
| 150799 | General physics | Phys | 15A | 2S | L |
| 150799 | General physics | Phys | 15B | 2S | L |
| 160302 | Intermediate algebra | Math | D | 2S | L |
| 160401 | Precalculus | Math | 9 | 2S | L |
| 160499 | First-yr anal geom & calc | Math | 1.1 | 3S | L |
| 160499 | First-yr anal geom & calc | Math | 1.2 | 3S | L |
| 160499 | First-yr anal geom & calc | Math | 1.3 | 3S | L |
| 160602 | Plane trigonometry | Math | C | 2S | L |
| 160802 | Intro statistical methods | Econ | 40 | 4Q | L |
| 160803 | Intro to statistics | Stat | 2 | 4S | L |
| 160803 | Intro to statistical meth | Stat | 40 | 4Q | L |
| 161199 | Advanced engineering math | Math | 114A | 3S | U |
| 161199 | Advanced engineering math | Math | 114B | 3S | U |
| 161199 | Advanced engineering math | Math | 114C | 3S | U |
| 161201 | Mathematics of finance | Bus | 432 | 3S | U |
| 180402 | History of philosophy | Philo | 20A | 3S | L |
| 180403 | History of philosophy | Philo | 20B | 3S | L |
| 180405 | History of Buddhist phil | Philo | 169 | 3S | U |
| 1807 | Individual morality & jus | Philo | 2 | 4S | U |
| 190311 | Competitive sport—youth | PhyEd | 125 | 3S | U |
| 200501 | Abnormal psychology | Psych | 163 | 4Q | U |
| 200504 | Adolescence | Psych | 139 | 3S | U |
| 200799 | Psych of communication | Psych | 156.1 | 3S | U |
| 200799 | Social psychology | Psych | 160 | 3S | U |
| 200804 | Learning & the learner | Educ | 110 | 2S | U |
| 2099 | General psychology | Psych | 1 | 3S | U |
| 220102 | Gen anthro: cultural | Anthr | 9 | 3S | L |
| 220102 | Folklore in America | Anthr | 193.1 | 3S | U |
| 220106 | Intro to physical anthro | Anthr | 1 | 3S | U |
| 220109 | Indians of California | Anthr | 174 | 3S | U |
| 220201 | Microeconomics | Econ | 1 | 5Q | U |
| 220201 | Econ principles, problems | Econ | 100 | 4Q | U |
| 220201 | Macroeconomics | Econ | 3 | 3S | U |
| 220208 | Taxation: myth & reality | Econ | 168 | 2S | U |
| 220211 | Labor econ & relations | Econ | 148 | 3S | U |
| 220214 | International economics | Econ | 190 | 4Q | U |
| 220432 | Amer intellectual history | Hist | 102.1 | 3S | U |
| 220432 | History of the US | Hist | 17A | 4Q | U |
| 220432 | History of the US | Hist | 17B | 4Q | U |
| 220432 | Western civilization | Hist | 21A | 3S | L |
| 220432 | Western civilization | Hist | 21B | 3S | L |
| 220432 | Western civilization | Hist | 21C | 3S | L |
| 220432 | The American West | Hist | 189.1 | 3S | U |

| NCES No. | Course Title | Dept. | Course No. | Credits | Level |
|---|---|---|---|---|---|
| 220453 | Hist of the Americas mod | Hist | 20 | 3S | L |
| 220501 | American institutions | PolSc | 100 | 3S | U |
| 220510 | Intro political theory | PolSc | 7 | 3S | L |
| 220601 | Introduction to sociology | Socio | 10 | 3S | L |
| 220602 | Crime, justice in America | Socio | 120 | 2S | U |
| 2299 | America & future of man | Hum | 101 | 3Q | U |
| 2299 | Making of Amer society | Hum | 106 | 3Q | U |
| | **Noncredit courses** | | | | |
| 020103 | Basic interior design | Des | 807 | NC | U |
| 030302 | Elements of music | Music | 800 | NC | |
| 040109 | Governmental accounting | Bus | | NC | |
| 040601 | English for business | Bus | 800 | NC | |
| 0499 | Govt contracts for bus | Bus | 807 | NC | |
| 060203 | Bus bkkping by computer | CmpSc | 802 | NC | |
| 0810 | Beginning engr drafting | EngAS | 800A | NC | |
| 0810 | Beginning engr drafting | EngAS | 800B | NC | |
| 0899 | Engineering fundamentals | EngAS | 843 | NC | |
| 090307 | Radiologic technology | HSci | 800A | NC | |
| 090307 | Radiologic technology | HSci | 800B | NC | |
| 120305 | Grammar for ESL students | Engl | 803 | NC | |
| 120310 | The writer within | Engl | 806 | NC | U |
| 120310 | Elementary composition | Engl | 804 | NC | |
| 120310 | Magazine article writing | Engl | 801 | NC | |
| 120310 | Advanced article writing | Engl | 808 | NC | |
| 120310 | Short story theory | Engl | 816 | NC | |
| 120310 | Short story writing | Engl | 817 | NC | |
| 120310 | Writing your own story | Engl | 802 | NC | |
| 120310 | Poetry writing | Engl | 815 | NC | |
| 160302 | Elementary algebra | Math | 852A | NC | |
| 160302 | Elementary algebra | Math | 852B | NC | |
| 160601 | Plane geometry | Math | M904 | NC | |
| 160601 | Plane geometry | Math | M905 | NC | |

## (37) UNIVERSITY OF COLORADO AT BOULDER

Dr. John R. Dunn
Program Manager of Continuing Education
Division of Continuing Education
University of Colorado
Campus Box 178
Boulder, Colorado 80309
Phone: 303-492-5145

Enrollment on a noncredit basis accepted in all credit courses. Gifted high school students are permitted to enroll in undergraduate courses for credit. Overseas enrollment accepted.

| NCES No. | Course Title | Dept. | Course No. | Credits | Level |
|---|---|---|---|---|---|
| | **High School courses** | | | | |
| 030502 | Beginning drawing & paint | Art | 001A | HF | H |
| 040101 | Beginning accounting | Bus | 024A | HF | H |
| 040101 | Beginning accounting | BusEd | 023A | HF | H |
| 040299 | Office procedures & pract | Bus | 013A | HF | H |
| 040299 | Office procedures & pract | BusEd | 014A | HF | H |
| 040302 | Consumer education | BusEd | 019A | HF | H |
| 040601 | Business English | Bus | 011A | HF | H |
| 0499 | General business | BusEd | 021A | HF | H |
| 070899 | Study skills | Study | 001A | HF | D |
| 080199 | Aerospace age | Aero | 001A | HF | H |
| 080999 | Basic elec & electronics | Sci | 009A | HF | H |
| 090119 | Health science | Sci | 001A | HF | H |
| 090119 | Health science | Sci | 002A | HF | H |
| 100699 | Persl adju, marriage, fam | HmEc | 011A | HF | H |
| 120305 | Ninth-grade English | Engl | 031A | HF | H |
| 120305 | Ninth-grade English | Engl | 032A | HF | H |
| 120305 | Tenth-grade English | Engl | 033A | HF | H |
| 120305 | Tenth-grade English | Engl | 034A | HF | H |
| 120305 | Eleventh-grade English | Engl | 035A | HF | H |
| 120305 | Eleventh-grade English | Engl | 036A | HF | H |
| 120305 | Twelfth-grade English | Engl | 037A | HF | H |
| 120305 | Twelfth-grade English | Engl | 038A | HF | H |
| 120305 | Basic English | Engl | 001N | HF | H |
| 120307 | The short story | EngLL | 009A | HF | H |
| 120307 | The novel | EngLL | 015A | HF | H |
| 120307 | Poetry | EngLL | 021A | HF | H |
| 120307 | American short story | Engl | 011N | HF | H |
| 120308 | Improvmt of reading skill | Engl | 003A | HF | H |
| 120308 | Improvmt of reading skill | Engl | 004A | HF | H |

| NCES No. | Course Title | Dept. | Course No. | Credits | Level |
|---|---|---|---|---|---|
| 120310 | Composition | Engl | 023N | HF | H |
| 150301 | Basic biology | Sci | 015A | HF | H |
| 150301 | Basic biology | Sci | 016A | HF | H |
| 150301 | Advanced biology | Sci | 019A | HF | H |
| 150799 | Physics | Sci | 035A | HF | H |
| 150799 | Physics | Sci | 036A | HF | H |
| 160199 | General mathematics | Math | 005A | HF | H |
| 160199 | General mathematics | Math | 006A | HF | H |
| 160301 | Remedial arithmetic | Math | 001A | HF | D |
| 160302 | Beginning algebra | Math | 031A | HF | H |
| 160302 | Beginning algebra | Math | 032A | HF | H |
| 160302 | Advanced algebra | Math | 035A | HF | H |
| 160302 | Advanced algebra | Math | 036A | HF | H |
| 160601 | Geometry | Math | 033N | HF | H |
| 160601 | Geometry | Math | 034N | HF | H |
| 160602 | Trigonometry | Math | 037N | HF | H |
| 161101 | Bus & consumer math | Math | 009X | HF | H |
| 161101 | Bus & consumer math | Math | 010X | HF | H |
| 200199 | Psychology | SocSt | 007N | HF | H |
| 220399 | World geography | SocSc | 021A | HF | H |
| 220421 | American history | SocSt | 033N | HF | H |
| 220421 | American history | SocSt | 034N | HF | H |
| 220433 | World history | SocSc | 031A | HF | H |
| 220433 | World history | SocSc | 032A | HF | H |
| 220501 | American government | SocSt | 035N | HF | H |
| 220502 | Civics | SocSt | 001N | HF | H |
| 220599 | Modern problems | SocSc | 037A | HF | H |
| 220606 | Sociology | SocSt | 003N | HF | H |
| | **College courses** | | | | |
| 030302 | Rudiments of music | Mus | 108 | 3S | L |
| 030503 | Art for elementary teachr | FA | 363 | 3S | U |
| 040106 | Cost accounting | Bus | 332 | 3S | U |
| 040111 | Intro to managerial acctg | Bus | 202 | 3S | L |
| 040113 | Intro to financial acctg | Bus | 200 | 3S | L |
| 0409 | Intro to business | BAd | 100 | 3S | L |
| 040905 | Child adm organ & mgt | ChEd | 45 | 2S | V |
| 040999 | Child adm parents & pers | ChEd | 43 | 2S | V |
| 041301 | Real estate appraisal I | RE | 21 | 1S | V |
| 041303 | Real estate basics | RE | 1 | 1S | V |
| 041306 | Real estate finance | RE | 22 | 1S | V |
| 041308 | Real estate law | RE | 12 | 1S | V |
| 070499 | Child curriculum planning | ChEd | 21 | 3S | V |
| 070512 | Lit for adolescents | TEd | 444 | 3S | U |
| 070512 | Children's literature | TEd | 456 | 3S | U |
| 070701 | Child guidance techniques | ChEd | 20 | 3S | V |
| 081502 | Occupational safety mgt | Eng | 400 | 3S | U |
| 090199 | Environmental health | PE | 295 | 3S | L |
| 100301 | Child adm nutrition | ChEd | 41 | 2S | V |
| 100601 | Child development 1 | ChEd | 10 | 3S | V |
| 100601 | Child development 2 | ChEd | 11 | 3S | V |
| 100601 | Child development 1 | ChEd | 10A | 3S | V |
| 100601 | Child development 2 | ChEd | 11A | 3S | V |
| 120103 | Hist & grammar of Eng lan | Engl | 484 | 3S | U |
| 120202 | Lit for adolescents | EngLL | 481 | 3S | U |
| 120304 | Studies in lang fiction | Engl | 382 | 3S | U |
| 120308 | Intro to fiction | EngLL | 120 | 3S | L |
| 120308 | Intro to drama | EngLL | 130 | 3S | L |
| 120308 | Intr to world literat I | Engl | 260 | 3S | L |
| 120308 | Intr to world literat II | Engl | 261 | 3S | L |
| 120308 | Modern short story | EngLL | 220 | 3S | L |
| 120308 | Contemporary literature | Engl | 253 | 3S | L |
| 120308 | Survey of American lit I | EngLL | 365 | 3S | U |
| 120308 | Bible as literature | Engl | 360 | 3S | U |
| 120308 | Chaucer | EngLL | 395 | 3S | U |
| 120308 | Shakespeare | EngLL | 397 | 3S | U |
| 120308 | Shakespeare | EngLL | 398 | 3S | U |
| 120308 | Survey of American lit II | EngLL | 366 | 3S | U |
| 120310 | General expository writng | A&S | 100 | 3S | L |
| 120310 | Advanced expository wrtng | A&S | 110 | 3S | L |
| 120310 | Intro to creative writing | Engl | 119 | 3S | L |
| 120310 | Intermediate fiction wksp | Engl | 305 | 3S | U |
| 120310 | Report writing | Engl | 315 | 3S | U |
| 120399 | Images of women | EngLL | 226 | 3S | L |
| 1299 | Intro to poetry | Engl | 140 | 3S | L |
| 130103 | Evidence & investigation | PlEd | 10 | 3S | V |
| 130199 | Litigation, civ proc, dis | PlEd | 11 | 3S | V |
| 131599 | Legal research | PlEd | 12 | 3S | V |
| 1505 | Intro to geology I | Geol | 103 | 3S | L |
| 160302 | College algebra | Math | 101 | 3S | L |
| 160499 | Analyt geom & calculus I | Math | 130 | 5S | L |
| 160499 | Analyt geom & calculus II | Math | 230 | 5S | L |

| NCES No. | Course Title | Dept. | Course No. | Credits | Level |
|---|---|---|---|---|---|
| 160602 | College trigonometry | Math | 102 | 2S | L |
| 160699 | College algebra & trig | Math | 110 | 5S | L |
| 1803 | Ethics | Phil | 102 | 3S | L |
| 1804 | Intro to philosophy | Phil | 100 | 3S | L |
| 180404 | Twentieth-cent philosophy | Phil | 404 | 3S | U |
| 181199 | Philosophy & religion | Phil | 105 | 3S | L |
| 200199 | Intro to psychology | Psych | 100 | 3S | L |
| 2002 | Intro to biopsychology | Psych | 205 | 3S | L |
| 200504 | Developmental psychology | Psych | 468 | 3S | U |
| 200505 | Psychology of adjustment | Psych | 230 | 3S | L |
| 200508 | Child & adolescent psych | Psych | 264 | 3S | L |
| 200799 | Social psychology | Psych | 440 | 3S | U |
| 220102 | Principles of anthro I | Anthr | 103 | 3S | L |
| 220102 | Principles of anthro II | Anthr | 104 | 3S | L |
| 220106 | Intro to physical anthr I | Anthr | 201 | 3S | L |
| 220106 | Intro to phys anthr II | Anthr | 202 | 3S | L |
| 220201 | Prin of economics I | Econ | 201 | 3S | L |
| 220201 | Prin of economics II | Econ | 202 | 3S | L |
| 220399 | Environ sys climate & veg | Geog | 100 | 3S | L |
| 220399 | Env sys landforms & soil | Geog | 101 | 3S | L |
| 220402 | Dipl his of Europe 20th c | Hist | 438 | 3S | U |
| 220428 | Hist of Colorado | Hist | 258 | 3S | L |
| 220431 | Hist of Russia thr 17th c | Hist | 493 | 3S | U |
| 220431 | Imperial Russia | Hist | 494 | 3S | U |
| 220431 | Russ Revolution & Sov reg | Hist | 495 | 3S | U |
| 220432 | Hist of US to 1865 | Hist | 151 | 3S | L |
| 220432 | Hist of US since 1865 | Hist | 152 | 3S | L |
| 220432 | Early American frontier | Hist | 457 | 3S | U |
| 220432 | Later American frontier | Hist | 458 | 3S | U |
| 220499 | Hist of Western civiliztn | Hist | 101 | 3S | L |
| 220499 | Hist of Western civiliztn | Hist | 102 | 3S | L |
| 220501 | American political system | PolSc | 110 | 3S | L |
| 220503 | Intro comparative politic | PolSc | 201 | 3S | L |
| 220505 | International relations | PolSc | 222 | 3S | L |
| 220606 | Intro to sociology | Soc | 211 | 3S | L |
| | **Noncredit courses** | | | | |
| 120399 | Vocabulary building | Engl | 108 | NC | L |

## ③⑧ UNIVERSITY OF FLORIDA

Dr. Harold Markowitz Jr.
Director
Department of Independent Study by Correspondence
University of Florida
1938 West University Avenue, Room 1
Gainesville, Florida 32603
Phone: 904-392-1711

Enrollment on a noncredit basis accepted in all credit courses. Gifted high school students are permitted to enroll in undergraduate courses for credit. Overseas enrollment accepted. University courses meet on-campus degree requirements. External degrees not offered. The Department of Independent Study by Correspondence represents all state universities and draws faculty and courses from several institutions. No additional charges for out-of-state students. DANTES and VA approved.

| NCES No. | Course Title | Dept. | Course No. | Credits | Level |
|---|---|---|---|---|---|
| | **High School courses** | | | | |
| 030602 | Art/2d comprehensive I | Art | 11A | HF | H |
| 030602 | Art/2d comprehensive II | Art | 11B | HF | H |
| 040104 | Bookkeeping 1st sem | Voc | 12A | HF | H |
| 040104 | Bookkeeping 2nd sem | Voc | 12B | HF | H |
| 120303 | English II 1st sem | Engl | 10A | HF | H |
| 120303 | English II 2nd sem | Engl | 10B | HF | H |
| 120304 | English III 1st sem | Engl | 11A | HF | H |
| 120304 | English III 2nd sem | Engl | 11B | HF | H |
| 120305 | English I 1st sem | Engl | 9A | HF | H |
| 120305 | English I 2nd sem | Engl | 9B | HF | H |
| 120307 | English IV 1st sem | Engl | 12A | HF | H |
| 120307 | English IV 2nd sem | Engl | 12B | HF | H |
| 120399 | Engl for spkrs other lang | Engl | 9C | HF | H |
| 130799 | Business law 1st sem | Voc | 11A | HF | H |
| 130799 | Business law 2nd sem | Voc | 11B | HF | H |
| 160302 | Algebra II 1st sem | Mat | 11A | HF | H |
| 160302 | Algebra II 2nd sem | Mat | 11B | HF | H |
| 160302 | Algebra I 1st sem | Mat | 10A | HF | H |
| 160302 | Algebra I 2nd sem | Mat | 10B | HF | H |
| 160599 | Mathematics analysis | Mat | 12A | HF | H |

| NCES No. | Course Title | Dept. | Course No. | Credits | Level |
|---|---|---|---|---|---|
| 1611 | General math I 1st sem | Mat | 9A | HF | H |
| 1611 | General math I 2nd sem | Mat | 9B | HF | H |
| 161201 | Business math I 1st sem | Mat | 11C | HF | H |
| 161201 | Business math I 2nd sem | Mat | 11D | HF | H |
| 190506 | Personal,soc,family relat | Hea | 11A | HF | H |
| 190509 | Health I life mngt skills | Hea | 12A | HF | H |
| 200505 | Peer couns II self-discov | PCn | 10A | HF | H |
| 220399 | World geography 1st sem | SSt | 9A | HF | H |
| 220399 | World geography 2nd sem | SSt | 9B | HF | H |
| 220432 | American history 1st sem | SSt | 11A | HF | H |
| 220432 | American history 2nd sem | SSt | 11B | HF | H |
| 220433 | World history 1st sem | SSt | 10A | HF | H |
| 220433 | World history 2nd sem | SSt | 10B | HF | H |
| 220501 | American government | SSt | 12A | HF | H |
| 220501 | Advanced American govt | SSt | 12B | HF | H |
| 220503 | Comparative political sys | SSt | 12C | HF | H |
| | **College courses** | | | | |
| 010199 | Prin of food & res econom | AEB | 3103 | 4S | U |
| 010406 | Beef cattle sci & rge mgt | AnSc | 4242C | 4S | U |
| 010702 | General soils | Agri | 3022C | 4S | U |
| 0199 | Introduction to agronomy | | 3005 | 3S | U |
| 040710 | Risk mgmt and insurance | Ins | 3015 | 3S | U |
| 040903 | Organizational behavior | Man | 3109 | 3S | U |
| 041001 | Basic marketing concepts | Mar | 3023 | 3S | U |
| 041104 | Mgmt of labor & ind rela | Man | 4407 | 3S | U |
| 041199 | Concepts of management | Man | 3010 | 3S | U |
| 041201 | Quantit meth of bus decs | QMB | 3200 | 3S | L |
| 0499 | Productivity work ana/dsg | FSS | 3423 | 3S | U |
| 0499 | Analysis of hospital comp | HFT | 3000 | 3S | U |
| 050101 | Elements of advertising | Adv | 3000 | 3S | U |
| 050102 | Radio-TV advertising | Adv | 4103 | 3S | U |
| 050104 | Copywriting & visualizatn | Adv | 4101 | 3S | U |
| 050201 | Survey of mass communictn | JMC | 1000 | 2S | L |
| 050605 | Magazine & feature writng | Jou | 4300 | 3S | U |
| 0508 | Writing for mass commun | JMC | 2100 | 3S | L |
| 0509 | Intro to public relations | PuR | 3000 | 3S | U |
| 051201 | Braille & methods of tch | EVI | 4211 | 3S | U |
| 070199 | Social foundations of ed | EdF | 3604 | 3S | U |
| 070199 | History of ed in the US | EdF | 3514 | 3S | U |
| 070303 | Expl cons ed for sec schl | Educ | 4930 | 2S | U |
| 070520 | Educational psychology | EdPsy | 3210 | 3S | U |
| 070522 | Pop dynamics & family pln | Educ | 4930 | 2S | U |
| 071103 | Measurement & eval in ed | EdF | 4430 | 3S | U |
| 082601 | Land surveying computatn | Sur | 3640 | 2S | U |
| 090255 | RN concpt bases-prof nurs | Nur | 3116 | 3S | U |
| 090255 | Case mngt of chil-chr ill | Nur | 4905A | | U |
| 090255 | Communication skills-nurs | Nur | 4905B | | U |
| 090255 | Facil grwth/dev in illchl | Nur | 4905C | | U |
| 090255 | Prac in case mngt illchil | Nur | 4905D | | U |
| 100103 | Textiles for consumers | CTe | 1401 | 3S | L |
| 100304 | Man's food | FoS | 2001 | 2S | L |
| 100312 | The science of nutrition | HuN | 1201 | 3S | L |
| 100312 | Fund of human nutrition | HuN | 2201 | 3S | L |
| 100601 | Child grwth & dev:adolesc | ChD | 4240 | 3S | U |
| 120202 | Amer fict: 1900 to WWII | Engl | 3124 | 3S | U |
| 120299 | Writing about literature | Lit | 1102 | 3S | L |
| 120299 | British authors to 1700 | Lit | 2011 | 3S | L |
| 120305 | English grammar | Engl | 2340 | 2S | L |
| 120307 | English novel: 18th cen | Engl | 3112 | 3S | U |
| 120307 | English novel: 19th cen | Engl | 3122 | 3S | U |
| 120307 | English novel: 20th cen | Engl | 3132 | 3S | U |
| 120310 | Imaginative writing: fict | CrW | 3110 | 3S | U |
| 120310 | Expos & argument writing | Engl | 1101 | 3S | L |
| 120310 | Techn writ & bus comm | BTWr | 3213 | 3S | U |
| 120310 | Advanced exposition | Engl | 3310 | 3S | U |
| 120310 | Advanced profes writing | Engl | 4260 | 3S | U |
| 1211 | Beginning German 1 | Ger | 1120 | 4S | L |
| 1211 | Beginning German 2 | Ger | 1121 | 3S | L |
| 1211 | Beginning German 3 | Ger | 1122 | 3S | L |
| 130799 | Business law | BuL | 4100 | 3S | U |
| 130799 | Business law | BuL | 4112 | 4S | U |
| 150102 | Surv of solar sys astron | Ast | 2003 | 3S | L |
| 150103 | Surv of stellar astronomy | Ast | 2004 | 3S | L |
| 150202 | Intro to the atmosphere | Met | 1010 | 3S | L |
| 150401 | Chemistry for lib studies | Chem | 1020 | 3S | L |
| 150599 | Expl the geological sci | Gly | 1000 | 3S | L |
| 150599 | Physical geology | Gly | 2015 | 3S | L |
| 150599 | Historical geology | Gly | 2100 | 3S | L |
| 160302 | College algebra | Mat | 1114 | 2S | L |
| 160302 | Basic college algebra | Mat | 1102 | 3S | L |
| 160305 | Precalculus: alg & trig | Mat | 1142 | 4S | L |

| NCES No. | Course Title | Dept. | Course No. | Credits | Level |
|---|---|---|---|---|---|
| 160603 | Analyt geometry & calc 1 | Mat | 3311 | 4S | U |
| 160603 | Analyt geometry & calc 2 | Mat | 3312 | 4S | U |
| 160802 | Stat proc for behav sci | Sta | 4122 | 4S | U |
| 180301 | Ethical iss & life choice | Phi | 2630 | 3S | L |
| 180599 | Intro to philosophy | Phi | 2010 | 3S | L |
| 180902 | The Christian tradition | Rel | 3505 | 3S | U |
| 181103 | Religion in America | Rel | 2120 | 3S | L |
| 181104 | Introduction to religion | Rel | 2000 | 3S | L |
| 181201 | Intro to Old Testament | Rel | 2210 | 3S | L |
| 181202 | Intro to New Testament | Rel | 2243 | 3S | L |
| 1899 | New religious mov in Amer | Rel | 3974 | 3S | U |
| 190599 | Contemporary health sci | HEd | 2000 | 3S | L |
| 200199 | Applied psychology | Psy | 3101 | 3S | U |
| 200199 | General psychology | Psy | 2013 | 3S | L |
| 200504 | Developmental psychology | DeP | 3003 | 3S | U |
| 200509 | Personality | PPe | 4004 | 3S | U |
| 200799 | Social psychology | SoP | 4004 | 3S | U |
| 200901 | Industrial psychology | Psy | 4004 | 3S | U |
| 220201 | Basic economics I | Econ | 2013 | 3S | L |
| 220201 | Basic economics II | Econ | 2023 | 3S | L |
| 220299 | Economic concepts & inst | Econ | 2000 | 3S | L |
| 220299 | Child grwth & dev foun yr | ChD | 3220 | 3S | U |
| 220302 | Conservation of resources | Geog | 3370 | 3S | U |
| 220399 | The face of Florida | Geog | 3271 | 3S | U |
| 220402 | US diplomacy to 1920 | AmH | 4510 | 3S | U |
| 220402 | US diplomacy since 1920 | AmH | 4511 | 3S | U |
| 220426 | 19th-century Europe:surve | EuH | 3004 | 3S | U |
| 220426 | 20th-century Europe:surve | EuH | 3005 | 3S | U |
| 220428 | Florida to 1845 | AmH | 3422 | 2S | U |
| 220428 | Florida since 1845 | AmH | 3423 | 3S | U |
| 220431 | Russia to Nicholas I | EuH | 3571 | 3S | U |
| 220431 | Hist of Russia, 1825-pres | EuH | 3572 | 3S | U |
| 220432 | United States to 1877 | AmH | 2010 | 3S | L |
| 220432 | United States since 1877 | AmH | 2020 | 3S | L |
| 220432 | Labor history of the US | AmH | 3501 | 3S | U |
| 220432 | American civilization | AmH | 1000 | 3S | L |
| 220450 | West hum:ancient-Renaissc | Hum | 2210 | 3S | L |
| 220453 | Modern world to 1815 | Hist | 1023 | 3S | L |
| 220453 | Modern world since 1815 | Hist | 1030 | 3S | L |
| 220501 | American govt: national | PolS | 1041 | 3S | L |
| 220501 | American federal govt | PolS | 2041 | 3S | L |
| 220505 | International relations | IntRe | 2002 | 3S | L |
| 220511 | Am state & local govt | PolS | 2112 | 3S | L |
| 220602 | Criminology | Crim | 3011 | 3S | U |
| 220602 | Law enforcement | Crim | 3101 | 3S | U |
| 220602 | Corrections | Crim | 3301 | 3S | U |
| 220605 | Marriage & the family | MAF | 2430 | 3S | L |
| 220606 | Principles of sociology | Soc | 2000 | 3S | L |
| 220614 | Urban sociology | Soc | 3410 | 3S | U |
| 2299 | Am cultural & soc institn | SocS | 2110 | 3S | L |
| 2299 | Emerg of Amer ec/pol inst | SocS | 2120 | 3S | L |
| 2299 | Law and society | IDS | 4900 | 3S | U |

**Noncredit courses**

| NCES No. | Course Title | Dept. | Credits |
|---|---|---|---|
| 040702 | Casualty ins: suretyship | Ins | NC |
| 040709 | Prop ins: fire & marine | Ins | NC |
| 040799 | Bail & bail bonds ins | Ins | NC |
| 040799 | Industrial fire | Ins | NC |
| 040799 | Motor veh phys damage ins | Ins | NC |
| 041106 | Intro to princ of superv | Sup | NC |
| 041106 | Supervision communication | Sup | NC |
| 041199 | Supervisory leadership | Sup | NC |
| 041199 | Managing problem employee | Sup | NC |
| 070599 | Prin of curriculum design | PCD | NC |
| 070703 | Princp of a job search | CR | NC |
| 081304 | Water treatment operat | WT | NC |
| 081304 | Wastewatr trtment plt opr | WW | NC |
| 100702 | Dietary manager course | DM | NC |
| 150327 | Guide for struct fumigat | PCI | NC |
| 190508 | Nutrition in diet modif | DM | NC |

(39) **UNIVERSITY OF GEORGIA**

Dr. Ernestine M. Copas
Assistant Director and Head of the University Credit Programs
Georgia Center for Continuing Education
University of Georgia
1197 South Lumpkin Street
Athens, Georgia 30602
Phone: 404-542-3243

Enrollment on a noncredit basis accepted in all credit courses. Gifted high school students are permitted to enroll in undergraduate courses for credit. Overseas enrollment accepted for college and noncredit courses.

| NCES No. | Course Title | Dept. | Course No. | Credits | Level |
|---|---|---|---|---|---|
| | **College courses** | | | | |
| 010603 | Agricultural entomology | Agri | 374 | 5Q | U |
| 030502 | Ancient and medieval art | ArHis | 287 | 5Q | L |
| 030502 | Renaissance to 18th cent | ArHis | 288 | 5Q | L |
| 030502 | 19th and 20th century art | ArHis | 289 | 5Q | L |
| 040101 | Principles of acctg I | Acctg | 110 | 5Q | L |
| 040101 | Principles of acctg II | Acctg | 111 | 5Q | L |
| 040114 | Tax I | Acctg | 540 | 5Q | U |
| 040201 | Office practice and proc | Bus | 506 | 5Q | U |
| 040201 | Principles of office mgmt | Bus | 507 | 5Q | U |
| 040208 | Business communication | Bus | 401 | 5Q | U |
| 040301 | Business finance | Bus | 330 | 5Q | U |
| 040306 | Investments | Bus | 431 | 5Q | U |
| 040308 | Money and banking | Bus | 326 | 5Q | U |
| 040399 | American financial system | Bus | 452 | 5Q | U |
| 040902 | Small-business management | Mgmt | 554 | 5Q | U |
| 040903 | Organizational behavior | Mgmt | 351 | 5Q | U |
| 041001 | Principles of marketing | Mktg | 360 | 5Q | U |
| 041001 | Principles of retailing | Mktg | 560 | 5Q | U |
| 041005 | Principles of advertising | Mktg | 351 | 5Q | U |
| 041203 | Operations analysis | Mgmt | 320 | 5Q | U |
| 050699 | Jrnlsm in secondry school | Jrnl | 566 | 5Q | U |
| 050699 | Law of communication | Jrnl | 504 | 5Q | U |
| 051108 | Psych of speech commu | Spch | 466 | 5Q | U |
| 100206 | Prin of family economics | HmEc | 364 | 5Q | U |
| 100313 | Nutrition fundamentals | HmEc | 251 | 5Q | L |
| 100503 | Interior design | HmEc | 381 | 5Q | U |
| 100601 | Intro to child developmnt | HmEc | 395 | 5Q | U |
| 100699 | Human growth and develop | Educ | 295 | 5Q | L |
| 120299 | Mythology in classicl lit | CILL | 150 | 5Q | L |
| 120303 | Derivatives frm Grk & Ltn | EngLL | 310 | 5Q | U |
| 120305 | Composition part I | Engl | 101 | 5Q | L |
| 120305 | Composition part II | Engl | 102 | 5Q | L |
| 120307 | Western world literature | Engl | 250 | 5Q | L |
| 120307 | Western world literature | Engl | 251 | 5Q | L |
| 120307 | English lit to 1700 | Engl | 231G | 5Q | L |
| 120307 | English lit after 1700 | Engl | 232G | 5Q | L |
| 120307 | Survey of American lit | Engl | 307 | 5Q | U |
| 120307 | Southern literature | Engl | 320 | 5Q | U |
| 120307 | Contemporary novel | Engl | 409 | 5Q | U |
| 120307 | Early American writing | Engl | 470T | 5Q | U |
| 120307 | Children's literature | Engl | 455 | 5Q | U |
| 120310 | Composition practicum | Engl | 100 | 5Q | L |
| 120310 | Technical writing | Engl | 302 | 5Q | U |
| 1210 | Elementary French | Frnch | 101 | 5Q | L |
| 1210 | Elementary French | Frnch | 102 | 5Q | L |
| 1210 | Beginning French | Frnch | 103 | 5Q | L |
| 1210 | Intermediate French | Frnch | 104 | 5Q | L |
| 1211 | Elementary German I | Ger | 151 | 5Q | L |
| 1211 | Elementary German II | Ger | 152 | 5Q | L |
| 1211 | Intermediate German I | Ger | 251 | 5Q | L |
| 1211 | Intermediate German II | Ger | 252 | 5Q | L |
| 1216 | Elementary Latin I | CILL | 101 | 5Q | L |
| 1216 | Elementary Latin II | CILL | 102 | 5Q | L |
| 1216 | Intermediate Latin | CILL | 203 | 5Q | L |
| 1216 | Readings in Latin | CILL | 304 | 5Q | U |
| 1225 | Elementary Spanish I | Span | 151 | 5Q | L |
| 1225 | Elementary Spanish II | Span | 152 | 5Q | L |
| 1225 | Intermediate Spanish I | Span | 251 | 5Q | L |
| 1225 | Intermediate Spanish II | Span | 252 | 5Q | L |
| 130799 | Business law part I | Bus | 370 | 5Q | U |
| 130799 | Business law part II | Bus | 576 | 5Q | U |
| 150304 | Ecology | Bio | 350 | 5Q | U |
| 150307 | Genetics | Bio | 440 | 5Q | U |
| 160199 | Finite mathematics I | Math | 101 | 5Q | L |
| 160203 | Finite mathematics | Math | 155 | 5Q | L |
| 160302 | Fundamentals of algebra | Math | 103 | 5Q | L |
| 160401 | Practical calculus | Math | 107 | 5Q | L |
| 160602 | Trigonometry | Math | 112 | 5Q | L |
| 160603 | Analyt geom & calculus | Math | 166 | 5Q | L |
| 1608 | Elementary Statistics | Math | 240 | 5Q | L |
| 160899 | Stat analysis for bus | Stat | 312 | 5Q | U |
| 180302 | Introduction to ethics | Philo | 305 | 5Q | U |
| 180501 | Intro to deductive logic | Philo | 110 | 5Q | L |
| 181199 | Intro to west rel traditn | Relig | 115 | 5Q | L |
| 181299 | New Testament literature | Relig | 411 | 5Q | U |
| 190501 | Effcts drug use and abuse | Educ | 521 | 5Q | U |

| NCES No. | Course Title | Dept. | Course No. | Credits | Level |
|---|---|---|---|---|---|
| 200199 | Elementary psychology | Psych | 101 | 5Q | L |
| 200406 | Learning and motivation | Psych | 304 | 5Q | U |
| 200501 | Psychology of abnormal | Psych | 423 | 5Q | U |
| 200504 | Psych of early childhood | Psych | 401 | 5Q | U |
| 200508 | Adolescent psychology | Educ | 305 | 5Q | U |
| 200509 | Theories of personality | Psych | 451 | 5Q | U |
| 200599 | Psych of sex & sex deviat | Psy | 326 | 5Q | U |
| 220102 | Cultural anthropology | Anthr | 452 | 5Q | U |
| 220201 | Prin of macroeconomics | Econ | 105 | 5Q | L |
| 220201 | Prin of microeconomics | Econ | 106 | 5Q | L |
| 220202 | Hist of economic thought | Econ | 473 | 5Q | U |
| 220207 | Econ development of US | Econ | 133 | 5Q | L |
| 220211 | Labor economics | Econ | 386 | 5Q | U |
| 220299 | Government and business | Econ | 478 | 5Q | U |
| 220302 | Economic geography | Geog | 358 | 5Q | U |
| 220305 | Earth science survey | Geog | 104 | 5Q | L |
| 220306 | Geography developed world | Geog | 101 | 5Q | L |
| 220306 | Underdeveloped world | Geog | 102 | 5Q | L |
| 220406 | Classical culture: Greece | ClCiv | 120 | 5Q | L |
| 220406 | Classical culture: Rome | ClCiv | 121 | 5Q | L |
| 220426 | Early modern western civ | Hist | 121 | 5Q | L |
| 220426 | Modern western civiliztn | Hist | 122 | 5Q | L |
| 220428 | History of Georgia | Hist | 470 | 5Q | U |
| 220432 | American history to 1865 | Hist | 251 | 5Q | L |
| 220432 | American hist since 1865 | Hist | 252 | 5Q | L |
| 220499 | The ancient world | ArHis | 210 | 3Q | L |
| 220499 | Mid Ages thru Renaissance | ArHis | 211 | 3Q | L |
| 220499 | Baroque to modern world | ArHis | 212 | 3Q | L |
| 220501 | American government | PolSc | 101 | 5Q | L |
| 220503 | Comparative politics | PolSc | 310 | 5Q | U |
| 220504 | American foreign policy | Polsc | 455 | 5Q | U |
| 220505 | International politics | PolSc | 210 | 5Q | L |
| 220511 | State and local governmnt | PolSc | 350 | 5Q | U |
| 220599 | Energy crisis and politic | PolSc | 390 | 5Q | U |
| 220599 | National security policy | PolSc | 375 | 5Q | U |
| 220599 | Minority politics | PolSc | 356 | 5Q | U |
| 220601 | Community organization | Socio | 403 | 5Q | U |
| 220602 | Criminology | Socio | 381 | 5Q | U |
| 220604 | Juvenile delinquency | Socio | 307 | 5Q | U |
| 220605 | Preparation for marriage | Socio | 103 | 5Q | L |
| 220605 | Sociology of the family | Socio | 410 | 5Q | U |
| 220606 | Introductory sociology | Socio | 105 | 5Q | L |
| 220607 | Social psychology | Socio | 371 | 5Q | U |
| 220607 | Personality & soc struct | Socio | 427 | 5Q | U |
| 220607 | Theories of social psych | Socio | 470 | 5Q | U |
| 220613 | Contemporary soc problems | Socio | 160 | 5Q | L |
| 220699 | Sociology of aging & aged | Socio | 412 | 5Q | U |
| 220699 | Sociology of occupations | Socio | 485 | 5Q | U |

**Noncredit courses**

| NCES No. | Course Title | Dept. | Course No. | Credits | Level |
|---|---|---|---|---|---|
| 040104 | Basic book for small bus | Acctg | | NC | L |
| 040203 | Records management | Bus | | NC | L |
| 040208 | Information processing | Bus | | NC | L |
| 061101 | Developng comput literacy | CmpSc | | NC | L |
| 090401 | Biopharmaceutics | Pharm | 002 | NC | L |
| 090411 | Effective pharmacy mgmt | Pharm | 004 | NC | L |
| 090499 | Drug interactions | Pharm | 001 | NC | L |
| 090499 | Disease states & therapeu | Pharm | 005 | NC | L |

④⓪ **UNIVERSITY OF IDAHO**

Ms. Carol Escapule
State Coordinator
Correspondence Study in Idaho
University of Idaho
Continuing Education Building, Room 116
Moscow, Idaho 83843
Phone: 208-885-6641

Enrollment on a noncredit basis accepted in all credit courses. Gifted high school students are permitted to enroll in undergraduate courses for credit. Overseas enrollment accepted.

| NCES No. | Course Title | Dept. | Course No. | Credits | Level |
|---|---|---|---|---|---|
| | **High School courses** | | | | |
| 040104 | Bookkeeping | FdAcg | I | HF | H |
| 040104 | Bookkeeping | FdAcg | II | HF | H |
| 100202 | Consumer economics | ConEd | I | HF | H |
| 120305 | Grammar and composition | FrEng | I | HF | H |

| NCES No. | Course Title | Dept. | Course No. | Credits | Level |
|---|---|---|---|---|---|
| 120305 | Grammar and composition | SoEng | I | HF | H |
| 120305 | English review grammar | SrEng | III | HF | H |
| 120307 | English lit and comp | FrEng | II | HF | H |
| 120307 | English lit and comp | SoEng | II | HF | H |
| 120307 | American lit and comp | JrEng | I | HF | H |
| 120307 | Modern lit and comp | JrEng | II | HF | H |
| 120307 | English lit and comp | SrEng | I | HF | H |
| 120307 | English novels and comp | SrEng | II | HF | H |
| 1503 | Biology | Bio | I | HF | H |
| 1503 | Biology | Bio | II | HF | H |
| 1508 | Physical science | Phys | I | HF | H |
| 1508 | Physical science | Phys | II | HF | H |
| 160301 | General mathematics | GnMth | I | HF | H |
| 160301 | General mathematics | GnMth | II | HF | H |
| 160302 | Algebra | Alg | I | HF | H |
| 160302 | Algebra | Alg | II | HF | H |
| 160604 | Geometry | Geom | I | HF | H |
| 160604 | Geometry | Geom | II | HF | H |
| 220432 | American history | AmHis | I | HF | H |
| 220432 | American history | AmHis | II | HF | H |
| 220501 | Problems in Amer democ | SocSc | II | HF | H |
| 220501 | American government | SocSc | I | HF | H |
| 220699 | Sociology | Socio | I | HF | H |

| NCES No. | Course Title | Dept. | Course No. | Credits | Level |
|---|---|---|---|---|---|
| | **College courses** | | | | |
| 010107 | Princ of farm/ranch mgmt | AgEc | C278 | 4S | L |
| 010199 | Ag in its soc/econ envir | AgEc | C101 | 3S | L |
| 010901 | Pub relations-nat resourc | Fores | C400 | 2S | U |
| 030302 | Survey of music | Music | C100 | 3S | L |
| 040101 | Principles of accounting | Acctg | C201 | 3S | L |
| 040101 | Intermediate accounting | Acctg | C301 | 4S | U |
| 040101 | Intermediate accounting | Acctg | C302 | 4S | U |
| 040111 | Managerial accounting | Acctg | C202 | 3S | L |
| 040203 | Local govt records mgmt | BusEd | C312 | 2S | U |
| 041001 | Marketing | Bus | C321 | 3S | U |
| 041303 | Fundamntls of real estate | RIEs | C201 | 3S | L |
| 041306 | Real estate finance | Bus | C465 | 3S | U |
| 041308 | Real estate law | Bus | C464 | 3S | U |
| 050199 | Promotional strategy | Bus | C420 | 3S | U |
| 060799 | Digital computer prog | Engr | C131 | 2S | L |
| 070306 | Princ of vocational ed | VocEd | C351 | 2S | U |
| 070309 | Devel/org of extension ed | AgEd | C248 | 2S | L |
| 070309 | Intro to adult education | VocEd | C473 | 3S | U |
| 070309 | Psych of adult learners | VocEd | C474 | 3S | U |
| 070309 | Principles of voc ed | AgEd | C351 | 2S | U |
| 070507 | Contemporary education | Ed | C468 | 3S | U |
| 070512 | Elementary language arts | Ed | C338 | 3S | U |
| 070515 | Elem school science meths | Educ | C344 | 3S | U |
| 070522 | Social studies methods | Educ | C421 | 3S | U |
| 070803 | Ed of exceptional child | SpEd | C275 | 3S | U |
| 070803 | Behavioral principles | SpEd | C323 | 3S | U |
| 0809 | Elem electrical theory | EE | C010 | 3S | L |
| 0810 | Engineering graphics | Engr | C101 | 2S | L |
| 0810 | Engineering graphics | Engr | C102 | 2S | L |
| 081102 | Fluid mechanics | EnSci | C320 | 3S | U |
| 081104 | Statics | EnSci | C210 | 3S | L |
| 081104 | Dynamics | EnSci | C220 | 3S | L |
| 0812 | Mechanics of materials | EnSci | C340 | 3S | U |
| 082699 | Elementary surveying | Engr | C201 | 3S | L |
| 090799 | El microbio/pub health | Bact | C154 | 3S | L |
| 100202 | Consumer education | ConEd | C471 | 3S | U |
| 100313 | Problems in nutrition | HmEc | C470 | 3S | U |
| 120305 | Composition | Engl | C101 | 3S | L |
| 120305 | Composition | Engl | C102 | 3S | L |
| 120307 | The novel for nonmajors | Engl | C321 | 3S | U |
| 1210 | Elementary French | Frnch | C101a | 4S | L |
| 1225 | Elementary Spanish | Span | C101 | 4S | L |
| 1225 | Elementary Spanish | Span | C102 | 4S | L |
| 1307 | Legal envir of business | Bus | C265 | 3S | L |
| 1307 | Business law | Bus | C467 | 3S | U |
| 1307 | Business law | Bus | C466 | 3S | U |
| 1402 | Introduction to museology | Anthr | C324 | 3S | U |
| 140305 | Museum administration | Anthr | C422 | 3S | U |
| 140401 | Cataloging & classificat | LibSc | C420 | 4S | U |
| 140408 | Acquisition & collect dev | LibSc | C421 | 3S | U |
| 150304 | General ecology | Bio | C331 | 3S | U |
| 150399 | Man and the environment | Bio | C200 | 3S | L |
| 1507 | General physics | Phys | C114 | 3S | L |
| 150799 | General physics | Phys | C113 | 3S | L |
| 160203 | Finite math | Math | C111 | 3S | L |
| 160301 | Math for elem teachers | Math | C135 | 3S | L |
| 160301 | Math for elem teachers | Math | C136 | 3S | L |

| NCES No. | Course Title | Dept. | Course No. | Credits | Level |
|---|---|---|---|---|---|
| 160302 | College algebra | Math | C140 | 3S | L |
| 160303 | Remedial mathematics | Math | C50 | | L |
| 160401 | Survey of calculus | Math | C160 | 4S | L |
| 160602 | Analytic trigonometry | Math | C179 | 2S | L |
| 160603 | Analytic geom and calc I | Math | C180 | 4S | L |
| 160801 | Intro to statistics | Math | C252 | 3S | L |
| 1803 | Ethics | Philo | C151 | 3S | L |
| 180401 | History of ancient philo | Philo | C309 | 3S | U |
| 180403 | History of modern philo | Philo | C310 | 3S | U |
| 200104 | Intro to psychology | Psych | C100 | 3S | L |
| 200501 | Abnormal psychology | Psych | C311 | 3S | U |
| 200504 | Developmental psychology | Psych | C205 | 3S | L |
| 200504 | Per/social devel in child | Psych | C309 | 3S | U |
| 200509 | Psychology of personality | Psych | C310 | 3S | U |
| 200599 | Human sexuality | Psych | C210 | 2S | L |
| 200603 | Meas and eval in psych | Psych | C402 | 3S | U |
| 200799 | Social psychology | Psych | C320 | 3S | U |
| 210102 | Public administration | PolSc | C451 | 3S | U |
| 210110 | Politics and energy | PolSc | C155 | 1S | L |
| 210111 | Politics and pollution | PolSc | C152 | 1S | L |
| 2201 | Study of man | Anthr | C301 | 3S | U |
| 220201 | Principles of economics | Econ | C151 | 3S | L |
| 220201 | Principles of economics | Econ | C152 | 3S | L |
| 220204 | Money and banking | Econ | C301 | 3S | U |
| 220423 | History of the Far East | Hist | C470 | 3S | U |
| 220424 | History of England | Hist | C271 | 3S | L |
| 220424 | History of England | Hist | C272 | 3S | L |
| 220428 | Idaho and the Pacific NW | Hist | C423 | 3S | U |
| 220432 | Intro to US history | Hist | C111 | 3S | L |
| 220432 | Intro to US history | Hist | C112 | 3S | L |
| 220450 | History of civilization | Hist | C101 | 3S | L |
| 220450 | History of civilization | Hist | C102 | 3S | L |
| 220501 | US govt: structure & func | PolSc | C101 | 3S | L |
| 220501 | US govt: policies & issue | PolSc | C102 | 3S | L |
| 220511 | American state government | PolSc | C275 | 3S | L |
| 220511 | American local government | PolSc | C276 | 3S | L |
| 220511 | Local govt/intergovt rel | PolSc | C461 | 3S | U |
| 220511 | County government | PolSc | C476 | 3S | U |
| 220602 | Intro to criminal just ad | Cr | C201 | 3S | L |
| 220604 | Juvenile delinquency | Socio | C330 | 3S | U |
| 220608 | Rural sociology | Socio | C310 | 3S | U |
| 220612 | Introduction to soc ser | Soc | C140 | 3S | L |
| 220613 | Social problems | Socio | C230 | 3S | L |
| 220699 | Introduction to sociology | Socio | C110 | 3S | L |

# (41) UNIVERSITY OF ILLINOIS

Dr. Robert W. Batchellor
Director of Guided Individual Study
1046 Illini Hall
University of Illinois
725 South Wright Street
Champaign, Illinois 61820
Phone: 217-333-1321

Enrollment on a noncredit basis accepted in all credit courses. Gifted high school students are permitted to enroll in undergraduate courses for credit. Overseas enrollment is not encouraged; each case is judged on an individual basis. Overseas enrollees need excellent English skills and dependable mail service. Credit courses meet on-campus degree requirements. External degrees are not offered. Enrollment by correspondence does not constitute admission to a degree program. Inquire about noncredit videotape courses in engineering.

| NCES No. | Course Title | Dept. | Course No. | Credits | Level |
|---|---|---|---|---|---|
| | **College courses** | | | | |
| 040101 | Principles of acctg I | Acctg | X201 | 3S | L |
| 040101 | Principles of acctg II | Acctg | X202 | 3S | U |
| 040101 | Intermediate accounting | Acctg | X211 | 3S | U |
| 040106 | Cost accounting | Acctg | X221 | 3S | U |
| 040109 | Governmental accounting | Acctg | X361 | 2S | U |
| 040304 | Financl markets & instit | Fin | X258 | 3S | U |
| 040601 | Bus & admin communication | BTWr | X251 | 3S | U |
| 040604 | Report writing | BTWr | X272 | 3S | U |
| 0408 | Intro to internationl bus | BusAd | X382 | 3S | L |
| 0408 | International management | BusAd | X384 | 3S | U |
| 0408 | Japanese managemt systems | BusAd | X294B | 3S | U |
| 0408 | International marketing | BusAd | X370 | 3S | U |

| NCES No. | Course Title | Dept. | Course No. | Credits | Level |
|---|---|---|---|---|---|
| 0409 | Intro to management | BusAd | X247 | 3S | U |
| 040901 | Business policy | BusAd | X389 | 3S | U |
| 040999 | Purchasing management | BusAd | X199A | 3S | U |
| 041001 | Principles of marketing | BusAd | X202 | 3S | U |
| 0501 | Introduction to advertisg | Adv | X281 | 3S | U |
| 050104 | Advert creative strategy | Adv | X382 | 3S | U |
| 050199 | Advert in contemp society | Adv | X393 | 3S | U |
| 070516 | Metrics educ for teachers | VoTec | X399B | 2S | U |
| 070516 | Math for elem teachers | Math | X202 | 5S | U |
| 070516 | Math for elem teachers | Math | X203 | 3S | U |
| 0706 | Tchg occ career prac arts | VoTec | X388 | 2S | U |
| 0707 | Indiv counslg & group wrk | EdPsy | X199 | 3S | L |
| 070799 | Mental hyg & the school | EdPsy | X312 | 2S | U |
| 071102 | Const & use of tests | EdPsy | X391 | 4S | U |
| 0810 | Engineering graphics | GEngr | X103 | 3S | L |
| 081104 | Analyt mechan–statics | TAM | X150 | 2S | L |
| 081104 | Engr mechanics I–statics | TAM | X152 | 3S | L |
| 081104 | Analyt mechan–dynamics | TAM | X212 | 3S | U |
| 081199 | Elem mech of deform body | TAM | X221 | 3S | U |
| 090114 | Immunochem-humoral resp | Micro | X329A | 2S | U |
| 090114 | Immunochem-cellular immun | Micro | X329B | 1S | U |
| 090114 | Immunochem-autoimmun | Micro | X329C | 1S | U |
| 090299 | Patient education | HIEd | X394 | 3S | U |
| 090504 | First aid | HIEd | X199 | 2S | L |
| 0907 | Public health | HIEd | X110 | 3S | L |
| 100601 | Child dev for elem teachr | EdPsy | X236 | 3S | U |
| 120307 | Introduction to drama | EngLL | X102 | 3S | L |
| 120307 | Masterpieces of Amer lit | EngLL | X116 | 3S | L |
| 120307 | Intro to Shakespeare | EngLL | X118 | 3S | L |
| 120307 | Modern short story | EngLL | X246 | 3S | U |
| 120307 | American fiction | EngLL | X249 | 3S | U |
| 120307 | Masterpieces of Engl lit | Engl | X115 | 3S | L |
| 120307 | The British novel | Engl | X247 | 3S | U |
| 120310 | Principles of composition | Rhet | X105 | 4S | L |
| 120310 | Advan narrative writing | Rhet | X205 | 3S | U |
| 1210 | Elementary French | Frnch | X101 | 4S | L |
| 1210 | Elementary French | Frnch | X102 | 4S | L |
| 1210 | Modern French | Frnch | X103 | 4S | L |
| 1210 | Modern French | Frnch | X104 | 4S | L |
| 1210 | Intro Fr lit 17th-18th ce | Frnch | X209 | 3S | U |
| 1210 | Intro Fr lit 19th-20th ce | Frnch | X210 | 3S | U |
| 1211 | Elementary German | Ger | X101 | 4S | L |
| 1211 | Elementary German | Ger | X102 | 4S | L |
| 1211 | Intermediate German | Ger | X103 | 4S | L |
| 1211 | Intermediate German | Ger | X104 | 4S | L |
| 1212 | Elementary Greek | Greek | X101 | 4S | L |
| 1216 | Latin composition | Latin | X113 | 2S | L |
| 1216 | Latin composition | Latin | X114 | 2S | L |
| 1216 | Elementary Latin | Latin | X101 | 4S | L |
| 1216 | Elementary Latin | Latin | X102 | 4S | L |
| 1216 | Intermediate Latin | Lat | X103 | 4S | L |
| 1216 | Intro to Latin literature | Lat | X104 | 4S | L |
| 1220 | First-year Russian | Rus | X101 | 4S | L |
| 1220 | First-year Russian | Rus | X102 | 4S | L |
| 1220 | Second-year Russian | Rus | X103 | 4S | L |
| 1220 | Second-year Russian | Rus | X104 | 4S | L |
| 1220 | 19th-cent Rus lit in tran | Rus | X315 | 3S | L |
| 1225 | Elementary Spanish | Span | X101 | 4S | L |
| 1225 | Elementary Spanish | Span | X102 | 4S | L |
| 1225 | Reading & writing Spanish | Span | X123 | 4S | L |
| 1225 | Reading & writing Spanish | Span | X124 | 4S | L |
| 1225 | Span lit: Mid Ages–18th c | Span | X240 | 3S | U |
| 1225 | Span lit: 19th cen to pres | Span | X241 | 3S | U |
| 1225 | Spanish-Amer literature | Span | X242 | 3S | U |
| 131102 | Law and planning implemtn | UrPl | X308 | 3S | U |
| 150311 | Immunochem–humoral resp | Micro | X329A | 2S | U |
| 150311 | Immunochem–cellular imm | Micro | X329B | 1S | U |
| 150311 | Immunochem–autoimm dise | Micro | X329C | 1S | U |
| 1507 | Gen phys: mech heat matte | Phys | X123 | 4S | L |
| 1507 | Gen phys: elec mag atm nu | Phys | X124 | 4S | L |
| 160302 | College algebra | Math | X111 | 5S | L |
| 160302 | College algebra | Math | X112 | 5S | L |
| 160306 | Elem linear alg with appl | Math | X125 | 3S | L |
| 160401 | Calc & analyt geom I | Math | X120 | 5S | L |
| 160401 | Calc & analyt geom II | Math | X132 | 3S | L |
| 160401 | Calc & analyt geom III | Math | X242 | 5S | L |
| 160406 | Differ eq & orthog funct | Math | X345 | 3S | U |
| 160602 | Plane trigonometry | Math | X114 | 2S | L |
| 1608 | Descriptive statistics | Psych | X233 | 3S | U |
| 1608 | Inferential statistics | Psych | X234 | 2S | U |
| 1611 | Finite math: bus & soc sc | Math | X124 | 3S | L |
| 1611 | Calculus-bus and soc sci | Math | X134 | 4S | L |

| NCES No. | Course Title | Dept. | Course No. | Credits | Level |
|---|---|---|---|---|---|
| 161101 | Economic statistics I | Econ | X172 | 3S | L |
| 161103 | Intro econ-bus statistics | Econ | X171 | 3S | L |
| 161108 | Statistical meth in psych | Psych | X235 | 5S | U |
| 1905 | Health and modern life | HlEd | X150 | 3S | L |
| 190501 | Drug-abuse education | HlEd | X393 | 2S | U |
| 190502 | Public health education | HlEd | X390 | 3S | U |
| 190503 | Consumer health education | HlEd | X396 | 2S | U |
| 190504 | Concepts of disease prev | HlEd | X283 | 3S | U |
| 190511 | Safety education | SEd | X280 | 3S | U |
| 190512 | Human sexuality | HlEd | X206 | 2S | U |
| 190515 | Sex educ for teachers | HlEd | X285 | 4S | U |
| 190515 | Hlth & safety ed elem sch | HlEd | X392 | 3S | U |
| 190599 | Patient education | HlEd | X394 | 3S | U |
| 2001 | Intro to psychology | Psych | X100 | 3S | L |
| 200401 | Behavior modification | Psych | X337 | 3S | U |
| 200406 | Introduction to learning | Psych | X248 | 3S | U |
| 200501 | Abnormal psychology | Psych | X238 | 3S | U |
| 200509 | Psychology of personality | Psych | X250 | 3S | U |
| 2007 | Intro to social psychol | Psych | X201 | 3S | U |
| 200804 | Educational psychology | EdPsy | X211 | 3S | U |
| 200901 | Industrial psychology | Psych | X245 | 3S | U |
| 220102 | Intro to cultural anthro | Anthr | X103 | 4S | L |
| 220105 | Intro to linguistic anthr | Anthr | X270 | 3S | U |
| 220201 | Introduction to economics | Econ | X101 | 4S | L |
| 220202 | Hist of econ thought | Econ | X306 | 3S | U |
| 220206 | Intro to public finance | Econ | X214 | 3S | U |
| 220305 | Physical geography I | Geog | X102 | 4S | L |
| 220305 | Physical geography II | Geog | X103 | 4S | L |
| 220401 | Const dev of US to 1865 | Hist | X369 | 3S | U |
| 220401 | Const dev of US snce 1865 | Hist | X370 | 3S | U |
| 220426 | Hist of West civ to 1660 | Hist | X111 | 4S | L |
| 220426 | Hist of West civ fr 1660 | Hist | X112 | 4S | L |
| 220432 | US history to 1877 | Hist | X151 | 4S | L |
| 220432 | US history 1877 to pres | Hist | X152 | 4S | L |
| 220432 | US in 20th century | Hist | X262 | 3S | U |
| 220470 | Afro-Amer hist to 1865 | Hist | X253 | 3S | U |
| 220470 | Afro-Amer hist since 1865 | Hist | X254 | 3S | U |
| 2205 | Intro to political sci | PolSc | X100 | 3S | L |
| 220501 | American government | PolSc | X150 | 3S | L |
| 220503 | Intro to compar politics | PolSc | X240 | 3S | U |
| 220505 | International relations | PolSc | X280 | 3S | U |
| 220510 | Contemp political theory | PolSc | X396 | 3S | U |
| 220511 | Municipal government | PolSc | X305 | 3S | U |
| 2206 | Introduction to sociology | Socio | X100 | 3S | L |
| 220612 | Stratification & soc clas | Socio | X223 | 3S | U |
| 220613 | Family violence | Soc | X242 | 3S | U |
| 220613 | Alcohol and society | Soc | X241 | 3S | U |
| 220699 | Collective behavior | Socio | X240 | 3S | U |

## (42) UNIVERSITY OF IOWA

Dr. Von V. Pittman
Director of Center for Credit Programs
W400 Seashore Hall
The University of Iowa
Iowa City, Iowa 52242
Phone: 319-353-4963
335-3500

Enrollment on a noncredit basis accepted in some credit courses. Gifted high school students are permitted to enroll in undergraduate courses for credit. Overseas enrollment accepted.

| NCES No. | Course Title | Dept. | Course No. | Credits | Level |
|---|---|---|---|---|---|
| | **College courses** | | | | |
| 030302 | Introduction to music | Music | 259 | 3S | L |
| 030401 | Basic playwriting | Theat | 49161 | 3S | B |
| 030401 | Advanced playwriting | Theat | 49167 | 3S | B |
| 040301 | Intro financial mgmt | Bus | 6F100 | 3S | B |
| 040306 | Investments | Bus | 6F111 | 3S | B |
| 040502 | Entrepreneurship new bus | Bus | 6F127 | 3S | B |
| 040502 | Managing new or small bus | bus | 6F128 | 3S | B |
| 040903 | Organizational behavior | Bus | 6K160 | 3S | B |
| 041104 | Collective bargaining | Bus | 6L153 | 3S | B |
| 050499 | Pop culture & mass comm | Jrnl | 19153 | 3S | B |
| 050605 | Free-lance writing | Jrnl | 1983 | 3S | L |
| 070401 | Intro to education | Educ | 7S101 | 3S | B |
| 070404 | Methods early child ed | Educ | 7E157 | 3S | B |
| 070404 | Classroom management | Educ | 7E170 | VC | B |
| 070505 | Methods sec sch journalsm | Jrnl | 19125 | 3S | B |

| NCES No. | Course Title | Dept. | Course No. | Credits | Level |
|---|---|---|---|---|---|
| 070512 | Lit for adolescents | Educ | 7S193 | 3S | B |
| 070512 | Methods high sch reading | Educ | 7S194 | 3S | B |
| 0708 | Exceptional persons | Educ | 7U130 | 3S | B |
| 070803 | Education of the gifted | Educ | 7U137 | 3S | B |
| 070806 | Mental retardation | Educ | 7U135 | 3S | B |
| 071299 | Ind study nonmajors | Educ | 7W193 | 3S | B |
| 0810 | Lettering | EngAS | 58105 | 1S | B |
| 0810 | Mechanical drawing | EngAS | 58105 | 2S | B |
| 090118 | Nrsng proc & pharmacology | Nrsng | 96111 | 3S | B |
| 090302 | Diet therapy | HmEc | 17147 | 3S | B |
| 090904 | Intro biomedical ethics | Relig | 32163 | 3S | B |
| 100313 | Nutrition | HmEc | 17142 | 3S | B |
| 100313 | Advanced nutrition | HmEc | 17145 | 3S | B |
| 100602 | Parent-child-teacher rel | HmEc | 17116 | 3S | B |
| 120202 | Maj 19th-cent Brit works | EngLL | 863 | 3S | L |
| 120202 | Amer works before 1900 | EngLL | 864 | 3S | L |
| 120202 | Chaucer | EngLL | 8120 | 3S | B |
| 120202 | Shakespeare | EngLL | 8122 | 3S | B |
| 120202 | Pop lits detective fictn | EngLL | 8142 | 3S | B |
| 120202 | Science fiction I | EngLL | 8181 | 3S | B |
| 120202 | Science fiction II | EngLL | 8182 | 3S | B |
| 120202 | Women in literature | EngLL | 8161 | 3S | B |
| 120202 | Chan concept women in lit | EngLL | 8169 | 3S | B |
| 120305 | Greek & Lat for vocab bld | Clas | 2010L | 2S | B |
| 120307 | Lit & cult 20th-cent Amer | EngLL | 8106 | 3S | B |
| 120307 | Eng novel Scott to Butler | EngLL | 8133 | 3S | B |
| 120307 | Lit of African peoples | Engl | 458 | 3S | L |
| 120307 | Prose by women writers | Engl | 8188 | 3S | B |
| 120307 | Interpret of literature | Engl | 8G1 | 3S | L |
| 120310 | Expository writing | EngLL | 8W10 | 3S | L |
| 120310 | Creative writing | EngLL | 8W23 | 3S | L |
| 120310 | Fiction writing | EngLL | 8W151 | 3S | B |
| 120310 | Advanced fiction writing | EngLL | 8W161 | 3S | B |
| 120310 | Writing for bus & indus | EngLL | 8W113 | 3S | B |
| 120310 | Adv fiction writing II | EngLL | 8W162 | 3S | B |
| 120310 | Writng for sciences-biomd | Engl | 8W112 | 3S | B |
| 120310 | Rhetoric | Rhet | 103 | 4S | L |
| 1207 | Chinese I | Asian | 391 | 4S | L |
| 1210 | Elementary French | Frnch | 91 | 4S | L |
| 1210 | Elementary French | Frnch | 92 | 4S | L |
| 1211 | First-semester German | Ger | 1311 | 3S | L |
| 1211 | Second-semester German | Ger | 1312 | 3S | L |
| 1216 | Elementary Latin | Clas | 201 | 4S | L |
| 1216 | Elementary Latin | Clas | 202 | 4S | L |
| 1221 | First-year Sanskrit I | Asian | 3921 | 4S | L |
| 1225 | Elementary Spanish I | Span | 351 | 4S | L |
| 1225 | Elementary Spanish II | Span | 352 | 4S | L |
| 1225 | Intermediate Spanish I | Span | 3511 | 3S | L |
| 1225 | Intermediate Spanish II | Span | 3512 | 3S | L |
| 1225 | Intens elem readg Spanish | Span | 357 | 3S | L |
| 150399 | Human biology | Zool | 1121 | 3S | L |
| 150401 | Principles of chemistry | Chem | 413 | 3S | L |
| 150599 | Introduction to geology | Geol | 125 | 4S | L |
| 160306 | Intro linear algebra | Math | 22M27 | 4S | L |
| 160308 | Elements of group theory | Math | 22M50 | 3S | L |
| 160399 | Basic math techniques | Math | 22M1 | 3S | L |
| 160399 | Mathematical techniques I | Math | 22M2 | 3S | L |
| 160399 | Math techniques II | Math | 22M3 | 3S | L |
| 160399 | Fundamentals college math | Math | 22M10 | 4S | L |
| 160399 | Fundamentals college math | Math | 22M11 | 4S | L |
| 160401 | Calculus I | Math | 22M25 | 4S | L |
| 160401 | Calculus II | Math | 22M26 | 4S | L |
| 160401 | Engineering calculus | Math | 22M35 | 4S | L |
| 160401 | Quantitative methods | Math | 22M7 | 4S | L |
| 160601 | Foundations of geometry | Math | 22M70 | 3S | L |
| 160603 | Elementary functions | Math | 22M20 | 3S | L |
| 160802 | Intro to stat methods | Educ | 7P143 | 3S | B |
| 161107 | Intro to biostatistics | PvMed | 63161 | 3S | B |
| 180905 | Modern Judaism | Relig | 32112 | 3S | B |
| 181104 | Religion and society | Relig | 3262 | 3S | L |
| 181199 | Religion & women | Relig | 32111 | 3S | B |
| 181301 | World of Old Testament | Relig | 32105 | 3S | B |
| 181302 | World of New Testament | Relig | 32122 | 3S | B |
| 181399 | Ind studies in relig (UG) | Relig | 32195 | 3S | U |
| 190299 | Human anatomy | PhyEd | 2753 | 2S | L |
| 190508 | Nutrition work wth childn | HmEc | 17124 | 3S | B |
| 190702 | Aging & leisure | RecEd | 162 | 3S | B |
| 190799 | Contemp issues rec & leis | RecEd | 146 | 3S | B |
| 200199 | Elementary psychology | Psych | 311 | VC | L |
| 200501 | Abnormal psychology | Psych | 31163 | 3S | B |
| 200503 | Behavior modification | Psych | 31170 | 3S | B |
| 200506 | Death and dying | Relig | 32193 | 2S | B |

| NCES No. | Course Title | Dept. | Course No. | Credits | Level |
|---|---|---|---|---|---|
| 200804 | Ed psych & measurement | Educ | 7P75 | 3S | L |
| 200804 | Educational psychology | Educ | 7P131 | 3S | B |
| 200804 | Adolescent & young adult | Educ | 7P133 | 3S | B |
| 200805 | Socialization sch child | Educ | 7P109 | 3S | B |
| 200901 | Psych in bus & industry | Psych | 3119 | 3S | L |
| 210199 | Intro to public admin | PolSc | 30120 | 3S | B |
| 210404 | Intro to social work | SocWk | 4222 | 4S | L |
| 210499 | Individual study aging | SocWk | 42191 | VC | B |
| 210499 | Perspectives on aging | SocWk | 42184 | 3S | B |
| 220101 | Intro Midwest prehistory | Anthr | 11320 | 3S | L |
| 220102 | Biblical archaeology | Relig | 32103 | 1S | B |
| 220102 | Intro study cult & soc | Anthr | 1133 | 4S | L |
| 220102 | Anthro & contemp world | Anthr | 11310 | 3S | L |
| 220107 | Women's roles cross-cult | Anthr | 156 | 3S | B |
| 220199 | Intro folklore studies | Anthr | 105 | 3S | B |
| 220201 | Principles of economics | Econ | 6E1 | 4S | L |
| 220201 | Principles of economics | Econ | 6E2 | 4S | L |
| 220216 | Problems in urban econ | Econ | 6E137 | 3S | B |
| 220305 | Intro physical geography | Geog | 443 | 4S | L |
| 220308 | Urban geography | Geog | 44135 | 3S | B |
| 220402 | US in world affairs 1900 | Hist | 16178 | 3S | B |
| 220408 | Relig & occult in antiqty | Relig | 20113 | 3S | B |
| 220423 | Civilizations of Asian | Hist | 165 | 3S | L |
| 220426 | Western civilization | Hist | 161 | 3S | L |
| 220426 | West civztn since 1792 | Hist | 162 | 3S | L |
| 220426 | 20th-cent Europe Nazi era | Hist | 16135 | 3S | B |
| 220426 | 19th-cent Eur: imper era | Hist | 16134 | 3S | B |
| 220432 | Amer history 1492-1877 | Hist | 1661 | 3S | L |
| 220432 | Amer history 1877-present | Hist | 1662 | 3S | L |
| 220432 | Contemp US 1940-present | Hist | 16168 | 3S | B |
| 220432 | Great Plains experience | Hist | 16109 | 3S | B |
| 220432 | New Deal/new era 1920-40 | Hist | 16167 | 3S | B |
| 220452 | Medieval civilization | Hist | 16110 | 3S | B |
| 220501 | Am const law & politics | PolSc | 30116 | 3S | B |
| 220511 | Munic govt & politics | PolSc | 30111 | 3S | B |
| 220511 | American state politics | PolSc | 30113 | 3S | B |
| 220511 | Urban administration | PolSc | 30121 | 3S | B |
| 220511 | Iowa govmt & politics | PolSc | 30112 | 3S | B |
| 220599 | Ind study in pol science | PolSc | 30190 | VC | B |
| 220602 | Sociology of corrections | Socio | 34145 | 3S | B |
| 220602 | Socio of law & crim just | Socio | 34182 | 3S | B |
| 220603 | World population problems | Socio | 34174 | 3S | B |
| 220605 | American family | Socio | 34161 | 3S | B |
| 220606 | Intro to socio principles | Socio | 341 | 3S | L |
| 220606 | Intro to socio problems | Socio | 342 | 3S | L |
| 220606 | Theories of sociology | Socio | 34191 | 3S | B |

**Graduate courses**

| NCES No. | Course Title | Dept. | Course No. | Credits | Level |
|---|---|---|---|---|---|
| 070701 | Intro rehabil services | Educ | 7C241 | 2S | G |
| 071103 | Educ measurement & eval | Educ | 7P257 | 3S | G |
| 071299 | Ind st insruct design | Educ | 7W293 | VC | G |
| 180999 | Rdgs in Asian religions | Relig | 32265 | 2S | G |
| 181299 | Rdg Jewish/Chrstn scripts | Relig | 32260 | 2S | G |
| 181399 | Rdgs theol & rel thought | Relig | 32263 | 2S | G |
| 181399 | Ind studies in relig grad | Relig | 32290 | 3S | G |
| 181599 | Rdgs in religious ethics | Relig | 32264 | 2S | G |
| 190107 | Phys ed program planning | PhyEd | 28260 | 3S | G |

**Noncredit courses**

| NCES No. | Course Title | Dept. | Course No. | Credits | Level |
|---|---|---|---|---|---|
| 090104 | Interp card arrhythmias I | Nrsng | 90676 | NC | V |
| 090104 | Interp card arrhythm II | Nrsng | 90677 | NC | V |
| 090104 | Intro cong heart failure | Nrsng | 90807 | NC | V |
| 090199 | Medical terminology | HSci | HS100 | NC | B |
| 090799 | Ag health probs in ind | Nrsng | 90808 | NC | V |
| 160301 | Practical math review | Math | SI30 | NC | D |

### ④③ UNIVERSITY OF KANSAS

Ms. Nancy Colyer
Director of Independent Study
Continuing Education Building
University of Kansas
Lawrence, Kansas 66045
Phone: 913-864-4792

Enrollment on a noncredit basis accepted in all credit courses. Gifted high school students are permitted to enroll in undergraduate courses for credit. Overseas enrollment accepted.

| NCES No. | Course Title | Dept. | Course No. | Credits | Level |
|---|---|---|---|---|---|
| **High School courses** | | | | | |
| 100604 | Project self-discovery | | | HF | H |
| 120308 | Fiction's world of horror | | | HF | H |
| 120308 | Short story reluct readrs | | | HF | H |
| 200408 | Straight thinking | | | HF | H |
| 200502 | Career planning | | | HF | H |
| **College courses** | | | | | |
| 040101 | Financial accounting | Bus | 240 | 4S | L |
| 040111 | Managerial accounting | Bus | 241 | 3S | L |
| 040601 | Business communication | Bus | 355 | 3S | U |
| 040903 | Organizational behavior | Mgmt | 443 | 3S | U |
| 040999 | Prod/operations managemnt | Mgmt | 423 | 3S | U |
| 041105 | Personnel management | Mgmt | 544 | 3S | U |
| 041106 | Supervisory management | Mgmt | 343 | 3S | U |
| 050199 | Elements of advertising | Journ | 240 | 3S | L |
| 050608 | Reporting I | Journ | 350 | 3S | U |
| 051102 | Intercultural communicatn | ComS | 246 | 3S | U |
| 051103 | Loving relationships | ComS | 455 | 3S | U |
| 051103 | Life shaping | ComS | 459 | 2S | U |
| 051103 | Dir hi schl forensic prog | ComS | 559 | 3S | U |
| 051103 | Dev child aware via commu | ComS | 741 | 3S | U |
| 070199 | Educational psychology | C&I | 324 | 2S | U |
| 070199 | Survey of American educ | EPA | 312 | 2S | U |
| 070201 | Teacher & school admin | EPA | 308 | 3S | U |
| 070404 | Teaching reading in sec s | C&I | 429 | 3S | U |
| 070699 | Educ in multicultural soc | C&I | 210 | 3S | U |
| 070899 | Intro to psyc & ed child | SpEd | 725 | 3S | U |
| 070899 | Psych excep child: comput | SpEd | 725 | 3S | U |
| 071103 | Intro educ measurements | EPR | 302 | 2S | U |
| 080101 | Space dynamics | AE | 655 | 3S | U |
| 100599 | Housing | FEcon | 420 | 3S | U |
| 100601 | Intro child behav & devel | HDFL | 160 | 3S | L |
| 100601 | Intro child behav & devel | HDFL | 432 | 3S | U |
| 100601 | Children and television | HDFL | 325 | 3S | U |
| 100602 | Marriage & family relatns | HDFL | 288 | 3S | L |
| 100604 | Analysis evryday behavior | HDFL | 180 | 3S | L |
| 100699 | Prin nutr & health in dev | HDFL | 220 | 3S | L |
| 100699 | Prin of env design & fam | HDFL | 102 | 3S | L |
| 100699 | Theories of human develop | HDFL | 480 | 3S | U |
| 120305 | Composition & literature | Engl | 101 | 3S | L |
| 120305 | Composition & literature | Engl | 102 | 3S | L |
| 120307 | Shakespeare | Engl | 332 | 3S | U |
| 120307 | Literature for children | Engl | 466 | 3S | U |
| 120307 | Directed readings: Austen | Engl | 495 | 1S | U |
| 120307 | Directed readings: Conrad | Engl | 495 | 1S | U |
| 120307 | Directed rdngs: Lawrence | Engl | 495 | 1S | U |
| 120307 | Post–World War II Am nov | Engl | 571 | 3S | U |
| 120307 | American literature I | Engl | 320 | 3S | U |
| 120307 | American literature II | Engl | 322 | 3S | U |
| 120307 | Dir readings: Hemingway | Engl | 495 | 1S | U |
| 120307 | Directed readings: Cather | Engl | 495 | 1S | U |
| 120307 | Kansas literature | Engl | 570 | 3S | U |
| 120310 | Technical writing | Engl | 362 | 3S | U |
| 120310 | Creative writing: fiction | Engl | 251 | 3S | U |
| 120399 | Grk & Lat elem in Eng lge | Clsx | 232 | 3S | L |
| 120399 | Grk & Lat elem in Eng lge | Clsx | 332 | 3S | U |
| 1210 | Elementary French I | Frnch | 110 | 5S | L |
| 1210 | Elementary French II | Frnch | 120 | 5S | L |
| 1210 | French for reading knowlg | Frnch | 100 | 3S | L |
| 1211 | Elementary German I | Ger | 104 | 5S | L |
| 1211 | Elementary German II | Ger | 108 | 5S | L |
| 1211 | German reading course | Ger | 100 | 4S | L |
| 1216 | Elementary Latin | Latin | 104 | 5S | L |
| 1216 | Latin reading & grammar | Latin | 108 | 5S | L |
| 1216 | Virgil's *Aeneid* | Latin | 124 | 3S | L |
| 1225 | Elementary Spanish I | Span | 104 | 5S | L |
| 1225 | Spanish reading course | Span | 100 | 3S | L |
| 1225 | Intermediate Spanish I | Span | 212 | 3S | L |
| 1225 | Elementary Spanish II | Span | 108 | 5S | L |
| 150202 | Meteorology | Metr | 320 | 3S | U |
| 150202 | Introductory meteorology | Metr | 105 | 3S | L |
| 150202 | Introductory meteorology | Metr | 105 | 5S | L |
| 150301 | Human reprod bio & behav | Bio | 303 | 3S | U |
| 150399 | Human physiology | Bio | 305 | 4S | U |
| 150399 | Can man survive? | Bio | 521 | 3S | U |
| 160299 | Modern elementary math I | Math | 109 | 3S | L |
| 160299 | Modern elementary math II | Math | 110 | 3S | L |
| 160302 | Algebra | Math | 101 | 3S | L |
| 160302 | Intermediate algebra | Math | 002 | 3S | L |
| 160302 | Algebra | Math | 102 | 5S | L |

| NCES No. | Course Title | Dept. | Course No. | Credits | Level |
|---|---|---|---|---|---|
| 160602 | Trigonometry | Math | 103 | 2S | L |
| 160603 | Calculus I | Math | 121 | 5S | L |
| 180404 | Intro to philosophy | Philo | 140 | 4S | L |
| 180599 | Intro to logic | Philo | 148 | 3S | L |
| 180905 | Introduction to Judaism | Relig | 320 | 3S | U |
| 181199 | Loving relationships | Relig | 475 | 3S | U |
| 190311 | Coaching of basketball | HPER | 252 | 2S | L |
| 190311 | Coaching of track & field | HPER | 390 | 2S | L |
| 190311 | Coaching of football | HPER | 240 | 3S | U |
| 190505 | Environmental health | HPER | 449 | 2S | U |
| 190599 | Personal & commun health | HPER | 260 | 3S | L |
| 190703 | Recreation program | HPER | 489 | 3S | U |
| 200199 | General psychology | Psych | 104 | 3S | L |
| 200399 | Environmental psychology | Psych | 467 | 3S | U |
| 200499 | Brain, mind, behavior | Psych | 390 | 3S | U |
| 200599 | Psych of adolescence | Psych | 626 | 3S | U |
| 200599 | Children and television | Psych | 325 | 3S | U |
| 200799 | Social psychology | Psych | 260 | 3S | L |
| 200804 | Educational psychology | EPR | 300 | 2S | U |
| 220106 | Intro physical anthropol | Anthr | 104 | 4S | L |
| 220106 | Intro physical anthropol | Anthr | 304 | 4S | U |
| 220201 | Introductory economics | Econ | 104 | 4S | L |
| 220305 | Intro physical geography | Geog | 106 | 5S | L |
| 220409 | History American family | Hist | 542 | 3S | U |
| 220432 | Hist US through Civil War | Hist | 128 | 3S | L |
| 220433 | Hist US since Civil War | Hist | 129 | 3S | L |
| 220470 | Black exper in Americas | AfAmS | 106 | 3S | U |
| 220471 | Hist of American Indian | Hist | 619 | 3S | U |
| 220499 | History of art | ArHis | 200 | 3S | L |
| 220499 | Hist of Second World War | Hist | 440 | 3S | U |
| 220499 | History of Kansas | Hist | 620 | 3S | U |
| 220501 | Intro to US politics | PolSc | 110 | 3S | L |
| 220503 | Intro to compar politics | PolSc | 150 | 3S | L |
| 220507 | Library res public policy | PolSc | 190 | 1S | L |
| 220602 | Causation of crime & deli | Soc | 661 | 3S | U |
| 220606 | Elements of sociology | Soc | 104 | 3S | L |
| 220612 | Sociology of health & med | Soc | 624 | 3S | U |
| 220613 | Sociology of aging | Soc | 523 | 3S | U |
| 220699 | Socio prob & Amer values | Soc | 160 | 3S | L |

(44) **UNIVERSITY OF KENTUCKY**

Dr. Earl Pfanstiel .
Director of Independent Study
Room 1, Frazee Hall
Independent Studies
University of Kentucky
Lexington, Kentucky 40506
Phone: 606-257-3466

Enrollment on a noncredit basis accepted in all credit courses. Gifted high school students are permitted to enroll in undergraduate courses for credit. Overseas enrollment is not encouraged; each case is judged on an individual basis.

| NCES No. | Course Title | Dept. | Course No. | Credits | Level |
|---|---|---|---|---|---|
| | **High School courses** | | | | |
| 040101 | Accounting I first half | BusHS | 01 | HF | H |
| 040101 | Accounting I second half | BusHS | 02 | HF | H |
| 049900 | Business math second half | BusHS | 04 | HF | H |
| 049900 | Business law | BusHS | 06 | HF | H |
| 049900 | Gen business first half | BusHS | 07 | HF | H |
| 049900 | Gen business second half | BusHS | 08 | HF | H |
| 049900 | Business math first half | BusHS | 03 | HF | H |
| 059900 | Mass media/print/radio/TV | EngHS | 21 | HF | H |
| 100602 | Family studies first hf | FamHS | 60 | HF | H |
| 100602 | Family studies second hf | FamHS | 61 | HF | H |
| 120305 | Grammar grade 9 | Engl | 13 | HF | H |
| 120305 | Grammar grade 10 | Engl | 15 | HF | H |
| 120305 | Grammar grade 11 | Engl | 17 | HF | H |
| 120305 | Grammar grade 12 | Engl | 19 | HF | H |
| 120307 | Literature grade 9 | Engl | 14 | HF | H |

| NCES No. | Course Title | Dept. | Course No. | Credits | Level |
|---|---|---|---|---|---|
| 120307 | Literature grade 10 | Engl | 16 | HF | H |
| 120307 | Literature grade 11 | Engl | 18 | HF | H |
| 120307 | Literature grade 12 | Engl | 20 | HF | H |
| 1210 | French I, II, III, IV | LanHS | 26 | 1U | H |
| 1211 | German I, II, III, IV | LanHS | 24 | 1U | H |
| 1211 | Greek I | LanHS | 22 | 1U | H |
| 1216 | Latin I, II | LanHS | 23 | 1U | H |
| 1225 | Spanish I, II, III, IV | LanHS | 25 | 1U | H |
| 1503 | Gen biology first half | SciHS | 50 | HF | H |
| 1503 | Gen biology second half | SciHS | 51 | HF | H |
| 1509 | Earth science first half | SciHS | 52 | HF | H |
| 1509 | Earth science second half | SciHS | 53 | HF | H |
| 160301 | General math first half | MatHS | 29 | HF | H |
| 160302 | General math second half | MatHS | 30 | HF | H |
| 160302 | Algebra I first half | MatHS | 31 | HF | H |
| 160302 | Algebra I second half | MatHS | 32 | HF | H |
| 160302 | Algebra II first half | MatHS | 33 | HF | H |
| 160302 | Algebra II second half | MatHS | 34 | HF | H |
| 160401 | Precalculus first half | MathS | 37 | HF | H |
| 160401 | Precalculus second half | MathS | 38 | HF | H |
| 160601 | Plane geometry first half | MatHS | 35 | HF | H |
| 160601 | Plane geometry second hf | MatHS | 36 | HF | H |
| 160602 | Trigonomety | MathS | 39 | HF | H |
| 190509 | Personal-community health | Hlth | 27 | HF | H |
| 190509 | Pers-comm hlth second hf | Hlth | 28 | HF | H |
| 200502 | Psychology | Psych | 43 | HF | H |
| 220399 | World geog first half | Geog | 39 | HF | H |
| 220399 | World geog second half | Geog | 40 | HF | H |
| 220432 | US history first half | Hist | 41 | HF | H |
| 220432 | US history second half | Hist | 42 | HF | H |
| 220433 | World civilization 1st hf | SocSt | 46 | HF | H |
| 220433 | World civilization 2nd hf | SocSt | 47 | HF | H |
| 220502 | Civics first half | SocSt | 48 | HF | H |
| 220502 | Civics second half | SocSt | 49 | HF | H |
| 220601 | Sociology first half | SocHS | 44 | HF | H |
| 220601 | Sociology second half | SocHS | 45 | HF | H |

| NCES No. | Course Title | Dept. | Course No. | Credits | Level |
|---|---|---|---|---|---|
| | **College courses** | | | | |
| 010199 | Economics of food and agr | Agri | 101 | 3S | L |
| 010402 | Agri animal science | Agri | 106 | 4S | L |
| 010407 | Agri feeds and feeding | Agri | 380 | 3S | U |
| 010604 | Agri plant science | Agri | 104 | 4S | L |
| 010607 | Field crop production | Agri | 386 | 3S | U |
| 010703 | Soil science management | Agri | 366 | 3S | U |
| 010901 | Elements of forestry | Fores | 100 | 2S | L |
| 030303 | Introduction to music | Music | 200 | 3S | L |
| 040101 | Principles of accounting | Acctg | 201 | 3S | L |
| 040101 | Prin of accounting II | Acctg | 202 | 3S | L |
| 040201 | Office admin and services | BOE | 445 | 3S | U |
| 040205 | Theory of shorthand I | BOE | 112 | 3S | L |
| 040207 | Beginning typewriting | BOE | 117 | 3S | L |
| 040301 | Corporate finance | Fin | 300 | 3S | U |
| 040902 | Business management | Mgmt | 300 | 3S | U |
| 040903 | Organizational behavior | Mgmt | 410 | 3S | U |
| 041003 | Marketing management | Mkt | 300 | 3S | U |
| 041104 | Personnel and industrial | Mgmt | 320 | 3S | U |
| 049900 | Law, business and society | Mgmt | 340 | 3S | U |
| 049900 | Business law I | Mgmt | 341 | 3S | U |
| 049900 | Business law II | Mgmt | 441 | 3S | U |
| 050608 | Princ of news writing | Jrnl | 203 | 3S | L |
| 070516 | Math for elem teachers I | Math | 201 | 3S | L |
| 070516 | Math for elem teachers II | Math | 202 | 3S | L |
| 0899 | Engineering tech writing | Engl | 204 | 3S | L |
| 100103 | Clothing awareness select | HmEc | 337 | 3S | U |
| 100199 | Introduction to textiles | HmEc | 120 | 3S | L |
| 100399 | Food nutrition for man | HmEc | 101 | 3S | L |
| 100499 | Personal/family finance | HmEc | 251 | 3S | L |
| 100602 | Individual marriage & fam | HmEc | 252 | 3S | L |
| 110503 | Basic engineering graphcs | Graph | 105 | 2S | L |
| 120201 | Western lit Greeks–1660 | Engl | 261 | 3S | L |
| 120201 | Western lit 1660–present | Engl | 262 | 3S | L |
| 120201 | Lit Old Testament | Engl | 270 | 3S | L |
| 120201 | Lit New Testament | Engl | 271 | 3S | L |
| 120201 | Shakespeare survey | Engl | 425 | 3S | U |
| 120201 | American lit 1800-1860 | Engl | 451 | 3S | U |
| 120201 | American lit 1860-1900 | Engl | 452 | 3S | U |
| 120201 | Women in literature | Engl | 375 | 3S | U |
| 120303 | English lit survey I | Engl | 221 | 3S | L |
| 120303 | English lit survey II | Engl | 222 | 3S | L |
| 120310 | Freshman composition | Engl | 101 | 3S | L |
| 120310 | Advanced freshman comp | Engl | 102 | 3S | L |
| 120310 | Writing for industry | Engl | 203 | 3S | L |

| NCES No. | Course Title | Dept. | Course No. | Credits | Level |
|---|---|---|---|---|---|
| 120399 | Etymology | Engl | 201 | 3S | L |
| 120399 | Medical terminology | Engl | 131 | 3S | L |
| 1210 | Elementary French I | Frnch | 101 | 3S | L |
| 1210 | Elementary French II | Frnch | 102 | 3S | L |
| 1210 | Intermediate French I | Frnch | 201 | 3S | L |
| 1210 | Intermediate French II | Frnch | 202 | 3S | L |
| 1211 | Elementary German I | Ger | 111 | 3S | L |
| 1211 | Elementary German II | Ger | 112 | 3S | L |
| 1212 | Beginning Greek | Greek | 151 | 3S | L |
| 1212 | Intermediate German I | Ger | 201 | 3S | L |
| 1212 | Intermediate German II | Ger | 202 | 3S | L |
| 1216 | Elementary Latin I | Latin | 101 | 3S | L |
| 1216 | Elementary Latin II | Latin | 102 | 3S | L |
| 1225 | Elementary Spanish I | Span | 141 | 3S | L |
| 1225 | Elementary Spanish II | Span | 142 | 3S | L |
| 1225 | Intermediate Spanish I | Span | 241 | 3S | L |
| 1225 | Intermediate Spanish II | Span | 242 | 3S | L |
| 150199 | Descriptive astronomy I | Astro | 191 | 3S | L |
| 150199 | Descriptive astronomy II | Astro | 192 | 3S | L |
| 150301 | Human biology | Bio | 110 | 3S | L |
| 150306 | Evolution | Bio | 508 | 3S | U |
| 150307 | Principles of genetics | Bio | 404 | 3S | U |
| 150311 | Principles of microbiol | Bio | 108 | 3S | L |
| 150316 | Plant biology | Bio | 106 | 3S | L |
| 150323 | Animal biology | Bio | 104 | 3S | L |
| 150399 | Animal-plant microbiology | Bio | 103 | 3S | L |
| 150399 | Economic botany | Bio | 465 | 3S | U |
| 160302 | Remedial algebra | Math | 108R | 3S | L |
| 160302 | College algebra | Math | 109 | 3S | L |
| 160401 | Calculus I: integral | Math | 113 | 4S | L |
| 160401 | Calculus II: differential | Math | 114 | 4S | L |
| 160401 | Elementary calculus | Math | 123 | 3S | L |
| 160602 | Trigonometry | Math | 112 | 2S | L |
| 160801 | Descriptive statistics | Stat | 292 | 1S | L |
| 160899 | Probability | Stat | 293 | 1S | L |
| 160899 | Sampling and inference | Stat | 294 | 1S | L |
| 161101 | Mathematics of finance | Math | 121 | 3S | L |
| 180399 | Introductory ethics | Philo | 130 | 3S | L |
| 180405 | Asian philosophy | Philo | 343 | 3S | U |
| 180501 | Elementary logic | Philo | 120 | 3S | L |
| 1807 | Intro to philosophy | Philo | 100 | 3S | L |
| 200199 | Intro to psychology | Psych | 100 | 4S | L |
| 200501 | Abnormal psychology | Psych | 533 | 3S | U |
| 200504 | Developmental psychology | Psych | 223 | 3S | L |
| 200901 | Industrial psychology | Psych | 502 | 3S | U |
| 200902 | Personnel psychology | Psych | 503 | 3S | U |
| 210401 | Social welfare | SocW | 222 | 3S | L |
| 210402 | Social work profession | SocW | 322 | 4S | U |
| 220201 | Principles of economics I | Econ | 260 | 3S | L |
| 220201 | Prin of economics II | Econ | 261 | 3S | L |
| 220204 | Monetary economics | Econ | 485 | 3S | U |
| 220305 | Physical geography | Geog | 151 | 3S | L |
| 220306 | Regional geography | Geog | 152 | 3S | L |
| 220399 | Weather and climate | Geog | 251 | 3S | L |
| 220399 | Environmental geography | Geog | 210 | 3S | L |
| 220399 | Human geography | Geog | 252 | 3S | L |
| 220424 | British people I | Hist | 202 | 3S | L |
| 220424 | British people II | Hist | 203 | 3S | L |
| 220426 | History of Europe to 1713 | Hist | 104 | 3S | L |
| 220426 | Europe 1713 to present | Hist | 105 | 3S | L |
| 220432 | US history through 1865 | Hist | 108 | 3S | L |
| 220432 | US history since 1865 | Hist | 109 | 3S | L |
| 220432 | US history since 1939 | Hist | 566 | 3S | U |
| 220432 | Civil War 1860-1877 | Hist | 567 | 3S | U |
| 220432 | History of the Old South | Hist | 578 | 3S | U |
| 220432 | History of the New South | Hist | 579 | 3S | U |
| 220499 | Afro-Amer history to 1865 | Hist | 260 | 3S | L |
| 220499 | Afro-Amer hist from 1865 | Hist | 261 | 3S | L |
| 220499 | History of Kentucky | Hist | 240 | 3S | L |
| 220501 | American government | PolSc | 101 | 3S | L |
| 220507 | Political parties | PolSc | 470 | 3S | U |
| 220511 | State government | PolSc | 255 | 3S | L |
| 220511 | Municipal government | PolSc | 452 | 3S | U |
| 220601 | The community | Socio | 220 | 3S | L |
| 220602 | Criminology | Socio | 437 | 3S | U |
| 220604 | Juvenile delinquency | Socio | 538 | 3S | U |
| 220605 | The family | Socio | 409 | 3S | U |
| 220606 | Introductory sociology | Socio | 101 | 3S | L |
| 220609 | Relations in administratn | Socio | 542 | 3S | U |
| 220609 | Dimensions of aging | Socio | 528 | 3S | U |
| 220610 | Deviant behavior | Socio | 436 | 3S | U |
| 220613 | Modern social problems | Socio | 152 | 3S | L |

## (45) UNIVERSITY OF MICHIGAN

Mr. Alfred W. Storey
Director of Extension Service
Department of Independent Study
University of Michigan
200 Hill Street
Ann Arbor, Michigan 48104
Phone: 313-764-5306

Enrollment on a noncredit basis accepted in all credit courses. Gifted high school students are permitted to enroll in undergraduate courses for credit. Overseas enrollment accepted.

| NCES No. | Course Title | Dept. | Course No. | Credits | Level |
|---|---|---|---|---|---|
| | **High School courses** | | | | |
| 040205 | Beginning shorthand | BusEd | 016N | HF | H |
| | **College courses** | | | | |
| 0199 | The environ & the citizen | NatrS | 485 | 2S | B |
| 0199 | The environ & the citizen | NatrS | 486 | 2S | B |
| 030399 | Topics in Amer cult: jazz | AmCul | 301 | 3S | L |
| 040101 | Principles of accounting | Acctg | 271 | 3S | L |
| 050299 | Tech & prof writing | Hums | 498 | 3S | U |
| 050399 | Intro to film | Spch | 220 | 3S | L |
| 070499 | Psych of tchg rdg & writg | Educ | C510 | 3S | B |
| 070512 | Tchng Engl as a for lang | Educ | D4481 | 2S | B |
| 090119 | Intro to physiology | Phys | 101 | 3S | L |
| 120304 | Lit & cult of Ireland | Engl | 317 | 3S | L |
| 120304 | Contemporary Am novel | Engl | 434 | 3S | U |
| 120307 | Great Books | GrBks | 201 | 4S | L |
| 120399 | Teach Eng as a forgn lang | Educ | D448 | 3S | B |
| 120399 | Major American authors | Engl | 475 | 3S | U |
| 120399 | Contemporary poetry | Engl | 441 | 3S | U |
| 1210 | First special rdg course | Fren | 111 | 4S | B |
| 1210 | Second special rdg course | Fren | 112 | 4S | B |
| 1211 | First special rdg course | Ger | 111 | 4S | B |
| 1211 | Second special rdg course | Ger | 112 | 4S | B |
| 1299 | Asia through fiction | As St | 441 | 3S | L |
| 160306 | Elementary linear algebra | Math | 117 | 2S | L |
| 160399 | Algebra & analyt trig | Math | 105 | 4S | L |
| 160602 | Analyt geom & calculus I | Math | 115 | 4S | L |
| 160602 | Analyt geom & calculus II | Math | 116 | 3S | L |
| 2099 | Intro to psychology | Psych | 172 | 4S | L |
| 2099 | Psychology of aging | Psych | 459 | 3S | U |
| 2099 | Intro to behavior modific | Psych | 474 | 3S | B |
| 220201 | Principles of economics | Econ | 201 | 4S | L |
| 220499 | Pales & Arab-Israeli conf | Hist | 592 | 3S | B |
| 2299 | Intro to women's studies | WmSt | 240 | 4S | L |
| 2299 | Cross-disci studies | WmSt | 342 | 3S | L |
| 2299 | Women and the arts | WmSt | 344 | 3S | L |
| | **Noncredit courses** | | | | |
| 0199 | The environ & the citizen | NatrS | 485 | NC | |
| 0199 | The environ & the citizen | NatrS | 486 | NC | |
| 040601 | Pract wrtg for business | BuC | I | NC | |
| 050605 | Writing nonfiction | Journ | 1 | NC | |
| 050605 | Wrtg fiction for mags | Journ | 2 | NC | |
| 070512 | Tchng Engl as a for lang | Educ | 04481 | NC | |
| 1199 | Fire service inst traing | Fire | I | NC | |
| 120307 | Great Books | GrBks | 201 | NC | |

## (46) UNIVERSITY OF MINNESOTA

Ms. Deborah Nelson
Associate Director of Independent Study
45 Wesbrook Hall
University of Minnesota
77 Pleasant Street, SE
Minneapolis, Minnesota 55455
Phone: 612-373-3803

Gifted high school students are permitted to enroll in undergraduate courses for credit. Overseas enrollment accepted.

| NCES No. | Course Title | Dept. | Course No. | Credits | Level |
|---|---|---|---|---|---|
| | **High School courses** | | | | |
| 040101 | Fundmntls of accountg A | Bus | 9813 | HF | H |
| 040101 | Fundmntls of accountg B | Bus | 9814 | HF | H |

| NCES No. | Course Title | Dept. | Course No. | Credits | Level |
|---|---|---|---|---|---|
| 040205 | Shorthand | Bus | 9901 | HF | H |
| 0499 | General business A | Bus | 9821 | HF | H |
| 0499 | General business B | Bus | 9822 | HF | H |
| 1299 | Ninth-grade English A | Engl | 9831 | HF | H |
| 1299 | Ninth-grade English B | Engl | 9832 | HF | H |
| 1299 | Tenth-grade English A | Engl | 9833 | HF | H |
| 1299 | Tenth-grade English B | Engl | 9834 | HF | H |
| 1299 | Eleventh-grade English A | Engl | 9835 | HF | H |
| 1299 | Eleventh-grade English B | Engl | 9836 | HF | H |
| 1299 | Twelfth-grade English A | Engl | 9847 | HF | H |
| 1299 | Twelfth-grade English B | Engl | 9848 | HF | H |
| 1299 | Straight thinking | Engl | 9839 | QT | H |
| 1299 | Youth in conflict | Engl | 9840 | QT | H |
| 1299 | Meaning/self-discov–lit | Engl | 9841 | QT | H |
| 1299 | Practical writing | Engl | 9842 | QT | H |
| 1299 | Advanced composition | Engl | 9845 | QT | H |
| 1299 | Comparative mythology | Engl | 9844 | QT | H |
| 1299 | Contemp lit and problems | Engl | 9843 | HF | H |
| 1299 | Black American experience | Engl | 9919 | QT | H |
| 1299 | American dream and drama | Engl | 9846 | HF | H |
| 1299 | Creative writing | Engl | 9849 | HF | H |
| 150399 | Biology A | Bio | 9801 | HF | H |
| 150399 | Biology B | Bio | 9802 | HF | H |
| 150899 | Physical science | Phys | 9891 | HF | H |
| 160199 | Math for consumer: basics | Math | 9881 | QT | H |
| 160199 | Math for consumer:banking | Math | 9882 | QT | H |
| 160199 | Math for consumer:spendng | Math | 9883 | QT | H |
| 160199 | Math for consumer:problms | Math | 9884 | QT | H |
| 160302 | Elementary algebra A | Math | 9871 | HF | H |
| 160302 | Elementary algebra B | Math | 9871 | HF | H |
| 160302 | Higher algebra A | Math | 9885 | HF | H |
| 160302 | Higher algebra B | Math | 9886 | HF | H |
| 160601 | Geometry A | Math | 9887 | HF | H |
| 160601 | Geometry B | Math | 9888 | HF | H |
| 160602 | Trigonometry | Math | 9876 | HF | H |
| 200399 | Environmental survival | Psych | 9894 | HF | H |
| 2099 | General psychology A | Psych | 9941 | HF | H |
| 2099 | General psychology B | Psych | 9942 | HF | H |
| 220432 | American history B | Hist | 9923 | HF | H |
| 220432 | American history A | Hist | 9922 | HF | H |
| 220433 | World history A | Hist | 9920 | HF | H |
| 220433 | World history B | Hist | 9921 | HF | H |
| 220501 | Probs of Amer democracy A | PolSc | 9911 | HF | H |
| 220501 | Probs of Amer democracy B | PolSc | 9912 | HF | H |

**College courses**

| NCES No. | Course Title | Dept. | Course No. | Credits | Level |
|---|---|---|---|---|---|
| 010103 | Agriculture mkts & prices | Agri | 1400 | 4Q | L |
| 010499 | Principles of beekeeping | AnSci | 0004C | 3V | L |
| 010499 | Horse production | AnSc | 1600 | 4Q | L |
| 010504 | Home landscape design | Hort | 1010 | 3Q | L |
| 010504 | Residential landscp desig | Hort | 3026 | 4Q | U |
| 0114 | Conserv of nat resources | For | 1201 | 3Q | L |
| 030302 | Ear trng & sight singing | Music | 1501 | 4Q | L |
| 030302 | Music appreciation | Music | 5950 | 4Q | L |
| 030402 | Hist of American theatre | Th | 5186 | 4Q | U |
| 030499 | Playwriting | Th | 5115 | 4Q | U |
| 030599 | Basic craft skills | ArHis | 1048 | 4Q | L |
| 0399 | Art in Western civilizati | ArHis | 1015 | 4Q | L |
| 040101 | Principles of acctg I | Acctg | 1024 | 3Q | L |
| 040101 | Principles of acctg II | Acctg | 1025 | 3Q | L |
| 040101 | Principles of acctg III | Acctg | 1026 | 3Q | L |
| 040101 | Accounting fundamentals I | GC | 1540 | 4Q | L |
| 040101 | Acct Fundamentals II | GC | 1542 | 4Q | L |
| 040114 | Income tax accounting | Acctg | 5135 | 4Q | U |
| 040302 | Consumer problems | Bus | 1731 | 5Q | L |
| 040302 | Personal finance | Bus | 1731 | 4Q | L |
| 040501 | Small business operations | Bus | 1513 | 4Q | L |
| 040703 | Estate planning | GC | 3583 | 4Q | U |
| 040710 | Risk mgmt and insurance | Ins | 3100 | 4Q | U |
| 041001 | Principles of marketing | Mktg | 3000 | 3Q | U |
| 0411 | Personnel administration | GC | 3560 | 4Q | U |
| 041106 | Applied supervision | GC | 3602 | 4Q | U |
| 041199 | Development administratn | PA | 5401 | 4Q | U |
| 0499 | Intro to modern business | Bus | 1511 | 5Q | L |
| 050199 | Principles of advertising | Jrnl | 1201 | 4Q | L |
| 0506 | Intro to mass communicatn | Jrnl | 1001 | 2Q | L |
| 050606 | History of journalism | Jrnl | 5601 | 4Q | U |
| 050699 | Communic & public opinion | Jrnl | 5501 | 4Q | U |
| 050699 | Mass media in dynamic soc | Jrnl | 5721 | 4Q | U |
| 050699 | Magazine writing | Jour | 3173 | 4Q | U |
| 051299 | Parliamentary procedure | Commu | 1226 | 1Q | L |
| 060199 | Intro to data processing | GC | 1535 | 3Q | L |

| NCES No. | Course Title | Dept. | Course No. | Credits | Level |
|---|---|---|---|---|---|
| 060404 | Microprocessors | EE | 3352 | 4Q | U |
| 060799 | Block diagram & programmg | CmpSc | 1572 | 5Q | L |
| 061104 | Data processing | GC | 1533 | 2Q | L |
| 070102 | Crit issues–contemp educ | Educ | 5141 | 3Q | U |
| 070199 | Intro to philos of educ | | EDUC | 4Q | L |
| 070199 | School and society | Educ | 3090 | 3Q | U |
| 070299 | Personal time management | Educ | 5128 | 2Q | U |
| 071199 | Intro to statistics | Educ | 3102 | 3Q | U |
| 0799 | How to study | Educ | 1001 | 2Q | L |
| 0799 | Efficient reading | Educ | 1147 | 3Q | L |
| 0799 | Vocabulary building | GC | 1401 | 3Q | L |
| 0799 | Multidisc aspects aging | Educ | 5440 | 4Q | U |
| 080399 | Amer architecture to 1860 | AmSt | 3970 | 4Q | U |
| 080999 | Logic and design | EE | 3351 | 4Q | U |
| 081502 | Indust rel: manpwr mgmt | IR | 3012 | 4Q | U |
| 081503 | Work measurment standards | IEOR | 0103 | 5V | L |
| 081599 | Supervision I | IR | 0001C | 3V | L |
| 081599 | Indust rel: labor mktg | IR | 3002 | 4Q | U |
| 081999 | Soils engineering | EngAS | 0001C | 4V | L |
| 081999 | Concrete materials | EngAS | 0302C | 3V | L |
| 090118 | Intelligent self medicat | Phar | 3001 | 2Q | U |
| 090199 | Aspects phys disability | HSU | 5008 | 4Q | U |
| 090199 | Multidisc aspects aging | HSU | 5009 | 4Q | U |
| 090706 | Child abuse & neglect | PubHl | 5642 | 3Q | U |
| 100301 | Tech of food processing | FScN | 1102 | 4Q | L |
| 100602 | Parent-child relationship | GC | 1722 | 4Q | L |
| 100602 | Minority families | FSoS | 3240 | 4Q | U |
| 100602 | Family stress & coping | FSoS | 5240 | 3Q | U |
| 100604 | Dating/courtship/marriage | FSoS | 1001 | 3Q | L |
| 100604 | Parenting: altern for 80s | FSoS | 5240 | 4Q | U |
| 100604 | American families in tran | FSoS | 5230 | 4Q | U |
| 100699 | Human sexual behavior | FSoS | 5001 | 4Q | U |
| 1199 | Hazardous mat & processes | FPro | 0002C | 3V | L |
| 1199 | Hazardous mat & processes | FPro | 0003C | 3V | L |
| 1199 | Hazardous mat & processes | FPro | 0004C | 3V | L |
| 1199 | Fire prevention & control | FPro | 0005C | 3V | L |
| 1199 | Life safety systems | FPro | 0006C | 3V | L |
| 1199 | Private fire prot systems | FPro | 0007C | 3V | L |
| 1199 | Private fire prot systems | FPro | 0008C | 3V | L |
| 1199 | Fire dept administration | FPro | 0009C | 3V | L |
| 120201 | European folk tales | Engl | 5414 | 4Q | U |
| 120299 | Ellery Queen detect stor | AmSt | 1920 | 4Q | U |
| 120299 | American popular culture | AmSt | 3920 | 4Q | U |
| 120299 | Tech terms–science med | Clas | 1048 | 3Q | L |
| 120299 | Magic/witchcraft/occult | Clas | 1019 | 4Q | L |
| 120299 | Religion: Greek & Helleni | Clas | 3071 | 4Q | U |
| 120299 | Madness/dev behav Greece | Clas | 5005 | 4Q | U |
| 120299 | Intro to mod lit: poetry | Engl | 1017 | 4Q | L |
| 120299 | Intro to mod lit: drama | Engl | 1019 | 4Q | L |
| 120299 | Intro to literature I | Engl | 1821 | 4Q | L |
| 120299 | Shakespeare I | Engl | 3241 | 4Q | U |
| 120299 | Shakespeare II | Engl | 3242 | 4Q | U |
| 120299 | American literature I | Engl | 3411 | 4Q | U |
| 120299 | American literature II | Engl | 3412 | 4Q | U |
| 120299 | American literature III | Engl | 3413 | 4Q | U |
| 120299 | 20th-century Engl novel | Engl | 5153 | 4Q | U |
| 120299 | Chaucer | Engl | 5221 | 4Q | U |
| 120299 | Literature for children | Engl | 1363 | 4Q | L |
| 120299 | Afro-American literature | Engl | 1816 | 3Q | L |
| 120299 | Reading short stories | Engl | 1371 | 3Q | L |
| 120299 | Philosophy through lit | Engl | 3352 | 4Q | U |
| 120299 | Humanities in mod world I | Hum | 1101 | 3Q | L |
| 120299 | Hum in modern world II | Hum | 1002 | 5Q | L |
| 120299 | Hum in modern world III | Hum | 1103 | 3Q | L |
| 120299 | Hum in modern world IV | Hum | 1104 | 3Q | L |
| 120299 | European heritage: Greece | Hum | 1011 | 5Q | L |
| 120299 | European heritage: Rome | Hum | 1012 | 5Q | L |
| 120299 | Mod sci fiction & fantasy | Engl | 1005 | 4Q | L |
| 120299 | Survey English lit I | Engl | 3111 | 4Q | U |
| 120299 | Survey English lit II | Engl | 3113 | 4Q | U |
| 120299 | American short story | Engl | 3455 | 4Q | U |
| 120299 | Am lit:major fig & themes | Engl | 1016 | 4Q | L |
| 120299 | Survey English lit II | Engl | 3112 | 4Q | U |
| 120307 | Nature writers | Engl | 3920 | 4Q | U |
| 120307 | Celtic world | Engl | 3910 | 4Q | U |
| 120307 | Modern drama: Piran-Pintr | Engl | 5175 | 4Q | U |
| 120310 | Intermed composition | Commu | 1027 | 4Q | L |
| 120310 | Fiction writing | Engl | 3101 | 4Q | U |
| 120310 | Business writing | Commu | 1531 | 4Q | L |
| 120310 | Business writing | Commu | 3531 | 4Q | U |
| 120310 | Journal & memoir writing | Engl | 5109 | 4Q | U |
| 120310 | Writing for publication | GC | 3484 | 4Q | U |

| NCES No. | Course Title | Dept. | Course No. | Credits | Level |
|---|---|---|---|---|---|
| 120310 | Writing practice I | Comp | 1011 | 5Q | L |
| 120310 | Writing about literature | Comp | 3011 | 4Q | U |
| 120310 | Writing about nonfiction | Comp | 3012 | 4Q | U |
| 120310 | Writing about science | Comp | 3012 | 4Q | U |
| 120310 | Writing for arts | Comp | 3013 | 4Q | U |
| 120310 | Writing for social scienc | Comp | | 4Q | U |
| 120310 | Advanced expository writi | Comp | 3027 | 4Q | U |
| 120310 | Tech writing for engineer | Comp | 3031 | 4Q | U |
| 120310 | Writing for business | Comp | 3032 | 4Q | U |
| 1207 | Religions in East Asia | Chi | 1032 | 4Q | L |
| 1207 | Asian civ: China | Chi | 3501 | 4Q | U |
| 1209 | Beginning Finnish I | Fin | 1101 | 5Q | L |
| 1210 | Beginning French I | Frnch | 1101 | 5Q | L |
| 1210 | Beginning French II | Frnch | 1102 | 5Q | L |
| 1210 | Beginning French III | Frnch | 1103 | 5Q | L |
| 1210 | French literary texts | Frnch | 3104 | 5Q | U |
| 1211 | Beginning German I | Ger | 1101 | 5Q | L |
| 1211 | Beginning German II | Ger | 1102 | 5Q | L |
| 1211 | Beginning German III | Ger | 1103 | 5Q | L |
| 1211 | Intermediate German | Ger | 1301 | 5Q | L |
| 1211 | Ger lit: Heinrich Böll | Ger | 1101 | 4Q | L |
| 1212 | Beginning classical Greek | Greek | 1101 | 5Q | L |
| 1214 | Beginning Italian I | Ital | 1101 | 5Q | L |
| 1215 | Religions of East Asia | Jap | 1032 | 4Q | L |
| 1216 | Beginning Latin I | CILL | 1101 | 5Q | L |
| 1216 | Beginning Latin II | CILL | 1102 | 5Q | L |
| 1216 | Beginning Latin III | CILL | 1103 | 5Q | L |
| 1216 | Cicero | CILL | 3105 | 3Q | U |
| 1216 | Vergil: *Aeneid* | CILL | 3106 | 5Q | U |
| 1216 | Latin readings | CILL | 1104 | 5Q | L |
| 1218 | Beginning Norwegian I | Nor | 1101 | 5Q | L |
| 1218 | Beginning Norwegian II | Nor | 1102 | 5Q | L |
| 1220 | Beginning Russian I | Rus. | 1101 | 5Q | L |
| 1220 | Beginning Russian II | Rus. | 1102 | 5Q | L |
| 1220 | Beginning Russian III | Rus. | 1103 | 5Q | L |
| 1220 | Scientific Russian I | Rus. | 1221 | 5Q | L |
| 1220 | Scientific Russian II | Rus. | 1222 | 2Q | L |
| 1220 | Scientific Russian III | Rus. | 1223 | 2Q | L |
| 1225 | Beginning Spanish I | Span | 1101 | 5Q | L |
| 1225 | Beginning Spanish II | Span | 1102 | 5Q | L |
| 1225 | Beginning Spanish III | Span | 1103 | 5Q | L |
| 1225 | Intermediate Spanish | Span | 1104 | 4Q | L |
| 1225 | Reading and composition | Span | 1105 | 5Q | L |
| 1225 | Civ: pre-Colamb to 1825 | Span | 1502 | 4Q | L |
| 1226 | Beginning Swedish I | Swed | 1101 | 5Q | L |
| 1226 | Beginning Swedish II | Swed | 1102 | 5Q | L |
| 1299 | Beginning Polish I | Plsh | 1101 | 5Q | L |
| 1299 | Modern Judaism | JwSt | 3126 | 4Q | U |
| 1299 | The Holocaust | JwSt | 3521 | 4Q | U |
| 1299 | Tales of H C Andersen | Scan | 3602 | 4Q | U |
| 130202 | Law of contracts & agency | Law | 3058 | 4Q | U |
| 130703 | Partner corp & real prope | Law | 3078 | 4Q | U |
| 130907 | Personal prop wills & est | Law | 3088 | 4Q | U |
| 131504 | Legal writing | GC | 3532 | 4Q | U |
| 1399 | Law in society | Law | 1235 | 5Q | L |
| 1399 | Practical law | Law | 1534 | 5Q | L |
| 150102 | Solar astronomy | Astro | 1161 | 5Q | L |
| 150103 | Stellar astronomy | Astro | 1162 | 5Q | L |
| 1503 | General biology | Bio | 1011 | 5Q | L |
| 150304 | Intro to ecology | EnvD | 3001 | 4Q | U |
| 150401 | Principles of chemistry | GC | 1166 | 5Q | L |
| 150599 | Physical geology | Geol | 1001 | 5Q | L |
| 150599 | Historical geology | Geol | 1006 | 3Q | L |
| 1507 | General physics | Phys | 1104 | 4Q | L |
| 1507 | General physics | Phys | 1105 | 4Q | L |
| 1507 | General physics | Phys | 1106 | 4Q | L |
| 150799 | Introduction to physics | Phys | 1031 | 5Q | L |
| 150799 | Introduction to physics | Phys | 1032 | 5Q | L |
| 150799 | General physics | Phys | 1281 | 4Q | L |
| 150799 | General physics | Phys | 1291 | 4Q | L |
| 150799 | General physics | Phys | 1271 | 4Q | L |
| 1508 | Changing physical world | Phys | 1003 | 4Q | U |
| 160199 | Precalculus | Math | 1201 | 5Q | L |
| 160302 | Intermediate algebra | GC | 1445 | 5Q | L |
| 160304 | College alg/analyt geom | Math | 1111 | 5Q | L |
| 160306 | Linear alg & lin diff equ | Math | 3221 | 5Q | U |
| 160401 | Intro to calculus | Math | 1142 | 5Q | L |
| 160402 | Analysis IV | Math | 3211 | 5Q | U |
| 160406 | Differential equations | Math | 3066 | 4Q | U |
| 160412 | Analysis I | Math | 1211 | 5Q | L |
| 160412 | Analysis II | Math | 1221 | 5Q | L |
| 160412 | Analysis III | Math | 1231 | 5Q | L |
| 160602 | Trigonometry | Math | 1008 | 3Q | L |
| 1608 | Intro to statistics | Stat | 1051 | 4Q | L |
| 180301 | Moral choices–contemp so | GC | 3355 | 4Q | U |
| 180399 | Ethics | GC | 1355 | 4Q | L |
| 180401 | Greek philosophy-history | Philo | 3001 | 5Q | U |
| 180402 | Descartes through Hume | Philo | 3003 | 5Q | U |
| 180403 | Kant through Nietzsche | Philo | 3004 | 5Q | U |
| 180501 | Logic | Philo | 1001 | 3Q | L |
| 180999 | Religions of East Asia | Relig | 1032 | 4Q | L |
| 181099 | Psychical phenom in relig | Relig | 3521 | 4Q | U |
| 181101 | Science and religion | Philo | 1011 | 4Q | L |
| 181103 | Women and religion | WoSt | 5123 | 4Q | L |
| 200501 | Abnormal psychology | Psych | 3604 | 4Q | U |
| 200501 | Underst & behavior disor | Psy | 5604 | 4Q | U |
| 200504 | Psych of human developmnt | Psych | 1283 | 5Q | L |
| 200504 | Maturity and aging | CPsy | 3304 | 4Q | U |
| 200504 | Infancy | CPsy | 3302 | 4Q | U |
| 200507 | Aspects phys disability | PMR | 5445 | 4Q | U |
| 200509 | Intro to personality | Psych | 3101 | 4Q | U |
| 200599 | Child psychology | Psych | 1301 | 4Q | L |
| 200599 | Adolescent psychology | Psych | 5303 | 4Q | U |
| 200599 | Multidisc aspects aging | CPsy | 5305 | 4Q | U |
| 200804 | Intelligence | EdPsy | 5110 | 3Q | U |
| 2099 | General psychology | Psych | 1001 | 5Q | L |
| 210405 | Family stress & coping | SWk | 8203 | 3Q | U |
| 220102 | Intro to soc & cult anthr | Anthr | 1102 | 5Q | L |
| 220102 | Culture and personality | Anthr | 5141 | 5Q | U |
| 220199 | Indians of North America | Anthr | 3211 | 5Q | U |
| 220199 | Human origins | Anth | 1101 | 5Q | L |
| 220201 | Principles of macroeconom | Econ | 1001 | 4Q | L |
| 220201 | Principles of microeconom | Econ | 1002 | 4Q | L |
| 220204 | Money and banking | Econ | 3701 | 4Q | U |
| 220211 | Labor mkt behav & regulat | Econ | 5537 | 4Q | U |
| 220299 | Macroeconomic theory | Econ | 3102 | 4Q | U |
| 220299 | Economic security | Econ | 5534 | 4Q | U |
| 220306 | Geog of US and Canada | Geog | 3101 | 4Q | U |
| 220306 | Geog of Minnesota | Geog | 3111 | 4Q | U |
| 220306 | Geog of South America | Geog | 3121 | 4Q | U |
| 220306 | Geog of USSR | Geog | 3181 | 4Q | U |
| 220306 | Minnesota resources | Geog | 3841 | 4Q | U |
| 220399 | Environmental problems | Geog | 3355 | 4Q | U |
| 220420 | African history | Hist | 1433 | 4Q | L |
| 220423 | Asian civilizations | Hist | 3452 | 4Q | U |
| 220423 | Asian civilizations | Hist | 3453 | 4Q | U |
| 220423 | Asian civilizations | Hist | 3451 | 4Q | U |
| 220426 | English history | Hist | 3151 | 4Q | U |
| 220426 | English history | Hist | 3152 | 4Q | U |
| 220426 | Dipl hist Eur: 19th-20th | Hist | 5284 | 4Q | U |
| 220426 | Dipl hist Eur: 19th-20th | Hist | 5285 | 4Q | U |
| 220426 | Dipl hist Eur: 19th-20th | Hist | 5286 | 4Q | U |
| 220426 | Europe during World W ll | Hist | 3224 | 4Q | U |
| 220428 | Minnesota history | GC | 1221 | 5Q | L |
| 220428 | Local history | Hist | 3955 | 4Q | U |
| 220432 | American history | Hist | 1301 | 4Q | L |
| 220432 | American history | Hist | 1302 | 4Q | L |
| 220450 | Ancient civilization I | Hist | 1051 | 3Q | L |
| 220450 | Ancient civilization II | Hist | 1052 | 3Q | L |
| 220450 | Ancient civilization III | Hist | 1053 | 3Q | L |
| 220450 | Readings in ancient civ | Hist | 1061 | 2Q | L |
| 220450 | Readings in ancient civ | Hist | 1062 | 2Q | L |
| 220450 | Readings in ancient civ | Hist | 1063 | 2Q | L |
| 220450 | Ancient Near East I | Hist | 5051 | 3Q | U |
| 220450 | Ancient Near East II | Hist | 5052 | 3Q | U |
| 220450 | Ancient Near East III | Hist | 5053 | 3Q | U |
| 220453 | Intro mod European hist | Hist | 1001 | 4Q | L |
| 220453 | Intro mod European hist | Hist | 1002 | 4Q | L |
| 220453 | Intro mod European hist | Hist | 1003 | 4Q | L |
| 220501 | American govt & politics | PolSc | 1001 | 5Q | L |
| 220504 | World politics | PolSc | 1025 | 3Q | L |
| 220507 | Political parties | PolSc | 5737 | 4Q | U |
| 220599 | American foreign policy | PolSc | 1026 | 4Q | U |
| 220599 | Govt & pol of Sov Union | PolSc | 5443 | 4Q | U |
| 220599 | Govt & pol–African count | PolSc | 5448 | 4Q | U |
| 220599 | Chinese govt and politics | PolSc | 5454 | 4Q | U |
| 220601 | American community | Socio | 1002 | 4Q | L |
| 220602 | Elements of criminology | Socio | 3103 | 4Q | U |
| 220603 | World population problems | Soc | 3551 | 4Q | U |
| 220607 | Intro to soc psychology | Socio | 5201 | 4Q | U |
| 220610 | Crime & justice in Amer | GC | 1236 | 4Q | L |
| 220699 | Introduction to sociology | Socio | 1001 | 4Q | L |
| 220699 | Death in America | Socio | 5960 | 4Q | U |
| 220699 | Soc of law & soc control | Soc | 3102 | 4Q | U |

| NCES No. | Course Title | Dept. | Course No. | Credits | Level |
|---|---|---|---|---|---|
| 220699 | Analytical social theory | Soc | 5701 | 4Q | U |
| 220699 | Multidisc aspects aging | Soc | 5960 | 4Q | U |
| | **Noncredit courses** | | | | |
| 030499 | Independent playwriting | ThArt | 0001 | NC | |
| 120310 | Preparatory composition | Commu | 0001 | NC | |
| 120310 | Grammar review | Commu | 0002 | NC | |
| 120310 | Writing of poetry | Commu | 0011 | NC | |
| 120310 | Advanced writg of poetry | Commu | 0012 | NC | |
| 120310 | Independent writing | Commu | 0017 | NC | |
| 120310 | Short manuscript criticsm | Commu | 0018 | NC | |
| 1210 | French for grad students | Frnch | 0001 | NC | |
| 1211 | German for grad students | Ger | 0221 | NC | |
| 1211 | German for grad students | Ger | 0222 | NC | |
| 1225 | Spanish for grad students | Span | 0221 | NC | |
| 160399 | Basic mathematics | Math | 0001 | NC | |
| 160399 | Basic mathematics | Math | 0002 | NC | |
| 160399 | Basic mathematics | Math | 0003 | NC | |
| 160399 | Basic mathematics | Math | 0004 | NC | |

## ㊼ UNIVERSITY OF MISSISSIPPI

Ms. Christine S. White
Coordinator of Independent Study
Department of Independent Study
University of Mississippi
Division of Continuing Education
University, Mississippi 38677
Phone: 601-232-7313

Enrollment on a noncredit basis accepted in some credit courses. Gifted high school students are permitted to enroll in undergraduate courses for credit. Overseas enrollment accepted for college courses. This department does not offer an external degree program.

| NCES No. | Course Title | Dept. | Course No. | Credits | Level |
|---|---|---|---|---|---|
| | **College courses** | | | | |
| 030302 | History of music | Music | 202 | 3S | L |
| 030302 | Music literature I | Music | 101 | 3S | L |
| 030399 | Opera | Music | 203 | 1S | L |
| 030402 | Survey of theatre history | ThArt | 321 | 3S | U |
| 030402 | Survey of theatre history | ThArt | 322 | 3S | U |
| 030502 | Art appreciation | Art | 281 | 3S | L |
| 030602 | Mat and tech of painter | Art | 105 | 1S | L |
| 040101 | Intro to accounting prin | Acctg | 201 | 3S | L |
| 040101 | Intro to accounting prin | Acctg | 202 | 3S | L |
| 040199 | Administrative accounting | Acctg | 301 | 3S | U |
| 040199 | Children's lit, K-8 | LibSc | 301 | 3S | U |
| 040201 | Admin practices & proced | OfAdm | 561 | 3S | U |
| 040206 | Office procedures | OfAdm | 351 | 3S | U |
| 040308 | Money and banking | Econ | 303 | 3S | U |
| 040308 | Money and banking | Fin | 303 | 3S | U |
| 040601 | Business communication | OfAdm | 271 | 3S | L |
| 040604 | Business reports | OfAdm | 372 | 3S | U |
| 040799 | Risk and insurance | Fin | 341 | 3S | U |
| 040902 | Found of voc bus educ | BusEd | 201 | 3S | L |
| 041001 | Marketing principles | Mktg | 351 | 3S | U |
| 041099 | Buyer-seller comm | Mktg | 354 | 3S | U |
| 041099 | Intro to retailing | Mktg | 361 | 3S | U |
| 041301 | Real estate valuatn & app | Fin | 353 | 3S | U |
| 041306 | Real estate fin mort bank | Fin | 355 | 3S | U |
| 041309 | Principles of real estate | Fin | 351 | 3S | U |
| 050199 | Intro to advertising | Mktg | 353 | 3S | U |
| 050699 | School publications | SecEd | 528 | 3S | U |
| 050699 | Intro to advertising | Jrnl | 385 | 3S | U |
| 050699 | School publications | Jrnl | 399 | 3S | U |
| 051199 | Ana and phy speech hear | ComDi | 205 | 3S | L |
| 061199 | Computer science survey | CmpSc | 103 | 3S | L |
| 070499 | Pub sch curriculum | SecEd | 401 | 3S | U |
| 070520 | Psychology of adolescence | Educ | 309 | 3S | U |
| 070522 | Science in the elem sch | ElEd | 303 | 3S | U |
| 070522 | Soc studies in the el sch | ElEd | 401 | 3S | U |
| 070599 | Arith in the elem school | ElEd | 403 | 3S | U |
| 070602 | Career education | Culns | 300 | 3S | U |
| 070610 | Found of elem reading | Read | 300 | 3S | U |
| 070610 | Tchng rdng in elem school | Read | 415 | 3S | U |
| 070610 | Diagnostic tchng of readg | Read | 417 | 3S | U |
| 070610 | Readg in the sec school | Read | 429 | 3S | U |
| 070701 | Principles of guidance | Educ | 539 | 3S | U |

| NCES No. | Course Title | Dept. | Course No. | Credits | Level |
|---|---|---|---|---|---|
| 070799 | Psyc of human grwth & dev | Educ | 333 | 3S | U |
| 0708 | Survey of except children | SpEd | 201 | 3S | L |
| 071199 | Elem statistics in educ | EdRes | 501 | 3S | U |
| 100313 | Nutrition | HmEc | 311 | 3S | U |
| 100601 | Child development | ElEd | 305 | 3S | U |
| 100601 | Child care and developmnt | HmEc | 321 | 3S | U |
| 100602 | Marriage and family rel | HmEc | 325 | 3S | U |
| 100699 | Human sexuality | HmEc | 435 | 3S | U |
| 120199 | Ana and phy speech hear | Ling | 205 | 3S | L |
| 120299 | Shakespeare | Engl | 301 | 3S | U |
| 120299 | Shakespeare | Engl | 302 | 3S | U |
| 120299 | Backgro of Am lit culture | Engl | 403 | 3S | U |
| 120299 | Am novel before 1914 | Engl | 573 | 3S | U |
| 120299 | Am novel after 1914 | Engl | 574 | 3S | U |
| 120299 | Survey of English lit | Engl | 308 | 3S | U |
| 120299 | Survey of English lit | Engl | 309 | 3S | U |
| 120299 | Sur of Am lit to Civ War | Engl | 303 | 3S | U |
| 120299 | Sur Am lit since Civ War | Engl | 304 | 3S | U |
| 120299 | Faulkner's fiction | Engl | 466 | 3S | U |
| 120299 | Intro to literature | Engl | 200 | 3S | L |
| 120302 | Hist of the English lang | Engl | 406 | 3S | U |
| 120302 | Hist of the English lang | Ling | 406 | 3S | U |
| 120305 | Advanced English grammar | Engl | 401 | 3S | U |
| 120305 | Advanced English grammar | Ling | 401 | 3S | U |
| 120307 | Masterworks of Engl lit | Engl | 205 | 3S | L |
| 120307 | Masterworks of Engl lit | Engl | 206 | 3S | L |
| 120310 | English composition | Engl | 101 | 3S | L |
| 120310 | English composition | Engl | 102 | 3S | L |
| 120310 | Advanced composition | Engl | 321 | 3S | U |
| 1210 | Second-year French | Frnch | 201 | 3S | L |
| 1210 | Second-year French | Frnch | 202 | 3S | L |
| 1211 | Elementary German | Ger | 101 | 3S | L |
| 1211 | Elementary German | Ger | 102 | 3S | L |
| 1211 | Second-year German | Ger | 201 | 3S | L |
| 1211 | Second-year German | Ger | 202 | 3S | L |
| 1216 | Intro to Latin | Latin | 101 | 3S | L |
| 1216 | Intro to Latin | Latin | 102 | 3S | L |
| 1216 | Intermediate Latin | Latin | 202 | 3S | L |
| 1216 | Latin review and reading | Latin | 203 | 3S | L |
| 1216 | Intermediate Latin | Latin | 201 | 3S | L |
| 1225 | Elementary Spanish | Span | 101 | 3S | L |
| 1225 | Elementary Spanish | Span | 102 | 3S | L |
| 1225 | Second-year Spanish | Span | 201 | 3S | L |
| 150102 | Descriptive astronomy | Astro | 101 | 3S | L |
| 150102 | Descriptive astronomy | Astro | 102 | 3S | L |
| 150399 | Survey of biology I | Bio | 102 | 3S | L |
| 150399 | Wildlife conservation | Bio | 215 | 3S | L |
| 150399 | Survey of botany | Bio | 211 | 3S | L |
| 150399 | Survey of biology II | Bio | 104 | 3S | L |
| 150499 | Environmental chemistry | Chem | 201 | 3S | L |
| 150499 | Environmental chemistry | Chem | 202 | 3S | L |
| 150799 | Phys of sound and music | Phys | 111 | 1S | L |
| 150799 | Phys of light color art | Phys | 112 | 1S | L |
| 150799 | Phys for sci and engr | Phys | 211 | 3S | L |
| 150799 | Phys for sci and engr | Phys | 212 | 3S | L |
| 150899 | Physical science | Phys | 105 | 3S | L |
| 160299 | Math for elem teachers I | Math | 245 | 3S | L |
| 160299 | Math for elem teachers II | Math | 246 | 3S | L |
| 160302 | College algebra | Math | 121 | 3S | L |
| 160401 | Unif calc & analyt geom | Math | 261 | 3S | L |
| 160401 | Unif calc & analyt geom | Math | 262 | 3S | L |
| 160401 | Unif calc & analyt geom | Math | 263 | 3S | L |
| 160401 | Unif calc & analyt geom | Math | 264 | 3S | L |
| 160406 | Elem differential equatns | Math | 353 | 3S | U |
| 160499 | Elem math analysis I | Math | 267 | 3S | L |
| 160499 | Elem math analysis II | Math | 268 | 3S | L |
| 160602 | Trigonometry | Math | 123 | 3S | L |
| 1608 | Elementary statistics | Math | 175 | 3S | L |
| 160899 | Elem statistics | Math | 175 | 3S | L |
| 180399 | Business ethics | Phil | 327 | 3S | U |
| 180499 | History of philosophy | Philo | 301 | 3S | U |
| 180499 | History of philosophy | Philo | 302 | 3S | U |
| 180599 | Logic | Philo | 203 | 3S | L |
| 180609 | Phil of religion | Philo | 307 | 3S | U |
| 1807 | Phil of contemporary soc | Philo | 102 | 3S | L |
| 180999 | World religions | Relig | 205 | 3S | L |
| 181299 | New Testament thought | Relig | 306 | 3S | U |
| 190509 | Personal and comm health | PhyEd | 191 | 3S | L |
| 190511 | Safety education | PhyEd | 507 | 3S | U |
| 190599 | First aid | PhyEd | 203 | 3S | L |
| 200804 | Educational psychology | Educ | 307 | 3S | U |
| 220201 | Principles of economics | Econ | 201 | 3S | L |

| NCES No. | Course Title | Dept. | Course No. | Credits | Level |
|---|---|---|---|---|---|
| 220201 | Principles of economics | Econ | 202 | 3S | L |
| 220299 | Economic fluctuations | Econ | 509 | 3S | U |
| 220402 | Am diplomacy to 1898 | Hist | 315 | 3S | U |
| 220402 | Am diplomacy since 1898 | Hist | 316 | 3S | U |
| 220409 | Reform movement in the US | Hist | 331 | 3S | U |
| 220426 | Modern Europe to 1660 | Hist | 151 | 3S | L |
| 220426 | Modern Europe since 1660 | Hist | 152 | 3S | L |
| 220428 | Miss 1540 to the present | Hist | 311 | 3S | U |
| 220432 | The US to 1877 | Hist | 105 | 3S | L |
| 220432 | The US since 1877 | Hist | 106 | 3S | L |
| 220472 | Women's movemnt in the US | Hist | 332 | 3S | U |
| 220499 | Women in the South | SSt | 303 | 3S | U |
| 220599 | Criminal investigation | PolSc | 333 | 3S | U |
| 220602 | Criminology | Socio | 431 | 3S | U |
| 220604 | Juvenile delinquency | Socio | 333 | 3S | U |
| 220615 | The prison community | Socio | 421 | 3S | U |
| | **Noncredit courses** | | | | |
| 1210 | PhD French | Frnch | 95 | NC | L |
| 1211 | PhD German | Ger | 95 | NC | L |

(48) **UNIVERSITY OF MISSOURI–COLUMBIA**

Dr. Roger G. Young
Director
Center for Independent Study
University of Missouri-Columbia
400 Hitt Street
Columbia, Missouri 65211
Phone: 314-882-6431

Enrollment on a noncredit basis accepted in all credit courses. Gifted high school students are permitted to enroll in undergraduate courses for credit. Overseas enrollment accepted.

| NCES No. | Course Title | Dept. | Course No. | Credits | Level |
|---|---|---|---|---|---|
| | **High School courses** | | | | |
| 010499 | Functional horsemanship | Agri | | HF | H |
| 0105 | Introductory horticulture | Agri | | HF | H |
| 0199 | Agriculture | Agri | | 1U | H |
| 030599 | Art | Art | | HF | H |
| 040104 | Bookkeeping | Acctg | | 1U | H |
| 040207 | Typing | BusEd | | HF | H |
| 040299 | Clerical practice | Bus | | HF | H |
| 041004 | Retail merchandising | Bus | | HF | H |
| 041099 | Retailing | Bus | | HF | H |
| 0499 | General business | Bus | | 1U | H |
| 0499 | Salesmanship | Bus | | 1U | H |
| 0499 | You & the world of work | Bus | | HF | H |
| 0506 | Intro to journalism | Engl | | HF | H |
| 061101 | Computer literacy | BusEd | | HF | H |
| 070703 | Career planning | HmEc | | HF | H |
| 070799 | Planning for college | PerDe | | HF | H |
| 0810 | General drafting | IndAr | | 1U | H |
| 0810 | Technical drafting | IndAr | | HF | H |
| 100202 | Consumer econ: econ envir | Bus | | HF | H |
| 100202 | Econ: making decisions | Bus | | HF | H |
| 100313 | Fund of nutrition | HmEc | | HF | H |
| 100601 | Chld dev concep to adoles | HmEc | | HF | H |
| 100602 | Marriage & parenting | HmEc | | HF | H |
| 100604 | Personal adj & dating | HmEc | | HF | H |
| 100604 | Project self-discovery | HmEc | | HF | H |
| 120305 | Ninth-grade English | Engl | | 1U | H |
| 120305 | Tenth-grade English | Engl | | 1U | H |
| 120305 | Eleventh-grade English | Engl | | 1U | H |
| 120305 | Twelfth-grade English | Engl | | 1U | H |
| 120307 | Afro-Amer lit: early year | Engl | | HF | H |
| 120307 | Amer envir through lit | Engl | | HF | H |
| 120307 | American lit to 1890 | Engl | | HF | H |
| 120307 | Contemp Afro-Amer prose | Engl | | HF | H |
| 120307 | Eng lit thru Shakespeare | Engl | | HF | H |
| 120307 | Man and myth | Engl | | HF | H |
| 120307 | Readings in short story | Engl | | HF | H |
| 120307 | Science fiction | Engl | | HF | H |
| 120307 | Search for iden thru lit | Engl | | HF | H |
| 120307 | Shrt stry reluc readers | Engl | | HF | H |
| 120307 | Readings in Amer novel | Engl | | HF | H |
| 120308 | Reading & study skills | Engl | | HF | H |
| 120399 | Thnkng clear: mkng sense | Engl | | HF | H |

| NCES No. | Course Title | Dept. | Course No. | Credits | Level |
|---|---|---|---|---|---|
| 1210 | French I | Lang | | HF | H |
| 1225 | Spanish I | Lang | | HF | H |
| 1302 | Consumer & business law | Law | | HF | H |
| 1399 | You and the law | Law | | HF | H |
| 1503 | Survey of living world | Bio | | HF | H |
| 150401 | Chemistry | Chem | | 1U | H |
| 150599 | Environmental geology | Geol | | HF | H |
| 150599 | Underground world caves | Sci | | HF | H |
| 1507 | Physics | Phys | | 1U | H |
| 150704 | AC electronics | Phys | | HF | H |
| 150704 | DC electronics | Phys | | HF | H |
| 1599 | Conserv of nat resources | EnvSc | | HF | H |
| 160301 | General mathematics | Math | | 1U | H |
| 160302 | Algebra I | Math | | HF | H |
| 160302 | Algebra II | Math | | HF | H |
| 160401 | Precalculus | Math | | HF | H |
| 160601 | Geometry | Math | | HF | H |
| 160899 | Fund of stat and probabil | Math | | HF | H |
| 161101 | Business mathematics | Math | | HF | H |
| 181002 | World religions | Relig | | HF | H |
| 1905 | Health | HSci | | HF | H |
| 1906 | Driver education | DriEd | | HF | H |
| 2001 | Psych: found human behavr | Psych | | HF | H |
| 2001 | Personal & social psych | Psych | | HF | H |
| 200508 | Youth in conflict | Psych | | HF | H |
| 2201 | Anthropology | Anthr | | HF | H |
| 220109 | Indians of Missouri | Anthr | | HF | H |
| 2203 | Geography | Geog | | HF | H |
| 220428 | Missouri history | Hist | | HF | H |
| 220432 | Amer history to 1865 | Hist | | HF | H |
| 220432 | Amer history since 1865 | Hist | | HF | H |
| 220433 | World history to Am Revol | Hist | | HF | H |
| 220433 | World hist since Am Revol | Hist | | HF | H |
| 220450 | Ancient history | Hist | | HF | H |
| 220452 | Medieval history | Hist | | HF | H |
| 220470 | Black Amer experience | Hist | | HF | H |
| 220501 | American government | PolSc | | HF | H |
| 220505 | International relations | PolSc | | HF | H |
| 220509 | Civics: natl/state/local | PolSc | | HF | H |
| 220509 | Civics: polit proc/prob | PolSc | | HF | H |
| 2206 | Sociology | Socio | | HF | H |
| 2299 | Contemporary world | SoSci | | HF | H |
| | **College courses** | | | | |
| 010103 | Gen agricultural mktng | AgEcn | 220 | 3S | B |
| 010301 | Planning farm buildings | AgEng | 103 | 3S | L |
| 0105 | Basic home horticulture | Hort | 20 | 3S | L |
| 040101 | Accounting I | Acctg | 36 | 3S | L |
| 040111 | Accounting II | Acctg | 37 | 3S | L |
| 040902 | Engineering economy | Engin | 208 | 3S | B |
| 040904 | Fundamentals of mgmt | Mgmt | 202 | 3S | B |
| 041001 | Principles of marketing | Mktg | 204 | 3S | B |
| 0411 | Personnel management | Mgmt | 310 | 3S | B |
| 050606 | Hist & prin of journalism | Jrnl | 309 | 3S | B |
| 050699 | High school journalism | Jrnl | 380 | 2S | B |
| 070199 | Hist found Amer education | Educ | B351 | 3S | B |
| 070503 | Art activ in elem school | Educ | T230 | 2S | B |
| 070509 | Elements of health educ | Educ | H65 | 2S | L |
| 070516 | Algebra for elem teachers | Math | 7 | 3S | L |
| 070516 | Geometry for el teachers | Math | 8 | 3S | L |
| 070516 | Teaching math elem school | Educ | T267 | 3S | B |
| 070519 | Org & adm of PE programs | Educ | H199 | 2S | L |
| 070599 | Special readings | Educ | T250 | VC | B |
| 070610 | Teaching of reading | Educ | T315 | 3S | B |
| 0708 | Psych ed exceptionl indiv | Educ | 313 | 3S | B |
| 070806 | Intro mental retardation | Educ | 330 | 3S | B |
| 071101 | Intro ed measure & eval | Educ | A280 | 2S | B |
| 071102 | Educational statistics I | Educ | R370 | 3S | B |
| 0799 | Problems | ExtEd | 400 | VC | B |
| 0810 | Gen engineering drawing | Engin | 11 | 3S | L |
| 081103 | Mech of materials | EngrM | 110 | 3S | L |
| 081104 | Engr mech: dynamics | EngrM | 150 | 2S | L |
| 081104 | Engr mech: dynamics | EngrM | 160 | 3S | L |
| 081104 | Engineer mechan-statics | EngrM | 50 | 3S | L |
| 090601 | Problems: hospital mgmt | HSMgt | 300 | 3S | B |
| 090602 | Amer health-care system | HSMgt | 210HM | 3S | B |
| 120299 | Classical mythology | Class | 60 | 3S | L |
| 120299 | Intro to folklore | Engl | 185 | 3S | L |
| 120299 | Womens exp in mod fiction | Engl | 101 | 3S | L |
| 120299 | Women in pop culture | WnStu | 201 | 3S | B |
| 120307 | Literary types | Engl | 12 | 3S | L |
| 120307 | Afro-American literature | Engl | 104 | 3S | L |

| NCES No. | Course Title | Dept. | Course No. | Credits | Level |
|---|---|---|---|---|---|
| 120307 | Intro to Shakespeare | Engl | 135 | 3S | L |
| 120307 | American literature | Engl | 175 | 3S | L |
| 120307 | Eng lit: begin to 1784 | Engl | 201 | 3S | U |
| 120307 | Gothic fiction | Engl | 101 | 3S | L |
| 120310 | Composition | Engl | 1 | 3S | L |
| 120310 | Creative wrtng: short str | Engl | 50 | 3S | L |
| 120310 | Technical writing | Engl | 161 | 3S | L |
| 120310 | Exposition | Engl | 60 | 3S | L |
| 120310 | Creative writing: poetry | Engl | 70 | 3S | L |
| 1210 | Elementary French I | Frnch | 1 | 5S | L |
| 1210 | Elementary French II | Frnch | 2 | 5S | L |
| 1225 | Elementary Spanish I | Span | 1 | 5S | L |
| 1225 | Elementary Spanish II | Span | 2 | 5S | L |
| 1225 | Elementary Spanish III | Rom | 3 | 3S | L |
| 1307 | Intro to business law | Mgmt | 254 | 3S | B |
| 150202 | Introductory meteorology | AtmSc | 50 | 3S | L |
| 150327 | Insects in environment | Entom | 101 | 3S | L |
| 150499 | Prep for general chem | Chem | 10 | 2S | L |
| 150599 | Physical geology | Geol | 2 | 4S | L |
| 160199 | Basic concepts mod math | Math | 12 | 3S | L |
| 160302 | Basic algebra | Math | 3 | 2S | L |
| 160302 | College algebra | Math | 10 | 3S | L |
| 160401 | Analytic geom & calculus | Math | 80 | 5S | L |
| 160401 | Calculus II | Math | 175 | 5S | L |
| 160401 | Calculus III | Math | 201 | 4S | B |
| 160602 | Trigonometry | Math | 9 | 2S | L |
| 160802 | Elementary statistics | Stat | 31 | 3S | L |
| 180501 | Logic | Philo | 15 | 3S | L |
| 1808 | General intro to philo | Philo | 1 | 3S | L |
| 190502 | Community health | FCMed | 25 | 2S | L |
| 1907 | Intro to leisure studies | RecPk | 10 | 3S | L |
| 190701 | Intro leisure serv mgmt | RecPk | 151 | 3S | L |
| 190703 | Problems | RecPA | 300 | VC | B |
| 2003 | Environmental psychology | Psych | 312 | 3S | B |
| 200406 | Human learning | Psych | 212 | 3S | B |
| 200501 | Abnormal psychology | Psych | 180 | 3S | L |
| 200504 | Child development | Educ | A207 | 2S | B |
| 200504 | Psychology of aging | Psych | 387 | 3S | B |
| 200599 | Child psychology | Psych | 170 | 3S | L |
| 200599 | Adolescent psychology | Psych | 271 | 3S | U |
| 2007 | Social psychology | Psych | 260 | 3S | B |
| 200901 | Industrial psychology | Psych | 212 | 3S | B |
| 200906 | Human factors engineering | Psych | 311 | 3S | B |
| 2101 | Intro to public admin | PolSc | 310 | 3S | B |
| 2201 | General anthropology | Anthr | 1 | 3S | L |
| 220102 | Cultural anthropology | Anthr | 153 | 3S | L |
| 220201 | Fund of microeconomics | Econ | 2 | 3S | L |
| 220302 | Economic geography | Geog | 100 | 3S | L |
| 220305 | Physical geography 1 | Geog | 111 | 3S | L |
| 220305 | Physical geography | Geog | 112 | 3S | L |
| 220306 | Reg & nations of world I | Geog | 1 | 3S | L |
| 220306 | Reg & nations of world II | Geog | 2 | 3S | L |
| 220306 | Geography of Missouri | Geog | 125 | 3S | L |
| 220407 | Am foreign policy sin WW2 | Hist | 173 | 3S | L |
| 220424 | Britain 1688 to present | Hist | 106 | 3S | L |
| 220426 | Contemporary Europe | Hist | 231 | 3S | B |
| 220428 | History of the Old South | Hist | 359 | 3S | B |
| 220428 | History of Missouri | Hist | 210 | 3S | B |
| 220432 | Foundations Western civ | Hist | 1 | 4S | L |
| 220432 | American history to 1865 | Hist | 3 | 3S | L |
| 220432 | American hist since 1865 | Hist | 4 | 3S | L |
| 220432 | Period of Amer Revolution | Hist | 364 | 3S | B |
| 220450 | Roman culture | Class | 116 | 3S | L |
| 220501 | American government | PolSc | 1 | 3S | L |
| 220505 | International relations | PolSc | 55 | 3S | L |
| 220510 | Amer political thought | PolSc | 360 | 3S | B |
| 220511 | State government | PolSc | 102 | 3S | L |
| 220599 | Intro to political sci | PolSc | 11 | 3S | L |
| 220601 | Collective behavior | Socio | 215 | 3S | B |
| 220606 | Intro to sociology | Socio | 1 | 3S | L |
| 220608 | Rural sociology | RuSoc | 1 | 3S | L |
| 220610 | Social deviance | Socio | 50 | 3S | L |
| 220615 | Sociology of aging | Socio | 322 | 3S | B |
| 220615 | Race and ethnic relations | Socio | 337 | 3S | B |
| 2299 | Intro to peace studies | Socio | 50 | 3S | L |
| **Graduate courses** | | | | | |
| 070309 | Prog devlpmt & evaluation | ExtEd | 403 | 3S | G |
| 0704 | Secondary school curric | Educ | T445 | 3S | G |
| 070404 | Fund of ext tchng of adul | ExtEd | 406 | 3S | G |
| 070610 | Issues & trends reading | Educ | T420 | 3S | G |
| 220432 | Special topics Amer hist | Hist | 400 | 3S | G |

| NCES No. | Course Title | Dept. | Course No. | Credits | Level |
|---|---|---|---|---|---|
| **Noncredit courses** | | | | | |
| 040703 | Family estate planning | BPA | | NC | |
| 080799 | City and county planning | CivEg | | NC | |
| 090103 | Blood gas interpretation | Nurs | | NC | |
| 090201 | EKG interpretation | Nurs | | NC | |
| 090201 | Nurs care ad chest pain | Nurs | | NC | |
| 090201 | Nurs care ad cong ht fail | Nurs | | NC | |
| 090201 | Nurs care ad myocar infar | Nurs | | NC | |
| 181002 | Major world religions | Relig | | NC | |
| 181202 | Intro to the Old Testmnt | Relig | | NC | |
| 181202 | Intro to the New Testmnt | Relig | | NC | |
| 181202 | Life & letters of Paul | Relig | | NC | |
| 210303 | Hazardous materials | Sfty | | NC | |
| 210304 | Criminal investigation | Law | | NC | |
| 210304 | Law enforcemnt patrol pro | Law | | NC | |
| 210503 | So you're a park bd memb | PubAd | | NC | |
| 220502 | Citizenship | PolSc | | NC | |

## 49 UNIVERSITY OF NEBRASKA–LINCOLN

Mr. Monty E. McMahon
Director of Independent Study
269 Nebraska Center for Continuing Education
University of Nebraska–Lincoln
33rd and Holdrege
Lincoln, Nebraska 68583
Phone: 402-472-1926

Enrollment on a noncredit basis accepted in all credit courses. Gifted high school students are permitted to enroll in undergraduate courses for credit. Overseas enrollment accepted. The UNL Independent Study High School program is accredited by the Nebraska State Department of Education and the North Central Association of Colleges and Schools and is authorized to grant a fully accredited high school diploma. A special diploma program for adults (18 years or older) is also available.

| NCES No. | Course Title | Dept. | Course No. | Credits | Level |
|---|---|---|---|---|---|
| **High School courses** | | | | | |
| 010599 | Horticulture | Agri | 009A | HF | H |
| 010599 | Horticulture | Agri | 011A | HF | H |
| 0199 | General agriculture | Agri | 001A | HF | H |
| 0199 | General agriculture | Agri | 002A | HF | H |
| 030302 | Beginning piano | Music | 001A | HF | H |
| 030302 | Intermediate piano | Music | 003A | HF | H |
| 030302 | Harmony | Music | 007A | HF | H |
| 030302 | Music theory | Music | 005N | HF | H |
| 030399 | History & apprec of music | Music | 011A | HF | H |
| 040101 | Beginning accounting | BusEd | 023A | HF | H |
| 040101 | Beginning accounting | BusEd | 024R | HF | H |
| 040205 | Beginning shorthand | BusEd | 015N | HF | H |
| 040205 | Begining shorthand | BusEd | 016N | HF | H |
| 040207 | Typing with one hand | BusEd | 001A | HF | H |
| 040207 | Beginning typing | BusEd | 003N | HF | H |
| 040207 | Beginning typing | BusEd | 004N | HF | H |
| 040207 | Advanced typing | BusEd | 005N | HF | H |
| 040207 | Advanced typing | BusEd | 006N | HF | H |
| 040299 | Office proced & practice | BusEd | 013A | HF | H |
| 040299 | Office proced & practice | BusEd | 014A | HF | H |
| 040699 | Business English | BusEd | 011A | HF | H |
| 0499 | General business | BusEd | 021N | HF | H |
| 061103 | Computer BASICS | CmpSc | 001A | HF | H |
| 0799 | Effective methds of study | StSki | 001A | HF | H |
| 090199 | Health science | Sci | 001A | HF | H |
| 090199 | Health science | Sci | 002A | HF | H |
| 100104 | Clothing construction | HmEc | 007N | HF | H |
| 100699 | Persl adju, marriage, fam | HmEc | 011A | HF | H |
| 1099 | Etiquette | HmEc | 001A | HF | H |
| 1099 | General homemaking | HmEc | 003A | HF | H |
| 1099 | General homemaking | HmEc | 004A | HF | H |
| 110412 | Small engine care/operatn | IndEd | 005A | HF | H |
| 110412 | Small engine maint/repair | IndEd | 006A | HF | H |
| 110413 | Automotive mechanics | IndEd | 007A | HF | H |
| 110503 | Beg drawing and painting | Art | 001A | HF | H |
| 110503 | Advanced drawing | Art | 007A | HF | H |
| 110503 | Advanced watercolor | Art | 009A | HF | H |
| 110504 | Photography | Photo | 001N | HF | H |
| 1199 | General shop | IndEd | 001A | HF | H |
| 1199 | General shop | IndEd | 002A | HF | H |

| NCES No. | Course Title | Dept. | Course No. | Credits | Level |
|---|---|---|---|---|---|
| 120305 | Basic English 1 | Engl | 001N | HF | H |
| 120305 | Basic English 2 | Engl | 002N | HF | H |
| 120307 | The short story | Engl | 009A | HF | H |
| 120307 | American short story | Engl | 011N | HF | H |
| 120307 | Poetry | Engl | 021N | HF | H |
| 120308 | Improvmt of readng skills | Engl | 003A | HF | H |
| 120308 | Improvmt of readng skills | Engl | 004A | HF | H |
| 120308 | General literature | Engl | 005N | QT | H |
| 120308 | General literature | Engl | 006N | QT | H |
| 120308 | General literature | Engl | 007N | QT | H |
| 120310 | Composition: basic expos | Engl | 023A | HF | H |
| 120399 | Eleventh-grade English | Engl | 035A | HF | H |
| 120399 | Eleventh-grade English | Engl | 036A | HF | H |
| 120399 | Twelfth-grade English | Engl | 037N | HF | H |
| 120399 | Twelfth-grade English | Engl | 038N | HF | H |
| 120399 | Ninth-grade English | Engl | 031N | HF | H |
| 120399 | Ninth-grade English | Engl | 032N | HF | H |
| 120399 | Tenth-grade English | Engl | 033N | HF | H |
| 120399 | Tenth-grade English | Engl | 034N | HF | H |
| 1210 | First-year French | Lang | F002A | HF | H |
| 1210 | Second-year French | Lang | F003A | HF | H |
| 1210 | Second-year French | Lang | F004N | HF | H |
| 1210 | First-year French | Lang | F001N | HF | H |
| 1211 | First-year German | Lang | G001A | HF | H |
| 1211 | First-year German | Lang | G002A | HF | H |
| 1211 | Second-year German | Lang | G003A | HF | H |
| 1211 | Second-year German | Lang | G004A | HF | H |
| 1216 | First-year Latin | Lang | L001A | HF | H |
| 1216 | First-year Latin | Lang | L002A | HF | H |
| 1216 | Second-year Latin | Lang | L003A | HF | H |
| 1216 | Second-year Latin | Lang | L004A | HF | H |
| 1216 | Third-year Latin | Lang | L005A | HF | H |
| 1216 | Third-year Latin | Lang | L006A | HF | H |
| 1225 | Second-year Spanish | Lang | S003X | HF | H |
| 1225 | Second-year Spanish | Lang | S004X | HF | H |
| 1225 | First-year Spanish | Lang | S001N | HF | H |
| 1225 | First-year Spanish | Lang | S002N | HF | H |
| 1503 | Basic biology | Sci | 007A | HF | H |
| 1503 | Basic biology | Sci | 008A | HF | H |
| 150399 | Advanced biology | Sci | 019A | HF | H |
| 150399 | Advanced biology | Sci | 020A | HF | H |
| 150401 | Chemistry | Sci | 031A | HF | H |
| 150401 | Chemistry | Sci | 032A | HF | H |
| 1507 | Gen physics (calc-based) | Sci | 051A | HF | H |
| 1507 | Gen physics (calc-based) | Sci | 052A | HF | H |
| 150704 | Bsc electrcty & electrncs | Sci | 009A | HF | H |
| 150799 | Physics | Sci | 035N | HF | H |
| 150799 | Physics | Sci | 036N | HF | H |
| 1508 | Physical science | Sci | 013A | HF | H |
| 1508 | Physical science | Sci | 014A | HF | H |
| 160301 | Basic mathematics 1 | Math | 001N | HF | H |
| 160301 | Basic mathematics 2 | Math | 002N | HF | H |
| 160302 | Beginning algebra | Math | 031A | HF | H |
| 160302 | Beginning algebra | Math | 032A | HF | H |
| 160302 | Advanced algebra | Math | 035A | HF | H |
| 160302 | Advanced algebra | Math | 036A | HF | H |
| 160399 | General mathematics | Math | 005A | HF | H |
| 160399 | General mathematics | Math | 006A | HF | H |
| 160399 | Precalculus | Math | 041A | HF | H |
| 160399 | Precalculus | Math | 042A | HF | H |
| 160601 | Geometry | Math | 034N | HF | H |
| 160601 | Geometry | Math | 033R | HF | H |
| 160602 | Trigonometry | Math | 037N | HF | H |
| 160603 | Analytic geom & calculus | Math | 051A | HF | H |
| 160603 | Analytic geom & calculus | Math | 052A | HF | H |
| 161299 | Business & consumer math | Math | 009X | HF | H |
| 161299 | Business & consumer math | Math | 010X | HF | H |
| 190699 | Driver education | Dr | 001A | HF | H |
| 200199 | Psychology | SocSt | 007N | HF | H |
| 220201 | Economics | BusEd | 027N | HF | H |
| 220208 | Consumer education | BusEd | 019A | HF | H |
| 220399 | World geography | SocSt | 021N | HF | H |
| 220399 | World geography | SocSt | 022N | HF | H |
| 220432 | American history | SocSt | 033N | HF | H |
| 220432 | American history | SocSt | 034N | HF | H |
| 220433 | World history | SocSt | 031A | HF | H |
| 220433 | World history | SocSt | 032A | HF | H |
| 220501 | American government | SocSt | 035N | HF | H |
| 220501 | American government | SocSt | 036N | HF | H |
| 220502 | Civics | SocSt | 001N | HF | H |
| 220606 | Sociology | SocSt | 003N | HF | H |
| 2299 | Modern problems | SocSt | 037A | HF | H |

| NCES No. | Course Title | Dept. | Course No. | Credits | Level |
|---|---|---|---|---|---|
| | **College courses** | | | | |
| 030599 | Intro art history & crit | Art | 167X | 3S | L |
| 040101 | Intermediate accounting | Acctg | 313X | 3S | U |
| 040101 | Introductory accounting | Acctg | 201X | 3S | L |
| 040101 | Introductory accounting | Acctg | 202X | 3S | U |
| 040111 | Managerial accounting | Acctg | 308X | 3S | U |
| 040311 | Finance | Fin | 361X | 3S | U |
| 040902 | Operatns & resourcs mgmt | Mgmt | 331X | 3S | U |
| 040999 | Administrative policy | Mgmt | 435X | 3S | B |
| 041001 | Marketing | Mktg | 341X | 3S | U |
| 041199 | Personnel administration | Mgmt | 361X | 3S | U |
| 0412 | Elem quantitative methods | Econ | 245X | 3S | L |
| 0412 | Elem quantitative methods | Mgmt | 245X | 3S | L |
| 041301 | Real estate appraisal | RIEs | 441X | 3S | U |
| 041303 | Real estate prin & prac | Fin | 382X | 3S | U |
| 041303 | Real est princ & practice | RIEs | 382X | 3S | U |
| 041304 | Real estate management | RIEs | 345X | 3S | U |
| 041306 | Real estate finance | Fin | 482X | 3S | U |
| 041306 | Real estate finance | RIEs | 482X | 3S | U |
| 041307 | Real estate investments | RIEs | 439X | 3S | U |
| 050401 | Adv broadcast writing | Brdcs | 474X | 3S | U |
| 070199 | Intro philosophy educ | AEdSF | 331X | 3S | U |
| 070404 | Tchng soc stud in ele sch | Crlns | 307X | 3S | U |
| 081503 | Intro industrial dcs mdls | IMSE | 206X | 3S | U |
| 090504 | Emergency health care | HPE&R | 170X | 3S | L |
| 090999 | Elements health promotion | HPE&R | 101X | 3S | L |
| 100313 | Introduction to nutrition | HNFSM | 151X | 3S | L |
| 120299 | Composition & short story | Engl | 103X | 3S | L |
| 120299 | Composition & lit survey | Engl | 100X | 3S | L |
| 120307 | Modern fiction | Engl | 205BX | 3S | L |
| 120307 | Shakespeare | Engl | 230AX | 3S | L |
| 120310 | Business writing | Engl | 255X | 3S | L |
| 120310 | Special topics in writing | Engl | 258X | 2S | L |
| 1299 | Scientific Greek & Latin | Clas | 116X | 2S | L |
| 150304 | Introductory ecology | BioSc | 220X | 3S | L |
| 150799 | Gen phys for life sci | Phys | 141X | 4S | L |
| 150799 | Gen phys for life sci | Phys | 142X | 4S | L |
| 150799 | General physics | Phys | 211X | 4S | L |
| 150799 | General physics | Phys | 212X | 4S | L |
| 160302 | Algebra | Math | 100X | 2S | L |
| 160302 | Algebra | Math | 101X | 2S | L |
| 160602 | Trigonometry | Math | 102X | 2S | L |
| 160603 | Analyt geom & calculus I | Math | 106X | 5S | L |
| 160603 | Analyt geom & calculus II | Math | 107X | 5S | L |
| 160603 | Analyt geom & calc III | Math | 208X | 4S | L |
| 180599 | Elementary logic | Philo | 110X | 3S | L |
| 190311 | Coaching of basketball | HPE&R | 311X | 2S | U |
| 200504 | Human dev and the family | HuDev | 160X | 3S | L |
| 200599 | Elementary psychology I | Psych | 170X | 3S | L |
| 200599 | Psychosocl aspcts alchlsm | Psych | 222X | 3S | L |
| 200804 | Learning in the classroom | EdPsy | 362X | 3S | U |
| 220201 | Principles of economics | Econ | 211X | 3S | L |
| 220201 | Principles of economics | Econ | 212X | 3S | L |
| 220299 | Statistics | Econ | 215X | 3S | L |
| 220301 | Intro human geography | Geog | 140X | 3S | L |
| 220302 | Intro economic geography | Geog | 120X | 3S | L |
| 220306 | Geography of US | Geog | 271X | 3S | L |
| 220306 | Geography of Asia | Geog | 375X | 3S | U |
| 220426 | History early mod Europe | Hist | 212X | 3S | L |
| 220426 | Western civ since 1715 | Hist | 101X | 3S | L |
| 220428 | Nebraska history | Hist | 359X | 3S | U |
| 220432 | American history to 1877 | Hist | 201X | 3S | L |
| 220432 | Amer history after 1877 | Hist | 202X | 3S | L |
| 220452 | History of Middle Ages | Hist | 211X | 3S | L |
| 220501 | Amer natl and state govt | PolSc | 100X | 3S | L |
| 220507 | Polit prties & elctn camp | PolSc | 230X | 3S | L |
| 220599 | Contemporary foreign govt | PolSc | 104X | 3S | L |
| 220602 | Delinquency and crime | Socio | 209X | 3S | L |
| 220605 | Marriage and the family | Socio | 225X | 3S | L |
| 220606 | Intro to sociology | Socio | 153X | 3S | L |
| 220608 | Rural sociology | AgEco | 276X | 3S | L |
| 220608 | Rural sociology | Socio | 241X | 3S | L |
| | **Noncredit courses** | | | | |
| 010399 | Irrigation theory-prac | Irr | 1X | NC | L |
| 210302 | Fire and arson invest | Arsln | 1X | NC | L |
| 210399 | Field inspec & plan rview | Blgln | 1X | NC | L |

## ㊿ UNIVERSITY OF NEVADA RENO

Ms. Catharine D. Sanders
Assistant Director
College Inn, Room 333
University of Nevada Reno
1001 South Virginia Street
Reno, Nevada 89557
Phone: 702-784-4652

Enrollment on a noncredit basis accepted in all credit courses. Gifted high school students are permitted to enroll in undergraduate courses for credit. Overseas enrollment accepted.

| NCES No. | Course Title | Dept. | Course No. | Credits | Level |
|---|---|---|---|---|---|
| | **College courses** | | | | |
| 040101 | Introductory accounting I | Acctg | C201 | 3S | L |
| 040101 | Introduct accounting II | Acctg | C202 | 3S | L |
| 0499 | Orientation to hotel ind | HoA | C101 | 3S | L |
| 050605 | The feature article | Jrnl | C468 | 2S | U |
| 0509 | Pub reltns, prin, pract | Jrnl | C301 | 2S | U |
| 060301 | Computer logic & architec | Math | C387 | 3S | U |
| 070404 | Science tchg & reasng dev | C&I | C481 | 3S | U |
| 070404 | Five teaching skills | C&I | C481 | 1S | U |
| 070404 | Tchg min comp arithmetic | C&I | C481 | 3S | U |
| 070599 | Curriculum dev in env ed | C&I | C449 | 3S | U |
| 070899 | Ed of the exceptnl child | C&I | C310 | 3S | U |
| 080999 | Computer logic & architec | EE | C333 | 3S | U |
| 090999 | Medical terminology | MedT | C111 | 1S | L |
| 100102 | Food-service operations I | HOA | C160 | 3S | L |
| 100313 | Human nutrition | HmEc | C121 | 3S | L |
| 100601 | Child development | HmEc | C131 | 3S | L |
| 100699 | Chld & fmls: multi-eth so | HmEc | C438 | 3S | U |
| 120301 | Introduction to fiction | Engl | C244 | 2S | L |
| 120399 | Vocabulary and meaning | Engl | C181 | 2S | L |
| 120399 | Introduction to drama | Engl | C253 | 3S | L |
| 120399 | Introduction to poetry | Engl | C261 | 2S | L |
| 1210 | Elementary French I | Frnch | C101 | 4S | L |
| 1210 | Elementary French II | Frnch | C102 | 4S | L |
| 1210 | Reading French I | Frnch | C205 | 2S | L |
| 1210 | Reading French II | Frnch | C209 | 2S | L |
| 1211 | Second-year German I | Ger | C203 | 3S | L |
| 1211 | Second-year German II | Ger | C204 | 3S | L |
| 1214 | Elementary Italian I | Ital | C101 | 4S | L |
| 1214 | Elementary Italian II | Ital | C102 | 4S | L |
| 1225 | Elementary Spanish I | Span | C101 | 4S | L |
| 1225 | Elementary Spanish II | Span | C102 | 4S | L |
| 1225 | Survey of Spanish lit | Span | C353 | 3S | U |
| 1225 | Reading Spanish I | Span | C205 | 2S | L |
| 1225 | Reading Spanish II | Span | C209 | 2S | L |
| 150323 | General zoology | Bio | C160 | 3S | L |
| 150399 | General biology | Bio | C103 | 3S | L |
| 160302 | Intermediate algebra | Math | C101 | 2S | L |
| 160399 | College algebra | Math | C110 | 3S | L |
| 160602 | Plane trigonometry | Math | C102 | 2S | L |
| 160603 | Analytic geometry | Math | C140 | 3S | L |
| 161101 | Mathematics of finance | Math | C210 | 3S | L |
| 1699 | Elementary school math I | Math | C173 | 3S | L |
| 1699 | Elementary school math II | Math | C174 | 3S | L |
| 1699 | Elements of calculus | Math | C265 | 3S | L |
| 200501 | Abnormal psychology | Psych | C441 | 3S | U |
| 200509 | Personality | Psych | C435 | 3S | U |
| 200599 | Psychology of adolescence | Psych | C234 | 3S | L |
| 200599 | Child psychology | Psych | C233 | 3S | L |
| 200804 | Educational psychology | Psych | C321 | 3S | U |
| 2099 | Introductory psychology | Psych | C101 | 3S | L |
| 220101 | Introdctn to archaeology | Anthr | C202 | 3S | L |
| 220199 | Introdctn to anthropology | Anthr | C101 | 3S | L |
| 220199 | Intr to hum evol & prehis | Anthr | C102 | 3S | L |
| 220299 | Princpls of statistics I | Econ | C261 | 3S | L |
| 220299 | Princpls of statistics II | Econ | C262 | 3S | L |
| 220299 | Prin of microeconomics | Econ | C102 | 3S | L |
| 220299 | Prin of macroeconomics | Econ | C101 | 3S | L |
| 220301 | Intro to cultural geog | Geog | C106 | 3S | L |
| 220424 | England & the British Emp | Hist | C393 | 3S | U |
| 220424 | England & the Brit Emp II | Hist | C394 | 3S | U |
| 220426 | European civilization | Hist | C105 | 3S | L |
| 220426 | European civilization | Hist | C106 | 3S | L |
| 220428 | Nevada history | Hist | C217 | 3S | L |
| 220501 | Prin of Amer const govt | PolSc | C103 | 3S | L |
| 220511 | Constitution of Nevada | PolSc | C100 | 1S | L |
| 220606 | Principles of sociology | Soc | C101 | 3S | L |

| NCES No. | Course Title | Dept. | Course No. | Credits | Level |
|---|---|---|---|---|---|
| | **Noncredit courses** | | | | |
| 070199 | Legal foundations of educ | Educ | CA | NC | |
| 090118 | Pharmacology by home sty | | | NC | |
| 161202 | Fund of the metric system | Math | CC | NC | D |
| 220502 | Citizenship for new Amer | PolSc | CA | NC | D |

## ⑤① UNIVERSITY OF NORTH CAROLINA

Mr. Norman H. Loewenthal
Associate Director for Independent Study
Division of Extension and Continuing Education
University of North Carolina at Chapel Hill
201 Abernethy Hall 002A
Chapel Hill, North Carolina 27514
Phone: 919-962-1106

Enrollment on a noncredit basis accepted in all credit courses. Gifted high school students are permitted to enroll in undergraduate courses for credit. Overseas enrollment accepted. Interinstitutional program within consolidated University of North Carolina system; institutional code precedes course number. C — University of North Carolina at Chapel Hill; A — Appalachian State University; S — North Carolina State University; G — University of North Carolina at Greensboro; E — East Carolina University; U — University of North Carolina at Asheville; W — Winston-Salem State University; Z — Elizabeth City State University; T — Western Carolina University.

| NCES No. | Course Title | Dept. | Course No. | Credits | Level |
|---|---|---|---|---|---|
| | **College courses** | | | | |
| 010406 | Poultry production | AnSci | S200 | 3S | L |
| 030302 | Fundamentals of music | Music | C21 | 3S | L |
| 030399 | Music appreciation | Music | C40 | 3S | L |
| 030402 | Intro to the theater | Drama | C15 | 3S | L |
| 030599 | History of Western art | ArHis | C31a | 3S | L |
| 030599 | History of American art | ArHis | S203 | 3S | L |
| 040101 | Acctg I concepts fin acct | Acctg | S260 | 3S | L |
| 040101 | Basic accounting princip | Bus | C72 | 3S | L |
| 040101 | Prin of accounting | Acctg | G201 | 3S | L |
| 040101 | Accounting principles | Acctg | G202 | 3S | L |
| 040111 | Elem management account | Bus | C72 | 3S | L |
| 040111 | Acctg II intro mgerl acct | Acctg | S261 | 3S | L |
| 040601 | Business writing | Engl | C32 | 3S | L |
| 040601 | Business writing | Engl | C32a | 2S | L |
| 040601 | Wrtg for business & indus | Commu | E3880 | 3S | U |
| 041001 | Principles of marketing | Mktg | A3050 | 3S | U |
| 041303 | Real estate prin & prac | RlEs | A2850 | 3S | L |
| 070199 | Educ in American society | CmpSc | C41 | 3S | L |
| 070303 | The secondary school | Educ | C99 | 3S | L |
| 070516 | Math in the elem school | Educ | C156 | 3S | U |
| 0708 | Intro to exceptional chil | Educ | C130 | 3S | U |
| 071103 | Educ measurement & eval | Educ | C106 | 3S | U |
| 0799 | Educational psychology | Educ | C71 | 3S | L |
| 0799 | Org & mgmt youth club act | Educ | S457 | 3S | U |
| 080901 | Electrical circuits I | EEg | S211 | 3S | L |
| 1199 | Technology and change | Int | W4604 | 3S | U |
| 120301 | Social dialects | Spch | C153 | 3S | U |
| 120305 | English grammar | Engl | C36 | 3S | L |
| 120307 | Brit lit Wordsworth-Eliot | Engl | C22 | 3S | L |
| 120307 | Contemporary literature | Engl | C24 | 3S | L |
| 120307 | Shakespeare | Engl | C58 | 3S | L |
| 120307 | Amer lit: beginning-1865 | Engl | C81 | 3S | L |
| 120307 | Brit lit Chaucer to Pope | Engl | C20 | 3S | L |
| 120310 | English comp & rhetoric | Engl | C1 | 3S | L |
| 120310 | Composition & rhetoric | Engl | S111 | 3S | L |
| 120310 | English comp & rhetoric | Engl | C2 | 3S | L |
| 120310 | Composition & reading | Engl | S112 | 3S | L |
| 120310 | Introduction to fiction | Engl | C23W | 3S | L |
| 120310 | Advanced creative writing | Engl | C35 | 3S | L |
| 120310 | Advanced poetry writing | Engl | C35P | 3S | L |
| 120310 | Foundation composition | Engl | T300 | 3S | L |
| 120310 | Composition & lit I | Engl | Z102 | 3S | L |
| 120310 | Composition & lit II | Engl | Z103 | 3S | L |
| 120310 | Writing for bus & indus | Engl | E3880 | 3S | U |
| 1210 | Elementary French | Frnch | C1 | 4S | L |
| 1210 | Beginning French | Frnch | G102a | 4S | L |
| 1211 | Elementary German | Ger | C1 | 3S | L |
| 1211 | Elementary German | Ger | C2 | 3S | L |
| 1211 | Intermediate German | Ger | C3 | 3S | L |

| NCES No. | Course Title | Dept. | Course No. | Credits | Level |
|---|---|---|---|---|---|
| 1211 | Intermediate German | Ger | C4 | 3S | L |
| 1214 | Elementary Italian | Ital | C1 | 3S | L |
| 1214 | Elementary Italian | Ital | C2 | 3S | L |
| 1214 | Intermediate Italian | Ital | C3 | 3S | L |
| 1214 | Intermediate Italian | Ital | C4 | 3S | L |
| 1216 | Intermediate Latin | Latin | C3 | 3S | L |
| 1216 | Intermediate Latin | Latin | C4 | 3S | L |
| 1216 | Elementary Latin | Latin | C1 | 3S | L |
| 1216 | Elementary Latin | Latin | C2 | 3S | L |
| 1220 | Elementary Russian | Rus | C1 | 3S | L |
| 1220 | Elementary Russian | Rus | C2 | 3S | L |
| 1220 | Intermediate Russian | Rus | C3 | 3S | L |
| 1220 | Intermediate Russian | Rus | C4 | 3S | L |
| 1225 | Intermediate Spanish | Span | C3 | 3S | L |
| 1225 | Intermediate Spanish | Span | C4 | 3S | L |
| 1299 | Medical word form & etym | Clas | C25 | 3S | L |
| 1299 | Word formation & etymol | Clas | C26 | 3S | L |
| 140804 | Research skills | LibSc | E1000 | 1S | L |
| 150199 | Conceptual astronomy | Phys | G203 | 3S | L |
| 150316 | Plants and life | Bio | C10 | 3S | L |
| 150401 | Gen descriptive chem | Chem | C11 | 3S | L |
| 150401 | Gen descriptive chem | Chem | C21 | 3S | L |
| 150401 | Intro to chemical concept | Chem | C10 | 2S | L |
| 150401 | General chemistry I | Chem | G111 | 3S | L |
| 150401 | General chemistry II | Chem | G114 | 3S | L |
| 1505 | Introduction geology | Geol | C11 | 4S | L |
| 1505 | General physical geology | Geol | S101 | 3S | L |
| 1505 | Physical geology | Geol | Z142 | 3S | L |
| 1506 | Surv coastal marine envmt | Ocean | E2125 | 3S | L |
| 1507 | General physics | Phys | S204 | 3S | L |
| 1507 | General physics | Phys | S207 | 3S | L |
| 150899 | Gen environmental science | EnvSc | 2101 | 3S | L |
| 160302 | Algebra & trigonometry | Math | S111 | 4S | L |
| 160401 | Analytic geom & calc I | Math | S102 | 4S | L |
| 160401 | Analytic geom & calc II | Math | S201 | 4S | L |
| 160401 | Analytic geom & calc III | Math | S202 | 4S | L |
| 160401 | Intro to calculus | Math | S113 | 4S | L |
| 160601 | Trig & analytic geometry | Math | C30 | 3S | L |
| 160602 | Trigonometry | Math | Z116 | 3S | L |
| 160699 | Pre-calculus | Math | Z118 | 3S | L |
| 1608 | Basic statistics | Stat | Z251 | 3S | L |
| 160899 | Intro stat for engineers | Stat | S361 | 3S | U |
| 161101 | Mathematics of finance | Math | S122 | 3S | L |
| 161199 | Calc for bus & social sci | Math | C22 | 3S | L |
| 170102 | American military history | Hist | C77 | 3S | L |
| 1803 | Introduction to ethics | Philo | C22 | 3S | L |
| 180502 | Introd symbolic logic | Philo | C21 | 3S | L |
| 181201 | Intro to Old Test lit | Relig | C21 | 3S | L |
| 181202 | Intro to New Test lit | Relig | C22 | 3S | L |
| 1899 | Main problems in phil | Philo | C20 | 3S | L |
| 1899 | Problems & types of philo | Philo | S205 | 3S | L |
| 190303 | Hist of American sport | Hist | S333 | 3S | U |
| 1907 | Intro to recreation | Rec | S152 | 3S | L |
| 1907 | Intro to comm recreation | Rec | C10 | 3S | L |
| 2001 | General psychology | Psych | C10 | 3S | L |
| 200501 | Abnormal psychology | Psych | G341 | 3S | U |
| 2201 | General anthropology | Anthr | C41 | 3S | L |
| 220102 | Cultural anthropology | Anthr | S252 | 3S | L |
| 220102 | Cultural anthropology | Anthr | G213 | 3S | L |
| 220201 | Economics I | Econ | S201 | 3S | L |
| 220201 | Intermediate microecon | Econ | S301 | 3S | L |
| 220217 | Econ & bus statistics | Econ | S350 | 3S | L |
| 220301 | Cultural geography | Geog | G201 | 3S | L |
| 220305 | Physical geography | Geog | C10 | 3S | L |
| 220305 | Environmental phys geog | Geog | S208 | 3S | L |
| 220306 | Geography of Anglo-Amer | Geog | C157 | 3S | U |
| 220402 | US foreign relations-1914 | Hist | C143 | 3S | U |
| 220402 | US foreign rel 1914-pres | Hist | C144 | 3S | U |
| 220421 | Amer history to 1865 | Hist | C21 | 3S | L |
| 220424 | English history to 1688 | Hist | C44 | 3S | L |
| 220424 | English hist since 1688 | Hist | C45 | 3S | L |
| 220426 | Mod Europ hist 1500-1815 | Hist | C48 | 3S | L |
| 220426 | Mod Europ hist since 1815 | Hist | C49 | 3S | L |
| 220427 | Latin Amer since 1826 | Hist | S216 | 3S | L |
| 220428 | North Carolina 1524-1835 | Hist | C161 | 3S | U |
| 220428 | North Carolina 1835-1976 | Hist | C162 | 3S | U |
| 220431 | Hist of Russia 1861-pres | Hist | C31 | 3S | L |
| 220432 | Amer history since 1865 | Hist | C22 | 3S | L |
| 220432 | United States 1845-1914 | Hist | S243 | 3S | L |
| 220450 | Ancient history | Hist | C41 | 3S | L |
| 220450 | Ancient world to 180 AD | Hist | S207 | 3S | L |
| 220499 | Hist of Western civ I | Hist | C11 | 3S | L |

| NCES No. | Course Title | Dept. | Course No. | Credits | Level |
|---|---|---|---|---|---|
| 220499 | Hist of Western civ II | Hist | C12 | 3S | L |
| 220499 | Western civ since 1400 | Hist | S205 | 3S | L |
| 220501 | Intro to Amer government | PolSc | C41 | 3S | L |
| 220501 | Amer national govt | PolSc | Z301 | 3S | L |
| 220505 | American foreign policy | PolSc | U280 | 3S | L |
| 220511 | State & local gov in US | PolSc | C42 | 3S | L |
| 220511 | Local govtl systems | PolSc | S202 | 3S | L |
| 220599 | Urban politics | PolSc | W3371 | 3S | U |
| 220599 | European politics | PolSc | C52 | 3S | L |
| 220602 | Criminology | Socio | S306 | 3S | U |
| 220604 | Juvenile delinquency | Socio | S425 | 3S | U |
| 220605 | Sociology of family | Socio | S204 | 3S | L |
| 220605 | Family & society | Socio | C30 | 3S | L |
| 220605 | Marriage & family | Socio | G355 | 3S | U |
| 220605 | The family | Socio | Z2401 | 3S | U |
| 220606 | Principles of sociology | Socio | S202 | 3S | L |
| 220606 | American society | Socio | C10 | 3S | L |
| 220606 | Intro to sociology | Socio | Z201 | 3S | L |
| 220606 | Intro to sociology | Socio | G211 | 3S | L |
| 220614 | Urban sociology | Socio | S402 | 3S | U |
| 220614 | Urban sociology | Socio | Z306 | 3S | L |
| 220699 | Black-white relat in US | Socio | C22 | 3S | L |
| 220699 | Population problems | Socio | C21 | 3S | L |
| 220699 | Human behavior | Socio | S301 | 3S | U |
| 220699 | Corrections & penology | Socio | G413 | 3S | U |
| 220699 | Population problems | Socio | G339 | 3S | U |
| 220699 | Race & ethnic relations | Socio | G327 | 3S | U |
| 2299 | West attitudes death & dy | Int | U301 | 3S | U |
| 2299 | Energy & man | UnStu | S495 | 3S | U |

**Noncredit courses**

| NCES No. | Course Title | Dept. | Course No. | Credits | Level |
|---|---|---|---|---|---|
| 0799 | Family day care mgmt | FDC | C1 | NC | V |
| 0799 | Buildg qual in fam daycar | FDC | C2 | NC | V |
| 090242 | Aging in America | Geron | | NC | V |
| 090253 | Professionalism | DA | C1 | NC | V |
| 090253 | Legal & ethical considtns | DA | C2 | NC | V |
| 090253 | Office management | DA | C3 | NC | V |
| 090253 | Anatomy & physiology | DA | C4 | NC | V |
| 090253 | Dental anatomy | DA | C5 | NC | V |
| 090253 | Pathology | DA | C6 | NC | V |
| 090253 | Pharmacology | DA | C7 | NC | V |
| 090253 | Microbiology & sterilztn | DA | C8 | NC | V |
| 090253 | Med emerg in dentl office | DA | C9 | NC | V |
| 090253 | Histology | DA | C10 | NC | V |
| 090253 | Oral pathology | DA | C11 | NC | V |
| 090253 | Communication | DA | C12 | NC | V |
| 090253 | Psychology | DA | C13 | NC | V |
| 090253 | Nutrition | DA | C14 | NC | V |
| 090253 | Preventive dentistry | DA | C15 | NC | V |
| 090253 | Dental radiology equipmt | DA | C16 | NC | V |
| 090253 | Radiographic anat & biol | DA | C17 | NC | V |
| 090253 | Dental radiograph techn | DA | C18 | NC | V |
| 090253 | Restorative materials | DA | C19 | NC | V |
| 090253 | Impressions & models | DA | C20 | NC | V |
| 090253 | Dental casting | DA | C21 | NC | V |
| 090253 | Denture prosthetics | DA | C22 | NC | V |
| 090253 | Dental practice orientatn | DA | C23 | NC | V |
| 090253 | Dental surgery | DA | C24 | NC | V |
| 090253 | Restorative dentistry | DA | C25 | NC | V |
| 090253 | Pedodontics/orthodontics | DA | C26 | NC | V |
| 090253 | Fundamentals in practice | DA | C27 | NC | V |
| 090253 | Dental surgery practice | DA | C28 | NC | V |
| 090253 | Restorative dent practice | DA | C29 | NC | V |
| 090253 | Pedo & ortho practice | DA | C30 | NC | V |
| 120310 | Engl composition & gramm | Engl | CO | NC | D |
| 160302 | Contemporary algebra | Math | CR | NC | D |
| 160601 | Plane geometry | Math | CA | NC | D |
| 220502 | Citizenship | Citz | C1 | NC | D |

㊼ **UNIVERSITY OF NORTH DAKOTA**

Ms. Rebecca C. Monley
Director of Correspondence Study
Department of Correspondence Study
University of North Dakota
Box 8277, University Station
Grand Forks, North Dakota 58202
Phone: 701-777-3044

Enrollment on a noncredit basis accepted in all credit courses. Only in exceptional cases are gifted high school students permitted to enroll in undergraduate courses for credit. No overseas enrollment accepted. Students in high school who have completed 14 units may enroll in undergraduate courses for credit.

| NCES No. | Course Title | Dept. | Course No. | Credits | Level |
|---|---|---|---|---|---|
| | **College courses** | | | | |
| 030599 | Art history survey | VisAr | 210 | 3S | L |
| 030599 | American art & architect | VisAr | 315 | 3S | U |
| 040101 | Elements of accounting | Acctg | 200 | 3S | L |
| 040101 | Elements of accounting | Acctg | 201 | 3S | L |
| 040106 | Cost accounting | Acctg | 305 | 3S | U |
| 040203 | Records management | BVEd | 315 | 3S | U |
| 040904 | Principles of management | Mgmt | 300 | 3S | U |
| 041001 | Principles of marketing | Mktg | 301 | 3S | U |
| 041005 | Retailing | Mktg | 303 | 3S | U |
| 041099 | Salesmanship | Mktg | 204 | 2S | L |
| 041099 | Marketing information | Mktg | 400 | 3S | U |
| 041099 | Consumer & market behav | Mktg | 401 | 3S | U |
| 0411 | Personnel management | Mgmt | 302 | 3S | U |
| 041301 | Real estate appraisal | Mgmt | 329 | 3S | U |
| 041303 | Principles of real estate | Mgmt | 324 | 3S | U |
| 0501 | Advertising and sales pro | Mktg | 302 | 3S | U |
| 061103 | Introduction to computers | CmpSc | 101 | 2S | L |
| 070803 | Career/voc ed of excep ch | Educ | 421 | 3S | U |
| 070899 | Prescriptive teaching | Educ | 318 | 3S | U |
| 0810 | Engineering graphics | Engr | 101 | 2S | L |
| 0810 | Descriptive geometry | Engr | 102 | 2S | L |
| 100313 | Fundamentals of nutrition | HmEc | 240 | 3S | L |
| 100313 | Geriatric nutrition | HmEc | 495 | 2S | U |
| 120305 | Modern grammar | Engl | 309 | 3S | U |
| 120307 | Survey of English lit | EngLL | 301 | 3S | U |
| 120307 | Survey of English lit | EngLL | 302 | 3S | U |
| 120307 | Survey of American lit | EngLL | 303 | 3S | U |
| 120307 | Survey of American lit | EngLL | 304 | 3S | U |
| 120307 | Shakespeare | EngLL | 315 | 3S | U |
| 120307 | Shakespeare | EngLL | 316 | 3S | U |
| 120308 | Introduction to fiction | EngLL | 211 | 2S | L |
| 120308 | Introduction to drama | EngLL | 217 | 2S | L |
| 120310 | Composition I | Engl | 101 | 3S | L |
| 120310 | Composition II | Engl | 102 | 3S | L |
| 120310 | Composition III | Engl | 203 | 2S | L |
| 120310 | Technical & business writ | Engl | 209 | 2S | L |
| 120310 | Creative writing | Engl | 305 | 2S | U |
| 1210 | Beginning French | CILL | 101 | 4S | L |
| 1210 | Beginning French | CILL | 102 | 4S | L |
| 1210 | Second-year French | CILL | 201 | 4S | L |
| 1210 | Second-year French | CILL | 202 | 4S | L |
| 1210 | Third-year French | CILL | 301 | 3S | U |
| 1210 | Third-year French | CILL | 302 | 3S | U |
| 1211 | Beginning German | CILL | 101 | 4S | L |
| 1211 | Beginning German | CILL | 102 | 4S | L |
| 1216 | First-year college Latin | CILL | 101 | 4S | L |
| 1216 | First-year college Latin | CILL | 102 | 4S | L |
| 1217 | American Indian lit | EngLL | 367 | 3S | U |
| 1218 | Beginning Norwegian | CILL | 101 | 4S | L |
| 1218 | Beginning Norwegian | CILL | 102 | 4S | L |
| 1218 | Second-year Norwegian | CILL | 201 | 4S | L |
| 1218 | Second-year Norwegian | CILL | 202 | 4S | L |
| 1225 | Beginning Spanish | CILL | 101 | 4S | L |
| 1225 | Beginning Spanish | CILL | 102 | 4S | L |
| 1225 | Second-year Spanish | CILL | 201 | 4S | L |
| 1225 | Second-year Spanish | CILL | 202 | 4S | L |
| 1225 | Survey of Span-Amer lit | CILL | 403 | 2S | U |
| 1305 | Business law I | Acctg | 315 | 3S | U |
| 1305 | Business law II | Acctg | 316 | 3S | U |
| 160302 | College algebra | Math | 103 | 3S | L |
| 160302 | Intermediate algebra | Math | 102 | 3S | L |
| 160401 | Calculus I | Math | 211 | 4S | L |
| 160401 | Calculus II | Math | 212 | 4S | L |
| 160401 | Calculus III | Math | 213 | 4S | L |
| 160602 | Trigonometry | Math | 105 | 2S | L |
| 1807 | Philosophy of voc ed | BVEd | 444 | 3S | U |
| 181002 | World religions | Relig | 203 | 3S | L |
| 181099 | Introduction to religion | Relig | 101 | 3S | L |
| 181502 | Contemporary moral issues | Relig | 205 | 3S | L |
| 181599 | Death and dying | Relig | 345 | 2S | U |
| 181599 | Intro to humanities | Hum | 101 | 4S | L |
| 190599 | School health education | PhyEd | 403 | 2S | U |
| 220201 | Principles of econ I | Econ | 201 | 3S | L |
| 220201 | Principles of econ II | Econ | 202 | 3S | L |

| NCES No. | Course Title | Dept. | Course No. | Credits | Level |
|---|---|---|---|---|---|
| 220301 | Cultural geography | Geog | 151 | 3S | L |
| 220306 | World regional geography | Geog | 161 | 3S | L |
| 220426 | Western civ to 1500 | Hist | 101 | 3S | L |
| 220426 | Western civ since 1500 | Hist | 102 | 3S | L |
| 220428 | History of North Dakota | Hist | 220 | 3S | U |
| 220501 | American government I | PolSc | 101 | 3S | L |
| 220501 | American government II | PolSc | 102 | 3S | L |
| 220602 | Criminology | Socio | 252 | 3S | L |
| 220605 | The family | Socio | 335 | 4S | U |
| 220606 | Introduction to sociology | Socio | 101 | 3S | L |
| 220607 | Social psychology | Socio | 361 | 4S | U |
| 220608 | Rural sociology | Socio | 331 | 3S | U |
| 220699 | Aging | Socio | 352 | 3S | U |
| | **Noncredit courses** | | | | |
| 040101 | Accounting fundamentals I | | | NC | |
| 040101 | Accounting fund II | | | NC | |
| 041304 | Real estate management | | | NC | |
| 090699 | Long-term-care admin | | | NC | |
| 100302 | Dietary managers course | | | NC | |
| 100309 | B & c nutrit for diet per | | | NC | |
| 100309 | School food service | | | NC | |
| 1299 | ESO reading course | | | NC | |
| 160301 | Elem concepts of math | | | NC | |
| 181599 | Relig values in marriage | | | NC | |
| 220599 | Naturalization course | | | NC | |

㊳ **UNIVERSITY OF NORTHERN COLORADO**

Ms. Alma Azama
University Program Specialist II
Frasier Hall, Room 11
University of Northern Colorado
Greeley, Colorado 80639
Phone: 303-351-2944

Enrollment on a noncredit basis accepted in all credit courses. Gifted high school students are permitted to enroll in undergraduate courses for credit. Overseas enrollment accepted.

| NCES No. | Course Title | Dept. | Course No. | Credits | Level |
|---|---|---|---|---|---|
| | **College courses** | | | | |
| 040101 | Principles of acctg I | Acctg | 220 | 4Q | L |
| 040101 | Principles of acctg II | Acctg | 221 | 4Q | L |
| 070899 | Hndcpd stu in reg clsrm | EdSE | 410 | 3Q | U |
| 070899 | Wkg w hndcp stu elem sch | EdSE | 406 | 2Q | U |
| 100504 | Cnsmr aspct of hshld equi | FND | 308 | 4Q | U |
| 120299 | Middle Ages & Renaissance | Hum | 112 | 4Q | L |
| 1503 | Biological science | Sci | 104 | 3Q | L |
| 160102 | Intro to history of math | Math | 464 | 3Q | U |
| 160302 | Intermediate algebra | Math | 123 | 5Q | L |
| 160602 | Plane trigonometry | Math | 125 | 5Q | L |
| 2007 | Psych of fam relations | Psy | 499 | 3Q | U |
| 220306 | World geography | Geog | 100 | 5Q | L |
| 220306 | Geography of Colorado | Geog | 350 | 3Q | U |
| 220501 | National govt of the US | PSci | 100 | 5Q | L |
| 220501 | President and bureaucracy | PSci | 302 | 3Q | U |
| 220511 | State & local government | PSci | 201 | 5Q | L |

㊴ **UNIVERSITY OF NORTHERN IOWA**

Dr. James E. Bodensteiner
Coordinator of Credit Programs
144 Gilchrist
University of Northern Iowa
Cedar Falls, Iowa 50614
Phone: 319-273-2121

Enrollment on a noncredit basis accepted in some credit courses. Gifted high school students are permitted to enroll in undergraduate courses for credit. Overseas enrollment accepted for college courses. Students cannot earn a degree solely through correspondence study.

| NCES No. | Course Title | Dept. | Course No. | Credits | Level |
|---|---|---|---|---|---|
| | **College courses** | | | | |
| 040101 | Principles of acctng I | Acctg | 12030 | 3S | L |

| NCES No. | Course Title | Dept. | Course No. | Credits | Level |
|---|---|---|---|---|---|
| 070199 | History of education | Educ | 26134 | 3S | B |
| 070404 | Methods in elem science | Educ | 21142 | 2S | B |
| 070404 | Social studies elem sch | Educ | 21143 | 2S | B |
| 070404 | Group eval techniques | Educ | 25181 | 3S | B |
| 100313 | Basic nutrition | HmEc | 31030 | 2S | L |
| 100604 | Personal relationships | HmEc | 31051 | 2S | L |
| 120307 | Modern drama | EngLL | 62115 | 3S | B |
| 120307 | 20th-cent British novel | EngLL | 62120 | 3S | B |
| 120307 | Shakespeare | EngLL | 62148 | 3S | B |
| 120307 | British novel thru Hardy | EngLL | 62156 | 3S | B |
| 120307 | Lit for young adults | EngLL | 62165 | 3S | B |
| 120307 | Intro to literature | EngLL | 62031 | 3S | L |
| 120310 | Writing exposition | EngLL | 62003 | 3S | L |
| 150202 | Elements of weather | ErSci | 87021 | 3S | L |
| 150599 | Fundamentals of geology | Geol | 87128 | 4S | B |
| 160103 | Survey of math ideas | Math | 80020 | 3S | L |
| 160103 | Metric system measurement | Math | 80136 | 2S | B |
| 160803 | Fund of statistical meth | Math | 80172 | 3S | B |
| 181104 | Religions of the world | Relig | 64124 | 3S | B |
| 181104 | Individual readings relig | Relig | 64189 | VC | B |
| 190509 | Personal health | Hlth | 41015 | 3S | L |
| 200199 | Intro to psychology | Psych | 40008 | 3S | L |
| 200804 | Child psychology | Educ | 20100 | 2S | B |
| 200804 | Development of young chld | Educ | 20109 | 3S | B |
| 200804 | Psych of adolescence | Educ | 20116 | 2S | B |
| 200804 | Social psychology educ | Educ | 20140 | 3S | B |
| 210499 | Amer social welfare inst | SocWk | 45040 | 3S | L |
| 220102 | Culture nature society | Anthr | 99011 | 3S | L |
| 220299 | Econ for general educ | Econ | 92024 | 3S | U |
| 220305 | Communicatng through maps | Geog | 97050 | 2S | L |
| 220306 | Regional geog Middle East | Geog | 97150 | 3S | B |
| 220308 | Urban geography | Geog | 97132 | 3S | U |
| 220399 | World geography | Geog | 97025 | 3S | U |
| 220399 | History of Iowa | Hist | 96130 | 3S | B |
| 220423 | Foreign area stdy: India | Hist | 68125 | 3S | U |
| 220426 | Modern Europe to 1815 | Hist | 96054 | 3S | L |
| 220426 | Modern Europe since 1815 | Hist | 96055 | 3S | L |
| 220432 | US history to 1877 | Hist | 96014 | 3S | U |
| 220432 | US history since 1877 | Hist | 96015 | 3S | U |
| 220432 | Recent US history | Hist | 96116 | 3S | B |
| 220432 | The black in US history | Hist | 96122 | 3S | B |
| 220432 | US foreign relations | Hist | 96138 | 3S | B |
| 220472 | Women's studies: intro | Hist | 68040 | 3S | L |
| 220499 | Humanities I | Hist | 68021 | 4S | U |
| 220499 | Humanities II | Hist | 68022 | 4S | U |
| 220501 | Intro to Amer politics | PolSc | 94014 | 3S | U |
| 220601 | Principles of sociology | Socio | 98058 | 3S | U |
| 220602 | Corrections & punishment | Socio | 98126 | 3S | B |
| 220605 | The family | Socio | 98105 | 2S | U |
| 220610 | Social deviance & control | Socio | 98123 | 3S | B |
| 220613 | Social problems | Socio | 98060 | 3S | U |
| 220615 | Minority group relations | Socio | 98130 | 3S | B |

## (55) UNIVERSITY OF OKLAHOMA

Mr. John Burgeson
Course Development Specialist
Independent Study Department
University of Oklahoma
1700 Asp Avenue, Room B-1
Norman, Oklahoma 73037
Phone: 405-325-1921

Enrollment on a noncredit basis accepted in all credit courses. Overseas enrollment accepted.

| NCES No. | Course Title | Dept. | Course No. | Credits | Level |
|---|---|---|---|---|---|
| | **High School courses** | | | | |
| 0114 | Conservatn nat resources | SocSt | | HF | H |
| 030502 | Art understanding | Art | D | HF | H |
| 040104 | Bookkeeping | Acctg | A | HF | H |
| 040104 | Bookkeeping | Acctg | B | HF | H |
| 040207 | Begin type for one hand | Typew | AH | HF | H |
| 040207 | Typewrit first yr fir sem | Typew | A | HF | H |
| 040207 | Typewrit first yr sec sem | Typew | B | HF | H |
| 040207 | Typewrit second yr fir se | Typew | C | HF | H |
| 040207 | Typewrit second yr sec se | Typew | D | HF | H |
| 040601 | Business Engl first sem | Engl | K | HF | H |
| 040604 | Business Engl second sem | Engl | L | HF | H |
| 0499 | General business | Bus | A | HF | H |
| 0499 | General business | Bus | B | HF | H |
| 0506 | Creative prose writing | Jrnl | | HF | H |
| 0506 | The school newspaper | Jrnl | | HF | H |
| 080102 | Aeronautics | Sci | A | HF | H |
| 100109 | Clothes | HmEc | B | HF | H |
| 100401 | General homemaking | HmEc | C | HF | H |
| 100501 | Home furnishings | HmEc | F | HF | H |
| 100601 | Relationships child grow | HmEc | A | HF | H |
| 110503 | Beginning lettering | Art | A | HF | H |
| 110503 | Beginning drawing | Art | C | HF | H |
| 110503 | Drawing II | Art | E | HF | H |
| 1203 | Engl ninth-gr first sem | Engl | A | HF | H |
| 1203 | Engl ninth-gr second sem | Engl | B | HF | H |
| 1203 | Engl tenth-gr first sem | Engl | C | HF | H |
| 1203 | Engl tenth-gr second sem | Engl | D | HF | H |
| 1203 | Engl eleventh-gr fir sem | Engl | E | HF | H |
| 1203 | Engl twelth-gr fir sem | Engl | G | HF | H |
| 1203 | Engl twelth-gr sec sem | Engl | H | HF | H |
| 120305 | Basic English grammar | Engl | | HF | H |
| 120310 | Advanced composition | Engl | J | HF | H |
| 1210 | French first-yr first sem | Frnch | A | HF | H |
| 1210 | French first-yr second se | Frnch | B | HF | H |
| 1210 | French second-yr first se | Frnch | C | HF | H |
| 1210 | French second-yr sec sem | Frnch | D | HF | H |
| 1216 | Latin first-yr first sem | Clas | A | HF | H |
| 1216 | Latin first-yr second sem | Clas | B | HF | H |
| 1216 | Latin second-yr first sem | Clas | C | HF | H |
| 1216 | Latin second-yr second se | Clas | D | HF | H |
| 1225 | Spanish first-yr fir sem | Span | A | HF | H |
| 1225 | Spanish first-yr sec sem | Span | B | HF | H |
| 1225 | Spanish second-yr fir sem | Span | C | HF | H |
| 1225 | Spanish second-yr sec sem | Span | D | HF | H |
| 140199 | Use of the library | LibSi | | HF | H |
| 1503 | Biology first sem | Bio | A | HF | H |
| 1503 | Biology second sem | Bio | B | HF | H |
| 160301 | General math first sem | Math | K | HF | H |
| 160301 | General math second sem | Math | M | HF | H |
| 160302 | Algebra first sem | Math | A | HF | H |
| 160302 | Algebra second sem | Math | B | HF | H |
| 160302 | Algebra third sem | Math | E | HF | H |
| 160302 | Algebra fourth sem | Math | F | HF | H |
| 160401 | Pre-calc & analytic geom | Math | H | HF | H |
| 160601 | Modern geometry first sem | Math | C | HF | H |
| 160601 | Modern geometry sec sem | Math | D | HF | H |
| 160602 | Trigonometry | Math | G | HF | H |
| 161201 | Business mathematics | Math | L | HF | H |
| 1905 | Modern health | Scien | C | HF | H |
| 2001 | Psychology | Psych | | HF | H |
| 220201 | Basic economics | Econ | | HF | H |
| 220208 | Consumer econ first sem | Econ | A | HF | H |
| 220208 | Consumer econ second sem | Econ | B | HF | H |
| 220208 | Democracy | Dem | | HF | H |
| 2203 | World geography first sem | Geog | A | HF | H |
| 2203 | World geography sec sem | Geog | B | HF | H |
| 220428 | Oklahoma history | Hist | O | HF | H |
| 220432 | American hist first sem | Hist | E | HF | H |
| 220432 | American hist second sem | Hist | F | HF | H |
| 220433 | World history first sem | Hist | J | HF | H |
| 220433 | World history second sem | Hist | K | HF | H |
| 220501 | American government | Govt | | HF | H |
| 2206 | Sociology | Socio | | HF | H |
| 2299 | Etiquette everyday mannrs | HmEc | | HF | H |
| | **College courses** | | | | |
| 030302 | Understanding of music | Music | 1113 | 3S | L |
| 030402 | History of the theater I | Drama | 2713 | 3S | L |
| 030402 | History of the theater II | Drama | 2723 | 3S | L |
| 040101 | Fund of financial acct | Acctg | 2113 | 3S | L |
| 040101 | Fund of managerial acct | Acctg | 2123 | 3S | L |
| 040106 | Cost accounting | Acctg | 3313 | 3S | U |
| 040108 | Intermed accounting I | Acctg | 3113 | 3S | U |
| 040108 | Intermed accounting II | Acctg | 3123 | 3S | U |
| 040301 | Business finance | Fin | 3303 | 3S | U |
| 040302 | Personal finance | Fin | 1203 | 3S | L |
| 040308 | Fncl intermediaries/mkts | Fin | 3403 | 3S | U |
| 040601 | Adv business communicatn | BuCom | 3223 | 3S | U |
| 040604 | Business report writing | BuCom | 3113 | 3S | U |
| 040904 | Prin orgn and management | Mgmt | 3013 | 3S | U |
| 041001 | Intro to marketing | Mktg | 3013 | 3S | U |
| 0411 | Personnel management | Mgmt | 3513 | 3S | U |

| NCES No. | Course Title | Dept. | Course No. | Credits | Level |
|---|---|---|---|---|---|
| 041303 | Real estate principles | Fin | 3503 | 3S | U |
| 0501 | Intro to advertising | Jrnl | 2303 | 3S | L |
| 0506 | Prof writing: fundamentals | Jrnl | 3504 | 4S | U |
| 0506 | Prof writ: appr to fiction | Jrnl | 3514 | 4S | U |
| 0506 | Prof writ: magazine writ | Jrnl | 3534 | 3S | U |
| 0506 | Prof writing: the novel | Jdur | 4514 | 4S | U |
| 0506 | Radio and TV regulation | Jdur | 4613 | 4S | U |
| 0509 | Prin of public relations | Jrnl | 3413 | 3S | U |
| 070402 | Supvsn sec sch publicat | Jrnl | 4703 | 3S | U |
| 070503 | Public school art | Art | 3142 | 2S | U |
| 070512 | Lang arts elementary schs | Educ | 4252 | 2S | U |
| 070512 | Teaching of English | Engl | 4913 | 3S | U |
| 070522 | Social studies elem schs | Educ | 4322 | 2S | U |
| 0708 | Educ exceptional children | Educ | 3412 | 2S | U |
| 080703 | Hydrology | EngAS | 5843 | 3S | U |
| 080901 | Electrical science | EngAS | 2613 | 3S | L |
| 081102 | Fluid mechanics | EngAS | 3223 | 3S | U |
| 081104 | Rigid-body mechanics | EngAS | 2113 | 3S | L |
| 0812 | Thermodynamics | EngAS | 2213 | 3S | L |
| 0815 | Intro to industrial engrg | EngAS | 2011 | 3S | L |
| 081503 | Fund of engrg economy | EngAS | 4223 | 3S | U |
| 0819 | Strength of materials | EngAS | 2153 | 3S | L |
| 0819 | Struct and prop materials | EngAS | 2313 | 3S | L |
| 1001 | Textiles | HmEc | 2443 | 3S | L |
| 100109 | Sociodynamics of fashion | HmEc | 3452 | 2S | U |
| 100313 | Elementary nutrition | HmEc | 1823 | 3S | L |
| 120201 | Classical mythology | Clas | 2383 | 3S | L |
| 120201 | World lit to 1700 | Engl | 2433 | 3S | L |
| 120201 | The Bible as literature | Engl | 2453 | 3S | L |
| 120201 | Mod Brit and cont drama | Engl | 4433 | 3S | U |
| 120201 | World lit since 1700 | Engl | 2443 | 3S | L |
| 120302 | Hist of English language | Engl | 4133 | 3S | U |
| 120305 | Prin English comp I | Engl | 1113 | 3S | L |
| 120305 | Prin English comp II | Engl | 1213 | 3S | L |
| 120307 | Engl lit 1375 to 1700 | Engl | 2543 | 3S | L |
| 120307 | Engl lit 1700 to present | Engl | 2653 | 3S | L |
| 120307 | American literature I | Engl | 2773 | 3S | L |
| 120307 | American literature II | Engl | 2883 | 3S | L |
| 120307 | Milton maj prose min poet | Engl | 4613 | 3S | U |
| 120307 | Milton maj poems Chr doct | Engl | 4623 | 3S | U |
| 120307 | Shakespeare's comedies | Engl | 4523 | 3S | U |
| 120307 | Shakespeare's tragedies | Engl | 4533 | 3S | U |
| 120307 | Milton | Engl | 4553 | 3S | U |
| 120307 | American drama | Engl | 4813 | 3S | U |
| 120307 | Ethnic literature | Engl | 2023 | 3S | L |
| 120310 | Prof writing: the novel | Jour | 4514 | 4S | U |
| 1210 | French civilization | Frnch | 4313 | 3S | U |
| 1210 | Beginning French I | Frnch | 1115 | 5S | L |
| 1210 | Beginning French II | Frnch | 1225 | 5S | L |
| 1210 | Sur Frnch lit to 1800 | Frnch | 4153 | 3S | U |
| 1210 | Sur Frnch lit 19th-20th c | Frnch | 4163 | 3S | U |
| 1210 | French reading I | Frnch | 2113 | 3S | L |
| 1210 | French reading II | Frnch | 2223 | 3S | L |
| 1210 | French composition I | Frnch | 2322 | 2S | L |
| 1210 | French composition II | Frnch | 2422 | 2S | L |
| 1210 | Advanced Frnch compositn | Frnch | 3423 | 3S | U |
| 1211 | Beginning German I | Ger | 1115 | 5S | L |
| 1211 | Beginning German II | Ger | 1225 | 5S | L |
| 1211 | Hist German lit to 1750 | Ger | 4153 | 3S | U |
| 1211 | Begin German for read I | Ger | 1013 | 3S | L |
| 1211 | Begin German for read II | Ger | 1023 | 3S | L |
| 1211 | Intermediate German I | Ger | 2113 | 3S | L |
| 1211 | Intermediate German II | Ger | 2223 | 3S | L |
| 1211 | Scientific German I | Ger | 3013 | 3S | U |
| 1211 | German composition I | Ger | 2322 | 2S | L |
| 1211 | German composition II | Ger | 2422 | 2S | L |
| 1211 | Hist German lit from 1750 | Ger | 4163 | 3S | U |
| 1212 | New Testament Greek | Greek | 2123 | 3S | L |
| 1213 | Beginning Hebrew I | Heb | 1113 | 3S | L |
| 1213 | Beginning Hebrew II | Heb | 1213 | 3S | L |
| 1213 | Intermediate Hebrew | Heb | 2113 | 3S | L |
| 1216 | Beginning Latin I | Latin | 1115 | 5S | L |
| 1216 | Beginning Latin II | Latin | 1215 | 5S | L |
| 1216 | Advanced poetry—Vergil | Latin | 3213 | 3S | U |
| 1216 | Interm prose—Cicero Orat | Latin | 2113A | 3S | L |
| 1216 | Interm prose—livy | Latin | 2113B | 3S | L |
| 1216 | Latin derivatives | Clas | 1112 | 2S | L |
| 1216 | Interm prose-Cicero essay | Latin | 2113 | 3S | L |
| 1220 | Beginning Russian I | Russ | 1115 | 5S | L |
| 1220 | Beginning Russian II | Russ | 1225 | 5S | L |
| 1220 | Scientific Russian I | Russ | 3023 | 3S | U |
| 1220 | Scientific Russian II | Russ | 3213 | 3S | U |
| 1225 | Spanish civilization | Span | 4313 | 3S | U |
| 1225 | Beginning Spanish I | Span | 1115 | 5S | L |
| 1225 | Beginning Spanish II | Span | 1225 | 5S | L |
| 1225 | Sur Sp-Am lit 1888-pres | Span | 4103 | 3S | U |
| 1225 | Sur Spanish lit to 1700 | Span | 4153 | 3S | U |
| 1225 | Sur Spanish lit from 1700 | Span | 4163 | 3S | U |
| 1225 | Spanish reading I | Span | 2113 | 3S | L |
| 1225 | Spanish reading II | Span | 2223 | 3S | L |
| 1225 | Spanish composition I | Span | 2322 | 2S | L |
| 1225 | Spanish composition II | Span | 2422 | 2S | L |
| 1225 | Advan Spanish comp | Span | 3423 | 3S | U |
| 1225 | Surv Sp/Amer lit to 1888 | Span | 4093 | 3S | U |
| 1299 | Soviet lit in English | MLang | 3533 | 3S | U |
| 1299 | Russian lit in translatn | Russ | 2003 | 3S | L |
| 1299 | Medical vocabulary | Clas | 2412 | 2S | L |
| 1304 | Elementary criminal law | PolSc | 4813 | 3S | U |
| 130402 | Criminal legal procedure | PolSc | 4803 | 3S | U |
| 1307 | Legal environ of business | BuLaw | 3323 | 3S | U |
| 1309 | Real property | BuLaw | 4613 | 3S | U |
| 1501 | General astronomy | Astro | 1504 | 4S | L |
| 1504 | Chemis for nonsci majors | Chem | 1614 | 4S | L |
| 150408 | Organic chemistry I | Chem | 3053 | 3S | U |
| 150408 | Organic chemistry II | Chem | 3153 | 3S | U |
| 1505 | Physical geology w/lab | Geo | 1114 | 4S | L |
| 1505 | Historical geology w/lab | Geo | 1124 | 4S | L |
| 160302 | Begin algebra for col stu | Math | 0133 | 5U | D |
| 160302 | Intermediate algebra | Math | 1213 | 3S | L |
| 160302 | College algebra | Math | 1513 | 3S | L |
| 160306 | Linear algebra | Math | 3333 | 3S | U |
| 160401 | Calculus I | Math | 1823 | 3S | L |
| 160401 | Calculus II | Math | 2423 | 3S | L |
| 160401 | Calculus III | Math | 2434 | 3S | L |
| 160602 | Trigonometry | Math | 1612 | 2S | L |
| 160603 | Analytic geometry | Math | 1812 | 2S | L |
| 160802 | Elements of statistics | Econ | 2843 | 3S | L |
| 160802 | Elementary statistics | Math | 3703 | 3S | U |
| 1611 | Calculus I: bus/life/so sc | Math | 1743 | 3S | L |
| 1611 | Engineering mathematics I | Math | 3114 | 4S | U |
| 1611 | Math for bus/life/soc sci | Math | 1443 | 3S | L |
| 1611 | Calculus for bus/life/soc | Math | 2123 | 3S | L |
| 1801 | Aesthetics: beauty and art | Philo | 3053 | 3S | U |
| 1803 | History of ethics | Philo | 3253 | 3S | U |
| 180401 | Hist Greek and Roman phil | Philo | 3313 | 3S | U |
| 180402 | Hist medieval philosophy | Philo | 3323 | 3S | U |
| 180403 | Hist modern philosophy | Philo | 3333 | 3S | U |
| 1805 | Introduction to logic | Philo | 1113 | 3S | L |
| 190106 | Org & admin health phy ed | PhyEd | 4943 | 3S | U |
| 190107 | Adaptive phy ed program | PhyEd | 3882 | 2S | U |
| 190110 | Tests and meas in phy ed | PhyEd | 4923 | 3S | U |
| 190205 | Kinesiology | PhyEd | 3713 | 3S | U |
| 190311 | Theory of baseball | PhyEd | 3052 | 2S | U |
| 190311 | Theory of basketball | PhyEd | 3072 | 2S | U |
| 190311 | Theory of track and field | PhyEd | 3082 | 2S | U |
| 190311 | Theory of wrestling | PhyEd | 3092 | 2S | U |
| 1905 | Health education | Educ | 2913 | 3S | L |
| 1905 | Health education | PhyEd | 2913 | 3S | L |
| 190704 | Leadership in recreation | PhyEd | 2932 | 2S | L |
| 2001 | Elements of psychology | Psych | 1113 | 3S | L |
| 200504 | Intro life-span dev psych | Psych | 1603 | 3S | L |
| 200509 | Intro to personality | Psych | 1193 | 3S | L |
| 200901 | Industrial psychology | Psych | 3363 | 3S | U |
| 2101 | Intro public administratn | PolSc | 2173 | 3S | L |
| 210111 | Conservation | Geog | 3253 | 3S | U |
| 210304 | Intro law enforcement | PolSc | 2803 | 3S | L |
| 210304 | Police administration I | PolSc | 3803 | 3S | U |
| 210304 | Prin criminal investigatn | PolSc | 3853 | 3S | U |
| 2201 | General anthropology | Anthr | 1113 | 3S | L |
| 220101 | Intro to archaeology | Anthr | 2113 | 3S | L |
| 220101 | Archaeology of N America | Anthr | 3813 | 3S | U |
| 220102 | Mythology and folklore | Anthr | 3043 | 3S | U |
| 220104 | High civiliz ancient Amer | Anthr | 3893 | 3S | U |
| 220104 | Nat people/western N Amer | Anthr | 3823 | 3S | U |
| 220107 | Intro to social anthropol | Anthr | 2203 | 3S | L |
| 220201 | Principles of economics I | Econ | 2113 | 3S | L |
| 220201 | Principles of economicsII | Econ | 2123 | 3S | L |
| 220214 | Internat econ problems | Econ | 3613 | 3S | U |
| 2203 | Human geography | Geog | 1103 | 3S | L |
| 220302 | Prin economic geography | Geog | 1213 | 3S | L |
| 220402 | US diplomat hist to 1900 | Hist | 3563 | 3S | U |
| 220402 | US diplomat hist to 1900 | PolSc | 3563 | 3S | U |
| 220403 | Econ development of US | Econ | 1013 | 3S | L |
| 220423 | East Asian civizn to 1800 | Hist | 1723 | 3S | L |

| NCES No. | Course Title | Dept. | Course No. | Credits | Level |
|---|---|---|---|---|---|
| 220423 | Mod East Asia since 1800 | Hist | 1733 | 3S | L |
| 220424 | England to 1603 | Hist | 2313 | 3S | L |
| 220424 | England since 1603 | Hist | 2323 | 3S | L |
| 220426 | Sur ancient medieval Euro | Hist | 1013 | 3S | L |
| 220426 | Europe 1500 to 1815 | Hist | 1223 | 3S | L |
| 220426 | Europe since 1815 | Hist | 1233 | 3S | L |
| 220427 | Hispanic Amer 1492-1810 | Hist | 2613 | 3S | L |
| 220427 | Hispanic Amer 1810-pres | Hist | 2623 | 3S | L |
| 220428 | History of Oklahoma | Hist | 3393 | 3S | U |
| 220429 | Hebrew civ in ancie times | Clas | 3413 | 3S | U |
| 220429 | Hebrew civ in ancie times | Hist | 3413 | 3S | U |
| 220432 | United States 1492-1865 | Hist | 1483 | 3S | L |
| 220432 | United States 1865-pres | Hist | 1493 | 3S | L |
| 220433 | World civilization-1600 | Hist | 1913 | 3S | L |
| 220433 | World civilization-1980 | Hist | 1923 | 3S | L |
| 220450 | Ancient history | Hist | 1033 | 3S | L |
| 2205 | Intro to political sci | PolSc | 1603 | 3S | L |
| 220501 | Govt of the United States | PolSc | 1113 | 3S | L |
| 220505 | Intro to internatl relat | PolSc | 2503 | 3S | L |
| 220507 | American polit parties | PolSc | 2403 | 3S | L |
| 220509 | Government of Oklahoma | PolSc | 3303 | 3S | U |
| 220511 | State government | PolSc | 2303 | 3S | L |
| 220511 | Urban govt and politics | PolSc | 3313 | 3S | U |
| 220602 | Sociology: crime and delin | Socio | 3523 | 3S | U |
| 220605 | The family | Socio | 3723 | 3S | U |
| 220606 | Intro to sociology | Socio | 1113 | 3S | L |

**Noncredit courses**

| NCES No. | Course Title | Dept. | Credits | Level |
|---|---|---|---|---|
| 0506 | Creative prose writing | Jrnl | NC | H |
| 0506 | Creative prose writing | Jrnl | NC | D |
| 0506 | Prof writ I fundamentals | Jrnl | NC | D |
| 0506 | Prof writ II appr fiction | Jrnl | NC | D |
| 0506 | Prof writ III fiction | Jrnl | NC | D |
| 0506 | Prof writ IV nonfiction | Jrnl | NC | D |
| 110503 | Calligraphy | Art | NC | D |
| 110503 | Drawing fundamentals | Art | NC | D |
| 110503 | Drawing methods | Art | NC | D |
| 120305 | English review | Engl | NC | D |
| 1212 | New Testament Greek | Greek | NC | L |

## (56) UNIVERSITY OF SOUTH CAROLINA

Ms. Sylvia A. Brazell
Director
Correspondence Study
University of South Carolina
915 Gregg Street
Columbia, South Carolina 29208
Phone: 803-777-2188

Only in exceptional cases are gifted high school students permitted to enroll in undergraduate courses for credit. Overseas enrollment accepted. Maximum period for completion of a course is one year from date of enrollment. For additional information, please contact the Correspondence Study Office and request a free catalog. External degrees are not offered.

| NCES No. | Course Title | Dept. | Course No. | Credits | Level |
|---|---|---|---|---|---|
| | **High School courses** | | | | |
| 040101 | High school acctg I | BAdm | BE023 | HF | H |
| 040101 | High school acctg II | BAdm | BE024 | HF | H |
| 040299 | Office proc & practices | BAdm | BE013 | HF | H |
| 040299 | Office proc & practices | BAdm | BE014 | HF | H |
| 040901 | General business I | BAdm | BE021 | HF | H |
| 040901 | General business II | BAdm | BE022 | HF | H |
| 100604 | Etiquette | HmEc | HE001 | HF | H |
| 1203 | Basic English I | Engl | EN001 | HF | H |
| 1203 | Basic English 2 | Engl | EN002 | HF | H |
| 120399 | Ninth-grade English I | Engl | EN031 | HF | H |
| 120399 | Ninth-grade English II | Engl | EN032 | HF | H |
| 120399 | Tenth-grade English I | Engl | EN033 | HF | H |
| 120399 | Tenth-grade English II | Engl | EN034 | HF | H |
| 120399 | Eleventh-grade English I | Engl | EN035 | HF | H |
| 120399 | Eleventh-grade English II | Engl | EN036 | HF | H |
| 120399 | Twelfth-grade English I | Engl | EN037 | HF | H |
| 120399 | Twelfth-grade English II | Engl | EN038 | HF | H |
| 120399 | Business English | Engl | BE011 | HF | H |
| 120399 | Remedial English | Engl | EN001 | HF | H |
| 150301 | Basic biology I | Sci | S1015 | HF | H |
| 150301 | Basic biology II | Sci | S1016 | HF | H |

| NCES No. | Course Title | Dept. | Course No. | Credits | Level |
|---|---|---|---|---|---|
| 1508 | Physical science | Sci | SI013 | HF | H |
| 1508 | Physical science | Sci | SI014 | HF | H |
| 160302 | Beginning algebra I | Math | MA031 | HF | H |
| 160302 | Beginning algebra II | Math | MA032 | HF | H |
| 160302 | Advanced algebra I | Math | MA035 | HF | H |
| 160302 | Advanced algebra II | Math | MA036 | HF | H |
| 160401 | Precalculus | Math | MA041 | HF | H |
| 160401 | Precalculus | Math | MA042 | HF | H |
| 160601 | Geometry I | Math | MA033 | HF | H |
| 160601 | Geometry II | Math | MA034 | HF | H |
| 160602 | Trigonometry | Math | MA037 | HF | H |
| 161201 | Business & consumer math | Math | MA009 | HF | H |
| 161201 | Business & consumer math | Math | MA010 | HF | H |
| 161299 | Basic math I | Math | MA001 | HF | H |
| 161299 | Basic math 2 | Math | MA002 | HF | H |
| 190599 | Health science I | Sci | S1001 | HF | H |
| 190599 | Health science II | Sci | S1002 | HF | H |
| 200104 | Psychology | SoStu | SS007 | HF | H |
| 220101 | Economics | SoStu | BE027 | HF | H |
| 220305 | World geography I | SoStu | SS021 | HF | H |
| 220305 | World geography II | SoStu | SS022 | HF | H |
| 220432 | American history I | SoStu | SS033 | HF | H |
| 220432 | American history II | SoStu | SS034 | HF | H |
| 220433 | World history I | SoStu | SS031 | HF | H |
| 220433 | World history II | SoStu | SS032 | HF | H |
| 220501 | American government | SoStu | SS035 | HF | H |
| 220501 | American government | SoStu | SS036 | HF | H |
| 220502 | Civics | SoStu | SS001 | HF | H |
| 220606 | Sociology | SoStu | SS003 | HF | H |

**College courses**

| NCES No. | Course Title | Dept. | Course No. | Credits | Level |
|---|---|---|---|---|---|
| 040101 | Fundamentals of acctg | BAdm | C-225 | 3S | L |
| 040101 | Fundamentals of acctg | BAdm | C-226 | 3S | L |
| 040103 | Auditing I | BAdm | C-438 | 4S | U |
| 040106 | Cost/managerial acctg I | BAdm | C-432 | 3S | U |
| 040108 | Financial accounting I | BAdm | C-431 | 4S | U |
| 040108 | Financial accounting II | BAdm | C-433 | 4S | U |
| 040108 | Financial accounting III | BAdm | C-436 | 3S | U |
| 040109 | Govern & nonprofit acctg | BAdm | C-533 | 3S | U |
| 040114 | Tax I | BAdm | C-434 | 3S | U |
| 040301 | Commer bank prac & policy | BAdm | C-465 | 3S | U |
| 040399 | Commer & central banking | BAdm | C-301 | 3S | U |
| 040710 | Prin of risk & insurance | BAdm | C-341 | 3S | U |
| 040904 | Prin of management | BAdm | C-371 | 3S | U |
| 040999 | Retailing management | BAdm | C-551 | 3S | U |
| 041001 | Marketing | BAdm | C-350 | 3S | U |
| 041004 | Marketing management | BAdm | C-558 | 3S | U |
| 041005 | Marketing communications | BAdm | C-352 | 3S | U |
| 041005 | Promot policies & strat | BAdm | C-454 | 3S | U |
| 041099 | Channels and institutions | BAdm | C-353 | 3S | U |
| 041099 | Consumer behavior | BAdm | C-455 | 3S | U |
| 041099 | Marketing research | BAdm | C-457 | 3S | U |
| 041099 | Marketing environment | BAdm | C-550 | 3S | U |
| 041303 | Intro real est & urb dev | BAdm | C-366 | 3S | U |
| 070401 | Organ & curr middle sch | Educ | C-451 | 3S | U |
| 070509 | Health educ elem schools | HEdu | C-331 | 3S | U |
| 070512 | Lang arts in elem school | Educ | C-507 | 3S | U |
| 070515 | Science in elem school | Educ | C-515 | 3S | U |
| 070516 | Basic concepts elem math | Math | C-501 | 3S | U |
| 070516 | Basic concepts elem math | Math | C-502 | 3S | U |
| 070520 | Intro to educ psychology | Educ | C-335 | 3S | U |
| 070803 | Psych of exceptnl child | Psych | C-528 | 3S | U |
| 070805 | Spec learn disab sch chil | Psych | C-531 | 3S | U |
| 090710 | Personal & commun health | HEdu | C-221 | 3S | L |
| 100206 | Personal finance | BAdm | C-369 | 3S | U |
| 110699 | Transportation | BAdm | C-549 | 3S | U |
| 120103 | Vocabulary & semantics | Engl | C-452 | 3S | U |
| 120201 | The short story | Engl | C-435 | 3S | U |
| 120205 | Studies in literary theor | Engl | C430a | 3S | U |
| 120307 | Composition & literature | Engl | C-102 | 3S | L |
| 120307 | American literature | Engl | C-287 | 3S | L |
| 120307 | Chaucer | Engl | C-401 | 3S | U |
| 120307 | Shakespeare's tragedies | Engl | C-405 | 3S | U |
| 120307 | Shakespeare's comedies | Engl | C-406 | 3S | U |
| 120307 | Children's literature | Engl | C-431 | 3S | U |
| 120307 | Adolescent literature | Engl | C-432 | 3S | L |
| 120307 | Fiction | Engl | C-282 | 3S | L |
| 120307 | English literature II | Engl | C-290 | 3S | L |
| 120307 | English literature I | Engl | C-289 | 3S | L |
| 120307 | Drama | Engl | C-284 | 3S | L |
| 120307 | Poetry | Engl | C-286 | 3S | L |
| 120310 | Composition | Engl | C-101 | 3S | L |

| NCES No. | Course Title | Dept. | Course No. | Credits | Level |
|---|---|---|---|---|---|
| 1210 | Intro French | ForLa | C-102 | 3S | L |
| 1210 | Intermediate French | ForLa | C-201 | 3S | L |
| 1210 | Intermediate French | ForLa | C-202 | 3S | L |
| 1210 | Intro French | ForLa | C-101 | 4S | L |
| 1211 | Intermediate German | ForLa | C-201 | 3S | L |
| 1211 | Intermediate German | ForLa | C-202 | 3S | L |
| 1216 | Intro Latin | ForLa | C-101 | 4S | L |
| 1216 | Intro Latin | ForLa | C-102 | 3S | L |
| 1225 | Intro Spanish | ForLa | C-101 | 4S | L |
| 1225 | Intro Spanish | ForLa | C-102 | 3S | L |
| 1225 | Intermediate Spanish | ForLa | C-201 | 3S | L |
| 1225 | Intermediate Spanish | ForLa | C-202 | 3S | L |
| 130202 | Survey of commercial law | BAdm | C-324 | 3S | U |
| 130202 | Commercial law I | BAdm | C-347 | 3S | U |
| 130202 | Commercial law II | BAdm | C-348 | 3S | U |
| 1501 | Descriptive astronomy IA | Astro | C111A | 1S | L |
| 1501 | Descriptive astronomy II | Astro | C-112 | 3S | L |
| 1501 | Descriptive astronomy IIA | Astro | C112A | 1S | L |
| 1501 | Descriptive astronomy I | Astro | C-111 | 3S | L |
| 150310 | Oceans and man | MSci | C-210 | 3S | L |
| 1507 | General physics I lab | Phys | C201L | 1S | L |
| 1507 | General physics II | Phys | C-202 | 3S | L |
| 1507 | General physics I | Phys | C-201 | 3S | L |
| 160199 | Precalculus mathematics | Math | C-125 | 3S | L |
| 160302 | College algebra | Math | C-121 | 3S | L |
| 160401 | Calc for b adm & soc sci | Math | C-122 | 3S | L |
| 160701 | Finite mathematics | Math | C-203 | 3S | L |
| 160803 | Elementary statistics | Math | C-201 | 3S | L |
| 161101 | Business mathematics | GStd | C-144 | 3S | L |
| 180499 | Hist of modern philosophy | Philo | C-202 | 3S | L |
| 180501 | Intro to logic I | Philo | C-110 | 3S | L |
| 180599 | Intro to philosophy | Philo | C-102 | 3S | L |
| 190105 | Phil & prin of physica ed | PEdu | C-232 | 3S | L |
| 190106 | Organ & admin of phy educ | PEdu | C-553 | 3S | U |
| 190110 | Measuremnt & eval phy edu | PEdu | C-545 | 3S | U |
| 190311 | Foundations of coaching | PEdu | C-302 | 3S | U |
| 190311 | Scientific bases for coac | PEdu | C-303 | 3S | U |
| 200104 | Intro to psychology | Psych | C-101 | 3S | L |
| 200499 | Psychological statistics | Psych | C-225 | 3S | L |
| 200501 | Abnormal psychology | Psych | C-410 | 3S | U |
| 200504 | Abnorm behavior in childn | Psych | C-510 | 3S | U |
| 200504 | Psych of child developmnt | Psych | C-520 | 3S | U |
| 200505 | Psychology of adjustment | Psych | C-103 | 3S | L |
| 200599 | Psychology of marriage | Psych | C-301 | 3S | U |
| 200599 | Human sexual behavior | Psych | C-300 | 3S | U |
| 200599 | Psych of adolescence | Psych | C-521 | 3S | U |
| 210101 | Intro to public admin | GInt | C-370 | 3S | U |
| 210103 | Public financial mgmt | GInt | C-571 | 3S | U |
| 210199 | Public personnel admin | GInt | C-572 | 3S | U |
| 220201 | Principles of economics | BAdm | C-221 | 3S | L |
| 220201 | Principles of economics | BAdm | C-222 | 3S | L |
| 220201 | The American economy | BAdm | C-123 | 3S | L |
| 220202 | History of econ thought | BAdm | C-408 | 3S | U |
| 220211 | Labor economics | BAdm | C-506 | 3S | U |
| 220299 | Gov policy toward bus | BAdm | C-379 | 3S | U |
| 220303 | Man's impact on environmt | Geog | C-343 | 3S | U |
| 220305 | Intro to weather & clim | Geog | C-202 | 4S | L |
| 220306 | Geog of North America | Geog | C-424 | 3S | U |
| 220426 | Intro European civilizat | Hist | C-101 | 3S | L |
| 220426 | Intro European civilizat | Hist | C-102 | 3S | L |
| 220426 | Contemporary Europe | Hist | C-321 | 3S | U |
| 220426 | Contemporary Europe | Hist | C-322 | 3S | U |
| 220428 | South Carolina | GStd | C-109 | 3S | L |
| 220428 | Hist of SC 1670-1865 | Hist | C-341 | 3S | U |
| 220428 | Hist of SC since 1865 | Hist | C-342 | 3S | U |
| 220432 | The United States | GStd | C-108 | 3S | L |
| 220432 | Hist of US discov to pres | Hist | C-201 | 3S | L |
| 220432 | Hist of US discov to pres | Hist | C-202 | 3S | L |
| 220432 | Civ War & reconstruction | Hist | C-334 | 3S | U |
| 220432 | Rise of indust America | Hist | C-335 | 3S | U |
| 220432 | US history since 1945 | Hist | C-337 | 3S | U |
| 220501 | American national govt | GInt | C-201 | 3S | L |
| 220501 | Contem US foreign policy | GInt | C-341 | 3S | U |
| 220501 | The legislative process | GInt | C-462 | 3S | U |
| 220504 | Comparative politics | GInt | C-316 | 3S | U |
| 220504 | Ideology & world politics | GInt | C-430 | 3S | U |
| 220504 | US & world prob: perspctv | GInt | C-101 | 3S | L |
| 220504 | US & world prob: perspctv | GInt | C-102 | 3S | L |
| 220505 | International relations | GInt | C-315 | 3S | U |
| 220601 | Socio of delin youth beha | Socio | C-350 | 3S | U |
| 220602 | Sociology of crime | Socio | C-353 | 3S | U |
| 220606 | Introductory sociology | Socio | C-101 | 3S | L |
| 220610 | Socio of deviant behavior | Socio | C-323 | 3S | U |
| 220613 | Intro to social problems | Socio | C-340 | 3S | U |
| 220699 | Sociology of sex roles | Socio | C-301 | 3S | U |

**Noncredit courses**

| NCES No. | Course Title | Dept. | Course No. | Credits | Level |
|---|---|---|---|---|---|
| 041303 | Fundmntls of real estate | BAdm | | NC | |
| 070301 | Guide for daycare centers | Educ | | NC | |
| 220502 | Citizenship | SoStu | | NC | |

(57) **UNIVERSITY OF SOUTH DAKOTA**

Ms. Sharon Brown
Director of Independent Study Division
126 Center for Continuing Education
University of South Dakota
414 East Clark
Vermillion, South Dakota 57069
Phone: 605-677-5281

Enrollment on a noncredit basis accepted in all credit courses. Gifted high school students are permitted to enroll in undergraduate courses for credit. Overseas enrollment accepted. Enrollment on a noncredit basis in credit courses offered at a reduced tuition rate. High school students may enroll in college-level honors program courses. Basic Math Review is a refresher course for updating math skills and prepares students to test out of freshman-level math courses required for most degrees.

| NCES No. | Course Title | Dept. | Course No. | Credits | Level |
|---|---|---|---|---|---|
| | **High School courses** | | | | |
| 030502 | Beg drawing and painting | Art | 001A | HF | H |
| 040101 | Beginning accounting 1 | BusEd | 023A | HF | H |
| 040101 | Beginning accounting 2 | BusEd | 024A | HF | H |
| 040205 | Beginning shorthand | BusEd | 015N | HF | H |
| 040207 | Beginning typing 1 | BusEd | 003N | HF | H |
| 040207 | Beginning typing 2 | BusEd | 004N | HF | H |
| 040207 | Advanced typing | BusEd | 005N | HF | H |
| 0499 | General business 1 | BusEd | 021A | HF | H |
| 0499 | General business 2 | BusEd | 022A | HF | H |
| 0499 | Business English | BusEd | 011A | HF | H |
| 070899 | Effective methods of stdy | StuSk | 001A | HF | H |
| 090199 | Health science 1 | HeaSc | 001A | HF | H |
| 090199 | Health science 2 | HeaSc | 002A | HF | H |
| 100104 | Clothing construction | HmEc | 007N | HF | H |
| 100604 | Personal adjustment | HmEc | 011A | HF | H |
| 100701 | Etiquette | Etiq | 001A | HF | H |
| 100701 | General homemaking 1 | HmEc | 003A | HF | H |
| 100701 | General homemaking 2 | HmEc | 004A | HF | H |
| 120299 | General literature 1 | Engl | 005N | QT | H |
| 120299 | General literature 2 | Engl | 006N | QT | H |
| 120305 | Ninth-grade English 1 | Engl | 031N | HF | H |
| 120305 | Ninth-grade English 2 | Engl | 032N | HF | H |
| 120307 | Tenth-grade English 1 | Engl | 033N | HF | H |
| 120307 | Tenth-grade English 2 | Engl | 034N | HF | H |
| 120307 | Eleventh-grade English 1 | Engl | 035A | HF | H |
| 120307 | Eleventh-grade English 2 | Engl | 036A | HF | H |
| 120307 | Twelfth-grade English 1 | Engl | 037N | HF | H |
| 120307 | Twelfth-grade English 2 | Engl | 038N | HF | H |
| 120307 | The short story | Engl | 009A | HF | H |
| 120308 | Improvemnt of rdg skill 1 | Engl | 003A | HF | H |
| 120308 | Improvemnt of rdg skill 2 | Engl | 004A | HF | H |
| 120310 | Composition | Engl | 023A | HF | H |
| 120399 | Basic English | Engl | 001N | HF | H |
| 1210 | Beginning French 1 | ForLa | 001N | HF | H |
| 1210 | Beginning French 2 | ForLa | 002A | HF | H |
| 1210 | Second-year French 1 | ForLa | 003A | HF | H |
| 1210 | Second-year French 2 | ForLa | 004X | HF | H |
| 1211 | Beginning German 1 | ForLa | 001A | HF | H |
| 1211 | Beginning German 2 | ForLa | 002A | HF | H |
| 1211 | Second-year German 1 | ForLa | 003A | HF | H |
| 1211 | Second-year German 2 | ForLa | 004A | HF | H |
| 1225 | Beginning Spanish 1 | ForLa | 001N | HF | H |
| 1225 | Beginning Spanish 2 | ForLa | 002N | HF | H |
| 1225 | Second-year Spanish 1 | ForLa | 003X | HF | H |
| 1225 | Second-year Spanish 2 | ForLa | 004X | HF | H |
| 1503 | Basic biology 1 | Sci | 007A | HF | H |
| 1503 | Basic biology 2 | Sci | 008A | HF | H |
| 150899 | Physical science 1 | Sci | 013A | HF | H |
| 150899 | Physical science 2 | Sci | 014A | HF | H |
| 160301 | General mathematics 1 | Math | 005A | HF | H |

| NCES No. | Course Title | Dept. | Course No. | Credits | Level |
|---|---|---|---|---|---|
| 160301 | General mathematics 2 | Math | 006A | HF | H |
| 160302 | Beginning algebra 1 | Math | 031A | HF | H |
| 160302 | Beginning algebra 2 | Math | 032A | HF | H |
| 160302 | Advanced algebra 1 | Math | 035A | HF | H |
| 160302 | Advanced algebra 2 | Math | 036A | HF | H |
| 160399 | Basic mathematics 1 | Math | 001N | HF | H |
| 160399 | Basic mathematics 2 | Math | 002N | HF | H |
| 160601 | Geometry 1 | Math | 033R | HF | H |
| 160601 | Geometry 2 | Math | 034N | HF | H |
| 160603 | Analytic geometry & calc | Math | 051A | HF | H |
| 161201 | Bus and consumer math 1 | Math | 009X | HF | H |
| 161201 | Bus and consumer math 2 | Math | 010X | HF | H |
| 200101 | Psychology | SocSt | 007N | HF | H |
| 220201 | Economics | BusEd | 027N | HF | H |
| 220299 | Economics | SocSt | 027N | HF | H |
| 2203 | World geography 1 | SocSt | 021N | HF | H |
| 2203 | World geography 2 | SocSt | 022A | HF | H |
| 220432 | American history 2 | Hist | 034N | HF | H |
| 220432 | American history 1 | Hist | 033N | HF | H |
| 220433 | World history 1 | SocSt | 031A | HF | H |
| 220433 | World history 2 | SocSt | 032A | HF | H |
| 220501 | American government 1 | Socio | 035N | HF | H |
| 220501 | American government 2 | Socio | 036N | HF | H |
| 220612 | Sociology | SocSt | 031A | HF | H |
| 220613 | Modern problems | SocSt | 037A | HF | H |
| 220699 | Personal adjustment | Socio | 011A | HF | H |

**College courses**

| NCES No. | Course Title | Dept. | Course No. | Credits | Level |
|---|---|---|---|---|---|
| 040101 | Principles of acctg 1 | Bus | 210 | 3S | L |
| 040102 | Principles of acctg 2 | Bus | 211 | 3S | L |
| 040601 | Professional writing | Engl | 300 | 3S | U |
| 051109 | Communication disorders | Commu | 131 | 3S | L |
| 070302 | Geography for elem tchrs | Educ | 162 | 2S | L |
| 070302 | Teaching art in elem sch | Educ | 206 | 4S | L |
| 070303 | Reading dev in content | Educ | 452 | 3S | U |
| 070309 | Ind std in adult & higher | Educ | 491 | 1S | U |
| 070509 | Personal health | Educ | 100 | 3S | L |
| 070509 | First aid | Educ | 250 | 2S | L |
| 070520 | Adol growth & development | Educ | 422 | 3S | U |
| 070613 | Safety education | Educ | 450 | 3S | U |
| 070701 | Guidance in elem schools | Educ | 415 | 3S | U |
| 120305 | English grammar | Engl | 203 | 3S | L |
| 120307 | Intro to literature | Engl | 163 | 3S | L |
| 120307 | Intro to British lit | Engl | 221 | 3S | L |
| 120307 | Intro to British lit 2 | Engl | 222 | 3S | L |
| 120307 | American literature 1 | Engl | 241 | 3S | L |
| 120307 | American literature 2 | Engl | 242 | 3S | L |
| 120307 | Masterpieces of lit 1 | Engl | 211 | 3S | L |
| 120307 | Masterpieces of lit 2 | Engl | 212 | 3S | L |
| 120307 | Classical mythology | Engl | 310 | 2S | U |
| 120310 | Advanced composition | Engl | 200 | 3S | L |
| 120310 | Composition | Engl | 101 | 3S | L |
| 1210 | First-year French 1 | Frnch | 101 | 4S | L |
| 1210 | First-year French 2 | Frnch | 102 | 4S | L |
| 1210 | Practical French | Frnch | 201 | 3S | L |
| 1210 | Read Frnch in arts & sci | Frnch | 203 | 3S | L |
| 1211 | German 1 | Ger | 101 | 4S | L |
| 1211 | German 2 | Ger | 102 | 4S | L |
| 1211 | Second-year German 1 | Ger | 203 | 3S | L |
| 1211 | Second-year German 2 | Ger | 204 | 3S | L |
| 1212 | Greek literature in trans | Clas | 362 | 3S | U |
| 1212 | Greek etymology | Clas | 103 | 2S | L |
| 1216 | Latin literature in trans | Clas | 363 | 3S | U |
| 1216 | Latin etymology | Clas | 102 | 2S | L |
| 1216 | Latin refresher & rdg 1 | Clas | 201 | 3S | L |
| 1216 | Latin refresher & rdg 2 | Clas | 202 | 3S | U |
| 1216 | Vergil: *The Aeneid* | Clas | 213 | 3S | L |
| 1216 | Vergil: *The Aeneid* | Clas | 214 | 3S | L |
| 1216 | Writing of Latin 1 | Clas | 301 | 1S | U |
| 1216 | Writing of Latin 2 | Clas | 302 | 1S | U |
| 1216 | Classical mythology | Clas | 361 | 2S | U |
| 1216 | Roman social institutions | Clas | 341 | 2S | U |
| 1225 | Intro to Hispanic culture | Span | 202 | 3S | U |
| 1225 | Intro to Hispanic lit | Span | 203 | 3S | L |
| 1225 | First year Spanish 1 | Span | 101 | 4S | L |
| 1225 | First year Spanish 2 | Span | 102 | 4S | L |
| 1225 | Review of Spanish grammar | Span | 201 | 3S | L |
| 150199 | Astronomy | Astro | 203 | 3S | L |
| 160103 | Foundations of math | Math | 351 | 3S | U |
| 160199 | Modern concepts for el ed | Math | 341 | 3S | U |
| 160199 | Basic math concepts | Math | 140 | 3S | L |
| 160203 | Finite mathematics | Math | 340 | 3S | U |

| NCES No. | Course Title | Dept. | Course No. | Credits | Level |
|---|---|---|---|---|---|
| 160302 | College algebra | Math | 111 | 4S | L |
| 160302 | Intro to finite math | Math | 112 | 4S | L |
| 160306 | Linear algebra | Math | 315 | 3S | U |
| 160401 | Elem calculus 1 | Math | 123 | 4S | L |
| 160401 | Elem calculus 2 | Math | 224 | 4S | L |
| 160401 | Elem calculus 3 | Math | 225 | 4S | L |
| 160406 | Differential equations | Math | 321 | 3S | U |
| 160602 | Trigonometry | Math | 120 | 2S | L |
| 160802 | Intro to statistics | Math | 381 | 3S | U |
| 161199 | Calc: mngmt life soc sci | Math | 222 | 4S | L |
| 200103 | General psychology | Psych | 101 | 3S | L |
| 200508 | Aging and the individual | Psych | 490 | 3S | U |
| 200509 | Personal adjustment | Psych | 165 | 3S | L |
| 210304 | Intro to criminal justice | CJus | 201 | 3S | L |
| 210304 | The police process | CJus | 203 | 3S | L |
| 210304 | Intro to crime & delin | CJus | 250 | 3S | L |
| 210304 | Criminology | CJus | 351 | 3S | L |
| 210304 | Penology | CJus | 352 | 3S | L |
| 210304 | Juvenile delinquency | CJus | 451 | 3S | L |
| 220101 | Greek art & archaeology | Clas | 331 | 3S | U |
| 220101 | South Dakota perhistory | Archy | 320 | 3S | U |
| 220101 | Roman art & archaeology | Clas | 332 | 3S | U |
| 220201 | Prin of economics–macro | Bus | 201 | 3S | L |
| 220201 | Prin of economics–micro | Bus | 202 | 3S | L |
| 220428 | South Dakota govt and pol | Socio | 315 | 3S | U |
| 220432 | American history 1 | Hist | 034N | 3S | L |
| 220432 | American history 2 | Hist | 252 | 3S | L |
| 220433 | Western civilization 1 | Hist | 121 | 3S | L |
| 220433 | Western civilization 2 | Hist | 122 | 3S | L |
| 220450 | Greek art and archaeology | AnHis | 311 | 3S | U |
| 220450 | Roman art and archaeology | AnHis | 312 | 3S | U |
| 220501 | American government | PolSc | 100 | 3S | L |
| 220602 | Intro to crime and delin | Socio | 250 | 3S | L |
| 220602 | Criminology | Socio | 351 | 3S | U |
| 220602 | Penology | Socio | 352 | 3S | U |
| 220604 | Juvenile delinquency | Socio | 451 | 3S | L |
| 220605 | Courtship & marriage | Socio | 280 | 3S | L |
| 220606 | Intro to sociology | Socio | 100 | 3S | L |
| 220609 | Methods of social res | Socio | 310 | 3S | U |
| 220613 | Social problems | Socio | 150 | 3S | L |
| 220615 | Racial & ethnic relations | Socio | 350 | 3S | U |
| 220699 | Field of social work | Socio | 200 | 3S | L |
| 220699 | Social work practice 2 | Socio | 330 | 3S | U |
| 220699 | Issues in social work | Socio | 401 | 3S | U |
| 220699 | Advanced social work prac | Socio | 485 | 3S | U |

**Noncredit courses**

| NCES No. | Course Title | Dept. | Course No. | Credits | Level |
|---|---|---|---|---|---|
| 040101 | Accounting: 6 components | Acctg | | NC | |
| 041303 | Real estate 1 | | | NC | V |
| 041303 | Real estate 2 | | | NC | V |
| 041309 | Real estate 3 | | | NC | V |
| 1501 | Backyard astronomy | Astro | | NC | |
| 160199 | Math review | Math | | NC | |
| 200508 | Understanding aging | Psych | | NC | |
| 220101 | Intro archy of South Dak | Archy | | NC | |

## (58) UNIVERSITY OF SOUTHERN MISSISSIPPI

Dr. William A. Lewis
Director of Independent Study
Southern Station
University of Southern Mississippi
P.O. Box 5056
Hattiesburg, Mississippi 39406
Phone: 601-266-4860

Enrollment on a noncredit basis accepted in all credit courses. Gifted high school students are permitted to enroll in undergraduate courses for credit. Overseas enrollment accepted.

**High School courses**

| NCES No. | Course Title | Dept. | Course No. | Credits | Level |
|---|---|---|---|---|---|
| 040601 | Business English | Bus | | HF | H |
| 0499 | General business 1st half | Bus | | HF | H |
| 0499 | General business 2nd half | Bus | | HF | H |
| 050699 | Journalism | Jrnl | | HF | H |
| 100199 | Homemaking II 1st half | HmEc | | HF | H |
| 100313 | Homemaking I 2nd half | HmEc | | HF | H |
| 100499 | Homemaking II 2nd half | HmEc | | HF | H |

| NCES No. | Course Title | Dept. | Course No. | Credits | Level |
|---|---|---|---|---|---|
| 100601 | Child development | HmEc | | HF | H |
| 100602 | Family living | HmEc | | HF | H |
| 100699 | Homemaking I 1st half | HmEc | | HF | H |
| 120299 | English IV 2nd half | Engl | | HF | H |
| 120305 | English I 1st half | Engl | | HF | H |
| 120307 | English I 2nd half | Engl | | HF | H |
| 120307 | English II 1st half | Engl | | HF | H |
| 120307 | English II 2nd half | Engl | | HF | H |
| 120307 | English III 1st half | Engl | | HF | H |
| 120307 | English III 2nd half | Engl | | HF | H |
| 120310 | English IV 1st half | Engl | | HF | H |
| 1210 | French I 1st half | Frnch | | HF | H |
| 1210 | French I 2nd half | Frnch | | HF | H |
| 1210 | French II 1st half | Frnch | | HF | H |
| 1210 | French II 2nd half | Frnch | | HF | H |
| 1225 | Spanish I 1st half | Span | | HF | H |
| 1225 | Spanish I 2nd half | Span | | HF | H |
| 1225 | Spanish II 1st half | Span | | HF | H |
| 1225 | Spanish II 2nd half | Span | | HF | H |
| 130799 | Business law | Bus | | HF | H |
| 150399 | Biology 1st half | Bio | | HF | H |
| 150399 | Biology 2nd half | Bio | | HF | H |
| 150401 | Chemistry 1st half | Chem | | HF | H |
| 150401 | Chemistry 2nd half | Chem | | HF | H |
| 1599 | General science 1st half | Sci | | HF | H |
| 1599 | General science 2nd half | Sci | | HF | H |
| 160299 | Fundamental math I 1st hf | Math | | HF | H |
| 160299 | Fundamental math I 2nd hf | Math | | HF | H |
| 160299 | Fundamental math II 1st hf | Math | | HF | H |
| 160299 | Fundamental math II 2nd hf | Math | | HF | H |
| 160302 | Algebra elem 1st half | Math | | HF | H |
| 160302 | Algebra elem 2nd half | Math | | HF | H |
| 160302 | Algebra adv 1st half | Math | | HF | H |
| 160302 | Algebra adv 2nd half | Math | | HF | H |
| 160601 | Geometry 1st half | Math | | HF | H |
| 160601 | Geometry 2nd half | Math | | HF | H |
| 161201 | Business arithmetic | Bus | | HF | H |
| 1699 | Senior math adv 1st half | Math | | HF | H |
| 1699 | Senior math adv 2nd half | Math | | HF | H |
| 220201 | Economics | Econ | | HF | H |
| 220399 | World geography | Geog | | HF | H |
| 220432 | American history 1st half | Hist | | HF | H |
| 220432 | American history 2nd half | Hist | | HF | H |
| 220433 | World history 1st half | Hist | | HF | H |
| 220433 | World history 2nd half | Hist | | HF | H |
| 220501 | American government | PolSc | | HF | H |
| 220502 | Civics | PolSc | | HF | H |
| 220511 | Mississippi history | Hist | | HF | H |
| 220599 | Problems in American dem | PolSc | | HF | H |
| 220699 | Sociology | Socio | | HF | H |

**College courses**

| NCES No. | Course Title | Dept. | Course No. | Credits | Level |
|---|---|---|---|---|---|
| 040101 | Prin of accounting I | Acc | 201 | 3S | L |
| 040101 | Prin of accounting II | Acc | 202 | 3S | L |
| 040199 | Personal finance | Fin | 320 | 3S | U |
| 040301 | Business finance | Fin | 389 | 3S | U |
| 040604 | Business writing | BEd | 300 | 3S | U |
| 040708 | General insurance | REI | 325 | 3S | U |
| 040999 | Managerial communications | GBA | 375 | 3S | U |
| 041001 | Principles of marketing | Mkt | 300 | 3S | U |
| 041199 | Principles of management | Mgt | 360 | 3S | U |
| 041303 | Real estate principles | REI | 330 | 3S | U |
| 041306 | Real estate finance | REI | 432 | 3S | U |
| 041308 | Real estate law | REI | 340 | 3S | U |
| 050605 | Feature writing | Jou | 301 | 3S | U |
| 061099 | Statistical methods I | CSs | 211 | 3S | L |
| 061099 | Statistical methods II | CSs | 212 | 3S | L |
| 070516 | Math for elem teachers II | Mat | 310 | 3S | U |
| 070516 | Math teach jr hi sch math | Mat | 410 | 3S | U |
| 070701 | Principles of guidance | REF | 336 | 3S | U |
| 071199 | Tests & measurements | REF | 469 | 3S | U |
| 0810 | Engineering drawing I | IVE | 323 | 3S | U |
| 0810 | Engineering drawing II | IVE | 324 | 3S | U |
| 090305 | Neurology | Thy | 454 | 3S | U |
| 090305 | Pathology | Thy | 455 | 3S | U |
| 1199 | Engineering economics | Int | 301 | 3S | U |
| 120201 | Shakespeare comedy & trag | Eng | 454 | 3S | U |
| 120299 | Literature of the South | Eng | 485 | 3S | U |
| 120305 | Language | Eng | 101 | 3S | L |
| 120307 | Literature | Eng | 102 | 3S | L |
| 120310 | Intro poetry writing | Eng | 322 | 3S | U |
| 120310 | Intro short fiction writg | Eng | 321 | 3S | U |

| NCES No. | Course Title | Dept. | Course No. | Credits | Level |
|---|---|---|---|---|---|
| 120310 | Short story writing | Eng | 421 | 3S | U |
| 120310 | Poetry writing | Eng | 422 | 3S | U |
| 120399 | Fiction | Eng | 201 | 3S | L |
| 120399 | Poetry | Eng | 202 | 3S | L |
| 1211 | Beginning German I | FL | 121 | 3S | L |
| 1211 | Beginning German II | FL | 122 | 3S | L |
| 1211 | Intermediate German | FL | 221 | 3S | L |
| 1211 | Intermediate German | FL | 222 | 3S | L |
| 130799 | Legal environment bus | GBA | 295 | 3S | L |
| 150301 | Biological science I | PS | 106 | 3S | L |
| 150301 | Biological science II | PS | 107 | 3S | L |
| 150399 | History of biology | Bio | 401 | 3S | U |
| 150399 | Biogeography | Bio | 460 | 3S | U |
| 150599 | Physical geology | Gly | 101 | 3S | L |
| 150599 | Historical geology | Gly | 103 | 3S | L |
| 150899 | Physical science I | PS | 104 | 3S | L |
| 1509 | Physical science II | PS | 105 | 3S | L |
| 160103 | Appl algebra prob solv | Mat | 112 | 3S | L |
| 160199 | Math for arts & hum | Mat | 120 | 3S | L |
| 160199 | Math for elem teachers I | Mat | 210 | 3S | L |
| 160302 | College algebra | Mat | 101 | 3S | L |
| 160401 | Calculus I & analyt geom | Mat | 277 | 3S | L |
| 160401 | Calculus I & analyt geom | Mat | 276 | 3S | L |
| 160602 | Plane trigonometry | Mat | 103 | 3S | L |
| 180599 | Introduction to logic | Phi | 253 | 3S | L |
| 1808 | Intro to philosophy | Phi | 151 | 3S | L |
| 181101 | Introduction to religion | Rel | 131 | 3S | L |
| 181202 | The Christian tradition | Rel | 335 | 3S | U |
| 190104 | Survey hist & phil of PE | PEd | 222 | 3S | L |
| 190106 | Organ & admin of PE | PEd | 426 | 3S | U |
| 190311 | Org & adm of athletics | AAC | 303 | 3S | U |
| 190311 | Adv tech of coach basktbl | AAC | 422 | 3S | U |
| 190502 | Community health | Hth | 321 | 3S | U |
| 190509 | Personal health | Hth | 101 | 3S | L |
| 190704 | Recreation leadership | Rec | 323 | 3S | U |
| 200199 | General psychology | Psy | 110 | 3S | L |
| 200408 | Mental hygiene | Psy | 231 | 3S | L |
| 200599 | Human growth & dev I: chi | EPy | 370 | 3S | U |
| 200599 | Hum growth & dev II: adol | EPy | 372 | 3S | U |
| 200805 | Educational psychology | EPy | 374 | 3S | U |
| 210304 | Traffic law | CJ | 332 | 3S | U |
| 220199 | Gen or intro anthropology | Ant | 101 | 3S | L |
| 220201 | Principles of economics I | Eco | 255 | 3S | L |
| 220299 | Introduction to economics | Eco | 200 | 3S | L |
| 220306 | World regional geography | Ghy | 103 | 3S | L |
| 220306 | Geography of US & Canada | Ghy | 402 | 3S | L |
| 220432 | United States to 1877 | His | 140 | 3S | L |
| 220432 | United States since 1877 | His | 141 | 3S | L |
| 220433 | World civ to AD 1648 | Hth | 101 | 3S | L |
| 220433 | World civ since AD 1648 | His | 102 | 3S | L |
| 220501 | American government | PS | 101 | 3S | L |
| 220505 | US foreign policy | PS | 330 | 3S | U |
| 220505 | Intro internatnl politics | PS | 331 | 3S | U |
| 220509 | State & local politics | PS | 301 | 3S | U |
| 220510 | Introduction to pol sci | PS | 220 | 3S | L |
| 220602 | Intro to criminal justice | CJ | 200 | 3S | L |
| 220602 | Criminology | Soc | 341 | 3S | U |
| 220605 | Marriage & human sex | Hth | 430 | 3S | U |
| 220605 | The family | Soc | 314 | 3S | U |
| 220606 | Intro to sociology | Soc | 101 | 3S | L |

(59) **UNIVERSITY OF TENNESSEE, KNOXVILLE**

Dr. Kenneth L. Burton
Director
Center for Extended Learning
University of Tennessee
420 Communications Building
Knoxville, Tennessee 37996
Phone: 615-974-5134

Enrollment on a noncredit basis accepted in all credit courses. Gifted high school students are permitted to enroll in undergraduate courses for credit. Overseas enrollment accepted. The Center for Extended Learning offers courses from all four of the University of Tennessee campuses.

## High School courses

| NCES No. | Course Title | Dept. | Course No. | Credits | Level |
|---|---|---|---|---|---|
| 030501 | Art: cartooning I | Art | 1HS | HF | H |
| 030501 | Art: cartooning II | Art | 2HS | HF | H |
| 04 | General business | Bus | 1HS | HF | H |
| 04 | General business | Bus | 2HS | HF | H |
| 040104 | Accounting | Acctg | 1HS | HF | H |
| 040104 | Accounting | Acctg | 2HS | HF | H |
| 0402 | Clerical practice | ClrPr | 1HS | HF | H |
| 040601 | Bus English 1st sem | BusEn | 1HS | HF | H |
| 040601 | Bus English 2nd sem | BusEn | 2HS | HF | H |
| 041001 | Salesmanship 1st sem | Sales | 1HS | HF | H |
| 041001 | Salesmanship 2nd sem | Sales | 2HS | HF | H |
| 100313 | Foods & nutrition | F&N | 1HS | HF | H |
| 100604 | Project self-discovery | SelfD | 1HS | HF | H |
| 120305 | Ninth-grade lang skills | Engl | F-1H | HF | H |
| 120305 | Tenth-grade lang skills | Engl | S-1H | HF | H |
| 120305 | Eleventh-grade lang skills | Engl | J-1H | HF | H |
| 120305 | Twelfth-grade lang skills | Engl | SR-1H | HF | H |
| 120305 | Ninth-grade English | Engl | 1HS | HF | H |
| 120307 | Ninth-grade English | Engl | 2HS | HF | H |
| 120307 | Tenth-grade English: lit | Engl | 4HS | HF | H |
| 120307 | Eleventh-gr Eng: Amer lit | Engl | 6HS | HF | H |
| 120307 | Twelfth-gr Eng: Brit lit | Engl | 8HS | HF | H |
| 120307 | British novel I | Engl | 12HS | HF | H |
| 120307 | British novel II | Engl | 2-12H | HF | H |
| 120308 | Ninth-grade rdg skills | Engl | F-2H | HF | H |
| 120308 | Tenth-grade rdg skills | Engl | S-2H | HF | H |
| 120308 | Eleventh-grade rdg skills | Engl | J-2H | HF | H |
| 120308 | Twelfth-grade rdg skills | Engl | SR-2H | HF | H |
| 120310 | Tenth-grade English | Engl | 3HS | HF | H |
| 120310 | Eleventh-grade English | Engl | 5HS | HF | H |
| 120310 | Twelfth-grade English | Engl | 7HS | HF | H |
| 120310 | Creative writ: articles | Engl | 9HS | HF | H |
| 120310 | Creative writ: stories | Engl | 10HS | HF | H |
| 120310 | Creative writ: poetry | Engl | 11HS | HF | H |
| 1210 | French I 1st sem | Frnch | 1HS | HF | H |
| 1210 | French I 2nd sem | Frnch | 2HS | HF | H |
| 1210 | French II 1st sem | Frnch | 3HS | HF | H |
| 1210 | French II 2nd sem | Frnch | 4HS | HF | H |
| 1216 | Latin I 1st sem | Lat | 1HS | HF | H |
| 1216 | Latin I 2nd sem | Lat | 2HS | HF | H |
| 1225 | Spanish I 1st sem | Span | 1HS | HF | H |
| 1225 | Spanish I 2nd sem | Span | 2HS | HF | H |
| 1225 | Spanish II 1st sem | Span | 3HS | HF | H |
| 1225 | Spanish II 2nd sem | Span | 4HS | HF | H |
| 1307 | Business law 1st sem | BusLw | 1HS | HF | H |
| 1307 | Business law 2nd sem | BusLw | 2HS | HF | H |
| 15 | General science | Sci | 1HS | HF | H |
| 15 | General science | Sci | 2HS | HF | H |
| 1503 | Biology | Bio | 1HS | HF | H |
| 1503 | Biology | Bio | 2HS | HF | H |
| 160301 | 9th-grade arith 1st sem | Math | 9HS | HF | H |
| 160301 | 9th-grade arith 2nd sem | Math | 10HS | HF | H |
| 160302 | Algebra I 1st sem | Math | 1HS | HF | H |
| 160302 | Algebra I 2nd sem | Math | 2HS | HF | H |
| 160302 | Algebra II 1st sem | Math | 3HS | HF | H |
| 160302 | Algebra II 2nd sem | Math | 4HS | HF | H |
| 160601 | Geometry: plane 1st sem | Math | 5HS | HF | H |
| 160601 | Geometry: plane 2nd sem | Math | 6HS | HF | H |
| 160602 | Trigonometry | Math | 7HS | HF | H |
| 161201 | Business arith 1st sem | BusAr | 1HS | HF | H |
| 161201 | Business arith 2nd sem | BusAr | 2HS | HF | H |
| 181202 | Bible: New Testament | Relig | 1HS | HF | H |
| 181202 | Bible: Old Testament | Relig | 2HS | HF | H |
| 1901 | Physical education | PhyEd | 1HS | HF | H |
| 190510 | Phys fitnss & hlth 1st s | Hlth | 7HS | HF | H |
| 190510 | Phys fitnss & hlth 2nd s | Hlth | 8HS | HF | H |
| 1906 | Driver ed: gen safety | Sfty | 1HS | HF | H |
| 2001 | Psychology | Psych | 1HS | HF | H |
| 2001 | Psychology | Psych | 2HS | HF | H |
| 2202 | Economics 1st sem | Econ | 1HS | HF | H |
| 2202 | Economics 2nd sem | Econ | 2HS | HF | H |
| 2203 | World geography 1st sem | Geog | 1HS | HF | H |
| 2203 | World geography 2nd sem | Geog | 2HS | HF | H |
| 2204 | Ancient & medieval hist | Hist | 1HS | HF | H |
| 2204 | Ancient & medieval hist | Hist | 2HS | HF | H |
| 220432 | American history | Hist | 8HS | HF | H |
| 220432 | American history | Hist | 7HS | HF | H |
| 220433 | World history | Hist | 5HS | HF | H |
| 220433 | World history | Hist | 6HS | HF | H |
| 220501 | American govrnmnt 1st sem | AmGvt | 1HS | HF | H |
| 220501 | American govrnmnt 2nd sem | AmGvt | 2HS | HF | H |
| 220502 | Civics 1st sem | Civ | 1HS | HF | H |
| 220502 | Civics 2nd sem | Civ | 2HS | HF | H |
| 2206 | Sociology | Socio | 1HS | HF | H |
| 220605 | Adjust & marriage prep | Socio | 2HS | HF | H |

## College courses

| NCES No. | Course Title | Dept. | Course No. | Credits | Level |
|---|---|---|---|---|---|
| 0101 | Land economics | AgEco | 4330K | 3Q | U |
| 010106 | World agriculture & trade | AgEco | 4240K | 3Q | U |
| 010999 | Introduction to forestry | For | 1620K | 3Q | L |
| 040103 | Theory & pract: auditing | Acctg | 4110M | 3Q | U |
| 040106 | Manager cost acctg survey | Acctg | 2130K | 3Q | L |
| 040106 | Managerial cost acctg | Acctg | 3210K | 3Q | U |
| 040106 | Managerial cost acctg | Acctg | 3220K | 3Q | U |
| 040108 | Fundamentals of acctg | Acctg | 2110K | 3Q | L |
| 040108 | Fundamentals of acctg | Acctg | 2120K | 3Q | L |
| 040108 | Intermed financial acctg | Acctg | 3110K | 3Q | U |
| 040108 | Intermed financial acctg | Acctg | 3120K | 3Q | U |
| 040108 | Intermed financial acctg | Acctg | 3130K | 3Q | U |
| 040114 | Federal income tax | Acctg | 3430K | 3Q | U |
| 040201 | Mgt: concepts/theo & prac | Bus | 315C | 3S | U |
| 040201 | Personnel management | Bus | 332C | 3S | U |
| 040308 | Money and banking | Econ | 301C | 3S | U |
| 050603 | Radio-TV news | Brdcs | 3610K | 3Q | U |
| 050605 | Writing feature articles | Jrnl | 3120K | 3Q | U |
| 050608 | Writing for mass media | Jrnl | 2210K | 3Q | L |
| 0701 | Education in the US | Educ | 201C | 3S | L |
| 0701 | School in society | Educ | 200C | 1S | L |
| 070201 | Principles of bus educatn | Educ | 4010M | 3Q | U |
| 070610 | Teaching readng: elem sch | Educ | 320C | 3S | U |
| 070610 | Teaching readng: seco sch | Educ | 321C | 3S | U |
| 070610 | Diag & presc teach readng | Educ | 423C | 3S | U |
| 0708 | Ed of exceptional childrn | Educ | 250C | 3S | L |
| 070804 | Psy & ed of hearng impair | Educ | 4250K | 3Q | U |
| 070804 | Curr: el/sec sch, hearg i | Educ | 4280K | 3Q | U |
| 080901 | Elec eng: circuits I | EEg | 2010K | 3Q | L |
| 080901 | Elec eng: circuits II | EEg | 2020K | 3Q | L |
| 081505 | Quality control | IndEg | 3440K | 3Q | U |
| 081599 | Engineering economy | IndEg | 4520K | 3Q | U |
| 100313 | Elementary nutrition | Nutrn | 1230M | 3Q | L |
| 1006 | Adult developmnt & aging | ChFam | 4260K | 3Q | U |
| 100601 | Lrng experiences w parent | ChFam | 4420K | 3Q | U |
| 100601 | Child-care staff comptncs | ChFam | 4710K | 3Q | U |
| 100602 | Sex roles and marriage | ChFam | 2120K | 3Q | L |
| 120302 | History of the Eng lang | Engl | 4420M | 3Q | U |
| 120305 | Modern English grammar | Engl | 4430M | 3Q | U |
| 120307 | Lit of the Western world | Engl | 2112M | 3Q | L |
| 120307 | Lit of the Western world | Engl | 2132M | 3Q | L |
| 120307 | English masterpieces | Engl | 2510K | 4Q | L |
| 120307 | English masterpieces | Engl | 2520K | 4Q | L |
| 120307 | American masterpieces | Engl | 2531K | 4Q | L |
| 120307 | Intro to drama | Engl | 2660K | 4Q | L |
| 120307 | Prose in the 18th century | Engl | 3630M | 3Q | U |
| 120307 | Women in literature | Engl | 3750M | 3Q | U |
| 120307 | Women in literature | Engl | 3760M | 3Q | U |
| 120307 | Shakespeare | Engl | 4010K | 3Q | U |
| 120307 | Shakespeare | Engl | 4020K | 3Q | U |
| 120307 | The British novel | Engl | 4340K | 3Q | U |
| 120307 | Intro study English lang | Engl | 4410M | 3Q | U |
| 120307 | Southern literature | Engl | 4650M | 3Q | U |
| 120307 | Poetry of John Milton | Engl | 4850M | 3Q | U |
| 120307 | Chaucer: *Canterbury Tales* | Engl | 4920M | 3Q | U |
| 120307 | Nineteenth-cen Amer novel | Engl | 4050K | 3Q | U |
| 120307 | American masterpieces | Engl | 2532K | 4Q | L |
| 120310 | English composition | Engl | 1010K | 3Q | L |
| 120310 | English composition | Engl | 1020K | 3Q | L |
| 120310 | English composition | Engl | 1031K | 3Q | L |
| 120310 | Technical writing | Engl | 2010M | 3Q | L |
| 120399 | Medical & scientif vocab | Engl | 3150M | 4Q | U |
| 1210 | Elementary French | Frnch | 1110K | 3Q | L |
| 1210 | Elementary French | Frnch | 1120K | 3Q | L |
| 1210 | Elementary French | Frnch | 1130K | 3Q | L |
| 1210 | Elementary French | Frnch | 1520K | 4Q | L |
| 1210 | French lit 17th century | Frnch | 4110K | 3Q | U |
| 1210 | French lit 17th century | Frnch | 4120K | 3Q | U |
| 1210 | French lit 17th century | Frnch | 4130K | 3Q | U |
| 1210 | French lit 18th century | Frnch | 4310K | 3Q | U |
| 1210 | French lit 18th century | Frnch | 4320K | 3Q | U |
| 1210 | French lit 18th century | Frnch | 4330K | 3Q | U |
| 1210 | Intermediate French | Frnch | 2110K | 3Q | L |

| NCES No. | Course Title | Dept. | Course No. | Credits | Level |
|---|---|---|---|---|---|
| 1210 | Intermediate French | Frnch | 2120K | 3Q | L |
| 1210 | Intermediate French | Frnch | 2130K | 3Q | L |
| 1210 | Aspects of French lit | Frnch | 3110K | 3Q | U |
| 1210 | Aspects of French lit | Frnch | 3120K | 3Q | U |
| 1210 | Aspects of French lit | Frnch | 3130K | 3Q | U |
| 1211 | Elementary German | Ger | 1110K | 3Q | L |
| 1211 | Elementary German | Ger | 1120K | 3Q | L |
| 1211 | Elementary German | Ger | 1130K | 3Q | L |
| 1211 | Intermediate German | Ger | 2110K | 3Q | L |
| 1211 | Intermediate German | Ger | 2120K | 3Q | L |
| 1211 | Intermediate German | Ger | 2130K | 3Q | L |
| 1214 | Elementary Italian | Ital | 1110K | 3Q | L |
| 1214 | Elementary Italian | Ital | 1120K | 3Q | L |
| 1214 | Elementary Italian | Ital | 1130K | 3Q | L |
| 1225 | Elementary Spanish | Span | 1510K | 4Q | L |
| 1225 | Elementary Spanish | Span | 1520K | 4Q | L |
| 1225 | Intermediate Spanish | Span | 2510K | 4Q | L |
| 1225 | Intermediate Spanish | Span | 2520K | 4Q | L |
| 1225 | Aspects of Spanish lit | Span | 3510K | 4Q | U |
| 1225 | Aspects of Spanish lit | Span | 3520K | 4Q | U |
| 1225 | Spanish civilization | Span | 4410K | 3Q | U |
| 1304 | Criminal law | CrJus | 4000M | 3Q | U |
| 140199 | Books & materials: child | Educ | 4510M | 3Q | U |
| 140199 | Books & matrls: yng peopl | Educ | 4520M | 3Q | U |
| 150401 | Chemistry & environment | Chem | 111C | 3S | L |
| 150599 | Elements of geology | Geol | 1110M | 4Q | L |
| 150599 | Elements of geology | Geol | 1120M | 4Q | L |
| 150599 | Elements of geology | Geol | 1130M | 4Q | L |
| 1602 | Logic & sets | Math | 3100K | 3Q | U |
| 1603 | Basic math skills | Math | 1140K | 3Q | L |
| 160302 | College algebra | Math | 1540K | 4Q | L |
| 160303 | Structure-number system | Math | 2110K | 3Q | L |
| 160303 | Structure-number system | Math | 2120K | 3Q | L |
| 160303 | Structure-number system | Math | 2130K | 3Q | L |
| 160401 | Introductory calculus | Math | 1550K | 4Q | L |
| 160401 | Single-variable calculus | Math | 1840K | 4Q | L |
| 160401 | Single-variable calculus | Math | 1850K | 4Q | L |
| 160401 | Single-variable calculus | Math | 1860K | 4Q | L |
| 160401 | Dif equations & infin ser | Math | 2840K | 4Q | L |
| 160401 | Multi cal & matrix algebr | Math | 2850K | 4Q | L |
| 160401 | Multi cal & matrix algebr | Math | 2860K | 3Q | L |
| 1611 | General mathematics | Math | 1560K | 4Q | L |
| 161108 | Psychological statistics | Psych | 3150K | 3Q | U |
| 180303 | Medical ethics | Phil | 3611K | 3Q | U |
| 180399 | Bioethics | Zool | 3410K | 3Q | U |
| 180902 | Images of Jesus | Relig | 3311K | 4Q | U |
| 181103 | Medical ethics | Relig | 3611K | 3Q | U |
| 181104 | Hist of West rel tho & in | Relig | 3060K | 3Q | U |
| 181104 | Hist of West rel tho & in | Relig | 3070K | 3Q | U |
| 190502 | Death, dying & bereavemnt | Hlth | 4140K | 3Q | U |
| 190509 | Princ of personal health | Hlth | 1110K | 3Q | L |
| 190509 | Personal hygiene | Hlth | 100C | 3S | L |
| 190511 | Princ of general safety | Hlth | 3520K | 3Q | U |
| 2001 | Psych as a social science | Psych | 2530K | 3Q | L |
| 2001 | General psychology | Psych | 2500K | 4Q | L |
| 2002 | Biology foundtns of behav | Psych | 2520K | 3Q | L |
| 2005 | Psych of the individual | Psych | 2540K | 3Q | L |
| 200501 | Abnormal psychology | Psych | 3650K | 3Q | U |
| 200508 | Child psychology | Psych | 3550K | 4Q | U |
| 2007 | Social psychology | Psych | 3120K | 3Q | U |
| 200804 | Human grth & devel—child | Educ | 203C | 3S | L |
| 200804 | Humn grth & devel—adoles | Educ | 204C | 3S | L |
| 200804 | Ed psych | Educ | 207C | 3S | L |
| 210304 | Intro to criminal justice | CrJus | 2000M | 3Q | L |
| 210304 | Scientific investigation | CrJus | 3110M | 3Q | U |
| 210304 | Criminal procedure | CrJus | 3210M | 3Q | U |
| 210304 | Police & community relatn | CrJus | 3300M | 3Q | U |
| 210304 | Organization & mgmt of CJ | CrJus | 3500M | 3Q | U |
| 210304 | Introduction to security | CrJus | 3900M | 3Q | U |
| 210304 | Senior semr in crim just | CrJus | 4600M | 3Q | U |
| 220102 | Human culture | Anthr | 2530K | 4Q | L |
| 220107 | Race, class, & power | Anthr | 3410K | 3Q | U |
| 220199 | Human origins | Anthr | 2510K | 3Q | U |
| 220201 | Princ of econ: microecon | Econ | 102C | 3S | L |
| 220201 | Intermed macroecon theory | Econ | 325C | 3S | U |
| 2203 | Introduction to geography | Geog | 1610K | 4Q | L |
| 2203 | Introduction to geography | Geog | 1620K | 4Q | L |
| 220302 | Economic geography | Geog | 2110K | 4Q | L |
| 220302 | Economic geography | Geog | 2120K | 4Q | L |
| 2204 | Dev of Western civilizatn | Hist | 1510K | 4Q | L |
| 2204 | Dev of Western civilizatn | Hist | 1520K | 4Q | L |
| 220408 | Westn relig thoght & inst | Hist | 3060K | 3Q | U |

| NCES No. | Course Title | Dept. | Course No. | Credits | Level |
|---|---|---|---|---|---|
| 220408 | Westn relig thoght & inst | Hist | 3070K | 3Q | U |
| 220428 | History of Tennessee | Hist | 3311 | 3Q | U |
| 220428 | History of Tennessee | Hist | 3321 | 3Q | U |
| 220432 | History of United States | Hist | 2510K | 4Q | L |
| 220432 | History of United States | Hist | 2520K | 4Q | L |
| 220501 | US gov & polit: fndatns | PolSc | 2510K | 4Q | L |
| 220501 | US gov & polit: institutn | PolSc | 2520K | 4Q | L |
| 220599 | International relations | PolSc | 3210M | 3Q | U |
| 2206 | General sociology | Socio | 1510K | 4Q | L |
| 220602 | Corrections | Socio | 4120M | 3Q | U |
| 220603 | Collective behavior | Socio | 3010K | 3Q | U |
| 220603 | Sociology of aging | Socio | 4730K | 4Q | U |
| 220605 | Marriage & family relatns | Socio | 2180M | 3Q | L |
| 220607 | Social psychology | Socio | 3130K | 4Q | U |
| 220610 | Sociology of deviant beha | Socio | 3510K | 3Q | U |
| 220612 | Social stratification | Socio | 3350K | 4Q | U |
| 220612 | Race, class, and power | Socio | 3410M | 3Q | U |
| 220613 | Socio of social problems | Socio | 1520K | 4Q | L |
| 220614 | Urban environment | Socio | 3410K | 4Q | U |
| 220699 | Intro to social research | Socio | 3910K | 4Q | U |
| 220699 | Elem statistical methods | Socio | 3920K | 4Q | U |
| 220699 | Formal organization | Socio | 4560K | 4Q | U |
| 220699 | Social movements | Socio | 4930K | 4Q | U |

**Noncredit courses**

| NCES No. | Course Title | Dept. | Course No. | Credits | Level |
|---|---|---|---|---|---|
| 030501 | Cartooning I: basic | | 1 | NC | H |
| 030501 | Cartooning II: advanced | | 2 | NC | H |
| 030501 | Intr to pencil drawing | | | NC | L |
| 040207 | Typing | | | NC | |
| 041301 | Real estate appraisal | RIEs | | NC | L |
| 061101 | Computers | | | NC | |
| 080301 | Building inspection | | | NC | |
| 090404 | Tennessee pharmacy laws | Pharm | 333 | NC | U |
| 090404 | Phamaceutcl jurisprudence | Pharm | 334 | NC | U |
| 090408 | Drug interactions | Pharm | 322 | NC | U |
| 090408 | Disease proc & app therap | Pharm | 327 | NC | U |
| 090411 | Cmnty pharm mgt/plng/dev | Pharm | 232 | NC | U |
| 090411 | Cmnty pharm mgt/op proc | Pharm | 313 | NC | U |
| 090411 | Nonprescription drugs I | Pharm | 335 | NC | U |
| 090411 | Nonprescription drugs II | Pharm | 336 | NC | U |
| 090411 | Intr to self-care consltg | Pharm | 337 | NC | U |
| 090411 | Weight-control counseling | Pharm | 338 | NC | U |
| 090411 | Patnt medcatn prof/phrmct | Pharm | 342 | NC | U |
| 090411 | Patnt medcatn recrd/nurse | Pharm | 343 | NC | U |
| 090411 | Hlth assess: self-care | Pharm | 339 | NC | U |
| 090411 | Self-care consult system | Pharm | 340 | NC | U |
| 090411 | Geriatric patient care | Pharm | 400 | NC | U |
| 090411 | Geriatric patient care | Pharm | 401 | NC | U |
| 090411 | Geriatric patient care | Pharm | 402 | NC | U |
| 090411 | Geriatric patient care | Pharm | 403 | NC | U |
| 090411 | Locating a practice | Pharm | 404 | NC | U |
| 090411 | Prescription pricing syst | Pharm | 405 | NC | U |
| 090411 | Effective inventry contrl | Pharm | 406 | NC | U |
| 090411 | Financial planning | Pharm | 407 | NC | U |
| 090411 | Marketing community pharm | Pharm | 408 | NC | U |
| C90411 | Home totl parenteral nutr | Pharm | 409 | NC | U |
| 100603 | Intro to gerontology | | | NC | U |
| 100604 | Project self-discovery | | | NC | H |
| 120308 | How to study | | | NC | L |
| 120310 | How to write almost anyth | | | NC | L |
| 120310 | Creative writng: articles | | 1 | NC | L |
| 120310 | Creative writng: stories | | 2 | NC | L |
| 120310 | Creative writng: poetry | | 3 | NC | L |
| 1212 | Greek | | 1 | NC | |
| 1212 | Greek | | 2 | NC | |
| 1212 | Greek | | 3 | NC | |
| 160302 | Refresher algebra | | | NC | |
| 160602 | Trigonometry | | | NC | |
| 1612 | Everyday mathematics | | | NC | |
| 181202 | Bible: What does Bble say | Bible | 1 | NC | |
| 181202 | Bible: mighty acts of God | Bible | 2 | NC | |
| 181202 | Bible: What's right | Bible | 3 | NC | |
| 181202 | Bible: New Testament | Relig | 4 | NC | |
| 181202 | Bible: Old Testament | Relig | 5 | NC | |
| 181202 | Bible:What's relig livng? | Relig | 6 | NC | |
| 181202 | Bible: life/lit New Testa | Relig | 7 | NC | |
| 181202 | Bible: life/lit Old Testa | Relig | 8 | NC | |
| 181202 | Bible: Protestnt denomins | Relig | 10 | NC | |

## (60) UNIVERSITY OF TEXAS AT AUSTIN

Ms. Olga Garza
Supervisor of Student Services
Education Annex F-38
The University of Texas at Austin
P.O. Box 7700
Austin, Texas 78713
Phone: 512-471-5616

Enrollment on a noncredit basis accepted in all credit courses. Gifted high school students are permitted to enroll in undergraduate courses for credit. Overseas enrollment accepted.

| NCES No. | Course Title | Dept. | Course No. | Credits | Level |
|---|---|---|---|---|---|
| | **High School courses** | | | | |
| 040104 | Accounting 1st sem | Acctg | | HF | H |
| 040104 | Accounting 2nd sem | Acctg | | HF | H |
| 0499 | Personal business mgt | PBM | PBMgt | HF | H |
| 120302 | Junior lit English IIIB | Engl | Eng3B | HF | H |
| 120305 | Sen grammar-comp Eng IVA | Engl | Eng4A | HF | H |
| 120307 | Freshman literature IB | Engl | Eng1B | HF | H |
| 120307 | Sophomore literature IIB | Engl | Eng2B | HF | H |
| 120307 | Junior literature IIIA | Engl | Eng3A | HF | H |
| 120307 | Senior literature IVB | Engl | Eng4B | HF | H |
| 120307 | Lit genre-Arthur legend | Engl | lit6r | HF | H |
| 120310 | Freshman grammar-comp IA | Engl | EnglA | HF | H |
| 120310 | Soph grammar-comp and IIA | Engl | Eng1A | HF | H |
| 120310 | Eng IV academic comp | Engl | | HF | H |
| 1211 | German I 1st sem | Ger | GerIA | HF | H |
| 1211 | German I 2nd sem | Ger | GerIB | HF | H |
| 1211 | German II 1st sem | Ger | Ger2A | HF | H |
| 1211 | German II 2nd sem | Ger | Ger2B | HF | H |
| 130799 | Business and consumer law | BL | | HF | H |
| 1503 | Biology I 1st sem | Bio | I | HF | H |
| 1503 | Biology I 2nd sem | Bio | I | HF | H |
| 1508 | Physical science 1st sem | PS | | HF | H |
| 1508 | Physical science 2nd sem | PS | | HF | H |
| 160301 | Fund of math 1st sem | FOM | | HF | H |
| 160301 | Fund of math 2nd sem | FOM | | HF | H |
| 160302 | Algebra I 1st sem | Alg | Alg1A | HF | H |
| 160302 | Algebra I 2nd sem | Alg | Alg2B | HF | H |
| 160302 | Algebra II 1st sem | Alg | Alg1A | HF | H |
| 160302 | Algebra II 2nd sem | Alg | Alg2B | HF | H |
| 160601 | Geometry 1st sem | Geo | | HF | H |
| 160601 | Geometry 2nd sem | Geo | | HF | H |
| 160602 | Trigonometry one semester | Trg | | HF | H |
| 161202 | Math of cons econ 2nd sem | MCE | | HF | H |
| 190312 | Physical educ I 1st sem | PEd | I | HF | H |
| 190312 | Physical educ I 2nd sem | PEd | I | HF | H |
| 190509 | Health education I | HEd | I | HF | H |
| 2202 | Economics | Econ | Eco | HF | H |
| 220301 | Wld geog studies 1st sem | WGS | | HF | H |
| 220301 | Wld geog studies 2nd sem | WGS | | HF | H |
| 220432 | US history 1st sem | USHis | USHA | HF | H |
| 220432 | US hist 2nd sem | USHis | USHB | HF | H |
| 220433 | Wld hist studies 1st sem | WHS | | HF | H |
| 220433 | Wld hist studies 2nd sem | WHS | | HF | H |
| 220501 | US government | USGov | USGov | HF | H |
| | **College courses** | | | | |
| 040604 | Bus rpt wrtng behav comm | BC | 324 | 3S | U |
| 0408 | International business | Mktg | 350 | 3S | U |
| 040903 | Organizational behav admn | Mgmt | 336 | 3S | U |
| 040999 | Operations management | Mgmt | 335 | 3S | U |
| 041001 | Principles of marketing | Mktg | 337 | 3S | U |
| 041199 | Personnel management | Mgmt | 325 | 3S | U |
| 041299 | Elementary business stat | Sta | 309 | 3S | L |
| 041299 | Intermed bus statistics | Sta | 362 | 3S | U |
| 041303 | Intr real est urb lnd dev | RE | 358 | 3S | U |
| 070199 | Psych found of elem educ | EdP | 332E | 3S | U |
| 070199 | Psych found of secnd educ | EdP | 332S | 3S | U |
| 070309 | Hum lrn dev: adult years | EdC | 371.3 | 3S | U |
| 070516 | Modern topics elem math I | Math | 316K | 3S | L |
| 070516 | Modern topics el math II | Math | 316L | 3S | L |
| 070516 | Tching problems geometry | Math | 333L | 3S | U |
| 070899 | Orietatn to teachng sp ed | SpEd | 101 | 1S | L |
| 070899 | Survey of exceptnalities | SpEd | 371 | 3S | U |
| 090499 | Pharm and med terminology | Pharm | 313K | 3S | L |
| 100313 | Introductory nutrition | HmEc | 311 | 3S | L |
| 120307 | Mstrwks Eng lit th 18th c | Engl | 312L | 3S | L |
| 120307 | Intro to literature I | Engl | 314K | 3S | L |

| NCES No. | Course Title | Dept. | Course No. | Credits | Level |
|---|---|---|---|---|---|
| 120307 | Shakespeare: selected ply | Engl | 321 | 3S | U |
| 120307 | American lit 1865 to pres | Engl | 338 | 3S | U |
| 120307 | Intro to lit II black lit | Engl | 314L | 3S | L |
| 120307 | Mstrwks of lit: English | Engl | 316K | 3S | L |
| 120310 | Rhetoric and composition | Engl | 306 | 3S | L |
| 120310 | Literature & composition | Engl | 307 | 3S | L |
| 120310 | Technical writing | Engl | 317 | 3S | L |
| 120310 | Creative writing | Engl | 325 | 3S | L |
| 1210 | First-year French I | Frnch | 506 | 5S | L |
| 1210 | First-year French II | Frnch | 507 | 5S | L |
| 1210 | Second-year French I | Frnch | 312K | 3S | L |
| 1210 | Second-year French II | Frnch | 312L | 3S | L |
| 1211 | First-year German I | Ger | 506 | 5S | L |
| 1211 | First-year German II | Ger | 507 | 5S | L |
| 1211 | Second-year German I | Ger | 312K | 3S | L |
| 1211 | Second-year German II | Ger | 312L | 3S | L |
| 1212 | First-year Greek I | Greek | 506 | 5S | L |
| 1212 | Greek poetry and prose | Greek | 312 | 3S | L |
| 1212 | New Testmnt Gk: The Gospe | Greek | 319 | 3S | L |
| 1212 | Nw Tst Gk: Gsp/Acts/Pl/Ep | Greek | 328 | 3S | U |
| 1216 | First-year Latin I | Latin | 506 | 5S | L |
| 1216 | First-year Latin II | Latin | 507 | 5S | L |
| 1222 | First-year Czech I | Czech | 506 | 5S | L |
| 1222 | First-year Czech II | Czech | 407 | 4S | L |
| 1225 | First-year Spanish I | Span | 506 | 5S | L |
| 1225 | First-year Spanish II | Span | 507 | 5S | L |
| 1225 | Second-year Spanish I | Span | 312K | 3S | L |
| 1225 | Second-year Spanish II | Span | 312L | 3S | L |
| 1225 | Advanced composition | Span | 327 | 3S | U |
| 130201 | Commercial transactions | BL | 366 | 3S | U |
| 130299 | Business law first course | BL | 323 | 3S | U |
| 140803 | Museum education | AEd | 376 | 3S | U |
| 150103 | Introductory astronomy | Astro | 302 | 3S | L |
| 150302 | Cellular & molecular biol | Bio | 302 | 3S | L |
| 150303 | Structure-fnctn organisms | Bio | 303 | 3S | L |
| 150803 | Mechanics | Phys | 301 | 3S | L |
| 150899 | Gen phys mech heat sound | Phys | 302K | 3S | L |
| 150899 | Gen phys elec mag lt nuc | Phys | 302L | 3S | L |
| 150899 | Elem phys nontech mech ht | Phys | 609A | 3S | L |
| 150899 | Elem phys nontech elec mg | Phys | 609B | 3S | L |
| 160302 | College algebra | Math | 301 | 3S | L |
| 160303 | First crs theory numbers | Math | 328K | 3S | U |
| 160307 | Lin alg and matrix theory | Math | 311 | 3S | L |
| 160401 | Calculus I | Math | 808A | 4S | L |
| 160401 | Calculus II | Math | 808B | 4S | L |
| 160401 | Math for bus/econ | Math | 403K | 4S | L |
| 160401 | Calculus II for bus/econ | Math | 403L | 4S | L |
| 160602 | Trigonometry | Math | 304E | 3S | L |
| 160603 | Analytic geometry | Math | 305E | 3S | L |
| 160699 | Elem fnctns coord geom | Math | 305G | 3S | L |
| 160702 | Probability I | Math | 362K | 3S | L |
| 161299 | Mathematics of investment | Math | 303F | 3S | L |
| 180501 | Introduction to logic | Philo | 312 | 3S | L |
| 200104 | Intro to psychology | Psych | 301 | 3S | L |
| 200403 | Stat methds in psychology | Psych | 317 | 3S | L |
| 200501 | Abnormal psychology | Psych | 352 | 3S | U |
| 200599 | Child psychology | Psych | 342 | 3S | U |
| 220102 | Cultural anthropology | Anthr | 302 | 3S | L |
| 220106 | Physical anthropology | Anthr | 301 | 3S | L |
| 220106 | Fossil man | Anthr | 348 | 3S | U |
| 220201 | Intro to econ I: macroecon | Econ | 302 | 3S | L |
| 220201 | Intro to econ II: microeco | Econ | 303 | 3S | L |
| 220212 | Global resources | Econ | 352M | 3S | U |
| 220301 | Geography of the world | Geog | 305 | 3S | L |
| 220302 | Economic geography | Res | 325 | 3S | U |
| 220302 | Econ geog and locatn thry | Geog | 335 | 3S | U |
| 220305 | Physical geography | Grg | 301C | 3S | L |
| 220424 | English civ before 1603 | Hist | 304K | 3S | L |
| 220424 | English civ since 1603 | Hist | 304L | 3S | L |
| 220427 | Latin America before 1810 | Hist | 346K | 3S | L |
| 220432 | The US 1492-1865 | Hist | 315K | 3S | L |
| 220432 | The US since 1865 | Hist | 315L | 3S | L |
| 220452 | Westrn civ in med times | Hist | 309K | 3S | L |
| 220453 | Westrn civ in mdrn times | Hist | 309L | 3S | L |
| 220501 | American government | Gov | 610A | 3S | L |
| 220501 | American government | Gov | 610B | 3S | L |
| 220504 | Intl politics snce 2nd WW | Gov | 323M | 3S | U |
| 220505 | American foreign relatns | Gov | 344 | 3S | U |
| 220511 | Texas government | Gov | 105 | 1S | L |
| 220603 | Population and society | Socio | 369K | 3S | U |
| 220606 | Intro to stdy of sociolgy | Socio | 302 | 3S | L |
| 220615 | Racial and ethnic rltns | Socic | 344 | 3S | U |

| NCES No. | Course Title | Dept. | Course No. | Credits | Level |
|---|---|---|---|---|---|
| 220699 | Sex roles | Socio | 333K | 3S | U |
| 220699 | Nuclear threat | Socio | 321K | 3S | U |
| | **Noncredit courses** | | | | |
| 090253 | Dental office procedures | DOP | | NC | V |
| 090253 | Dental charting | DC | | NC | V |
| 090253 | Dental chairside techniqs | DCT | | NC | V |
| 220502 | Citizenship I | Cit | I | NC | D |
| 220502 | Citizenship II | Cit | II | NC | D |

## ⑥① UNIVERSITY OF UTAH

Mrs. Donna F. Moore
Administrative Assistant
1152 Annex Building
University of Utah
Division of Continuing Education
Salt Lake City, Utah 84112
Phone: 801-581-6485

Enrollment on a noncredit basis accepted in some credit courses. Gifted high school students are permitted to enroll in undergraduate courses for credit. Overseas enrollment accepted.

| NCES No. | Course Title | Dept. | Course No. | Credits | Level |
|---|---|---|---|---|---|
| | **College courses** | | | | |
| 030302 | Poetry, prose & music | Music | 511 | 3Q | U |
| 030302 | The elements of music | Music | 200 | 3Q | L |
| 030303 | Music fund for elem tchrs | Music | 159 | 2Q | L |
| 030303 | Music ed in elem school | Music | 371 | 3Q | U |
| 030502 | Intro to the visual arts | Art | 100 | 5Q | L |
| 040101 | Elementary accounting | Acctg | 121 | 3Q | L |
| 040101 | Elementary accounting | Acctg | 122 | 3Q | L |
| 040111 | Management accounting | Acctg | 350 | 3Q | U |
| 040114 | Federal tax accounting | Acctg | 509 | 4Q | U |
| 040114 | Federal tax accounting | Acctg | 510 | 4Q | U |
| 040205 | Gregg shorthand | SecTr | 161 | 4Q | L |
| 040206 | Business gramm and punct | SecTr | 100 | 2Q | L |
| 040207 | Fundmntls of typewriting | SecTr | 130 | 2Q | L |
| 040207 | Intermediate typewriting | SecTr | 131 | 2Q | L |
| 040301 | Business finance | Finan | 303 | 4Q | U |
| 040302 | Personal finance | Finan | 120 | 4Q | L |
| 040306 | Investment principles | Finan | 336 | 4Q | U |
| 040308 | Money and banking | Econ | 320 | 3Q | U |
| 040601 | Bus comm & research des | Mgmt | 518 | 4Q | U |
| 040708 | Risk and insurance | Finan | 324 | 4Q | U |
| 041001 | Principles of marketing | Mktg | 301 | 4Q | U |
| 050103 | Principles of advertising | Mktg | 350 | 4Q | U |
| 050601 | The editing process | Commu | 301 | 4Q | U |
| 050605 | Magazine article writing | Commu | 451 | 3Q | U |
| 070204 | Public school finance | EdAdm | 628 | 3Q | U |
| 070206 | Educational law | EdAdm | 633 | 3Q | U |
| 070399 | Introduction to education | Educ | 151 | 2Q | L |
| 070399 | Conceptual prob in educ | Educ | 652 | 3Q | U |
| 070401 | Kindergarten/early ch ed | Educ | 520 | 3Q | U |
| 070404 | Storytelling in elem sch | Educ | 102 | 3Q | L |
| 070404 | Tching science in el sch | Educ | 449 | 3Q | U |
| 070404 | Social studies in el sch | Educ | 450 | 3Q | U |
| 070404 | Creative tchg of art elsc | Educ | 581-1 | 3Q | U |
| 070404 | Mathematics in el school | Educ | 408 | 3Q | U |
| 070404 | Language arts in el sch | Educ | 430 | 3Q | U |
| 070404 | Reading as develop prcess | Educ | 420 | 4Q | U |
| 070404 | Tching reading early chil | Educ | 421 | 5Q | U |
| 070404 | Tching reading inter grds | Educ | 422 | 5Q | U |
| 070404 | Tching reading content ar | Educ | 558 | 4Q | U |
| 070404 | Child dev curriculum chge | Educ | 624 | 3Q | U |
| 070404 | Modern pro in dev reading | Educ | 670 | 3Q | U |
| 070404 | Tching reading secon schs | Educ | 423 | 5Q | U |
| 070404 | Gen secondary tching meth | Educ | 575 | 3Q | U |
| 070404 | Art for secondary schs | Art | 491 | 3Q | U |
| 070404 | Math for elementary tchrs | Math | 405 | 4Q | U |
| 070404 | The use of books & librs | EduM | 102 | 2Q | L |
| 070404 | Methods/skills arts/craft | RecLe | 320 | 3Q | U |
| 070404 | Child literature in sch | Educ | 440 | 3Q | U |
| 070599 | Behavior prob in school | Educ | 646 | 3Q | U |
| 070613 | Intro to driver education | HEdu | 350 | 3Q | U |
| 070613 | Organ and admin driver ed | HEdu | 351 | 3Q | U |
| 070613 | Driver ed: internship | HEdu | 692 | VC | U |
| 070613 | Driver education invd std | HEdu | 392 | VC | U |

| NCES No. | Course Title | Dept. | Course No. | Credits | Level |
|---|---|---|---|---|---|
| 070801 | Intro to special educ | SpEd | 502 | 3Q | U |
| 071203 | Intro to instruction tech | EduM | 561 | 3Q | U |
| 071203 | Intro to instruction tech | EduM | 561 | 5Q | U |
| 071203 | Prin of graphic communica | EduM | 562 | 4Q | U |
| 071204 | Mgt comput/lrn res center | EduM | 565 | 3Q | U |
| 071205 | Instructional TV programg | EduM | 566 | 3Q | U |
| 071299 | Eval and sel of ed media | EduM | 503 | 3Q | U |
| 071299 | Cat and class: non-print | EduM | 658 | 3Q | U |
| 0810 | Engineering drawing | CivEg | 101 | 2Q | L |
| 082199 | Elements of metallurgy | MetEg | 361 | 3Q | U |
| 090403 | Alcohol and drugs | HEdu | 548 | 3Q | U |
| 090901 | Personal health problems | HEdu | 101 | 3Q | L |
| 090901 | School health program | HEdu | 312 | 3Q | U |
| 100312 | Fundmntls of nutrition | FdNut | 144 | 3Q | U |
| 120299 | Amer lit 1900-1945 | Engl | 519 | 5Q | U |
| 120299 | Amer lit since 1945 | Engl | 520 | 4Q | U |
| 120299 | Shakespeare: early plays | Engl | 540 | 5Q | U |
| 120299 | American folklore | Engl | 573 | 5Q | U |
| 120305 | Modern English grammar | Engl | 343 | 5Q | U |
| 120310 | Intro to college writing | Writ | 101 | 4Q | U |
| 1299 | First-year Persian | Persi | 101 | 5Q | L |
| 1299 | First-year Persian | Persi | 102 | 5Q | L |
| 130799 | Business law | Mgmt | 341 | 4Q | U |
| 140199 | Cataloging and classifica | EduM | 564 | 4Q | U |
| 140804 | Reference work | EduM | 351 | 4Q | U |
| 140899 | Selection of lib material | EduM | 563 | 4Q | U |
| 1409 | Library work with child | EduM | 326 | 5Q | U |
| 150199 | Popular astronomy | Phys | 106 | 4Q | L |
| 150202 | Intro to meteorology | Meteo | 101 | 4Q | L |
| 150304 | Human ecology | Bio | 175 | 3Q | L |
| 150307 | Human genetics | Bio | 335 | 4Q | U |
| 150399 | Human physiology | Bio | 201 | 5Q | L |
| 150799 | Elementary physics | Phys | 101 | 5Q | L |
| 150799 | General mechanics sound | Phys | 111 | 4Q | L |
| 150799 | General heat elec magneti | Phys | 112 | 4Q | L |
| 150799 | General light modern phy | Phys | 113 | 4Q | L |
| 150799 | For sc eng: mechanics | Phys | 171 | 4Q | L |
| 150799 | For sc eng: elec magneti | Phys | 172 | 4Q | L |
| 150799 | For sc eng: heat/lght/sd | Phys | 173 | 4Q | L |
| 150799 | Science and soc futurism | Phys | 100 | 3Q | L |
| 160302 | Intermediate algebra | Math | 101 | 5Q | L |
| 160302 | College algebra | Math | 105 | 5Q | L |
| 160401 | Calculus I | Math | 111 | 4Q | L |
| 160401 | Calculus I | Math | 112 | 4Q | L |
| 160401 | Calculus I | Math | 113 | 4Q | L |
| 160602 | Plane trigonometry | Math | 106 | 5Q | L |
| 160803 | Elementary statistics | Math | 107 | 4Q | L |
| 190199 | Intro to physical educ | PhyEd | 250 | 2Q | L |
| 190203 | Physiology of exercise | PhyEd | 282 | 2Q | L |
| 190203 | Medical aspects | PhyEd | 283 | 2Q | L |
| 190306 | Sport psychology | PhyEd | 278 | 2Q | L |
| 190511 | Home school commun safety | HEdu | 304 | 3Q | U |
| 190512 | Human sexuality | HSci | 300 | 3Q | U |
| 190704 | The recreation program | RecLe | 332 | 5Q | U |
| 190709 | Outdoor recreation | RecLe | 350 | 3Q | U |
| 190799 | Recreat and leisure mod s | RecLe | 192 | 5Q | L |
| 200199 | Psychology | Psych | 101 | 5Q | L |
| 200501 | Psych of abnormal behav | Psych | 340 | 4Q | U |
| 200503 | Survey of clinical psych | Psych | 332 | 3Q | U |
| 200599 | Psychology of adolescence | Psych | 123 | 3Q | L |
| 200603 | Elementary statistics | Psych | 150 | 4Q | L |
| 200799 | Social psychology | Psych | 341 | 4Q | U |
| 220101 | Prehistory of No America | Anthr | 381-4 | 3Q | U |
| 220101 | Archaeology of Southwest | Anthr | 381-3 | 3Q | U |
| 220102 | Intro to cultural anthro | Anthr | 101 | 5Q | L |
| 220106 | Intro to physical anthro | Anthr | 102 | 5Q | L |
| 220109 | Civiliz of the Aztecs | Anthr | 381-1 | 5Q | U |
| 220109 | Indians of North America | Anthr | 303 | 5Q | U |
| 220109 | Civilization of the Maya | Anthr | 381-2 | 5Q | U |
| 220201 | Economics as social sci | Econ | 105 | 5Q | L |
| 220202 | Economic history of US | Econ | 274 | 4Q | U |
| 220211 | Labor economics | Econ | 310 | 4Q | U |
| 220301 | World cultural geography | Geog | 160 | 5Q | L |
| 220306 | Geography of Utah | Geog | 360 | 5Q | U |
| 220408 | Age of the Reformation | Hist | 326 | 5Q | U |
| 220426 | Europe since 1914 | Hist | 310 | 5Q | U |
| 220428 | History of Utah | Hist | 478 | 5Q | U |
| 220432 | American civilization | Hist | 170 | 5Q | L |
| 220450 | Hist of civilizat: ancien | Hist | 101 | 5Q | L |
| 220453 | Hist of civilizat: modern | Hist | 103 | 5Q | L |
| 220501 | American national govt | PolSc | 110 | 5Q | L |
| 220505 | Intro to intl politics | PolSc | 210 | 5Q | L |

| NCES No. | Course Title | Dept. | Course No. | Credits | Level |
|---|---|---|---|---|---|
| 220599 | Intro to political sci | PolSc | 101 | 5Q | L |
| 220606 | Intro to sociology | Socio | 101 | 5Q | L |
| | **Noncredit courses** | | | | |
| 040104 | Simplified accounting | Acctg | 5R | NC | V |
| 040999 | Effective writing in bus | Mgmt | 7R | NC | V |
| 040999 | Retail management | Mgmt | 79R | NC | V |
| 041303 | Real estate principles | Finan | 24 | NC | V |
| 071299 | Church & synagogue libr | EduM | 10R-1 | NC | V |
| 160302 | Preparatory algebra | Math | 50 | NC | L |
| 1906 | Motor vehicle acc reconst | | | NC | L |
| 220502 | Naturalization | | | NC | V |

## ⑥ UNIVERSITY OF WASHINGTON

Dr. Harry L. Norman
Department Head
University Extension—Distance Learning GH-23
University of Washington
5001 25th Avenue, NE, Room 109
Seattle, Washington 98195
Phone: 206-543-2350

Enrollment on a noncredit basis accepted in all credit courses. Gifted high school students are permitted to enroll in undergraduate courses for credit. Overseas enrollment accepted.

| NCES No. | Course Title | Dept. | Course No. | Credits | Level |
|---|---|---|---|---|---|
| | **College courses** | | | | |
| 010901 | Interp the environment | ForM | C353 | 5Q | U |
| 020104 | History of urban design | ArPlg | C471 | 3Q | U |
| 030302 | History of jazz | Music | C331 | 3Q | U |
| 040311 | Money, natl income, price | B Ecn | C301 | 4Q | U |
| 0408 | Interntnl enviro business | IntBu | C300 | 3Q | U |
| 0408 | Bus in indust countries | IntBu | C340 | 4Q | U |
| 041001 | Marketing concepts | Mktg | C301 | 4Q | U |
| 041004 | Retailing | Mktg | C470 | 4Q | U |
| 041005 | Advertising | Mktg | C340 | 4Q | U |
| 060701 | Intro FORTRAN programming | Engr | C141 | 4Q | L |
| 070812 | Beginning Braille | Rehab | C496 | 3Q | U |
| 071103 | Basic educ statistics | EdPsy | C490 | 3Q | U |
| 081104 | Engineering statics | Engr | C210 | 4Q | L |
| 090299 | Seizure disorders | Nurs | C353 | 3Q | U |
| 090999 | Biolog aspects of aging | UConj | C440 | 3Q | U |
| 100601 | Normal devel & atypic inf | Psych | C498 | 3Q | U |
| 120103 | Intro to linguistics | Ling | C200 | 5Q | L |
| 120299 | Mod Europ lit in translat | Engl | C371 | 5Q | U |
| 120307 | Popular literature | Engl | C221 | 5Q | L |
| 120307 | Chldrn's lit reconsidered | Engl | C223 | 5Q | L |
| 120307 | Late Renaissance | Engl | C321 | 5Q | U |
| 120307 | Milton | Engl | C322 | 5Q | U |
| 120307 | Amer lit: early nation | Engl | C352 | 5Q | U |
| 120307 | Amer lit: later 19th cent | Engl | C353 | 5Q | U |
| 120307 | Amer lit: early modern | Engl | C354 | 5Q | U |
| 120307 | Amer lit: contemp America | Engl | C355 | 5Q | U |
| 120307 | Utopias and social ideals | Engl | C417 | 5Q | U |
| 120307 | Shakespeare: survey | Engl | C231 | 5Q | L |
| 120307 | Shakespeare to 1603 | Engl | C314 | 5Q | U |
| 120307 | Shakespeare after 1603 | Engl | C315 | 5Q | U |
| 120307 | Reading literature | Engl | C200 | 5Q | L |
| 120307 | The contemporary novel | Engl | C359 | 5Q | U |
| 120307 | The modern novel | Engl | C340 | 5Q | U |
| 120307 | Fantasy | Engl | C370 | 5Q | U |
| 120307 | The Bible as literature | Engl | C309 | 5Q | U |
| 120307 | Studies in autobiog lit | Engl | C489 | 5Q | U |
| 120310 | Begin verse writing | Engl | C274 | 5Q | L |
| 120310 | Intermediate verse writng | Engl | C386 | 5Q | L |
| 120310 | Advanced verse writing | Engl | C422 | 5Q | U |
| 120310 | Begin short story writing | Engl | C277 | 5Q | L |
| 120399 | Technical writing | Engr | C331 | 3Q | U |
| 1208 | Elem Danish | Dan | C101 | 5Q | L |
| 1208 | Elem Danish | Dan | C102 | 5Q | L |
| 1208 | Elem Danish | Dan | C103 | 5Q | L |
| 1209 | Elem Finnish | Finn | C101 | 5Q | L |
| 1209 | Elem Finnish | Finn | C102 | 5Q | L |
| 1210 | Elem French | Fren | C111 | 5Q | L |
| 1210 | Elem French | Fren | C112 | 5Q | L |
| 1210 | Elem French | Fren | C113 | 5Q | L |

| NCES No. | Course Title | Dept. | Course No. | Credits | Level |
|---|---|---|---|---|---|
| 1210 | Elem French reading | Fren | C105 | 5Q | L |
| 1211 | First-year German | Germ | C111 | 5Q | L |
| 1211 | First-year German | Germ | C112 | 5Q | L |
| 1211 | First-year German | Germ | C113 | 5Q | L |
| 1211 | Advan 2nd-year German | Germ | C203 | 3Q | L |
| 1211 | Basic 2nd-year German | Germ | C201 | 5Q | L |
| 1211 | Inter 2nd-year German | Germ | C202 | 5Q | L |
| 1213 | Biblical Hebrew | Hebr | C400 | 5Q | U |
| 1214 | Elem Italian | Ital | C111 | 5Q | L |
| 1214 | Elem Italian | Ital | C112 | 5Q | L |
| 1214 | Elem Italian | Ital | C113 | 5Q | L |
| 1218 | Elem Norwegian | Norw | C101 | 5Q | L |
| 1218 | Norwegian contemp novel | Norw | C300 | 3Q | U |
| 1218 | Elem Norwegian | Norw | C102 | 5Q | L |
| 1218 | Elem Norwegian | Norw | C103 | 5Q | L |
| 1222 | First-year Russian | Russ | C101 | 5Q | L |
| 1222 | First-year Russian | Russ | C102 | 5Q | L |
| 1225 | Cultural bkground lit | Span | C461 | 5Q | U |
| 1225 | Elem Spanish | Span | C111 | 5Q | L |
| 1225 | Basic grammar review | Span | C122 | 5Q | L |
| 1225 | Elem Spanish | Span | C112 | 5Q | L |
| 1225 | Elem Spanish | Span | C113 | 5Q | L |
| 1225 | Inter Spanish | Span | C211 | 5Q | L |
| 1225 | Inter Spanish | Span | C212 | 5Q | L |
| 1225 | Inter Spanish | Span | C213 | 5Q | L |
| 1225 | Advan syntax and comp | Span | C301 | 5Q | U |
| 1225 | Advan syntax and comp | Span | C302 | 5Q | U |
| 1226 | Elem Swedish | Swed | C101 | 5Q | L |
| 1226 | Elem Swedish | Swed | C102 | 5Q | L |
| 130199 | Intro to law | Law | C200 | 5Q | L |
| 130899 | Women and the law | WomS | C310 | 5Q | U |
| 150101 | Astronomy | Astr | C101 | 5Q | L |
| 150102 | The planets | Astro | C150 | 5Q | L |
| 150201 | Survey of the atmosphere | AtmSc | C101 | 5Q | L |
| 150306 | The universe & orig life | Astro | C201 | 5Q | L |
| 150401 | Chemical science | Chem | C100 | 5Q | L |
| 150401 | General chemistry | Chem | C140 | 4Q | L |
| 150401 | General chemistry | Chem | C150 | 4Q | L |
| 1506 | Survey of oceanography | Ocean | C101 | 5Q | L |
| 160399 | Appl of algebra to busin | Math | C156 | 5Q | L |
| 160403 | Calculus with analyt geom | Math | C124 | 5Q | L |
| 160406 | Appl of calculus to busin | Math | C157 | 5Q | L |
| 160406 | Calculus with analyt geom | Math | C125 | 5Q | L |
| 160407 | Calculus with analyt geom | Math | C126 | 5Q | L |
| 160408 | Elem diff equations | Math | C238 | 3Q | L |
| 160507 | Elementary functions | Math | C105 | 5Q | L |
| 160802 | Basic statistics | Stat | C220 | 5Q | L |
| 160802 | Basic statistics wth appl | Stat | C301 | 5Q | U |
| 160802 | Elements of stat methods | Stat | C311 | 5Q | U |
| 161299 | Math for elem schl tchrs | Math | C170 | 3Q | L |
| 180502 | Introduction to logic | Phil | C120 | 5Q | L |
| 1807 | Phil issues in the law | Phil | C114 | 5Q | L |
| 181002 | Intro to Eastern religion | Relig | C202 | 5Q | L |
| 200501 | Deviant personality | Psych | C305 | 5Q | U |
| 200504 | Normal devel & atypic inf | Psych | C498 | 3Q | U |
| 200504 | Developmental psychology | Psych | C306 | 5Q | U |
| 200509 | Intro to pers and ind dif | Psych | C205 | 4Q | U |
| 200702 | Social psychology | Psych | C345 | 5Q | U |
| 200799 | Psych as a social science | Psych | C101 | 5Q | L |
| 210501 | Adv park & rec mgmt | ForM | C454 | 3Q | U |
| 220102 | Intro to study of man | Anthr | C100 | 5Q | L |
| 220102 | Anthro studies of women | Anthr | C353 | 5Q | U |
| 220107 | Principles social anthro | Anthr | C202 | 5Q | L |
| 220201 | Intro to economics | Econ | C200 | 5Q | L |
| 220201 | Principles of economics | Econ | C100 | 5Q | L |
| 220202 | Econ hist of Westrn world | Econ | C260 | 5Q | L |
| 220213 | Intro microeconomics | Econ | C200 | 5Q | L |
| 220302 | Economic geography | Geog | C207 | 5Q | L |
| 220308 | Geography of cities | Geog | C277 | 5Q | L |
| 220406 | North Amer Ind Pac NW | AInSt | C311 | 5Q | U |
| 220428 | Hist Washington and NW | Hist | C432 | 5Q | U |
| 220472 | Anthrop study of women | WomS | C353 | 5Q | U |
| 220504 | Pub bureauc in pol order | PolSc | C470 | 5Q | U |
| 220505 | American foreign policy | PolSc | C321 | 5Q | U |
| 220505 | Intro to intntl policy | PolSc | C203 | 5Q | L |
| 220506 | Intro to Amer politics | PolSc | C202 | 5Q | L |
| 220507 | Politics & mass communic | PolSc | C305 | 5Q | U |
| 220510 | Intro to politics | PolSc | C101 | 5Q | L |
| 220605 | The family | Socio | C352 | 5Q | U |
| 220606 | Survey of sociology | Socio | C110 | 5Q | L |
| 220610 | Sociology of deviance | Socio | C271 | 5Q | L |
| 220612 | Intr to tech as so/po phn | SMT | C401 | 3Q | U |

| NCES No. | Course Title | Dept. | Course No. | Credits | Level |
|---|---|---|---|---|---|
| | **Noncredit courses** | | | | |
| 160302 | Intermediate algebra | Math | C101 | NC | H |
| 160399 | Elementary algebra: survey | Math | CA | NC | H |
| 160399 | Elementary algebra: survey | Math | CB | NC | H |
| 160602 | Plane trigonometry | Math | C104 | NC | H |
| 160603 | Analytic geometry: survey | Math | CC | NC | H |
| 160603 | Analytic geometry: survey | Math | CD | NC | H |

63 **UNIVERSITY OF WISCONSIN–EXTENSION**

Dr. Donald F. Kaiser
Director of
Independent Study
University of Wisconsin-Extension
432 North Lake Street
Madison, Wisconsin 53706
Phone: 608-263-2055

Enrollment on a noncredit basis accepted in some credit courses. Gifted high school students are permitted to enroll in undergraduate courses for credit. Overseas enrollment accepted.

| NCES No. | Course Title | Dept. | Course No. | Credits | Level |
|---|---|---|---|---|---|
| | **High School courses** | | | | |
| 020402 | Architectural drawing | Arch | A88 | HF | H |
| 030302 | Beginning music theory I | Music | H30 | 1U | H |
| 030302 | Beginning music theory II | Music | H31 | 1U | H |
| 030599 | Basic drawing | VisAr | A20 | HF | H |
| 040104 | Basic bookkeeping I | Bus | A30 | HF | H |
| 040104 | Basic bookkeeping II | Bus | A31 | HF | H |
| 0499 | General business I | Bus | H25 | HF | H |
| 0499 | Stocks, bonds & investing | Bus | A69 | QT | H |
| 0804 | Automotive mechanics I | EngAS | A60 | HF | H |
| 0804 | Automotive mechanics II | EngAS | A61 | HF | H |
| 080999 | Electricity fundamentals | EngAS | W72 | HF | H |
| 090799 | Personal & family health | HSci | H30 | HF | H |
| 120305 | First-yr high sch Engl I | Engl | H10 | HF | H |
| 120305 | First-yr high sch Eng II | Engl | H11 | HF | H |
| 120307 | American literature | Lit | H30 | HF | H |
| 120307 | American literature | Lit | H31 | HF | H |
| 120307 | English literature | Lit | H41 | HF | H |
| 120310 | Second-yr high sch Eng I | Engl | H20 | HF | H |
| 120310 | Second-yr high sch Eng II | Engl | H21 | HF | H |
| 120310 | Writing & grammar review | Engl | H42 | HF | H |
| 120310 | Creative writing | Engl | H45 | HF | H |
| 1210 | First-sem high sch French | Frnch | H10 | HF | H |
| 1210 | Second-sem h s Frnch | Frnch | H11 | HF | H |
| 1210 | Third-sem high sch French | Frnch | H20 | HF | H |
| 1210 | Fourth-sem high sch French | Frnch | H21 | HF | H |
| 1210 | Fifth-sem high sch French | Frnch | H30 | HF | H |
| 1210 | Sixth-sem high sch French | Frnch | H31 | HF | H |
| 1210 | Seventh-sem h s French | Frnch | H40 | HF | H |
| 1210 | Eighth-sem high sch Frnch | Frnch | H41 | HF | H |
| 1211 | First-sem high sch German | Ger | H10 | HF | H |
| 1211 | Second-sem high sch Ger | Ger | H11 | HF | H |
| 1211 | Third-sem h s German | Ger | H20 | HF | H |
| 1211 | Fourth-sem high sch Ger | Ger | H21 | HF | H |
| 1211 | Fifth-sem high sch German | Ger | H30 | HF | H |
| 1211 | Sixth-sem high sch German | Ger | H31 | HF | H |
| 1211 | Eighth-sem high sch Ger | Ger | H41 | HF | H |
| 1216 | First-sem high sch Latin | CILL | H10 | HF | H |
| 1216 | Second-sem high sch Latin | CILL | H11 | HF | H |
| 1216 | Third-sem high sch Latin | CILL | H20 | HF | H |
| 1216 | Fourth-sem high sch Latin | CILL | H21 | HF | H |
| 1220 | First-sem high sch Russn | Rus | H10 | HF | H |
| 1220 | Second-sem h s Russian | Rus | H11 | HF | H |
| 1220 | Third-sem h s Russian | Rus | H20 | HF | H |
| 1220 | Fourth-sem h s Russian | Rus | H21 | HF | H |
| 1220 | Russian conversation/comp | Rus | A70 | 1U | H |
| 1220 | Fifth-sem h s Russian | Rus | H30 | HF | H |
| 1220 | Sixth-sem h s Russian | Rus | H31 | HF | H |
| 1220 | Seventh-sem h s Russian | Rus | H40 | HF | H |
| 1220 | Eighth-sem h s Russian | Rus | H41 | HF | H |
| 1225 | First-sem h s Spanish | Span | H10 | HF | H |
| 1225 | Second-sem h s Spanish | Span | H11 | HF | H |
| 1225 | Third-sem h s Spanish | Span | H20 | HF | H |
| 1225 | Fourth-sem h s Spanish | Span | H21 | HF | H |
| 1225 | Seventh-sem h s Spanish | Span | H40 | HF | H |

| NCES No. | Course Title | Dept. | Course No. | Credits | Level |
|---|---|---|---|---|---|
| 1225 | Eighth-sem h s Spanish | Span | H41 | HF | H |
| 1225 | Fifth-sem h s Spanish | Span | H30 | HF | H |
| 1225 | Sixth-sem h s Spanish | Span | H31 | HF | H |
| 150302 | General biology I | Bio | H20 | HF | H |
| 150303 | General biology II | Bio | H21 | HF | H |
| 150899 | Gen physical science I | Meas | H20 | HF | H |
| 150899 | Gen physical science II | Meas | H21 | HF | H |
| 160301 | Practical arithmetic | Meas | A52 | HF | H |
| 160302 | First-semester algebra | Math | H10 | HF | H |
| 160302 | Second-semester algebra | Math | H11 | HF | H |
| 160302 | Advanced algebra I | Math | H30 | HF | H |
| 160302 | Advanced algebra II | Math | H31 | HF | H |
| 160302 | College algebra | Math | H39 | HF | H |
| 160601 | Geometry I | Math | H20 | HF | H |
| 160601 | Geometry II | Math | H21 | HF | H |
| 160602 | Plane trigonometry | Math | H40 | HF | H |
| 161299 | Math for electricity I | Meas | A56 | HF | H |
| 161299 | Math for electricity II | Meas | A57 | HF | H |
| 220299 | Contemporary economics | Econ | H40 | HF | H |
| 220305 | Physical geography | Geog | H22 | HF | H |
| 220432 | US history to 1877 | Hist | H30 | HF | H |
| 220432 | US history since 1877 | Hist | H31 | HF | H |
| 220501 | American govt today | PolSc | H30 | HF | H |
| | **College courses** | | | | |
| 010104 | Cooperation | Agri | 422 | 3S | L |
| 010902 | Introduction to forestry | Bio | 100 | 2S | L |
| 030302 | Apprec & history of music | Music | 101 | 2S | L |
| 030302 | Apprec & history of music | Music | 102 | 2S | L |
| 030599 | Creative design | Art | 131 | 3S | L |
| 030699 | History of Western art | ArHis | 105 | 4S | L |
| 040101 | Elementary accounting I | Bus | 201 | 3S | L |
| 040101 | Elementary accounting II | Bus | 202 | 3S | L |
| 040101 | Intermediate accounting I | Bus | 301 | 3S | L |
| 040101 | Intermediate acctg II | Bus | 302 | 3S | L |
| 040106 | Cost accounting I | Bus | 323 | 3S | U |
| 040106 | Advanced cost accounting | Bus | 413 | 3S | U |
| 040111 | Managerial accounting | Bus | 300 | 3S | L |
| 040306 | Investments | Bus | 322 | 3S | L |
| 040306 | Principles of finance | Bus | 320 | 3S | U |
| 040307 | Financial management | Bus | 427 | 3S | U |
| 040710 | Prin of risk management | Bus | 560 | 3S | U |
| 040903 | Organization behavior | Bus | 346 | 3S | L |
| 040905 | Organization & mgt | Bus | 233 | 3S | L |
| 040999 | Production management | Bus | 341 | 3S | L |
| 040999 | Purchasing—matrls mgmt | Bus | 436 | 3S | U |
| 041001 | Principles of marketing | Bus | 311 | 3S | L |
| 041199 | Management of personnel | Bus | 361 | 3S | L |
| 0499 | Business law I | Bus | 305 | 3S | U |
| 050103 | Advertising copy & layout | Jrnl | 450 | 4S | L |
| 050605 | Writing feature articles | Jrnl | 305 | 3S | L |
| 050608 | Newswriting | Jrnl | 203 | 3S | L |
| 0507 | Publications design | Jrnl | 207 | 2S | L |
| 0509 | Public relations | Jrnl | 525 | 3S | L |
| 060799 | FORTRAN programming | EngAS | 211 | 2S | U |
| 070309 | Voc tech adult education | Educ | 502 | 2S | L |
| 070499 | School curriculum design | Educ | 300 | 3S | L |
| 070499 | Early childhood education | Educ | 482 | 1S | L |
| 070509 | Health info for teachers | Educ | 501 | 3S | L |
| 070512 | Children's literature | Educ | 649 | 3S | L |
| 070602 | Career education | Educ | 498 | 3S | L |
| 070899 | The exceptnl individual | Educ | 300 | 3S | L |
| 070899 | Children with handicaps | Educ | 496 | 2S | L |
| 070902 | Human relation-education | Educ | 465 | 3S | L |
| 070999 | Family day care | Educ | 481 | 1S | L |
| 080799 | Critical path network | EngAS | 590 | 2S | L |
| 081104 | Dynamics | EngAS | 222 | 3S | U |
| 081104 | Statics | EngAS | 221 | 3S | U |
| 081199 | Mechanics of materials | EngAS | 303 | 3S | U |
| 081799 | Economic analysis—engr | EngAS | 312 | 3S | U |
| 082099 | Intro numerical control | EngAS | 428 | 2S | L |
| 082199 | Intro to materials sci | EngAS | 360 | 3S | L |
| 090799 | Health care in school | Nurs | 470 | 2S | U |
| 100206 | Consumer education | Bus | 344 | 3S | L |
| 100601 | Development in adolescenc | Educ | 321 | 3S | L |
| 100604 | Human ability & learning | Educ | 301 | 3S | U |
| 110119 | Art & science of welding | EngAS | 137 | 3S | L |
| 120103 | Intro to linguistics | Engl | 320 | 3S | L |
| 120201 | Fantasy & science fiction | Lit | 357 | 3S | L |
| 120302 | Hist of English language | Engl | 323 | 3S | L |
| 120305 | Structure of English lang | Engl | 329 | 3S | L |
| 120307 | Intro to literature | Engl | 200 | 3S | L |

| NCES No. | Course Title | Dept. | Course No. | Credits | Level |
|---|---|---|---|---|---|
| 120307 | American literature | Engl | 211 | 3S | L |
| 120307 | American literature | Engl | 212 | 3S | L |
| 120307 | Shakespearian drama | Engl | 217 | 3S | L |
| 120307 | Shakespearian drama | Engl | 218 | 3S | L |
| 120307 | Saul Bellow | Engl | 311 | 1S | L |
| 120307 | Willa Cather | Engl | 312 | 1S | L |
| 120307 | Doris Lessing | Engl | 313 | 1S | L |
| 120307 | Eudora Welty | Engl | 314 | 1S | L |
| 120307 | Virginia Woolf | Engl | 315 | 1S | L |
| 120307 | Sherwood Anderson | Engl | 365 | 1S | L |
| 120307 | Ernest Hemingway | Engl | 431 | 1S | L |
| 120307 | William Faulkner | Engl | 433 | 1S | L |
| 120307 | Graham Greene | Engl | 434 | 1S | L |
| 120307 | The English novel | Engl | 460 | 3S | L |
| 120307 | Campus in translation | Engl | 230 | 1S | L |
| 120307 | De Beauvoir in translatio | Engl | 231 | 1S | L |
| 120307 | Colette in translation | Engl | 232 | 1S | L |
| 120307 | Malraux in translation | Engl | 260 | 1S | L |
| 120307 | Thomas Mann | Engl | 190 | 1S | L |
| 120307 | Günter Grass | Engl | 191 | 1S | L |
| 120307 | Scandinavian experience | Engl | 295 | 1S | L |
| 120307 | Unamuno | Engl | 256 | 1S | L |
| 120307 | Wisconsin authors | Engl | 216 | 3S | L |
| 120310 | Technical writing | EngAS | 279 | 3S | L |
| 120310 | Technical writing I | EngAS | 273 | 1S | L |
| 120310 | Technical writing II | EngAS | 274 | 1S | L |
| 120310 | Technical writing III | EngAS | 275 | 1S | L |
| 120310 | Intermediate composition | Engl | 201 | 2S | L |
| 120310 | Intro to creative writing | Engl | 203 | 2S | L |
| 120399 | Freshman English | Engl | 102 | 3S | L |
| 1205 | First-semester Arabic | Heb | 101 | 4S | L |
| 1210 | First-semester French | Frnch | 103 | 4S | L |
| 1210 | Second-semester French | Frnch | 104 | 4S | L |
| 1210 | Third-semester French | Frnch | 203 | 3S | U |
| 1210 | Fourth-semester French | Frnch | 204 | 3S | U |
| 1210 | French-lit: 17th & 18th c | Frnch | 221 | 3S | U |
| 1210 | French-lit: 19th century | Frnch | 222 | 3S | U |
| 1210 | French-lit: 20th century | Frnch | 223 | 3S | U |
| 1210 | Modern French dramatists | Frnch | 644 | 3S | U |
| 1210 | André Malraux | Frnch | 360 | 1S | U |
| 1210 | Camus | Frnch | 441 | 1S | U |
| 1210 | Simone de Beauvoir | Frnch | 442 | 1S | U |
| 1210 | Colette | Frnch | 443 | 1S | U |
| 1210 | Intermediate composition | Frnch | 227 | 2S | U |
| 1210 | Advanced composition | Frnch | 324 | 2S | U |
| 1210 | Business French | Frnch | 219 | 2S | U |
| 1211 | Applied German philology | Ger | 662 | 3S | U |
| 1211 | First-semester German | Ger | 101 | 4S | L |
| 1211 | Second-semester German | Ger | 102 | 4S | L |
| 1211 | Third-semester German | Ger | 203 | 3S | U |
| 1211 | Fourth-semester German | Ger | 204 | 3S | U |
| 1211 | Intro German literature | Ger | 221 | 3S | U |
| 1211 | Intro German literature | Ger | 222 | 3S | U |
| 1211 | The classical period | Ger | 302 | 3S | U |
| 1211 | Contemporary German lit | Ger | 305 | 3S | U |
| 1211 | Goethe's *Faust* | Ger | 633 | 3S | U |
| 1211 | Thomas Mann | Ger | 699A | 1S | U |
| 1211 | Günter Grass | Ger | 699B | 1S | U |
| 1211 | Intermediate composition | Ger | 223 | 3S | U |
| 1211 | Intermediate composition | Ger | 224 | 3S | U |
| 1212 | Elementary Greek | Greek | 103 | 4S | L |
| 1212 | Elementary Greek | Greek | 104 | 4S | L |
| 1212 | Plato | Greek | 104P | 2S | L |
| 1212 | Homer: *The Iliad* | Greek | 210 | 3S | L |
| 1212 | Xenophon & New Testament | Greek | 204 | 3S | L |
| 1213 | First-sem Hebrew—bibl | Heb | 101B | 4S | L |
| 1213 | Scnd-sem Hebrew—bibl | Heb | 104 | 2S | L |
| 1213 | Biblical texts: Esther | Heb | 201 | 2S | L |
| 1213 | Exodus & Leviticus | Heb | 321 | 2S | L |
| 1213 | Biblical texts: Joshua | Heb | 322 | 2S | L |
| 1213 | Aramaic: Daniel & Ezra | Heb | 501 | 2S | U |
| 1213 | First-sem Hebrew—modern | Heb | 101M | 4S | L |
| 1213 | Scnd-sem Hebrew—modern | Heb | 103 | 2S | L |
| 1213 | Mod Hebrew conversation | Heb | 225 | 3S | L |
| 1213 | Sefarad-Spanish Jewry | Heb | 365 | 3S | U |
| 1213 | Jewish cultural hist I | Heb | 471 | 3S | L |
| 1213 | Jewish cultural hist II | Heb | 472 | 3S | L |
| 1214 | First-semester Italian | Ital | 103 | 4S | L |
| 1214 | Second-semester Italian | Ital | 104 | 4S | L |
| 1214 | Third-semester Italian | Ital | 203 | 3S | L |
| 1216 | Elementary Latin | Clas | 103 | 4S | L |
| 1216 | Elementary Latin | Clas | 104 | 4S | L |
| 1216 | Cicero's *Orations* | Clas | 203 | 4S | L |
| 1216 | Vergil | Clas | 204 | 4S | L |
| 1216 | General survey (Latin) | Clas | 301 | 3S | U |
| 1216 | General survey (Latin) | Clas | 302 | 3S | U |
| 1216 | Intermediate Latin comp | Clas | 505 | 2S | U |
| 1216 | Advanced Latin comp | Clas | 506 | 2S | U |
| 1216 | Horace: *Sat & Epis* | Clas | 512 | 3S | U |
| 1216 | Medieval Latin | Clas | 563 | 2S | U |
| 1218 | Beginning Norwegian I | Ger | 101 | 4S | L |
| 1218 | Beginning Norwegian II | Ger | 102 | 4S | L |
| 1219 | First-sem Portuguese | Span | 101 | 4S | L |
| 1219 | Second-sem Portuguese | Span | 102 | 4S | L |
| 1220 | First-semester Russian | Rus | 101 | 4S | L |
| 1220 | Second-semester Russian | Rus | 102 | 4S | L |
| 1220 | Third-semester Russian | Rus | 203 | 4S | U |
| 1220 | Fourth-semester Russian | Rus | 204 | 4S | U |
| 1225 | First-semester Spanish | Span | 101 | 4S | L |
| 1225 | Second-semester Spanish | Span | 102 | 4S | L |
| 1225 | Third-semester Spanish | Span | 203 | 3S | U |
| 1225 | Fourth-semester Spanish | Span | 204 | 3S | U |
| 1225 | Spanish literature | Span | 221 | 3S | U |
| 1225 | Spanish literature | Span | 222 | 3S | U |
| 1225 | Modern Spanish readings | Span | 228 | 3S | U |
| 1225 | Modern Spanish readings | Span | 229 | 3S | U |
| 1225 | Miguel de Unamuno | Span | 407 | 1S | U |
| 1227 | First-semester Yiddish | Heb | 101 | 4S | L |
| 1227 | Second-semester Yiddish | Heb | 102 | 4S | L |
| 1299 | Greek & Latin medical trm | Clas | 205 | 3S | L |
| 1299 | Greek drama in English | Clas | 313 | 2S | L |
| 1299 | Classical mythology | Clas | 370 | 3S | L |
| 150202 | Weather & climate | EngAS | 100 | 2S | L |
| 150316 | Survey of botany | Bio | 100 | 3S | L |
| 150401 | General chemistry I | EngAS | 103 | 3S | L |
| 150401 | General chemistry II | EngAS | 104 | 3S | L |
| 150599 | General geology | Geol | 100 | 3S | L |
| 150799 | General physics I | EngAS | 103 | 3S | L |
| 150799 | General physics II | EngAS | 104 | 3S | L |
| 160302 | Intermediate algebra | Math | 101 | 4S | L |
| 160302 | College algebra | Math | 112 | 3S | L |
| 160302 | College algebra | Math | 112A | 3S | L |
| 160306 | Matrix & linear algebra | Math | 340 | 3S | U |
| 160399 | Algebra & trigonometry | Math | 114 | 5S | L |
| 160399 | Algebra & trigonometry | Math | 114A | 5S | L |
| 160401 | Calculus & related topics | Math | 211 | 5S | U |
| 160406 | Differential equations | Math | 305 | 2S | U |
| 160499 | Calculus & analyt geom I | Math | 221 | 5S | U |
| 160499 | Calculus & analyt geom II | Math | 222 | 5S | U |
| 160499 | Calculus & analyt geo III | Math | 223 | 5S | U |
| 160602 | Plane trigonometry | Math | 113 | 2S | L |
| 160899 | Intro statistical methods | Math | 301 | 3S | U |
| 180199 | Intro to philosophy | Philo | 101 | 4S | L |
| 180301 | Introduction to ethics | Philo | 241 | 4S | L |
| 180502 | Beginning logic | Philo | 211 | 4S | L |
| 190599 | Women & their bodies | WomSt | 103 | 3S | L |
| 200504 | Child psychology | Psych | 560 | 3S | L |
| 200599 | Intro to psychology | Psych | 202 | 3S | L |
| 200701 | Intro to socl psychology | Psych | 530 | 3S | L |
| 210401 | Social welfare programs | SocWk | 205 | 3S | L |
| 210499 | Child welfare services | SocWk | 462 | 3S | U |
| 220102 | Intro to anthropology | Anthr | 100 | 3S | L |
| 220201 | Introductory economics | Econ | 101 | 4S | L |
| 220201 | Principles of economics | Econ | 103 | 3S | L |
| 220302 | Economic geography | Geog | 102 | 3S | L |

(64) **UNIVERSITY OF WYOMING**

Dr. Heikki I. Leskinen
Coordinator
Correspondence Study Department
University of Wyoming
Box 3294, University Station
Laramie, Wyoming 82071
Phone: 307-766-5631

Enrollment on a noncredit basis accepted in all credit courses. Gifted high school students are permitted to enroll in undergraduate courses for credit.

Overseas enrollment accepted. Enrollment period is one year. A one-year extension is permitted with $5 fee. Minimum time for course completion is six weeks. With instructor's permission, students may return assignments for a maximum of three lessons a week. Sixty percent of tuition refundable if student withdraws within one month, 40% within two months, 20% within three months.

| NCES No. | Course Title | Dept. | Course No. | Credits | Level |
|---|---|---|---|---|---|
| | **High School courses** | | | | |
| 010902 | Intro to forestry sem 1 | Sci | E1 | HF | H |
| 010902 | Intro to forestry sem 2 | Sci | E2 | HF | H |
| 030502 | Introduction to art | Art | A1 | HF | H |
| 040104 | Bookkeeping I sem 1 | Acctg | A1 | HF | H |
| 040104 | Bookkeeping I sem 2 | Acctg | A2 | HF | H |
| 0499 | Business law | Bus | C1 | HF | H |
| 100202 | Consumer living | HmEc | C1 | HF | H |
| 100308 | Food for everyday life | HmEc | B1 | HF | H |
| 100699 | Interpersonal relations | HmEc | A1 | HF | H |
| 120305 | Grammar | Engl | A1 | HF | H |
| 120307 | Comp & lit: 10th gr sem 1 | EngLL | D1 | HF | H |
| 120307 | Comp & lit: 10th gr sem 2 | EngLL | D2 | HF | H |
| 120307 | Comp & lit: 11th gr sem 1 | EngLL | E1 | HF | H |
| 120307 | Comp & lit: 11th gr sem 2 | EngLL | E2 | HF | H |
| 120307 | Comp & lit: 12th gr sem 1 | EngLL | F1 | HF | H |
| 120307 | Comp & lit: 12th gr sem 2 | EngLL | F2 | HF | H |
| 1210 | First-year French sem 1 | Frnch | A1 | HF | H |
| 1225 | First-yr Spanish sem 1 | Span | A1 | HF | H |
| 150304 | Environmental science | Sci | C1 | HF | H |
| 160301 | General mathematics | Math | A1 | HF | H |
| 160302 | Algebra I sem 1 | Math | C1 | HF | H |
| 160302 | Algebra II sem 1 | Math | E1 | HF | H |
| 160302 | Algebra I sem 2 | Math | C2 | HF | H |
| 161201 | Business mathematics | Bus | B1 | HF | H |
| 200199 | Intr to psychology | SocSt | K1 | HF | H |
| 220215 | Economics | SocSt | B1 | HF | H |
| 220401 | United States Constituton | SocSt | F1 | HF | H |
| 220432 | History of the US sem 1 | SocSt | E1 | HF | H |
| 220432 | History of the US sem 2 | SocSt | E2 | HF | H |
| 220501 | United States government | SocSt | G1 | HF | H |
| 220613 | Social problems | SocSt | J1 | HF | H |
| | **College courses** | | | | |
| 010106 | Econ of world food & agri | Agri | 686 | 3S | U |
| 010199 | Econ with applic to agr I | Agri | 370 | 3S | L |
| 010407 | Animal nutrition | AnSci | 510 | 3S | U |
| 010407 | Feeds and feeding | AnSc | 410 | 4S | L |
| 010603 | Agricultural entomology | Agri | 555 | 3S | U |
| 030302 | Introduction to music | Music | 300 | 3S | L |
| 030302 | Theory I—written | Music | 301 | 3S | L |
| 030399 | America's ethnic music | Music | 312 | 2S | L |
| 030402 | Intro to theater | ThArt | 391 | 3S | L |
| 030502 | Intro to hist & crit art | ArHis | 380 | 3S | L |
| 040101 | Principles of account I | Acctg | 401 | 3S | L |
| 040101 | Principles of account II | Acctg | 402 | 3S | L |
| 040106 | Cost accounting | Acctg | 511 | 3S | U |
| 040203 | Indexing and filing | EdBus | 324 | 2S | L |
| 040203 | Records management | EdBus | 524 | 3S | U |
| 040207 | Intermediate typing | EdBus | 321 | 3S | L |
| 040301 | Managerial finance | Fin | 625 | 3S | U |
| 040306 | Intro investment mgt | Fin | 601 | 3S | U |
| 040904 | Management & organization | Mgmt | 621 | 3S | U |
| 041001 | Elements of marketing | Mktg | 621 | 3S | U |
| 041099 | Advertising | Mktg | 623 | 3S | U |
| 041199 | Personnel management | Mgmt | 641 | 3S | U |
| 0499 | Introduction to business | Bus | 300 | 3S | L |
| 050605 | Journalistic writing | Jrnl | 311 | 3S | L |
| 051001 | Broadcast fundamentals | Radio | 405 | 3S | L |
| 051108 | Intro to human communcatn | Commu | 304 | 3S | L |
| 0599 | Intr to mass media | Bdcst | 300 | 3S | L |
| 061103 | Intro to computer science | CmpSc | 301 | 3S | L |
| 070199 | Issues in contempry educ | Educ | 626 | 2S | U |
| 070299 | Tchr & elemen sch adminis | Educ | 621 | 2S | U |
| 070299 | Tchr & second sch adminis | Educ | 622 | 2S | U |
| 070302 | Educ trends in elem educ | Educ | 707 | 2S | U |
| 071102 | Educ tests & measurements | Educ | 606 | 2S | U |
| 071203 | Intro to educ comun & tec | Educ | 612 | 3S | U |
| 080703 | Hydrology | CivEg | 680 | 3S | U |
| 081104 | Statics | EngAS | 401 | 3S | L |
| 081104 | Dynamics | EngAS | 402 | 3S | L |

| NCES No. | Course Title | Dept. | Course No. | Credits | Level |
|---|---|---|---|---|---|
| 090102 | Intro comparative biochem | Bioch | 401 | 4S | L |
| 100206 | Personal finance | HmEc | 511 | 3S | L |
| 100305 | Intr to food science | FSc | 453 | 3S | L |
| 100313 | Nutrition | HmEc | 360 | 2S | L |
| 100503 | Applied design | HmEc | 301 | 3S | L |
| 100601 | Child development | HmEc | 454 | 4S | L |
| 100602 | Foundations of marriage | HmEc | 442 | 3S | L |
| 120305 | Freshman English I | Engl | 300 | 3S | L |
| 120305 | Freshman English II | Engl | 301 | 3S | L |
| 120307 | Amer lit: colonial-Melvil | EngLL | 435 | 3S | L |
| 120307 | Amer lit: Whitman-Faulkne | EngLL | 436 | 3S | L |
| 120307 | Shakespeare: comedies | EngLL | 611 | 3S | U |
| 120307 | Shakespeare: trag/Rom his | EngLL | 612 | 3S | U |
| 120310 | Critical read & writing | Engl | 467 | 3S | L |
| 120310 | Scientific & tech writing | Engl | 601 | 3S | U |
| 1210 | First-year French | Frnch | 301 | 4S | L |
| 1210 | Second-year French | Frnch | 420 | 4S | L |
| 1211 | Second-year German | Ger | 420 | 4S | L |
| 1225 | First-year Spanish I | Span | 301 | 4S | L |
| 1225 | First-year Spanish II | Span | 302 | 4S | L |
| 1225 | Second-year Spanish | Span | 420 | 4S | L |
| 130202 | Business law I | Bus | 431 | 3S | L |
| 140303 | Libraries & librarianship | LibSc | 452 | 2S | L |
| 140307 | Admin of sch lib/med cntr | LibSc | 634 | 3S | U |
| 140401 | Cataloging & classficatn | LibSc | 638 | 3S | U |
| 140408 | Selectn of instruc matrls | LibSc | 632 | 3S | U |
| 1409 | Literature for children | LibSc | 412 | 3S | L |
| 150103 | Descriptive astronomy | Astro | 302 | 2S | L |
| 150403 | Food biochemistry | FSc | 672 | 3S | U |
| 150501 | Introduction to geology | Geol | 300 | 2S | L |
| 160301 | Theory of arith I | Math | 407 | 3S | L |
| 160301 | Theory of arith II | Math | 408 | 3S | L |
| 160302 | Precalculus algebra | Math | 301 | 3S | L |
| 160306 | El linear alg & matrix ty | Math | 401 | 3S | L |
| 160399 | Precalculus mathematics | Math | 303 | 5S | L |
| 160401 | Calculus I | Math | 311 | 4S | L |
| 160401 | Calculus II | Math | 312 | 4S | L |
| 160602 | Precalculus trigonometry | Math | 302 | 3S | L |
| 160802 | Fundmntls of statistics | Stat | 405 | 4S | L |
| 161201 | Math analysis for busines | Math | 313 | 4S | L |
| 190502 | Personl & commun hlth | Hlth | 306 | 3S | L |
| 200199 | General psychology | Psych | 302 | 4S | L |
| 200504 | The child | Psych | 430 | 3S | L |
| 200504 | Exceptional children | Psych | 431 | 2S | L |
| 200504 | Adjustment | Psych | 433 | 3S | L |
| 200702 | Social psychology | Psych | 575 | 3S | U |
| 220101 | Intro to archaeology | Anthr | 303 | 3S | L |
| 220102 | Expl of cultural diversty | Anthr | 302 | 3S | L |
| 220106 | Human origins | Anthr | 301 | 3S | L |
| 220201 | Prin of macroeconomics | Econ | 301 | 3S | L |
| 220201 | Prin of microeconomics | Econ | 302 | 3S | L |
| 220213 | Interm microeconomics | Econ | 602 | 3S | L |
| 220301 | Intro to human geography | Geog | 302 | 3S | L |
| 220426 | Foundation of W Eurpn civ | Hist | 310 | 3S | L |
| 220426 | Hist of Westn Eurpn civza | Hist | 311 | 3S | L |
| 220428 | History of Wyoming | Hist | 360 | 2S | L |
| 220428 | Hist of the American West | Hist | 363 | 2S | L |
| 220432 | Gen survey of US history | Hist | 341 | 3S | L |
| 220432 | Gen survey of US history | Hist | 342 | 3S | L |
| 220471 | Hist of Indians of the US | Hist | 465 | 3S | L |
| 220501 | Gov of the US & Wyo const | PolSc | 305 | 3S | L |
| 220606 | Sociological principles | Socio | 301 | 3S | L |
| 220607 | Human interaction | Socio | 410 | 3S | L |
| 220613 | Social problems | Socio | 305 | 3S | L |
| | **Noncredit courses** | | | | |
| 040502 | Intr to small-bus retail | Bus | 10 | NC | |
| 040502 | Practicum: small-bus ret | Bus | 11 | NC | |
| 040502 | Design small-bus retail | Bus | 12 | NC | |
| 0508 | Handwriting analysis | GnKno | 10 | NC | |
| 0799 | The school board | Educ | 10 | NC | |
| 160199 | Metric system | Math | 10 | NC | |
| 180901 | Buddhism | Rel | 10 | NC | |
| 180902 | Christianity | Rel | 11 | NC | |
| 180903 | Hinduism | Rel | 12 | NC | |
| 180904 | Islam | Rel | 13 | NC | |
| 180905 | Judaism | Rel | 14 | NC | |
| 220510 | Capitalism | PolSc | 10 | NC | |
| 220510 | Communism | PolSc | 11 | NC | |
| 220510 | Socialism | PolSc | 12 | NC | |

## ⑥⑤ USDA GRADUATE SCHOOL

Ms. Norma L. Harwood
Director of Correspondence Study
Room 1404, South Building
US Department of Agriculture Graduate School
14th and Independence Avenue, SW
Washington, District of Columbia 20250
Phone: 202-447-7123

Gifted high school students are permitted to enroll in undergraduate courses for credit. Overseas enrollment accepted. Courses are designed to meet the specific needs of federal government employees. Most courses are applicable to the private sector. The US Office of Personnel Management accepts credits for examination and qualification purposes on the same basis as those from accredited colleges and universities.

| NCES No. | Course Title | Dept. | Course No. | Credits | Level |
|---|---|---|---|---|---|
| | **College courses** | | | | |
| 040101 | Prin of accounting I | Acctg | 101 | 4Q | L |
| 040101 | Prin of accounting II | Acctg | 102 | 4Q | L |
| 040101 | Intermediate acctg I | Acctg | 201 | 4Q | L |
| 040101 | Intermediate acctg II | Acctg | 202 | 4Q | L |
| 040101 | Prin of accounting III | Acct | 103 | 4Q | L |
| 040103 | Internal auditing I | Acctg | 301 | 3Q | U |
| 040103 | Internal auditing II | Acctg | 302 | 3Q | U |
| 040106 | Cost accounting I | Acctg | 250 | 2Q | L |
| 040106 | Cost accounting II | Acctg | 251 | 2Q | L |
| 040106 | Cost accounting III | Acctg | 252 | 2Q | L |
| 040109 | REA accounting—electric | Acctg | 211 | 4Q | L |
| 040109 | REA accounting—telephone | Acctg | 212 | 4Q | L |
| 040109 | Federal govt acctg I | Acctg | 260 | 3Q | L |
| 040109 | Federal govt acctg II | Acctg | 261 | 3Q | L |
| 040203 | Inf and records mgmt | Mgmt | 301 | 3Q | U |
| 041106 | Modern supervisory prac | Mgmt | 201 | 3Q | L |
| 041106 | Success-oriented supervis | Mgmt | 202 | 4Q | L |
| 041199 | Federal personnel proc | Mgmt | 130 | 3Q | L |
| 0508 | Principles of editing | Commu | 140 | 4Q | L |
| 0508 | Intermediate editing | Commu | 230 | 3Q | L |
| 0508 | Printing, layout & design | Commu | 270 | 3Q | L |
| 0508 | Basic indexing | Commu | 360 | 3Q | U |
| 0508 | Applied indexing | Commu | 361 | 4Q | U |
| 0508 | Publishing management | Commu | 375 | 3Q | U |
| 0508 | Proofreading | Commu | 160 | 3Q | L |
| 0508 | Adu practice in editing | Commu | 310 | 3Q | U |
| 0508 | Editing technical ms | Commu | 350 | 3Q | U |
| 060799 | Intro computer programmng | CmpSc | 102 | 3Q | L |
| 061104 | Concepts of data processg | CmpSc | 101 | 3Q | L |
| 080703 | Hydrology I | CivEg | 501 | 4Q | B |
| 080703 | Hydrology II | CivEg | 502 | 4Q | B |
| 080903 | Basic electronics | EEg | 201 | 4Q | L |
| 080907 | Basic electricity | EEg | 101 | 3Q | L |
| 080907 | Elec trans and dist | EEg | 202 | 3Q | L |
| 080907 | Electrical wiring | EEg | 203 | 3Q | L |
| 081104 | Hydraulics I: hydrostatic | EngAS | 204 | 3Q | L |
| 100604 | Individualized retirement | Socio | 100 | 3Q | L |
| 120305 | Punctuation | Engl | 030 | 1Q | D |
| 120305 | Spell and capitalization | Engl | 031 | 1Q | D |
| 120305 | Nouns pronouns adj adverb | Engl | 032 | 1Q | D |
| 120305 | Verb tenses | Engl | 033 | 1Q | D |
| 120310 | Better letters | Engl | 101 | 1Q | L |
| 120310 | Writing for govt & bus | Engl | 102 | 3Q | L |
| 120310 | Report writing | Engl | 201 | 3Q | L |
| 120310 | Regulations writing | Engl | 350 | 3Q | U |
| 120310 | Effectve writing—profess | Engl | 501 | 4Q | B |
| 120399 | Intro to speech writing | Engl | 103 | 3Q | L |
| 130101 | Admin law and procedure | Law | 310 | 3Q | U |
| 1303 | Constitutional law | Laws | 251 | 3Q | L |
| 130799 | Business law I | Law | 120 | 3Q | L |
| 130799 | Business law II | Laws | 121 | 3Q | L |
| 131502 | Legal research | Law | 550 | 3Q | B |
| 131599 | Intro law for paralegals | Law | 110 | 3Q | L |
| 131599 | Legal writing I | Law | 555 | 2Q | U |
| 131599 | Legal writing II | Law | 556 | 2Q | U |
| 1401 | Intro to library tech | LibSc | 110 | 3Q | L |
| 140401 | Cataloging and classif I | LibSc | 120 | 3Q | L |
| 140701 | Use of archives & manusct | LibSc | 211 | 3Q | L |
| 140703 | Intro to bibliographies | LibSc | 225 | 3Q | L |
| 140709 | Library media services | LibSc | 210 | 4Q | L |
| 140799 | Legal literature | LibSc | 255 | 3Q | L |
| 140804 | Basic ref service & tools | LibSc | 245 | 3Q | L |
| 150202 | Dynamic meteorology I | Meteo | 161 | 4Q | L |

| NCES No. | Course Title | Dept. | Course No. | Credits | Level |
|---|---|---|---|---|---|
| 150202 | Dynamic meteorology II | Meteo | 162 | 4Q | L |
| 1508 | General physics I | Phys | 201 | 4Q | L |
| 1508 | General physics II | Phys | 202 | 4Q | L |
| 160302 | College algebra I | Math | 201 | 3Q | L |
| 160302 | College algebra II | Math | 202 | 3Q | L |
| 160401 | Calculus I | Math | 210 | 4Q | L |
| 160401 | Calculus II | Math | 211 | 4Q | L |
| 160602 | Trigonometry | Math | 103 | 3Q | L |
| 160802 | Elements of statistics | Stat | 301 | 3Q | U |
| 160802 | Adv agricultural statist | Stat | 401 | 6Q | U |
| 160809 | Sample survey methods | Stat | 501 | 4Q | B |
| 161107 | Stat meth in biol & agric | Stat | 502 | 3Q | B |
| 161199 | Basic mathematics | Math | 101 | 3Q | L |
| 2101 | Fed procurement/contract | PrPM | 108 | 3Q | L |
| 2101 | Intro to property mgmt | PrPM | 107 | 3Q | L |
| | **Noncredit courses** | | | | |
| 0409 | Work objectives | Mgmt | 001 | NC | D |
| 120305 | Refresher English I | Engl | 001 | NC | D |
| 120305 | Refresher English II | Engl | 002 | NC | D |
| 161201 | Everyday mathematics | Math | 011 | NC | D |

## ⑥⑥ UTAH STATE UNIVERSITY

Mrs. Shirley Andreason
Program Administrator
Independent Study Division
Utah State University
Eccles Conference Center
Logan, Utah 84322
Phone: 801-750-2131

Enrollment on a noncredit basis accepted in all credit courses. Gifted high school students are permitted to enroll in undergraduate courses for credit. Overseas enrollment accepted.

| NCES No. | Course Title | Dept. | Course No. | Credits | Level |
|---|---|---|---|---|---|
| | **College courses** | | | | |
| 010102 | Farm bsns decision making | AgEd | 210 | 3Q | L |
| 010103 | Marketing farm products | AgEc | 260 | 3Q | L |
| 010107 | Farm & ranch management | AgEc | 410 | 3Q | U |
| 010402 | Horse production practice | AnSci | 219 | 3Q | L |
| 010402 | Breeding farm animals | AnSci | 456 | 4Q | U |
| 010404 | Prin of reproduction | AnSci | 520 | 3Q | U |
| 010406 | Funds of livestock produc | AnSci | 110 | 3Q | L |
| 010406 | Livestock industries | AnSci | 111 | 2Q | L |
| 010406 | Lactation of farm animals | AnSci | 535 | 3Q | U |
| 010407 | Feeding farm animals | AnSci | 245 | 3Q | L |
| 010407 | Animal feeds & feeding | AnSci | 245 | 5Q | L |
| 010604 | Intro to agric plant sci | PlSci | 100 | 4Q | L |
| 010701 | General soils | Soils | 358 | 4Q | U |
| 010801 | General fishery biology | WlfSc | 350 | 5Q | U |
| 010901 | Principles of conservatn | For | 410 | 3Q | U |
| 011299 | Wildlife law enforcement | WlfSc | 410 | 3Q | U |
| 020102 | Intro to landscape archit | LAEP | 103 | 5Q | U |
| 030502 | Survey of Western art | Art | 275 | 3Q | L |
| 030502 | Survey of Western art | Art | 276 | 3Q | L |
| 030502 | Survey of Western art | Art | 277 | 3Q | L |
| 030602 | Exploring art | Art | 101 | 3Q | L |
| 030602 | Basic lettering | Art | 330 | 3Q | U |
| 040101 | Introductory accounting | Acctg | 201 | 3Q | L |
| 040101 | Introductory accounting | Acctg | 202 | 3Q | L |
| 040106 | Industrial cost acctg | Acctg | 331 | 4Q | U |
| 040111 | Managerial accounting | Acctg | 203 | 3Q | U |
| 040201 | Intro to business | BusAd | 135 | 3Q | L |
| 040301 | Corporation finance | BusAd | 340 | 4Q | U |
| 040399 | Managing personal finan | BusEd | 314 | 3Q | U |
| 040502 | Entrepren/new venture mgt | BusAd | 435 | 4Q | U |
| 040601 | Business correspondence | ASBE | 155 | 3Q | L |
| 040902 | Management concepts | BusEd | 311 | 4Q | U |
| 040902 | Administrative sys mgt | BusEd | 541 | 3Q | U |
| 040999 | Retailing management | BusAd | 454 | 4Q | U |
| 041001 | Fundmntls of marketing | BusAd | 350 | 4Q | U |
| 041103 | Behav dimensions in mgt | BusAd | 360 | 4Q | U |
| 041203 | Operations research | BusAd | 308 | 4Q | U |
| 050102 | Basic advertising design | Art | 331 | 3Q | U |
| 070516 | Metric educ for teachers | SecEd | 345 | 1Q | U |
| 070516 | Math for elem teachers | Math | 201 | 3Q | L |
| 070516 | Math for elem teachers | Math | 202 | 3Q | L |

| NCES No. | Course Title | Dept. | Course No. | Credits | Level |
|---|---|---|---|---|---|
| 070516 | Math for elem teachers | Math | 203 | 3Q | L |
| 070522 | Teaching social studies | ElEd | 420 | 3Q | U |
| 070610 | Teaching of reading | ElEd | 415 | 3Q | U |
| 070803 | Educ of exceptnl children | SpEd | 301 | 3Q | U |
| 070803 | Intro instr for excp chld | SpEd | 305 | 3Q | U |
| 070803 | Ed of gifted & talented | ElEd | 584 | 3Q | U |
| 070804 | Educational audiology | ComD | 528 | 3Q | U |
| 070805 | Developing IEPS | SpEd | 535 | 2Q | U |
| 070806 | Etiology of devel disabil | SpEd | 590 | 3Q | U |
| 071103 | Measurement & eval in edu | SecEd | 604 | 5Q | U |
| 080205 | Soils, water & environmnt | Soils | 200 | 2Q | L |
| 080703 | Water res eng hydraulics | CEE | 352 | 4Q | U |
| 080703 | Engineering hydraulics | CEE | 553 | 5Q | U |
| 081102 | Elem fluid mechanics | CEE | 350 | 5Q | U |
| 081104 | Engr mechanics statics | Engr | 200 | 3Q | L |
| 081104 | Engr mechanics dynamics | Engr | 202 | 3Q | L |
| 090106 | Fundmntls of epidemiology | Bio | 430 | 3Q | U |
| 090111 | Personal health | Bio | 115 | 2Q | L |
| 090113 | Communicable disease cont | Bio | 412 | 3Q | U |
| 090114 | Elementary microbiology | Bio | 111 | 4Q | L |
| 090119 | Human physiology | Bio | 130 | 5Q | L |
| 090301 | Phonetics | ComD | 275 | 3Q | L |
| 090702 | Environmental health | Bio | 410 | 4Q | U |
| 090702 | Insect/rodent vector cont | Bio | 413 | 3Q | U |
| 090702 | Waterborne-disease contrl | Bio | 414 | 3Q | U |
| 090702 | Foodborne-disease control | Bio | 416 | 3Q | U |
| 090799 | School health program | Bio | 457 | 4Q | U |
| 100312 | Nutrition update | NFS | 585 | 3Q | U |
| 100312 | Nutrition for men | NFS | 122 | 3Q | U |
| 120299 | Children's literature | Engl | 416 | 3Q | U |
| 120299 | Lit for adolescents | Engl | 417 | 3Q | U |
| 120305 | Elements of grammar | Engl | 109 | 3Q | L |
| 120305 | Vocabulary | Engl | 110 | 3Q | L |
| 120305 | Grammar | Engl | 410 | 3Q | U |
| 120308 | Intro to short stories | Engl | 118 | 3Q | L |
| 120310 | Writing poetry | Engl | 501 | 3Q | U |
| 140499 | Cataloging & classificatn | IM | 521 | 3Q | U |
| 140799 | Eval & sel of instr mater | IM | 511 | 3Q | U |
| 150301 | Biology & the citizen | Bio | 101 | 5Q | L |
| 150302 | General biology | Bio | 120 | 5Q | L |
| 150304 | General ecology | RngSc | 384 | 5Q | U |
| 150327 | Insects affecting man | Bio | 190 | 4Q | L |
| 150327 | Biology of honeybees | Bio | 191 | 2Q | L |
| 150599 | Introductory geology | Geol | 101 | 5Q | L |
| 160301 | Basic mathematics | Math | 001 | 5Q | L |
| 160302 | Elementary algebra | Math | 002 | 5Q | L |
| 160302 | Intro to college algebra | Math | 101 | 5Q | L |
| 160302 | College algebra | Math | 105 | 5Q | L |
| 160401 | Calculus I | Math | 215 | 3Q | L |
| 160602 | Plane trigonometry | Math | 106 | 3Q | L |
| 160801 | Business statistics | BusAd | 296 | 5Q | L |
| 190510 | Dynamic fitness | HPER | 300 | 3Q | U |
| 220201 | Economics I | Econ | 200 | 5Q | L |
| 220201 | Economics II | Econ | 201 | 5Q | L |
| 220208 | Microeconomics | Econ | 501 | 4Q | U |
| 220208 | Consumer behavior | BusAd | 451 | 4Q | U |
| 220432 | American civilization | Hist | 170 | 5Q | L |
| 220432 | Civil War & Reconstructn | Hist | 438 | 3Q | U |
| 220452 | Comp civil: anc & medievl | Hist | 101 | 3Q | L |
| 220453 | Comp civilizs: modern | Hist | 103 | 3Q | L |
| 220453 | Comp civs: early modern | Hist | 102 | 3Q | L |
| 220453 | Recent America 1945-pres | Hist | 446 | 3Q | U |

## 67 WASHINGTON STATE UNIVERSITY

Ms. Ellen Krieger
Independent Study Coordinator
208 Van Doren Hall
Washington State University
Pullman, Washington 99164
Phone: 509-335-3557

Enrollment on a noncredit basis accepted in all credit courses. Gifted high school students are permitted to enroll in undergraduate courses for credit. Overseas enrollment accepted.

| NCES No. | Course Title | Dept. | Course No. | Credits | Level |
|---|---|---|---|---|---|
| | **High School courses** | | | | |
| 090101 | Basic health | He | 1X | HF | H |
| 1225 | Spanish I first semester | ForL | 5X | HF | H |
| 1225 | Spanish I second semester | ForL | 6X | HF | H |
| 1507 | Physics first semester | Sc | 1X | HF | H |
| 1507 | Physics second semester | Sc | 2X | HF | H |
| 160302 | Algebra I first semester | Math | 1X | HF | H |
| 160302 | Algebra I second semester | Math | 2X | HF | H |
| 160302 | Algebra II first semester | Math | 3X | HF | H |
| 160302 | Algebra II second sem | Math | 4X | HF | H |
| 160399 | Precalculus first sem | Math | 5X | HF | H |
| 160399 | Precalculus second sem | Math | 6X | HF | H |
| | **College courses** | | | | |
| 010407 | Animal nutrition | AS | 307X | 3S | U |
| 010505 | Turfgrass culture | Agron | 301X | 2S | U |
| 010599 | Plants and gardens | Hort | 101X | 3S | L |
| 010603 | Agricultural entomology | Entom | 340X | 3S | U |
| 010604 | Commercial veg crops | Hort | 320X | 3S | U |
| 010702 | Soils | Soils | 201X | 3S | L |
| 030399 | Survey of music literat | Mus | 160X | 3S | L |
| 040101 | Prin of accounting I | Acctg | 230X | 3S | L |
| 040101 | Prin of accounting II | Acctg | 231X | 3S | L |
| 0403 | Finance | Fin | 325X | 3S | U |
| 040601 | Business communications | Engl | 265X | 3S | L |
| 040710 | Risk and insurance | Ins | 320X | 3S | U |
| 040903 | Organizational behavior | Mgt | 401X | 3S | U |
| 040904 | Principles of management | Mgt | 301X | 3S | U |
| 041099 | Consumer behavior | Mktg | 367X | 3S | U |
| 0412 | Statistics | QMeth | 215X | 4S | L |
| 041303 | Real estate | RE | 305X | 3S | U |
| 041308 | Law of real estate | BLaw | 414X | 3S | U |
| 041309 | Real estate administratn | RE | 406X | 3S | U |
| 051103 | Language/human behavior | Spe | 325X | 3S | U |
| 0599 | Mass communications & soc | Com | 101X | 3S | L |
| 080799 | Statics | CE | 211X | 3S | L |
| 090115 | Human nutrition | FSHN | 233X | 3S | L |
| 100313 | Human nutrition | FSHN | 233X | 3S | L |
| 100399 | Nutrition for man | FSHN | 130X | 3S | L |
| 120103 | Language/human behavior | Spe | 325X | 3S | U |
| 120202 | Reading literature | Engl | 108X | 3S | L |
| 120299 | Topics in Eng/detect fict | Engl | 495X | 3S | U |
| 120299 | Contemporary Amer fiction | Engl | 250X | 1S | L |
| 120299 | Women in literature | Engl | 338X | 3S | U |
| 120307 | English lit to 1750 | Engl | 209X | 3S | L |
| 120307 | English lit 1750 to 1900 | Engl | 210X | 3S | L |
| 120307 | American lit to 1855 | Engl | 245X | 3S | L |
| 120307 | American lit since 1855 | Engl | 246X | 3S | L |
| 120307 | Shakespeare | Engl | 305X | 3S | U |
| 120307 | Shakespeare | Engl | 306X | 3S | U |
| 120307 | English Romantic lit | Engl | 416X | 3S | U |
| 120307 | Victorian literature | Engl | 417X | 3S | U |
| 120310 | English composition | Engl | 101X | 3S | L |
| 120310 | Expository writing | Engl | 201X | 3S | L |
| 120310 | Business communications | Engl | 265X | 3S | L |
| 1210 | First-semester French | Fren | 101X | 4S | L |
| 1210 | Second-semester French | Fren | 102X | 4S | L |
| 1211 | First-semester German | Ger | 101X | 4S | L |
| 1211 | Second-semester German | Ger | 102X | 4S | L |
| 1225 | First-semester Spanish | Span | 101X | 4S | L |
| 1225 | Second-semester Spanish | Span | 102X | 4S | L |
| 130401 | Criminal law | CrmJ | 320X | 3S | U |
| 130403 | Intro to juvenile justice | CrmJ | 240X | 3S | L |
| 130799 | Law and business I | BLaw | 210X | 3S | L |
| 160302 | Intermediate algebra | Math | 101X | 3S | L |
| 160306 | Intro linear algebra | Math | 220X | 2S | L |
| 160401 | Calculus I | Math | 171X | 4S | L |
| 160401 | Calculus II | Math | 172X | 4S | L |
| 160406 | Differential equations | Math | 315X | 3S | U |
| 160602 | Precalculus trigonometry | Math | 108X | 2S | L |
| 160802 | Statistics | QMeth | 215X | 4S | L |
| 180302 | Ethics in contemp society | Phil | 260X | 3S | L |
| 180401 | Hum in ancient world | Hum | 101X | 3S | L |
| 180499 | Intro to philosophy | Phil | 101X | 3S | L |
| 190599 | Sci concepts for nurs I | Nurs | 305X | 3S | U |
| 190599 | Sci concepts for nurs II | Nurs | 315X | 3S | U |
| 2001 | Intro Psych human behavr | Psych | 102X | 3S | L |
| 200501 | Abnormal psychology | Psych | 333X | 3S | U |
| 200504 | Developmental psychology | Psych | 361X | 3S | U |
| 200509 | Intro to personality | Psych | 321X | 3S | U |
| 2007 | Social psychology | Psych | 350X | 3S | U |
| 2099 | Human sexuality | Psych | 230X | 3S | L |
| 220107 | Human issues int'l dev | Anth | 462X | 3S | U |
| 220201 | Contemporary economics | Econ | 201X | 4S | L |

| NCES No. | Course Title | Dept. | Course No. | Credits | Level |
|---|---|---|---|---|---|
| 220423 | Challenge of China & Japn | Hist | 274X | 3S | L |
| 220423 | Challenge of China & Japn | AsSt | 274X | 3S | L |
| 220426 | Classcl/Christian Europe | Hist | 101X | 3S | L |
| 220426 | Europe since Louis XIV | Hist | 102X | 3S | L |
| 220432 | American history to 1865 | Hist | 110X | 3S | L |
| 220432 | American hist since 1865 | Hist | 111X | 3S | L |
| 220450 | Hum in ancient world | Hum | 101X | 3S | L |
| 220501 | Amer national government | PolS | 101X | 3S | L |
| 220505 | Human issues in int'l dev | PolS | 462X | 3S | U |
| 220511 | State-local government | PolS | 206X | 3S | L |
| 220602 | Criminology | Soc | 361X | 3S | U |
| 220605 | Marital sexual lifestyles | Soc | 150X | 3S | L |
| 220605 | The family | Soc | 351X | 3S | U |
| 220606 | Intro to sociology | Soc | 101X | 3S | L |
| 220607 | Social psychology | Soc | 350X | 3S | U |
| 220613 | Human issues in int'l dev | Soc | 462X | 3S | U |
| 220699 | Sociology of sex roles | Soc | 384X | 3S | U |
| 2299 | Intro women studies | WSt | 200X | 3S | L |
| 2299 | Human sexuality | WSt | 230X | 3S | L |
| 2299 | The family | WSt | 351X | 3S | U |
| 2299 | Marital & sex, lifestyles | WSt | 150X | 3S | L |
| 2299 | Sociology of sex roles | WSt | 384X | 3S | U |
| | **Noncredit courses** | | | | |
| 040999 | Stress & effective mgmt | Mgt | 089 | NC | U |
| 100207 | Nutrition: What's for you | HNF | 078X | NC | V |
| 100312 | Nutrition: What's for you? | HNF | 078X | NC | V |

## ⑥⑧ WEBER STATE COLLEGE

Dr. Richard F. Thomas
Associate Dean
Division of Continuing Education
3750 Harrison Boulevard
Ogden, Utah 84408
Phone: 801-626-6600

Enrollment on a noncredit basis accepted in all credit courses. Gifted high school students are permitted to enroll in undergraduate courses for credit. Overseas enrollment accepted for college courses. Open enrollment with one year to complete, matriculation not required, reduced fees, instructor consultation by appointment, field-proctored examinations, audio- and video-assisted materials.

| NCES No. | Course Title | Dept. | Course No. | Credits | Level |
|---|---|---|---|---|---|
| | **College courses** | | | | |
| 0106 | Plants in human affairs | Bot | NS101 | 4Q | L |
| 0303 | Music essentials | Music | 169 | 3Q | L |
| 030302 | Introduction to music | Music | HU101 | 3Q | L |
| 030302 | Introduction to jazz | Music | HU102 | 3Q | L |
| 0501 | Principals of advertising | Mktg | 340 | 4Q | U |
| 0599 | Intro mass communication | Commu | HU112 | 3Q | L |
| 0599 | Mass media society | Commu | 328 | 3Q | U |
| 0901 | Biomedical science core | HeaSc | 111 | 5Q | L |
| 0901 | Biomedical science core | HeaSc | 112 | 5Q | L |
| 0901 | Biomedical science core | HeaSc | 113 | 5Q | L |
| 090299 | Pathophysiology | HeaSc | 130 | 3Q | L |
| 090702 | Comnty hlth promotion | HeaEd | 315 | 3Q | U |
| 090799 | Patient education | HeaEd | 319 | 3Q | U |
| 090799 | Dev of hlth promot prog | HeaEd | 415 | 3Q | U |
| 090799 | Foundtns of hlth promot | HeaEd | 310 | 3Q | U |
| 0999 | Medical terminology | HeaSc | 101 | 3Q | L |
| 100206 | Plan indiv family finance | ChFam | PD115 | 3Q | L |
| 100313 | Princples of nutrition | ChFam | PD101 | 3Q | L |
| 100601 | Human development | ChFam | PD150 | 5Q | L |
| 100603 | Intro to gerontology | Geron | SS101 | 5Q | L |
| 120307 | Introduction to fiction | Engl | HU232 | 5Q | L |
| 120310 | English composition | Engl | 102 | 5Q | L |
| 120310 | English composition | Engl | 103 | 3Q | L |
| 120399 | Vocabulary building | Engl | 107 | 2Q | L |
| 120399 | Fiction writing | Engl | 225 | 3Q | L |
| 120399 | Poetry writing | Engl | 326 | 3Q | U |
| 150202 | Intro to meteorology | Geog | NS113 | 4Q | L |
| 1504 | Introduction to chemistry | Chem | NS101 | 5Q | L |
| 160302 | First course in algebra | Math | 101 | 5Q | L |
| 160302 | Intermediate algebra | Math | 105 | 5Q | L |
| 1999 | Personal health | Hlth | 101 | 2Q | L |
| 2001 | Intro to psychology | Psych | SS101 | 5Q | L |
| 200505 | Psych of adjustment | Psych | SS154 | 3Q | L |

| NCES No. | Course Title | Dept. | Course No. | Credits | Level |
|---|---|---|---|---|---|
| 2101 | Intro to public administ | PolSc | 370 | 5Q | U |
| 2103 | Criminal justice | CLEE | SS101 | 5Q | L |
| 210304 | Police process | CLEE | 101 | 3Q | L |
| 2201 | Introduction anthropology | Anthr | SS101 | 5Q | L |
| 220305 | Physical geography | Geog | NS101 | 5Q | L |
| 220402 | Diplomatic history of US | Hist | 425 | 5Q | U |
| 220420 | History of Africa | Hist | 374 | 5Q | U |
| 220423 | History of the Far East | Hist | 470 | 5Q | U |
| 220426 | Twentieth-century Europe | Hist | 433 | 5Q | U |
| 220427 | Latin American-modern | Hist | 461 | 5Q | U |
| 220429 | Hist of the Middle East | Hist | 473 | 5Q | U |
| 220432 | American civilization | Hist | SS170 | 5Q | L |
| 220433 | World civilization begin | Hist | SS101 | 4Q | L |
| 220433 | World civilization-1871 | Hist | SS102 | 4Q | L |
| 220433 | World civilization-presnt | Hist | SS103 | 4Q | L |
| 220472 | Women in American history | Hist | 415 | 3Q | L |
| 220499 | Far Western history | Hist | 427 | 5Q | U |
| 220499 | Utah history | Hist | 428 | 3Q | U |
| 220501 | American national govermt | PolSc | SS110 | 5Q | L |
| 220501 | The constitution | PolSc | 492 | 4Q | U |
| 2206 | Intro to sociology | Socio | SS101 | 5Q | L |
| 220602 | Criminology | Socio | SS327 | 3Q | U |
| 220613 | Social problems | Socio | SS102 | 5Q | L |
| 220699 | Social stratification | Socio | 301 | 3Q | U |

## ⑥⑨ WESTERN ILLINOIS UNIVERSITY

Dr. Joyce E. Nielsen
Director of Independent Study Program
318 Sherman Hall
Western Illinois University
West Adams Road
Macomb, Illinois 61455
Phone: 309-298-2496

Only in exceptional cases are gifted high school students permitted to enroll in undergraduate courses for credit. Overseas enrollment is not encouraged; each case is judged on an individual basis. Registration for courses follows the on-campus semester timetable. Please request course listings for future terms. External degree program available.

| NCES No. | Course Title | Dept. | Course No. | Credits | Level |
|---|---|---|---|---|---|
| | **College courses** | | | | |
| 040111 | Managerial accounting | Acctg | 343 | 3S | U |
| 040301 | Business finance | Mktg | 312 | 3S | U |
| 040308 | Money, banking and credit | Econ | 325 | 3S | U |
| 040399 | Personal investing | Mktg | 305 | 3S | U |
| 040710 | Risk mgmt & insurance | Mktg | 351 | 3S | U |
| 0408 | International business | IntBu | 317 | 3S | U |
| 040903 | Organizational behavior | Mgmt | 350 | 3S | U |
| 040904 | Principles of management | Mgmt | 349 | 3S | U |
| 040999 | Management and society | Mgmt | 481 | 3S | U |
| 040999 | Intro to operations mgmt | Mgmt | 352 | 3S | U |
| 041001 | Principles of marketing | Mktg | 327 | 3S | U |
| 041004 | Retailing management | Mktg | 343 | 3S | U |
| 041005 | Advtg & promotional conc | Mktg | 331 | 3S | U |
| 041099 | Consumer market behavior | Mktg | 333 | 3S | U |
| 0411 | Personnel management | PAIR | 353 | 3S | U |
| 041103 | Personnel management | Mgmt | 353 | 3S | U |
| 041303 | Principles of real estate | Fin | 361 | 3S | U |
| 051001 | Broadcasting and society | CA&S | 323 | 3S | U |
| 070602 | Career educ & persnl devl | Educ | 241 | 2S | U |
| 100312 | Child nutrition & health | HmEc | 303 | 3S | U |
| 100313 | Intro to nutrition | HmEc | 109 | 3S | L |
| 100699 | Marriage and family | HmEc | 321 | 3S | U |
| 120305 | Modern English grammar | Engl | 370 | 3S | U |
| 120307 | Women and literature | Engl | 301 | 3S | U |
| 120307 | Spec studies in English | Engl | 309 | 3S | U |
| 120307 | Romantic literature | Engl | 320 | 3S | U |
| 120310 | Writing in humanities | Engl | 380 | 3S | U |
| 120399 | Scientific & tech writing | Engl | 381 | 3S | U |
| 150103 | Astronomy | Geog | 325 | 3S | U |
| 150301 | Biology | Bio | 303 | 4S | U |
| 150303 | Human biology | Bio | 304 | 4S | U |
| 150306 | Intro to organ evolution | Bio | 319 | 4S | U |
| 150599 | Environmental geology | Geol | 375 | 3S | U |
| 180301 | Moral philosophy | Philo | 330 | 3S | U |
| 180501 | Logic & reasoning | Philo | 115 | 3S | L |
| 180999 | Religion in America | Relig | 395 | 3S | U |

| NCES No. | Course Title | Dept. | Course No. | Credits | Level |
|---|---|---|---|---|---|
| 190799 | Tourism | Rec | 362 | 3S | U |
| 200799 | Fire-related human behavr | Psych | 481 | 3S | U |
| 210302 | Fire protect struc design | InArt | 443 | 3S | U |
| 210302 | Pol & legal fnd fire prot | LEA | 485 | 3S | U |
| 210302 | Adv fire administration | LEA | 481 | 3S | U |
| 210302 | Anlyt appr to fire protec | LEA | 482 | 3S | U |
| 210302 | Psnl mgmt for fire serv | LEA | 483 | 3S | U |
| 210302 | Fire-prvn organ & mgmt | LEA | 484 | 3S | U |
| 210302 | Disaster & fire def plang | HSci | 477 | 3S | U |
| 210302 | Applic of fire research | Socio | 475 | 3S | U |
| 210302 | Fire dynamics | InArt | 475 | 3S | U |
| 210302 | Incen fire analy & inves | Lea | 475 | 3S | U |
| 210302 | Community and fire threat | Lea | 475 | 3S | U |
| 210401 | Soc serv & welfare policy | Socio | 311 | 3S | U |
| 210501 | Outdoor recreat perspect | Rec | 376 | 3S | U |
| 220199 | Anthropology of religion | Anthr | 324 | 3S | U |
| 220211 | Labor instit & pub policy | Econ | 340 | 3S | U |
| 220299 | Intro health economics | Econ | 390 | 3S | U |
| 220299 | Managerial economics | Econ | 332 | 3S | U |
| 220399 | Climatology | Geog | 424 | 3S | U |
| 220399 | Population geography | Geog | 443 | 3S | U |
| 220399 | Conserv and mgmt nat res | Geog | 426 | 3S | U |
| 220432 | American history to 1877 | Hist | 105 | 3S | L |
| 220432 | American hist since 1877 | Hist | 106 | 3S | L |
| 220432 | Business in Am history | Hist | 302 | 3S | U |
| 220432 | US military history | Hist | 304 | 3S | U |
| 220432 | The American West | Hist | 308 | 3S | U |
| 220432 | Am Revol & the new nation | Hist | 413 | 3S | U |
| 220499 | Germany under Hitler | Hist | 438 | 3S | U |
| 220501 | Int to Am govt & politics | PolSc | 122 | 3S | L |
| 220599 | Supreme Court | PolSc | 319 | 3S | U |
| 220602 | Criminology | Socio | 355 | 3S | U |
| 220604 | Juvenile delinquency | Socio | 425 | 3S | U |
| 220605 | The family | Socio | 460 | 3S | U |
| 220615 | Minority peoples | Socio | 411 | 3S | U |

⑦⓪ **WESTERN MICHIGAN UNIVERSITY**

Mrs. Geraldine A. Schma
Director of Self-Instructional Programs
Ellsworth Hall, Room B-102
Western Michigan University
West Michigan Avenue
Kalamazoo, Michigan 49008
Phone: 616-383-0788

Enrollment on a noncredit basis accepted in all credit courses. Gifted high school students are permitted to enroll in undergraduate courses for credit. Overseas enrollment is not encouraged; each case is judged on an individual basis. All courses offered for undergraduate credit only. Western Michigan University does not offer an external degree. Courses meet on-campus degree requirements and may also be transferred to other universities.

| NCES No. | Course Title | Dept. | Course No. | Credits | Level |
|---|---|---|---|---|---|
| | **College courses** | | | | |
| 010699 | Plants of SW Michigan | Bio | 599 | 3S | L |
| 010699 | Trees & shrubs | Bio | 599 | 2S | L |
| 010699 | Economic botany | Bio | 599 | 3S | U |
| 020699 | Energy & the way we live | AmSt | 333 | 2S | L |
| 020699 | Connections: tec & change | A&Sci | 501 | 2S | U |
| 050299 | Mass media: messgs/manip | GHum | 316 | 4S | U |
| 050401 | Photography workshop | Educ | 550 | 3S | U |
| 050402 | Technical communication | InEg | 102 | 3S | L |
| 050499 | Popular literature | AmSt | 333 | 1S | L |
| 050608 | Newswriting | Engl | 264 | 4S | L |
| 060199 | Intro to info processing | Bus | 102 | 3S | L |
| 060199 | Intro to computers | CmpSc | 105 | 3S | L |
| 070306 | Prin of vocational educat | IndEd | 512 | 3S | U |
| 070511 | Teach pract arts & voc ed | IndEd | 344 | 3S | L |
| 070515 | Biological sci in elem ed | Bio | 107 | 4S | L |
| 070599 | Course planng & construct | IndEd | 342 | 3S | L |
| 070603 | Coord techniq in co-op ed | IndEd | 543 | 3S | U |
| 070799 | Prin & phil of guidance | CP | 580 | 2S | L |
| 090199 | Medical terminology | OT | 436 | 2S | U |
| 090259 | Computers in radiology | H&HS | 560 | 1S | U |
| 090303 | Hm grth devlmnt & aging | OT | 225 | 3S | L |
| 090303 | Orientat to occup therapy | OT | 202 | 3S | L |
| 090303 | Psychiatric conditions | OT | 436 | 3S | U |

| NCES No. | Course Title | Dept. | Course No. | Credits | Level |
|---|---|---|---|---|---|
| 100699 | Amer families in transitn | AmSt | 333 | 2S | L |
| 100699 | Working: changes/choices | AmSt | 333 | 2S | L |
| 100699 | Death & dying: ch/change | A&Sci | 501 | 2S | U |
| 120299 | The British novel | Eng | 344 | 4S | U |
| 120299 | World of mystery fiction | AmSt | 499 | 2S | L |
| 120299 | Children's literature | Eng | 282 | 4S | L |
| 120308 | Personal readg efficiency | Educ | 103 | 2S | L |
| 120310 | Thought & language: expos | Eng | 105 | 4S | L |
| 120310 | Preprofessional writing | Engl | 305 | 4S | L |
| 120399 | Personal vocabulary devel | Educ | 101 | 2S | L |
| 120399 | Effctv rdg for coll stu | Educ | 104 | 2S | L |
| 1503 | Biological science | Bio | 107 | 4S | L |
| 150316 | Applied botany | Bio | 220 | 4S | L |
| 150316 | Medical botany | Bio | 599 | 3S | U |
| 150399 | Environmental biology | Bio | 105 | 3S | L |
| 150499 | History of chemistry | Chem | 580 | 3S | U |
| 160202 | Logic | Phil | 520 | 4S | U |
| 160301 | Computational skills | Math | 109 | 2S | L |
| 1608 | Intro to statistics | Math | 366 | 4S | L |
| 1807 | Intro to humanities | GHum | 101 | 4S | L |
| 1807 | American culture | GHum | 302 | 4S | L |
| 1807 | Depression and war | GHum | 401 | 4S | U |
| 181303 | Monasticism and reform | MdvSt | 500 | 2S | U |
| 190504 | Healthful living | Bio | 599 | 2S | U |
| 200501 | Abnormal psychology | Psych | 250 | 3S | U |
| 200508 | Child psychology | Psych | 160 | 3S | L |
| 200599 | Intro to human behavior | Psych | 150 | 3S | L |
| 200599 | Human sexuality | Psych | 524 | 3S | U |
| 200901 | Organizational psychology | Psych | 344 | 3S | L |
| 220201 | Principles of econ: micro | Econ | 201 | 3S | L |
| 220201 | Principles of econ: macro | Econ | 202 | 3S | L |
| 220204 | Money & credit | Econ | 420 | 4S | U |
| 220211 | Labor problems | Econ | 410 | 3S | U |
| 220299 | Contemp econ problems | Econ | 100 | 3S | L |
| 220306 | Geography of Michigan | Geog | 311 | 3S | U |
| 220472 | Women: past, pres, future | GHum | 409 | 4S | U |
| 220499 | Intro to non-Westrn world | GenS | 304 | 4S | U |
| 220505 | International relations | PolSc | 250 | 4S | U |
| 220599 | Poli topics: admin behavr | PSci | 270 | 1S | U |
| 220599 | Prct appl of mgmt prin | PolSc | 270 | 1S | U |
| 220601 | American society | Soc | 100 | 3S | L |
| 220602 | Criminology | Socio | 362 | 3S | U |
| 220604 | Juvenile delinquency | Socio | 564 | 3S | U |
| 220606 | Principles of sociology | Socio | 200 | 3S | L |
| 220607 | Intro to social psych | Soc | 320 | 3S | L |
| 220615 | Intro to social gerontol | Soc | 352 | 3S | U |
| 220699 | Intro to criminal justice | Soc | 264 | 3S | L |
| 220699 | Soc impacts of sci & tech | Soc | 171 | 3S | L |
| 220699 | Computer usage | Soc | 182 | 3S | L |
| 2299 | Modern Japanese society | Soc | 336 | 3S | L |

⑦① **WESTERN WASHINGTON UNIVERSITY**

Ms. Janet Howard
Independent Study Coordinator
Old Main 400
Western Washington University
Bellingham, Washington 98225
Phone: 206-676-3320

Gifted high school students are permitted to enroll in undergraduate courses for credit. Overseas enrollment is not encouraged; each case is judged on an individual basis.

| NCES No. | Course Title | Dept. | Course No. | Credits | Level |
|---|---|---|---|---|---|
| | **College courses** | | | | |
| 040101 | Prin of financial acctg | Acctg | 241 | 4Q | L |
| 040101 | Prin of financial acctg | Acctg | 242 | 4Q | L |
| 040109 | Fund and governmental acc | Acctg | 367 | 3Q | U |
| 040111 | Prin of managerial acctg | Acctg | 243 | 4Q | L |
| 070199 | Foundation of education | Educ | 411 | 4Q | U |
| 070199 | History of American educ | Educ | 413 | 4Q | U |
| 070899 | Intro to exceptional chld | Educ | 360 | 3Q | U |
| 071102 | Eval in secondary school | Psych | 371 | 3Q | U |
| 071102 | Eval in elementary school | Psych | 372 | 2Q | U |
| 100313 | Human nutrition | HmEc | 250 | 3Q | U |
| 1199 | Hist and phil of voc ed | Tech | 491 | 3Q | U |
| 1199 | Community/indus resources | Tech | 496 | 1Q | U |
| 120305 | Language and exposition | Engl | 101 | 4Q | L |

| NCES No. | Course Title | Dept. | Course No. | Credits | Level |
|---|---|---|---|---|---|
| 120307 | Bible as literature | Engl | 336 | 5Q | U |
| 150201 | Climatology | Geog | 331 | 5Q | U |
| 160102 | Intro to mathematics | Math | 151 | 3Q | L |
| 160302 | College algebra I | Math | 103 | 3Q | L |
| 160302 | College algebra II | Math | 105 | 3Q | L |
| 160401 | Calc with app to bus/econ | Math | 156 | 4Q | L |
| 160602 | Trigonometry | Math | 104 | 3Q | L |
| 160603 | Calc/analytic geometry | Math | 124 | 5Q | L |
| 160801 | Intro to statistics | Math | 240 | 3Q | L |
| 200406 | Psych: human lrng/instruc | Psych | 351 | 3Q | U |
| 200504 | Developmental psychology | Psych | 316 | 5Q | U |
| 200504 | Child development & educ | Psych | 352 | 3Q | U |
| 200508 | Adolescent psychology | Psych | 353 | 4Q | U |
| 220102 | Intro to cultural anthrop | Anthr | 201 | 5Q | L |
| 220423 | Traditional Korea | SEAs | 311 | 5Q | U |
| 220426 | Modern Europe 1914-1945 | Hist | 428 | 5Q | U |
| 220428 | Hist/govern of Washington | Hist | 391 | 3Q | U |
| 220428 | History of Hawaiian Islds | Hist | 417C | 3Q | U |
| 220428 | Survey of community hist | Hist | 491 | 2Q | U |
| 220432 | American history to 1865 | Hist | 103 | 5Q | L |
| 220432 | American hist since 1865 | Hist | 104 | 5Q | L |
| 220470 | Intro to Asian-Amer study | EthSt | 205 | 3Q | L |
| 220470 | Comparative minority st | EthSt | 301 | 3Q | U |
| 220605 | Sociology of the family | Socio | 360 | 5Q | U |
| 220699 | Sociology of sexual behav | Socio | 338 | 5Q | U |

# ALPHABETICAL LISTING OF SUBJECT-MATTER AREAS

*Use this alphabetical listing to quickly locate the name of any subject-matter area in the Index; then turn to the section of the Index that corresponds to the number following the subject listing. For example, if you are interested in advertising, find Advertising below (Advertising 0501), and then (after carefully reading the key to the Index on its first page) turn to section 0501 of the Index to determine which colleges and universities offer courses in that area.*

| | |
|---|---|
| Abnormal Psychology | 200501 |
| Accident and Health Insurance | 040705 |
| Accounting | 0401 |
| Accounting Principles | 040101 |
| Accounting Systems | 040102 |
| Administration of Health Education | 190513 |
| Administration of Libraries and Museums | 1403 |
| Administrative and Office Services | 0402 |
| Administrative Law | 130101 |
| Administrative Management | 210103 |
| Administrative Procedures | 040201 |
| Administrative Theory | 210101 |
| Adult-Continuing Education Systems | 070309 |
| Advertising | 0501 |
| Advertising Evaluation | 050101 |
| Advertising Media | 050102 |
| Advertising Production | 050103 |
| Aerodynamics | 080101 |
| Aeronautics | 080102 |
| Aerospace and Aeronautical Engineering and Technology | 0801 |
| Aesthetics | 1801 |
| African History | 220420 |
| Agency Law | 130701 |
| Agricultural Credit and Finance | 010102 |
| Agricultural Design, Construction, and Maintenance | 010301 |
| Agricultural Economics | 0101 |
| Agricultural Engineering | 0102 |
| Agricultural Engineering and Technology | 0802 |
| Agricultural Marketing | 010103 |
| Agricultural Organizations | 010104 |
| Agricultural Technology | 0103 |
| Agriculture and Renewable Natural Resources | 01 |
| Algebra | 160302 |
| Algebraic Geometry | 160304 |
| Algebraic Structures | 160305 |
| American Colonial History | 220421 |
| American Government | 220501 |
| American Military History | 170102 |
| Analytic Geometry | 160603 |
| Ancient History | 220450 |
| Ancient Near East Theology | 181301 |
| Ancient Western Philosophy | 180401 |
| Animal Anatomy | 150324 |
| Animal Diseases, Parasites, and Insects | 010403 |
| Animal Genetics | 150326 |
| Animal Genetics and Reproduction | 010404 |
| Animal Management and Production | 010406 |
| Animal Nutrition | 010407 |
| Animal or Animal Products Selection and Evaluation | 010402 |
| Animal Sciences | 0104 |
| Antarctic History | 220422 |
| Anthropology | 2201 |
| Applications in Computer Science and Data Processing | 0601 |
| Applications of Mathematics (General) | 1611 |
| Applied Linguistics | 120101 |
| Applied Statistics | 160802 |

| | |
|---|---|
| Appraisal and Valuation | 041301 |
| Arabic | 1205 |
| Archaeology | 220101 |
| Architectural Design | 020101 |
| Architectural Drafting | 020402 |
| Architectural Engineering and Technology | 0803 |
| Architecture and Environmental Design | 02 |
| Archives | 140701 |
| Arithmetic | 160301 |
| Arithmetic and Algebra | 1603 |
| Arts, Visual and Performing | 03 |
| Arts, Visual and Performing | 070503 |
| Asian History | 220423 |
| Assemblers | 060801 |
| Astronomy | 1501 |
| Astrophysics | 150702 |
| Atmospheric Sciences | 1502 |
| Attitudes | 200701 |
| Audiology and Speech Pathology | 090301 |
| Auditing | 040103 |
| Automotive Engineering and Technology | 0804 |
| Bacteriology | 150317 |
| Banking and Finance | 0403 |
| Basic Concepts of Computer Science | 061103 |
| Basic Concepts of Data Processing | 061104 |
| Basic Health-Care Sciences | 0901 |
| Behavior Analysis | 200401 |
| Bibliographies | 140703 |
| Bilingual Education Programs | 070611 |
| Biochemistry | 090102 |
| Biochemistry | 150403 |
| Biological Behavior | 150301 |
| Biology | 1503 |
| Biopharmaceutics | 090401 |
| Biopsychology | 2002 |
| Bookkeeping | 040104 |
| Braille | 051201 |
| British History | 220424 |
| Buddhism | 180901 |
| Building Construction | 080301 |
| Business | 04 |
| Business | 070504 |
| Business and Corporate Finance | 040301 |
| Business and Industrial Economics | 220213 |
| Business Communication | 040601 |
| Business Mathematics | 161201 |
| Business Policy | 040901 |
| Business Report Writing | 040604 |
| Business Research Methods | 041201 |
| Calculus | 160401 |
| Calculus of Variations | 160412 |
| Canadian History | 220425 |
| Cardiology | 090201 |
| Career Development | 200502 |
| Career Education | 070602 |
| Career Information and Counseling | 070703 |
| Casualty Insurance | 040702 |
| Cataloging of Collections | 140401 |
| Cell Biology | 150302 |
| Chemical Engineering and Technology | 0806 |
| Chemistry | 1504 |
| Child Development | 100601 |
| Chinese | 1207 |
| Christianity | 180902 |

| | | | |
|---|---|---|---|
| Electrical Engineering and Technology | 0809 | Food Service | 100309 |
| Electrical Instrumentation | 080906 | Food-Service Management | 100702 |
| Electrical Power | 110303 | Forest Biology | 010902 |
| Electricity | 150704 | Forest Management and Administration | 010901 |
| Electromechanical Circuits | 080901 | Forestry | 0109 |
| Electronic Journalism | 050603 | Foundations of Education | 0701 |
| Electronics | 080903 | Foundations of Probability | 160706 |
| Elementary Education Systems | 070302 | Foundations of Psychology | 2001 |
| Emergency Services | 0905 | French | 1210 |
| Engineering and Construction Surveying | 082602 | Functional Analysis | 1605 |
| Engineering and Engineering Technology | 08 | | |
| Engineering Mechanics | 0811 | General Accounting | 040108 |
| Engineering Science | 0812 | General Botany | 150316 |
| English Language and Civilization | 120303 | General Chemistry | 150401 |
| English Language and Contemporary Culture | 120304 | General Earth-Space Science | 1509 |
| English Language Literature | 120307 | General Genetics | 150307 |
| English Language Structure and Grammar | 120305 | General Marketing | 041001 |
| English Language, The Study and Uses of | 1203 | General Perspectives of Health Care and Health Sciences | 0909 |
| Entomology | 150327 | General Physical Sciences | 1508 |
| Entrepreneurship | 0405 | General Zoology | 150323 |
| Environmental Design | 0201 | Geography | 2203 |
| Environmental Engineering and Technology | 0813 | Geology | 1505 |
| Environmental Health Administration | 090703 | Geometrics | 160604 |
| Environmental-Health Education | 190505 | Geometry and Topology | 1606 |
| Environmental Psychology | 2003 | Geomorphology | 150501 |
| Environmental Technology | 0206 | German | 1211 |
| Epidemiology | 090106 | Gerontology | 090242 |
| Epistemology | 1802 | Gerontology | 100603 |
| Estate Planning | 040703 | Gifted and Talented | 070803 |
| Ethical Principles of Psychology | 200101 | Governmental and Institutional Accounting | 040109 |
| Ethics | 1803 | Governmental Regulation of Business | 1305 |
| Ethics and Jurisprudence in Health Care and Health Sciences | 090904 | Graphic Arts | 1105 |
| Ethics of Professions | 180303 | Graphics and Drafting for Engineering and Technology | 0810 |
| Ethnography | 220103 | Graph Theory | 160204 |
| Ethnology | 220104 | Greek | 1212 |
| European History | 220426 | Group Games, Contests, and Self-Testing Activities | 190103 |
| Evidence | 130103 | Group Processes | 200702 |
| Evolution | 150306 | Group Theory | 160308 |
| Exercise | 190102 | | |
| Experimental Psychology | 2004 | Health-Care Anatomy | 090101 |
| Experimentation and Innovation | 071001 | Health Care and Health Sciences | 070509 |
| | | Health Care and Health Sciences | 09 |
| Fabric Maintenance and Repair | 110406 | Health-Care Assisting | 090253 |
| Family Development | 100602 | Health-Care Delivery Systems | 090602 |
| Family-Health Education | 190506 | Health-Care Nutrition | 090115 |
| Family Medicine | 090272 | Health-Care Physiology | 090119 |
| Farm and Ranch Management | 010107 | Health Education | 1905 |
| Feature and In-Depth Writing | 050605 | Health-Education Instruction | 190515 |
| Fields and Waves | 080904 | Health Planning | 090901 |
| Film as Art | 0302 | Hearing Handicapped | 070804 |
| Film as Communication | 0503 | Hebrew | 1213 |
| Financial Institutions | 040304 | Hinduism | 180903 |
| Finite Differences and Functional Equations | 160408 | Historical Geography | 220303 |
| Finite Probability | 160701 | Historical Perspectives of Psychology | 200102 |
| Finite Sets | 160203 | Historical Theology | 1813 |
| Finnish | 1209 | History and Traditions of Philosophy | 1804 |
| Fire Protection | 210302 | History of Economics | 220202 |
| First Aid | 090504 | History of Food and Nutrition | 100311 |
| Fisheries | 0108 | History of Health Care and Health Sciences | 090902 |
| Fisheries Biology | 010801 | History of Leisure Studies | 190706 |
| Flight Operations | 110601 | History of Mathematics | 160102 |
| Fluid Mechanics | 081102 | History of Physical Education | 190104 |
| Food and Nutrition | 1003 | History of Science | 220405 |
| Food Habits and Patterns | 100304 | History of the English Language | 120302 |
| Food-Production Technology | 100305 | | |
| Food Selection | 100308 | | |

| | |
|---|---|
| Measure and Integration | 160403 |
| Measurement and Evaluation in Physical Education | 190110 |
| Mechanical Design | 082006 |
| Mechanical Engineering and Technology | 0820 |
| Mechanics | 150803 |
| Medical Hygiene | 090111 |
| Medieval History | 220452 |
| Medieval Theology | 181303 |
| Medieval Western Philosophy | 180402 |
| Mediterranean History | 220429 |
| Mentally Handicapped | 070806 |
| Metallurgical Engineering and Technology | 0821 |
| Metaphysics | 1806 |
| Meteorology | 150202 |
| Methodology | 071102 |
| Microbiology | 090114 |
| Microbiology | 150311 |
| Microprocessors | 060404 |
| Military History | 1701 |
| Military Sciences | 17 |
| Minority Enterprises | 040501 |
| Minority Group History | 220470 |
| Missiology | 181608 |
| Modern History | 220453 |
| Modern Theology | 181304 |
| Modern Western Philosophy | 180403 |
| Monetary and Fiscal Policy | 040307 |
| Monetary and Fiscal Theory and Institutions | 220204 |
| Money and Banking | 040308 |
| Moral and Ethical Issues | 181502 |
| Moral and Ethical Studies | 1815 |
| Motivation | 200404 |
| Museology | 1402 |
| Museum Administration | 140305 |
| Music | 0303 |
| Music in Education | 030303 |
| Music Studies | 030302 |
| Music Studio and Performance | 030301 |
| | |
| National Income | 220205 |
| Native American | 1217 |
| Native American History | 220471 |
| News Reporting and Writing | 050608 |
| Noise-Pollution Control | 081302 |
| Nonprint Materials | 140709 |
| Nonprint Media | 050401 |
| Norwegian | 1218 |
| Nuclear Engineering and Technology | 0823 |
| Nuclear Medicine | 090276 |
| Number Theory | 160303 |
| Numerical Analysis | 160901 |
| Numerical Analysis and Approximation Theory | 1609 |
| Nursing | 090255 |
| Nutrition | 100313 |
| Nutrition Education | 100312 |
| Nutrition Education | 190508 |
| | |
| Occupational Therapy | 090303 |
| Oceanology | 1506 |
| Operating Systems | 060806 |
| Operations Research | 041203 |
| Operations Research | 081503 |
| Optics | 150706 |
| Ordinary Differential Equations | 160406 |
| Organic Chemistry | 150408 |

| | |
|---|---|
| Organizational Communication | 051104 |
| Organizational Development and Behavior | 040903 |
| Organizational Psychology | 200703 |
| Organizational Theory and Behavior | 210102 |
| Organization of Marketing | 041007 |
| Oriental Philosophy | 180405 |
| Ornamental Horticulture | 0105 |
| Outdoor Recreation | 0110 |
| | |
| Paleontology | 150504 |
| Partial Differential Equations | 160407 |
| Pastoral Studies | 1816 |
| Performance Physiology | 190203 |
| Personal and Family Finance | 100206 |
| Personal Development | 100604 |
| Personal-Health Education | 190509 |
| Personal Insurance | 040712 |
| Personal Moralities | 180301 |
| Personnel Management and Administration | 0411 |
| Personnel Psychology | 200902 |
| Perspectives on Law | 1308 |
| Petroleum Engineering | 0825 |
| Petroleum Exploration | 082501 |
| Pharmaceutical Sciences | 0904 |
| Pharmaceutics | 090408 |
| Pharmacology | 090118 |
| Pharmacy Practices and Management | 090411 |
| Phenomenology of Religion | 1810 |
| Philosophical Anthropology | 180605 |
| Philosophical Foundations | 1808 |
| Philosophy of Art | 180101 |
| Philosophy of Language | 180504 |
| Philosophy of Mathematics | 160101 |
| Philosophy of Natural Science | 180202 |
| Philosophy of Physical Education | 190105 |
| Philosophy of Religion | 180609 |
| Philosophy, Religion, and Theology | 18 |
| Photography | 110504 |
| Physical Anthropology | 220106 |
| Physical Chemistry | 150409 |
| Physical Education | 1901 |
| Physical Education Administration | 190106 |
| Physical Education Curriculum | 190107 |
| Physical Education, Health Education, and Leisure | 070519 |
| Physical Education, Health Education, and Leisure | 19 |
| Physical Education Instruction | 190108 |
| Physical Education Supervision | 190109 |
| Physical Fitness | 190510 |
| Physical Geography | 220305 |
| Physical Therapy | 090305 |
| Physics | 1507 |
| Physiological Hygiene | 090709 |
| Plane and Solid Geometry | 160601 |
| Planning | 0209 |
| Plant Anatomy and Physiology | 010601 |
| Plant Genetics and Reproduction | 010602 |
| Plant Insects and Control | 010603 |
| Plant Management and Production | 010604 |
| Plant or Plant Products Selection and Evaluation | 010607 |
| Plant Pathology | 150321 |
| Plant Sciences | 0106 |
| Political Behavior | 220506 |
| Political History | 220407 |
| Political Parties and Public Opinion | 220507 |
| Political Science and Government | 2205 |

| | |
|---|---|
| Political Structures | 220509 |
| Political Theory | 220510 |
| Populations and Leisure Services | 190702 |
| Portuguese | 1219 |
| Power and Energy | 080907 |
| Power Systems | 1103 |
| Pragmatic Communication | 051106 |
| Pre-Elementary Education Systems | 070301 |
| Principles and Theories of Counseling and Guidance | 070701 |
| Principles and Theories of Curriculum and Instruction | 070401 |
| Principles and Theories of Educational Administration | 070201 |
| Principles and Theory of Economics | 220201 |
| Principles and Theory of Evaluation and Research | 071103 |
| Principles and Theory of Finance | 040311 |
| Principles and Theory of Management | 040904 |
| Principles and Theory of Organization | 040905 |
| Principles and Theory of Sociology | 220606 |
| Principles of Insurance | 040708 |
| Principles of Real Estate | 041303 |
| Print Media | 0507 |
| Private Ownership | 040502 |
| Probability | 1607 |
| Procedure-Oriented Languages | 060705 |
| Product Service (Maintenance) | 1104 |
| Professional Development | 070708 |
| Professional Practices in Communication | 0508 |
| Professional Practices in Health Care and Health Sciences | 090903 |
| Professional Responsibility | 131401 |
| Programming Languages | 0607 |
| Programming Systems | 0608 |
| Programming Techniques | 060903 |
| Property Insurance | 040709 |
| Property Law | 1309 |
| Property Management | 041304 |
| Protective Services | 210305 |
| Psychological Programs (Applied and Professional) | 2008 |
| Psychological Sociology | 220607 |
| Psychological Testing | 200603 |
| Psychology | 070520 |
| Psychology | 20 |
| Psychology in Economics, Industry, and Government | 2009 |
| Psychology of Adjustment | 200505 |
| Psychology of Death | 200506 |
| Psychology of Disadvantaged Persons (Culturally or Physically Handicapped) | 200507 |
| Psychology of Identifiable Sets (Women, Blacks, Others) | 200508 |
| Psychology of Learning | 200406 |
| Psychology of Personality | 200509 |
| Psychology of the Individual | 2005 |
| Psychology of Thinking and Problem Solving | 200408 |
| Psychometrics | 2006 |
| Public Address | 051107 |
| Public Administration | 2101 |
| Public Administration and Social Services | 21 |
| Public Education Services and Functions | 140803 |
| Public Finance | 040312 |
| Public Finance | 220206 |
| Public Health | 0907 |
| Public-Health Administration | 090710 |
| Public-Policy Analysis and Evaluation | 210113 |
| Public Policy and Natural Resources and Environment | 210111 |
| Public Policy and Science and Technology | 210110 |
| Public Recreation | 2105 |

| | |
|---|---|
| Public-Recreation Administration | 210503 |
| Public Relations | 0509 |
| | |
| Quality Assurance | 081505 |
| Quantitative Economics | 220217 |
| Quantitative Methods | 0412 |
| Quantitative Methods | 220609 |
| | |
| Radiation Control | 082303 |
| Radiation Therapy | 090307 |
| Radio | 0510 |
| Radio and Public Policy | 051001 |
| Radiobiology | 090121 |
| Radiology | 090259 |
| Radio Production | 051002 |
| Reading and Language Arts Programs | 070610 |
| Reading in the English Language | 120308 |
| Real Analysis | 160402 |
| Real Estate | 0413 |
| Real-Estate Economics | 041305 |
| Real-Estate Finance | 041306 |
| Real-Estate Investments | 041307 |
| Real-Estate Law | 041308 |
| Real-Estate Practice | 041309 |
| Recordkeeping | 040113 |
| Records Management | 040203 |
| Recreation Activities | 190705 |
| Recreational Environments | 210501 |
| Recreation Therapy | 090308 |
| Recruitment, Selection, and Separation | 041105 |
| Reference and Retrieval | 140804 |
| Regional Geography | 220306 |
| Regulation of Employment Relations | 1310 |
| Regulation of the Environment | 1311 |
| Rehabilitation and Therapy | 0903 |
| Related Arts | 0306 |
| Related Arts and Aesthetic Education | 030603 |
| Related-Arts Studies | 030602 |
| Religion and Culture | 181104 |
| Religion and Human Experience | 1811 |
| Religion and Personality Studies | 181102 |
| Religion and Science | 181101 |
| Religion and Social Issues | 181103 |
| Religious Education | 181603 |
| Religious History | 220408 |
| Renewable Natural Resources | 0114 |
| Resource Management | 100402 |
| Resource Management in Leisure Studies | 190701 |
| Rhetorical and Communication Theory | 051108 |
| Risk Management | 040710 |
| Rural Sociology | 220608 |
| Russian | 1220 |
| Russian History | 220431 |
| | |
| Sacred Writings | 1812 |
| Sacred Writings of the Christian Faith | 181202 |
| Sacred Writings of the Jewish Faith | 181201 |
| Safety and Correctional Services | 2103 |
| Safety and Health Law | 131004 |
| Safety Education | 190511 |
| Sample Surveys | 160809 |
| Sanskrit | 1221 |
| School-Library and Media-Center Administration | 140307 |
| School Psychology | 200805 |
| Secondary Education Systems | 070303 |
| Selection and Acquisition of Collections | 140408 |

| | |
|---|---|
| Sex Education | 190512 |
| Shorthand and Transcription | 040205 |
| Slavic Languages | 1222 |
| Small-Engine Repair | 110412 |
| Social and Political Philosophy | 1807 |
| Social Anthropology | 220107 |
| Social Control and Deviance | 220610 |
| Social Economics | 220215 |
| Social Environments and Human Behavior | 210405 |
| Social Ethics | 180302 |
| Social History | 220409 |
| Social Institutions | 220611 |
| Social Organization and Change | 220612 |
| Social Problems | 220613 |
| Social Psychology | 2007 |
| Social Sciences and Social Studies | 070522 |
| Social Sciences and Social Studies | 22 |
| Social Welfare | 210401 |
| Social Work | 2104 |
| Social Work, Fields of | 210404 |
| Social-Work Methods | 210403 |
| Social-Work Practice | 210402 |
| Socioeconomic Foundations | 070103 |
| Sociology | 2206 |
| Sociology of Groups | 220615 |
| Sociopsychological Aspects of Clothing and Textiles | 100109 |
| Software Methodology | 0609 |
| Soil and Water Resources | 080205 |
| Soil Chemistry | 010701 |
| Soil Classification | 010702 |
| Soil Conservation and Land Use | 010703 |
| Soil Fertility | 010704 |
| Soil Mechanics and Foundations | 080706 |
| Soil Sciences | 0107 |
| Solar Astronomy | 150102 |
| Solid Mechanics | 081103 |
| Spanish | 1225 |
| Speaking the English Language | 120309 |
| Special Communication | 0512 |
| Special Education | 0708 |
| Special Functions | 160405 |
| Specialized Secretarial Services | 040206 |
| Specific Religions | 1809 |
| Speech Communication | 0511 |
| Speech Communication Education | 051109 |
| Speech Handicapped | 070811 |
| Sport | 1903 |
| Sport Activities | 190312 |
| Sport History | 190303 |
| Sport in Schools and Colleges | 190301 |
| Sport Psychology | 190306 |
| Sports Medicine | 190205 |
| State and Local Government | 220511 |
| Statics and Dynamics | 081104 |
| Statistics | 1608 |
| Stellar Astronomy | 150103 |
| Structural Engineering | 080707 |
| Structural Technology | 0205 |
| Supervision | 041106 |
| Supervision and Regulation of Banking and Finance | 040314 |
| Surface Chemistry | 150410 |
| Surveying and Mapping | 0826 |

| | |
|---|---|
| Swedish | 1226 |
| Symbolic and Algebraic Manipulation Languages | 060707 |
| Symbolic Logic | 180502 |
| Systematic Theology | 1814 |
| Systems Analysis | 060904 |
| Systems of Education | 0703 |
| Systems of Psychology | 200103 |
| | |
| Tax Accounting | 040114 |
| Teacher Methods | 070404 |
| Teacher Training | 070403 |
| Technical Communication | 050402 |
| Television | 0513 |
| Television Applications to Education | 071205 |
| Theater Arts | 0304 |
| Theater Arts Studio and Performance | 030401 |
| Theater in Education | 030403 |
| Theater Studies | 030402 |
| Theories in Psychology | 200104 |
| Theory of Computation | 0610 |
| Theory of Probability | 160702 |
| Thermodynamics and Kinetics | 080603 |
| Topical Anthropology | 220109 |
| Training and Development | 041107 |
| Transfer-of-Property Law | 130902 |
| Transportation | 1106 |
| Transportation Geography | 220307 |
| Trigonometry | 160602 |
| Turf Grass | 010505 |
| Typewriting | 040207 |
| | |
| United States History | 220432 |
| Universal Algebra | 160307 |
| Urban and Rural Economics | 220216 |
| Urban Design | 020104 |
| Urban Geography | 220308 |
| Urban Sociology | 220614 |
| User-Oriented Mathematics | 1612 |
| | |
| Vehicle Maintenance and Repair | 110413 |
| Visual Arts | 0305 |
| Visual Arts in Education | 030503 |
| Visual-Arts Studies | 030502 |
| Visual-Arts Studio and Production | 030501 |
| Visually Handicapped | 070812 |
| Vocational-Technical Education Systems | 070306 |
| | |
| Water and Sewage Control | 081304 |
| Welding | 110119 |
| Welfare and Safety | 041108 |
| Wildlife | 0112 |
| Wildlife Management | 011202 |
| Word Processing | 040208 |
| World History | 220433 |
| Writing for Television | 051303 |
| Writing the English Language | 120310 |
| | |
| Yiddish | 1227 |

# INDEX TO SUBJECT-MATTER AREAS

**Key to the Index**

*This index is based on the classification of educational subject-matter areas prepared by the National Center for Education Statistics (NCES). Listed in alphabetical order are twenty-two broad subject-matter areas, representing major academic disciplines, with more specific areas grouped under them in two levels of subordination. Each main index line has three elements:*

- The NCES subject-area identification number, which appears at the left. (NCES numbers also appear in numerical order next to the names of courses in the "Institutions and Correspondence Courses Offered" section, so that the names of courses in an area can be quickly identified in an institution's entry.)
- The name of the subject-matter area.
- The code number for the name of each institution offering one or more courses in the area, plus a code letter for each kind of course the institution offers in that area (E = Elementary, H = High School, C = College, G = Graduate, N = Noncredit). The institution represented by each code number can be identified by a quick glance at the back cover foldout.

Example:

| NCES No. | Subject-Matter Area | Institutional Code No. |
|---|---|---|
| 040101 | Accounting Principles | 1C, 2C, 11EHCN |

*To find the names of specific courses an institution offers in an area, make a note of the NCES number and institutional code number, including the letter code for the kind of course, and identify the institution's name and page number in the Contents, where institutional code numbers and corresponding names are listed in numerical and alphabetical order. Or turn directly to the "Institutions and Correspondence Courses Offered" section, where code numbers and corresponding names are listed numerically and alphabetically at the beginning of institutional entries and—in dictionary fashion—at the top of pages.*

*(If you have difficulty locating a subject-matter area in this Index, refer first to the Alphabetical Listing of Subject-Matter Areas, which precedes the Index.)*

## 01 AGRICULTURE AND RENEWABLE NATURAL RESOURCES

Agricultural Engineering is listed in the subject-matter area of Engineering and Engineering Technology, but Agricultural Technology is included here. Animal Sciences includes the general care of animals as factors of production. The medical treatment of animals is included in Veterinary Medical Sciences in the subject-matter area of Health Care and Health Sciences. Agricultural Economics is included in this area, but the broad subject matter of Economics is included under Social Sciences and Social Studies. The elements within Plant Sciences are differentiated from similar elements in the area of Life Sciences and Physical Sciences by their emphasis on food and fiber production.

**0101 Agricultural Economics** 35C, 59C
010102 Agricultural Credit and Finance 31C, 66C
010103 Agricultural Marketing 46C, 48C, 66C
010104 Agricultural Organizations 31C, 63C
010106 Economic Development and International Trade 59C, 64C
010107 Farm and Ranch Management 31H, 40C, 66C
010199 Other Agricultural Economics 17C, 31C, 38C, 40C, 44C, 64C

**0102 Agricultural Engineering (See 08—Engineering and Engineering Technology)**

**0103 Agricultural Technology**
010301 Agricultural Design, Construction, and Maintenance 48C
010399 Other Agricultural Technology 49N

**0104 Animal Sciences** 20C
010402 Animal or Animal Products Selection and Evaluation 44C, 66C
010403 Animal Diseases, Parasites, and Insects 26N
010404 Animal Genetics and Reproduction 35C, 66C
010406 Animal Management and Production 17C, 22C, 24C, 38C, 51C, 66C
010407 Animal Nutrition 9CN, 22C, 44C, 64C, 66C, 67C
010499 Other Animal Sciences 34C, 46C, 48H

**0105 Ornamental Horticulture** 48HC
010504 Landscaping 46C
010505 Turf Grass 67C
010599 Other Ornamental Horticulture 36H, 49H, 67C

**0106 Plant Sciences** 16H, 20C, 68C
010601 Plant Anatomy and Physiology 22C
010602 Plant Genetics and Reproduction 6C
010603 Plant Insects and Control 9CN, 39C, 64C, 67C
010604 Plant Management and Production 44C, 66C, 67C
010607 Plant or Plant Products Selection and Evaluation 44C
010699 Other Plant Sciences 31C, 35C, 70C

**0107 Soil Sciences**
010701 Soil Chemistry 22C, 66C
010702 Soil Classification 38C, 67C
010703 Soil Conservation and Land Use 44C
010704 Soil Fertility 31C

**0108 Fisheries**
010801 Fisheries Biology 66C

**0109 Forestry** 20C
010901 Forest Management and Administration 40C, 44C, 62C, 66C
010902 Forest Biology 63C, 64H
010999 Other Forestry 59C

**0110 Outdoor Recreation** 9CN

**0112 Wildlife**
011202 Wildlife Management 19C
011299 Other Wildlife 9C, 19C, 66C

**0114 Renewable Natural Resources** 34C, 35C, 46C, 55H

**0199 Other Agriculture and Renewable Natural Resources** 38C, 45CN, 48H, 49H

## 02 ARCHITECTURE AND ENVIRONMENTAL DESIGN

Subject-matter elements in this area deal with the design of environments as well as the management of construction. Virtually all subject matter related to environmental planning has been included in this subject-matter area. Engineering theory and design involved in building and environmental systems are found in the area of Engineering and Engineering Technology. Elements relating to construction skills can be found in the subject-matter area of Industrial Arts, Trades, and Technology.

**0201  Environmental Design**
020101  Architectural Design   25N
020102  Landscape Architectural Design   66C
020103  Interior Design   6H, 9N, 36N
020104  Urban Design   62C
020199  Other Environmental Design   9C

**0202  Design and Planning Technology**
020299  Other Design and Planning Technology   24C
020402  Architectural Drafting   63H

**0205  Structural Technology**
020599  Other Structural Technology   22N

**0206  Environmental Technology**
020699  Other Environmental Technology   70C

**0209  Planning**
020902  Housing Planning   17C

**0299  Other Architecture and Environmental Design**

## 03  ARTS, VISUAL AND PERFORMING

Dance is listed in this area as an aesthetic art form. It is also listed in the area of Physical Education, Health Education, and Leisure, where the emphasis is on the physical activity. Film as an artistic medium is included in this area. The knowledge of Film for the transmission of messages is included in the subject-matter area of Communication. Arts Therapy in this subject-matter area should be differentiated from the formalized medical therapy that is included in the area of Health Care and Health Sciences.

**0301  Dance (See 1904—Dance)**

**0302  Film as Art (See 0503—Film as Communication)**

**0303  Music   68C**
030301  Music Studio and Performance   30C, 36C
030302  Music Studies   6HN, 10C, 14HC, 16H, 21C, 36HCN, 37C, 40C, 42C, 46C, 47C, 49H, 51C, 55C, 61C, 62C, 63HC, 64C, 68C
030303  Music in Education   44C, 61C
030399  Other Music   3C, 16C, 17C, 22C, 32C, 36C, 45C, 47C, 49H, 51C, 64C, 67C

**0304  Theater Arts   5C**
030401  Theater Arts Studio and Performance   42C
030402  Theater Studies   5C, 22C, 25CN, 32C, 35C, 46C, 47C, 51C, 55C, 64C
030403  Theater in Education   6HC
030499  Other Theater Arts   8C, 17C, 25N, 35C, 46CN

**0305  Visual Arts**
030501  Visual-Arts Studio and Production   16HC, 24C, 25C, 30C, 36HC, 59HN
030502  Visual-Arts Studies   6C, 16HC, 21C, 36C, 37H, 39C, 47C, 55H, 57H, 61C, 64HC, 66C
030503  Visual Arts in Education   37C
030599  Other Visual Arts   8C, 17H, 24N, 36C, 46C, 48H, 49C, 51C, 52C, 63HC

**0306  Related Arts   27C**
030602  Related-Arts Studies   22C, 38H, 47C, 66C
030603  Related Arts and Aesthetic Education   6C, 16C, 36C
030699  Other Related Arts   25N, 63C

**0399  Other Arts, Visual and Performing   6C, 15C, 25C, 46C**

## 04  BUSINESS

Subject matter that is a part of Distributive Education and Career Education Programs can be found in this area under Marketing. Also, selected subject matter in this classification is applicable to office occupations. Although the knowledge of Economics is an integral part of business, it is listed in the subject-matter area of Social Sciences and Social Studies and not here. The knowledge of the skills involved in many occupational programs is found in this area even though differences may exist in the form and substance of the subject matter as it is presented to students. This is particularly true for elements listed under Administrative and Office Services, such as Typewriting.

**0401  Accounting   5C**
040101  Accounting Principles   8C, 16C, 17CN, 19C, 20C, 21C, 22HCN, 24HC, 25C, 28C, 31C, 32C, 33C, 34C, 35C, 36HC, 37H, 39C, 40C, 41C, 43C, 44HC, 45C, 46HC, 47C, 48C, 49HC, 50C, 51C, 52CN, 53C, 54C, 55C, 56HC, 57HCN, 58C, 61C, 63C, 64C, 65C, 66C, 67C, 71C
040102  Accounting Systems   14H, 21C, 57C
040103  Auditing   17C, 24CN, 36C, 56C, 59C, 65C
040104  Bookkeeping   6H, 17H, 18H, 32HC, 34H, 35H, 38H, 39N, 40H, 48H, 55H, 59H, 60H, 61N, 63H, 64H
040106  Cost Accounting   16C, 17C, 19C, 24C, 32C, 36C, 37C, 41C, 52C, 55C, 56C, 59C, 63C, 64C, 65C, 66C
040107  Data-Processing Accounting   5C
040108  General Accounting   3C, 6C, 16H, 31H, 55C, 56C, 59C
040109  Governmental and Institutional Accounting   6C, 16C, 24CN, 32C, 36CN, 41C, 56C, 65C, 71C
040111  Managerial Accounting   3C, 8C, 17C, 21C, 25C, 37C, 40C, 43C, 48C, 49C, 51C, 61C, 63C, 66C, 69C, 71C
040113  Recordkeeping   37C
040114  Tax Accounting   6H, 16C, 17C, 20C, 32C, 36C, 39C, 46C, 56C, 59C, 61C
040199  Other Accounting   6H, 16C, 31C, 47C, 58C

**0402  Administrative and Office Services   20C, 59H**
040201  Administrative Procedures   17C, 35H, 39C, 44C, 47C, 59C, 66C
040203  Records Management   5C, 17C, 19C, 20C, 34C, 35HN, 39N, 40C, 52C, 64C, 65C
040205  Shorthand and Transcription   6HC, 16H, 17HC, 24C, 35H, 44C, 45H, 46H, 49H, 57H, 61C
040206  Specialized Secretarial Services   19C, 24C, 47C, 61C
040207  Typewriting   6HC, 14EHC, 16H, 17HC, 18H, 35H, 44C, 48H, 49H, 55H, 57H, 59N, 61C, 64C
040208  Word Processing   39CN
040299  Other Administrative and Office Services   10C, 15N, 16HC, 17H, 19C, 20C, 24C, 37H, 48H, 49H, 56H

**0403  Banking and Finance   6H, 67C**
040301  Business and Corporate Finance   3C, 16N, 17C, 19C, 21C, 32C, 39C, 42C, 44C, 55C, 56C, 58C, 61C, 64C, 66C, 69C
040302  Consumer Finance   16C, 24H, 25C, 37H, 46C, 55C, 61C
040304  Financial Institutions   16C, 31C, 41C
040306  Investments and Securities   16CN, 25C, 31C, 32C, 33C, 36C, 39C, 42C, 61C, 63C, 64C
040307  Monetary and Fiscal Policy   63C
040308  Money and Banking   10C, 17C, 19C, 29C, 32C, 39C, 47C, 55C, 59C, 61C, 69C
040311  Principles and Theory of Finance   6C, 25C, 49C, 62C
040312  Public Finance   3C, 13C, 16C, 32C

## 05 COMMUNICATION

Film as Communication in this subject-matter area is considered as a means of transmitting messages. In contrast, Film as Art in the area of Arts, Visual and Performing, is considered as an artistic medium. Journalism and Speech Communication are both found in this subject-matter area and not in the area of Language, Linguistics, and Literature with which they are closely related and often reported.

**06 COMPUTER SCIENCE AND DATA PROCESSING**

Most of the mathematical logic upon which computer systems are based is included in the subject-matter area of Mathematical Sciences. Knowledge of the engineering design and construction of computing equipment is found in the category of Electrical Engineering and Technology within the subject-matter area of Engineering and Engineering Technology. Knowledge about the ways in which computers and data-processing equipment are utilized can be classified under other subject-matter areas if the emphasis is on the application and not upon the computer or data-processing system.

**07 EDUCATION**

The subject matter in this area is concerned with the knowledge that is needed to teach and to otherwise carry out the process of education.

**0815**  **Industrial Engineering and Technology**  55C
081502   Human Factors in Industry   37C, 46C
081503   Operations Research (See 041203—Operations
            Research)   46C, 49C, 55C
081505   Quality Assurance   59C
081599   Other Industrial Engineering and Technology   25C,
            46C, 59C

**0817**  **Manufacturing Engineering and Technology**
081799   Other Manufacturing Engineering and Technology
            63C

**0819**  **Materials Engineering and Technology**  55C
081999   Other Materials Engineering and Technology   25C,
            46C

**0820**  **Mechanical Engineering and Technology**
082006   Mechanical Design   25C
082099   Other Mechanical Engineering and Technology   25C,
            63C

**0821**  **Metallurgical Engineering and Technology**
082199   Other Metallurgical Engineering and Technology
            61C, 63C

**0823**  **Nuclear Engineering and Technology**
082303   Radiation Control   22CN

**0825**  **Petroleum Engineering**  33C
082501   Petroleum Exploration   25N
082599   Other Petroleum Engineering   22CN, 25N

**0826**  **Surveying and Mapping**
082601   Land Surveying and Subdivision   38C
082602   Engineering and Construction Surveying   36C
082699   Other Surveying and Mapping   40C

**0899**  **Other Engineering and Engineering Technology**  6C,
            22CN, 25C, 35C, 36CN, 44C

## 09   HEALTH CARE AND HEALTH SCIENCES

Under Basic Health-Care Sciences are those elements of
knowledge that come from the Biological Sciences but whose
emphasis is directed toward the care and treatment of humans
and animals. General knowledge, not specific to the restoration
or preservation of health, is included in the subject-matter area
of Life Sciences and Physical Sciences. Where appropriate,
cross-references are shown in this structure.

Clinical Health Sciences lists those elements of knowledge that
are related to diseases, injuries, or deformities. The list is
divided into five subjectively established categories: (1)
knowledge related to body organs or localized parts of the body,
(2) knowledge of disorders or general conditions of the body,
(3) knowledge that is specific to an age group or type of patient,
(4) knowledge of health care approaches that are not unique to
areas of the body or type of patient but focus instead on the
treatment itself, and (5) knowledge of special-purpose health
care and health sciences.

Many of the elements in this subject-matter area can apply to
either humans or animals.

**0901**  **Basic Health-Care Sciences**  19H, 68C
090101   Health-Care Anatomy   6H, 32H, 67H
090102   Biochemistry (See 150403—Biochemistry)   64C
090103   Clinical Chemistry   48N
090104   Diagnostics   42N
090106   Epidemiology   66C
090111   Medical Hygiene   66C
090113   Infectious Diseases   66C
090114   Microbiology (See 150311—Microbiology)   19C, 41C,
            66C
090115   Health-Care Nutrition   16C, 67C

090118   Pharmacology   16C, 42C, 46C, 50N
090119   Health-Care Physiology   37H, 45C, 66C
090121   Radiobiology   22C
090199   Other Basic Health-Care Sciences   19C, 37C, 42N,
            46C, 49H, 57H, 70C

**0902**  **Clinical Health Sciences**
090201   Cardiology   48N
090242   Gerontology   51N
090253   Health-Care Assisting   51N, 60N
090255   Nursing   16C, 23N, 38C
090259   Radiology   70C
090272   Family Medicine   6HC
090276   Nuclear Medicine   25CN
090299   Other Clinical Health Sciences   41C, 62C, 68C

**0903**  **Rehabilitation and Therapy**
090301   Audiology and Speech Pathology   66C
090302   Dietetics and Nutrition   42C
090303   Occupational Therapy   70C
090305   Physical Therapy   58C
090307   Radiation Therapy   36N
090308   Recreation Therapy   16N
090399   Other Rehabilitation and Therapy   16N

**0904**  **Pharmaceutical Sciences**
090401   Biopharmaceutics   39N
090403   Drug and Drug-Abuse Information   6HC, 61C
090404   Drug Regulation and Control   59N
090408   Pharmaceutics   59N
090411   Pharmacy Practices and Management   26N, 39N, 59N
090499   Other Pharmaceutical Sciences   39N, 60C

**0905**  **Emergency Services**
090504   First Aid   6C, 22C, 23N, 41C, 49C
090599   Other Emergency Services   35C

**0906**  **Hospital and Health-Care Administration**
090601   Hospital Organization and Management   28C, 48C
090602   Health-Care Delivery Systems   27C, 28C, 48C
090699   Other Hospital and Health-Care Administration   16C,
            27C, 28C, 32C, 52N

**0907**  **Public Health**   28C, 41C
090702   Community Medicine   6C, 27C, 66C, 68C
090703   Environmental Health Administration   3C, 28C
090704   Human Ecology   21C, 28C
090705   Industrial-Health Administration   21C
090706   Maternal and Child Health Administration   23N, 46C
090709   Physiological Hygiene   25H
090710   Public-Health Administration   27C, 56C
090799   Other Public Health   6C, 12C, 36C, 40C, 42N, 63HC,
            66C, 68C

**0909**  **General Perspectives of Health Care and Health
            Sciences**
090901   Health Planning   16H, 18H, 22C, 27C, 61C
090902   History of Health Care and Health Sciences   6C
090903   Professional Practices in Health Care and Health
            Sciences   34C
090904   Ethics and Jurisprudence in Health Care and Health
            Sciences   28C, 42C
090905   Clinical Practices in Health Care and Health Sciences
            26N
090999   Other General Perspectives of Health Care and Health
            Sciences   3C, 16HC, 30C, 34C, 49C, 50C, 62C

**0999**  **Other Health Care and Health Sciences**  6C, 68C

120308 Reading in the English Language  6HCN, 16HC, 18H, 21C, 22H, 25H, 34C, 35H, 36H, 37HC, 43H, 48H, 49H, 52C, 57H, 59HN, 66C, 70C
120309 Speaking the English Language  16C, 18N
120310 Writing the English Language  3C, 6HCN, 11C, 13C, 14C, 15C, 16HC, 17CN, 20C, 21C, 22C, 24C, 25C, 27C, 28C, 31C, 32C, 33C, 34H, 35C, 36HCN, 37HC, 38C, 39C, 41C, 42C, 43C, 44C, 46CN, 47C, 48C, 49HC, 51CN, 52C, 54C, 55HC, 56C, 57HC, 58HC, 59HCN, 60HC, 61C, 62C, 63HC, 64C, 65C, 66C, 67C, 68C, 69C, 70C
120399 Other Study and Uses of the English Language  6HCN, 14EH, 16HCN, 17HC, 18HN, 24C, 32C, 35HC, 36HC, 37CN, 38H, 43C, 44C, 45C, 48H, 49H, 50C, 56H, 57H, 58C, 59C, 62C, 63C, 65C, 68C, 69C, 70C

**1205**   **Arabic**   63C

**1207**   **Chinese**   6HN, 42C, 46C

**1208**   **Danish**   62C

**1209**   **Finnish**   46C, 62C

**1210**   **French**   2C, 3C, 6C, 8C, 14HC, 16HC, 17HC, 18H, 19HC, 22C, 24C, 25C, 31H, 32C, 34C, 35HC, 36HC, 39C, 40C, 41C, 42C, 43C, 44HC, 45C, 46CN, 47CN, 48HC, 49H, 50C, 51C, 52C, 55HC, 56C, 57HC, 58H, 59HC, 60C, 62C, 63HC, 64HC, 67C

**1211**   **German**   2C, 6C, 8C, 14HC, 16H, 17C, 21C, 22C, 24C, 25C, 32HC, 34C, 35C, 36HC, 38C, 39C, 41C, 42C, 43C, 44HC, 45C, 46CN, 47CN, 49H, 50C, 51C, 52C, 55C, 56C, 57HC, 58C, 59C, 60HC, 62C, 63HC, 64C, 67C

**1212**   **Greek**   14C, 21C, 25C, 36C, 41C, 44C, 46C, 55CN, 57C, 59N, 60C, 63C

**1213**   **Hebrew**   6C, 55C, 62C, 63C

**1214**   **Italian**   16C, 36C, 46C, 50C, 51C, 59C, 62C, 63C

**1215**   **Japanese**   6N, 46C

**1216**   **Latin**   6C, 16HC, 17C, 18H, 19H, 21C, 25C, 32C, 35H, 36H, 39C, 41C, 42C, 43C, 44HC, 46C, 47C, 49H, 51C, 52C, 55HC, 56C, 57C, 59H, 60C, 63HC

**1217**   **Native American**   33C, 52C

**1218**   **Norwegian**   46C, 52C, 62C, 63C

**1219**   **Portuguese**   63C

**1220**   **Russian**   25C, 41C, 46C, 51C, 55C, 63HC

**1221**   **Sanskrit**   42C

**1222**   **Slavic Languages**   60C, 62C

**1225**   **Spanish**   2C, 6HCN, 8C, 14HC, 16HC, 17HC, 18H, 19HC, 25C, 32C, 34C, 35HC, 36HC, 39C, 40C, 41C, 42C, 43C, 44HC, 46CN, 47C, 48HC, 49H, 50C, 51C, 52C, 55HC, 56C, 57HC, 58H, 59HC, 60C, 62C, 63HC, 64HC, 67HC

**1226**   **Swedish**   46C, 62C

**1227**   **Yiddish**   63C

**1299**   **Other Language, Linguistics, and Literature**   34C, 35H, 36C, 37C, 45C, 46HC, 49C, 51C, 52N, 55C, 61C, 63C

## 13   LAW

**1301**   **Civil and Administrative Procedure**
130101 Administrative Law  65C

130103 Evidence  37C
130199 Other Civil and Administrative Procedure  24C, 37C, 62C

**1302**   **Commercial Law**   3C, 35C, 48H
130201 Law of Commercial Paper  60C
130202 Law of Contracts  46C, 56C, 64C
130299 Other Commercial Law  16C, 21C, 60C

**1303**   **Constitutional Law**   65C
130399 Other Constitutional Law  21C, 29C

**1304**   **Criminal Law**   55C, 59C
130401 Crimes  67C
130402 Criminal Procedure and Evidence  21C, 24C, 55C
130403 Juvenile Justice  16C, 67C
130499 Other Criminal Law  32C

**1305**   **Governmental Regulation of Business**   52C

**1307**   **Law of Business and Other Organizations**   20C, 21C, 25C, 28C, 40C, 48C, 55C, 59H
130701 Agency Law  33C
130702 Law of Associations  33C
130703 Law of Corporations  46C
130799 Other Law of Business and Other Organizations  16H, 18H, 21C, 22C, 31HC, 32C, 36C, 38HC, 39C, 58HC, 60H, 61C, 65C, 67C

**1308**   **Perspectives on Law**
130899 Other Perspectives on Law  62C

**1309**   **Property Law**   55C
130902 Transfer-of-Property Law  21C
130907 Law of Wills and Estates  46C
130999 Other Property Law  32C

**1310**   **Regulation of Employment Relations**
131004 Safety and Health Law  16C, 21C
131099 Other Regulation of Employment Relations  16C

**1311**   **Regulation of the Environment**
131102 Law of Land-Use Planning  41C

**1314**   **Legal Profession**
131401 Professional Responsibility  16N

**1315**   **Legal Skills**
131502 Legal Bibliography  65C
131504 Drafting of Legal Instruments  46C
131599 Other Legal Skills  37C, 65C

**1318**   **Law of State and Local Governments**   18N

**1399**   **Other Law**   46C, 48H

## 14   LIBRARIES AND MUSEUMS
The elements in this subject-matter area represent the substance of knowledge that has been determined to be appropriate to Libraries and Museums.

**1401**   **Library Science**   65C
140199 Other Library Science  6C, 32C, 55H, 59C, 61C

**1402**   **Museology**   40C

**1403**   **Administration of Libraries and Museums**
140303 Library Administration  64C
140305 Museum Administration  40C
140307 School-Library and Media-Center Administration  64C

**1404**   **Collection Management**
140401 Cataloging of Collections  40C, 64C, 65C
140408 Selection and Acquisition of Collections  40C, 64C
140499 Other Collection Management  66C

## 15      LIFE SCIENCES AND PHYSICAL SCIENCES

The arrangement of elements within the subject-matter category of Biology includes those that could be aggregated into Botany and Zoology as well. To have broken them out would have required another level of coding and two additional digits.

Many of the elements within Biology have been cross-referenced to identical titles in Health Care and Health Sciences. The related elements differ in that the subject matter of Health Care and Health Sciences emphasizes the restoration and preservation of health. Subject matter in Life Sciences and Physical Sciences is not as specific and can be related to a broad range of units of instruction.

## 16      MATHEMATICAL SCIENCES

Every attempt was made to include in this subject-matter area all subject-matter elements that have their genesis in mathematics. Accordingly, the elements within Probability and Statistics, in particular, will be combined with several other elements in other subject-matter areas.

160302  Algebra   1C, 2C, 4C, 6HCN, 8C, 10C, 11C, 14HC, 15C, 16HC, 17HCN, 18H, 19HC, 20C, 21C, 22HC, 24HC, 25HC, 29C, 31HC, 32HC, 33C, 34HC, 35HC, 36HCN, 37HC, 38HC, 39C, 40HC, 41C, 43C, 44HC, 46HC, 47C, 48HC, 49HC, 50C, 51CN, 52C, 53C, 55HC, 56HC, 57HC, 58HC, 59HCN, 60HC, 61CN, 62N, 63HC, 64HC, 65C, 66C, 67HC, 68C, 71C

160303  Number Theory   21C, 25C, 40C, 59C, 60C

160304  Algebraic Geometry   32H, 46C

160305  Algebraic Structures   17C, 38C

160306  Linear and Multilinear Algebra   21C, 24C, 25C, 41C, 42C, 45C, 46C, 55C, 57C, 63C, 64C, 67C

160307  Universal Algebra   60C

160308  Group Theory   42C

160399  Other Arithmetic and Algebra   6H, 15C, 16CN, 18N, 19C, 32C, 42C, 45C, 46N, 49H, 50C, 57H, 62CN, 63C, 64C, 67H

**1604   Classical Analysis**   4C

160401  Calculus   3C, 6H, 16HC, 17C, 19C, 21C, 22C, 24C, 25C, 31HC, 32C, 33C, 34C, 35C, 36C, 39C, 40C, 41C, 42C, 44HC, 46C, 47C, 48HC, 51C, 52C, 55HC, 56HC, 57C, 58C, 59C, 60C, 61C, 63C, 64C, 65C, 66C, 67C, 71C

160402  Real Analysis   46C

160403  Measure and Integration   32C, 62C

160405  Special Functions   62C

160406  Ordinary Differential Equations   1C, 3C, 6C, 25C, 41C, 46C, 47C, 57C, 62C, 63C, 67C

160407  Partial Differential Equations   62C

160408  Finite Differences and Functional Equations   35C, 62C

160412  Calculus of Variations   6C, 46C

160499  Other Classical Analysis   21C, 36C, 37C, 47C, 63C

**1605   Functional Analysis**

160507  Distributions (Generalized Functions)   62C

160599  Other Functional Analysis   38H

**1606   Geometry and Topology**   6C, 21C

160601  Plane and Solid Geometry   6H, 14H, 16H, 18H, 19H, 22H, 24H, 25H, 31H, 34H, 35H, 36HN, 37H, 42C, 44H, 46H, 48H, 49H, 51CN, 55H, 56H, 57H, 58H, 59H, 60H, 63H

160602  Trigonometry   2C, 3C, 6HC, 8C, 10C, 16HC, 17HC, 19HC, 22C, 24C, 25HC, 31HC, 32HC, 33C, 34HC, 35C, 36HC, 37HC, 39C, 40C, 41C, 43C, 44HC, 45C, 46HC, 47C, 48C, 49HC, 50C, 51C, 52C, 53C, 55HC, 56H, 57C, 58C, 59HN, 60HC, 61C, 62N, 63HC, 64C, 65C, 66C, 67C, 71C

160603  Analytic Geometry   6C, 16C, 17C, 21C, 31HC, 38C, 39C, 40C, 42C, 43C, 49HC, 50C, 55C, 57H, 60C, 62N, 71C

160604  Geometrics   40H

160606  Differential Geometry   22C

160699  Other Geometry and Topology   6C, 21C, 37C, 51C, 60C

**1607   Probability**

160701  Finite Probability   21C, 56C

160702  Theory of Probability   60C

160706  Foundations of Probability   6C

**1608   Statistics**   3C, 39C, 41C, 46C, 47C, 51C, 70C

160801  Descriptive Statistics   6C, 8C, 15C, 17C, 25C, 32C, 40C, 44C, 66C, 71C

160802  Applied Statistics   5C, 6C, 17C, 21C, 22C, 36C, 38C, 42C, 48C, 55C, 57C, 62C, 64C, 65C, 67C

160803  Mathematical Statistics   17C, 36C, 54C, 56C, 61C

160809  Sample Surveys   65C

160899  Other Statistics   16C, 19C, 29C, 34C, 39C, 44C, 47C, 48H, 51C, 63C

**1609   Numerical Analysis and Approximation Theory**

160901  Numerical Analysis   2C

160999  Other Numerical Analysis and Approximation Theory   34C

**1611   Applications of Mathematics (General)**   38H, 41C, 55C, 59C

161101  Mathematics of Business and Finance   3C, 6H, 8C, 15C, 21C, 35HC, 37H, 41C, 44C, 48H, 50C, 51C, 56C

161103  Mathematics of Economics   17C, 41C

161107  Mathematical and Statistical Biology   42C, 65C

161108  Mathematical and Statistical Psychology   6C, 31C, 41C, 59C

161199  Other Applications of Mathematics   3C, 14E, 15C, 34C, 35H, 36C, 51C, 57C, 65C

**1612   User-Oriented Mathematics**   59N

161201  Business Mathematics   1C, 6H, 16H, 17H, 18H, 36C, 38H, 55H, 56H, 57H, 58H, 59H, 64HC, 65N

161202  Consumer Mathematics   14H, 16H, 17H, 31H, 32H, 50N, 60H

161299  Other User-Oriented Mathematics   18H, 30C, 33C, 49H, 56H, 60C, 62C, 63H

**1699   Other Mathematical Sciences**   3C, 50C, 58H

## 17   MILITARY SCIENCES

**1701   Military History**

170102  American Military History   51C

## 18   PHILOSOPHY, RELIGION, AND THEOLOGY

**1801   Aesthetics**   22C, 55C

180101  Philosophy of Art   21C

180199  Other Aesthetics   63C

**1802   Epistemology**

180202  Philosophy of Natural Science   16C

**1803   Ethics**   37C, 40C, 51C, 55C

180301  Personal Moralities   5C, 17C, 38C, 46C, 63C, 69C

180302  Social Ethics   19C, 21C, 22HC, 32C, 39C, 67C

180303  Ethics of Professions   21C, 59C

180399  Other Ethics   16C, 44C, 46C, 47C, 59C

**1804   History and Traditions of Philosophy**   5C, 28C, 31C, 37C

180401  Ancient Western Philosophy   16C, 21C, 40C, 46C, 55C, 67C

180402  Medieval Western Philosophy   36C, 46C, 55C

180403  Modern Western Philosophy   35C, 36C, 40C, 46C, 55C

180404  Contemporary Western Philosophy   25C, 37C, 43C

180405  Oriental Philosophy   3C, 36C, 44C

180499  Other History of Philosophy   16C, 25C, 34C, 47C, 56C, 67C

**1805   Logic and Philosophical Methodology**   3C, 55C

180501  Informal Logic   21C, 25C, 39C, 44C, 46C, 48C, 56C, 60C, 69C

180502  Symbolic Logic   17C, 25C, 30C, 31C, 34C, 51C, 62C, 63C

180504  Philosophy of Language   6C

180599  Other Logic and Philosophical Methodology   22C, 32C, 35C, 38C, 43C, 47C, 49C, 56C, 58C

**1806    Metaphysics**
180605    Philosophical Anthropology    21C
180609    Philosophy of Religion    21C, 47C

**1807    Social and Political Philosophy**    32C, 34C, 36C, 44C, 47C, 52C, 62C, 70C

**1808    Philosophical Foundations**    16C, 21C, 48C, 58C

**1809    Specific Religions**
180901    Buddhism    64N
180902    Christianity    32C, 38C, 59C, 64N
180903    Hinduism    64N
180904    Islam    64N
180905    Judaism    42C, 43C, 64N
180999    Other Specific Religions    14C, 42G, 46C, 47C, 69C

**1810    Phenomenology of Religion**
181002    Comparative Religions    24C, 28C, 48HN, 52C, 62C
181099    Other Phenomenology of Religion    46C, 52C

**1811    Religion and Human Experience**
181101    Religion and Science    19C, 46C, 58C
181102    Religion and Personality Studies    32C
181103    Religion and Social Issues    38C, 46C, 59C
181104    Religion and Culture    16C, 38C, 42C, 54C, 59C
181199    Other Religion and Human Experience    37C, 39C, 42C, 43C

**1812    Sacred Writings**
181201    Sacred Writings of the Jewish Faith    38C, 51C
181202    Sacred Writings of the Christian Faith    6C, 31HC, 38C, 48N, 51C, 58C, 59HN
181299    Other Sacred Writings    6C, 31C, 39C, 42G, 47C

**1813    Historical Theology**
181301    Ancient Near East Theology    42C
181302    Early Christian and Rabbinic Theology    42C
181303    Medieval Theology    70C
181304    Modern Theology    25C
181399    Other Historical Theology    42CG

**1814    Systematic Theology**
181406    Christology    14C

**1815    Moral and Ethical Studies**
181502    Moral and Ethical Issues    52C
181599    Other Moral and Ethical Studies    42G, 52CN

**1816    Pastoral Studies**
181603    Religious Education    6C
181608    Missiology    6C

**1899    Other Philosophy, Religion, and Theology**    14EHC, 25C, 38C, 51C

# 19    PHYSICAL EDUCATION, HEALTH EDUCATION, AND LEISURE

Dance is listed both in Physical Education, Health Education, and Leisure and in Arts, Visual and Performing. As an art form, it is more concerned with aesthetics than with physical movement, although both factors are involved.

Health Education deals with the knowledge that individuals use to maintain good health as members of society. Specific knowledge relating to the restoration and preservation of health is included in the subject-matter area of Health Care and Health Sciences.

**1901    Physical Education**    20C, 59H
190102    Exercise    6HCN
190103    Group Games, Contests, and Self-Testing Activities    6H
190104    History of Physical Education    4C, 8C, 15C, 21C, 25C, 58C

190105    Philosophy of Physical Education    56C
190106    Physical Education Administration    16C, 21C, 35C, 55C, 56C, 58C
190107    Physical Education Curriculum    25C, 42G, 55C
190108    Physical Education Instruction    6C, 9C, 25C
190109    Physical Education Supervision    15C
190110    Measurement and Evaluation in Physical Education    25C, 35C, 55C, 56C
190199    Other Physical Education    6C, 19C, 32C, 61C

**1902    Kinesiology**    21C
190203    Performance Physiology    61C
190205    Sports Medicine    55C
190299    Other Kinesiology    42C

**1903    Sport**
190301    Sport in Schools and Colleges    25C
190303    Sport History    5C, 51C
190306    Sport Psychology    61C
190311    Instruction and Coaching of Sport    6C, 16N, 25C, 36C, 43C, 49C, 55C, 56C, 58C
190312    Sport Activities    60H

**1904    Dance (See 0301—Dance)**
190401    Dance Choreography    6C
190405    Dance History    8C
190499    Other Dance    6C

**1905    Health Education**    4C, 41C, 48H, 55HC
190501    Drugs and Other Substances    13C, 25C, 31C, 39C, 41C
190502    Community-Health Education    8C, 10HC, 16C, 17C, 19C, 21C, 41C, 48C, 58C, 59C, 64C
190503    Consumer-Health Education    19C, 25C, 41C
190504    Disease Prevention and Control    15C, 19C, 25C, 31C, 41C, 70C
190505    Environmental-Health Education    8C, 43C
190506    Family-Health Education    38H
190508    Nutrition Education    16C, 38N, 42C
190509    Personal-Health Education    8C, 16C, 24HC, 31HC, 32C, 35H, 36H, 38H, 44H, 47C, 54C, 58C, 59C, 60H
190510    Physical Fitness    59H, 66C
190511    Safety Education    10C, 15C, 17C, 19C, 41C, 47C, 59C, 61C
190512    Sex Education    6C, 17C, 22C, 31C, 41C, 61C
190513    Administration of Health Education    16C, 34C
190515    Health-Education Instruction    14H, 41C
190599    Other Health Education    8C, 14C, 15C, 17HC, 19C, 38C, 41C, 43C, 47C, 52C, 56H, 63C, 67C

**1906    Driver and Safety Education**    48H, 59H, 61N
190603    Development of Driving Judgment    36H
190699    Other Driver Education    25H, 49H

**1907    Leisure Studies**    48C, 51C
190701    Resource Management in Leisure Studies    8C, 31C, 48C
190702    Populations and Leisure Services    16C, 42C
190703    Leisure and Recreation Planning    8C, 16C, 43C, 48C
190704    Leadership in Leisure Studies    4C, 55C, 58C, 61C
190705    Recreation Activities    6C
190706    History of Leisure Studies    25C, 31C
190709    International and Comparative Leisure Studies    61C
190799    Other Leisure Studies    4C, 25N, 42C, 61C, 69C

**1999    Other Physical Education, Health Education, and Leisure**    16N, 32C, 68C

# ARTventure
## Down the Mekong

Easy-to-Make Art Projects

**Creative Artistic Director & Primary Author**
Trami Nguyen Cron

**Senior Art Director**
Smita Garg, Ed.D

**Art Lessons by**
Smita Garg, Ed.D
Cynthia Cao
Amanda Pascual

**Designed by**
Cynthia Cao

**Illustrated by**
Ashley Hin

**Photographed by**
Jackie Huynh
Trami Nguyen Cron

*Chopsticks Alley Art team*

**Edited by**
Esther Young
Harleen Kaur
Minh Trương

**Translated by**
Liên Hương Cao

**Bibliography by**
Vani M. Garg

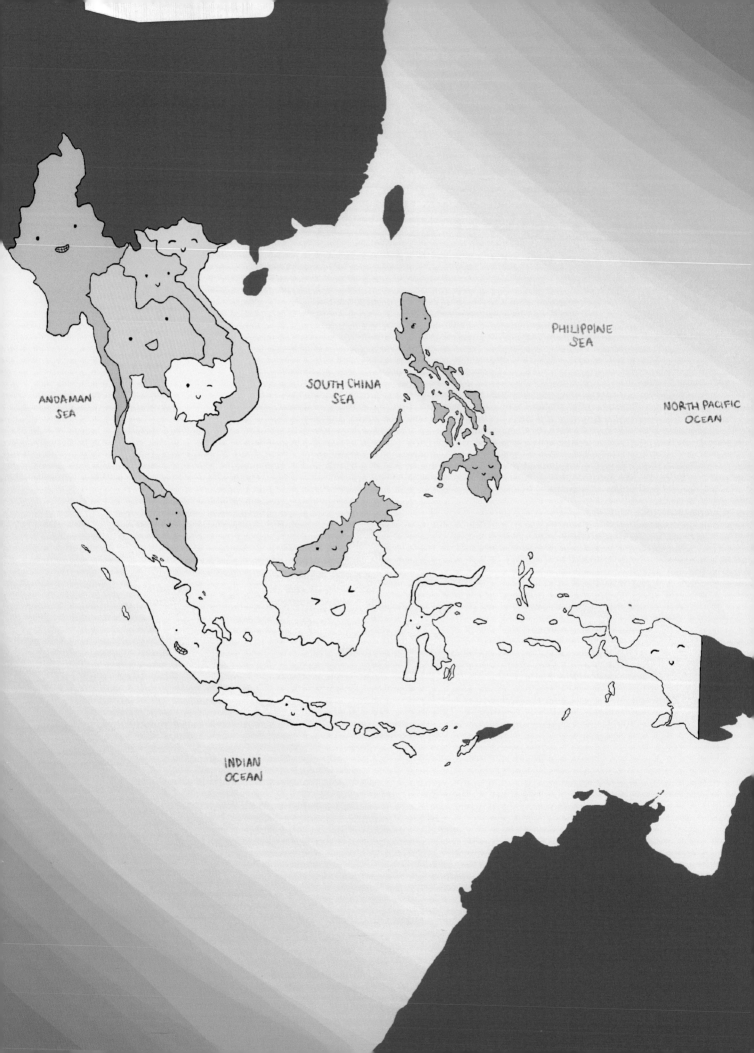

ANDAMAN
SEA

SOUTH CHINA
SEA

PHILIPPINE
SEA

NORTH PACIFIC
OCEAN

INDIAN
OCEAN

# Dedication

*ARTventure Down the Mekong* is a labor of love dedicated to the indomitable spirit of pan-Asian immigrants and their families. We dedicate this book to our elders and parents. Their resilience enabled us to become leaders, artists, and changemakers.

This book is also a tribute to the artisans of Southeast Asia who have preserved ancient traditions in the face of war, genocide, hunger, colonialism, and displacement from their homeland.

Their sacrifices have kept these art forms alive and vibrant for all of us.

# Tri Ân

*ARTventure Down the Mekong*, Cuộc Phiêu Lưu Nghệ Thuật Theo Dòng Sông Mekong, là một tác phẩm đầy tình yêu thương dành cho tinh thần bất khuất của những người và gia đình nhập cư vào nước Mỹ từ châu Á. Chúng tôi dành tặng cuốn sách này cho các cô các bác lớn tuổi và cha mẹ của chúng tôi. Khả năng chống chỏi và phục hồi của các bậc này đã giúp chúng tôi trở thành những nhà lãnh đạo, nghệ sĩ và người cải tiến nhiệt huyết.

Cuốn sách này cũng là một lời tri ân các nghệ nhân Đông Nam Á, những người đã gìn giữ truyền thống cổ xưa qua các vấn nạn chiến tranh, diệt chủng, nạn đói, chủ nghĩa thực dân và di dời khỏi quê hương.

Sự hy sinh của họ đã giúp cho các loại hình nghệ thuật được chia sẻ dưới đây luôn sống động cho chúng ta.

# Table of Contents

**Myanmar (Burma)**
Pathein Hti, Pathein Parasol
page 14

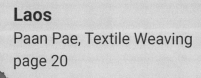

**Laos**
Paan Pae, Textile Weaving
page 20

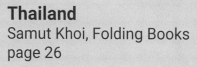

**Thailand**
Samut Khoi, Folding Books
page 26

**Cambodia (Khmer)**
Krueng Smaun, Pottery
page 32

# Mục Lục

**Vietnam**
Sơn Mài, Lacquer Painting
page 38

**Malaysia**
Wau Bulan, Moon Kite
page 44

**Philippines**
Bulul, Male Rice Deity Statue
page 50

**Indonesia**
Batik on Paper
page 56

River of Flowers, Ho Chi Minh City (Saigon), Vietnam

Chopsticks Alley Art is a non-profit organization promoting Southeast Asian cultural heritage through the shared creative expression of art. We support and promote artists through art exhibits, classes, performances, events, and now, an art book!

We serve emerging Southeast Asian artists, low-income families, youth, elders, the LGBTQ+ community, and individuals with differing abilities. We celebrate Southeast Asian contemporary art to foster greater understanding and connect different communities through the arts.

In March 2020, Chopsticks Alley's operational model was dramatically challenged by the pandemic, like all other arts groups in the San Francisco Bay Area. Our fundamental offerings—classes, exhibits, performances, and festivals—were placed on hold indefinitely with shelter-in-place orders prohibiting gatherings of any kind. The impact was immediate and somewhat shocking.

San Jose is the tenth-largest city in the United States. The Asian community represents nearly a third of the population. In the early days of the shelter-in-place order, the City of San Jose and the County of Santa Clara contacted Chopsticks Alley to quickly create public service announcements in the Vietnamese language, providing urgently needed health protocols and warnings about COVID-19. We are uniquely equipped to provide timely and direct information to the Vietnamese community. It was an easy request for us to accommodate; moreover, it also illuminated critical elements of our mission.

In light of the new reality for arts groups and our society, Chopsticks Alley Art has shifted our planning. We are responding to what the world looks like now and in the near future. The health crisis has re-ignited the agile and entrepreneurial spirit of the Chopsticks Alley team and illuminated new opportunities to engage and serve marginalized communities. We recognize that some groups, especially our elders, lack access to virtual technology and programming. The creation of an art kit and the publication of an art book will help serve this population. With the Asian Googlers Network's help and private donations, these lessons are translated into Vietnamese, and 500 free art kits will be distributed to Vietnamese seniors throughout

Santa Clara County. Our goal is to keep the art lessons simple and easy to follow; the art supplies we chose are intentionally low-cost to make them affordable for everyone.

The artists and writers involved in producing this artbook did extensive research to identify unique artistic traditions to highlight from each Southeast Asian country. The loss of culture and contextual identity through assimilation is widespread throughout Southeast Asia. We believe the resilience of our ancient cultures is relevant, now more than ever, as the younger generations find their way back to their roots to reclaim their identities and find strength in their heritage and traditions. In this era of globalization, we must prepare our youth with a solid foundation to help them restore pride in their history.

Huế Imperial City (The Citadel), Huế, Vietnam

Trami Nguyen Cron
*Creative Artistic Director*
Chopsticks Alley Art

4

Chopsticks Alley invites you on an ARTventure along the Mekong River as we introduce you to eight Southeast Asian countries and their traditional art. Our team of artists is led by Dr. Smita Garg, an artist and arts educator with 30 years of expertise in developing culturally inclusive arts programs for diverse populations.

The Mekong River is one of the largest rivers in the world. It serves as the crossroads of many peoples who have settled in the area for centuries. The river originates in the icy headwaters of the Tibetan highlands. It flows through China's steep canyons down to Myanmar, Laos, Thailand, and Cambodia before fanning across an expansive delta in Vietnam and emptying into the South China Sea, where you will find Malaysia, Indonesia, and the Phillippine Islands. The Mekong is also known by the Vietnamese as *Sông Cửu Long*, River of Nine Dragons—it splits into nine smaller rivers as it reaches the Southern regions of Vietnam before emptying into the South China Sea. It is a biological treasure trove of over a thousand animal species and plants. Unfortunately, due to climate change and human carelessness, the region's low-lying coastalce geography is vulnerable to the rise in sea levels, coastal erosion, saltwater intrusion, and pollution.

ARTventure is an introductory journey to the art and culture of Southeast Asia. You will get a glimpse of eight countries, discover unique aspects of their culture, and brief history through each art lesson. These art activities created by Chopsticks Alley Artists intentionally draw inspiration from each country's rich culture and simplify them into easy-to-do art projects.

Hop aboard Chopsticks Alley's *Thuyền Thúng*, Basket Boat, and enjoy your ARTventure Down the Mekong River with us.

## Thuyền Thúng

Basket boats are a symbol of independence in the hearts of Vietnamese fishermen. The origin story of these boats is still unclear, but our favorite one began with fishermen from Đà Nẵng wanting to guard their boats against unfair taxation imposed by the French government. The fishermen could not afford these exorbitant fees, so they designed a circular woven basket—simple, but perfect for floating and fishing. These *Thuyền Thúng* quickly became popular along the coast and are still being used today. Its unique engineering and shape have cleverly outmaneuvered French colonial tax rules.

Hang tight and join An Thạnh as he guides you through *ARTventure Down the Mekong* in his Thuyền Thúng.

Làng Lụa Hội An, Vietnam (Hoi An Silk Village)

Chopsticks Alley Art là một tổ chức phi lợi nhuận để quảng bá di sản văn hóa Đông Nam Á bằng cách cùng nhau sáng tạo nghệ thuật. Chúng tôi hỗ trợ và quảng bá các nghệ sĩ thông qua các cuộc triển lãm nghệ thuật, lớp học, buổi biểu diễn, sự kiện, và giờ đây là một cuốn sách về nghệ thuật!

Chúng tôi phục vụ các nghệ sĩ Đông Nam Á mới nổi, các gia đình có thu nhập thấp, thanh niên, người cao tuổi, cộng đồng LGBTQ+ và các cá nhân có nhu cầu và năng khiếu đặc biệt. Chúng tôi tôn vinh nghệ thuật Đông Nam Á đương đại, quảng bá kiến thức và kết nối các cộng đồng thông qua kênh nghệ thuật.

Vào tháng 3 năm 2020, mô hình hoạt động của Chopsticks Alley, cũng như của các nhóm nghệ thuật khác trong vùng Vịnh San Francisco, gặp nhiều khó khăn vì đại dịch COVID-19. Các dịch vụ cơ bản, các lớp học, các cuộc triển lãm trực tiếp, buổi trình diễn và lễ hội bị hoãn vô thời hạn vì lệnh cấm tụ họp dưới bất kỳ hình thức nào. Tác động ngay sau đó rất mạnh và tạo ra ít nhiều bất ngờ. Nhưng nó cũng làm sáng lên một phần quan trọng trong khối nhiệm vụ của Chopsticks Alley.

San Jose là thành phố lớn thứ mười ở Hoa Kỳ. Cộng đồng Châu Á đại diện cho gần một phần ba dân số. Trong những ngày đầu của lệnh đóng cửa, Thành phố San Jose và Quận Santa Clara đã liên hệ với Chopsticks Alley, yêu cầu nhanh chóng thông báo các dịch vụ cho cộng đồng bằng tiếng Việt, cung cấp các giao thức y tế cần thiết và cảnh báo về COVID-19. Chopsticks Alley là cơ quan duy nhất được trang bị để cung cấp thông tin kịp thời và trực tiếp cho cộng đồng Việt Nam bị bỏ quên. Đó là một yêu cầu dễ dàng đối với chúng tôi; hơn thế nữa, nó cũng phản ánh những yếu tố quan trọng trong nhiệm vụ của chúng tôi.

Trước thực trạng mới cho các nhóm nghệ thuật và cho xã hội, Chopsticks Alley Art đã điều chỉnh chương trình kế hoạch. Chúng tôi muốn đáp ứng cho thế giới hiện tại và trong tương lai gần. Cuộc khủng hoảng y tế đã khơi dậy tinh thần phát triển sáng tác nhanh nhẹn của nhóm Chopsticks Alley và thắp sáng những cơ hội mới để gắn kết và phục vụ các cộng đồng bị thiệt thòi. Chúng tôi nhận thấy rằng một số nhóm, đặc biệt là những người cao tuổi, thiếu cơ hội tiếp cận với công nghệ ảo và lập trình. Chúng tôi quyết định tạo ra một bộ nghệ thuật, và xuất bản một cuốn sách nghệ thuật để phục đối tượng này. Với sự trợ giúp của

Googlers Châu Á, những bài học nghệ thuật được dịch sang tiếng Việt và 500 dụng cụ nghệ thuật được phân phát miễn phí cho người Việt Nam cao tuổi trên toàn Quận Santa Clara. Mục tiêu của chúng tôi là đưa ra các bài học nghệ thuật đơn giản và dễ hiểu; các vật liệu dụng cụ nghệ thuật được chọn lọc với chủ ý chi phí thấp để phù hợp với túi tiền của tất cả mọi người.

Các nghệ sĩ và nhà văn tham gia biên soạn cuốn sách nghệ thuật này đã nghiên cứu sâu rộng để xác định được các truyền thống nghệ thuật độc đáo nổi bật từ mỗi quốc gia Đông Nam Á. Khắp Đông Nam Á, chúng ta đã từ từ mất dần đi văn hóa và bản sắc dân tộc vì quá trình đồng hóa đã được phổ biến rộng rãi. Chúng tôi tin rằng khả năng chống chỏi và phục hồi của các nền văn hóa cổ đại rất là quan trọng, giờ đây và hơn bao giờ hết, khi các thế hệ trẻ tìm về cội nguồn để lấy lại bản sắc và tìm thấy sức mạnh trong di sản truyền thống của mình. Trong thời đại toàn cầu hóa này, chúng ta phải chuẩn bị cho lớp trẻ một nền tảng vững chắc để giúp họ khôi phục lại niềm tự hào về lịch sử của mình.

Trami Nguyen Cron
*Giám Đốc Nghệ Thuật*
Chopsticks Alley Art

Kompong Phluk on Tonle Sap Lake, Cambodia

8

Chopsticks Alley mời bạn tham gia một cuộc phiêu lưu nghệ thuật truyền thống của tám quốc gia Đông Nam Á nằm dọc theo sông Mekong. Đội ngũ nghệ sĩ của chúng tôi được dẫn dắt bởi tiến sĩ Smita Garg, một nghệ sĩ và nhà giáo dục nghệ thuật với 30 năm chuyên môn trong việc phát triển các chương trình nghệ thuật hòa nhập văn hóa cho các sắc dân đa dạng.

Sông Mekong là một trong những con sông lớn nhất thế giới. Cũng là ngã tư của nhiều dân tộc đã định cư trong khu vực này trong nhiều thế kỷ qua. Sông bắt đầu từ nguồn băng giá của vùng cao nguyên Tây Tạng, chảy qua các hẻm núi dốc của Trung Quốc xuống Myanmar, Lào, Thái Lan và Campuchia trước khi rẽ qua một vùng đồng bằng rộng lớn ở Việt Nam, và đổ ra Biển Đông, nơi chúng ta gặp các nước Malaysia, Indonesia và quần đảo Philippin. Sông Mekong còn được người Việt Nam gọi là Sông Cửu Long, sông của chín con rồng - chia thành chín con sông nhỏ đổ về các vùng phía Nam của Việt Nam, trước khi đổ ra biển Đông. Đây là một kho tàng sinh học của hơn một nghìn loài động thực vật. Không may, do biến đổi khí hậu và sự bất cẩn của con người, địa lý ven biển thấp của khu vực đã bị ảnh hưởng bởi sự gia tăng của mực nước biển, xói mòn bờ biển, ngập mặn và ô nhiễm.

*ARTventure* là một cuộc hành trình giới thiệu về nghệ thuật và văn hóa vùng Đông Nam Á. Bạn sẽ làm quen với tám (8) quốc gia, khám phá những phần độc đáo của các nền văn hóa và lịch sử, qua những bài học nghệ thuật ngắn gọn cho từng quốc gia. Những bài học này được thiết kế bởi các nghệ sĩ Chopsticks Alley, lấy cảm hứng từ nền văn hóa phong phú của mỗi quốc gia, và hoàn thành những dự án nghệ thuật độc đáo và dễ thực hiện.

Mời bạn hãy cùng chúng tôi lên *Thuyền Thúng* của Chopsticks Alley và cùng thưởng thức *ARTventure, Cuộc Phiêu Lưu Nghệ Thuật Trên Dòng Sông Mekong.*

Thuyền thúng là biểu tượng của sự độc lập trong lòng ngư dân Việt Nam. Nguồn gốc của những chiếc thuyền này không được rõ, nhưng câu chuyện chúng tôi yêu thích bắt đầu từ việc ngư dân Đà Nẵng muốn bảo vệ thuyền của họ chống lại việc đánh thuế bất công của chính phủ Pháp. Những người đánh cá không thể chi trả những khoản phí cắt cổ này, vì vậy họ đã thiết kế một chiếc giỏ đan hình tròn - đơn giản, nhưng hoàn hảo để thả nổi và câu cá. Những chiếc thuyền thúng này nhanh chóng trở nên phổ biến dọc theo bờ biển, và vẫn được sử dụng cho đến ngày nay. Kỹ thuật độc đáo của thuyền thúng vượt xa các quy định về thuế của thực dân Pháp.

Hãy cùng theo anh An Thạnh, anh sẽ hướng dẫn bạn qua *ARTventure Down the Mekong* trong thuyền thúng của anh.

# Art Materials

Here are the basic supplies you will need to create the art projects in this book.

- Beads - 9mm pony bead
- Chopsticks (disposable)
- Coffee filter
- Construction paper (9x12 inches) - 10 white, 2 black, and 4 assorted colors and patterns
- Crayons
- Eraser
- Foam brush
- Glue
- Marker - black/medium point
- Paintbrush (small)
- Pencil
- Pencil sharpener
- Polymer clay - 1 oz (or more)
- Ruler
- Tempera paints set
- Thread - thin for embroidery or sewing
- Toothpicks
- Washi tape roll
- Wooden stylus

Additional household items:

- Bowl, cup, and plate for mixing glue, water, and paint
- Craft items - ribbons, beads, bells, glitter, etc.
- Dish soap
- Empty jars or vessels (small to medium size)
- Hairdryer
- Iron
- Newspaper
- Paper towels
- Pen
- Rags
- Rubber Band
- Scissors
- Stapler
- Water

# Tips for Beginners

**Keep yourself clean**

- **Wash your hands** well before and after working on any art projects.

- **Wear an apron** or an old shirt to prevent your clothes from getting dirty.

- **Never put your fingers or any art materials in your eyes or mouth.** Should this happen, wash your eyes and rinse your mouth thoroughly with water.

**Prepare your work surfaces**

- To prepare your art surface, **wipe it clean before you begin or line your table with clean newspapers.**

- **Have extra rags** or towels handy to wipe off any spills.

- **Keep extra materials** handy while working such as newspapers, scrap paper, a cup of clean water, and a couple of empty plastic bowls.

**Take care of your art materials**

- Always **put back caps on markers and cover your paints** to prevent them from evaporating to help them last longer.

- When waiting for your work to dry, **place items on a dry surface or tray and away from foot traffic.**

- **Do not leave brushes soaking** in water for too long.

- When you are done using your brushes, **wash them thoroughly with soapy water** immediately until the water runs clear.

- **Lay them out flat to dry** on a newspaper or a towel.

# Dụng Cụ Và Cách Làm

Đây là danh sách các dụng cụ cần thiết cho tất cả các bài học nghệ thuật trong cuốn sách này.

- Hạt cườm lớn (Pony 9mm)
- Đũa (loại dùng một lần rồi bỏ đi)
- Giấy lọc cà phê
- Giấy thủ công, nhiều màu (9x12 inches) - 10 trắng, 2 đen và 4 màu và hoa văn các loại
- Bút sáp màu, nhiều màu
- Tẩy bút chì
- Cọ xốp
- Chai / que keo
- Bút lông (cỡ trung bình màu đen)
- Cọ sơn (nhỏ)
- Bút chì
- Đồ chuốt bút chì
- Đất sét polyme - (1 oz trở lên)
- Thước
- Bộ sơn tempera
- Chỉ - (mỏng để thêu hoặc may)
- Tăm
- Cuộn băng keo Washi
- Bút stylus bằng gỗ

Các đồ dùng trong nhà:

- Bát, ly, và đĩa trộn keo, nước và sơn
- Đồ thủ công - các loại ruy băng, hạt cườm, chuông, kim tuyến, v.v.
- Xà bông rửa chén
- Lọ hoặc bình rỗng (cỡ nhỏ đến vừa)
- Máy sấy tóc
- Bàn là (ủi)
- Giấy báo
- Khăn giấy
- Bút mực

- Giẻ rách
- Dây thun
- Kéo
- Đồ bấm giấy
- Nước

**Hãy giữ gìn sạch sẽ**

- **Rửa tay sạch trước** và sau khi thực hiện mỗi dự án.

- **Mặc tạp dề hoặc áo sơ mi** cũ để tránh làm bẩn quần áo.

- **Không bao giờ đưa ngón tay hoặc bất kỳ vật liệu nghệ thuật nào vào mắt hoặc miệng.** Nếu điều này xảy ra, hãy rửa mắt và súc miệng kỹ bằng nước.

**Chuẩn bị mặt bàn làm việc**

- Chuẩn bị bàn làm việc **bằng cách lau sạch bàn trước khi bắt đầu hoặc lót bàn bằng báo sạch.**

- **Chuẩn bị thêm giẻ hoặc khăn** để lau sạch các vết đổ hoặc dơ.

- **Chuẩn bị thêm** báo, giấy vụn, một cốc nước sạch và một vài bát nhựa trống khi làm việc.

**Cẩn thận gìn giữ các dụng cụ nghệ thuật**

- **Luôn đậy nắp các bút mực, và phủ lớp sơn của bạn** để ngăn bay hơi, giữ bền hơn.

- Khi chờ cho tác phẩm của bạn khô ráo, hãy đặt tác **phẩm trên một bề mặt hoặc khay khô ráo, tránh xa lối đi lại.**

- **Không để cọ ngâm trong nước** quá lâu.

- Khi sử dụng cọ xong, hãy **rửa kỹ bằng nước xà bông** ngay lập tức cho đến khi nước trong.

- **Đặt cọ phẳng** trên một tờ báo hoặc một chiếc khăn để phơi khô.

# MYANMAR

The Golden Land of Myanmar, formerly known as Burma, is named for its glistening golden pagodas sprinkled throughout the country. About 135 ethnic groups make up the population of this rich and varied landscape with its beautiful beaches. Myanmar is a colorful country, and their parasols, known as *Hti*, reflect this vibrant culture. They are used as decorations throughout the nation and also symbolize honor in monastic life. Within the pagodas temples, they are a decorative finial.

Hti is best known from the town of Pathein, formerly known as Bassein. It's a picturesque tree-lined city combined with colonial-era buildings along the Pathein River and serves as the capital of the deltaic region dating back to the 12th century. It was the main port for ships from India and Southeast Asia, and today it is still a vibrant entrepôt for passengers and cargo from various parts of Myanmar. It is also home to the famous Bhuddhist Shwemokhtaw Pagoda.

Initially, Hti was made of paper, but eventually, they were replaced by oil-soaked cotton, silk, and taffeta to lengthen the life of each Hti. Traditional parasols are made of bamboo soaked in water to prevent insect infestation. These umbrellas are sized differently for men and women, and decorations on these parasols also have masculine and feminine interpretations. Women's parasols tend to feature nature and floral designs, while the men's parasols are painted with two white hands cupping royal cities. Golden umbrellas are reserved for use in Buddhist temples and monasteries. In pre-colonial Myanmar, the color white was an indicator of social status. The white Hti were used exclusively by noble families or by those who were granted permission to do so.

*Kyaiktiyo Pagoda, Thaton District, Myanmar*

Though Hti is made everywhere throughout Myanmar, the colorful parasols from Pathein are widely known and are treasured souvenirs. Beyond their function to protect the people from sun and rain, they are artistic expressions and serve as an icon for Myanmar.

"My great-grandparents lived in Myanmar, and this project made me think of the stories they shared with me."

—Dr. Smita

# Pathein Hti, Pathein Parasol

Dr. Smita Garg

## Project

Make a colorful miniature Hti.

## Materials

Bead
Chopstick
Coffee filter
Construction paper - white
Foam brush
Glue
Paintbrush
Pencil
Rubber band

Scissors
Sharpie
Tape or stapler
Tempera paint
Toothpick

**Optional Materials**
Hairdryer

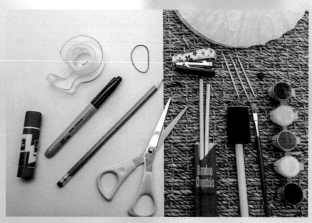

## STEPS

1. Lay the coffee filter flat on top of construction paper.

2. Glue filter onto the paper and smooth out wrinkles. Place aside for a few minutes to dry.

3. Once the filter has dried, use the foam brush to paint bright colors such as yellow and orange onto the filter with gentle dabbing motions. Make it as colorful as you like. Wait for the paint to dry.
Tip: For quick drying, use a hairdryer.

4. Once the paint has dried, draw a design with a sharpie or pencil on it. **Make sure to draw lines radiating out from the center of your parasol to the edge of the filter—you will use these lines to assemble your parasol.** Add as many design elements as you wish.

5. Next, cut out the circular parasol. Then cut along one of the lines from the outer edge to the center.

6. Take both cut ends and overlap them together, making a cone, but not too sharp.

7. Staple or tape the ends to secure them.

8. Poke a toothpick through the top center of the cone to make a hole.

9. Use a rubber band or tape to secure the chopstick, then poke the skinny end of the chopstick through the hole underneath the parasol.

10. Secure the top of the chopstick by gluing a bead to the tip.

### MORE IDEAS!
- Try different colors and sizes.
- Display your parasol next to small sculptures of Buddha or any deity.
- Decorate by gluing embellishments like sequins or adding a border.
- Add small bells to your parasol.

# MYANMAR

Vùng đất vàng của Myanmar, trước đây gọi là Miến Điện, được đặt tên này vì có nhiều ngôi chùa vàng lấp lánh rải khắp đất nước. Khoảng 135 dân tộc tạo nên dân số của cảnh quan đa dạng và phong phú này, với nhiều bãi biển tuyệt đẹp. Myanmar là một đất nước đầy màu sắc, và những chiếc dù che nắng, được gọi là *Hti*, phản ánh một nền văn hóa sôi động. Dù được sử dụng làm đồ trang trí trên khắp nước, Hti cũng là biểu tượng cho danh dự trong đời sống tu viện, dùng để trang trí các đỉnh chùa.

Hti được biết đến nhiều nhất từ thị trấn Pathein, trước đây được gọi là Bassein. Đây là một thành phố rợp bóng cây đẹp như tranh vẽ, kết hợp với các tòa nhà thời thuộc địa dọc theo sông Pathein, và là thủ phủ của vùng châu thổ có từ thế kỷ 12. Đây là cảng chính cho các tàu bè đến từ Ấn Độ và Đông Nam Á, và ngày nay vẫn là một cảng trung chuyển sôi động cho hành khách và hàng hóa từ nhiều vùng của Myanmar. Đây cũng là nơi có chùa Buddhist Shwemokhtaw nổi tiếng. Ban đầu, Hti làm bằng giấy, nhưng rồi thì người ta thay

bằng bông tẩm dầu, lụa và taffeta (một loại lụa cứng) để dùng Hti được lâu hơn. Những chiếc lọng truyền thống được làm bằng tre ngâm nước để chống côn trùng phá hoại. Những chiếc dù Hti có kích thước khác nhau cho nam và nữ, và trang trí trên dù cũng thể hiện nam hay nữ. Dù che của phụ nữ thường vẽ cảnh thiên nhiên và hoa lá, trong khi dù che của nam giới được vẽ hai bàn tay trắng ôm lấy các thành phố hoàng gia. Những chiếc dù bằng vàng được dành để sử dụng trong các ngôi chùa và tu viện Phật giáo.

Ở Myanmar thời kỳ tiền thuộc địa, màu trắng biểu hiệu cho địa vị xã hội. Chỉ có gia đình quý tộc hoặc những người được phép, mới được dùng Hti trắng.

Mặc dù ô dù Hti được làm ở khắp mọi nơi trên đất Myanmar, những chiếc lọng đầy màu sắc từ Pathein vẫn nổi tiếng khắp nơi và là món quà lưu niệm quý giá. Ngoài chức năng che mưa nắng cho người dân, Hti còn là hình tượng nghệ thuật và biểu tượng cho Myanmar.

*"Ông bà cố của tôi sống ở Myanmar, và dự án này làm tôi nghĩ đến những câu chuyện ông bà đã kể cho tôi nghe."*

—Ts. Smita

# Pathein Hti, Pathein Parasol

Ts. Smita Garg

**Dự án**

Làm một Hti nhỏ đầy màu sắc.

**Nguyên vật liệu**

Hạt cườm

Đũa

Giấy lọc cà phê

Giấy thủ công - trắng

Cọ xốp

Keo dán

Cọ sơn

Bút chì

Dây thun

Kéo

Bút lông đen

Băng keo hoặc đồ bấm giấy

Sơn tempera

Tăm xỉa răng

**Vật liệu tùy chọn**

Máy sấy tóc

**Hướng dẫn cách làm**

1. Đặt giấy lọc cà phê phẳng lên trên giấy thủ công.

2. Dùng keo dán giấy lọc lên giấy thủ công, làm phẳng các nếp nhăn. Đặt sang một bên vài phút để khô.

3. Khi giấy lọc đã khô, hãy sử dụng cọ xốp để sơn các màu sáng như vàng và cam lên giấy lọc, thoa đánh nhẹ. Cho nhiều màu sắc theo ý bạn. Chờ sơn khô.Mẹo vặt: Có thể dùng máy sấy tóc sấy thêm cho mau khô.

4. Sau khi sơn khô, hãy vẽ lên một hình tượng bằng bút lông đen hoặc bút chì.
**Nhớ vẽ các đường tỏa ra từ tâm dù che nắng đến mép giấy lọc—bạn sẽ sử dụng các đường này để lắp ráp chiếc dù.**
Vẽ thêm theo ý của bạn.

5. Kế tiếp, cắt theo đường dù tròn. Sau đó, cắt dọc theo một đường từ mép ngoài vào giữa.

6. Lấy hai đầu đã cắt, chồng lên nhau, tạo thành hình nón, không quá nhọn.

7. Bấm giấy hoặc dùng băng dán hai đầu cho chặt.

8. Chọc một chiếc tăm qua tâm hình nón để làm một lỗ.

9. Dùng dây thun hoặc băng dính để giữ chặt một chiếc đũa bên dưới dù.

10. Dán một hạt cườm vào đầu đũa để giữ chắc.

**VÀI Ý TƯỞNG KHÁC**

- Bạn có thể thử nhiều màu sắc và kích cỡ khác nhau.

- Bạn có thể trưng bày chiếc dù bên cạnh các tác phẩm điêu khắc nhỏ của Đức Phật hoặc bất kỳ vị thần nào.

- Bạn có thể trang trí bằng cách dán các phụ kiện như kim tuyến, hoặc vẽ đường viền.

- Bạn có thể dán thêm vài chuông nhỏ xung quanh dù.

# LAOS

As we flow down the Mekong River, we find ourselves in Laos. The country is geographically isolated and has mountainous terrains. There are over 47 ethnic groups, 149 sub-groups, and 80 different languages. The Mekong River forms much of Laos' western borders and serves as a significant trade route.

*Pha That Luang, Vientiane, Laos*

Across many ethnic groups in Laos, *Paan Pae*, or textile, is the dominant artistic and cultural expression. *Paan Pae* has been traditionally passed down from mother to daughter for centuries and is still practiced by villagers throughout the country. Textiles in Laos are more than beautiful garments; they also carry the Lao people's history. Instead of sharing their history through written and oral traditions, they are woven into fabrics. Archeologists can decipher between different ethnic groups, families, and regions by studying symbols and motifs, myths, stories, values, and beliefs that are woven into these textiles.

Some symbols date back over a thousand years ago and can be found in ancient poetry, proverbs, and literature. These textiles are hand-dyed in red, pink, yellow, and green hues from plants extracted from the forests.

Textile art is slowly losing its personalization due to mass production and commercialization, but the younger generation is still preserving it while also creating new designs to reflect their experience. You can now find motifs that are "war-related" to record the Lao people's lives during recent years.

"*The process of weaving is meditative.*"

—Cynthia

# Paan Pae, Textile Weaving

Cynthia Cao

## Project
Weaving project using paper and geometric designs.

## Materials
Construction paper - 2 different colors
Glue
Pencil
Ruler
Scissors
Tape

## Optional materials for embellishments
Color pencils
Glitter
Magazines, customized painted paper, or tissue paper
Markers
Strings or ribbons

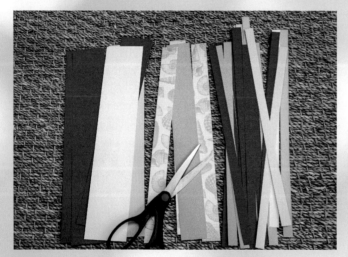

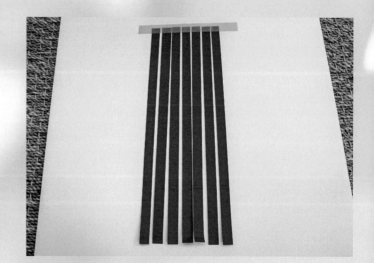

# STEPS

1.  Decide which paper you will use for the vertical strips and the horizontal strips.

2.  Using a ruler and pencil, measure and mark paper to make ¼ - 1 inch wide strips. For beginners, try starting with strips of the same size.

3.  Cut strips with scissors.

4.  Lay the vertical strips onto a hard surface and use tape to hold down one end. Leave a little space in between to make the weaving process easier.

5. Take one strip of paper, and weave it horizontally through the vertical strips by going under and over until it reaches the end.

6. Try creating a pattern by alternating the over/under to make a simple checkerboard pattern.

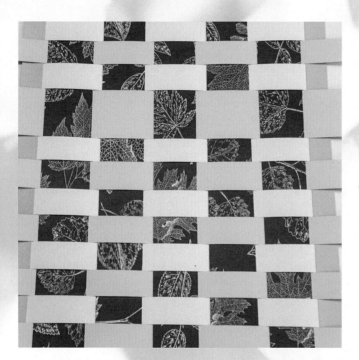

7. Start building shapes—you can draw each strip with a pencil and then weave in the strips. It works best if the edges are woven under to keep the strips in place.

8. To finish the piece, fold over the edges and glue them down. Or glue down the strips to a separate sheet of paper to make a sturdy backing.

**MORE IDEAS!**
- Add more details by drawing on the paper with colored pencils or markers.
- Embellish the edges with strings, ribbons, or tissue paper.
- Add embellishments with other media such as string, tissue paper, or glitter.

# LÀO

Đi xuôi dòng sông Mekong, chúng ta đến đất Lào. Đất nước này bị cô lập về mặt địa lý và có nhiều đồi núi. Có hơn 47 nhóm dân tộc, 149 nhóm nhỏ hơn, và 80 ngôn ngữ khác nhau. Sông Mekong, biên giới phía tây của Lào, là một tuyến đường thương mại quan trọng.

Trong nhiều nhóm dân tộc ở Lào, *Paan Pae*, hay dệt vải, biểu hiện văn hóa và nghệ thuật đặc trưng. Paan Pae được truyền từ mẹ đến con gái qua nhiều thế kỷ, và vẫn được dân làng trên khắp nước thực dụng. Hàng dệt ở Lào không chỉ là hàng may đẹp, mà còn mang hình ảnh lịch sử của dân tộc Lào. Thay vì được truyền đạt theo lối truyền thống như bằng văn bản và truyền khẩu, lịch sử Lào đã được dệt vào các tấm vải. Các nhà khảo cổ học có thể giải mã các nhóm dân tộc, gia đình và khu vực qua nghiên cứu các biểu tượng và mô típ, thần thoại, câu chuyện, giá trị và niềm tin được dệt trên những tấm vải này. Một số biểu tượng có từ hơn một nghìn năm trước và được thấy trong thơ ca, tục ngữ và văn học cổ đại. Những hàng dệt được nhuộm bằng tay với các màu đỏ, hồng, vàng và xanh lá cây từ các loại thực vật đều được khai thác trong rừng.

Nghệ thuật dệt đang dần dần mất đi tính cách cá nhân do việc sản xuất hàng loạt và thương mại hóa, tuy nhiên thế hệ trẻ hiện nay vẫn gìn giữ, đồng thời tạo ra thêm những mẫu thiết kế mới để phản ánh kinh nghiệm đời sống của họ. Giờ đây, bạn có thể tìm thấy các họa tiết liên quan đến chiến tranh, ghi lại cuộc sống của người dân Lào trong những năm gần đây.

*"Khi dệt là một cách thiền."*

—Cynthia

# Paan Pae, Hàng Dệt

Cynthia Cao

### Dự án

Sử dụng giấy để dệt và thiết kế hình học.

### Nguyên vật liệu

Giấy thủ công - 2 màu khác nhau

Keo dán

Bút chì

Thước

Kéo

Băng dính

### Vật liệu tùy chọn

Bút chì màu

Kim tuyến

Tạp chí, giấy tự sơn hoặc giấy mỏng

Bút lông

Dây hoặc ruy băng

### Hướng dẫn cách làm

1. Quyết định loại giấy bạn muốn dùng cho các dải dọc và các dải ngang.

2. Dùng thước kẻ và bút chì, đo và đánh dấu giấy để tạo thành các dải rộng từ ¼ inch đến 1 inch. Người mới bắt đầu nên thử với các dải cùng kích thước.

3. Cắt các dải bằng kéo.

4. Đặt các dải dọc lên một bề mặt cứng và dùng băng dính để giữ một đầu. Chừa một khoảng trống ở giữa các dải để dệt dễ hơn.

5. Lấy một dải giấy và dệt theo chiều ngang qua các dải dọc bằng cách luồn qua lại cho đến khi hết.

6. Hãy thử tạo một mẫu bằng cách xen kẽ trên và dưới để tạo thành một mẫu bàn cờ đơn giản.

7. Bắt đầu tạo hình—bạn có thể vẽ từng dải bằng bút chì và sau đó dệt các dải. Nên dệt các cạnh bên dưới để giữ cho các dải ở đúng vị trí.

8. Để hoàn thành miếng vải, gấp các mép lại và dán xuống. Hoặc dán các dải xuống một tờ giấy khác để làm lớp nền vững chắc.

### VÀI Ý TƯỞNG KHÁC!

- Thêm các chi tiết khác bằng cách vẽ trên giấy bằng bút chì màu hoặc bút lông.

- Tô điểm các cạnh bằng dây, ruy băng hoặc giấy mỏng.

- Làm một tấm thảm lớn bằng cách dán (dùng băng dán hoặc keo dán) các tấm dệt vuông nhỏ với nhau lên một tờ giấy lớn.

- Tô điểm thêm, dùng vật dụng khác như dây, ruy băng, giấy mỏng hoặc kim tuyến.

# THAILAND

Thailand encompasses some of the oldest settled areas in the world. The Mekong River supports Thailand's agricultural economy. It is known as *Maè Nam Khong* or Mother of All Rivers in Lao and Thai. In 1932, Siam became a constitutional monarchy and changed its official name to Thailand. The institution of the monarchy in Thailand is unique in Southeast Asia, and its history goes back more than 700 years. It has managed to preserve its relevance in today's contemporary world. Although royal institutions of the Chakri Dynasty maintain Siamese culture, societal values in Thailand are more collectivist and are influenced by western colonization.

Art and culture in Thailand are heavily shaped by India and ancient civilizations from Cambodia, Laos, Burma, Malaysia, Indonesia, and to a lesser extent, China. Perhaps the two most significant influences on Thai culture are Buddhism and Ramakien. Hindu traditions are also often seen in Thai art.

*The Grand Palace Bangkok, Thailand*

*Samut Khoi* is an illustrated manuscript often used in Buddhist cultures throughout Southeast Asia. They are usually used for texts and illustrations to record the history of the royals, literature works, or religious texts. The earliest surviving manuscripts date back to the late eighteenth century, and they are usually written in Khom script. They are made of paper from the Khoi Tree, which is not bound like western books but folded in horizontal accordion-style, with black or white paper. Antique books are often lacquered in black and decorated with gold leaves. The Thai people consider Samut Khoi national treasures from their ancestors. They are held in monasteries, museums, universities, and private collections.

"I love handmade books, which is why I picked this artform!"

—Dr. Smita

# Samut Khoi, Folding Books

Dr. Smita Garg

## Project

Create your own Samut Khoi to write your favorite poems, songs, or personal thoughts in.

## Materials

Construction paper - 4 white
Crayons
Eraser
Glue bottle/stick
Pen
Pencil
Ruler
Scissors
Sharpener
Washi tape

### Optional materials

Colored markers
Colored pencils
Colorful papers or pictures

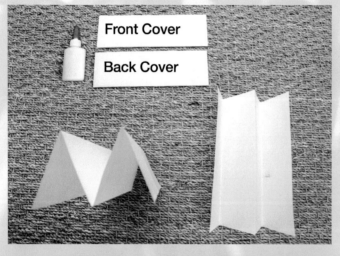

Front Cover

Back Cover

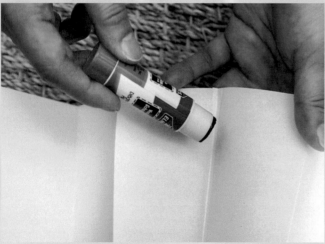

## STEPS

1. Take the shorter edge of a construction paper, fold it in half, then fold it again to make it into a 4-fold.

2. To make the book's front cover, glue all the folds together to create a thicker piece. Take a second piece of paper and repeat steps 1 and 2. Now you have the back cover of the book. Set front and back covers aside.

3. Take two more sheets of white construction paper. Repeat step 1.

4. Gently press along the edges of the folds with your fingers to make the folds sharp and neat. Each piece of paper should look like an accordion.

5. To make a long book, glue the edges of the two sheets of paper together by slightly overlapping the top shorter edge of the other and glue them together.

6. To attach the front and back covers, glue the front cover, made in step 2, to the first fold of the accordion book. Glue the back cover to the last fold of the book. **Both covers should be glued on the same side of the book when you lay everything flat.**

7. Check to see if the book is folding correctly and can be opened and closed easily like an accordion.

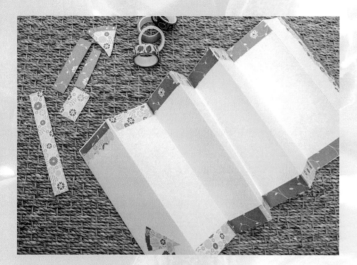

8. Open the book and draw a wide margin on both sides, leaving the middle section empty for writing. Borders can be decorated with washi tape, crayons, pictures, or textured or patterned paper.

9. Next, embellish both covers. It is totally up to you how you want to decorate your book.

10. Each fold of the book can be used to write a poem, song, or even your thoughts! You may use this book for other purposes too. Let your imagination fly!

**MORE IDEAS!**
- Although a traditional Samut Khoi is typically horizontal, your book can also be vertical.
- Use black paper and metallic ink pens for a more elaborate book.
- Make a picture book for kids.
- Make a simple photo album.

# THÁI LAN

Thái Lan bao gồm một số khu vực định cư lâu đời nhất trên thế giới. Sông Mekong hỗ trợ nền kinh tế nông nghiệp của Thái Lan. Sông có tên Maè Nam Khong hay Mẹ Của Tất Cả Các Dòng Sông trong tiếng Lào và tiếng Thái. Năm 1932, Xiêm trở thành quốc gia quân chủ lập hiến và đổi tên chính thức thành Thái Lan. Thái Lan là nước duy nhất ở Đông Nam Á có thể chế quân chủ, đã có từ hơn 700 năm trước, và vẫn cố gắng tự duy trì trong thế giới đương đại ngày nay. Mặc dù chế độ quân chủ và thể chế hoàng gia của Vương triều Chakri vẫn duy trì văn hóa Xiêm, nhưng

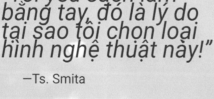

*"Tôi yêu sách làm bằng tay, đó là lý do tại sao tôi chọn loại hình nghệ thuật này!"*
—Ts. Smita

các giá trị xã hội ở Thái Lan mang tính tập thể và bị ảnh hưởng bởi quá trình thực dân hóa của phương Tây.

Nghệ thuật và văn hóa ở Thái Lan được ảnh hưởng rất nhiều bởi Ấn Độ và các nền văn minh cổ đại từ Campuchia, Lào, Miến Điện, Malaysia, Indonesia, và ở một mức độ ít hơn là Trung Quốc.

Có lẽ hai ảnh hưởng đáng kể nhất đến văn hóa Thái Lan là Phật giáo và Ramakien. Truyền thống Ấn Độ giáo cũng thường thấy trong nghệ thuật Thái Lan.

*Samut Khoi* là một bản thảo minh họa thường được sử dụng trong các nền văn hóa Phật giáo khắp Đông Nam Á. Thường được sử dụng cho các văn bản và hình ảnh minh họa để ghi lại lịch sử của các hoàng gia, các tác phẩm văn học hoặc các văn bản tôn giáo. Những bản viết tay sớm nhất còn sót lại có niên đại vào cuối thế kỷ thứ mười tám, và thường được viết bằng chữ Khôm. Những bản viết tay này được làm bằng giấy cây Khôi, không đóng sách như sách tây mà gấp ngang theo kiểu đàn accordion cùng với giấy màu đen hoặc trắng. Sách cổ thường được sơn mài đen và trang trí bằng vàng lá. Người

Thái coi Samut Khoi là bảo vật quốc gia từ tổ tiên của họ và được giữ trong các tu viện, viện bảo tàng, trường đại học và các bộ sưu tập tư nhân.

## VÀI Ý TƯỞNG KHÁC!

- Thêm các chi tiết khác bằng cách vẽ trên giấy bằng bút chì màu hoặc bút lông.
- Tô điểm các cạnh bằng dây, ruy băng hoặc giấy mỏng.
- Làm một tấm thảm lớn bằng cách dán (dùng băng dán hoặc keo dán) các tấm dệt vuông nhỏ với nhau lên một tờ giấy lớn.
- Tô điểm thêm, dùng vật dụng khác như dây, ruy băng, giấy mỏng hoặc kim tuyến.

# Samut Khoi, Sách gấp

Ts. Smita Garg

**Dự án**

Tạo Samut Khoi để viết những bài thơ, bài hát yêu thích hoặc suy nghĩ cá nhân của bạn.

**Nguyên vật liệu**

Giấy thủ công - 4 tờ trắng

Bút sáp màu
Cục tẩy
Keo dán
Bút mực
Bút chì
Thước
Kéo
Đồ chuốt bút chì

Băng keo washi

**Vật liệu tùy chọn**

Bút lông
Bút chì màu
Giấy hoặc hình ảnh đầy màu sắc

**Hướng dẫn cách làm**

1. Lấy cạnh ngắn của một tờ giấy thủ công, gấp đôi rồi lại gấp đôi để tạo thành nếp gấp 4.

2. Để làm bìa trước của cuốn sách, hãy dán tất cả các nếp gấp lại với nhau để tạo ra một miếng dày hơn. Lấy một mảnh giấy thứ hai và lặp lại các bước 1 và 2. Bây giờ bạn đã có bìa sau của cuốn sách. Đặt bìa trước và sau sang một bên.

3. Lấy thêm hai tờ giấy trắng thủ công. Lặp lại bước 1.

4. Dùng ngón tay ấn nhẹ dọc theo các mép của nếp gấp để nếp gấp sắc nét và gọn gàng. Mỗi mảnh giấy sẽ giống như một chiếc đàn accordion.

5. Để làm một cuốn sách dài, hãy dán các mép của hai tờ giấy lại với nhau bằng cách chồng hai mép ngắn của hai tờ lên nhau và dán lại.

6. Để gắn bìa trước và bìa sau, hãy dán bìa trước, đã thực hiện ở bước 2, vào nếp gấp đầu tiên của cuốn sách accordion. Dán bìa sau vào nếp gấp cuối cùng của cuốn sách. **Cả hai bìa phải được dán trên cùng một mặt của cuốn sách khi bạn đặt mọi thứ bằng phẳng.**

7. Kiểm tra xem sách có gấp đúng cách và có thể đóng mở dễ dàng như đàn accordion hay không.

8. Mở sách và kẻ một lề rộng ở hai bên, để trống phần giữa để viết. Các đường viền có thể được trang trí bằng băng washi, bút màu bằng sáp, tranh ảnh, hoặc giấy có họa tiết hoặc hoa văn.

9. Tiếp theo, tô điểm hai tấm bìa. Bạn muốn trang trí cuốn sách của mình như thế nào là hoàn toàn tùy ý bạn.

10. Mỗi nếp gấp của cuốn sách có thể được sử dụng để viết một bài thơ, bài hát, hoặc suy nghĩ của bạn! Bạn cũng có thể sử dụng cuốn sách này cho các mục đích khác. Hãy để trí tưởng tượng của bạn bay bổng.

# CAMBODIA

Cambodia, formally known as Khmer, is an ancient civilization that flourished in the Mekong Delta region between the 9th and the 13th centuries. The Khmer empire was a powerful state in Southeast Asia. It covered much of today's Cambodia, Thailand, Laos, and southern Vietnam at its peak.

The Mekong River is called Mékôngk or *Tonle Thom*, which means the Great River. As the center of the Khmer empire, it was the life force of trade and agriculture. Excavations of ancient sites revealed functional *Kreung Smaun*— pottery that reflected the people's daily lives, giving us a glimpse into their culture, religion, economy, architecture, and social structure.

*Angkor Wat,
Siem Reap, Cambodia*

Khmer's arts were nearly wiped out during the genocidal years of the Khmer Rouge, a radical communist movement that ruled Cambodia from 1975 to 1979. Led by Pol Pot, the communist forces claimed they wanted to create "Year Zero." They intended for the people to return to the "Golden Age" where people were agricultural workers and not city dwellers. Religions were banned; music and radios were prohibited; the use of money was abolished. All aspects of life were subject to regulation. People were not allowed to choose their marriage partners or even select their clothes. Under Pol Pot's leadership, millions of educators, artists, musicians, and dancers were killed. Their civilization was nearly wiped out in this destruction of their art, education systems, and values. On December 25, 1978, Communist Vietnamese overran the Khmer Rouge and ended Pol Pot's regime.

Before his regime, there were 380,000 artists, but only 300 artists survived at the end of this dark period. During the 1980s, a movement to revive Khmer's thousand-year-old cultural heritage emerged. The few remaining artists regrouped and reestablished the University of Fine Arts. Among them are three surviving master potters working against the clock to pass on this tradition to the new generation.

The uniqueness of Khmer Krueng Smaun is in its simplicity of designs. Unlike other Southeast Asian ceramics, Khmer potteries reflect an indigenous culture free of influences from other Asian and Middle Eastern cultures. Their shapes and decorations feature characteristics specific to Khmer pottery. Some vessels are molded into animal forms such as elephants, fish, horses, and frogs.

*"Cambodian pottery is elegant in its simple beauty."*

—Cynthia

# Kreung Smaun, Pottery

Cynthia Cao

## Project

Make a vessel inspired by Kreung Smaun with paper mache.

## Materials

Bowl to hold paper mache glue
Container to make the vessel (Example: glass jar,
yogurt cup, empty can, bowl, or paper cup)
Newspaper, scrap paper, or magazines
Paintbrush
Paper mache paste
Plastic wrap or bag
Tempera paint

**Optional materials**
Embellishments
Scissors

## STEPS

1. Cover your working surface with newspaper to protect it.

2. Prepare the paper mache paste (See instructions).

3. Tear newspaper in 1-2 inches strips in a variety of lengths. You can also cut the strips, but the edges of the torn paper will adhere better.

## HOW TO MAKE PAPER MACHE PASTE

**Ingredients**
Flour or white glue
Water

**No Heat**
Mix 1/2 cup white glue with 1/2 cup water. Stir until well combined. Adjust by adding 1 tablespoon of glue or water until the mixture thickens, similar to the consistency of heavy cream.

**In the Microwave**
Mix 1/2 cup flour and 1 cup water in a microwave-safe container. Heat for 30 seconds. Remove and stir to remove all lumps. Repeat 1-2 times until the mixture thickens, similar to the consistency of heavy cream. Set aside to cool before using.

**On the Stovetop**
Mix 1/2 cup of flour and 1 cup of water in a small bowl. Mix until there are no lumps. Transfer the mixture to a small pot and heat it on the stove over low heat. Continue to stir to remove all lumps until the mixture thickens, similar to the consistency of heavy cream. Set aside to cool before using.

4. Cover the glass jar with plastic wrap or bag. The plastic will make it easier to remove the paper mache after it has dried.

5. Dip one paper strip into the paper mache paste, and use two fingers to squeeze the excess paste back into the bowl.

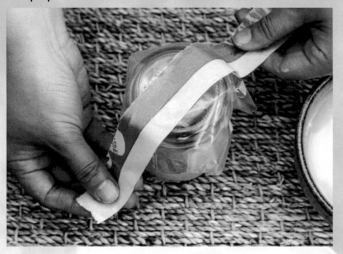

6. Lay the strip of paper over the bottom of the vessel and smooth it out with your fingers. Continue overlapping the strips of paper for the first layer until the object is completely covered. Let it dry for 24 hours.

7. Repeat the process three times, allowing each layer to dry completely, to get the desired shape of your vessel. You can also shape your piece to resemble an animal.

8. Once the paper mache layers are completely dry, gently remove the plastic.

9. Decorate and paint your object. Start by painting the vessel all white to help the remaining colors pop. Now it's ready for display!

**MORE IDEAS!**
Experiment with different containers for new shapes and add embellishments as desired.

# CAMPUCHIA (KHMER)

Campuchia, tên chính thức là Khmer, là một nền văn minh cổ đại phát triển mạnh ở khu vực đồng bằng Sông Cửu Long từ thế kỷ thứ IX đến thế kỷ thứ XIII. Đế chế Khmer là một quốc gia hùng mạnh ở Đông Nam Á, vào thời đỉnh cao đã bao phủ phần lớn Campuchia, Thái Lan, Lào và miền nam Việt Nam ngày nay.

Sông Mekong được gọi là *Mêkôngk* hay *Tonle Thom*, có nghĩa là Sông Lớn. Là trung tâm của đế chế Khmer, sông Mekong là động lực sống của thương mại và nông nghiệp. Các cuộc khai quật các địa điểm cổ đại cho thấy *Kreung Smaun*—đồ gốm phản ánh cuộc sống hàng ngày của người dân, cho chúng ta cái nhìn về văn hóa, tôn giáo, kinh tế, kiến trúc và cấu trúc xã hội của họ.

Nghệ thuật Khmer gần như bị xóa sổ trong những năm diệt chủng của thời Khmer Đỏ, một phong trào cộng sản cấp tiến cai trị Campuchia từ năm 1975 đến năm 1979. Dưới sự lãnh đạo của Pol Pot,

các lực lượng cộng sản tuyên bố muốn tạo ra "Year Zero". Họ muốn mọi người quay trở lại "Thời Kỳ Hoàng Kim", nơi mọi người là công nhân nông nghiệp chứ không phải cư dân thành phố. Các tôn giáo bị cấm; âm nhạc và radio bị cấm; việc sử dụng tiền bị bãi bỏ. Tất cả các khía cạnh

*"Gốm Campuchia thanh lịch trong vẻ đẹp đơn giản của nó."*
—Cynthia

của cuộc sống đều phải tuân theo quy định. Mọi người không được phép chọn đối tác kết hôn hoặc thậm chí chọn quần áo để mặc. Dưới sự lãnh đạo của Pol Pot, hàng triệu nhà giáo, nghệ sĩ, nhạc sĩ và vũ công đã bị giết chết. Nền văn minh của họ gần như bị xóa sổ trong sự phá hủy nghệ thuật, hệ thống giáo dục và giá trị sống. Ngày 25 tháng 12 năm 1978, Việt Nam đem quân vào Campuchia đánh bại Khmer Đỏ và chấm dứt chế độ Pol Pot. Trước chế độ Khmer Đỏ, nước này có

380.000 nghệ sĩ, nhưng chỉ có 300 nghệ sĩ còn sống sót vào cuối thời kỳ đen tối này. Trong những năm 1980, một phong trào phục hưng di sản văn hóa hàng nghìn năm tuổi của người Khmer đã nổi lên. Số ít họa sĩ còn sót lại đã tập hợp và tái lập trường Đại Học Mỹ thuật. Trong số đó có ba nghệ nhân đồ gốm còn sống sót, họ làm việc miệt mài để truyền lại di sản văn hoá này cho thế hệ mới.

Khmer *Krueng Smaun* độc đáo vì thiết kế rất đơn giản. Không giống như các đồ gốm sứ Đông Nam Á khác, gốm sứ Khmer phản ánh một nền văn hóa bản địa không bị ảnh hưởng bởi các nền văn hóa Châu Á và Trung Đông khác. Hình dạng và trang trí mang những đặc điểm đặc trưng cho gốm Khmer. Một số bình gốm được đúc thành các hình dạng động vật như voi, cá, ngựa, và cả ếch nữa.

## VÀI Ý TƯỞNG KHÁC!
Thử nghiệm với các thùng chứa khác nhau để có hình dạng mới và thêm các phần tô điểm theo ý muốn.

# Kreung Smaun, Đồ gốm
## Cynthia Cao

**Dự án**
Làm một chiếc bình lấy cảm hứng từ Kreung Smaun bằng giấy bồi.

**Nguyên vật liệu**
Bát để đựng keo dán giấy bồi
Vật chứa để làm bình

(Ví dụ: Hũ thủy tinh, ly sữa chua, lon rỗng, bát hoặc ly giấy)
Báo, giấy nháp hoặc tạp chí
Cọ sơn
Keo dán giấy bồi (Xem hướng dẫn)

Giấy hoặc túi nhựa (nylon)
Sơn tempera

**Vật liệu tùy chọn**
Vật liệu trang trí
Kéo cắt giấy

### HƯỚNG DẪN CÁCH LÀM KEO GIẤY BỒI

**Thành phần:**
Bột mì hay keo
Nước

hỗn hợp đặc lại, tương tự như độ đặc của kem đặc. Để nguội trước khi sử dụng.

tương tự như độ đặc của kem đặc. Để nguội trước khi sử dụng.

**Nếu làm trên bếp/nấu:**
Trộn 1/2 ly bột mì và 1 ly nước vào một cái bát nhỏ. Trộn cho đến khi không còn vón cục. Chuyển hỗn hợp vào một chiếc nồi nhỏ và bắc lên bếp đun với lửa nhỏ. Tiếp tục khuấy để loại bỏ hết vón cục cho đến khi

**Nếu làm trong lò vi sóng:**
Trộn 1/2 ly bột mì và 1 ly nước trong bát nhỏ đựng an toàn cho lò vi sóng. Đun nóng trong 30 giây. Lấy ra và khuấy đều để loại bỏ tất cả vón cục. Lặp lại 1-2 lần cho đến khi hỗn hợp đặc lại,

**Làm không cần nhiệt:**
Trộn 1/2 ly keo trắng với 1/2 ly nước. Khuấy cho đến khi hết vón cục. Điều chỉnh bằng cách thêm 1 thìa keo hoặc nước cho đến khi hỗn hợp đặc lại, tương tự như độ đặc của kem đặc.

### Hướng dẫn cách làm

1. Đặt giấy báo bao phủ bề mặt làm việc tránh để bàn bị bẩn.
2. Chuẩn bị keo dán giấy bồi (Xem hướng dẫn).
3. Xé giấy báo thành dải 1 inch - 2 inch với độ dài khác nhau. Cũng có thể cắt các dải giấy, nhưng các mép giấy bị rách sẽ bám dính tốt hơn.
4. Bao phủ lọ bạn đã chọn bằng giấy nhựa hoặc túi nhựa. Nhựa sẽ giúp bạn lấy giấy bồi ra dễ hơn sau khi khô.
5. Nhúng một dải giấy vào keo dán, dùng hai ngón tay miết phần keo thừa trở lại bát.
6. Đặt dải giấy lên đáy bình và dùng ngón tay vuốt phẳng. Tiếp tục chồng các dải giấy lên nhau cho đến khi vật thể được bao phủ hoàn toàn. Để khô ít nhất 24 tiếng.
7. Lặp lại quy trình ba lần, để mỗi lớp khô hoàn toàn, để có được hình dạng của chiếc bình. Bạn cũng có thể tạo hình giống một con vật.
8. Sau khi các lớp giấy bồi hoàn toàn khô, nhẹ nhàng lấy giấy nhựa ra.
9. Trang trí và sơn bình. Bắt đầu bằng cách sơn toàn bộ màu trắng, các màu khác sẽ nổi hơn. Bạn đã sẵn sàng để trưng bày!

# VIETNAM

The interconnectedness between the Vietnamese, Khmer, and Chinese cultures makes it difficult to determine where the technique of *Sơn Mài*, lacquer painting, originated.

In the 1620s, Khmer King Chey Chettha II allowed the Vietnamese to settle in Prey Nokor, an area known as Sài Gòn in the Mekong Delta. The Khmer empire eventually lost control of this area due to years of war with Thailand. By 1691, Mạc Cửu, a Chinese general, expanded Vietnamese and Chinese settlements deeper into Khmer lands. In 1698, *Nguyễn Hữu Cảnh*, a Vietnamese noble, was sent by the Nguyễn Lords of Huế to establish Vietnamese administrative structures in the area. This action formally detached the Mekong Delta from the Khmer empire.

During the Tây Sơn wars and the subsequent Nguyễn Dynasty, Vietnam's boundaries were pushed as far as the Cape of Cà Mau. In 1802, Nguyễn Ánh crowned himself the first emperor of the Nguyễn Dynasty and renamed himself, Gia Long. He unified all the territories comprising modern Vietnam, including the Mekong Delta, also known as *Sông Cửu Long* or River of Nine Dragons. The name embodies the majesty of the Mekong as the giant river empties into the South China Sea through a network of nine distributaries in South Vietnam.

Sơn Mài began over 4000 years ago in China and made its way to Vietnam between 930-950 AD during the Đinh Dynasty. Traditional sơn mài is used on furniture and household objects, whereas golden lacquer is found inside wealthy homes, churches,

*Temple of Literature, Hanoi, Vietnam*

communal houses, pagodas, and royal tombs and palaces. The most well-known technique is embossed lacquer, designed in eye-catching patterns of the four benevolent spirit animals—the dragon, phoenix, turtle, and lân (a unicorn lion). Vietnam has been seeking UNESCO's recognition of the traditional craft of Sơn Mài as part of the world's intangible cultural heritage since 2016.

Lacquer is a clear sap coming from any of six species of trees growing in Vietnam. Black lacquer

comes from stirring the lacquer with an iron rod for a few days. The chemical reaction between lacquer and iron produces black lacquer. Clear lacquer can also be mixed with various natural or artificial dyes to create the desired color. It should be noted that it is a skin irritant and can cause contact dermatitis and be potentially carcinogenic.

Making Sơn Mài paintings is a long and arduous process. It may take several months to complete, depending on the artist's specific technique and how many lacquer and cotton cloth layers are included. The process consists of numerous layers of painting and sanding until the desired thickness is achieved. The weather also plays a significant role in when these paintings can be made. High humidity or heat can cause the wood to crack or bend. When Sơn Mài paintings are done correctly, they last for generations.

*"Learning about Sơn Mài made me appreciate the richness of my heritage."*

—Cynthia

# Sơn Mài, Lacquer Painting

Cynthia Cao

## Project

Create a scratchboard painting inspired by Vietnamese Sơn Mài.

## Materials

Chopsticks
Construction paper - white or light color
Crayons
Liquid dish soap
Paintbrush
Pencil
Small bowl or plate
Sponge brush
Stylus
Tempera paint - black
Toothpicks

**Optional materials**
Eggshells
Glitter
Glue
Gold or copper paint
Oil Pastels
Seashells

## STEPS

1.  Cut construction paper in half to about 4x6 inches.

2.  With a pencil, sketch a simple design on the paper.

3.  Color in your design with crayons. Press hard, so the color adheres to the paper. It's okay to color in different directions to cover the entire sheet of paper. If the white paper is exposed, the paint we will apply later in step 5 will stick to the exposed areas and cause the paper to tear.

4. In a small bowl or plate, mix 2 tablespoons of black tempera paint with 1 tablespoon of dish soap  (2 to 1 ratio).

5. Use a paint or sponge brush to apply the black paint evenly on the colored paper to cover it completely. The paint will look shiny. Set it aside to dry for about 30 minutes to 1 hour.

6. Repeat step 5 until the paper is completely covered in black. Apply 2 to 3 coats of paint. Remember to wait for each layer to dry before applying the next layer. When the last layer of black paint has dried, you now have a scratchboard ready for carving.

7. Use a pencil, toothpick, or chopsticks to gently scratch off a new design on the black painted paper to reveal the color underneath.

**MORE IDEAS!**
- Color the paper using multiple color crayons for a more vibrant drawing.
- Mix different paint colors with the black paint to create a colorful painting.
- Experiment with different scratching tools around the house for other effects.

- Embellish your final drawing with gold paint and glitter.
- Try different designs. Sơn Mài paintings usually have intricate patterns.
- Embellish with textural materials by gluing glitter, sand, crushed eggshells, or small beads on top of the painting.

# VIỆT NAM

Nền văn hóa Việt Nam, Khmer và Trung Quốc tương tác với nhau rất nhiều nên rất khó xác định được nguồn gốc của kỹ thuật vẽ tranh *Sơn Mài*.

Vào những năm 1620, Vua Khmer Chey Chettha II cho phép người Việt Nam đến định cư ở Prey Nokor, khu vực bây giờ gọi là Sài Gòn ở Đồng Bằng Sông Cửu Long. Đế chế Khmer cuối cùng mất quyền kiểm soát khu vực này do nhiều năm chiến tranh với Thái Lan. Đến năm 1691, Mạc Cửu, một vị tướng Trung Quốc, mở rộng các khu định cư của người Việt và người Hoa vào sâu hơn vùng đất của người Khmer. Năm 1698, Nguyễn Hữu Cảnh, một quý tộc Việt Nam, được chúa Nguyễn ở Huế cử đến để thiết lập các cơ cấu hành chính của Việt Nam trong khu vực. Hành động này chính thức tách Đồng Bằng Sông Cửu Long khỏi đế chế Khmer.

Trong các cuộc chiến tranh Tây Sơn và triều Nguyễn sau

*"Học về sơn mài giúp tôi trân quý di sản phong phú của mình."*
—Cynthia

đó, ranh giới của Việt Nam được đẩy xa đến tận Mũi Cà Mau. Năm 1802, Nguyễn Ánh lên ngôi hoàng đế đầu tiên của triều Nguyễn và đổi tên là Gia Long. Ông thống nhất tất cả các lãnh thổ thành Việt Nam hiện đại, bao gồm Đồng Bằng Sông Mekong, còn được gọi là Sông Cửu Long hoặc Sông Chín Rồng. Cái tên thể hiện sự hùng vĩ của sông khổng lồ Mekong khi đổ ra Biển Đông qua một mạng lưới gồm chín phân lưu ở miền Nam Việt Nam.

Sơn Mài bắt đầu cách đây hơn 4000 năm trước ở Trung Quốc và đến Việt Nam khoảng năm 930-950 sau Công Nguyên dưới thời nhà Đinh. Sơn mài truyền thống được sử dụng làm đồ nội thất và đồ gia dụng, trong khi sơn mài vàng được sử dụng trong các ngôi nhà giàu có, nhà thờ, đình, chùa, lăng mộ và cung điện. Kỹ thuật nổi tiếng nhất là sơn mài chạm nổi, được thiết kế theo hoa văn của bốn con vật nhân từ - rồng, phượng, rùa và lân. Năm 2016, Việt Nam đệ đơn yêu cầu UNESCO công nhận

truyền thống Sơn Mài là một phần của di sản văn hóa thế giới.

Sơn ta là một loại nhựa cây trong, đến từ một trong số sáu loài cây mọc ở Việt Nam. Khi quấy sơn ta bằng que sắt vài ngày, phản ứng hóa học giữa sơn ta và sắt tạo ra sơn mài đen. Sơn mài trong cũng có thể được trộn với các loại hàng nhuộm tự nhiên hoặc nhân tạo để tạo ra màu sắc. Cần lưu ý đây là một chất kích ứng da, có thể gây viêm da, và có khả năng gây ung thư.

Làm tranh Sơn Mài là một công việc lâu dài và khó nhọc, có thể cần vài tháng để hoàn thành, tùy theo kỹ thuật của nghệ nhân và bao nhiêu lớp sơn mài và vải bông được dùng. Công việc dùng nhiều lớp sơn và chà nhám cho đến khi đạt được độ dày mà nghệ sĩ muốn. Cũng cần phải để ý đến thời tiết trong công việc này. Độ ẩm cao hoặc nhiệt độ cao có thể làm cho gỗ bị nứt hoặc cong. Những bức tranh Sơn Mài thực hiện một cách kỹ lưỡng có thể tồn tại qua nhiều thế hệ.

# Sơn Mài
Cynthia Cao

## Dự án

Tạo một bức tranh vẽ bằng giấy khắc lấy cảm hứng từ Sơn Mài Việt Nam.

## Nguyên vật liệu

Đũa

Giấy thủ công - màu trắng hoặc màu nhạt

Bút sáp màu

Xà phòng rửa bát dạng lỏng

Cọ sơn

Bút chì

Bát hoặc đĩa nhỏ

Cọ xốp

Bút stylus bằng gỗ

Sơn Tempera - đen

Tăm

## Vật liệu tùy chọn

Vỏ trứng

Kim tuyến

Keo dán

Sơn vàng hoặc đồng

Bút màu bằng dầu

Vỏ sò

## Hướng dẫn cách làm

1. Cắt giấy thủ công làm đôi, mỗi tờ khoảng 4x6 inch.
2. Dùng bút chì, phác thảo một hình ảnh đơn giản trên giấy.
3. Tô màu hình ảnh bằng bút sáp màu. Nhấn mạnh để màu bám vào giấy. Bạn có thể tô màu theo vài hướng khác nhau để phủ toàn bộ tờ giấy. Nếu phần giấy trắng bị lộ ra, lớp sơn mà chúng ta sẽ thoa sau đó ở bước 5 sẽ dính vào những chỗ bị hở và làm giấy dễ bị rách.
4. Trong một bát hoặc đĩa nhỏ, trộn 2 thìa sơn tempera đen với 1 thìa xà phòng rửa bát (tỷ lệ 2:1).
5. Dùng cọ quét sơn hoặc cọ xốp quét đều sơn đen lên giấy màu để phủ hoàn toàn. Lớp sơn trông sẽ sáng bóng. Đặt sang một bên để khô khoảng 30 phút đến 1 giờ.
6. Lặp lại bước 5 cho đến khi giấy được bao phủ hoàn toàn bằng màu đen. Sơn 2 đến 3 lớp. Nhớ đợi từng lớp khô trước khi thoa lớp tiếp theo. Khi lớp sơn đen cuối cùng khô, bạn có một tấm bìa cứng sẵn sàng để khắc.
7. Dùng bút chì, tăm xỉa răng hoặc đũa, cào nhẹ theo hình ảnh trên giấy sơn đen, để lộ màu bên dưới.

## VÀI Ý TƯỞNG KHÁC!

- Tô giấy dùng nhiều bút màu bằng sáp khác nhau để có một bức tranh sống động hơn.
- Trộn các màu sơn khác nhau với sơn đen để tạo ra một bức tranh đầy màu sắc.
- Thử nghiệm với các dụng cụ cào khác trong nhà để có các hiệu ứng khác.
- Tô điểm bản vẽ cuối cùng bằng sơn vàng lấp lánh.
- Hãy thử vài hình ảnh khác nhau. Tranh sơn mài thường có hoa văn tinh xảo.
- Tô điểm bằng cách dán kim tuyến, cát, vỏ trứng nghiền hoặc các hạt nhỏ lên bức tranh.

# MALAYSIA

As the Mekong River empties into the South China Sea, we find ourselves in Malaysia situated north of the equator and composed of two noncontiguous regions, East and West. At the same time, its northern border is connected to Thailand.

Malaysia's culture is made up of indigenous tribes as well as Chinese, Indian, Persian, Arabic, and British migrants. Though they each maintain their distinctive cultural identities, a few crossovers have created artistic and cultural expressions unique to Malaysia. Malaysian society has been described as "Asia in miniature." An import from China is the kite, where the art of kite making originated. In Malaysia, they are called *Wau Bulan* or Moon Kites. Though it is a dying art, there are a few Malaysian master craftsmen left. The name Wau Bulan came from its shape: the lower body resembles that of a crescent moon. Traditionally, leaves from the Buri palm tree are attached to the kite as embellishments. When the kite begins to take flight, the leaves' rustling makes a rhythmic sound "wau... wau...wau," hence Wau Bulan's name.

Malay wood carvings may have inspired the designs of early kites. Cut out by hand, each layer creates colorful patterns depicting nature scenes. The colorful design is a sight to be seen! Thin strips of bamboo, soaked in mud for nearly two weeks to increase flexibility, make a lightweight frame for the kite's structure. In the center of most of these kites is a prominent flowery symbol. If it's not there, the kite may not be considered "traditional" because leaves and flowers are called the *Ibu* or Mother of all Life.

The average Wau Bulan is large compared to other kites. Its average size is about 2.5 meters in width and 3.5 meters in length. Wau Bulan are icons of celebration and are sometimes flown following a successful harvest. During the day, the kites are also flown over rice fields during planting season to frighten off birds, and at night, they raise the Spirit of the Rice Paddy to help ensure a bountiful season.

*Menara Kuala Lumpur
Kuala Lumpur, Malaysia*

*"Making Wau brought back good memories from my childhood."*

—Amanda

# Wau Bulan, Moon Kite
Amanda Pascual

**Project**
Create a paper Wau Bulan to decorate your home or porch.

**Materials**
Construction paper - white
Crayons
Glue
Scissors
Thread
Toothpick

## STEPS

1.  Cut the paper in half lengthwise.

2.  Fold one of the cut halves of paper half lengthwise and draw the Wau Bulan shape on it.

3.  Cut the Wau Bulan shape on the open edge of the folded paper. Open the kite and set it aside.

4.  To make the tail, cut four long thin strips from leftover paper.

5. Glue ends of the strips together to make a long tail, then glue the strands to the bottom center of the Wau.

6. Decorate your Wau Bulan with different colors and embellishments.

7. **How to tie a string on your kite:**

a. Fold the Wau in half and make a hole using a toothpick where the nose and large wings meet. Make the holes larger by gently wiggling the toothpick through the holes in circular motions.

b. Cut 2 strands of thread, each measuring about 6 inches long. (Strands A and B)

c. Cut 1 strand of thread measuring about 12 inches or longer. (Strand C)

d. Tie strand A to hole #1.

e. Tie strand B to hole #2.

f. Connect the ends of strand A and B together by tying a loose knot (#3).

g. Attach strand C to the knot #3 to connect all 3 threads.
   Your Wau Bulan is ready for display!

**MORE IDEAS!**

- To stiffen the kite, tape a chopstick or stylus to the back at the center of the kite.
- Decorate using the Batik process as described in the lesson on Indonesia. Batik is also common in Malaysia.
- Make a giant kite with larger paper.
- Add embellishments or different strings.
- Make tassels to decorate the tips of the wings using strips of paper or excess thread.

# MALAYSIA

Khi Sông Mekong đổ ra Biển Đông, chúng ta thấy Malaysia nằm ở phía bắc đường xích đạo và bao gồm hai khu vực không tiếp giáp, Đông và Tây. Đồng thời, biên giới phía bắc kết nối với Thái Lan.

Văn hóa của Malaysia được tạo thành từ các bộ lạc bản địa cũng như những người di cư từ Trung Quốc, Ấn Độ, Ba Tư, Ả Rập và Anh Quốc. Mặc dù mỗi nhóm đều duy trì bản sắc văn hóa đặc trưng, một vài sự giao thoa đã tạo nên những nét nghệ thuật và văn hóa độc đáo cho Malaysia. Xã hội Malaysia được ví như "Châu Á thu nhỏ."

Nghệ thuật làm cánh diều khởi nguồn từ Trung Quốc, rồi được nhập vào Malaysia. Dân Malaysia gọi là *Wau Bulan* hoặc Diều Trăng. Ngày nay nghệ thuật làm diều không còn phổ biến, nhưng ở Malaysia vẫn còn một số nghệ nhân. Cái tên Wau Bulan xuất phát từ hình dạng của diều bay: phần thân dưới giống như mặt trăng lưỡi liềm. Theo truyền thống, những chiếc lá từ cây cọ Buri được gắn vào cánh diều để trang trí. Khi cánh diều cất cánh, tiếng xào xạc của lá tạo ra âm thanh nhịp nhàng "wau...wau...wau," do đó có tên Wau Bulan.

Các tác phẩm chạm khắc bằng gỗ của người Mã Lai có thể đã truyền cảm hứng cho các thiết kế ban đầu của diều Wau Bulan. Cắt bằng tay, mỗi lớp tạo nên những hoa văn sặc sỡ miêu tả cảnh thiên nhiên. Thiết kế đầy màu sắc, một cảnh tượng đáng chiêm ngưỡng! Những thanh tre mỏng được ngâm trong bùn gần hai tuần để tăng độ mềm dẻo, làm khung nhẹ cho kết cấu của diều bay. Ở trung tâm của diều bay có một biểu tượng hoa nổi bật. Nếu không có hoa, con diều không được coi là "truyền thống" vì lá và hoa được gọi là Ibu hoặc Mẹ Của Mọi Sự Sống.

Wau Bulan trung bình lớn hơn các loại diều khác. Kích thước trung bình là khoảng 2,5 mét chiều rộng và 3,5 mét chiều dài. Wau Bulan là biểu tượng của ngày lễ, đôi khi dân làng thả Wau Bulan để ăn mừng khi được mùa. Ban ngày thả diều trên ruộng lúa trong mùa gieo cấy để xua đuổi chim chóc, ban đêm thả diều cho Thần Lúa để được một mùa bội thu.

*"Làm Wau làm tôi nhớ lại bao nhiêu kỷ niệm đẹp từ thời thơ ấu."*

—Amanda

# Wau Bulan, Diều Trăng

Amanda Pascual

**Dự án**

Tạo một Wau Bulan bằng giấy để trang trí nhà hoặc hiên nhà của bạn.

**Nguyên vật liệu**

Giấy thủ công - trắng

Bút sáp màu

Keo dán

Kéo

Chỉ

Tăm

**Hướng dẫn cách làm**

1. Cắt giấy làm đôi theo chiều dọc.
2. Gấp một nửa giấy đã cắt theo chiều dọc và vẽ hình Wau Bulan trên đó.
3. Cắt hình Wau Bulan trên mép mở của giấy đã gấp. Mở diều bay và đặt sang một bên.
4. Để làm đuôi, hãy cắt bốn dải hẹp từ giấy thừa.
5. Dán các đầu của các dải với nhau để tạo thành đuôi dài, sau đó dán các sợi vào tâm dưới của Wau.
6. Trang trí Wau Bulan với nhiều màu sắc và đồ trang trí.
7. **Cách thắt dây trên diều bay:**

a. Gấp đôi Wau Bulan và tạo một lỗ bằng tăm xỉa răng, nơi mũi và cánh lớn gặp nhau. Làm cho các lỗ lớn hơn bằng cách quay que tăm xỉa răng qua các lỗ theo chuyển động tròn.

b. Cắt 2 sợi chỉ, mỗi sợi dài khoảng 6 inch. (Sợi A và B)

c. Cắt 1 sợi chỉ dài khoảng 12 inch hoặc dài hơn. (Sợi C)

d. Buộc sợi A vào lỗ số 1.

e. Buộc sợi B vào lỗ số 2.

f. Nối các đầu của sợi A và B với nhau bằng cách buộc một nút lỏng (# 3).

g. Gắn sợi C vào nút số 3 để kết nối cả 3 sợi. Wau Bulan của bạn đã sẵn sàng đem ra để trưng bày!

**VÀI Ý TƯỞNG KHÁC!**

- Để làm cứng cánh diều, hãy dán một chiếc đũa hoặc bút stylus vào mặt sau, chính giữa cánh diều.
- Trang trí dùng quy trình Batik như được mô tả trong bài học về Indonesia. Batik cũng phổ biến ở Malaysia.
- Làm một con diều khổng lồ bằng giấy lớn hơn.
- Thêm phần tô điểm hoặc thêm giây khác.
- Trang trí các đầu cánh bằng tua, làm bằng các dải giấy và sợi chỉ còn thừa.

# PHILIPPINES

Before the Spanish colonization of the Philippine Islands, its different nations, tribes, and islands were ruled by kings and sultans. Each province had its own identity. Ferdinand Magellan claimed the islands, and between 1521–1898 the islands fell under the rule of the Spanish Empire. In 1898, the United States took the Philippines as its territory, and during World War II (1942–1945), Imperial Japan occupied the islands. Finally, on July 4, 1946, complete independence was granted to the Republic of the Philippines by the U.S. Though the Filipino identity was created primarily due to hundreds of years of colonization, its indigenous culture is still embedded within the Filipino tradition.

One example of rooted native culture is practiced by the mountain people of Ifugao who live in Northern Luzon, a part of the Cordillera region. Rice is at the center of the Ifugao culture. Their rice terraces are designated as a UNESCO World Heritage Site for their living cultural landscape of unparalleled beauty. Before colonization, the Ifugaos were one of the most sophisticated and

*Chocolate Hills*
*Bohol Province, Philippines*

prosperous highlands. The people existed for over 2,000 years, ruled by elders with the belief of leading with peace. Because

of this philosophy, this area fostered the best agricultural technology in Asia at that time. Due to their geographical location combined with their determination, the Ifugaos have resisted assimilation and preserved their ancient wisdom and traditions.

In Central Cordillera, the people hold different rice ceremonies for their spiritual well-being. Artistic creations also play an essential part in their everyday lives. Carving ancestral and religious figurines is a common practice. Carving is primarily practiced by men, but the highly revered *Bulul* is inherited by the first child of the family, regardless of the child's gender. Bulul statues are carved from a single piece of wood depicting a male figure in a standing or sitting position. They embody the spirits of the family's ancestors, and their primary purpose is to protect, increase rice harvests, and provide healing. Priests also bless the statues with care and respect to ward off any evil spirits from the Bulul.

These indigenous ideologies have been copied and diluted by assimilation and mass production for tacky souvenir shops as decorations. They have lost their ritual meaning and cultural significance and demonstrate yet another form of cultural degradation. However, the Bulul is still used today in rice rituals and is recognized as a cultural property of the Ifugao people. It is a physical manifestation of indigenous knowledge that should be preserved and respected.

*"I admire the Ifugaos' stubborness and strength."*

—Amanda

# Bulul, Male Rice Deity Statue
Amanda Pascual

**Project**
Carve and sculpt a Bulul out of clay.

**Materials needed**
Pencil
Polymer clay
Small knife
Toothpicks

**Optional materials**
Foil
Oven

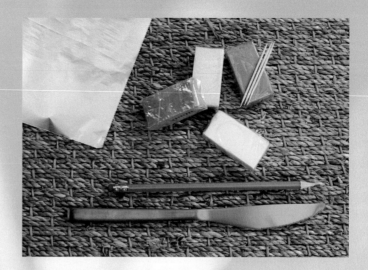

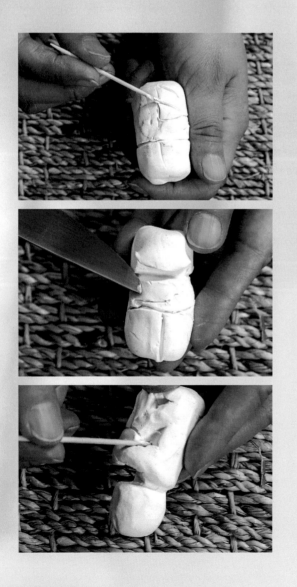

## STEPS

1. Choose a seating or standing position for your Bulul. Knead your clay to soften it into a rounded column around 2.5 inches tall.

2. Use a toothpick to draw an outline of the entire figure, starting from the head by marking a line around 1/3 of the clay. Then mark out the neck, arms, and legs. Don't worry about the size of the head, as you can always modify the shape later.

3. Cut or carve out a flat face with your knife or toothpick by removing less than half of the head shape. Round out the edges with your fingers. Dig out excess clay from the open areas between limbs.

4. Smooth out the edges and adjust the form to your liking. You can pinch off the clay with your fingertips or toothpick from the base or areas with too much clay and add it to areas that need more clay.

5. Place the sculpture on the table to check if it is balanced and stand or sit independently.

6. Flatten the base by gently pushing the figure onto the table to flatten the bottom. Use your fingers to smooth out any cracks or uneven areas gently.

7. Once satisfied with the body, pinch the center of the face to make a nose and poke two holes to create eyes. Smooth out the rest of the head.
**NOTE: The clay will not solidify until you bake it!**

8. Your Bulul is ready to be displayed as is or you can continue to the next step to solidify the clay.

9. **Baking Instructions:**
a. Place the Bulul on a piece of foil to protect it from burning. Place the second piece of foil to cover it loosely.
b. Set your oven at 275 degrees Fahrenheit (130 Celsius). Bake it for 15 minutes for every 1/4 inch. If you have a thick Bulul, bake for at least 30 minutes.

10. Place the Bulul near your rice dispenser, rice cooker, or in an auspicious space so he can help protect your rice and family.

**MORE IDEAS!**
- Use playdough for kids.
- Use more clay for a larger Bulul.
- Once baked, you can sand and paint your Bulul.

# PHILIPPINES

Trước khi Tây Ban Nha đô hộ Quần đảo Philippines, các quốc gia, bộ lạc và đảo được cai trị bởi các vị vua. Mỗi tỉnh có một bản sắc riêng biệt. Ông Ferdinand Magellan tuyên bố chủ quyền các đảo, và trong khoảng thời gian từ năm 1521–1898, các quần đảo nằm dưới sự cai trị của Đế chế Tây Ban Nha. Năm 1898, Hoa Kỳ lấy Philippines làm lãnh thổ, và trong thời kỳ Chiến tranh thế giới thứ hai (1942–1945), Đế quốc Nhật Bản chiếm đóng quần đảo này. Cuối cùng, ngày 4 tháng 7 năm 1946, Hoa Kỳ trao độc lập hoàn toàn cho Cộng Hòa Philippines. Mặc dù bản sắc của người Philippines là kết quả của hàng trăm năm thuộc địa, nhưng văn hóa bản địa vẫn gắn liền với truyền thống của họ.

Một ví dụ về văn hóa bản địa gốc đã được thực hiện bởi những người miền núi Ifugao sống ở Bắc Luzon, một phần của vùng Cordillera. Lúa gạo là trọng tâm của nền văn hóa Ifugao. Những cánh ruộng bậc thang được UNESCO công nhận là di sản thế giới vì cảnh quan văn hóa sống có vẻ đẹp vô song. Trước khi bị thuộc địa hóa, người Ifugao là một trong những dân vùng cao nguyên tinh vi và thịnh vượng nhất. Dân tộc họ tồn tại hơn 2.000 năm và được cai trị bởi những người lớn tuổi có niềm tin vào lãnh đạo trong hòa bình. Chính vì triết lý này, khu vực này có một nền công nghệ nông nghiệp bậc nhất Châu Á lúc bấy giờ. Do vị trí địa lý kết hợp với trí quyết tâm, người Ifugao đã chống lại sự đồng hóa và đã gìn giữ bảo tồn sự khôn ngoan và truyền thống cổ xưa.

*"Tôi ngưỡng mộ sức mạnh kiên trì của người dân Ifugaos."*
—Amanda

Ở Trung Tâm Cordillera, người dân tổ chức các nghi lễ cúng gạo, cầu mong được sức khỏe tâm linh. Sáng tạo nghệ thuật cũng đóng một phần thiết yếu trong cuộc sống hàng ngày của họ. Khắc tượng tổ tiên và tôn giáo là một việc làm phổ biến. Nghề chạm khắc chủ yếu được thực hiện bởi nam giới, nhưng tượng *Bulul* rất được tôn kính, và được truyền cho người con đầu trong gia đình, bất kể giới tính của đứa trẻ. Tượng Bulul được tạc từ một mảnh gỗ khắc họa hình tượng nam giới trong tư thế đứng hoặc ngồi. Họ là hiện thân của các linh hồn của tổ tiên trong gia đình, và mục đích chính của họ là bảo vệ, tăng thu hoạch thóc lúa và chữa bệnh. Các linh mục cũng tôn trọng và ban phước cho các bức tượng để xua đuổi mọi linh hồn xấu ra khỏi tượng Bulul.

Những ý thức hệ bản địa này đã bị sao chép và pha loãng bởi quá trình đồng hóa và sản xuất Bulul hàng loạt cho các cửa hàng lưu niệm làm vật trang trí. Chúng đã mất đi ý nghĩa nghi lễ và ý nghĩa văn hóa và vì đó thể hiện một hình thức suy thoái văn hóa. Tuy nhiên, Bulul ngày nay vẫn được sử dụng trong các nghi lễ cúng gạo và được công nhận là tài sản văn hóa của người Ifugao. Đó là một biểu hiện vật chất của tri thức bản địa cần được bảo tồn và tôn trọng.

# Bulul, Tượng thần lúa nam giới

Amanda Pascual

**Dự án**

Khắc và điêu khắc một bức tượng Bulul từ đất sét.

**Nguyên vật liệu**

Bút chì

Đất sét polymer

Dao nhỏ

Tăm

**Không bắt buộc:**

Giấy bạc

Lò nướng

**Hướng dẫn cách làm**

1. Chọn vị trí ngồi hoặc đứng cho bức tượng Bulul.

2. Dùng tăm để vẽ đường viền của toàn bộ hình, bắt đầu từ đầu tượng bằng cách đánh dấu một đường xung quanh 1/3 miếng đất sét. Sau đó đánh dấu cổ, tay và chân. Đừng quá lo về kích thước của đầu, bạn luôn có thể sửa đổi hình dạng sau này.

3. Dùng dao hoặc tăm, cắt hoặc khắc bộ mặt tượng cho phẳng, loại bỏ ít hơn một nửa hình dạng cái đầu. Dùng ngón tay để làm mịn các cạnh.

4. Làm mịn các cạnh và điều chỉnh hình tượng theo ý muốn. Hãy dùng đầu ngón tay hoặc tăm xén bớt đất sét ra khỏi nền hoặc những chỗ nào có quá nhiều đất, rồi thêm vào những chỗ cần nhiều đất sét hơn.

5. Đặt tác phẩm điêu khắc trên bàn để kiểm tra xem có cân bằng và đứng hoặc ngồi vững chắc.

6. Ấn nhẹ bức tượng xuống bàn để làm phẳng phần đế. Sử dụng ngón tay để nhẹ nhàng làm phẳng các vết nứt hoặc các chỗ không bằng phẳng.

7. Khi đã ưng ý với bức tượng, bạn hãy véo giữa khuôn mặt để làm mũi và chọc hai lỗ để tạo mắt. Làm mịn phần còn lại trên đầu. **LƯU Ý: Đất sét sẽ không cứng cho đến khi nướng!**

8. Bulul của bạn đã sẵn sàng để hiển thị hoặc bạn có thể tiếp tục bước tiếp theo để làm rắn chắc đất sét.

9. **Hướng dẫn nung đất sét:**

a. Đặt Bulul trên một miếng giấy bạc để khỏi bị cháy. Đặt miếng giấy bạc thứ hai lên Bulul để che hờ.

b. Đặt lò nung ở nhiệt độ 275 độ F (130 độ C). Nung 15 phút cho mỗi 1/4 inch. Nếu bạn có một Bulul dày, hãy nung ít nhất 30 phút.

10. Đặt Bulul gần bao gạo, nồi cơm điện, hoặc ở một chỗ tốt để giúp bảo vệ gạo của gia đình.

**VÀI Ý TƯỞNG KHÁC!**

- Sử dụng bột nặn của trẻ em.
- Sử dụng nhiều đất sét hơn để làm một bức tượng lớn hơn.
- Sau khi nung xong, bạn có thể chà nhám và sơn bức tượng.

# INDONESIA

Indonesia is a country in Southeast Asia and Oceania between the Indian and Pacific oceans with over 17,000 islands. Influences from the Middle East, Far East, and South Asia arrived in Indonesia to create a complex cultural mix that varies vastly from its original indigenous cultures. Despite these influences, there are still remote Indonesian regions that have preserved their unique traditions. The Mentawai, Asmat, Dani, Dayak, and Toraja are a few of these groups. They continue to wear traditional clothing using the same artisanal methods.

Making *Batik* fabric originated from the island of Java and is a symbol of Indonesian culture. Batik is derived from the Javanese *amba*, meaning to write, and the Javanese word for dot or point is *titik*. It is a particular artisanal method employed by dripping beads of hot wax onto cotton or silk fabric to block off designs before dyeing them. The material is hand-dyed with vegetables

*Ulu Danu Beratan Temple Bali, Indonesia*

and natural dyes by soaking the cloth in one color then removing the wax with boiling water. This process is repeated several times until multiple colors are achieved. Batik fabric can take as long as six months to make, and they are highly prized items. These techniques can also be used on different mediums such as paper, wood, leather, and ceramic.

The diversity in Indonesian textile is an excellent representation of its rich cultural heritage. Some motifs were restricted to the royal families' use while other

complex symbols such as palm leaves and local fruits depicted the simple daily lives of the Javanese people.

The culture of Batik making goes well beyond the handdyes and wax design techniques. They are handed down from generation to generation and form the cultural identity of the Indonesian people, and are a UNESCO-recognized art tradition.

*"This project brought back memories of my mother's beautiful Batik artwork!"*

—Dr. Smita

# Batik on Paper

Dr. Smita Garg

## Project

To create a Batik-inspired artwork using paper and crayons.

## Materials

Construction paper - white
Construction paper - black
Crayons
Foam brush and paintbrush

| | |
|---|---|
| Glue | Scissors |
| Iron and ironing board | Small plate or lid to |
| Newspaper | trace a circle (6-7 inches) |
| Paper towel | Tempera paint - black |
| Pencil | Water |

## STEPS

1. Take white construction paper, place the lid or round paper plate on it, and draw a circle around it with a pencil.

2. Draw inside the circle. Draw anything you like, such as a flower, geometric patterns, or scenery. Leave out small details from the drawing. Instead, draw wide spaces so you can color them in later.

3. Outline all parts of the drawing with black or dark-colored crayon. Color in the spaces with a combination of light and bright colored crayons. The more colorful, the better!

4. Crumple the paper into a ball. Don't worry, this is the fun part!

5. Uncrumple the ball and straighten the paper, laying it flat on a couple of sheets of newspaper or paper towel.

6. Take black paint, dip your foam brush or paintbrush in a bit of water, and dab a thin layer of black paint gently over the entire drawing. You can also use a paper towel instead of a brush. The black color will stick over the crumpled and cracked parts giving it the Batik effect. DO NOT let the paper dry out!

7. **Iron your painting to melt the wax and straighten out the paper:**
a. Turn your iron ON to the MEDIUM setting.
b. Cover your work surface with a paper towel or newspaper.
c. Place your drawing on top of a paper towel or newspaper.
d. Place a couple more sheets of newspaper on top of your drawing for padding to protect it.
e. With the hot iron, go over the top of the newspaper padding only. Avoid directly ironing over your painting. The heat will straighten out your artwork, and the black paint will stay in the crumpled creases.
f. If the color has dulled due to ironing, go over the areas with colored crayons again and retrace the outline with the black crayon as needed.
g. Cut out your artwork and glue it on a sheet of black construction paper to create a background. You can cut the black piece to make a square or rectangle. You now have a Batik artwork ready to be framed!

**MORE IDEAS!**
- Create different shapes and sizes of your drawing.
- Make a bookmark, greeting cards, or even larger-sized projects.
- Try out this technique on a piece of fabric.

59

# INDONESIA

Indonesia là một quốc gia ở Đông Nam Á và Châu Đại Dương nằm giữa Ấn Độ Dương và Thái Bình Dương, với hơn 17.000 hòn đảo lớn nhỏ. Ảnh hưởng từ Trung Đông, Viễn Đông và Nam Á đến Indonesia đã tạo ra một hỗn hợp văn hóa phức tạp khác với các nền văn hóa bản địa ban đầu rất nhiều. Tuy nhiên, vẫn có những vùng xa xôi của Indonesia vẫn bảo tồn được những truyền thống độc đáo. Mentawai, Asmat, Dani, Dayak và Toraja là một vài đảo trong nhóm này. Họ tiếp tục mặc trang phục truyền thống được dệt bằng phương pháp thủ công xưa. Làm vải *Batik* có nguồn gốc từ đảo Java và là biểu tượng của văn hóa Indonesia. Batik có nguồn gốc từ ngữ Java

*amba* có nghĩa là viết, và từ tiếng Java *titik* nghĩa là dấu chấm hoặc điểm. Đây là một phương pháp thủ công đặc biệt làm bằng cách nhỏ các hạt sáp nóng lên vải cotton hoặc lụa thành hình ảnh trước khi mang đi nhuộm. Vải được nhuộm bằng tay với nguyên liệu rau củ và hàng nhuộm tự nhiên bằng cách ngâm vải vào một màu, rồi lấy sáp ra bằng nước sôi. Việc này được lặp lại nhiều lần cho đến khi đạt được nhiều màu. Làm vải Batik có thể mất đến sáu tháng, và Batik là mặt hàng có giá trị cao.

Kỹ thuật này cũng có thể được sử dụng trên các nguyên liệu khác như giấy, gỗ, da và gốm.

Sự đa dạng trong ngành dệt may biểu hiện di sản văn hóa phong phú của Indonesia một cách xuất sắc. Một số họa tiết được hạn chế dành cho gia đình hoàng gia sử dụng, trong khi các biểu tượng khác ít phức tạp hơn như lá cọ và trái cây địa phương mô tả cuộc sống hàng ngày đơn giản của người dân Java.

Văn hóa làm Batik không chỉ bao gồm các loại thuốc nhuộm thủ công và kỹ thuật thiết kế bằng sáp. Các kỹ thuật được lưu truyền từ thế hệ này sang thế hệ khác, tạo thành bản sắc văn hóa của người dân Indonesia, cũng là một truyền thống nghệ thuật đã được UNESCO công nhận.

*"Dự án này làm tôi nhớ đến những tác phẩm nghệ thuật Batik tuyệt đẹp của mẹ tôi!"*

—Ts. Smita

## VÀI Ý TƯỞNG KHÁC!

- Tạo các hình dạng và kích thước khác nhau.
- Làm dấu trang sách, thiệp chúc mừng hoặc tác phẩm lớn hơn.
- Hãy thử kỹ thuật này trên một mảnh vải.

# Batik trên giấy

Ts. Smita Garg

### Dự án
Tạo ra một tác phẩm nghệ thuật lấy cảm hứng từ Batik, sử dụng giấy và bút sáp màu.

### Nguyên vật liệu
Giấy thủ công - trắng
Giấy thủ công - đen
Bút sáp màu
Cọ xốp và cọ sơn
Keo dán
Bàn ủi và bàn để ủi
Giấy báo
Khăn giấy
Bút chì
Kéo
Đĩa hoặc nắp nhỏ để vạch đường tròn (6-7 inch)
Sơn tempera - đen
Nước

### Hướng dẫn cách làm

1. Lấy giấy thủ công màu trắng, đặt nắp hoặc đĩa tròn lên và dùng bút chì vẽ một vòng tròn xung quanh.

2. Bên trong hình tròn, vẽ bất cứ điều gì bạn thích, chẳng hạn như một bông hoa, các hoạ tiết hình học hoặc phong cảnh. Không cần vẽ chi tiết nhỏ, mà nên để những khoảng rộng để tô màu.

3. Tô viền lên nét vẽ bằng bút sáp màu đen hoặc màu tối. Tô hình vẽ bằng bút sáp màu sáng và đậm.

4. Vò tờ giấy thành một quả bóng. Đừng ngại, đây là phần thú vị!

5. Mở rộng quả bóng và làm phẳng tờ giấy, đặt lên một vài tờ báo hoặc khăn giấy.

6. Lấy sơn đen, nhúng cọ xốp hoặc cọ vẽ vào một chút nước, và nhẹ nhàng chấm một lớp sơn đen mỏng lên toàn bộ bản vẽ. Bạn cũng có thể dùng khăn giấy thay cho cọ. Màu đen sẽ bám trên các phần nhàu nát và nứt nẻ, tạo hiệu ứng Batik. ĐỪNG để giấy bị khô!

7. **Dùng bàn ủi, ủi bức tranh của bạn để làm chảy sáp và làm phẳng giấy:**

a. Bật bàn ủi sang số MEDIUM.

b. Che bàn làm việc bằng khăn giấy hoặc báo.

c. Đặt bản vẽ lên trên khăn giấy hoặc báo.

d. Đặt thêm một vài tờ báo lên trên bản vẽ làm đệm bảo vệ.

e. Với bàn ủi nóng, ủi qua mặt trên của lớp giấy báo. Tránh ủi trực tiếp lên bức tranh. Sức nóng sẽ làm tác phẩm nghệ thuật thẳng ra, và lớp sơn đen sẽ lưu lại trong các nếp nhăn.

f. Nếu màu bị xỉn vì ủi, hãy vẽ lại những vùng đó với bút màu sáp và vẽ lại đường viền bằng bút màu sáp đen nếu cần.

g. Cắt tác phẩm nghệ thuật và dán lên một tờ giấy thủ công màu đen để tạo nền. Bạn có thể cắt giấy đen thành hình vuông hoặc hình chữ nhật. Bây giờ bạn có một tác phẩm nghệ thuật Batik đã sẵn sàng để đem đi đóng khung!

# Meet Our Chopstickers

**Trami Nguyen Cron**

Trami was born in Saigon, Vietnam, and when she was eight years old left Vietnam with her family for France. Three years later, they settled in the United States. She is the author of *VietnamEazy*, a novel about mothers, daughters, and food, published in 2016.

She is the Founder and Executive Artistic Director of Chopsticks Alley Art. *ARTventure Down the Mekong* is her second book and is a collaborative project with a team of Asian Bay Area artists to create a unique art-making experience for our readers. Trami is also Chief Editor for Chopsticks Alley Publication, a multimedia platform for Vietnamese and Filipino Americans. She is a community leader, producer, and host of talk shows and podcasts.

Trami has a Business Marketing degree from the University of Utah and currently serves as the City of San Jose's Arts Commissioner. She works tirelessly behind the scenes to seek change and equality for minorities, low-income families, elders, and youth.

**Smita Garg, Ed.D.**

Smita Garg is an artist and arts educator with 30 years of expertise in developing culturally inclusive arts programs for diverse populations. She earned her BFA in Applied Art from the College of Arts, New Delhi, studied Art History at the National Museum Institute, and received her doctorate in Arts Education from the University of Illinois, Urbana-Champaign.

Dr. Smita grew up listening to her great-grandmother and grandmother's stories of their life in Myanmar. Consequently, she has always felt a deep affinity with Southeast Asia. Working on this book gave her a deeper understanding of the rich cultural and artistic traditions of the countries located along the Mekong river. Dr. Smita loves to support diverse communities in the Bay Area with her creative gifts and talents. She is currently Chair of San Jose's Art Commission.

## Amanda Pascual

Amanda is a Bay Area artist from Vallejo California with a BA in Art Studio from Sacramento State University. She explores her Filipino American identity through painting and printmaking. Her works feature cozy interior spaces, textiles, and imagery from her cultures, such as her mother's Filipino Folk dance costumes and her grandparent's giant wooden fork and spoon with Bulul carved on the handles. Through her art, she develops images that speak to that feeling of being part of a culture but still trying to find one's place within it. In 2019, her work was exhibited at the City of San Jose's City Hall with Chopstick Alley's Salt Stained: Home and RAW Sacramento's ARISE showcase at Ace of Spades.

## Cynthia Cao

Cynthia is a Vietnamese American artist who works as a printmaker and painter. She earned her BFA in Pictorial Arts with a Minor in Art History from San José State University. She has taught at the San Jose Museum of Art and other private art studios in the Bay Area. At Chopsticks Alley Art, she is an Exhibit Designer, Art Teacher, and Book Designer. Cynthia believes everyone can enjoy creativity and art in their everyday life. Her favorite subjects to teach are woodblock printing and watercolor painting because the process is fun and messy. She currently lives in the Bay Area with a parrot and a cat.

## Jackie Huynh

Jackie is a first-generation Chinese Vietnamese American and the first in his family to attend college. He has a Graphics Design degree from San José State University and is an aspiring artist with diverse skills in different visual arts forms; however, photography is one of his main passions. His role for this project was to capture images for the book. He learned more about the Vietnamese culture through working on *ARTventure* than ever before, and it has helped him embrace his Vietnamese roots even more.

## Ashley Hin

Ashley is a Chinese Vietnamese American visual artist and landscape architecture student from the Bay Area. After graduating from the Oakland School for the Arts with an emphasis in Digital Media, she attended De Anza College before transferring to the University of California, Davis. She believes activism, arts, and culture all go hand-in-hand. As a student intern with Chopsticks Alley Art, Ashley helped in art shows, design posters, social media posts, brochures, and graphics for the organization. She wanted to work on *ARTventure* to improve her illustration skills and connect with her Southeast Asian roots. Outside of art, Ashley enjoys swimming, petting stray cats, gardening, and reading.

## Esther Young

Esther Young is a Chinese-American writer with a passion for the arts, especially facilitating and promoting culturally conscious presentations of art. After graduating from Santa Clara University with a BA in English and Music, she leaned into the nonprofit world. This path has opened rewarding opportunities to serve cultural and artistic organizations in the Bay Area, including the Oshman Family Jewish Community Center and Djerassi Resident Artists Program. As a writer, she has profiled local creatives for Content Magazine and served in various editorial roles. She is proud to support Chopsticks Alley's mission by co-producing events and programs. On the side, Esther finds meaning in writing songs and reconnecting to her roots through language studies.

## Harleen Kaur

Harleen is a first-generation Indian American, a copy-editing intern at Chopsticks Alley Art, and an upcoming second-year student at Foothill College. She is currently a Philosophy major who plans to become an immigration lawyer to help her community receive opportunities for a better life. As a San Jose native, she loves writing and editing stories that empower and highlight the prominent Southeast Asian community. Harleen is excited to be a part of the *ARTventure* team since she enjoys learning about new cultures, especially Southeast Asia's beautiful cultures. While copy-editing the lessons and attending team meetings, she was fascinated by the Indian influence and syncretism seen in the Mekong River civilizations.

## Liên Hương Cao

Cô Liên is the Vietnamese translator for *ARTventure Down the Mekong*. Her understanding of the local language pre and post-1975 is essential to this book written for Vietnamese Americans. Cô Liên is a licensed Marriage Family Therapist, a lecturer in the Masters in Leadership program at St. Mary's College, and a teaching assistant at Stanford Business School. She contributed to *"Synergic Inquiry: A Collaborative Action Methodology"* published by Sage Publications. Through her work in providing therapy for middle schools, high schools, community colleges, and clinics throughout California, Cô Liên explores Asian acculturation issues and struggles the community experiences.

# Gặp Các Bạn Chopstickers

## Trami Nguyen Cron

Cô Trà Mi sinh ra tại Sài Gòn, Việt Nam, và cô rời Việt Nam cùng gia đình sang Pháp năm 8 tuổi. Ba năm sau, gia đình định cư tại Hoa Kỳ. Cô là tác giả của *VietnamEazy*, một cuốn tiểu thuyết về mẹ, con gái và thực phẩm, xuất bản năm 2016.

Cô là người sáng lập và là Giám Đốc Nghệ Thuật Điều Hành của Chopsticks Alley Art. ARTventure Down the Mekong là cuốn sách thứ hai của cô và là một dự án hợp tác với nhóm các nghệ sĩ Châu Á ở khu vùng Vịnh để cống hiến cho các độc giả muốn làm nghệ thuật. Cô Trà Mi cũng là Trưởng ban biên tập cho Chopsticks Alley Publication, một nền diễn đàn đa phương tiện dành cho người Mỹ gốc Việt và Phi-lip-pin. Cô là một nhà lãnh đạo cộng đồng, nhà sản xuất và người dẫn chương trình trên TV, radio và podcast.

Cô Trà Mi có bằng Cử Nhân Tiếp Thị Kinh Doanh của Đại Học Utah và hiện là Ủy Viên Nghệ Thuật của Thành Phố San Jose. Cô làm việc không mệt mỏi, đi tìm cải tiến và bình đẳng cho người thiểu số, hộ gia đình có thu nhập thấp, người cao tuổi và thanh niên.

## Smita Garg, Ed.D.

Cô Smita Garg là một nghệ sĩ và nhà giáo dục nghệ thuật với 30 năm chuyên môn trong việc phát triển các chương trình nghệ thuật hòa nhập về văn hóa cho các nhóm dân cư đa dạng. Cô có bằng BFA về Nghệ Thuật Ứng dụng tại Đại Học Nghệ Thuật, New Delhi, và cô học Lịch Sử Nghệ Thuật tại Viện Bảo Tàng Quốc Gia và nhận bằng tiến sĩ về Giáo Dục Nghệ Thuật Tại Đại Học Illinois, Urbana-Champaign.

Ts. Smita lớn lên, lắng nghe những câu chuyện của bà và bà cố về cuộc đời của họ ở Myanmar. Do đó, cô luôn cảm thấy có mối quan hệ sâu sắc với Đông Nam Á. Thực hiện cuốn sách này đã giúp cô hiểu sâu hơn về truyền thống văn hóa và nghệ thuật phong phú của các quốc gia nằm dọc theo sông Mekong. Ts. Smita rất thích hỗ trợ các cộng đồng đa dạng trong khu vùng Vịnh qua tài năng và năng khiếu sáng tạo. Cô hiện là Chủ Tịch Ủy Ban Nghệ Thuật của San Jose.

## Amanda Pascual

Amanda là một nghệ sĩ Vùng Vịnh đến từ Vallejo, California với bằng Cử Nhân về Nghệ Thuật của Đại Học Bang Sacramento. Cô khám phá bản sắc Philippin và Mỹ của mình thông qua hội họa và in ấn. Các tác phẩm của cô có không gian nội thất ấm cúng, hàng dệt may và hình ảnh từ các nền văn hóa, chẳng hạn như trang phục múa dân gian Phi-lip-pin của mẹ, và chiếc thìa và đĩa gỗ khổng lồ của ông bà chạm khắc Bulul trên tay cầm. Thông qua nghệ thuật, cô phát triển những hình ảnh nói lên cảm giác trở thành một phần của văn hóa nhưng vẫn cố gắng tìm kiếm vị trí riêng của mình trong đó. Năm 2019, tác phẩm của cô được trưng bày tại Tòa Thị Chính của Thành Phố San Jose với Chopstick Alley Salt Stained: Home và RAW Sacramento's ARISE showcase tại Ace of Spades.

## Cynthia Cao

Cô Cynthia là một nghệ sĩ người Mỹ gốc Việt, làm nghề in và họa sĩ. Cô đã giảng dạy tại Bảo Tàng Nghệ Thuật San Jose và các xưởng nghệ thuật tư nhân khác ở Vùng Vịnh. Tại Chopsticks Alley Art, cô là nhà thiết kế triển lãm, giáo viên nghệ thuật và nhà thiết kế bố cục sách. Cô Cynthia tin rằng mọi người đều có thể tận hưởng sự sáng tạo và nghệ thuật trong cuộc sống hàng ngày. Các môn học yêu thích của cô là in khắc gỗ và vẽ màu nước vì công việc này rất bề bộn và vui nhộn. Cô hiện đang sống ở Bay Area, CA, với một con vẹt và một con mèo.

## Jackie Huynh

Anh Jackie là người Mỹ gốc Việt Hoa thế hệ thứ nhất và là người đầu tiên trong gia đình theo đại học. Anh có bằng Thiết Kế Đồ Họa của Đại Học Bang San Jose và là một nghệ sĩ đầy tham vọng với các kỹ năng đa dạng trong các loại hình nghệ thuật thị giác; tuy nhiên, nhiếp ảnh là một trong những niềm đam mê chính của anh. Vai trò của anh trong dự án này là chụp ảnh cho cuốn sách. Làm việc cho *ARTventure* giúp anh học thêm về văn hóa Việt Nam hơn bao giờ hết, giúp anh hiểu về cội nguồn Việt Nam của mình.

## Ashley Hin

Cô Ashley là một nghệ sĩ thị giác người Mỹ gốc Việt Hoa và là sinh viên kiến trúc cảnh quan ở vùng Vịnh. Sau khi tốt nghiệp Trường Nghệ Thuật Oakland với chuyên ngành Truyền Thông Kỹ Thuật Số, cô theo học tại Cao Đẳng De Anza trước khi chuyển sang Đại Học California, Davis. Cô tin rằng hoạt động, nghệ thuật và văn hóa luôn đi chung với nhau. Cô Ashley là sinh viên thực tập với Chopsticks Alley Art, cô giúp trong các buổi biểu diễn nghệ thuật, thiết kế áp phích, bài đăng trên mạng xã hội, tài liệu quảng cáo và đồ họa. Cô muốn làm việc trên *ARTventure* để nâng cao kỹ năng minh họa và kết nối với nguồn gốc Đông Nam Á của mình. Ngoài nghệ thuật, cô còn thích bơi lội, chơi với mèo hoang, làm vườn và đọc sách.

## Esther Young

Cô Esther Young là một nhà văn người Mỹ gốc Hoa có niềm đam mê nghệ thuật, đặc biệt là tạo điều kiện và thúc đẩy các bài thuyết trình có ý thức văn hóa về nghệ thuật. Sau khi tốt nghiệp Đại Học Santa Clara với bằng Cử Nhân Tiếng Anh và Âm Nhạc, cô đã tham gia vào thế giới phi lợi nhuận, nơi nghệ thuật và đối thoại gặp nhau. Con đường này đã mở ra những cơ hội bổ ích để phục vụ các tổ chức văn hóa trong Vùng Vịnh bao gồm Trung Tâm Cộng Đồng Do Thái Gia Đình Oshman và Chương Trình Nghệ Sĩ Thường Trú Djerassi. Trong sự nghiệp ban đầu, cô đã viết về các chương trình địa phương có tính cách sáng tạo cho Nội Dung Tạp Chí, và đảm nhiệm nhiều vai trò biên tập viên khác. Cô tự hào ủng hộ sứ mệnh của Chopsticks Alley bằng cách đồng sản xuất các chương trình và sự kiện bằng kỹ thuật số. Cô cũng thấy ý nghĩa trong việc viết bài hát và kết nối lại với cội nguồn của mình thông qua các nghiên cứu về ngôn ngữ.

## Harleen Kaur

Cô Harleen là một người Mỹ gốc Ấn thế hệ thứ hai và là thực tập sinh biên tập tại Chopsticks Alley Art, đồng thời là sinh viên năm thứ hai ở Đại Học Foothill. Cô hiện là sinh viên chuyên ngành Triết Học, có kế hoạch trở thành luật sư nhập cư để giúp cộng đồng mình nhận được cơ hội có cuộc sống tốt đẹp hơn. Là người gốc San Jose, cô thích viết và biên tập những câu chuyện truyền sức mạnh và làm nổi bật cộng đồng Đông Nam Á. Cô Harleen rất hào hứng khi là thành viên của nhóm *ARTventure* vì cô thích tìm hiểu về các nền văn hóa mới, đặc biệt là các nền văn hóa tươi đẹp của Đông Nam Á. Trong khi sao chép, biên tập các bài học và tham dự các cuộc họp nhóm, cô bị cuốn hút bởi ảnh hưởng của Ấn Độ và chủ nghĩa đồng bộ trong các nền văn minh dọc sông Mekong.

## Liên Hương Cao

Cô Liên là người dịch cuốn *ARTventure Down the Mekong* sang tiếng Việt. Sự hiểu biết của cô về ngôn ngữ địa phương trước và sau năm 1975 là điều cần thiết cho cuốn sách viết cho người Mỹ gốc Việt này. Cô Liên là Chuyên Gia Trị Liệu Tâm Lý, giảng viên trong chương trình Thạc sĩ về Lãnh Đạo Tại Đại Học St. Mary's, và trợ giảng tại Đại Học Stanford. Cô đã đóng góp vào cuốn sách *"Synergic Inquiry: A Collaborative Action Methodology"*, của nhà xuất bản Sage. Thông qua công việc cung cấp liệu pháp cho các trường trung học cơ sở, trung học phổ thông, trường cao đẳng cộng đồng, đại học và phòng khám trên khắp Vùng Vịnh California, Cô Liên tìm hiểu và tìm cách hỗ trợ trong các vấn đề văn hoá liên quan đến việc nhập cư của người gốc Châu Á, và các khó khăn tâm lý của những cộng đồng này.

# Acknowledgements
# Công Đóng Góp

**Chopsticks Alley Art Board of Directors**
Dinh Ly
Jeff Bordona
Jessica Savage
Kalpana Handu Guha
Marie Millares
Thomas Vo aka An Thạnh

**Advisory Board**
David Bonaccorsi, LLP
Jeff Ruster
Van Lan Truong

**Special Thanks**
Alyssa Byrkit
Julie Henley
Sophea Ork
Steve Arounsack
Thiri Zaw

**We wish to thank our donors for making**
***ARTventure Down the Mekong* possible.**
Lucia Cha
Asian Googlers Network: Trena Luong, Alice Lee, Hana Do
Silicon Valley Community Foundation
Vietnamese American Professional Women Association of Silicon Valley

**Community Partners**
Starting Arts
Mosaic America

# Bibliography
# Thư Mục

**SOUTHEAST ASIA**
"Southeast Asian Arts." Encyclopædia Britannica, Encyclopædia Britannica, Inc., britannica.com/art/Southeast-Asian-arts

**MYANMAR**
*Patheininfo*. Traveltopathein, 17 Dec. 2018, Traveltopathein.wordpress.com
"Mongolia, Bhutan, Burma/Myanmar, Nepal, Sri Lanka & India Tailor-Made Holidays, Tours, Expeditions and Media Fixing. - Panoramic Journeys." Panoramicjourneys.com/
"Myanmar." Wikipedia, Wikimedia Foundation, 3 Feb. 2021, www.en.wikipedia.org/wiki/Myanmar
"Myanmar Tours, Tours in Myanmar." Best Tailor Made Myanmar Tours with Unique Experiences, www.toursinmyanmar.com
"Under Maintenance." Myanmartravelinformation.com, www.myanmartravelinformation.com

**LAOS**
"Luxury Travel in Asia: Private Jets & Yachts." Remote Lands, www.remotelands.com
"House of Wandering Silk: Ethically Hand Crafted Clothing & Accessories." Houseofwanderingsilk, www.wanderingsilk.org
"Asia InCH – Encyclopedia of Intangible Cultural Heritage –…. Crafts and Textiles and Their Practitioners and Transmitters in South Asia." Asia InCH Encyclopedia of Intangible Cultural Heritage, www.asiainch.org
"Motifs in Hilltribe Weaving Design." Motifs of Hill Tribe Traditional Art | Above The Fray, www.hilltribeart.com/motifs-weaving-design
"Laos." Wikipedia, Wikimedia Foundation, 23 June. 2021, https://en.wikipedia.org/wiki/Laos

**THAILAND**
"About." Past Perfect, www.pastperfectsf.com
"LinkFang." Welcome to - En.LinkFang.org, www.en.linkfang.org
"Thailand." Wikipedia, Wikimedia Foundation, 23 June. 2021, https://en.wikipedia.org/wiki/Thailand
*Facts and Details*, www.factsanddetails.com
*Blogs Uk*, www.blogs.bl.uk/asian-and-african

**CAMBODIA**
Index, www.cambodiamuseum.info
Index of /Books/khmer_ceramics, www.rooneyarchive.net/books/khmer_ceramics
"News and Current Affairs from Germany and around the World: DW." DW.COM, www.dw.com
"Homepage." Homepage | Cultural Survival, www.culturalsurvival.org
"Holocaust Memorial Day Trust." Trust, www.hmd.org.uk
*WBUR*, www.wbur.org

**VIETNAM**
Sonmaivietnam.vn, www.sonmaivietnam.vn
"The Best Collection to Discover Mekong River." Luxury Mekong River Cruise, www.
luxurymekongrivercruise.com
"Vietnam." Wikipedia, Wikimedia Foundation, 3 Feb. 2021, www.en.wikipedia.org/wiki/Vietnam
"Vietnam Paintings & Artworks: Top 100 Talented Artists - Buy Online." Nguyen Art Gallery,
www.nguyenartgallery.com
*National Geographic*, nationalgeographic.com
*Vietnam Plus*, www.en.vietnamplus.vn

**MALAYSIA**
"The World Standard in Knowledge since 1768." Encyclopædia Britannica, Encyclopædia
Britannica, Inc., www.britannica.com
The Commonwealth, www.Thecommonwealth.org
"Main Page." Wikipedia, Wikimedia Foundation, 3 Feb. 2021, www.en.wikipedia.org
Jenius. "LegacyTimes 传城时代." Legacy Times, 29 Aug. 2019, www.legacytimesmedia.com
"Malaysia." Wikipedia, Wikimedia Foundation, 3 Feb. 2021, www.en.wikipedia.org/wiki/
Malaysia

**PHILIPPINES**
"Main Page." Wikipedia, Wikimedia Foundation, 3 Feb. 2021, www.en.wikipedia.org
Critical Filipinx American Histories, www.uw.pressbooks.pub/criticalfilipinxamericanhistories
"Where Good Ideas Find You." Medium, www.medium.com
"HISTORY | Watch Full Episodes of Your Favorite Shows." History.com, A&E Television
Networks, www.history.com
"Homepage." Homepage | Cultural Survival, www.culturalsurvival.org
"New York City." American Museum of Natural History, www.amnh.org
Digital Commons, www.digitalcommons.unl.edu
UNESCO, www.whc.unesco.org/en/list/722

**INDONESIA**
"Indonesian Batik." UNESCO, ich.unesco.org/en/RL/indonesian-batik-00170
"Main Page." Wikipedia, Wikimedia Foundation, 3 Feb. 2021, www.en.wikipedia.org
"By Expats ... for Expats." Home - Living in Indonesia: A Site for Expatriates - Helping Expats
Transition to Live in Indonesia, www.expat.or.id
"Main Page." Wikipedia, Wikimedia Foundation, 3 Feb. 2021, www.en.wikipedia.org
"Info:Main Page." Info:Main Page - New World Encyclopedia, www.newworldencyclopedia.org

# Photo Credits

1. Cover Photo by Tony Pham from Unsplash.

2. River of Flowers, Ho Chi Minh City (Saigon), Vietnam, Photo by Tony Pham from Unsplash. (Page 2).

3. Huế Imperial City (The Citadel), Huế, Vietnam, Photo by Trami Nguyen Cron (Page 4).

4. Làng Lụa Hội An, Vietnam (Hoi An Silk Village), Photo by Trami Nguyen Cron. (Page 6).

5. Kompong Phluk on Tonle Sap Lake, Cambodia, Photo by Trami Nguyen Cron. (Page 8).

6. All photos of art materials and art projects by Jackie Huynh.

7. Background photos by Trami Nguyen Cron.

8. Photos of Smita Garg, Amanda Pascual, Jackie Huynh, Esther Young, Harleen Kaur, and Liên Hương Cao by Trami Nguyen Cron. (Page 63 - 67).

9. Photo of Trami Nguyen Cron by Thomas Vo. (Page 62).

10. Photo of Cynthia Cao by Qian Wang. (Page 64).

All images reproduced with permission from the artists.